In Her Own Words

New Perspectives on Gender in Music

Editorial Advisors

Susan C. Cook
Beverley Diamond

In Her Own Words

Conversations with Composers in the United States

JENNIFER KELLY

University of Illinois Press
Urbana, Chicago, and Springfield

First Illinois paperback, 2014
Publication of this book was supported by a grant from the Henry and Edna Binkele Classical Music Fund.

Manufactured in the United States of America
1 2 3 4 5 C P 5 4 3 2 1
♾ This book is printed on acid-free paper.

The Library of Congress cataloged the cloth edition as follows:
Kelly, Jennifer (Musician)
In her own words: conversations with composers in the United States / Jennifer Kelly.
pages cm. — (New perspectives on gender in music)
Includes bibliographical references and index.
ISBN 978-0-252-03759-7 (cloth : alk. paper)
ISBN 978-0-252-09483-5 (e-book)
1. Women composers—United States—Interviews.
2. Composers—United States—Interviews.
I. Title.
ML390.K33 2013
780.92'520973—dc23 [B] 2012049961
PAPERBACK ISBN 978-0-252-08049-4

Contents

Acknowledgments

This book was possible because of the creative and generous women contained in its pages. These twenty-five composers were gracious with their time; they have a sincere respect for their craft and a desire to share their art with others. I am grateful for their trust and their valuable time. Special thanks to Libby Larsen, the first woman composer whose work I ever performed. Her music eventually led to my dissertation on her *Love Songs: Five Songs on Texts by Women Poets.* My work with Libby taught me that composers are indeed generous, and much can be learned by going to the source.

It has been my good fortune to have been taught by gifted and stimulating teachers: Susan McClary, who, through thoughtful and challenging questions, emphasized cultural connection and alternative perspective; Robert Winter, who stressed the benefits of being a studied, thinking performer; Donald Neuen, who taught the importance of honoring the score and the composer; and David Chase, in whose choir I was first introduced to music composed by women. I am also deeply indebted to the scholars of women in music who came before me. Their work was groundbreaking, and their representation of my own gender was inspiring. It is because of these women that I felt empowered and challenged to add to their body of work.

Thanks are also due to Susan Frykberg, Robert Winter, Byron Eicher, and Irene Harwood for their encouragement of this project when it was still just an idea, and I thank Janet Whittington and Hilary Tann for their continued encouragement.

Special thanks to three fabulous young women and scholars—Caitlin Flood, Shannon Moran, and Jackie Macri—who helped in the preliminary stages with obtaining background information, transcribing interviews, gathering works lists when many of these composers did not yet have published or contemporary repertoire lists assembled, and offering feedback from the perspective of young women in the twenty-first century. I am also grateful for my colleagues and friends: Rosie Bukics, Jorge Torres, Skip Wilkins, Tony Cummings, and Mary Kresna Yasa, who read some of the chapters in their preliminary stages and offered valuable criticism. Sincere thanks to Beth Seetch and Janet Whittington, whose editorial eyes and significant feedback made this book possible.

I am tremendously grateful to the University of Illinois Press and Laurie Matheson, editor-in-chief. Laurie's guidance throughout the process was sincere and invaluable. Additionally, Jane Bowers and Judith Tick's book, *Women Making Music: The Western Art Tradition, 1150–1950,* had a significant impact on my life as a young woman, and I feel proud that my first book is published by the same press. Finally, Michele Edwards and the other anonymous readers of drafts were challenging and meticulous, and I will be ever grateful for their input. This book would not have been possible without the generosity of Lafayette College and their support of this project through the Richard King Mellon Foundation Summer Research Fellowship Grant. Special thanks to the head of the music department, Larry Stockton, for his respect and his constant encouragement of my work.

Above all, I give my highest appreciation and respect to Greg Eicher. His unending support, numerous readings of drafts, honest criticism, and understanding of late nights, travel, and my need for intense focus throughout this project is more appreciated than words can express. He never questioned the work even when I wondered what was possible. This book exists, in part, because of Greg.

Chronological List of Birthdates

Alice Parker	1925
Emma Lou Diemer	1927
Toshiko Akiyoshi	1929
Pauline Oliveros	1932
Joan Tower	1938
Meredith Monk	1942
Tania León	1943
Hasu Patel	1947
Hilary Tann	1947
Mary Jane Leach	1949
Shulamit Ran	1949
Libby Larsen	1950
Beth Anderson	1950
Chen Yi	1953
Janika Vandervelde	1955
Pamela Z	1956
Laura Karpman	1959
Maria Schneider	1960
Jeanine Tesori	1961
Jennifer Higdon	1962
Augusta Read Thomas	1964
Svjetlana Bukvich	1967
Gabriela Lena Frank	1972
Deborah Lurie	1974
Winifred Phillips	declined to include date of birth

Introduction

This sourcebook contains interviews with twenty-five contemporary women composers in the United States. With interesting personal anecdotes and sometimes surprising intimacy and humor, these conversations represent the range of women composing music in the United States from the mid-twentieth century into the twenty-first.

As a conductor, performer, and teacher, I am keenly interested in exploring musical intention, with the goal of bringing a more informed performance to an audience and more informed discussion into the classroom. In these interviews, composers expound on the details of compositional technique, inspiration, creative process, and the composer-performer relationship. Beyond the details of bringing musical ideas to fruition in a compositional sense, these conversations also explore the composers' sense of time and place; the influences of their education and training; their family and cultural identity; their paths to finding their voices; their views of creativity; their takes on the business of composition; and the importance or irrelevance of gender issues for twenty-first-century American composers who are women.

This book is shaped by a conductor's sensibilities, as the interviews have been modeled upon the kinds of questions that conductors and teachers pose when creating programs for performers and audiences on concert stages or creating the arc of a semester's discussions. I studied all preparatory materials as if I were selecting works to conduct and then rehearsing them for live performance or experiencing them in the classroom. Desiring a broad understanding of each compositional voice, I asked general questions about inspiration and intention while deliberately avoiding detailed inquiry into specific works. The range of twenty-five composers aims to portray the scene for women—varying in age, birthplace, ethnicity, and education—who are composing music in the United States and to represent the kinds of music they compose, be it classical, jazz, multimedia, or collaborative forms for the stage, film, and video games. This collection intends to provide a more accurate picture than has previously been available of women's participation in the field of composition.

Several motivations converged in the assembling of this book, beginning with my own traditional formal education. As late as the 1980s in my high-school curriculum, women were not addressed as creators of music, and into the 1990s, when discussing women composers in college, the professors brought in "special" books. When I later became a professor of music myself, the standard textbooks still did not yet adequately represent my own gender; so I, too, brought in "special" books for the class.

Inspiration for this book also came from my high regard for the photographer Annie Leibovitz's work in *Women,* a book she coauthored with Susan Sontag. Leibovitz's portraits of women placed side-by-side convey a sense of distinctiveness and individuality, as when Alabama coal miners appear on the page next to ladies lunching in Houston—they illustrate both connection and contrast. This juxtaposition reminded me of a concert program and of the unique voice of a given composer, surrounded by voices of other composers and brought to life by conductors, instrumentalists, and singers. As I leafed through the pages of Leibovitz and Sontag's book, I became the audience reacting emotionally to the artistic interpretation of the women depicted there.

As a conductor, I have found that published compositions by women can be difficult to come by, and, when located, they must be purchased because the scores do not exist in most rehearsal libraries. Although I was advocating for the importance of women composers, I found that I was not programming their music in my own concerts.

The problems with concert programming were (and to some extent still are) problems of awareness and budget. First, without the benefit of having studied women composers as a matter of course throughout my education, I mistakenly believed that the number of talented women in music was small and their few musical scores worthy of study were already available on library shelves. Second, I was unaware of the publication challenges faced by composers throughout the centuries and into the present day. Unless a publisher with resources to market the compositions championed a composer, I had no initial access to the scores; nor did I possess the knowledge of where to find what I did not yet know existed. Third, the few works to which I was exposed were still quite expensive to perform because they tended to be composed or arranged for full orchestra and were usually new to musicians; added financial support would be required for new scores and additional rehearsal time. Fourth, for many women composers, recordings were frequently unavailable or unknown, and once again I was under the distinct impression that the women-composer pool from which to choose was rather small.

Awareness is powerful. As I began to seek further information, I learned about the wealth of music composed by women in numerous genres. Like other under-represented populations, women did not fill the pages of common textbooks or music-score libraries; women composers did indeed exist, but they were not yet fully recognized.

In our effort to choose which musical experiences to share with audiences, conductors and musicians rely in great measure upon current scholarship about composers to design our programs. Scholarship on composers utilizes scores, recordings, reviews, theoretical and musicological analyses, biographies, and interviews, yet, with notable exceptions, most such resources discuss either male composers or the same handful of women.

With some exceptions (see the list of Selected Resources at the end of the book), the expanded role of women composers in U.S. music starting in the second half of the twentieth century is not reflected in the available scholarship. To pave the way for more fully representative studies, this collection aims to reveal some of the additional resources that do exist for the study of women composers and to compare and contrast these composers' experiences, thus spurring continued discovery and publication of such material. As the twenty-first century develops new platforms for music, the nature of composed American music itself is being redefined, and this collection may also suggest approaches to the activity of redefinition.

New information about all of the composers interviewed appears here, in many cases filling voids where little to no information previously existed in published scholarship. Taken together, the interviews address the creative processes of U.S. women composing in the twentieth century and beyond by posing questions consistently across boundaries of musical genre, generation, birthplace, ethnic background, musical origin, education and training, and date of professional emergence through public performance or recording. Readers may appreciate the opportunity to identify potentially meaningful patterns, form hypotheses about the direction of composition in the United States, and draw conclusions that lead to pertinent scholarly projects and performances.

To reflect the breadth of women's participation in the field, I worked to identify composers of all ages, be they women whose contributions are well known in scholarly circles (e.g., Pauline Oliveros, Meredith Monk, and Libby Larsen) or within the narrower confines of their musical genres (e.g., Toshiko Akiyoshi, Jeanine Tesori, and Laura Karpman). Because of the influx of musicians into the United States from around the world in the twentieth century and with the influence of so-called world music, this project has sought to represent composers—including creators of improvised music—who have resided and worked permanently in the United States regardless of birthplace (e.g., Hilary Tann, Svjetlana Bukvich, and Hasu Patel). In assembling the list of potential interview subjects, I included composers who have earned recognition in the conventional hierarchy of composed music (e.g., Joan Tower, Shulamit Ran, and Jennifer Higdon) and those who challenge that hierarchy (e.g., Alice Parker, Deborah Lurie, and Pamela Z).

I selected interviewees based upon my research into concert programs and playbills across the country; university music-department rosters, ensembles, and courses; conference-circuit presentations; music-publishing catalogs; trade-magazine news and reviews, in print and online; as well as in the accepted scholarly listings of accomplished composers (see Selected Resources). A composer's compositional productivity and success have traditionally been measured by her or his representation in publishing houses, concert halls, the recording industry, and public reviews. But contemporary scholarship has uncovered a plethora of works by women of past centuries, and the discovery of these works creates a space for questioning the traditional measures of compositional productivity and the belief that women composers remain at the margins of success or, worse, of worthiness. Similarly, this collection of interviews with living composers aims to invite readers to give their work a listen in order to seek meaningful measures of its worth.

I also desired to represent as accurately as possible the abundance or scarcity of working women composers within various genres and identifications. For example, it would not be authentic to fill this book equally with composers of traditional instrumental music and composers of commercial media. While a wealth of women composers write for instrumental ensembles and use familiar structural forms, there is a scarcity of women writing for film, stage productions, and video games; consequently, fewer commercial composers appear in this book. Likewise, more composers of Western European heritage are making a living in music in the United States than are women composers of Eastern European, Asian, African, Middle Eastern, or Latin American ancestry; the included composers also reflect those findings.

Preparing for the interviews involved composing a list of general topics applicable to all the subjects as well as immersing myself in the available music and career information for every subject in order to craft questions appropriate for each individual. Some noteworthy challenges presented themselves in the gathering of materials for these living artists. For instance, it was fairly simple to gather materials on the few composers presented here who have numerous recordings and scores commercially available; they have been the subjects of articles, dissertations, chapters, and, in a few cases, books. Gathering materials for others was problematic, either because few, if any, commercial recordings of their work were available or because little written material, such as musical reviews or analyses, existed. While recorded music was more readily available for some composers, the scores of other composers' work were often more accessible than recordings. Sometimes, when a composer is handled through a large publisher, her or his larger works are available for rental or high-priced score purchase. Moreover, approaching an established publisher for several perusal scores at one time is seldom a straightforward process, whereas directly approaching a composer whose work is less often recorded or more often self-published frequently yields scores or recordings for perusal via their personal Web site. Making these materials accessible is in those composers' best interest, as they are almost solely responsible for the promotion and marketing of their work. Likewise, for composers whose work does not follow the conventional path of creation, such as Pauline Oliveros, Pamela Z, or Svjetlana Bukvich, available scores and recordings do not necessarily provide the most illuminating view of their work.

In studying composers like Oliveros, Z, or Bukvich, I relied more on written documents, my own experience, and others' interpretations of their work, as well as interviews and the composers' own discussion of their art, than on conventional recordings or scores. Composers of commercial or media music (film, television, theater, video games) have entirely different contexts for publication and access because their music serves or collaborates with the visual experience of a creation as a whole. Consequently, the act of simply gathering materials spawned useful questions regarding publication, recording, promotion, marketing, and legacy as currently understood.

Even though scholars pore over the letters of Mozart and Beethoven and recently discovered documents about Amy Beach or Franz Joseph Haydn searching for evidence about states of mind, points of view, and compositional intention, negative assumptions have been made for centuries about a composer's worthiness on the basis of the number of published, performed, and reviewed works. This book aims to help rebalance this picture. Fanny Mendelssohn Hensel's compositional output is a commonly discussed example of such a misleading notion. Understanding gender and class issues in nineteenth-century Western Europe enlightens comparison of the Mendelssohn siblings and may affect a conductor's subsequent programming. (It certainly affected mine.)

For many women composers today, recordings remain few, unavailable, or unknown. In the early years of the twenty-first century, making accurate recordings of music is paramount, for they help performers select material for concert programs, aid teachers in planning lectures, and create another compositional footprint to leave behind for future generations. Commissioned work is often generated through recordings, either on compact disc or online digital media. As several composers express in the pages of this book, the musical art as it exists through time is lost when no recording is made. It bears repeating that the number of recorded performances is still often used as a measure of compositional success. However, recording an ensemble of one's own music is usually cost-prohibitive without sponsorship or a grant. A recording output for a woman composer is a competitive accomplishment, but a lack of recording output does not necessarily preclude worthiness.

Primary sources, such as concert programs and trade magazines, were essential in providing leads to discovering composers and their music. Like any conductor wishing to expand the offerings for her or his audiences and musicians, I relied not only upon standard sources like Karin Pendle's *Women and Music,* Judith Lang Zaimont's *Musical Woman* volumes, and James Briscoe's anthologies of music by women, but also on word of mouth and unconventional sources like *Film Score Monthly, DownBeat,* and *GameSpot* to acquire information about and compositions by my subjects. Devising both the general questions and questions particular to a given composer, I anticipated moments in the script—or score—where I might leave room for spontaneity. What questions needed to be answered to interpret the music authentically? To how many of these questions could I find answers in the music, and which needed to be asked of the composer herself? Could there be varied interpretations from the available musicological analyses commonly used for this composer's work? The goal was to become fully immersed in the artistic identity of a single composer at a time, seeking both her voice and her potential audience. While I resisted categorizing style for purposes of this book, I did require an understanding of individual compositional technique to craft appropriate questions.

Some composers in this collection—such as Joan Tower, Meredith Monk, Pauline Oliveros, and Libby Larsen—have been interviewed, analyzed, and discussed for decades. Still, I asked questions of these often-studied composers to which I could not find answers in other sources. I grew interested in how their views might either have changed or become more rooted over time. For less well-known composers, I wished to develop a basic understanding of their histories and experiences, seeking information on identity and culture. Similar topics emerged in each interview, including inspiration and influence, creative process, the influence of gender, balance of work and family, ideas on education and training, composition, legacy, and the business of living a life making music. Readers at all levels of expertise or experience of varied genres will find in this book both well-known and unknown composers, and there lies some of its excitement. Certain questions I asked of everyone, such as whether she thought that there is a need for women-only concerts, festivals, and recordings. Yet no interview began like any other or comprised all of the same questions. It was my goal to find questions uniquely appropriate to each individual.

An interview is a kind of a performance. For this book, each interviewee was aware that she was being recorded and that her words would be published. Nevertheless, a composer's compositional voice is a product of her expression, and our conversation, although guided by me, was an alternate expression of her compositional voice.

Like any performance, each interview encountered moments of surprise. Because the subjects and I regarded each interview as a performance to be shared with you, the audience, the process of editing interview transcripts included each composer's review of our conversation. After my initial editing for length and cohesion, seldom did a subject request any deletion, and clarification was the usual result of any editing. Although the editing process clarified some phrasings and usages that might confuse readers, I deliberately retained characteristic language traits for multilingual composers such as Tania León, Toshiko Akiyoshi, and Chen Yi because their spoken language, like their music, is characterized by the amalgams of first and later languages. For example, Akiyoshi's linguistic profile expresses her deliberate and unique amalgamation of Japanese heritage with the medium of American big-band jazz.

Inspired by the composers in this book, I have ordered the chapters in the manner of a concert program. Composers spend years, often decades, shaping a unique artistic voice. Conductors and performers thoughtfully program concerts by combining these artistic voices in meaningful ways. Many consider programming an art in itself, as ensemble, audience, season trajectory, tone, and shape of musical experiences can be melded into a performance arc.

The interviews collected in this book constitute a performance programmed by a conductor with twenty-five compositional voices. Readers are invited to consider the program as intentionally beginning with Joan Tower to articulate these themes: humanizing classical music for an audience, nourishing the composer, communicating creative process, grasping the role of performers, evaluating new music, and considering women as a subject for research. Tower signals the theme of gender in this way: "Women have had a different experience than men, different history, different everything." The subsequent six interviews (Shulamit Ran, Jennifer Higdon, Gabriela Lena Frank, Alice Parker, Chen Yi, and Tania León) build upon and complicate Tower's themes while introducing the complexities of notation issues, cultural inspirations and identity, and various paths to finding one's compositional voice. The emerging composer Hasu Patel's life experience bridges this first section into the next, where Pauline Oliveros and Meredith Monk introduce alternative creative processes. Their processes can be viewed as alternatives to convention, for they expand accepted definitions of composition and venue and continue the forward-thinking of their career paths into the future. The multimedia composers Svjetlana Bukvich and Pamela Z join that section via their own alternative composing processes, and their interviews build upon the earlier discussion of cultural identity as it relates to their art.

Interviews with Toshiko Akiyoshi and Maria Schneider provide an interlude to refresh and reflect as an intermission might, while revealing commonalities and contrasts between these two composers of jazz born thirty years apart. Augusta Read Thomas, Hilary Tann, and Libby Larsen expand on Schneider's discussion of the business of composing and the changing role of technology for composers, followed by a series of four interviews (Laura Karpman, Winifred Phillips, Deborah Lurie, and Jeanine Tesori) with composers in the collaborative arts of cinema, stage, and video games. Finally, Beth Anderson, Janika Vandervelde, and Mary Jane Leach touch upon some of the gender and technological themes introduced earlier while articulating their own artistic developments. Our concert of compositional voices concludes with Emma Lou Diemer, who has been actively composing for over seventy years, reflecting on a life in music while still looking toward the future.

As with any musical program or exhibit of portraits, other conductors and curators might suggest different orders and paces to emphasize or introduce different themes—that is how some readers of this book might enter and leave it, with new approaches to questions about the women creating American music and how American music could be redefined and cultivated. Other readers may shuffle through the collection simply as music lovers expecting or hoping for discoveries.

While attending the biennial conference of the National Collegiate Choral Organization in 2011, I sat in the audience for a panel session about the process of commissioning composers. The topic of encouraging young, emerging composers was brought up and enthusiastically discussed. After spending years researching contemporary women in composition, I commented that not all emerging composers are young. Many women enter the field later in life due to circumstances or changing priorities, and encouragement for emerging composers would be welcome at any age. After the panel session ended, a woman older than I am thanked me for my comment. I asked her name, and she shyly mentioned that she was in college studying to be a composer. One day we may follow her emerging career from the vantage points introduced in this volume. I feel honored that these composers have trusted me with their words.

Bernard Mindich

1

Joan Tower

Numerous composers, including Jennifer Higdon, credit Joan Tower with helping to eradicate the glass ceiling for contemporary women composers. Born in New York in 1938 and spending most of her youth in South America, Tower has become a respected composer, performer, conductor, and educator. With degrees from Bennington College and Columbia University, her earliest works in the mid-twentieth century incorporated serial techniques. Thereafter, Tower developed an approach based in lyricism, colorful orchestration, and a rhythmic energy derived in part from her years in South America. With a productive career spanning over fifty years and with abundant recordings of her music, Tower has been studied and interviewed for decades.

Our conversation begins with the acknowledgment of her place in American music history as she discusses a composer's continued need for nourishment. She finds much of her nourishment through teaching as the Asher B. Edelman Professor of Music at the Bard College Conservatory of Music. She explains her love for her students, referring to them as her children, and discusses why she divides her time equally between teaching and composing.

Tower's interview reminds readers of the intensely personal job of a composer when she uses her characteristic humor to describe the anxiety she still feels delivering a composition to a performer. An accomplished pianist with a great respect for musicians, Tower believes strongly in the composer-performer connection; she explains why she encourages all musicians to compose and all composers to perform. She learned the benefits of this balance when she cofounded the New York–based Da Capo Chamber Players as a pianist in 1969 and composed several works for that ensemble. After decades composing for major ensembles, soloists, and orchestras, Tower continues to challenge herself. During our conversation, she recounts her process composing for the Ford *Made in America* consortium commission and the unique demands of composing for sixty-five community orchestras throughout all fifty states. Leonard Slatkin and the Nashville Symphony recorded *Made in America* along with the additional Tower works *Tambor* and *Concerto for Orchestra* in 2008. That album received three Grammy awards: Best Classical Contemporary Composition, Best Classical Album, and Best Orchestral Performance.

Like many of the composers in this book, Tower thinks about the future of her art and the compositional art form. She invests in her students, providing tiered listening experiences for their compositional development. Beyond discussing the skill of composition, she explains the need for performers and composers to humanize classical music for modern audiences. She encourages audience members likewise to feel empowered to form their own opinions of living composers and contemporary music. Acknowledging that she is called a "woman composer," she uses her professional positions to advocate for women and living composers. A recent example is her three-concert 2007 series "Unsung," "Unbound," and "Unleashed," supported by the St. Luke's Chamber Ensemble.

Tower's numerous awards include the Alfred I. Dupont Award for Distinguished Composers and Conductors, and she was the first woman to win the prestigious Grawemeyer Award for *Silver Ladders* in 1999. Tower was elected to the American Academy of Arts and Letters in 1998. Over five hundred different ensembles have played her popular *Fanfares for the Uncommon Woman,* and she continues to be an actively commissioned and performed composer while also devoting her time to teaching. Her music is published by Associated Music Publishers.

***

April 2010, at her home in Red Hook, New York

JOAN TOWER: We, as living composers, need to be fed some kind of nourishment for the work that we do, which is difficult work. It's not for the faint of heart because of the challenge involved. I tell my students who are struggling to be composers that it is a tough business for young composers (and older composers, too). I say, "Find something that gives you nourishment while you're composing. Is it playing soccer, cooking, teaching kids? Find that, and make sure you do that every day along with composing, because composing is not designed, at least initially, to give you much nourishment. Especially when you're young, because no one knows your music, and it's not getting played. As your music gets picked up, that could become the nourishment if it's working for you. That's what happened for me. That's how I got away from playing the piano and started composing more: my music started to get picked up. People were saying, "I want to play your clarinet piece, your flute piece, your string quartet." I was like, "Really?" It happened more and more and more over time. Soon I was getting invited to places, and it became a fantastically nourishing thing for me. Players actually liked to play my music, and audiences really were drawn to some of the pieces—not all. So that's become hugely important to me in my life.

JENNIFER KELLY: Given all that, is there some kind of expectation, or even a feeling of responsibility, that comes with being Joan Tower?

JT: It gets . . . it's hard. For example, the *Made in America* project was a huge challenge because I knew that that piece was going to be played by sixty-five orchestras all over the United States in hugely different communities. That was a big challenge. Writing for the Chicago Symphony, and New York, and now Pittsburgh—these are huge challenges. Or writing for soloists or the Tokyo Quartet or Emerson Quartet. But you take it one step at a time, and what you fundamentally realize is that you just have to write the best piece you can.

JK: Everything else be damned.

JT: Everything else be damned. You just hope the piece has life, and that's the real burden.

JK: In your mind's ear, when you're composing and the ideas start flowing, what do you hear first? Is it the piece in its entirety or the rhythm and tempo?

JT: It's like writing a novel. The idea might be a person who walks into the room who is funny and lively and outgoing but unhappy because of negative circumstances in their life. And then this person meets another person with a contrasting personality, and the interaction starts. And there's a tension between the two, or maybe a connection. It's like two ideas now are starting to work together. And to me, it's like a whole organic narrative story that has to take a realistic shape—a motivating shape, a shape that has a musical logic to it. That's the way I compose. And I listen a lot. I listen and listen and listen, because it has to tell me what to do rather than the other way around. You're in charge in a way, but you're actually not. This thing is starting to tell you what to do, but you have to listen carefully to let it tell you what to do. So there's that shift of creative authority, which takes a long time to give in to.

JK: Do you have to separate yourself out of it so you can listen?

JT: Exactly.

JK: What kind of parameters do you give yourself at the very beginning?

JT: I have two given parameters: medium and length. For example, an orchestra piece of approximately twenty minutes.

JK: And then do you always start at the beginning?

JT: Always. I could never start in the middle or the end. Some composers can do that—not me. There's no way I could start in the middle, because I view the process as an organic one.

JK: How can you tell if a piece is making an impact?

JT: I can't tell. I have no control over that. I just try to do the best job I can. And if it has a life, fantastic. I'm thrilled. And if it doesn't, I feel the piece has somehow failed.

JK: Do you compose with the audience in mind?

JT: I am the first listener, and it's me and the music and my perception. Is this working or not? That's all I have. It's not anybody else's perspective but mine. I have to say, "Is this working? Change that." So it's a lonely activity, because you're stuck really with your own perceptions. No one can tell you how this is really working. Not really. You have to do it yourself. That's why composition can't be taught. So this thing goes on the page into this highly defined notation. It's like an architectural blueprint. It is, "Eighth note equals this, and crescendo to the B-flat in that register on that instrument." It is very precise. The second listeners are the performers, and you've put this soul of yours in the architectural blueprint, and it comes out the other side, and there are these players, and they start reading it. Does it come to life for them? Does it engage them? Does it make them want to do something a certain way? Is the rhythm really important here, or is the color right? Being a member of the Da Capo Chamber Players for fifteen years, I learned a lot about that process from the point of view of being the player—the triangle relation between the creator, the page, and the performer/conductor. That's a very tricky pathway, and some pages are very clear about their intentions and may be wrong but still are clear. The composers would come into Da Capo and talk about their pieces, and sometimes there was a huge discrepancy between what we were doing and what they were talking about, and other times we didn't even need them there because the piece would just come alive off the page. The third listener is the audience.

JK: Being a player must enlighten your experience as a composer because you also have such experience as the second listener.

JT: Playing with Da Capo was a hugely important education for me because I got on the other side of the fence, and I saw the problems with notation. For me the composer, the second listener—the performer—is incredibly anxiety-provoking. I hand a piece to the players, and then I wait. They have no idea yet whether they like it or not, because they have to really learn the piece. That whole waiting time is very scary. I have a story about that. . . . I wrote this violin concerto for Elmar Oliveira. He's a very good violinist who has played all the traditional repertoire. So when he asked me for a piece, I was honored because he had heard several of my pieces and liked my music. (That's the best way to be asked by a performer: because they like what they're hearing.) So I started this violin concerto, and I sweated bullets over it. He's a virtuosic player, so I had to make it challenging and lyrical at the same time. I wrote this piece with sweat, blood, and tears. I sent it to him, and there was no answer. No answer. And in my paranoia, I read that as he thinks this is unplayable or he didn't like it. Another two months later, I go to rehearse with him [on the piano]. He says nothing about my concerto. All I could think of was the piece was unplayable. He hates it. So we start playing. We get finished, and he turns to me, and he says, "So, how did I do?" I thought, "How did *you* do?" I asked if there was anything awkward in the piece that he wanted to tell me about, and he told me about one double stop. I said, "Anything else?" And he said, "No, as a matter of fact it's beautifully written for the violin. It really is beautiful, and it's a great piece, Joan" [*laughs*].

JK: You've been vetted by musicians, audiences, and critics, and yet you are still quite critical of your own music.

JT: The most talented players I know are the ones that are the most vulnerable, because they still care about what the audience thinks. There are some very slick performers who can do anything at any time and impress you with their experience and their image and their facility . . . chops. But it's the ones who are really vulnerable that make the difference, because they care deeply about communicating. It's like they reach out to you and pull you in.

JK: While you're composing, do you think about the second and third listener, or are you really engrossed in the first listener?

JT: What I try and do is have giant ears. The whole thing about composing is you cannot assume anything. We try to create the biggest perceptual grid we can to make it really work. It's very complicated, but, sure, I care about the third and fourth and fifth listeners very much.

JK: Does it affect the way you write when you're in the process of writing? Or does it happen later?

JT: It happens during. I'm writing and creating a character, and I want that character to speak to a lot of people. I want them to speak to everybody: to older people, Latinos, bankers, dancers, whatever. I want them to be heard, so I work hard on making this character be heard. It has to do with communication. I think there are three types of composers. The first type is the one that wants to communicate in a big way to you the listener. They want you totally engaged, and they will go out and wrap around you and bring you in: examples are Tchaikovsky and John Corigliano. The second type is the one that sort of wants to communicate, but it's okay if you don't like it. They would like you to like it, but it's sort of live and let live. In this category I would put Schubert, because he is a beautiful composer who cares very much about what he's doing, but he's not going to grab you by the collar. Also John Harbison. The third type is, they don't care whether you like it or not, they're not interested in that at all. And those types are usually the ones who want to tell you what they know. They're usually smart, and they usually lecture: examples are middle and late Arnold Schoenberg and Milton Babbitt.

JK: So where do you put you?

JT: First.

JK: Do you allow yourself the kind of freedom to go back after a piece is completed and mess with it?

JT: Oh, sure. Anything to make it better. I mean, you can't change everything. Because once you change one thing, that changes another. It's like a mobile. You have to be careful how much you change.

JK: With regard to notation, when a conductor looks at a Tower score, is everything we need to know in the score?

JT: The notation is only a blueprint for the sound. Some are very notation-specific, and some are not, but that doesn't necessarily mean that the music is less strong or stronger. I learned that from playing in Da Capo. I think the strongest music will suggest all kinds of things no matter how it's notated. It jumps off of the page to you immediately and says, "This is what I need. This is what I need you to think about." Other music is much subtler. You need to pull it out to really get it. So I don't think it's a question of notation so much. It's a question of, "What is the notation yielding? What is this thing trying to be?" The notation is very tough for composers.

JK: What about you? What about when your music is played a hundred years from now?

JT: My music is not that abstract. My music is pretty instrumentally based and fairly visceral, so the tempos are important, but there is a leeway. The dynamics are important, but again, there is a leeway. But my notation is pretty specific, and some players go against it. If it works, I'm thrilled.

JK: Earlier, you brought up *Made in America.* That was truly a wonderful project.

JT: It was amazing, and it just kept multiplying. It started with Robert Rosoff, executive director of the Glens Falls Symphony Orchestra. He said, "I want to commission a major composer, but I don't have the money. So I'm going to get twenty-two of my colleagues in community orchestras." He was a go-getter type, and everybody knew who he was in the community-orchestra world, and he got twenty-two colleagues immediately. So the American Symphony Orchestra League [ASOL] saw this project and said, "This is fantastic. We're going to help you get more orchestras." They were each willing to pay one thousand dollars, because that's all they could afford. So the ASOL brought it up to thirty-six orchestras, and then the Ford Motor Company Fund said, "This is fantastic. If you can get this into fifty states, we'll pay for most of it." So the ASOL went to work, and they got it into fifty states with sixty-five orchestras.

JK: Within what time period was this played?

JT: 2005 to 2007.

JK: So within two years it was played by sixty-five orchestras in all fifty states? That's amazing. What did you learn as a composer? Even though you were a successful composer, that was a new experience, right?

JT: Well, I had never written for a community orchestra. I had been writing for major orchestras, and I didn't know the community-orchestra scene. I knew I was representing living composers, so I had to do something really good, and I wanted to make sure it worked for everybody. So I made two really good choices. What would appeal to all these people? I incorporated the tune "America the Beautiful" into this piece. That was my first good choice. My second good choice had to do with knowing that amateur orchestras were playing this piece, so I had to make sure they could play it. Because if they couldn't play it, I was on losing ground. So I went around to all my player friends with my score and asked if it was playable by a community orchestra. And they totally saved my butt.

JK: What kind of relationship would you ideally like to have with a performer? Can you give up a piece of work and say, "Thank you very much," or do you want to have a close relationship with them throughout the process?

JT: I care very much about who I'm writing for. All my friends are performers. I have a very close relationship with many of them, and it's very important to me that they like the piece, because then they feel empowered. So it's really a joint venture. It's them and me working together, and if they have suggestions, I respect their instincts enormously. If they say, "I think this should be a whole note instead of a dotted half," I am all ears. Or, "It doesn't quite go over the hump there." That's a deep kind of change they're suggesting, but I'm very respectful of that, and I would welcome it, actually. But most performers are intimidated and will not make that kind of change because they treat the page as if it's the Bible. "I can't change that. I just have to make it work somehow." If a player says to me, "I'd like to change the dotted half to a whole note," that is big-time. I really love the idea that they even suggested it.

JK: When you started teaching, did you do it because it was a steady gig or because you really wanted to teach?

JT: Oh, I really wanted to teach. I love to teach. These kids are like my children. I really care about them. I would die without them. Half of my life is making music, and the other half is teaching. And I divide the week up that way, actually. It's just a wonderful, nourishing energy to give these kids a life in music. It's so rewarding, and I'm good at it.

JK: Yet one can't teach composition?

JT: You can't. In my composition workshop for beginning composers, I am basically a traffic cop. I help them with the notation, with understanding the instruments, and with setting up situations where they hear their music being played. I tell them right away that I don't want an assignment, but I want something they care about, and that means a little bit of work. So I try to get them closer and closer to what they are composing by caring and being excited about the music, and then we talk about it, and the class talks about it and develops a dialogue of criticism which is fair and educational. Alongside of that path, I provide constant hearing situations at higher and higher levels. First it's me playing their pieces, and then they start working with players in the class. Then there's a professional group, the Da Capo Players, that comes up at the end of the semester. So there's this whole "tiering of hearing." It's a giant ear-training class, actually. But it's deep ear training. It's about hearing connections and continuity and perceptions of register, use of space, harmony, rhythm. It's not just about identifying pitch.

JK: What kind of music education is needed?

JT: The whole package of what makes music. Whatever makes music needs to be studied: rhythm, pitch, instruments, register, timbre, and dynamics. The whole package has to be studied. And the best way to do it is to play an instrument and play lots of different kinds of music. That's the best way: to actually play the music. You start composing, but it helps to play an instrument and conduct, because you have to understand rhythm and how to notate if you're involved in notating music. If you're involved in improvisation, that's a whole different ballgame, but an important one for developing an ear and generating your own voice. But I have students who are active improvisors who feel that it is important to write their music down so others could play it. Of course, composing is improvisation, because you have to decide whether you're going to write it all down or not. That's a big choice. But I think the first thing you have to do is learn to play an instrument and read music. Then you start composing right away. I don't think you have to wait until you're in college. When I started teaching at the Greenwich House School in New York, I started teaching composition to seven- and eight-year-olds. I was teaching piano, but I asked the director of the school if I could teach some composers. And before he knew it, I had this whole concert of compositions by these young kids. I remember there were seven of them, and out of that class, four are composers today. This is like sixty years later.

JK: What's the importance of composer mentoring?

JT: Well, I act as a role model by example because I'm an active composer, and I love to teach. It's a good combination for them, because I'm not just talking words. I do it myself.

JK: [Looking at a room full of scores, books, and notes.] This is an archive of the life of a great composer. Where are you going to put all of this?

JT: It's going to Bard [College] in my will.

JK: It would make Bard a destination to study Joan Tower.

JT: I have a person there who would take care of it, which is very important.

JK: Especially with so much music out there, it's so easy for things to get lost.

JT: Especially for women composers, who were, until recently, lost throughout history. And the only ones to survive were attached to a man in some way or other. The ones that were not were in a convent somewhere.

JK: I think about Hildegard von Bingen a lot, actually. I really wonder what it would have been like had she lived in the twentieth or twenty-first century.

JT: She had economic power. She could call the shots on a lot of things. Most women did not have economic power. That was the key at that time. You know, Nancy Reich, biographer of Clara Schumann, is the person who changed my life. She came [to Bard] for a semester to teach and taught a course called Women in Music. I was totally naïve, and I knew nothing about this subject, so I asked to sit in on her class knowing I couldn't take too much of it because I was so busy. I went the first day, she opened her mouth, and I was like, "Excuse me?" My hand was up in the air, and I was at every class. I learned so much. At Columbia, the history-of-music courses were very heavy, incredibly "serious stuff." A lot of it at that time was boring to me, because I was more into playing and composing and being out there doing music. So when [Nancy Reich's] course was offered, I was assuming it would go like that. But it had a totally different effect on me because the historical information was so fascinating to me—maybe because it was part of "my" history as a woman. I started understanding more about where I came from—the history of women composers.

JK: Is there still a need then for women's-only festivals and concerts?

JT: Absolutely, because to me it's like a research thing. It's like going to a festival of electronic music to learn more about the latest technology. It's a subject, and if you're part of that subject, I think it's important to know that history. I think at a women's festival you can do that. For instance, you can hear about the all-women's orchestras in the 1920s.

JK: What do you think about the argument that it becomes a subcategory? Instead of labeling it as simply "composer," we're marginalizing it by saying "woman composer."

JT: I never got the connection between the word "marginalization" and women. The fact that it's a gender-related subject to me is not the issue. The issue is that women have had a different experience than men, different history, different everything. It's a subject for research and understanding, and the more you know about it, the more tools you have to talk about it and understand where you came from. I think there's a hugely important thing there. And I came from Beethoven. I played Beethoven my whole life, and I played Chopin, because they were my favorites. I loved them, and they were my teachers in a way. But that's only one part of it. There's another whole part of it that has to do with my thinking as a woman composer.

JK: Are events like women's music festivals going to put more women in the textbooks and in publishing houses and on the big-money concerts?

JT: I don't think festivals actually fulfill that kind of function. I think the music fulfills that kind of function. The music has to be strong enough that it will be heard and repeated and played a lot. If it has that kind of power, then it will go into the books. I think the music is the driving force behind everything.

JK: So, we're just beyond the first decade of the twenty-first century. What is women's place in the textbook and concert hall?

JT: You know, my first thought about that is a very interesting one. Men are good at taking positions. That's a generalization, I know, but women don't normally like to do that, at least historically speaking and musicologically speaking. There are some of us who will take positions on panels, but I find writing about taking a position much harder unless you're a really good writer. So, either the dialogue has to change, or women have to learn to take positions in the male language or in their own language. Susan McClary took a position and was one of the very first to take a very strong, very radical position, and she got shot down from every side you could imagine and probably got hurt by that and probably retreated somewhat, is my guess. Of course, some of her positions were out there. But in a way it was like the radical feminists of the sixties, where they took these extreme positions, and they moved the entire dialogue over to the center by taking those positions. I think that's what she did, actually: she played a huge role in moving that dialogue over. I really have to hand it to her, because it must have been pretty devastating for her. She was the moving target.

JK: So you're saying we need more people willing to take a position like that?

JT: We need more people like her.

JK: What do you think about the labels? What do you think when somebody labels you as an "American composer" or "woman composer"?

JT: The American thing is interesting, because I actually resented that more than I resented the woman thing, because the word "American" conjured up all these ideas of Wonder Bread and "unsubtle." I grew up in South America, so I have a certain perspective on what "American" means, and it's not always good. I actually now understand why I'm called an American composer. I understand more about why that stylistic thing happens. The label "woman," I don't mind at all. In fact, I'm proud of it. They also call me "traditional" because I am retro compared to Pauline

[Oliveros] or Terry Riley or John Adams. Traditional? Yes, I guess so. Beethoven and Chopin (but also Latin music and jazz) have had big impacts on my voice and kept me in the "midtown" culture of music. (I left the "uptown" one in the 1970s.)

JK: So many composers and women in music refer to you as one of the few women composers on whose shoulders they stand.

JT: Well, that's nice. I like to hear that. I just had lunch with Jennifer [Higdon], and she said that to me. And it's a real compliment to know that you're affecting later generations.

JK: Do you stand on anybody's shoulders?

JT: Of women? No, because I didn't grow up with them at all, because they weren't around. The ones that were around, Miriam Gideon and Louise Talma, I liked them as people, and I knew them a lot, and we played their music constantly. But the music is not strong enough for me to stand on their shoulders. I didn't know Ruth Crawford Seeger or Amy Beach at all at the time. The shoulders I stood on were Beethoven, Stravinsky, Chopin, then Messiaen, Tchaikovsky. And I was married to a jazz musician, so I heard a lot of jazz people. That had an unconscious effect on me, particularly [Thelonius] Monk and Bill Evans, pianists. Then there was a lot of Latin music I was influenced by, because I spent a lot of time dancing and going to parties in Latin America and playing percussion, so a lot of that came into my music unconsciously. It's there, but in a subtle way.

JK: Your emphasis on rhythm and percussion.

JT: Absolutely. That all came from Latin American music.

JK: What did you get from jazz?

JT: Harmonies. There are a lot of jazz harmonies, but again it's not jumping out at you as jazz. Particular things coming from particular pieces in my music. I could practically tell you where every motive came from. It came from every piece of music that influenced me in some way or another. But the package comes out as my music, not as their music.

JK: No, your music definitely has a personality. It's Tower music.

JT: Thank you.

JK: Do you like conducting your own works?

JT: Yeah, I love it, actually. But it's a lot of work, and it takes a lot of time. I started conducting full-length concerts with Beethoven and all kinds of other people's, and I was in way over my head. I thought, "That's it, you cannot stand up in front of an orchestra and conduct something. You're not prepared. You don't have the time to learn these scores. Just do your own music." So I just do my own music.

JK: So how is it when you sit in the audience and hear another conductor perform your piece?

JT: It depends on several things. It depends on what a conductor's relationship is to my piece, what their relationship is to the orchestra, and how good they are—how musical they are and how good they are at conducting. For example, I've traveled a lot with Leonard Slatkin with the same piece, but different orchestra and different performance. Why? Because basically his relationship to the orchestra changed. This orchestra loves him, and they will do anything, and he loves the piece. Again, there's the conductor's relationship with the orchestra, which is significant. It affects the way they play my piece.

JK: When you first started being programmed on large orchestra concerts, they would often put you alongside Beethoven, yes?

JT: I don't like being next to Beethoven. No!

JK: Why don't you like it?

JT: Well, Beethoven is probably my biggest influence. And I think he's a really major-league strong musician. I don't like being next to him. I don't mind being next to Mozart, and I don't mind being next to Haydn.

JK: Because there's enough contrast?

JT: Yeah. And because it's lower-keyed, viscerally. And Bach—love being next to Bach. Perfect. When I went on tour with Orpheus, Bach preceded my piece. Perfect, because Bach is everything I am not. So it depends on who you're with on the program.

JK: It must affect an audience, the reaction to your music depending on who it's paired with.

JT: Exactly—who is before, and who is after. I've been killed many times by being in the wrong place among pieces that are too big.

JK: Are you conscious of the fact that composers who are starting out get excited about being paired next to a Tower piece?

JT: If I appear with another living composer, it's a miracle. It's always me and a lot of dead composers. Once in a great while there will be another living composer.

JK: So, where would you like to see classical music go?

JT: I have my own theory of why classical music is in trouble, and I think a part of it is that the composer and performer have split. This did not happen in the pop world. The singer/songwriter is the same person. Sometimes they're even the record producer. They do the whole package together, so you see the person who wrote the song. In classical music, the split of composers and performers has created a huge problem, because now the composers don't perform that much, and certainly the performers don't compose. You've got two different relationships to music, which are not codependent the way they are in the pop world. So composers forget what the performers are thinking about because they're not doing it themselves, and the performers forget what the composers are thinking about because they're not doing the composing. So they just follow directions. They learn how to follow directions really well. They learn how to sight-read and how to play their instrument really well. But they don't learn to think about how to make music. And they also go off into different institutions, conservatories, or universities. The other problem is, we are losing the people in the schools teaching violin and the other string instruments. Why? Because mostly they don't care about teaching their students how to play violin because they don't consider it that culturally significant anymore. So we've lost that audience, actually. That young audience is disappearing fast. (The winds are doing better because of the preservation of bands.)

JK: Do composers have a responsibility to write for the people who are able to play new music?

JT: Absolutely. Composers can write anything. . . . I tell my students, "If you have a triangle to write for, or two triangles would help [*laughs*], then that's what you have. And if they only know half-notes, then that's what you have. You have half-notes for triangles." That's not the problem. The problem is the person's attitude towards the person they are asking. That's the problem. I've discovered in the community orchestras that there's not a lot of living composers played. They think the music is too hard for them. It's a myth, the same way the choral world has this myth of "I can't count." I spent all my time through the *Made in America* program (and working with twenty out of sixty-five orchestras) trying to get them to change their attitude about, "Hey, there are composers in your community who would love to write for you." "Really they would love to write for us?" "Yes, and then you have to tell them what you can handle. And you talk to them. You negotiate it." I've spent hours doing that with them. There's a mythological connection all over the place on both sides.

JK: Well, maybe that's one of the keys, then: get everybody together, and start talking to one another and playing music.

JT: But then there's the perception of the audience. "Oh, but the audience isn't going to like the music." I gave a preconcert lecture once to a very conservative audience of two thousand people. I said, "How many of you expect to dislike my piece? And be honest." Ninety percent of the hands went up. I said, "Okay, thank you for your honesty. Now you don't know me at all. How many of you think that's unfair?" Ninety percent went back up again. I said, "You're judging me, and you don't even know me." End of story. Standing ovation. The guilt level was so high [*laughs*].

JK: You set that up well. Besides, Beethoven's music wasn't easy to listen to at the beginning, either.

JT: No, and the players hated it. "This is too high, and this is too hard." Except there was a big difference. He was already famous.

JK: So what about the evaluation of music? There's so much music out there.

JT: That's the biggest problem, right there. That's what we've lost. Performers and conductors don't know how to pick new music because they don't know how to evaluate it. They're not practicing the idea of evaluation. They're lost because they haven't been picking new pieces. It's a skill, and it's an experience that you have to keep doing. It's a muscle you have to keep using.

And also we're told, "This is a very famous composer, so who are you not to like this?" We're put into a passive evaluative position because we're told this music is very important music, and if you don't understand it, then that's your problem.

JK: Right, so even if there's something about it you don't like, you're told you're wrong.

JT: And then that brings in the women issue, which we're coming full circle to. "This woman isn't really known. There must be something wrong with Fanny because she hasn't done very well." Who is going to replace that idea that Fanny Mendelssohn is an important composer? Who is going to bring that idea up to fill in that historical gap? "Well, she hasn't been played very much." Well, neither was Bach for a hundred years.

JK: I think classical would appeal to the younger generation if they felt they were allowed to have a real opinion about it.

JT: That's exactly what I say to audiences. I say, "You're empowered to sit in your seat and have an opinion about me. You are allowed to say, 'I don't like those cow bells.'" With Beethoven, it's like you're too small to have an opinion about Beethoven. So I welcome that. I welcome the opinions—the human component. That's what we need to do with classical music: humanize it again.

JK: Speaking of being human, you've written so much. Is there a time when the music just doesn't come, and you're stuck?

JT: Oh yeah, all the time.

JK: How do you get unstuck?

JT: You just wait. And you wait. And you wait. Or I draw. This is what I do. It's my activity away from the activity [shows her drawings].

JK: Do these go to Bard with your music?

JT: Yes. It's just a colored pencil. Nothing fancy. If I get frustrated with something, I'll start drawing, just as a way to change the energy line. I have ones I like and then ones I distinctly don't like. And I always identify the music I'm writing at the time.

JK: Wow. I'm not attempting to analyze it, but there is distinct foreground and background, measured detail, circular, geometric shapes. I can definitely see how one may find connections to your music.

JT: I usually have a wavy thing versus a geometric thing. Contrast. I like that because the tension is really strong there.

JK: Thank you for sharing those with me. As someone who gives advice to her students all the time, what advice would you give a young person thinking of going into composition?

JT: Start your own group, and have everyone in the group compose pieces for the group. That's the best piece of advice I can give. Because that way, they're building something creative that they can do their own work with, without relying on other people—rejections and stuff like that. They can make it themselves. And most of the composers that are quite successful now have done that. [Steve]

Reich did it, [Philip] Glass, Bang on a Can All-Stars, I did it. We all started our own groups. You can also control the style of music. The vision of what you want to do musically. You just have to spend some time raising money and getting a place to perform. There are details that you have to take care of. You have to learn how to do it. But at least you're controlling your musical environment that way. That's my best piece of advice.

JK: You must have frequent commission offers. How do you know which ones to take?

JT: I am very, very lucky. I choose from a lot of considerations. What am I going to learn from it? Because you're always learning. So that's very important to me—that the person who is calling knows my music, loves my music, and is playing an instrument that I want to learn about or that I already love.

JK: So are you still trying to get better as a composer?

JT: Oh, sure. It's a constant struggle. I don't think you ever stop with that. And any composer that says you do is not a very good composer.

JK: What are you most proud of?

JT: That's an interesting question. I've been extremely hard on myself all my life. I'm hard on my music. I think I'm proud of my work. I've worked hard, and it's about time I pat myself on the back and stop saying, "That's not good enough." In a way, that becomes a fuel line for doing better, which I find in my students. The ones who are hardest on themselves are the ones who are doing the best work because, like I said before, they don't assume anything. And it's a tough road. But I'm proud that I've persevered against a lot of odds that I didn't know existed. As a composer—as a woman composer—I've done pretty well, actually, and I need to pat myself a little more on the back for what I've accomplished. And I think it's because I stuck my sights on the right things.

JK: What do you mean?

JT: I didn't go for the credentials or the prizes. I didn't go for the money. I went for the music. I think that's what I'm most proud of, that I kept my sights on the music.

***

Works by Joan Tower

All works published by Associated Music Publishers unless otherwise noted.

ORCHESTRAL ENSEMBLES

Amazon II, orchestra version (original *Amazon I* for five instruments), (1979).
Amazon III, for chamber orchestra (original *Amazon I* for five instruments), (1982).
Chamber Dance, for chamber orchestra (2006).

Clarinet Concerto (1988).
Composition for Orchestra (unpublished, 1967, 1972).
Concerto for Orchestra (1991).
Duets, for chamber orchestra (1994).
Fanfare for the Uncommon Woman No. 4 (1992).
Flute Concerto (1989).
In Memory, for string orchestra or string quartet (2002).
Island Prelude, for oboe and string orchestra (1989).
Island Rhythms (1985).
The Last Dance (2000).
Made in America (2005).
Music for Cello and Orchestra (1984).
Paganini Trills: Yet Another Set of Variations (on a Theme by Paganini) (1996).
Piano Concerto No. 1 (Homage to Beethoven) (1985).
Purple Rhapsody: Concerto for Viola and Orchestra (2005).
Rapids (Piano Concerto No. 2) (1996).
Sequoia (1979–81).
Silver Ladders (1986).
Strike Zones (Percussion Concerto) (2001).
Stroke (2010).
Tambor (1998).
Valentine Trills for Orchestra, originally for flute (1998).
Violin Concerto (1991).

BALLET

Stepping Stones: A Ballet, for ballet and orchestra or arranged for two pianos (1993, 1995).

BAND

Celebration Fanfare (from *Stepping Stones*), (1993).
Fascinating Ribbons (2001).

CHAMBER ENSEMBLE

Amazon I, for flute, clarinet, violin, cello, and piano (1977).
And . . . They're Off! for violin, cello, and piano (1997).
Angels (String Quartet No. 4), for string quartet (2008).
Aspect I–V, for violin, cello, and clarinet (unpublished, 1960s).
Big Sky, for violin, cello, and piano (2000).
Black Topaz, for piano, flute, clarinet, trumpet, trombone, and percussion (1976).
Breakfast Rhythms I and II, for solo clarinet, flute/piccolo, violin, cello, piano, and percussion (1983).
Brimset, for two flutes and percussion (American Composers Alliance, 1965).
Catching a Wave, for cello and piano (2012).

Copperwave, for brass quintet (2005).
DNA, for five percussion (2003).
Dumbarton Quintet, for piano and string quartet (2008).
Elegy (. . . Forgive These Wild and Wandering Cries . . .), for trombone and string quartet (1994).
Fanfare for the Uncommon Woman
No. 1, for brass and percussion (1986).
No. 2, for brass and percussion (1989, 1997).
No. 3, for double brass quintet (1991).
No. 5, for trumpet quartet (1993).
Fantasy . . . (Those Harbor Lights), for clarinet and piano (1983).
Five Pieces, for violin and piano (unpublished, 1969).
For Daniel, for violin, cello, and piano (2004).
Gift, for flute/piccolo, clarinet, bassoon, horn, and piano (2007).
In Memory, for string quartet or string orchestra (2002).
Incandescent, for string quartet (2003).
Island Prelude (1989).
oboe and string quartet
oboe and wind quartet
A Little Gift, for flute and clarinet (2006).
Movements, for flute and piano (American Composers Alliance, 1968).
Night Fields, for string quartet (1994).
Noon Dance, for flute, clarinet, violin, cello, piano, and percussion (1982).
Octet, for flute, clarinet, violin, viola, cello, bass, vibraphone or marimba, and piano (unpublished, 1968).
Opa Eboni, for oboe and piano (American Composers Alliance, 1967).
Percussion Quartet (American Composers Alliance, 1963, 1969).
Petroushskates, for flute, clarinet, violin, cello, and piano (1980).
Pillars, for two pianos and percussion (unpublished, 1961).
Prelude, for woodwind quartet and piano (unpublished, 1971).
Prelude for Five Players, for flute, oboe/violin, clarinet, bassoon/cello, and piano (American Composers Alliance, 1970).
Quintet, for two flutes, two clarinets, and bass clarinet (unpublished, 1960s).
Rain Waves, for violin, clarinet, and piano (1997).
Rising, for flute and string quartet (2009).
Snow Dreams, for flute and guitar (1986).
Study I, for horn, violin, clarinet, and cello (unpublished, 1965).
Toccanta, for oboe and harpsichord (1997).
Très Lent (Hommage à Messiaen), for cello and piano (1994).
Trio Cavany, for piano trio (2007).
Turning Points, for clarinet and string quartet (1999).
White Granite, for piano, violin, viola, cello (2010).
White Water, for string quartet (2011).

SOLO INSTRUMENTS

Ascent, for organ (1996).
Big Steps (Homage to Debussy's Pas Sur la Neige*),* for piano (unpublished, 2004).
Circles, for piano (American Composers Alliance, 1964).
Clocks, for guitar (1985).
Composition for Oboe, for oboe (American Composers Alliance, 1965).
Fantasia, for piano (American Composers Alliance, 1966).
For Marianne, for flute (2010).
Hexachords, for flute (American Composers Alliance, 1972).
Holding a Daisy, for piano (1996).
Ivory and Ebony, for piano (2009).
No Longer Very Clear: A Suite for Piano (includes *Holding a Daisy, Or Like a . . . an Engine,* and *Vast Antique Cubes/Throbbing Still*), (2005).
Or Like a . . . an Engine, for piano (1994).
Piano Piece (1964).
Platinum Spirals, for violin (1976).
Red Garnet Waltz, for piano (C. F. Peters, 1978).
Simply Purple, for viola (2008).
Six Variations, for cello (American Composers Alliance, 1971).
Stepping Stones, for two pianos (1993).
Steps, for piano (2011).
String Force, for violin (2010).
Valentine Trills for Flute, (Associated Music Publishers, 1996/Carl Fischer, 1999).
Vast Antique Cubes/Throbbing Still, for piano (2000).
Wild Purple, for viola (1998).
Wings, for clarinet or bass clarinet (1981).
Wings, arranged for alto saxophone (1991).

VOCAL

Can I? for youth chorus SSAA and percussion (2007).
Descent, for a cappella chorus (2012).
Motet, for two sopranos, tenor, bass or violin, clarinet, viola, and bassoon (unpublished, 1963).

Valerie Booth O.

2

Shulamit Ran

Born in Tel Aviv, Israel, in 1949, Shulamit Ran was awarded the Pulitzer Prize in Music in 1991 for *Symphony.* She was the second of only four women to be given this award by 2012. Spending most of her youth in Israel, Ran came to the United States at age fourteen for advanced musical study while on scholarship from the Mannes College of Music in New York and the America Israel Cultural Foundation. Today, she is an active composer and the Andrew MacLeish Distinguished Service Professor of Music at the University of Chicago. During our conversation, she expounds on the fulfillment she gets from teaching and her process of fostering creativity in her students. Like Joan Tower, Pauline Oliveros, and Augusta Read Thomas, Ran emphasizes the valuable skill of being able to listen to one's own music and to the music that surrounds us.

Ran is a composer and a pianist, at one time performing extensively in the United States, Europe, and her native Israel. Her experience as a professional performer has given Ran a deep respect for performing artists, and she explains why she considers them her closest collaborators. At the same time, she acknowledges the responsibility she feels to an audience as she demands their attention for the time it takes to listen to a piece. Her own performing experience enables her to approach composition knowing what the most skilled performers can accomplish.

Like other composers in this book, Ran feels a strong connection to her birth country. Her devotion to her Jewish faith can be found within her musical subjects and chosen texts, such as her first opera, *Between Two Worlds (The Dybbuk),* commissioned by the Lyric Opera of Chicago in 1999. Ran discusses the experience of composing the trilingual choral work *Das Was Geschah (That Which Happened),* which premiered at the sacred music festival International Orgel Woche in Nuremberg, Germany.

The theme of balance is a powerful thread in Ran's conversation. She describes the agony and ecstasy of performing and composing and her eventual choice to focus exclusively on composition. Her awareness of the need for balance influences her decisions on how to be a working composer, professor, and mother. Her musical catalog is diverse, including acoustical works for instrumental and vocal mediums, and her descriptions emphasize the beauty of the creative process.

Ran has a positive outlook for the future of art music. Like Tania León, she recognizes music as a human need; and like Augusta Read Thomas, she believes that there will always be people studying at the top of their field who want to be challenged to compose and perform great music. As the artistic director for Contempo, the Contemporary Chamber Players of the University of Chicago, Ran explains her thought process for programming the best music in part to foster dialogue among music communities.

In addition to her Pulitzer Prize, Ran is the recipient of numerous awards, fellowships, and commissions, including the Kennedy Center Friedheim Award, the Martha Baird Rockefeller Fund, Chamber Music America, and the music foundations of Ford, Guggenheim, Koussevitzky, and Fromm. She has served as vice president for music in the American Academy of Arts and Letters, was composer-in-residence for the Chicago Symphony Orchestra and the Lyric Opera of Chicago, and was elected to the American Academy of Arts and Sciences (1992) and the American Academy of Arts and Letters (2003). Her commissions for orchestral works, chamber music, solo, and choral ensemble continue to be plentiful. The recipient of five honorary doctorates, Shulamit Ran's works are published by the Theodore Presser Company and by the Israeli Music Institute.

***

July 2010, at the University of Chicago

JENNIFER KELLY: In so much of what I read about you, you discuss balance: balance between the intuition and fantasy parts of the creation, and then balance within the discipline side of the creation. Is that a skill somebody taught you or you learned over time?

SHULAMIT RAN: I think it's something that just happens over time—striving to create music that, to me, seems to have a sense of necessity and rightness about it. I think at almost any point a really creative, imaginative mind can take us in any number of unforeseen and unpredictable directions for which there is an infinite number of possibilities. Yet, ultimately, it needs to feel as though nothing there is arbitrary. Nothing could be exchanged or replaced by something else. You want the final result to have a sense of inevitability, and for that you need to balance intuition and letting yourself really go with a measure of discipline. Let the mind take you into unknown excursions and detours. If it's been a productive, fertile day, I'm not going to miss out on anything my mind imagines. But at the same time, often I'm not ready to commit myself, and it will be on the next day that I will ask myself, "Is this really what I want it to be?" So that balancing act happens at the unconscious and intuitive level, and at the same time I am applying the best of my critical facilities to it.

JK: You are an advocate for exploration, so is it easy to go back and throw something away when you decide it doesn't work?

SR: It's never easy. At the extreme end of the spectrum, I've had situations where I had composed a fair chunk of a piece and developed it with great care, only to get to a point where I realized it was not what I was really aiming for, and I would be keeping myself in chains if I stayed wedded to it, trying to make it work no matter what. Sometimes the best strategy is to go back to an earlier point, and after weeks of work, start back at the beginning, but then usually it flows much more quickly. It's as though I had to go through a field of thorns in order to find my rose. So I often say to my students, "A day where you've spent time composing and then ended up trashing it all is not a day wasted." It's all part of the creative process—going through many roads before the right path is revealed. You would not necessarily find it without going through various other possibilities and explorations.

JK: It almost sounds like an agonizing process.

SR: Oh yes, it can be. It's the agony and the ecstasy. The agony part can sometimes take much more of the time than those moments of sheer ecstasy where you know everything is right.

JK: You had a very promising recital career, but then you decided to go away from performance and move toward composition. Was the process of learning a piece, interpreting it and performing it on stage—was that also agony and ecstasy?

SR: Sometimes. I really think that being in the arts, whether it is creating art or re-creating it, which has its own distinctive level of creativity, often involves struggling with the elements, or willing the materials, which can be torturous. You're striving for what, at least in your own mind, is perfection. A wholeness. And one can certainly make the case that perfection is an imagined ideal, but that's okay. You are still striving for it. You would have no goal if you weren't in search for that imagined ideal, and that's certainly true for performance as well.

JK: So what did your performance side give to your composition side?

SR: It allowed me the closest access, the greatest intimacy, with great music. There is no better way to know music and understand its inner workings than to be, physically, the vessel through which music happens. It made me the musician that I am. It also gave me a firsthand understanding of the reality of sound and what it takes to produce it.

JK: Why did you ultimately choose composition over performance as your life's work?

SR: For one, I started out as a composer. My first intuition was composing. And as important as performance became at some times in my life, deep inside I always knew it was really composition that I was meant to be doing. Concert life, with its practice and travel, got to the point where there was very little left in terms of time and mental and emotional energy. Little was left for composition. The busier I got as a performer, the less I was composing.

JK: Given that you had a professional performance career, do you think about the performers while you compose because you know what they experience?

SR: Absolutely. Having been immersed as I was in performance was one of the most valuable lessons life had given me towards my work as a composer. I have a deep respect for performers. I never think they are just there to execute what I'm putting down on the paper. I see them as my closest collaborators. There is great intimacy in the whole process. I've composed something, and it's on paper in the form of dots and lines. It is very much alive in my mind, and yet it needs the performer so that it won't just live in my mind or on paper. It becomes a reality. And so performers are my closest allies, and it's an extraordinary relationship. For me, it's the greatest compliment and fulfillment to know that there are people out there who are waiting for a certain date when I will be delivering a new work for them, and they will delve into it and turn it into the reality of sound. The performers are the ones who make the biggest leap in terms of a work becoming something of meaning that will have a life. And if the performer brings conviction and passion to the performance of a work, then the audience will come along—I am convinced.

JK: So when you give up a piece to a performer or conductor, how much freedom do they have for interpretation?

SR: In my scores I try to provide all the information that will allow an inspired and accomplished performer to take flight with it, making it their own. I want as much as I'm imagining, every musical choice I make, to be clear through its notation. I also add descriptive, expressive remarks very often.

JK: In the vernacular.

SR: Right. I think that helps the performer place him- or herself in a certain frame of mind as to what it is that I'm hearing, and as to what it is they should try to bring to the listener.

JK: Your direction "as a hushed prayer" is still interpretable, but much more descriptive than *pianissimo.*

SR: Exactly. You really cannot pin down everything. And at a certain point, if you do an excessive amount of notation and information, it becomes a blur. You have to know the balance between giving a lot of information and giving too much, threatening to take away from the spontaneity that the performer can bring. You want the performers to bring themselves into the act of performing. I certainly know that from my own experience. So if you're going to put articulation and explanation on every single note, then in a way you've stripped the player of the ability to make the kind of decisions that also involve intuition that a gifted performer brings naturally. There's a balance there, too. We get back to that word "balance." I want to help put one's imagination in motion in ways that correlate with how I hear a piece. At the same time, I hope that the performer will then look at the music, learn the notes, attain the command at a technical level, know what it is that I'm searching for, and, based on all of that, it can become a blueprint in a sense for a personal interpretation.

JK: A truly educated and informed interpretation.

SR: Knowing your performers and their special strengths, and letting that be a source of inspiration as well, is also very exciting and beautiful. And when you actually get to the moment where they are rehearsing and you see it come alive, this is the best that life has to offer for me, the composer.

JK: Is it an enjoyable process for you to sit back and listen to someone else interpret your music? Or can it be frightening?

SR: It can be both. I think the good news is that my music is self-selective in terms of its difficulty. It is difficult music to perform. So by and large, a certain caliber of performer will approach it. And consequently I think I've had really a lot of wonderful performances that have been profoundly gratifying.

JK: You also have an active family life. So how do you balance the work and non-work parts of your life?

SR: Well, that is definitely a big challenge, too. And a sea change, if there ever was one. Life becomes infinitely more complicated. I was in a fortunate position of being fairly established when having my children. So scaling down on some things, such as the number of commissions I accepted at any given time, or taking far fewer, shorter engagements that involved travel, was a choice that I made quite willingly. Before having children, when I was not actively composing, my mind was still working out musical ideas at all hours of the day. Without a doubt, having children changes all that. And priorities change, too. It's a huge juggling act, but there's none more gratifying and wonderful.

JK: That reminds me about your own story of youth, when you moved from Israel to the United States. I was struck by how supportive your parents were of your artistry and goals.

SR: I was extraordinarily fortunate. I chose the best home in which to be born [*laughs*]. My parents were extraordinary people. Their approach was, "The sky's the limit." This is what I wanted to do, so if I put the necessary hard work and effort, and really took it seriously, then I would do it. And my parents were not musicians. They had no professional knowledge of the field, though they had a wonderful intuitive understanding.

JK: I wonder if you have a similar approach to your composition students, letting them explore and go where it seems they need to go.

SR: Well, one of the great privileges of teaching in an institution such as [the University of Chicago] is that, really, the quality of young composers that we get here is amazing. When they come for interviews, I try to get to the bottom of it. Do they really understand what they're getting into and why they are doing it? Because the only good reason to go into composition is if you feel your life otherwise would not be the life you want to live. There has to be a depth of passion and need and desire. Otherwise you should not be doing this. If it is the case that you're considering options, then this is not the option that you should be taking.

JK: It has to be a calling.

SR: Yes, that's exactly right. For the most part, these students come with a sense of vision. I try to support and encourage that vision while developing and refining tools. I try to help by giving an objective set of eyes and ears to lend a perspective they haven't thought of. So it's a combination of encouraging their vision, listening deeply, and instilling a sense of objectivity.

JK: So it's more like fostering thought about their own work or helping to encourage their own creativity rather than dictating what to do.

SR: Right.

JK: That nuance of teaching would take balance. What does your teaching give to your compositions?

SR: There's no question in my mind that my connection to my students is an inspiring experience in itself. They bring such wonderful, imaginative minds and different perspectives of things. With that, as with any teaching at a high level, it keeps one on one's toes and stretches one. But in past years I also loved teaching the perennial Introduction to Music to students who came to the university with none or next to no formal music training. My biggest goal was to teach people to listen to music. I thought you could teach a bit of theory and some idea of history and some concepts, but more than anything else I felt the challenge was to make people listen, because so often music is considered background.

JK: It's everywhere. It's as though we're almost taught to passively listen. Active listening is tricky.

SR: Precisely. The very idea of active listening is foreign to people, for the most part. My aim was to help my students discover ways of listening to music differently. Every once in a while I still hear from someone who was here thirty years ago and lets me know of their experience in a class they took of mine. And that's gratifying. You feel you left a mark. Very often they have achieved things in other fields besides music.

JK: I want to go back to communication for a minute, because you talked about your music being difficult. I find it interesting that you chose that particular word.

SR: Well, I certainly don't come from the point of view that I want to consciously write difficult music. That would be self-defeating.

JK: But I do know people who consciously write accessible music to ensure it is played and heard.

SR: That is not my approach. And that doesn't mean it needs to be incredibly obtuse. Complex and obtuse are not one and the same. There are things that, on the face of it, are simple and direct, and yet there is a level of complexity in them, a depth, which gives more when you come back again and again. I just write the music that I hear developing in my head. Sure, sometimes that means the music will be difficult. I could use the word "demanding" or "challenging"—challenging technically or challenging rhythmically, any number of things. Fortunately, we're lucky to have performers with a high level of capability all around. And I always hope that there is a humanity and an emotional presence in the music that will transcend the difficulties.

JK: It is clear that you truly respect the performers. You respect their time and their effort and the fact that they're going to put that time and effort into a work of yours. I read that you include in that respect the listeners as well.

SR: Yes. As a composer I take—I command—the listener's time for the duration of the composition. I'm in charge of their time, and that's a big responsibility, because what is there that is more precious than one's time? It's the one thing that is not replenishable, so I never forget that. So, on the one hand, I write music for myself. I also write music for the performers, knowing they are the intermediary between the creator and the listener. They are also the ones who are going to be most intimately involved with the music, who are giving their time, talent, years of training, their soul. But then there's also the audience. That sense of capturing the listener's imagination and thought, perhaps pushing them in ways I did not even imagine, is incredibly meaningful.

JK: It seems that a piece doesn't seem finished until there's been a performance.

SR: There's a continuum. Let's say you're part of a rehearsal process, and you hear the piece as it is coming to life in rehearsal. That is deeply fulfilling in itself. At times you yourself reach a new level of awareness of what it is you have created. Especially with the first performance, I try to be present for the rehearsals. And I think it's very helpful if there is a sense of the composer's conception of the piece, and we're going to try to fulfill that as closely as possible. But at some point, you have to let it take on its own life. It's a special, joyous feeling.

JK: You bring up an interesting point with regard to having a life beyond the first performance. As a living composer of music that isn't necessarily accessible for your average college ensemble, do you worry whether the piece does have life beyond the first performance?

SR: I don't worry about it, because I think much more about the next piece I am writing. I'm incredibly fortunate that for most of my life, I've written works by commission. Just about everything I wrote was for an organization or a person who wanted me to write it. We talk about music that is difficult—and that has not stood in the way. But that is not the only way I want to have the opportunity to make an imprint. I also accept the challenge to write for situations that would not involve the top new music ensemble of the big city. And you don't necessarily want to write for an audience of only musically educated people. You want to write for people. But at the same time, you want music that you can say, "That's me." The challenge is how to make my voice sing and soar and dance in ways that cut across boundaries.

JK: I notice that you don't shy away from sophisticated texts.

SR: I think, at the end, a creator of any kind wants to leave some small mark on the universe. Some way of saying, "I was here." And I was here in all sorts of ways. I was here as a human being, a mother, a Jew, an Israeli, a person who cares about issues, and that's all part and parcel of the same thing. I am an heir to an extraordinarily rich heritage.

JK: When I listen to your music of text, it seems very important to you that as we continue into the future, we make sure we don't forget sins of the past.

SR: Yes, that's a very strong and accurate way of putting it. With today's media and technology, it sometimes feels as though we go through an evolutionary phase once a week. What was huge news becomes ho-hum five days later. But of course that's an illusion, a very dangerous one, as far as how we perceive life and what we need to learn from the past.

JK: In almost everything I read of you, despite the fact that you came to the United States when you were fourteen, you are described as an Israeli-born composer or even an Israeli composer. Is that a label you use yourself or others have given to you?

SR: It's very often given to me, yet I have never stopped thinking of myself as an Israeli. In terms of simple factual data, I'm a dual citizen. I am enormously grateful to the United States for giving me extraordinary opportunities and continuing to do so. At the same time, my Israeliness and connectedness to Israel continues to be incredibly important to me and expresses itself in many ways. It so happens that the most recent big work that I wrote was a work that was commissioned by and first performed in a festival in Nuremberg, Germany.

JK: Wow. Was it a difficult commission to accept?

SR: Well, the initial invitation was from the Rascher Saxophone Quartet for a collaboration with a twelve-person choir of Paul Hillier, the conductor. Later, they approached the Nuremberg festival, with which they had worked before, a fact that had an immediate impact on my vision of this work.

JK: Did you have control over the text?

SR: Yes, and my text choices had everything to do with the place where this work was having its first hearing. The piece is a trilingual text, with a fair amount of English, and also Hebrew, and German. It has biblical text and modern poetry as well. The title is *Das Was Geschah (That Which Happened)*. That was how the poet Paul Celan—a fragment of whose poem begins my piece—referred to the Holocaust in a speech he gave in the 1950s.

JK: And the piece was performed in Nuremberg. That's powerful. How was it received?

SR: I have to say, the performance and also the process of writing the piece was a really moving experience. The creative process was flowing in a very fervent manner and filling me with a sense of . . . awe. It was incredibly meaningful to write this piece. And to feel that through music I was able to make a human statement on things that matter to me greatly. There's no greater privilege.

JK: I certainly hope at some point the piece is professionally recorded for release, because hearing you talk, it seems like a real statement of your music. Do you think about things like legacy yet?

SR: One's life's work is one's legacy, and of course you hope it has the power to survive. And yet you must just keep on doing it and not dwell on that. You hope to have the good fortune of having the time to do more. Paradoxically, I sometimes feel that the deeper I delve into myself, the more I can connect with others. I think about the enormity of contribution that sacred Christian music has made to music. And I say to myself, we [people of Jewish faith] have an incredible reservoir of riches that I want to see known to the world through music.

JK: That sounds like you're headed toward even more choral music, vocal music.

SR: I want to write all kinds of music. At the same time, I am struck by how much has not been tapped on, and I want to be one of those tapping. It gives me a great sense of meaning to do something in that realm. I want to write more opera. Also, I love writing for multiple languages.

JK: So what is your relationship with text? How do you approach it?

SR: I come to it for its content, for what it says to me by reading it. I choose texts because I am interested in making a text come to life in music. I love setting Hebrew and really enjoy the different resonance that different languages give to the same word. I find that exciting to work with. Using different languages and translations gives you a richer pool from which to draw. Of course, the rhythm and the sound of words is very important, but for me it's all in the service of making the meaning of the text come to the foreground.

JK: Going back to the labels for a moment, what about adding other labels? What about "woman composer"?

SR: I think least about that, actually. Of course, I'm a woman. I like being a woman. I love being a mother and a daughter. All of it allows unique experiences, and I'm sure that in all sorts of ways it's part of my identity. But it has never really been a central issue for me for self-deliberation. Or doubts, for that matter. When I said before that my parents always instilled in me a sense of the sky being the limit, this was it. It was never about being a girl and "girls don't do this or that." I think I became much more aware of this being an issue when I came to this country, because this is where people asked me, "What's it like being a woman composer?" Really, no one in Israel asked me that question. There was Golda Meir, some women composers I was familiar with, and women went into the army as a matter of course. I grew up in a society where not a whole lot was made of that. I think the first person that made me aware of it was an American conductor who came to conduct in Israel. I was introduced as a composer and he said, "And what will the husband say?"

JK: Now in this country today, do you think there is still a need for things like women-only concerts, women-only CDs, or is there no longer a need for that?

SR: In a way I feel it is not for me to say, because I've been able to do what I wanted to do from a very young age and received a lot of support and confidence instilled in me, not having to worry about that issue, and am married to a wonderfully supportive husband. But I cannot, and should not, speak for others growing up with other circumstances and home environments. To me, of continuing concern is that contemporary music is still only one tiny corner of a corner. That corner happens to be very vibrant and exciting, and, in that sense, any way to bring music to people's attention, okay. If doing a concert with only women composers will get some new audiences to come who otherwise wouldn't, so be it. I think at one point Ellen Zwilich spoke very eloquently, not long after she received the first Pulitzer Prize in music composition awarded to a woman, about how in the past women did not have access to power. The power in this case is the power to have an orchestra play your music. I don't feel there's that kind of gender divide today, though for *any* living composer, male or female, getting orchestral performances is tough. I have many women composers that studied with me, and on the rare occasion that a young woman composer would make the case, "Oh, women composers have to keep together," what I say is, "Just concentrate on composing. Just write the best music you can write. Don't worry about the other issues because it's really about making the most of your abilities and time."

JK: When you're in a position to create a program, for instance with the Chicago Symphony Orchestra or Music Series, is there a sense of responsibility or need to present an egalitarian program? I don't necessarily mean as a gender-only issue.

SR: I am the artistic director of Contempo, the Contemporary Chamber Players of the University of Chicago. One annual event in the last several seasons since I've been doing this is a Double-Bill. The Double-Bill is a concert where it's almost two concerts with an intermission in between. One is of the type of music we are talking about, and the other one is music of a different genre—outside what people think of as concert art music. It's mostly been jazz. We've had some fabulous jazz. The idea being that it's a dialogue of listening, of audiences coming together. Various people have come up to me after a concert saying that they came here because of the artist in the second half, often a very well-known and well-established jazz artist, but this is the first time they have ever heard classical contemporary music, they really like it, and they're going to look for more. That's the idea behind moving across these boundaries. And the jazz artists I choose are ones I think would draw audiences that are likely to be receptive to contemporary music even if they may not have encountered it before. And I try to create a program that has the best musical flow, with pieces reflecting off one another in some way by contrast or by commonality.

JK: Programming is an art in itself.

SR: Exactly. And I always say to people that the program is not complete until every detail is put into it. One change can throw everything topsy-turvy. So it is a type of performance too, putting together a program. My first goal is to choose the best music I can find—music that I'm excited by and that I want to share with other listeners. It has been incredibly easy to program music by women composers because there's such a wealth of wonderful music being written by women. Every once in a while, someone will say that they are teaching a course on women's music and picking from our program. That makes me feel very happy, because it wasn't chosen for that reason. My only criterion is choosing music of top quality, and there's just so much nowadays.

JK: As a contemporary composer and as a professor, you make yourself aware of the other contemporary music that's out there.

SR: Of course. It is one of my tasks to be as aware as I can. I'm in a situation where I do residencies at different universities, so I hear other music. My music is performed on programs, so I hear music I wouldn't have encountered otherwise. My students have made recommendations. So I get to hear a lot. There is so much that is happening that deserves a wider hearing, and definitely a good amount of it is being written by women.

JK: So what can we, as the creators, composers, and conductors, do to ensure that art music is going to continue?

SR: Yes, that's the million-dollar question. One can get severely depressed about it. Or one can look around and see the incredible number of young people who have this passion to compose and to perform, and you say to yourself that music is going to survive. There's no way it would not. Making music is a human need. And I think, for me, that's the core of it.

JK: That's a very positive way to be.

SR: I wasn't necessarily always looking at it this way. Every year we get a pool of applicants hoping to become students here at the university and a long list of people wanting to study composition. And for a long while, I wondered if they knew what they were getting themselves into. Do they have any idea? What did they have in mind? And suddenly, at a certain point, I just stopped worrying about it. It's the opposite. This is the reason for hope, because there are so many and they need to do it. They are doing it with idealism and fresh hope and ideas. They are going to make it happen. I don't have answers except a sense of hope that comes from the doing.

JK: Is there a sense of responsibility that comes with being a Pulitzer Prize–winner?

SR: I think there's a sense of responsibility that comes with being alive [*laughs*] and indeed fortunate, having been given wonderful opportunities. A sense of responsibility that comes with being entrusted to teach and work with splendid young people. There is a responsibility that comes with every privilege. The Pulitzer Prize has certainly helped with gender identification, because I no longer get letters to *Mr.* Shulamit [*laughs*]. I continue to feel incredibly honored to have been given the Pulitzer Prize, but the sense of responsibility comes from a much larger desire to speak to those issues of human concern that we consider important. There is a calling.

JK: If you were starting out today as a composer at the beginning of this twenty-first century, do you have a sense of how your path might be different? I ask because you are constantly teaching young composers.

SR: My compositional life has intersected a good bit with a very difficult period in music. A period where twelve-tone [method or technique] became total serialism, and it got to the point where every dot and speck on the page was part of some matrix. On the other extreme, people were finding different ways of thinking about what music meant and what sound meant and how they all came together. There was all this music out there, some of which made absolutely no sense to me. Anti-establishment becomes an establishment in itself. It really was a difficult time in music to be growing up in. And I think that's different for people growing up in this generation—there is far, far greater freedom, it seems. Am I sorry that I went through it? That I was born at a particular point in time and had to grow through that? Actually not. Because I think it made me stronger, having to be more cognizant of knowing what really mattered to me. Also staying really curious, wanting to find my own way through the "anything is possible" and "nothing is possible" concepts. I found a way into something meaningful and coherent to me as a composer. That was a major challenge, and having to do it so young was especially challenging. It contributed to important things in my musical thinking. Now, we're at an age with far fewer barriers. There is no more of that kind of doctrinaire approach and far less dogma.

JK: You're very fortunate in that you are a living composer who has active commissions, an active musical creative life, and the opportunity to teach the next generation.

SR: Yes. On balance, I would not have wanted a different life.

JK: Today, as you are very accomplished and have been vetted on concert stages all over the world, do you still have the occasional moments of self-doubt?

SR: Oh, of course. Every day.

JK: How do you go through those?

SR: With each piece you start, you're starting with a blank piece of paper. There is a part of you that says maybe you already put it all in previous works. But that same voice also tells you that if you found it in other works, there is probably something left. So it comes eventually. Sometimes quickly, sometimes laboriously. Sometimes the laborious part is prolonged and intense. But this has been a good year, so I'm feeling good.

JK: What are you most proud of so far?

SR: You ask what I'm most proud of. My sons really, but at the same time that's a work in progress [*laughs*]. As a mother, you just keep hoping.

JK: I ask now about your sense of pride in music, in career, in work.

SR: There are moments like rehearsals of the recent piece *Das Was Geschah* and moments of my opera *Between Two Worlds (The Dybbuk)*, or the piece I am composing right now, where it all seems to come together. This evolves all the time. I mean, why write another piece if you don't feel that you have more you are inspired by? I always want to do the next piece really well. So I am proud of believing that the real accomplishment is still in the future.

***

Works by Shulamit Ran

All works published by Theodore Presser Company unless otherwise noted.

ORCHESTRAL ENSEMBLES

Capriccio, featuring piano (unpublished, 1963).
Concert Piece, featuring piano (1970, 1973).
Concerto for Orchestra (1986).
Legends (1993, 2001).
Piano Concerto (unpublished, 1977).
The Show Goes On (Ha'hatzaga Nimshechet), featuring clarinet (Israeli Music Institute, 2008).
Symphonic Poem, featuring piano (unpublished, 1967).
Symphony (1989–90).
Ten Children's Scenes (Carl Fischer, 1970).
Vessels of Courage and Hope (1998).
Violin Concerto (2002–3).
Voices, featuring flute (2000).
Yearning, for violin and string orchestra (available from the composer, 1995).

OPERA

Between Two Worlds (The Dybbuk), opera in two acts (1995–97).

CHAMBER MUSIC

Another Wedding March, for piano four hands (1986).
Bach-Shards, for string quartet (2002).
Chicago Skyline, for brass and percussion (1991).
Concerto da Camera I, for woodwind quintet (Israeli Music Institute, 1985).
Concerto da Camera II, for clarinet, string quartet, and piano (1987).
Double Vision, for two quintets (woodwinds, brass) and piano (1976).
Excursions, for violin, cello, and piano (1981).
For Dear Life (Linda's Music), for string sextet (available from the composer, 2011).
Invocation, for horn, timpani, and chimes (1994).
Lyre of Orpheus, for string sextet and cello solo (2009).
Mirage, for flute, clarinet, violin, cello, and piano (1990).
A Prayer, for horn, clarinet, bass clarinet, bassoon, and timpani (1981).
Private Game, for clarinet and cello (1979).
Quartet, for flute, clarinet, cello, and piano (unpublished, 1967).
Silent Voices, for fourteen players with optional reader (2010).
Soliloquy, for violin, cello, and piano (1997).
Sonatina, for two flutes (1961).
Song and Dance, for saxophones and percussion (2007).

String Quartet No. 1 (Israeli Music Institute, 1984).
String Quartet No. 2, "Vistas" (1989).
Three Fantasy Pieces, for cello and piano (1971).
Under the Sun's Gaze (Concerto da Camera III), for chamber ensemble (2003–4).

SOLO INSTRUMENTS

East Wind, for flute (1987).
Fantasy Variations, for cello (1979, 1984).
For an Actor, monologue for clarinet (1978).
Ha'llel, for organ (2005).
Hyperbolae, for piano (Israeli Music Institute, 1976).
Inscriptions, for violin (1991).
Perfect Storm, for viola (2010).
Piano Sonata No. 2 (Israeli Music Institute, 1963).
Short Piano Pieces, for piano (Israeli Music Institute, 1963).
Sonata Brevis, for harpsichord (unpublished, 1975).
Sonata Waltzer, for piano (1983).
Structures, for piano (1968).
Three Scenes, for clarinet (2000).
Verticals, for piano (1982).

CHORAL/VOCAL

Adonai Malach (Psalm 93), for cantor, horn, piccolo, oboe, and clarinet (1985).
Amichai Songs, for mezzo-soprano, oboe, bass, and harpsichord (1985).
Apprehensions, for voice, clarinet, and piano (Israeli Music Institute, 1979).
Credo/Ani Ma'amin, for twelve-voice chorus (2006).
Das Was Geschah (That Which Happened), for twelve-person chorus and saxophone quartet (available from the composer, 2010).
Ensembles for 17, for soprano and instrumental ensemble (1975).
Fanfare, for two multitracked sopranos; five-voice adaptation for live performance (1981).
Fault Line, for soprano and chamber ensemble (2005–6).
Hatzvi Israel Eulogy, for mezzo-soprano, flute, harp, and string quartet (1969).
Moon Songs: A Song Cycle in Four Acts, for soprano, flute/piccolo, cello, and piano (available from the composer, 2011).
O the Chimneys, for mezzo-soprano and chamber ensemble (in preparation for release, 1969).
Shirim L'Yom Tov (Four Festive Songs), for a cappella choir (2003, 2005).
Seven Japanese Love Songs, for mezzo-soprano and piano (Israeli Music Institute, 1968).
Supplications, for chorus and orchestra (1979, 2002).

J. D. Scott

3

Jennifer Higdon

Jennifer Higdon shares the company of Shulamit Ran as two of only four women recipients to date of the Pulitzer Prize in music. Higdon was awarded the Pulitzer in 2010 for her *Violin Concerto,* and she credits Joan Tower and Libby Larsen as composers who helped eradicate the glass ceiling for women. Born in Brooklyn in 1962, Higdon spent most of her formative years in the southern United States, and she grew up with the culture of the South and the sounds of popular music on the radio. Her youthful attendance at contemporary "art happenings" with her family inspired discussions with her father about the parameters that define music and art. These early experiences helped Higdon to define her own ideas of music and art and to develop an artistic style.

Recognizing the power of popular music to connect to people, Higdon shares an affinity with Joan Tower in humanizing classical music for general audiences. She is a strong advocate for art music and living composers, believing that the future of classical music relies on people's education about and exposure to the music. During our conversation, Higdon discusses the importance of granting guest appearances, live interviews, radio spots, and print and media information, all adding a human face to the compositional voice. Her music speaks to her advocacy, as she recognizes that people need to be invited into new music. She is regarded as an open and listenable composer with a musical reputation that includes high-energy, percussively charged, and tonal works. Higdon is among the most played living orchestral composers in the United States, at one time having one of the most performed contemporary works for orchestra in the United States, *blue cathedral.* Her approachable and down-to-earth demeanor matches her musical style.

Like Tower and Ran, Higdon openly discusses her great respect for musicians and for the composer-performer relationship, calling it a "complex dance" in which all partners participate. A trained flutist and conductor, she recognizes the needs and challenges of any musician who approaches new music. Her scores are easy to read, well marked and edited, and designed to avoid wasting rehearsal time with basic questions. Musically, Higdon writes for everyone in the ensemble, often passing melodic lines throughout the orchestra.

Since age twenty-one, Higdon has been consistently composing and having her works performed. Championed early in her career by the Philadelphia Orchestra with the commission *Concerto for Orchestra* in 2002, Higdon has developed a catalog that includes a number of large orchestral works, chamber music, vocal music, and an upcoming opera, *Cold Mountain,* commissioned by the Santa Fe Opera and the Opera Company of Philadelphia. In addition to the Pulitzer Prize, Higdon was awarded a Grammy for Best Contemporary Classical Composition in 2010 for *Percussion Concerto* featuring Colin Currie and the London Philharmonic Orchestra, conducted by Marin Alsop on the album *Marin Alsop Conducts MacMillan, Adès, and Higdon.* Other Grammy-winning albums that feature Higdon's music include *Jennifer Higdon: City Scape/Concerto for Orchestra,* performed by Robert Spano conducting the Atlanta Symphony Orchestra; *Strange Imaginary Animals,* performed by eighth blackbird; and *Transmigration,* performed by the Atlanta Symphony Orchestra and Choruses, conducted by Robert Spano. Over 250 orchestras have played Higdon's larger works, and much of her work is recorded.

Years ago, she made the decision to self-publish, and all of her works are now self-published through Lawdon Press, operated by Higdon and her partner Cheryl Lawson. In our conversation, Higdon discusses the pros and cons of self-publishing. She currently holds the Milton L. Rock Chair in Composition Studies at the Curtis Institute of Music in Philadelphia.

***

April 2009, at her home in Philadelphia

JENNIFER KELLY: Do you still conduct?

JENNIFER HIGDON: I conduct occasionally. I'm going to do that more down the road. I discovered that it took a certain part of my brain really learning the repertoire the way I needed to, and it was actually interfering with the composing. It's different parts of the brain, but they don't seem to work in conjunction. And even when you're conducting your own pieces, you have to study them with a different mind.

JK: Are you a good conductor of your own works?

JH: I don't know. I don't know if composers are ever the best conductors of their own works. I really have doubts about that. I actually trust other people much more than I trust my interpretations [*laughs*].

JK: What's the ideal relationship between you and a conductor or an ensemble?

JH: I always depend on the conductor to let me know what works for them, because every one of the conductors I've worked with is really different. So I take my cue from the conductor. I ask them before we start, "What do you want from me?" I usually only comment on balances, because I figure they know their ensemble well enough to know. . . . I can hear the inaccuracies and things like rhythm and things that are out of tune, but I know that stuff will get fixed. So I try to give them interpretive freedom. I try to assist with whatever hall we're in and what the balance is, which really changes dramatically from hall to hall. For example, we did my *Percussion Concerto* with the Philadelphia Orchestra, and we did five performances here in Philadelphia in the Kimmel Center, one at the Kennedy Center, and one at Carnegie Hall. So I got a chance to hear that piece with all the same players, but in three different halls. And I could not believe how different it was. It was staggering, it's so different. From that experience, I realize that I need to leave more up to the conductor and not put my hands in it so much.

JK: So when you finish a piece, when you give it over to an ensemble, are you someone who can let it go?

JH: Yeah, I'm able to do that. There are so many elements in a performance you cannot control, and you also want it to be a good experience for the performers. I'm lucky, because I always get repeat performances. The only time I worry about it is if we're recording the work. That's actually when I worry about it. But I try to get it right, because I know that pieces are going to get done a lot, so I do it. It's known as "bulletproofing" a piece. I try to make sure all the notation is correct, and that all the orchestration things are the best judgment for the greatest number of people involved—whether it's wind ensemble, one on a part, or three on a part. Then I send the piece out into the world. It's very labor-intensive, but it's worth it.

JK: What does the fact that you're a conductor do for your compositional side?

JH: Having sat in a lot of ensembles, and having played, and having conducted, the biggest thing for me is getting everything clearly down on the page, so that if I can't be there, it's an interpretive-friendly experience for the conductor. Because most of the time, I can't be there. I can remember being on the other side, sitting there [as a player] struggling through pieces trying to figure out, "What do they want? I can't even tell what this is." So I have a tendency to try to make it as clear as possible. It's a lot of labor on my part, because even in the notation you have to tweak everything. So if you have an orchestra score, you're going to have to tweak about half the stuff that's on the page to get it aligned correctly. It's clarity to help the people who have to interpret the music. If they don't have to battle the notation, you're that much further along on the journey of getting a good performance.

JK: Your tempi are printed large. Is that to help the conductor or because your tempi are concrete?

JH: I make large marks like that just to make it easier for the conductor. I'm not a strict tempo person. In fact, sometimes I'm telling people to do a different tempo than what I have marked, because I've discovered that ensembles change and the halls change a lot, and it really changes the piece. Actually, I was talking to Hilary Hahn about this the other day, because I've got her violin concerto, and we just started doing the first movement. The tempo was just too fast. I know why it's happening. It's the computers.

JK: In what way are computers affecting tempo?

JH: The music-notation programs. I've always written fast tempos, even before we were notating things in computers, so that's my internal rhythm, and I notice that I always have to pull everything down. But I have also noticed every student that I have—and even the works when I have to judge a competition—the tempi are always pretty far out of the reach of what they've written for the instruments. And a lot of the composers have never played, so I think they're playing it back in MIDI and think that it's a realistic tempo, and it's not.

JK: They hear it through the speakers and assume it must be possible.

JH: Yeah. So I think it's the computers. I think it's because everyone is doing computer notation now. No one is hand-writing anything out, so it's causing a real shift.

JK: Do you think that's happening with dynamics too? Are things getting louder?

JH: I think louder, yes, just because our whole world is louder. All the kids I talk to are iPod-savvy. I always ask the question, "Who has iPods in here, and what's on your iPod?" I asked this at a convocation at OSU [Ohio State University], and the whole room put their hands up. It was hundreds and hundreds of people. They all have iPods, and they have almost no classical on their iPods, so they're listening to a lot of rock and stuff like that that I think is just a lot louder. So their expectations in music are louder. It is shifting, and it's shifting fast.

JK: As well accepted as you are now, do you still have "freakout" moments?

JH: [*Laughs*] Oh yeah! It's in everything. The first couple of weeks are just a nightmare until I get the language of the piece down. We get into premieres, and I worry about things going wrong. Have I over-orchestrated? Is the orchestra covering the violin? We actually did a premiere of Hilary Hahn's *Violin Concerto* in February, and the violin part is hard. So I worry about how hard it is. Although Hilary is so amazing, she nailed everything. I worry about the balances. Have I written something that's too thick? So I obsess about that stuff. And I knew we were recording that piece. We were recording it in a couple of weeks, so I was really careful about trying to get the adjustments in with the two orchestras prior to the recording session. And little things like dynamics. The *pizzicato* needed to go from *mezzo forte* to *mezzo piano*. So yeah, I have lots of freakout moments [*laughs*].

JK: Do you allow yourself to change something drastic in the middle of a rehearsal process?

JH: No, I don't, because that's usually too difficult to deal with. I've had a couple of situations where I've only had one rehearsal.

JK: One rehearsal for a contemporary piece, really?

JH: For a huge orchestra piece, yeah, so you can't really change. It has to be minor—really minor changes. That's actually very stressful. Yeah, I've had quite a few performances with one run-through, and that was it. And that's not enough time to really learn a new piece; I don't care who it is. But sometimes that's all you get.

JK: So even though you're writing so much music, do you proof your own parts?

JH: I do. I do all the music copying. That's a little unusual, but I know how it needs to be, what the MOLA guidelines are—the Major Orchestra Librarians Association. I'm also very aware of what works for the orchestra players, so every time that I've actually farmed that out, I've had to go back and adjust so much that it was easier for me to just go ahead and do it. I don't get complaints about the parts, so it's worth putting the time in. And sometimes I find things there. I won't realize it until I'm doing parts, and I'm like, "Wait a minute. I have too many people playing on this chord. This is liable to cover the soloist."

JK: So it actually helps your music.

JH: It does, and sometimes I find things, and I'm like, "Oh, I forgot to put dynamics in this spot." Things that I might not have caught if I was actually just proofing it. The fact that I'm going through it really makes it a little easier to catch that stuff.

JK: Do you allow yourself to throw anything away?

JH: Oh, yeah. I throw stuff away all the time. Pieces. Sections.

JK: Put it in a drawer?

JH: Not only in a drawer, but away [*laughs*]. Burn it in the fireplace! Quick, before anyone discovers it! I do, because I think it's possible, no matter how experienced you are, to write a clunker. It really is. I've actually thrown away whole movements. There could be three movements, and I'm like, "It's too much." And I've just thrown out one of the movements, and it sounded so much better, too. But that's hard. It's not natural, but it works. You have to be able to do it.

JK: You allow yourself to write several hours every day, yes?

JH: On an ideal day, I'll get in four to six hours. If I'm traveling a lot, it gets harder to write, because I get more tired. I used to be able to work into the evening in the hotel. But I'm not able to do that so much anymore. I guess that comes with age.

JK: What's your basic creative process? Where do you start?

JH: Because I'm always working on commissions, I know my players pretty well. I find out what they want—duration, instrumentation. I get to know the group or the soloist. I remember sitting in on a particular grant process where a group had submitted a bunch of pieces fourteen minutes long. So when they asked me to write something for them, I said, "I know exactly what you need. You need a little piece. Just something kind of fast to grab your attention."

JK: That's your conducting side coming out.

JH: Yeah, it is. The practical. The programming is a nightmare. I think that is one of the things composers don't understand—what you have to balance when you program. It's serious, and you have to think about a lot of things. Can you afford to hire the extra players? What's going to balance a program? There are pieces that work well on a lot of programs, and there are some pieces that are not going to work with many other pieces. So I do think about that. I try to get to know the players, and then I go off and daydream a lot. I figure out what works for their instrument, because the pieces tend to change quite a bit from instrument to instrument. The players are different, the instruments are different, and their needs, where they have to breathe, and the way they do their phrasing. I do a lot of sketching by hand, and I usually start writing the piece out in manuscript, but at some point, not too far into the process, usually about twenty, thirty, or forty measures, I start entering it into the computer. Now, I don't have my computer set up to play back like an orchestra. It will play everything back, but it sounds like a piano, which is not a very accurate assessment, so I use my imagination a lot. And then it's just tweaking. I write and write and write, and I'll go back the next day, and I'll look at what I wrote the day before, and I'll say, "This is not good." So I end up deleting a lot of stuff, reworking, changing the rhythms, changing pitches. And I'll go back to a section three or four or five days in a row and keep adding on to that, and you slowly build up measures, an accumulation of music.

JK: Do you play through it yourself?

JH: No, I'm not a pianist. And my stuff doesn't always fit on piano if I'm not writing for piano. I hear it differently in my head, so I'm thinking about what this instrument is capable of doing.

JK: So it's all what you can think you hear?

JH: In my head, yeah. It's a good thing to be able to do. Although I'm discovering that a lot of people can't do it anymore, because computers do play things back. So they're not used to looking at scoring and hearing what it sounds like.

JK: Does the phrase "First thought, best thought" apply to you?

JH: Sometimes, but not always. And I'm often in the situation where I'm looking at what I've written, and I'm like, "Something doesn't sound right. This doesn't feel right. It doesn't look right on the page. What is it?" So I have to sit there and analyze. Is it the rhythm? Is it the counterpoint? Is it the harmony? Is it when the colors are changing? You know, I do so much rewriting, so I don't think [First thought, best thought] applies to me. I rarely get it in one chunk, and I always worry when that happens.

JK: How do you know when a piece is finished?

JH: I don't know if I've ever felt like anything was truly finished. There are probably a few pieces that I could say, "You know what? That's finished." But there are not many of them. You do have to let it go, especially if the piece is being recorded. You better get it as close to finished as you think you can and then just say, "Okay, I've got to live with it."

JK: You mentioned that the beginning of your process is often difficult. My husband often has to talk me down off of what I call the "artistic ledge."

JH: We call it the ledge. It's Cheryl. Cheryl's like, "Get off the window ledge" [*laughs*].

JK: So what sticks you first of all, and then how does she get you unstuck?

JH: I think anything can stick me. And she always comes back with, "You know it's going to be okay. You know you always get through this stage. You know it's going to be all right. And if it's not all right, it's still not the end of the world" [*laughs*]. I don't know if I ever come all the way off the ledge. Sometimes that slim element of fear, I think, is a good motivator. It's like staying hungry so you're hungry enough to keep pushing yourself.

JK: You write that music is communication. Could that be one of the reasons why you compose?

JH: Yes, absolutely. Because I noticed last week when I lost my voice for three days, I thought I was going to go nuts, not being able to utter a sound. I'm so used to doing preconcert talks and radio interviews, and I'm adamant about doing it, because I feel like anything that will help the audience or the performers or both understand the creative process and get them enthused about it is worth doing.

JK: It sounds like one of your goals is to help nonartists get excited about art.

JH: Yes, I do that all the time. I think actually we all need to be doing that, because I think the audiences are shrinking. I think, if we don't do that, we may not survive. There is less recording and less press coverage. Quite a few newspapers have folded in the past couple of months, and quite a few music critics have been let go.

JK: So it's not just in the publishing house and in the performance hall that we need to make the effort.

JH: It's everywhere. I didn't grow up around classical music, so I tend to look at this differently than the people who have always been in classical music. If you talk to college students, the thing they love about the music on their iPods—which is usually nonclassical—is that it feels very relevant to their lives today. So every day that goes by, we're that much farther from Beethoven. They've got so much other music that is, in fact, relevant because it reflects their current heart situation, their soul situation. Last week I had a performance with a high-school honors orchestra in Arizona, and the piece the kids got excited about was *blue cathedral.* They were excited because there was a living composer on the program. That's what they got excited about! They weren't as excited about the older stuff. I realized from the number of conversations I've had with youth orchestras that that is a much bigger element for young people than I think everyone working in the field may realize.

JK: Because the older generation does not have the same respect for living composers?

JH: Right! They have got opposite thinking. But the younger people aren't going to make their way into the concert hall, and that's who they need to be getting into the concert hall. The way an orchestra views it and the way the general public views it are really in different places. And I feel like I have to be an advocate.

JK: So what do we need to do? How do we save it?

JH: I think about it all the time. I do it by going out with orchestras and talking to anyone who will listen. Six concerts in five days. I did preconcerts for all of them and postconcerts for quite a few, and then I did a couple of public talks. And then I did a radio show and newspaper interviews. It was a lot of music, and it was a lot of talking, but I think that's what it takes.

JK: You're a strong advocate.

JH: Yeah, but we've got to get lots of people advocating. We need to teach that in school. I actually think that needs to be added—advocating. The business of music: running your own ensemble or selling yourself or convincing the radio station to do something. It's advocating in your business aspect of your music.

The younger artists that are coming out say that they have to have those skills. The older artists I know, soloists who play, they don't do it. I recently spoke with [an eighty-year-old musician] who said that when he was performing, they did the concert and they went home. They didn't have to do preconcerts, postconcerts, autographs, or anything like that.

JK: Because it's assumed that everyone will come back, and they assume it will be reviewed.

JH: That's exactly it. Hilary Hahn makes real effort to Twitter. She has her own YouTube channel. So when we did the concerto, we did an entire thing on her YouTube channel. She always signs autographs. She will do CDs. She goes out on the road and plays with pop musicians. She is always thinking, "What can I do to get this into people's hands to empower them?" So I think we need more thinking like that—new ways to present the art. And we also have to update the art. It speaks to some of us, but it doesn't speak to young people.

JK: I have musician friends who enjoy playing but are uncomfortable speaking to an audience.

JH: And you have to speak. I don't think it's possible for you to have a career and not do that today. Because I think enough people look at classical music as a stuffy experience and not a living experience. They think of it as a museum experience and not something relevant to their lives today. And that's the problem.

JK: How, in your opinion, do we build audiences?

JH: I think we build audiences by people going out and doing newer stuff in unusual venues. Bars. Street corners. The classical-music culture needs to change. That's a massive statement. The fact is that most classical music in this country is consumed through video games or movies. Those are the two places. That's why, when an orchestra announces they're going to do a video-game concert, they sell out immediately, and the audience is different than what anyone has ever seen. It's the same for the movie music. So there's got to be some way to jump on that. Also, things do best in concerts where there's a mix. I don't even like going to concerts where it's all my music. I'd really rather hear other things. So a mix is much better.

JK: What about when you're mentoring as a composition teacher? What do you encourage your students to study?

JH: I have a student who is writing a string quartet. I had him go do a comparison of Beethoven's string quartets, Bartók's string quartets, and then a list of really contemporary things written in the past couple of years. It was quite an illuminating experience.

JK: Your music has a contagious energy about it, and I can imagine that both artists and nonartists get excited about it. Are you told that a lot?

JH: All the time. The nonartists are the ones who bring it up the most, actually. To me, it's a priority. I take very seriously the commitment of their time when someone comes to a concert hall, pays the money, and sits during a concert. So if you're going to say something, be adamant. That's my philosophy.

JK: The visual arts are clearly a place of inspiration for you. *Piano Trio, Impressions,* there are so many. Can you tell me about visual arts and where that came from?

JH: Yeah, you see this painting up here?

JK: It's wonderful. I noticed it right away.

JH: Yeah, my dad did that. I grew up around so many painters, visual artists, and people doing experimental film, I think as a child my orientation of the world had a visual element to it. I'm always aware of how colors are put together. Shapes and where things are placed on a canvas. And I think I tend to think of that musically. But in music I do it with the instruments and what the instruments are doing. I think we absorb so much growing up. I remember in the sixties attending an awful lot of art happenings in Atlanta.

JK: Oh yes, didn't you attend an art happening where a gentleman strapped himself to a canvas with rubber cement?

JH: [*Laughs*] Yes! He passed out! He was wearing black clothes and a black canvas. The idea was that they were going to blow white feathers with a fan, and theoretically they would stick on him. But he didn't think it through. Rubber cement gets you really high really fast [*laughs*]. I was only six or seven, and I kept looking at the adults on the stage who were putting these things together, and I kept thinking, "What are they doing? They look ridiculous." I realize now that, for me, my art has to have a little more form to it, and that you really should think things out. I'm pretty sure it's because of going through those experiences.

JK: You learned your own boundaries.

JH: That's it. So, those were good learning experiences. Note to self: Really think this stuff out [*laughs*].

JK: Did that translate to you architecturally?

JH: Well, I take note of everything. It's totally piece-specific and what I want to do in the piece.

JK: So you know where you want to go, you're just not sure how you're going to get there.

JH: That's right. I know what the end destination is, but I may take a bunch of back-country roads. Because sometimes I know part of it is going to be a fast-moving highway, and sometimes I want it to be riding a mule down a country lane. So I tend to think in those terms.

JK: I read that you think a lot about the mountains when you compose. Which mountains?

JH: Smoky Mountains in East Tennessee. Part of my childhood was living at the base of the Smoky Mountains. I just find them fascinating, beautiful, exquisite. The power. The running creeks. The sounds the insects make when you're hiking. The stones when they knock against each other in the creeks. Everything about them. The smell. What it feels like when you're hiking after you've been camping for several days with a forty-pound backpack on. And it's the early morning, and no one is up yet in the woods. There's something about the mountains, especially the Smoky Mountains. There's majesty there and a peacefulness that I think it's good to have permeate a part of your soul. Nature pops up quite a bit in my pieces. Not so much in the past couple of years, but it has previously. I think not so much lately because I've been doing so many concerti, and those are usually so instrument-specific that I tend not to think about nature. But I do have quite a few instances where nature is really the inspiration.

JK: Where do you find your inspiration beyond that?

JH: The performers, always. That's the first place I go. The character and personality of the performer, what they're playing like. Ninety percent is the performer.

JK: How do you relate it to the drive to compose?

JH: I have to compose. It's some sort of therapy. It's just some form of expression.

JK: Going back to your beginnings, with all the blues and rock 'n' roll, country and gospel that you grew up with, how did you end up a concert-music composer? Where did it start?

JH: I started noticing it with the *Star Wars* movies. The soundtracks of John Williams had an effect on me. I was really struck by the power of that music. When I went on to study classical music in college, I hardly knew any classical music.

JK: So who said, "Hey Jennifer, listen to this"?

JH: Assignments as an undergraduate. And my flute teacher, Judith Bentley, who to this day I still think of as probably the most prominent composition teacher I had. She really had a profound effect on all her students. Her enthusiasm just pulled you in. And she was one of those teachers where you learned a lot of stuff about life. It wasn't just the music lesson. And she also wasn't proprietary in the same way that some teachers say, "You're only going to play flute and that's it." She would say, "I think you should try writing a piece," or, "I'm going to have you conduct a flute choir."

JK: Try everything.

JH: Yeah, try everything. Question everything. Always stop and think what works in a particular situation because what works for one person wouldn't work for another. You know what a good sign about her was? Not all of her students went on to become flute players. Some of them went on to make really incredible flutes, great flute companies. Some of them play in major orchestras. Some of them don't do anything in music, but whatever they tackle, they tackle with full enthusiasm.

JK: And Robert Spano? How has he influenced your life and work?

JH: Robert came to Bowling Green [University] the last year I was a student there. He was the new conductor of the orchestra. I had gotten into a couple of graduate schools, including Curtis, and he had just come out of Curtis. I wanted to get his advice, because I really respected him. And he said, "I'm not letting you out of this office until you agree to go to Curtis." He was so convincing that he convinced me, which is what a good conductor does. They pull everyone along on the ride. So I went to Curtis. And he was right. I can't even imagine what my life would have been like had I not done that. *Blue cathedral* was a piece that launched a lot for me, and Curtis commissioned that from me. They said, "Robert Spano is the one who'll be conducting this." He had just gotten the Atlanta Symphony post. Then, at the premiere, he said he wanted to record it. So he did, and that really kind of got the ball rolling for me with a lot of things. I learned from him that you better be serious about what you're doing if you're going to get up in front of a group. I realized that composing felt truer to me than playing or conducting, so I needed to actually go more down that path. If I was up on the podium, it would cause problems with the writing, and I didn't feel like a responsible citizen being on the podium unless I really, really, really knew the scores. I realized how important it was to be completely filled with whatever you were going to be standing on that podium conducting.

JK: Through this process, has your family always been supportive, even before you were a sought-after composer?

JH: My parents never said to me at any point in time, "No, you can't do that." They never said, "You can't do art. You can't be a freelancer." My parents never said I had to have a backup plan, and I'm very grateful because it never occurred to me that I might fail.

JK: I'd like to know your view on the labels. What goes through your mind when others identify you as a woman composer?

JH: I don't ever think about it. I don't, only because I'm always thinking about the music. When I'm writing, I don't think about the fact that I'm a woman composer writing this. I often think, "Is this the best I can do?" I'm only thinking about the quality of the music. So I'm not sure if it's an issue or not. In the very early days of my starting to get pieces performed, I did have quite a few instances where someone would come up to me, and they'd say, "I can't believe a woman wrote that." To me, that statement made no sense whatsoever. And I can't complain about not getting performances because I'm a woman because I get so many performances, so I don't have any room to complain.

JK: You said once you can really thank women such as Joan Tower and Libby Larsen for eradicating the issue. What did they do?

JH: They kept at it. They didn't stop. They kept right on going. I don't know how people think now. It doesn't really come up as an issue. I had performances with the Columbus Symphony Orchestra, and the conductor on the podium was Alondra de la Parra, a wonderful woman conductor. And I somehow did not realize until we got to one of the postconcert talks that it was a woman composer and woman conductor. It just hadn't clicked in my head until an audience member stood up and said, "Do you realize how big this is?" It was like an elephant in the room.

JK: Can you understand how that might still strike people?

JH: Yeah, I guess they haven't seen a woman composer. Now, when I do master classes with young people, a lot of times they're startled if there isn't a woman involved. The generation change is happening so fast with women, minorities of any sort, and even being gay. I think for the younger generation these are all nonissues. But this is the thing I worry about: classical music. Are we figuring that out also? Classical could be a nonissue to young people if it felt more relevant to them. It's just that we're not used to thinking that way.

JK: I know what kind of an influence my husband is on me. What kind of influence is Cheryl on you?

JH: Huge. I think Cheryl, first of all, is the one who talks me off the ledge [*laughs*], which is a very big thing! But I often think that, because Cheryl provides a safe space for me, it's easier for me to expose more emotion in the pieces. It makes it safer for me to be more emotional in general in the works themselves. It's got to be some psychological emotional balance, because I think composing feels hazardous. It feels like you're putting your heart out there.

JK: And now, you're tethered.

JH: It feels exactly like that.

JK: How do you feel about being called an American composer? What does that mean?

JH: Yeah, I guess I am. I've heard so many critics say that my music sounds American that I think I'm repeating it back. I suspect it has something to do with the rhythm and the clear sense of pulse, but, other than that, I don't know what makes it American.

JK: When you hear yourself on concerts, are you the only woman?

JH: I'm frequently the only woman, but I'm also usually the only alive person on the concert. I think it is a matter of living composers more than a woman-composer issue. I'm almost always on with Beethoven, Brahms, Bach, Mozart, and Haydn. So I think it is a living-composer issue. I don't know if it's an issue that I'm a woman or not.

JK: I wanted to ask about your sense of place in the world. You have a reputation of being very comfortable, friendly, and approachable. Your music is often also very welcoming. Is that natural communication for you, or is that a conscious decision?

JH: Oh, it's both. I think it happens naturally, but it's also my belief of what it should do. It's the southern upbringing. You go to someone's house, and you bring a pie. You wave to everyone on the road, whether you know them or not. You just do.

JK: Is self-publishing a blessing or a curse?

JH: I think it's a blessing. It's a lot of work. It's a whole lot of work but totally worth it. I've discovered it gets the music out there better because people can afford the music. They get a really fast response when they contact us. Sometimes we've had situations where we only had a couple hours to get the music out to someone. A good example of that was [when] the Minnesota Orchestra had a percussion festival going on, and they found out twenty-four hours before the first rehearsal that the soloist that they had engaged could not get a visa. So they tried to think of a backup plan. They looked at who was coming later in the week. Colin Currie was coming. He's a wonderful percussionist who lives in London, and Colin is the guy I wrote the *Percussion Concerto* for. So the librarian called and said, "If you can get the music here by 10:00 A.M. tomorrow, we're going to do your concerto." I did it, and they performed it. It helps if you have enough control over the music that you can get it out yourself. I've had quite a few performances with less than a twenty-four-hour turnaround to get them the music. Those performances wouldn't have happened had I not been able to get them the music in time. So I think that's completely a blessing.

JK: How do you keep the curiosity in the music alive?

JH: You work at that. I always refer to it as keeping the flame alive. I think keeping it alive is always being open to explore new things. I try not to allow myself to get into any kind of rut. So when I got asked to do a bluegrass concerto, I thought, "That's really different. I think I'll try that." I think you have to be willing to fail, too. And be willing to say, "That was awful. Let's throw that one away." I call it "staying hungry/staying foolish." It's something you do when you're younger and less when you're older, but I try to keep that attitude, the younger attitude. And so far it's worked. I don't know if it will work a decade from now, but it's working for now.

JK: What do you want an audience to go away with after they leave the concert hall and one of your pieces is on the program?

JH: I hope they leave with some sort of impression. I always tell audiences that I design my pieces so that you don't have to know anything about classical music. I mean not only do you not have to know anything about contemporary music, but also you shouldn't even have to know anything about classical music. What if this is your very first classical concert? I want the music to be able to speak to you even in that circumstance. So it's always my hope that the audience will come out moved in some manner and say "Wow." The "wow" is the best experience you can ask for. The best test of a piece, I think, is the conversations that happen out in the hall when I'm not around and people are having a spontaneous reaction, even a negative reaction. When you have a critic writing in a paper, "Holy mackerel!" and you're hearing all these spontaneous comments, that's a real compliment.

JK: That's how you know you made an impact.

JH: Yeah! I also know the performers did a good job. The performers have to believe enough that they cause that reaction, too. It's not just me, the composer. They're a part of the dance. I look at it as a complex dance, and there are a lot of us dancing. When all the elements line up, it can be an amazing experience. The fact is, most people don't know there are living composers. They tend to think of classical music as dead, and I think that's been the hardest thing for classical music in many respects. It's kind of made it less relevant. But it is incredible when you see people get so excited that there's a living person on the program. They want to tell you about how it affected them, and sometimes they say, "You know, I've got a cousin who wants to be a composer," or, "I've got a son who is interested in music." You can see this light in their eyes, and that's the best thing. It's the best job in the world.

***

Question asked later of Jennifer Higdon after she won the 2010 Pulitzer Prize for her *Violin Concerto*:

JK: Do you feel a sense of responsibility that comes with being a Pulitzer Prize winner?

JH: I do feel a sense of responsibility on behalf of all living composers. I sometimes (frequently) feel we are a minority (composers who are alive) in a minority group (classical music), and I think it's very important for me to speak out on behalf of the works of living artists. So I take very seriously every interaction that I have with audiences, within classical music and outside of it, to explain the importance of what we do when we create a new piece of music. I try to do all radio and media requests, preconcert and postconcert engagements, and donor and board-meeting requests, so that I can help folks feel more comfortable with the music of their own time. It's imperative for us all, and I've found that with a Pulitzer attached to my name, people tend to listen more carefully. So it is a responsibility that I take very seriously.

***

Works by Jennifer Higdon

All works self-published by Lawdon Press unless otherwise noted.

ORCHESTRAL ENSEMBLES

All Things Majestic (2011).
blue cathedral (1999).
Celebration Fanfare, for string orchestra (2003).

City Scape (2002).
Peachtree Street
river sings a song to trees
SkyLine
Concerto 4-3, for two violins, bass, and orchestra (2008).
Concerto for Orchestra (2002).
Dooryard Bloom, for baritone vocalist and orchestra (2004).
Fanfare Ritmico (1999).
Light (2006).
Loco (2004).
Machine (2002).
Oboe Concerto (2005).
On a Wire, for soloists: flute, clarinet, violin, viola, cello, marimba, piano, and orchestra (2010).
On the Death of the Righteous, for SATB chorus and orchestra (2009).
Percussion Concerto (2005).
Piano Concerto (2006).
Shine (1995).
The Singing Rooms, for violin, SATB chorus, and orchestra (2007).
Soliloquy, for various ensembles (1989). (See also Chamber Music.)
cello and string orchestra (version A)
clarinet and string orchestra (version B)
English horn and string orchestra (version E)
Soprano Sax Concerto (2007).
Spirit, for orchestral brass and percussion (2006).
String (from *Concerto for Orchestra*), for string orchestra (2002).
TenFold, for orchestral brass and percussion (2011).
To the Point, for string orchestra (2004).
Violin Concerto (2008).
Wind Shear, for orchestral winds and horns (2000).

BAND/WIND ENSEMBLE

Fanfare Ritmico, for wind ensemble (2002). (Orchestra original: 1999.)
Kelly's Field, for concert band (2006).
Mysterium, for concert band (2010).
Oboe Concerto, arranged for oboe and wind ensemble (2008). (Orchestra original: 2005.)
Percussion Concerto, arranged for percussion solo and symphonic band (2009). (Orchestra original: 2005.)
Rhythm Stand, for young concert band (Hal Leonard Publishing, 2004).
Road Stories, for wind ensemble (2012).
Soprano Sax Concerto, for soprano saxophone and wind ensemble (2009).
Spirit, for orchestral brass and percussion (2006).
TenFold, for orchestral brass and percussion (2011).
Wind Shear, for orchestral winds and horns (2000).

CHAMBER MUSIC/INSTRUMENTAL SOLO

Amazing Grace, for flute choir (2002).
Amazing Grace, for string quartet (2003).
Autumn Music, for woodwind quintet (1995).
Autumn Reflection, for flute and piano (1994).
Blue Hills, for flute and piano (2010).
Bop, for saxophone quartet (2004).
Celestial Hymns, for clarinet, violin, and viola (2000).
Ceremonies, for organ and brass (2001).
Clarinet Sonata, for clarinet and piano (2011).
Dark Wood, for bassoon and violin (2001).
DASH, for varied ensembles (2001).
  clarinet, violin, piano (version A)
  flute, clarinet, piano (version B)
  flute, soprano saxophone, piano (version C)
  soprano saxophone, violin, piano (version D)
An Exaltation of Larks, for string quartet (2005).
Fanfare Quintet, for brass quintet (2002).
Flute Poetic, for flute and piano (2010).
Impressions, for string quartet (2003).
The Jeffrey Mode, for flute and piano (1984).
Legacy (1999).
  flute and piano (version A)
  violin and piano (version B)
Light Refracted, for clarinet, violin, viola, cello, and piano (2002).
Lullaby, for various ensembles (1991). (See also Choral/Vocal.)
  two flutes, piano (version B)
  flute quartet (version C)
  soprano saxophone, flute, piano (version D)
  two alto saxophones, piano (version E)
  soprano saxophone, alto saxophone, piano (version F)
  flute, clarinet, piano (version H)
Mountain Songs, for flute choir (1985).
Music Box of Light, for three C flutes and harp (2009).
Nocturne, for violin and piano (2006).
Piano Trio, for violin, cello, and piano (2003).
Quiet Art, for string octet (four violins, two violas, and two cellos), (2006).
running the edgE, for two flutes and piano (1996).
Sax Sonata, for alto saxophone and piano (2001).
Scenes from the Poet's Dreams, for piano quintet (piano left hand, string quartet), (1999).
Short Stories, for saxophone quartet (1996).
Sky Quartet, for string quartet (1997, 2001).

Smash (2005).
flute, clarinet, violin, viola, cello, piano (version A)
flute, clarinet, violin, cello, piano (version B)
Soliloquy, for various ensembles (1989). (See also Orchestral Ensembles.)
clarinet, string quartet (version C)
English horn, string quartet (version D)
flute, string quartet (version F)
English horn, flute quartet (version G)
flute quartet (version H)
Sonata for Viola and Piano (1990).
Southern Harmony, for string quartet (2003).
Splendid Wood, for marimba ensemble (2006).
Steeley Pause, for four C flutes (1988).
String Poetic, for violin and piano (2006).
String Trio, for violin, viola, and cello (1988).
Summer Shimmers, for piano and woodwind quintet (2004).
Trio Song, for two C flutes and cello (2003).
Trumpet Songs, for trumpet and piano (2004).
Voices, for string quartet (1993).
Wedding Hymn, for various ensembles (1995). (See also Choral/Vocal.)
two flutes, piano (version B)
flute, clarinet, piano (version C)
soprano saxophone, violin, piano (version D)
wissahickon poeTrees, for flute, clarinet, violin, cello, piano, and percussion (1998).
Zaka, for flute, clarinet, violin, cello, piano, and percussion (2003).
Zango Bandango, for flute, clarinet, violin, cello, marimba, and piano (2003).
ZONES (1991).
percussion quartet and CD (version A)
percussion quintet and CD (2003), (version B)

SOLO INSTRUMENTS

Ceremonies Suite, for solo organ (2001).
Gilmore Variation, for piano, based on the "Goldberg" Variations by J. S. Bach (BWV 988) (Edition Peters, 2004).
rapid.fire, for solo flute (1992).
Secret and Glass Gardens, for solo piano (2000).
Song, for solo flute (1995).

CHORAL/VOCAL

Bentley Roses, for mezzo-soprano, flute, and piano (2002).
breaking, for soprano and piano (1999).
Deep in the Night, for SATB chorus (1997).

Dooryard Bloom, for baritone and orchestra (2004).
Falling, for voice and piano (2003).
Falling Deeper, for voice and piano (2004).
Hop and Toe Dance, for soprano and piano (2001).
In Our Quiet, for soprano or mezzo-soprano and piano (1992).
Lullaby (1991). (See also Chamber Music/Instrumental Solo.)
  mezzo-soprano, flute, and piano (version A)
  soprano, alto saxophone, and piano (version G)
Morning Opens, for soprano and piano (1997).
Notes on Love, for soprano, flute, and piano (1992).
O magnum mysterium (2002 original).
  SATB chorus, two flutes, two crystal glasses, chimes (version A)
  SATB chorus, organ (version B)
  SATB chorus, a cappella (version C)
On the Death of the Righteous, for SATB chorus and orchestra (2009).
A Quiet Moment (1999).
  TTBB chorus (version A)
  SSAA chorus (version B)
  SATB chorus (version C)
Red, for bass-baritone and piano (2004).
Sanctus, for SSAATTBB chorus (2001).
Sing, Sing, for SATB chorus (1999).
The Singing Rooms, for solo violin, SATB chorus, and orchestra (2007).
The Solid Rock Song, for voice and piano (2005).
somewhere i have never travelled, gladly beyond, for SATB chorus, vibraphone, and piano (2006).
Southern Grace, for SATB chorus (1998).
Threaded, for mezzo-soprano and piano (2003).
To Home, for soprano and piano (1998).
Voice of the Bard, for TTBB chorus (2005).
Wedding Hymn (1995). (See also Chamber Music.)
  soprano, flute, piano (version A)

Sabina Frank

4

Gabriela Lena Frank

A self-described "old-fashioned" composer, Gabriela Lena Frank writes for acoustic instruments in familiar forms and takes inspiration from her Latin American roots. Born in Berkeley, California, in 1972, she has a strong connection to her family identity, especially her Andean/Peruvian heritage as passed down through her mother. Frank considers the exploration of her Latin roots a lifetime project, and she recognizes the responsibility that project instills when her works inspired by Andean music are held up as authentic examples. During our conversation, Frank expresses why and how she holds women and other historically underrepresented groups to higher standards, having experienced firsthand the assumptions about and expectations of a composer with these gender and cultural identities.

Like Hasu Patel and Chen Yi, Frank's desire to create authentic work inspired by cultures outside of the United States is a source of inspiration.

As an artist, she collects ideas and images in binders, executes daily creative tasks, and rarely begins a composition with a blank page. Influential teachers such as William Bolcom, Jeanne Fischer, and Logan Skelton taught Frank that the notes on the page are only the beginning of music. A respected pianist specializing in contemporary repertoire, she interprets a score from a place of cultural understanding. Likewise, to interpret one of Frank's own compositions, one must seek the roots of its culture, for they are the essence of her work.

Frank was fortunate to be picked up early in her career by the publishing company G. Schirmer. Working with such an established publisher has introduced her to the challenges of modern notation. She explains during our conversation how balancing the sound one hears with the accepted language on the page is often a challenging task. Further, the sounds of culture are not necessarily easy to notate within a traditional European-influenced notation system.

As a twenty-first-century freelance composer, Frank is aware of the business of her profession and actively shares her developing knowledge with emerging composers. She describes thoughtfully and with a sense of humor how she balances her creative side with the necessities of organization and planning. Like Jennifer Higdon, she is a strong proponent of teaching essential business and promotion skills in schools. Urgently invested in the future of the art, Frank mentors young composers and performers of new music on a regular basis, modeling paths to creativity, exploring one's own compositional philosophy, and articulating the high stakes of composing as a member of an underrepresented population.

Among Gabriela Lena Frank's awards are a John Simon Guggenheim Memorial Foundation Fellowship, a United States Artists Fellowship, and the Brillante Prize awarded by the Hispanic Scholarship Foundation. She won a 2009 Latin Grammy for Best Classical Contemporary Composition for *Inca Dances,* featuring Manuel Barrueco and Cuarteto Latinoamericano, and *Gabriela Lena Frank: Hilos,* featuring Alias Chamber Ensemble, was nominated for a 2011 Grammy for Best Small Ensemble Performance. Frank's recent commissions include Yo Yo Ma and the Silk Road Ensemble, the Chiara Quartet, the Los Angeles Master Chorale with the Andean group Huayucaltia, the Indianapolis Symphony, the Kronos Quartet, the Los Angeles Philharmonic Green Umbrella new music series, Dawn Upshaw and the Saint Paul Chamber Orchestra, the San Francisco Chamber Orchestra, and Ballet Hispanico. She has been artist-in-residence with the San Francisco Chamber Orchestra and the Los Angeles Philharmonic and served as creative advisor for the Berkeley Symphony in California.

***

June 2010, at a café in Berkeley, California

GABRIELA LENA FRANK: Things have changed so much. I look at the women coming into the profession now, and they have completely different challenges from me. Personally, I'm not about electronics at all. I'm very old-fashioned, and you see these women that don't have any fear about going into technology. And some are hardcore gaming chicks. It's an identity that's easier for them, and I find that very encouraging. There are also more women of color who are doing very interesting things, and not just women who were born here but women born elsewhere.

JENNIFER KELLY: You're still a relatively young composer, and yet you talk about the difference between you and young composers today. I guess twenty years really does make a difference in today's world.

GLF: I think it is technology. These kids grew up with the internet, and that has changed everything. Look at social media and how people connect. One downside is that this has produced a kind of dilettante art, where you have people who listen to a piece with African drumming on YouTube or Pandora and then write a piece about it. But they really don't understand the traditions. I think these things take years to understand the DNA of the music. For instance, Finale and Sibelius notation software have fairly realistic playback now, and young composers are writing pieces on the computer using this software and then are shocked when they hear their music played by real musicians.

JK: So is all this technology that they're growing up with a detriment?

GLF: It's a mixed bag, like any tool. It's your responsibility to do your own homework, but technology can also open a lot of possibilities that are very exciting. So it depends on the artist having the wherewithal and the awareness to use these tools well. I find myself increasingly asked to mentor this younger generation of composers, whether they are people of color that come and find me (because still there are not a lot of us), or perhaps because I'm young enough that an emerging composer can relate to me. That has encouraged me to go and understand what it means to be an electronic-music artist even though I'm not one myself, so I can find the common ground to understand what their reality is.

JK: I find it interesting that younger composers, having grown up with technology and knowledge of electronics as compositional tools, come to you, a self-proclaimed old-fashioned composer of acoustic instruments. So whose responsibility is it to understand the other generation? Do you need to understand where they are coming from, or do they need to put the electronics away for a minute and experience acoustic sound?

GLF: Both are necessary. I don't think that artistry is a linear path. You're still getting to the same place once you walk that road to great music. If there's a lot of percussion and a lot of sound and excitement, you might realize there isn't a lot of substance behind the razzle-dazzle. Or it could be electronic music with cool sounds panning from the right and left along with a visual light show, but really there is not a lot to it. You break it down to the fundamentals always. I think what I have sometimes seen from people who haven't been represented well (women, ethnic minorities, et cetera), is that in an effort to advance their demographic, there is sometimes a particular kind of stink to their work when they're going for a quick, easy fix. But there's almost more of a responsibility, because there are not enough of us. There's more responsibility to really have your stuff down.

JK: When you say "not enough of us," whom do you mean?

GLF: Say you have a situation where you have shallow music being written by a woman of color, and shallow music being written by a young hot-shot white guy. I'm more bothered by the first scenario.

JK: Why?

GLF: Because it's a missed opportunity. There are not enough of us around. She committed the same sin; it's not worse. I can't blame her. But I have a personal connection to what this person embodies to me. She had a chance to overcome skepticism that is in place against a certain demographic. In that respect, I do have higher expectations. I have higher hopes.

JK: I have the exact same feeling for choral conductors with orchestra. I recently participated as a singer in a major-work concert where the conductor just didn't know the music well enough to command the choir and orchestra. He wasn't doing his job. And I heard the horn section say, "It's okay. He's only a choral conductor." Missed opportunity that hurt the rest of us.

GLF: Oh! We just reinforced something unfortunate, even if it's just by a little bit. People are fairly and unfairly predisposed to believe that about the choral world. It's not as valued as other music by many. And this could hold true for any group that is not well represented. When I coach chamber music with all-Latin groups, if they can't play in tune, I sit down and talk to them about the big picture. "Look, you've got to have these fundamentals down. You don't want to be playing the race card where you only champion a certain kind of rep and you can't play the rep in tune, and you're going to make it worse for us in the long term. And everyone will say they can't point it out because they'll be racist, so you're making it bad for everybody. So don't give this concert until you can play the music in tune."

JK: Do they hear you when you say that?

GLF: Some do, some don't. It's up to them how they handle it. I would do it with women composers too, but I might not make it as obvious a point as I do with the race thing. I do hold these two in slightly different positions, and it's not quite clear to me why. I don't want to just be on all-Latin concerts and all-women concerts. I do have colleagues that are largely programmed on all-women concerts. It's good to make a point, but you need to be out in the larger arena. It's a Catch-22. You are reinforcing the idea that this kind of concert is the only place for us. I understand that we're still in transition, and I think in some parts of the world there's a need for all-women concerts, and in other parts of the world there isn't. I have had the response on all-women concerts where everyone is so excited about it because some had never seen something like that, so it made an impact. Other places like New York City—why do it? We don't have to carry a big flag about it; we just do it. And no one blinks an eye. They hold us to the same criteria as anyone else.

JK: So are you consciously aware of being a woman composer?

GLF: Only when somebody else brings it up. You don't bring it up in a hostile or surprised way. And I understand that we need to keep talking about it, because there are still causes to be advanced.

JK: That is part of the reason for this book. And I have direct experience where my musical interpretation of a work was better informed after talking with the composer.

GLF: That makes sense, because I don't think understanding somebody's music is an academic question. Having played a lot of new music myself, I totally understand that. And I think it's what makes me a good coach. Because I know the kind of information that a performer needs to hear. Sometimes it's technical, but sometimes it's the context of it. For example, if I have a phrase, I may have an image of a vendor going down and selling his knives in the street in Spain. He's shouting, "Knives! Knives!" in the music. If the performers become aware of that, you suddenly see them bringing out the accents, or changing their bowings, or they're holding notes a little longer and are freer because you gave them something to hook into. Now they have multiple different ways of doing it. Before, they were doing it one way on the page, and now it has blood and life in it.

JK: Cultural context seems very important in your music.

GLF: Yeah, I think the questions I often receive from people I am coaching have to do with a culture they are not familiar with, so they can be very hands-off. They want to be respectful, which I really appreciate, but then they don't interpret because they don't want to go against a style or sound too "gringo." So what I try to do is explain the style and then tell them where the wiggle room is to interpret. "Look, you can hold it here. Try something. If it's offensive, I'll tell you." And they try something, and then I say, "Do too much. Do what you think is distasteful. Rewire your neurons. Hold the notes too long and make the fortes too loud. Then we'll scale back." I also tell them when it's great and it was their chosen way of doing it. It encourages them to have a real relationship with the culture.

JK: Going beyond the piece.

GLF: Absolutely. Encourage them to play other pieces. They start researching more online. They ask me, and then they'll research, and even correct me sometimes, which is wonderful! I'm not the "be all, end all." I wasn't born in Peru, so it helps me if I feel people are also on the journey with me, but that also means humility.

JK: It's obvious that you like to be there for a premiere if you can and work with the performers, but what if that is not possible? Do you think about that when you're writing a piece?

GLF: The majority of my performances I'm not there for. That started about five or six years ago when I really started to get very busy. But I've always had that expectation, not because I thought a career was going to happen but because I was emulating my own experience of playing the masters. I mean, Beethoven is not around. At the University of Michigan, I studied with a piano teacher (Logan Skelton) who loved Bartók and was a good model to me because looking at the Bartók sonata was only 10 percent of his preparation. The other 90 percent was him researching, trying to find out what Bartók was inspired by. So I thought that was normal that the score was just a starting point. Bartók was meticulous. He put in accents and phrases. He had six different kinds of accents for piano. Right from the very beginning, before I was even aware of how problematic it is to notate performance practice, I was already on that path of a very clear score that could communicate without the composer being there.

JK: How much freedom does a performer or conductor have to interpret your score?

GLF: I think I'm very permissive, because I'm very curious about what others will turn up, and because I did so much playing on my own.

JK: You come with a performer's perspective.

GLF: I really do. I do more composing now because that's how my career has pushed me, but my primary teachers were composer-performers. I am a stickler about tempi, partly because if you slow down the tempo of certain traditional songs, they become an entirely different song altogether. You can't really change the tempo or the feel of it. It becomes a different genre.

JK: So your tempi are going to be accurate in the score.

GLF: Yeah, I give you a range, the flexibility. But if the tempo is basically the same, and your holding moments are free—if you're playing with the time that way—I like that. *Rubato*—that gives it blood.

JK: What do you hope that a conductor can bring to your work?

GLF: That they can allow the music to breathe, since they're not actually playing the music. They're actually the middlemen. And my expectations are exactly the same as with performers, but they have to do all of that and be a middleman. I want them to own it and recompose it with their interpretation. I want them to find another reason for this piece to be alive.

JK: Is it easy for you to give it up to the performer and the conductor?

GLF: Well, the thing about contemporary music is that we need a good performance more than Beethoven does. People trust Beethoven because they know he had something to say despite a bad performance. But contemporary music? If we get a bad performance, people are equally likely to blame the piece, not just the performance, because it's harder to tell the difference. It's a new language, and the audience is experiencing this for the first time. They get one stab at it, and then it's gone. I like people who hold the moments longer and who set things. They get the foreground separated from the background. You have to perform the piece in a more exaggerated way than you might think in order to make the story really come through.

JK: Some composers say that the score has everything one needs to know. It sounds like for your music, the printed score is only the beginning.

GLF: It's only the beginning. That's my view. That's my music. You need to be flexible in what kind of study mind you put on. I was trained how Bartók was so meticulous, so I've become very meticulous with my notation. An old-school publisher, G. Schirmer, signed me up very early, and I learned that publishing language changes very slowly. Notational language—there are certain symbols that they use. For example, for a solo piano work I'm writing, they may not have a symbol for a particular way I want to break a guitar-inspired chord according to Peruvian Andean traditions. So, we're trying to work with what's already in the notational vocabulary, and we'll spend months trying to work this out before we'll use something new. Schirmer made me very aware of legacy. They have been publishing composers from hundreds of years ago, and when they start talking about your music that way, you start working with them in that. What I have also found is that people that are not familiar with Peruvian or Bolivian music and come across its influence in my music will then define that song or that genre according to what I say. So it's a big responsibility. And I'm at the beginning of understanding the culture. It's going to be a lifelong endeavor. I'm not the go-to girl that some people might paint me to be for all things Latino. So that's another reason the whole longevity thing is a very serious question, because my music is being printed, sent off to Europe, and people are performing and writing about it. I think it goes back to why I'm harder on the all-Latino string quartet. I can see that responsibility coming their way. They're going to be defining their country to parts of the world that they can't anticipate yet, and they have to be in the habit of doing it well right from the beginning.

JK: So you're thinking about audience even from the very early stages of the creation process.

GLF: I'm always trying to connect, but I also don't want to be tacky about it. And it feels tacky if you're doing something that you're not truly excited by but you think other people are going to like. You should try to do things everyone is going to like, including yourself. I'm old enough now to see the life-cycle of my pieces that have been around ten or twelve years. Smart composers understand the industry as well as where it can match up with what they want to do artistically over the long haul.

JK: When you first start composing, when the idea first hits your mind's ear, what do you hear?

GLF: I don't have one usual way a piece gets started. Sometimes it's a beautiful image, and I know I can do something with that. I'll write down the image and put it in my binder of ideas. I keep these binders, so I never start with a blank piece of paper anymore. Like writers are always writing things down, I have a binder with beautiful lines or images.

JK: You collect inspiration.

GLF: That's very much in my family. We have fertile imaginations. Sometimes it's a sound. It could be the way a performer plays one moment. I'll go write down what that moment is. Then I think it's like testing food to try and taste what the ingredients are so you can make it at home.

JK: How do you feel about musicologists analyzing your music?

GLF: I'm very open to what people have to say. As long as it's not, "She was inspired by the Aztecan culture," and I haven't done anything with Aztecs. That's not music analysis; it's more programmatic definition that they give something. There are a lot of inaccuracies in that way. In terms of musical analysis, sometimes I'm surprised, but it's valid. I often think that writing a piece of music is like having a kid. So they're *through* you but are not *of* you. And when they're about three or four, they start having their own little opinions about something they saw in the playground. And you didn't tell them that. They become their own identity. So I'm very hopeful that my music can do that too. I don't know everything there is to know about it. It also keeps my interest alive in the piece itself. And there are certain pieces that have been picked up. If there continues to be a need for a piece to be played, and if there are recordings of it, and if I can do that for ten years, maybe that's the same thing that has happened for composers who have longevity for two hundred, three hundred years.

JK: I've noticed you haven't entered many of those young-artists competitions.

GLF: I hate them. That's why a viable career working out for me is a blessing. Maybe a reeducation is needed. We were always told that's what you had to do if you wanted a career. You encourage that just by putting up competition flyers on the bulletin boards in the music schools and reminding people about the deadlines. That's the message that you're getting: that competitions are everything, not just icing on the cake. But I hate those kinds of competitions. So, I thought I was going to be a well-loved teacher somewhere. I wasn't really looking at the concert world. And when this route opened up, I just took one step at a time. Now I'm fully in it.

JK: As a twenty-first-century concert-music composer, how do you sustain it beyond fifteen minutes of fame?

GLF: I think it's rooted in the work. The work will survive the environment. People will find a way to play your music if they believe in it, whether it's in a museum or in an old-person's home or in academia.

JK: Would it be okay with you if your music were played only in those venues?

GLF: I mistrust the accolades, and I'm making money now, but I'm socking it all away. I know it may not last. When I first signed up with Schirmer, I thought if I only get five years with them for some reason, I'll come away with friendships and a perspective I didn't have knowing this part of the world, and I'll survive, so it's all a plus. One of the challenges is that you don't want to write for a world that may not endure. I'm on the board of several organizations that are asking this question with a new sense of urgency: What is the future of classical music? We've been saying for a long time that classical music is dying, and yet we're still here. There's a new concern for the viability of orchestras, for instance. Big, dinosaur-huge orchestras. I think the model may have to change. The old guys may go down kicking and screaming, but the new ones may not, partly because a lot of musicians are already in this apocalypse we've been talking about. The ones that are complaining about it are the ones that have been very privileged. I'm someone in between. I caught some of that good fortune being signed up by Schirmer, but I cut my teeth on the way most of my peers are making music. Some of my projects are in one world, and some of my projects are in the other. I'm always very careful, and I want to maintain my skills in the apocalyptic world so that if that happens, I'm not going to be helpless.

JK: Sounds like a lot of necessary management. It's not just sitting down to compose and create. There's a lot of business.

GLF: There is. About two years ago, I realized I needed to protect the part of me that's unrealistic, that's just creating. I read a couple of business manuals and set myself up as a business. On my computer, I have inventory, which is my scores, then my marketing, then I have my creative team. Once a month I have a meeting with the head of the creative department, that's me [*laughs*]. I just sit down, and my creative team digs up my music ideas. So my four hours a day where I just create I'm completely free. I feel like I've built up my net so I don't have to worry about anything, and that's my one rule to myself. I need to do that. So I'll talk to young composers and say, "You have to be able to write grants. You have to be able to talk to administrators so they don't make decisions for you not knowing what it's like being in the trenches. You have to be articulate and well-read in the arts." Again, I demand more of my women students and people of color. "This is an opportunity for you to make a difference, because you're going to have information which is not generally as known. So, do your homework. There's something to protect." My company is Gabriela Inc. You have to be a smart manager, which is different from a businessperson. It's not so much the money thing.

JK: What does it mean to be a composer today in the twenty-first century?

GLF: What I have found that it means is this piece of music that I write ends up being a starting point for a lot of different endeavors, so some sort of discussion happens. It can be verbal. It can be musical in the context that performers jump into the conversation. But they talk about it with emotion because it's not a lecture. There's that extra power that a lecture doesn't have. For example, if I did a set of songs about the indigenous experience, I could tell you about it, or I could sing it for you. And then you see it not done by panpipes, but you see it done by string quartets. Then the "discussion" is about the connection between cultures, and it's much more powerful. There's also the idea of the artist as citizen. You're almost by default put on the path of civic initiative just by being an artist. So what actually went along with my discovery of Latin American music was volunteer work. I tried to find a way to bring music into that. It started off very humbly, with my giving free lessons to African American and Latino kids in Houston. There was extra pride or joy in the parents if I found a little mariachi tune. The kid would add to it, compose around it, and they owned it. I think that for me, composing has led to an identity quest, a personal discussion that way, a way to engage in a civic capacity. Later on in grad school, I did volunteer work in a men's prison. At first, all my presentations were on Latino topics, but it branched off to other subjects. I would find articles in the *New York Times,* and we would bring it back to music making, and they could display their creativity. And these were guys that never thought about that; they were just trying to survive. But the fact that they could tell a story and someone would actually listen? There's something creative in that expression, claiming your space. I think composers seize attention because you're going to listen to us and interpret us. You're going to listen to us not just on the stage but also in your own private practice time, owning it. As a composer, you're taking up somebody's life when you do that. That's a type of civic responsibility, too.

JK: I want to talk about the notion of creativity. We all understand the validity of training and practice to hone our skills. But what can a teacher do to foster creativity and vision in a student?

GLF: That is often neglected.

JK: Who's done that for you?

GLF: Logan Skelton, my piano teacher at Michigan; Jeanne Fischer, my first piano teacher at Rice; and my main teacher, William Bolcom. The thing about the way these guys talked about creativity and vision was almost as a by-product. They talked about their lives. They talked about how practicing was just the beginning, 10 percent. My best chamber-music coaches were highly imaginative and really demanded, "What is your take on Beethoven, and why are you doing this particular interpretation on this quartet and not in this other quartet?" They demanded that you weren't just copying somebody else's interpretation that you heard on a recording. Most of my efforts to hone vision came about in a concerted, conscious way after I left school. I talk about that all the time when I get my chances to talk to a young composer. I tell them to all write artistic statements. What's your philosophy? If it's beautiful and a life story, how is that going into your music? So some of them I encourage to start journaling.

JK: About their music?

GLF: About their music. About their lives. You're going to tell a story. The translation from a diary entry into a piece of music may not be obvious, but get in the habit of always shining a light on yourself, as uncomfortable as it is right now. Then I have them look at artists that are visionary. It could be Frida Kahlo, Leonardo da Vinci, Mark Twain, Bartók. People that cut a real personality. Picasso, Martha Graham, Bill Gates, even though he's not technically an artist. What are the circumstances in your life that will help you? Then change it up—just do one little thing; do something goofy or silly. You're trying to rewire stuff. For instance, instead of warming up on scales every day, I open a book, and I will write a short little song. I give myself fifteen minutes, and it gets my ideas going. Sometimes I flesh out something really good, and even if it doesn't go with the project of the day, I'll put it in my binder. So my brain is used to reacting and turning out a lot of material.

JK: So you actively work on being creative.

GLF: That's right. And I say I have two paths. I have one where I'm slapping down notes on the page. That's maybe a quarter of my work. The other 75 percent is the stuff behind the scenes. I'm feeding my ideas, and then I'm ready to go. It's not a linear path. I just start, and I have this huge wealth of material, spillage left over from other pieces.

JK: You also have a physical challenge to being a music composer: hearing loss. How have you managed that?

GLF: I was born with hearing loss, so I don't know what normal hearing is. And kids are really resilient. So I've never thought of that as a serious handicap. I lip-read very well, and my hearing aids work well for me. I have perfect pitch, so in some ways I hear better than normal hearing people.

JK: I'm fascinated with the connections between the brain and the body and how that manifests itself in the arts. Your brother is a neuroscientist. Do you see a creative connection between art and science?

GLF: There's been a lot of interesting research in that field. My brother is one of the most creative people I've ever met. He could have gone into art, but instead he went into science, because he has an analytical brain as well. I absolutely believe there is a connection between the body and what comes out as ephemeral art. Look at something like Beethoven's piano sonatas. Those are a beautiful documentary of his hearing loss in progression. We know that his hearing loss disappeared from the inside out. And for the sonatas, the hands basically get farther and farther apart. If you look at the energy between the two hands, they begin very similar in the early sonatas, but with the *Waldstein* sonata you have thick versus very thin. You can study the contrast and the density of notes. They use that technique in speech therapy and deaf therapy for kids. And that comes out in Beethoven's music, which influenced all these hearing composers afterwards. I find it highly ironic. He started forming all these harmonies. Dissonances are easier to feel, vibration-wise. They have done studies in neuroscience about how deaf people mark time differently with events. We tend to like to fill up space with events, a chord or whatnot. When I read about the deaf stuff, it translates. And that came out in the sonatas. It's a physical perception that he had of the world.

JK: Your hearing loss is not officially classified as "deaf," but do you see that connection in your music?

GLF: Yes and no. It has to be there. I prefer to compose and practice without my hearing aids. I find that sound can be a distraction in many ways. And when I need to hear exactly what I think, my hearing aids are choosing to realize for me. I don't single out the deafness. It's a part of me the same way that Latina is a part of me and being a woman is a part of me. If I were a man, I think my music would be different, but not from some female gene. It's more the experiences I had as a woman traveling in Latin America as opposed to a man traveling in Latin America, for instance.

JK: I agree with you that we as human beings are the collectives of our experience. And our creative output is a result of our collective experience. So when it comes to storytelling, I hear women tell stories differently than I hear men telling stories. If music is a way of telling stories, then why wouldn't it come out in our femaleness as well?

GLF: The experiences of being a woman from how society has perceived us and treated us—those are stories right there. I could draw on myths that are female-oriented, like the crying woman. There's so much there. I have a viola concerto that's based on the crying woman. I have instrumental songs based on the crying woman that's professionally hired to make funeral services sadder. But that's not because it's a female gene. I also don't think there is a Latin gene, but there are Latin sounds and experiences. So I agree with you wholeheartedly. I'm not sure how I feel about the whole feminine-endings and masculine-endings thing. I've been to a few feminist musicology conferences, just as a fly on a wall. I do think you need to be pushing the boundaries. I'm not sure how pertinent a lot of this stuff is, but for the value of pushing the boundaries and doing it well, I absolutely support it.

JK: I like the fact that questions are being asked. It's promoting discussion and exploration, which then encourages people to listen to the music.

GLF: Exactly. As far as that having a direct impact on me, I don't see that at this point in my life. I have found that the syllabi for Women in Music courses that seem the most interesting to me are classes that listen to composers' music and talk about their lives and challenges. It's like a good documentary that moves you. It doesn't shy away. They show you something more thoughtful.

JK: I teach a Women in Music class at Lafayette, and the students are most interested when we talk about the lives and cultures of composers, the nature of power, and the nature of class—exploring whether nineteenth-century class issues still affect us, and other similar topics.

GLF: Because it pertains to today. I think it is good for women to know the issues are still here, and that might affect the music we write. We may actually feel more responsibility to conquer certain subjects as a result, to promote discussion. I continue to be educated by performer friends of mine about some topic that I've never really thought about before. They want to show me something, or they think I can tackle something.

JK: Was there a defining moment when you realized you were a composer?

GLF: When I chose composing, I was almost seventeen, and on a whim I took a summer program at the San Francisco Conservatory of Music. I didn't know that even existed. Music making had been so private, and I didn't realize there was this world. I think that's a common story for a lot of people. They don't realize that classical composers are alive. So, I did this summer program, and I walked into a music building—I had never seen a music building before. It had a piano in every room. There were staff lines painted and textbook music. And I remember my heart started pounding. And I went home and knew this was it. I had no idea what the life meant. I just knew the endeavor. I also saw that I had talent.

JK: So what can we as composers, conductors, and performers of classical music do to help concert music continue well into the twenty-first century?

GLF: Performers need to take on the role of educating us composers. Before I write a violin piece, I should have played [Nicolo] Paganini Caprices. I should be going in with all that training, but it's not possible, so I need someone to workshop with me. We don't instill that sense of responsibility in performers in a conservatory. It's primarily our responsibility, but we need to be educated. Conductors, same thing. Don't be passive. I was always fascinated to sit in on conducting master classes and listen. There are so many things you have to do. I would sit in on timpani-tuning master classes, and it was fascinating. It gave me a lot to write towards. So I think that's one thing that's very important. The other is for performers to educate the audiences, commentary, and your personal connection. You get their trust, and it makes the contemporary piece something real. Take five minutes out and play the main themes. I think, with a little bit of information, audiences can listen to difficult music and enjoy it. It also educates other musicians in the audience who may be resistant to contemporary music. I think that's important. And the composers themselves are so often not cognizant of our overall responsibilities. We need to do more than just write a piece of music.

It could be serving as creative advisor for an orchestra. We have all of this perspective we can give to them from our experience. We have to learn how to talk performer lingo. We have to know how rehearsals work. We need to listen to the great recordings. Ten different interpretations of the Bach cello suites—we need to know why each one is necessary. There's just so much that young composers need to be stepping up so we have something to offer.

JK: Who is in the audience nowadays?

GLF: I don't think our audiences have changed that much, to be perfectly honest. I get a little bit of an anxiety attack when I see it's still largely an older audience, certain demographics, certain income level. We need them. But trying to get a more diverse audience has been very challenging. I've done some things with the San Francisco Chamber Orchestra that have actually worked out really well—a concert series where the first half was classical, and the second half was Peruvian/Bolivian folkloric. The classical music had Haydn, and my stuff, and Bartók. We tried to show a connection. And you see in one fell swoop people of different backgrounds in the audience talking with one another. We had a little reception, and it worked out really well. We were in a couple of traditional music halls, but then we went into Latin American cultural centers. This is something we need to bring together—the different styles and audiences. Going out for diverse audiences and being in tune with what the younger generation is doing and include that. Going smaller rather than bloated. Rather than a hundred musicians, why not use the extra money to go into new environments? We were saying about educating our peers. We're ambassadors born into certain environments. We need to have these discussions in the places of training. It needs to be more accessible, and the only way to do that is to be daring. It's not to be safe and do more Bach and Beethoven. And I'm traditional; I love these guys. For instance, why can't we say bad words in our choral texts? That's the reality of today. Be human. Talk to the audience. Be a human face. It's okay to not play all the repeats.

JK: I read once that you're on a quest to find out who you are. Where are you today in your quest?

GLF: I think one way I've nuanced the whole Latina thing in recent years is to keep pointing out my clumsiness. I remember when I first embarked on this I was embarrassed that I didn't know as much about my mom's culture as I thought I should. I was holding myself to the standard of Bartók, daunted by the work he did, how much knowledge he had of the cultures. So I started to gain that knowledge, and it has taken me in a slightly different way of writing music as a result. I realized this is who I am as the daughter of an immigrant. Having been able to nuance and accept all the rough edges of being of mixed heritage has been liberating in the last few years. So I think having a more honest view of my identity has allowed me to acknowledge the whole picture.

JK: What did it mean for you to win a Latin Grammy?

GLF: That was a big surprise, because I didn't go after that. I didn't realize I had been nominated because my performers are the ones that put the CD in the running. The piece that won has Peruvian and Bolivian influence that is very subtle. That's why I'm very surprised it won. It didn't fit my perception of what I thought they would look for. So when that piece won, I realized I had some freedom in what it means to be belonging to a Latin persuasion. So getting that award educated me, too.

JK: How would you like your music to evolve?

GLF: I have a long list. I would like to write better. I want to do more fusion with indigenous instruments from the Andes and classical. I haven't gotten into the depths of all my binders yet. I would like the stuff that I do to be a schoolwide event with connections between different departments. This whole community involvement is more meaningful. I want to design projects in which a writer and I get to offer something on that scale. We can cause a ripple in this way, which is a starting point, and other people can come in, and they offer a lot also. I never anticipated that when I was seventeen. Even something like what you've done. I didn't realize that by putting my stuff out there, somebody was going to come along and make a place for it in her work or her passion. And I despair when composers stop composing. They say they don't have projects, and I say just do it. It will attract things, and you will be attracted to what it generated.

***

Works by Gabriela Lena Frank

All works published by G. Schirmer unless otherwise noted.

ORCHESTRAL ENSEMBLES

La Centinela y la Paloma (The Keeper and the Dove), featuring soprano (2010).
Compadrazgo, featuring piano and cello (2007).
Concertino Cusqueño (2012).
Elegía Andina (2000).
Escaramuza, for strings, percussion, harp, and piano (2010).
Havana Jila, featuring violin (2003).
Illapa: Tone Poem for Flute and Orchestra (2004).
Isicha and the Pistaqo (2013).
Leyendas: An Andean Walkabout, arranged for string orchestra (2001).
La Llorona: Tone Poem for Viola and Orchestra (2007).
Manchay Tiempo (Time of Fear), for strings, percussion, harp, and piano (2005).
Peregrinos (2009).

Raíces (2012).
Three Latin American Dances for Orchestra (2003).
Two American Portraits (2008).

OPERA

A Night at the Alhambra Café: Act I Finale, for Latina soprano, tenor, baritone, onstage violin, with guitar, percussion, and piano (2006).

BAND

Requiem for a Magical America: El Día de los Muertos, for orchestral winds and percussion (2006).

CHAMBER MUSIC

Adagio para Amantani, for cello and piano (2007).
Canto de Harawi "Amadeoso," for flute, clarinet, and piano (2005).
Canto y Danza, for flute, oboe, and piano (2009).
¡Chayraq! for violin, cello, percussion, and pipa (2010).
Cinco Danzas de Chambi, for viola and piano (2006).
Cuatro Bosquejos Pre-Incaicos (Four Pre-Inca Sketches), for flute and cello (2006).
Danza de los Saqsampillos, for two pianos or two marimbas (2006).
Danza Peruana, for two flutes, two alto flutes, marimba, and percussion (2008).
Ghosts in the Dream Machine, piano quintet for two violins, viola, cello, and piano (2005).
Haillí Lírico, for solo violin, strings, flutes, and percussion (2010).
Hilos, for clarinet, violin, cello, and piano (2010).
Hypnagogia, for two violins, two violas, and two cellos (2008).
Inca Dances, for guitar, two violins, viola, and cello (2008).
Inkarrí (Inca Rey), for string quartet (2005).
Leyendas: An Andean Walkabout, for string quartet (2001).
Manhattan Serenades, for cello and piano (1995).
Milagros, for string quartet (2010).
Mititos, for violin and piano (2011).
Puntos Suspensivos, for violin, viola, and cello (2010).
Quijotadas, for string quartet (2007).
Rapsodia Andina, for flute, harp, viola, and cello (2011).
Ríos Profundos, for cello and piano (1999).
Ritmos Anchinos, for string quartet, sheng, and pipa (2006).
Las Sombras de los Apus, for cello quartet (1998–99).
Sonata Andina, for piano (2000).
Sueños de Chambi: Snapshots for an Andean Album (original), for violin and piano (2002).
Sueños de Chambi: Snapshots for an Andean Album, arranged for alto flute and piano (2002).
Tres Homenajes: Compadrazgo, for two violins, viola, cello, and piano (2007).

SOLO INSTRUMENTS

Barcarola Latinoamericana, for piano (2007).
Khazn's Recitative: Elu D'vorim, for violin (2003).
Soliloquio Serrano, for pipa (2007).
Sonata Andina, for piano (2000).
Vendaval (Storm), for piano (2010).

CHOIR/VOCAL

Collanan María, for a cappella chorus (2004).
Compadre Huashayo, for three male voices, three quenilla, two flauta de pan, two zampoña, six toyo, six percussion, four charango, four bandolín, four bandola, six guitarra, arpa andina, and contrabass (2012).
Cuatro Canciones Andinas, for mezzo-soprano and piano (1999).
Holy Sisters: Part 1, for soprano, SSAA, and orchestra (2012).
Hombre Errante, for a cappella chorus (2002).
Jalapeño Blues, for a cappella chorus (2007).
New Andean Songs, for soprano, mezzo-soprano, two percussion, and two pianos (2007).
Pollerita Roja, for SSAA a cappella (2006).
San Joaquin, for a cappella chorus (2008).
The Singing Mountaineers, for SATB and five instruments (2011).
Songs of Cifar and the Sweet Sea, for soprano, baritone, and piano (more songs in progress), (2004, 2007).
Tres Mitos de Mi Tierra, for men's vocal ensemble (2009).
Two Mountain Songs, for SSAA youth choir; SSAA women's choir (2008).
Why Am I So Brown? for SATB children's chorus (2005).

5

Alice Parker

Alice Parker was born in Boston in 1925. The bulk of her catalog is composing and arranging for choir. Having grown up with the sounds of past centuries based on tonality, melody, and folk song, Parker was college-educated in twelve-tone technique (emphasizing the absence of a tonal center). She did not enjoy composing in this atonal manner, and she questioned what she had to offer twentieth-century musical language. Influenced at first by a teacher who said that she should not compose unless her intention was to write great works, Parker turned to choral conducting and earned a master's degree from the Juilliard School in 1949, studying with Robert Shaw. Her continued work with Shaw and her studies with the theorist and musicologist Julius Herford affected the rest of her life's work in music, and she collaborated as arranger for the Robert Shaw Chorale, publishing hundreds of melodic folk songs, hymns, spirituals, and carols. To date, she has been awarded five honorary doctorates and is known as one of the most important figures in choral music of the twentieth century.

While Parker is often characterized as having a traditional sound within a traditional field, her motivation has always been forward-thinking. In college, she chose modern dance as her athletic elective, influenced by Martha Graham's idea that all movement comes from the core. Her dance experience affected her later work with Shaw, as Parker honed her keen sense of rhythm and pulse. Her music, like her pattern of speech, is filled with movement, fluidity, and a sense of journey. Parker's fluidity of speech is apparent in our conversation as she discusses compositional process and the significance of the natural flow of spoken text. Additionally, her understanding that folk music endures into our later years as other speech and memory may fail is connected to new understandings about neurology. (Pauline Oliveros addresses similar issues in her interview.). Parker found her own compositional voice in part through realizing the function of song, and she begins our conversation by explaining that singing is an inborn way to express emotion. She insists that those natural expressions should be cultivated and advocates the teaching of folk songs to children and inviting their participation in the act of music making.

Through song and song-text, Parker works from a center of melody. Recognizing the limitations of notating speech, she expects her sparsely marked score to be the beginning of interpretation. Like the composers Gabriela Lena Frank, Chen Yi, and Tania León, Parker believes that understanding the culture of a song leads a performer toward an effective interpretation. She discusses how she has spent much of her life arranging folk songs, learning the cultural similarities expressed through songs around the world, and experiencing the joy and power of melody. Parker has published books on melodic styles, choral improvisation, and *Good Singing in Church* (Liturgy Training Publications, 1991). Her detailed analysis, *The Anatomy of Melody,* was released in 2007 by GIA Publications.

Parker's passion for teaching has kept her busy for decades, leading workshops and community sings, conducting, and offering composition seminars. She is a natural teacher who speaks with the gentle authority of wisdom and experience. Quick to acknowledge mentors in her own life, Parker credits Shaw and Herford with introducing her to the essence of music. Much like Meredith Monk, Pauline Oliveros, and Svjetlana Bukvich, Parker consciously works with the energy that is present at any given time.

Parker continues to compose, teach, and make countless professional appearances as a clinician, conductor, and teacher of choral music. Through Melodious

Accord Incorporated, she and her board of directors organize her workshops, produce a newsletter, and publish her writings, while the Musicians of Melodious Accord record her music.

***

October 2009, at her home in Hawley, Massachusetts

JENNIFER KELLY: You say that when we use our voices, we enrich our lives. How?

ALICE PARKER: Our voices are part of who we are, and I think that our society has a very funny take on, "You shouldn't sing unless you have a voice"—meaning a trained voice or a good voice or something like that. When we separate out that singing is something only for special people to do, it's almost turning on its ear what the rest of the world (particularly the Third World) knows and what we've gotten away from. For instance, I'm positive that we sing before we speak, and that every baby is born knowing how to sing. Singing is as natural as speaking, which any kid will do if they are sung with from the very beginning. Not sung *to* or music in the background, sung *with*. You have to be doing it so that you are releasing a very, very inborn way of expressing your emotions.

JK: I remember you saying that we need to teach songs to the children because when they are in their very old age it may be the only thing they have left.

AP: Absolutely. We see it over and over again in stories about people in nursing homes who have Alzheimer's. The song totally focuses them, which shows how deep it is in the mind. The mind can literally be eaten away by disease, but the songs stay in there. What do you have to draw on if all you have is the latest hit, which was written to be disposed of? Whether they are religious or secular or from the church-anthem world, if they are written to be the latest hit they are like Kleenex—you use them once and then throw them away. That's not what lasts. People will ask me where I found "that wonderful song," and I'll show them a source book they've seen all their lives, or I'll show them one of those graded music books you use in school. For example, in a first-grade book, I found a beautiful spiritual, *Father's Got a Home*. It's like a seed: it develops, and things grow out of it. Nobody looking at an acorn would suspect an oak tree.

JK: What role does folk song today play in our culture?

AP: Well, you have to define folk song. Because a whole lot of what is called folk song now isn't anywhere near close to it. So first of all, folk song isn't a list of notes, or scales, or rhythm, or chords. But it is function, like lullaby. I had a wonderful trip around the world, and if I had a chance to talk to someone with a child, I'd say, "Sing me one of the earliest songs that your children learned, or you sang to your children, like a lullaby." And it was always something I could sing back. I might not be able to get the language, but the melodies were very similar. First of all, they are all governed by human breath, so the phrases are similar in length, and there's always a certain symmetry about it. And when they would tell me what they were about, it was also remarkably similar. There were the animal songs, transportation songs, songs of the year, baby sleep, and the counting games for kids. All over the world it's just fantastically similar. Also, it is the function of the children song, growing-up song, love song, and the work song. Folk song is a living thing. It's not what you can print on the page. My view on music arranging is that you decide who you are as you are singing, and you write that arrangement. You don't just do an all-purpose one. I teach a course in melody because I'm just fascinated with the single-line melody. One year we looked at melodies from different centuries of Western culture, and when you came right down to the music, they were fantastically similar.

JK: When you say "similar," do you mean similar in pentatonic scale or. . . .

AP: They were very simple. They could be pentatonic, or they could be within one of the modes. And it was always half steps or whole steps. Another thing that fascinates me now . . . I think we should all be singing songs in Arabic, because we need to know about that part of the world, especially if we're going to be in there fighting. That means that we've really got to get involved with quarter steps. Learning a language through learning songs is a no-brainer. All language classes should start with songs, because you learn the flow of the language through the song. You lose the flow when we learn one word and then another and then the grammar. You know how awkward it feels when we begin translating. But we hear the musical language of speech in what any baby can babble.

JK: I notice in your musical works that you consider all the different voice parts instead of always giving melody to the soprano line.

AP: That was one of the great discoveries I made in all those years when [Robert] Shaw and I were working together. I learned so much about composition, much more than what I had learned in college majoring in composition. And Shaw never had a theory course; he heard what he heard. He never heard it through a set of rules and regulations. One of the things we discovered was that we shared a hatred of modulating up for the last verse. It just seems so corny. It's kind of saying this melody isn't interesting enough in itself to carry it, so I'm going to goose it up somehow. Modulating up for the last verse is about applying harmony, and far-out harmony at that, because you might not have had a single accidental in the whole piece until then. And we discovered that you get much more of a goose by keeping it in the key. For instance, if the melody is sung by soprano for three verses, and then in the last verse you give the melody in the same key to the altos: *Whooom!* You all of a sudden not only have all that extra weight on the melody, but you've released the sopranos to go above it. It's a much more organic way of developing it. You decide when you start on the version of the melody you're going to use, and you don't switch major to minor, or something else strange halfway through. You decide at the beginning. Then I would always memorize it, all the words. Choose the words you're going to use carefully. Memorize it, and sing it all the way through. And then I would end up writing what I sang, and sometimes I was very startled to go back and see what I was working from, the original source. I would discover changes in my creation, but they were changes from my working it through over and over again.

JK: So, if it were an arrangement, then would you feel comfortable to use what you worked through and sang through?

AP: Yes, absolutely. Because the whole point of the song, one of the definitions of folk song is there has to be more than one version of it. If there is only one version of it, it is probably a composed song.

JK: So in your own compositions, when you're writing your own melodies, how do you arrive at that melody with your understanding and respect toward the traditional folk song?

AP: I always start with the text. Getting those words right, knowing everything from the first verse to the last verse. All the time I'm working with words, I feel like I'm mining for the music that's hidden within them, saying them over and over, then starting to sing them, to see if there's some little bit of pitch phrase that attaches itself at some point. Sing it over and over. Don't write it down until you can really sing it in your mind, and keep it in your mind, the same words and melody, for several days. As long as you haven't written it down, it's fluid. If you write it down too soon, you get tangled in it just like a spider web. Writing it down is at the very end of the process of finding the melody and then finding the arrangement.

JK: How do you present it to others?

AP: With the realization that it's a conversation between two people, the singer and the listener. There are three ways of singing a song. One is to yourself, so the singer and the listener are one. The next way is to sing to somebody else, as if I'm going to sing you a song, and you're going to listen while I sing. That is most vocal recitals: sit still and listen. The third way is to sing in such a way that you're singing, but your song is going around and in back of the person to whom you're singing and enveloping them, so they just have to sing with you. Which is very different from sit still and listen.

JK: Inviting.

AP: Yes. And so it is the inviting way that gets people involved in the whole process. You've got to set it in motion, and it's people that have got to get it going. If you have it in motion, people can get on.

JK: Feeling the pulse.

AP: Yeah, exactly. We gave up folk dancing, so people don't move. They don't have any conception of carrying a tempo.

JK: When you are conducting your chorus, the Musicians of Melodious Accord, what is your role as conductor?

AP: The singers are really colleagues, professional singers who teach me quickly the limitations of notation: what interpretive markings need to be added. The main part is re-creating the piece, which is like the seed. It's going to be different every single time. I'm not going to try to make it come out the way it is on the page, or the way anyone else has done it. How does it work right now, with this group, in this hall?

JK: So you don't want it to be exactly what's on the page?

AP: I want it to be alive. The primary interpreter, the conductor, should really work at becoming the song. It's a position of trust between the writer and reader of the page to know that what is written is there for a reason. If you can't figure out why on earth there's an accent over that note, then probably you're not pursuing the same path the composer did when they wrote it. And that's your job to try and find that. What did the composer have in mind? How can I get myself in confluence with what the original creator was asking for to make this live interpretation? And then, if you want to do something really different, or if you have to do something really different, there's a reason for your choice, and you realize why you're doing it.

JK: I noticed when I visually look at your scores, you do have tempo and dynamic markings, but it's still very minimalistic.

AP: Overmarking is totally self-defeating. It's contradictory. The minute I hear people singing from an overmarked score, I know they're not listening, and they're not respecting the language. I like to see the nice clean page, because for me it's coming from the words, and I can't imagine anybody singing it without paying attention to the words. But over and over these choirs are taught the pitches and the rhythm, putting the words in later, so they don't get the kind of fluidity they need. There's no way of notating speech. For instance, the minute you go into blues or jazz, where you get a little bit of freedom, you can't write it. It's not a triplet, and it's not a dotted eighth and sixteenth. It's something in between. It's what we do all the time while we're speaking. I call singing overmarked words being corseted. It just sounds terrible.

JK: By interpreting the phrase based on text and how we would naturally speak, you also know that's going to change, depending on where we are in the world.

AP: Absolutely. And the spiritual. Are you in Alabama? Virginia? Texas? The language is totally different, so decide where you are.

JK: The music itself will change.

AP: Yes, because the rhythm is fluid, and the pitches are fantastically fluid. "Blue notes," we call them. Any violinist or clarinetist knows all those in-between pitches and how you can alter a note because of the melodic line. Do you want it sharp so you can get up to that next step, or flat because you're sinking down? Teaching [my music to] Melodious Accord, I start by singing the first phrase. I can teach them all the things I can't notate just by singing the first phrase. The way I'm handling the words, the basic tempo—is it a strong beat, or is it kind of liquid? The emotive content—what's the attitude toward it? Am I weeping or laughing? I can't notate any of that. I can notate 5 percent of the information I would like you to have. So you, as the person looking at the page, bring 95 percent. This is the swerving together. Be sure that your 95 percent doesn't overwhelm my 5 percent, so you are aware of where I was starting.

JK: There's still a balance.

AP: If you can figure out why I wrote it, then you can do it.

JK: That's a tremendous responsibility on the conductor to know the music so well to be able to teach.

AP: Absolutely. You have to be able to feel as if you can literally re-create it.

JK: How do you work with breath? When you compose, do you constantly think breath?

AP: I always think breath. Certainly. Breath is to the singer as the floor is to a dancer. You can't do without it.

JK: Which is more important, the words or the music?

AP: For me, if you're singing it, the music trumps. But we must continually balance the claims of the music against those of the words and make decisions about how to honor both. There's a joint where one line meets another. It's like fine woodwork: you don't want people to see the joint or be aware of it. For example, "Good Morning, Brother Pilgrim" is a nice jaunty tune, but there's not much time to breathe. In reading aloud, I should pause after each comma, but there's no time in the ongoing march rhythm. "Good morning, Brother Pilgrim, / What, bound for Canaan's coast?" There's no time to breathe or pause after "Pilgrim," so I must make a second syllable very short and light to infer the comma. "What" must also be very short; and "coast" finally gets two beats, with another for a full breath. So you're always balancing these things out—easing into it, allowing that breath to be there without interrupting the musical line, while not interrupting the speech line, still allowing the breath to come through the music.

JK: So it's like dovetailing. A dovetail joint.

AP: Exactly.

JK: In your work, and even when you speak, you have an absolute sense of story and sense of journey. Movement, motion, constantly. Is that conscious or simply innate?

AP: Shaw brought a lot of that out of me, sharpening the whole sense of rhythm and faithfulness to the beat . . . when there is a beat. What's the most important part of this song? Is it the pitches, rhythm, harmony, text? Obviously it's going to be some combination of them. But if, for example, you're arranging "Camp Town Races," you can't let that beat go for one single minute. You can't do a little *rubato* or something like that. The other side of that is if the beat wants to be free, like "Shenandoah," it will resist like mad if you're harnessing it down. Another one of my teaching devices is the clothesline. I like housewifely images. With the clothesline, there are two opposites—strictly rhythmic metric music here, and totally free music there, like my vision of Gregorian chant. Where does each song hang on the clothesline? Is it right smack in the middle of the two? Or does it lean toward the strictly rhythmic, or does it lean towards wanting to be free? How do you get a signal in our notation of a piece that wants to be free?

JK: Even hearing you sing and watching you speak, there's always, even on a pause, there's motion.

AP: Absolutely, because it's dance. I'm absolutely convinced that song and dance come from the same place. Song and dance and poetry. They come from the same part of our mind. Asking kids to sit still when they're hearing music is cruel. It's terrible. There's that elementary connection to dancing, and I think we've lost it. Martha Graham said, "It all comes from here," as she pointed to her abdomen, meaning the core of all movement. I did modern dance all the way through college, because it was the only athletic program that I could really sympathize with, and I realized how much that was part of what I was developing into being later.

JK: Is there room for new folk songs?

AP: Oh, they're developing all the time. You can't hold them down. They're like weeds in a field. The distinction that I make is between one that has lasted and been tested by time, and one that has not. So I decided long ago that I wanted to associate myself with melodies that had lasted. The kind of melody I wanted to write had the possibility of lasting rather than perhaps being a big hit. That was my conscious decision.

JK: You are a natural teacher. I feel like I'm going to school. What role can we play today in music education?

AP: Oh, get rid of all those tests. I look at a kid or a baby as if their head is a piggy bank and my function is to drop songs in there. And once they have several hundred or thousand songs, then they have the raw material with which to go to college and take a course in music appreciation. I drew up a list once of evaluation for this kind of teaching. How many songs can your class sing without any book? Can they improvise on them, dance to them, make a play out of them? How do they sound when they sing it, look when they sing it? How easily do they learn a new song? Can they keep a round going? All of these things have to do with sound, not with the page. The minute you get a test, you're divorced from sound. It's "unmusic."

JK: So how do you introduce that notation? Because I know you believe in notation.

AP: I do. By having the kids write. Begin by handing the whole class a piece of music paper on which you've written the first phrase of a song they learned in first grade and say, "Can you finish it?" And you get all kinds of answers back, including kids who can do it because they've taken music lessons before, and kids who say they can't do it at all. Talk them through it, beginning with writing the words, putting in the rhythmic notation layer by layer. Then add the moveable "do," so you are singing functions. I remember the first time that I mentioned some folk song [to Robert Shaw], and he said, "Which one?" And I sang, "The water is wide, you cannot go in." He said, "What?" I sang again, more carefully, "The water is wide, you cannot go in." And he made me do it about five times until I sang the song as if I meant it. And it made me realize that this is what I'm after. You don't ever do it carelessly. Anytime you do it, do it right, because when you do it wrong, you're doing "unmusic."

JK: You've been bringing up Shaw many times. Obviously, he had a great influence on you.

AP: Yes. He made me realize what music really is. I was studying at the same time with another superb musician, Julius Herford, for analysis and piano. The two of them working together gave me an initiation into the world of sound so complete that I finally realized that music is *only* sound—not words about sound, or notes on a page. So that you realize there's no such thing as music divorced from sound. Anytime you're talking about it, you have to have that sound in your ear or you're talking about "unmusic." I find that it is rare to have a sound-based conversation about music. Most people, when they look at music, are recapitulating their own learning experience, which is largely page-based, so they're caught in the page. Shaw had a remarkable sensitivity to language; he was 95 percent more text-oriented than other choral conductors. And then working with Julius Herford on piano sonatas was just a revelation. You have to orchestrate the entire time you're playing. There's this little French horn that comes in here, and this is violin, and this is oboe and clarinet . . . so that you're not a bit harnessed by the notes you see on the page. Your imagination is released by what you see on the page while you're trying to get all these different sounds out of the piano. Also, there is no way we can repeat what we have done or what somebody else has done. If I were to sing a song right now, and we were to measure every little nuance, I still couldn't do it exactly the same the next minute, because I would be starting from a different place. It's just like dance. Each time you do it, you're working with the energy that's in the room *now.* So a whole lot of what we're doing is basically following the laws of physics and the laws of energy.

JK: There is speculation that although it says Parker/Shaw on the music, the relationship was not very equal, and given the time it was written, it had to say Parker/Shaw on the music. Could you clarify that?

AP: I'm always happy to do that because, if it has both of our names on it, we both worked on it. These arrangements were always a part of a recording project. When the songs were all on tape, we'd go back over each title and try to decide how to split that 5 percent royalty. And it would be absolutely wild sometimes, a good-humored exchange. The general pattern was that either RCA Victor or Shaw would give me a topic for the album to do a year from now, or as time went on I chose it. I would research in the public library until I had eighty possible tunes to use for a project, and there might be sixteen in the final album. Then I would just keep singing them. Eventually, the first sketch would always go through from the first note to the last line. Once your time is basically set and your big divisions within the time form the whole, you can go back and fill it in. I would only write what I heard, and so the basic outline would have been mine. Then, I would play it [for Shaw]. He heard everything, and I learned that each piece must have a point of view. He taught me to self-edit, which none of my teachers in school had been able to do. And the reason that we lasted so long together was that we worked so differently. I was all intuitive, the sweep all the way through. He could write a perfectly wonderful arrangement, but it was like chipping it out of solid granite. I came up with multiple ideas, and he would discipline and finish them. So that is what he taught me and why we worked so well together.

JK: That must have been a great evolution in your composition, working through all that.

AP: Well, I was not yet composing. I got out of college with a composition degree, but if I continued on to Eastman I would have had to start at the beginning again, as a freshman. I thought, I'll just be miserable. So I wasn't composing at all. I was just hating what I was writing anyway, what I was trying to do with twelve-tone music and stuff like that. I couldn't see how I fit into the twentieth century, because all I heard in my head was from past centuries, and I wasn't supposed to write anything that could have been written in the previous century. All that time working with Shaw was the same time I was getting married and having children and being fascinated with how the kids were learning and responding to music and speech.

JK: Your family was also an influence on you.

AP: Oh, my word, yes. My husband was a wonderful singer. And he also was just a dear of a human being, a genius with people, understanding where they were coming from. Unfailingly polite, that southern kind of courtesy, which is rare in the New York professional world. And it was wonderful to live with the basic inner quietness and also sense of order. I'm not awfully orderly in life.

JK: Yet when I read any of your reflections, the way you describe nature, the way you describe your chores, and the way you describe the way you work is tremendously organized.

AP: [*Laughs*] I can have something that sits in the front hallway on that bench for months at a time, and I just don't see that it's there. (I learned that in New York with the five kids.) Now, the music, Shaw taught me how to really finish a score. I've never forgotten one time, I was expecting a week of working together, and I had this whole sheaf of arrangements, about eighteen. I played them all the way through, and he hadn't said anything, no pencil or anything. I was not supposed to talk in that process, not supposed to protest, so I was thinking, What's going on here? He took up the whole sheaf, turned it over on the piano, and said, "Again." So I played through about the first three, and he said, "The second time through they sound absolutely natural. We'll leave them just the way they are." I felt as if I had been cheated. "We're not going to work on them?" He said, "No, I wouldn't change anything in them." My first reaction was total disappointment, and then later I realized that was like passing the final exam.

JK: You just graduated.

AP: I graduated, exactly. It was empowering, but I also realized that I had found a way of dealing with these modal melodies that I just loved. One of the sound images that I always have in my ear is that you're in a sound chamber, and the only notes in the universe are the ones in this sound chamber. So you find different ways of combining them that have nothing to do with traditional chords. It does actually have a lot to do with Hindemith, relative dissonance between different intervals, and the way you use seconds and sevenths or fourths and fifths, and that thirds and sixths are to be avoided mostly because they throw you back over into the tonal. I had found a way of doing this while writing continuously, melodically, allowing each voice part to go where it wanted to go.

JK: It's very horizontal.

AP: That's part of my melody thing again. One of the crosses I have to bear now is people that come to me doing an analysis of one of my pieces for a graduate course, but they refuse to analyze it on my terms. They are analyzing it from a point of modality. I'm not working from that. Why can't you work from where I'm coming from? They are trying to make it fit some other pattern they want it to fit, or what their advisor wants them to focus on. It drives me crazy.

JK: Now how did you balance it all? Working, raising kids, a husband, going on tour?

AP: Well, I wasn't doing anything else in those years. I wasn't traveling at all. But I was still finding my way and teaching when I needed to. And Tom and I had an agreement from the beginning. Anytime a professional opportunity came along for either of us, the other one would work to underwrite it so that these opportunities were taking precedence. The only steady job I had ended in 1951. I taught school for two years. So I've been independent ever since then, teaching piano, teaching children's music classes first, and then leading seminars and composing and conducting in different places. I was able to build a much better career for myself being self-employed rather than staying in one position that was not so independent.

JK: How do you think the United States is doing with regard to music education and supporting artists? How are we doing in the beginning of the twenty-first century?

AP: We're so overloaded with rules and regulations. I'm always traveling around the country, and I see wonderful people who aren't famous and aren't celebrated and are doing wonderful work in their communities. But in school, the rules and regulations, we're doing almost everything in the country to discourage community and discourage parenting. The whole idea that mothers should get out and work—there's no honor to staying home and educating the young. I'm so glad, looking back, that I had those years that felt at times musically stifled, but I learned so much about myself as a human being and also what was important to me in music.

JK: How did you find your way back into composition?

AP: That thing that I was struggling with in music all those years of arranging with Shaw was thinking I had nothing to offer to the twentieth-century musical language. And I got around to this other way of thinking of the function of the song. We need songs to sing at different times in our lives, and can I write a song to fill that function? The first piece I wrote when I started composing again after twelve years of really not composing at all was in answer to a good friend who needed a children's church anthem for Mother's Day. I said to myself, "I can certainly do that. I can find a text that has some dignity to it, and I can set it in a way that the kids will enjoy singing and the parents will enjoy listening, and I won't have violated anybody's musical or poetic sensibilities." So I did. And I found I was writing just as easily as I ever did, and I wasn't agonizing, trying to rationalize everything I did. It was as if this dam had been opened, and I found out how to use all that I had been learning from Shaw and feed it into this compositional thing that had been in me but had been literally dammed up by all this rational way of manipulating notes.

JK: In a different direction, do you think that now, in the beginning of the twenty-first century, there is still a need for women's-only concerts, women's-only CDs?

AP: I don't like them myself. I compare a women's-only concert to serving a dinner with only green food. It's irrelevant and limiting. I don't want to be a woman composer; I want to be a composer. On the one hand, I think there are nurturing qualities that women can bring to most of the occupations that have been dominated by men. On the other hand, my husband was one of the most nurturing people I know, so it's not a gender difference. I think that there's a good reason that composing has so few women in it. When you think of Fanny Mendelssohn, one of the strong social issues was against women doing men's work. Also, just women's lives, the endless childbearing and the fact that you never have any time, no time. Our society is really the first one to come along that really makes it possible for women to be independent. The huge danger there is that as women taste power, they become more and more what we think of as masculine but really is a human fallibility about power, and power sometimes destroys. The thing we have to resist is assuming that mantle, because it gives us more scope. Those gals that are making it as conductors, I just hand it to them, keeping this kind of balance. But then in the whole conducting profession there's a real movement away from the traditional German taskmaster and the total disregard of any human relationships.

JK: I'm glad we're leading away from that.

AP: Oh, me too. It's just more collaborative and democratic today. But that's both men and women. I don't see anything that's any different in the brain of a man or woman that would make a woman unsuitable as a composer. I can see all kinds of things, like the traditional nurturing of children, that would open up avenues. One of the things I remember being told in college was that I shouldn't think about being a composer unless I'm going to write important music, great music. Idiocy! I like to take any of those ridiculous pronouncements about music and transfer it to food, because I'm feeding people's ears with what I write, and I want people to have that immediate sense of community from it. So if you say you shouldn't cook unless you're going to cook an important meal like Thanksgiving and Christmas, if I shouldn't do anything else, then what do I feed the kids when we've just come in from a long trip and they're starving, *now*?!

JK: Whom do you listen to?

AP: I love chamber music, string quartets, and trios, and things like that. I love Renaissance music. Love chant, but I don't often hear versions of it that I love. One of my pieces that's being premiered this year is at Smith College's Christmas program. It's a chant of Hildegard of Bingen, and they wanted a setting of it. I had a wonderful time working on it, because I'm trying to stay out of the way of this melody. You can't put much against a chant melody and keep it free. It's struggling against notation because we imprison it in notation. I'm just fascinated with chant, with the stuff that's "unnoteable."

JK: Now, you're still actively composing and actively teaching and actively doing everything.

AP: Yes. I have a piece to finish that's due November 1, and I'm finally getting conversant with the computer program Sibelius, which is a huge help, because my hand shakes now as I write. So I've got that and then three more. I only write on commission. That was another thing from the early Shaw years: You don't sit down and work for years on a piece that nobody is ever going to rehearse and perform. You don't cook a meal and then try to find somebody to eat it. You set up your contract first and find out whom you are writing for. And I've always tried to keep some kind of a balance between a piece for a small choir, or church choir, or young choir, and the ones for the professionals or community groups, so that I'm doing different kinds of things.

JK: When you are no longer here, what is it that you want to make sure to leave behind?

AP: I'm going back to the basic meal exchange, trying to put food on the table. I want to leave food that is healthy and nourishing and inviting. While I'm here,

I want to be in personal contact with as many people as possible because I just don't think that this particular thing can get taught. You certainly can't get it from a book. A book is the same every time you play it, yet the real music is different every time.

JK: Is that partially why you teach so many seminars?

AP: Yes, and that is why I have the classes here at my home. They're fun because I can teach what is important to me, and not what someone else believes. I'm trying to pass along the things that I've learned, and I'm not really concerned with what happens after I go. I'm very interested in recording now as much as possible because the page is only one kind of passing it along to another generation. But there are so many different ways you can read the page. Recording is another way. It shows one possible performance. And people can make the strangest miscalculations about what I have on the page. They haven't really looked at the text, or they don't understand the genre. Also, I have this organization, Melodious Accord, which is wonderful for me. It gave me a center in my life, since I don't have a church or a school that's behind me. They are a wonderful board that advises me, raises money, and makes it possible for me to do what I do. But it's been quite clear to me from the beginning that there's not much point in what I say after I go. We have a newsletter that perhaps can find a functional way to continue, and [we have] the publishing company that is mostly making available things that have gone out of print. Seminars, symposia. . . .

JK: All working toward continuing your ideas.

AP: Yes, continuing my ideas. But I can't imagine it going on for very long once I am no longer here. I see these choruses that are started by one person who has a very clear vision—Dale Warland, for instance. He wanted to stop while he was still ahead, and the singers all survived. They thought their world was ending, but they were all singing in choruses before the year was out. And there is always somebody saying, "There are so many women. There's no place for me." You have to start your own chorus. Just do it. Invite a few people over to your house, tell them what you want to do, and just start. Build it! Because it's not a bit easy trying to fit into somebody else's pattern.

***

Works by Alice Parker

In addition to the works below, Parker has also arranged 298 sacred choral pieces, 137 secular choral pieces, and thirty-four musical editions and translations.

All works self-published by Alice Parker Music Company unless otherwise noted.

OPERAS

The Family Reunion, for SATB, SSA, children, flute, ten instruments including guitar and banjo, melodies and libretto by Parker and traditional sources (Carl Fischer, 1976).

The Martyrs' Mirror, in two acts, for SATB/SATB and children, two recorders, oboe, bassoon, trumpet, three trombones, harmonica, percussion, melodies and libretto taken from early Reformation hymns (ECS, 1971).

The Ponder Heart, in two acts, for SATB with multiple divisi, twelve instruments, including guitar and banjo, melodies and libretto by Alice Parker and traditional sources (1982).

Singers Glen, in two acts, for SATB with divisi, children, string quartet, bass, flute, trumpet, trombone, guitar, harmonica, melodies and libretto by Parker and traditional sources (Hinshaw, 1978).

CHORAL WORKS WITH ORCHESTRA

And Sing Eternally, New England Hymn Tunes, for SATB(T) and orchestra (Lawson Gould, 2000).

Commentaries, for SSA/SSAA and orchestra (Hinshaw, 1978).

Earth, Sky, Spirit, for soprano, children, and orchestra (ECS, 1986).

Gaudete: Six Latin Christmas Hymns, for SATB and orchestra (ECS, 1977).

Journeys: Pilgrims and Strangers, for SATB, baritone, and orchestra (Hinshaw, 1976).

Our Native Land, for SATB and orchestra or piano (1992).

Revolutionary Overture, for SATB and orchestra (ECS, 1983).

Seven Carols, for SATB and orchestra (Carl Fischer, 1972–73).

Songs from the Dragon Quilt, for SATB, narrator, and orchestra (ECS, 1984).

That Sturdy Vine: Mennonite Singing, for SATB, children, and orchestra (1994).

The World's One Song, for SATB and orchestra (1990).

CANTATAS WITH INSTRUMENTS

And Sing Eternally, New England Hymn Tunes, for SATB and chamber group (Lawson Gould, 2000).

Angels and Challengers, for SATB, soloists, oboe, two clarinets, bassoon, and piano (1990).

The Babe of Bethlehem, for SSAA, handbells, or piano (1986).

Charity and Love, for SATB, harp, and strings (1986).

Children, Saints, and Charming Sounds, for SATB, children, woodwind trio, and brass quartet (1980).

Christopher Dock, for SATB, children(STB), recorder quartet, trumpet, string quartet, and percussion (1966).

Clearings, Poems of Wendell Berry, for soprano, baritone, SATB/SATB, and reader (1992).

The Day-Spring, for SATB, children, flute, and organ (1979).

An Easter Rejoicing, for SATB, harp, organ, and percussion (1972).

Ellington: Songs from the Sacred Concerts, for SATB and solo, piano, bass, and percussion (1986).

The Feast of Ingathering, for SATB and organ (Carl Fischer, 1972).
From the Zeeland Psalter, for SATB, two oboes, horn, and bassoon (1989).
Harmonious Herbst, for SATB, flute, oboe, bassoon, and strings (Hinshaw, 1994).
In Praise of Singing, for SATB and string quartet (1981).
Kentucky Psalms, for SATB, string quartet, and flute (1987).
Listen, Lord, for SATB, bass, percussion, and piano (1991).
Melodious Accord, for SATB/SSATB soli, harp, and brass quartet (ECS, 1977).
Naomi and Ruth, for SSA, flute, violin, cello, and organ (1987).
Partings, for SATB, flute, oboe, harp, percussion, and strings (1993).
Pleasure in the Flowers, for SATB, oboe, harp, and organ (1989).
Sacred Symphonies, for SATB, flute, violin, cello, and organ (1984).
A Sermon from the Mountain: Martin Luther King, for SATB chorus, and SATB soli, narrator, strings, and improvisatory jazz (ECS, 1971).
The Sing-Song of Old Man Kangaroo, for SATB, oboe, English horn, bassoon, and percussion (1971).

CHORAL SUITES (MULTIPLE MOVEMENTS)

Alaskan Totems, for SA, piano, flute, oboe, clarinet, cello, and percussion (2011).
American Dances, for SA and piano (1989).
Angels Visit When We Sing, for SATB and piano (2007).
Anniversary Hymns, for SATB (1989).
Back-Woods Ballads, for SAB and piano (Hinshaw, 1983).
Brief Seasons, for four voices and four instruments (1973).
Cantata 1, 2, for SSA and piano (1949).
Carols to Play and Sing, for SATB, percussion, and organ (ECS, 1971).
Circles, for S, SA, SATB, cello, and percussion (2005).
Colorado, Santy Ano, Shenandoah, for SA (2003).
Dancing Songs, for SAB and piano (ChoralQuest, 2011).
Dem Bells, for SATB(B), handbells, or keyboard (Lawson Gould, 1992).
Dickinson: On "Nature," for SSAA (2005).
Die Bacherie, for soprano, tenor with audience, continuo, and percussion (1986).
An Easter Triptych, for SATB and organ (Selah, 2007).
Ecumenical Praise, for SATB, brass sextet, timpani, and percussion (1990).
Elinor Wylie: Incantations, for SSA, clarinet, and piano (Treble Clef, 1997).
An English Mass, for two equal voices (1976).
An Exultation of Birds, SATB and optional children's chorus (2002).
Frontier Suite, SATB/ST (Lawson Gould, 1970–73).
A Garland of Carols, for two-part children's voices and keyboard (Lawson Gould, 1968).
Green Dances, for SATB (Lawson Gould, 1998).
Hollering Sun, for SATB (Lawson Gould, 1994).
The King Shall Come, for SATB, with two unison choirs and organ (Cantate/Can, 1998).
G. M. Hopkins: This Juice, This Joy, for SATB/TB (1999).
Love Songs, for SATB and piano (Hinshaw, 1979).

The Lover Tells of the Rose in His Heart (Four Yeats Songs), for TTBB and viola (G. Schirmer, 2002).
"Magnificat," We Sing, SATB, piano or strings (2007).
Mass for Young Children, for two choruses S-SA and SA-SATB (2000).
Millay Madrigals, for SATB (1985).
Mystic Mooring, for SATB (1998).
Phonophobia, for SATB and piano (1977).
A Play on Numbers, for SA and piano (ECS, 1972).
Play-Party Songs, for SATB and piano (Hinshaw, 1982).
Prayer and Praise, for SATB, soprano and baritone, and harp (1965).
Psalms of Praise, for TB and percussion (Lawson Gould, 1968).
The Rock and the River, for SATB, and jazz combo (2008).
Roll Round with the Year, for TTBB, and guitar or piano (1989).
Runes, SA, SSAA, SSA (Treble Clef/APMC, 2004).
Schutz: Psalms for Barbara, for SATB (Selah, 2006).
Shepherds and Angels, for SATB (ECS, 2002).
Sing Now of Peace, for SATB, vibes, and percussion (1999).
Six Hymns to Dr. Watts, for SATB (ECS, 1977).
SongStream, for SATB, piano solo or duet (ECS, 1986).
Stars and Stones, for SATB, oboe, bassoon, and piano (1990).
Stevenson Songs, for SA and piano (1987).
Street Corner Spirituals, for SATB, trumpet, drums, and guitar (Lawson Gould, 1971).
There and Back Again, for SATB and woodwind quartet (1978).
Three Christmas Carols, for SA and harp (Lawson Gould, 1971).
Three Circles, for SATB and percussion (C. Fischer, 1972).
Three Mennonite Christmas Hymns, for SATB (Lawson Gould, 1969).
Wesley Madrigals, for SSATB (1989).
Women on the Plains, for SSA and piano (Treble Clef, 1996).
Wren Songs, for SATB (Hope, 1992).
Zimre Chayim, for SATB (Transcontinental, 1995).

SACRED CHORAL COMPOSITIONS

All Earth, Shout with Joy, for SATB and piano (2004).
An American Kedushah, for SATB (Transcontinental, 2002).
And Are We Yet Alive, SATB (1999).
Angels Supposedly, for SA and piano (1975).
The Animals' Christmas, for SATB (ECS, 2008).
The Anointing, for SATB, flute, violin, cello, and organ (1983).
Ave Maria, for TTBB (1993).
Away, Melancholy, for SSA/SSAA and tambourine (ECS, 1972).
Blessings, for SATB (Lawson Gould, 1971).
Beauty and Blessing, for SATB (ECS, 2009).
Brotherly Love, for two to five voices in canon and guitar (ECS, 1972).
Centering, for SATB (Selah, 2002).

The Children's Call for Peace: Three Beatitudes, for SA and piano or organ (Treble Clef, 2001).
Christmas Stars, SA and piano (Choristers Guild, 1991).
Come, and Let Us Sweetly Join, for SATB, brass, timpani, and organ (2010).
Composer of the World, for SATB (2010).
Consecration, for SATB, handbells, and organ (ECS, 2009).
The Daughter, for SATB, flute, violin, cello, and organ (1984).
De Profundis, for TTBB (2005).
Direct Us, Lord, through Darkness, for SATB (1993).
Distant Goal: A Peace, for SATB and organ (2004: Earthsongs, pending).
Earth Now Is Green, for SATB (1972).
Earth Woman, for SATB (Lawson Gould, 1994).
Easter Days, for SATB, children, and organ (GIA, 2005).
Enlarge the Limits of Your Home, for SATB and organ (2002).
An Evening Service, for soprano, SA, organ, flute, and cello (2001).
First the Wind upon the Water, for SATB (1995).
For the Fruit of All Creation, for children and adult chorus (GIA, 2005).
Gabriel's Message, for SSA, soprano, harp, and percussion (1972).
Gifts of the Spirit, for SATB (2011).
Glorious God (A Canonic Mass), for cantor and congregation (1993).
Glory to God Is the Song of the Stars, for SATB, children, congregation, bells, brass quintet, percussion, and organ (2010).
God of Grace and God of Laughter, for SATB (GIA, 2005).
The Good Shepherd, for TT/TTBB (ECS, 1988).
Grace and Glory, for SATB, bells, and percussion (ECS, 1978).
Great Our Joy, for SATB/SA and bells (1985).
Great Trees, for SATB and keyboard (Frank Warren, 2000).
Happy Choristers of Aire, for SSATBB (1986).
Harvest Days, for SATB and organ (Unitarian Universalist, 1992).
He Is Alive (from *An Easter Triptych*), for SATB (Selah, 2007).
Heart, Hold Fast, for SATB and organ (Waterloo Music, 1993).
Holy Manna, for SATB, youth, and organ (2010).
Holy Michael, for two voices, guitar, harp, or keyboard (ECS, 1987).
A Hymn for Confirmation, for SAB/SATB and organ (Agape, 1982).
I Saw a Stable, for SATB, organ, and percussion (ECS, 1971).
I Will Lift Up Mine Eyes, for SATB and organ (1990).
I Will Sing and Give Praise, for SATB/S and organ (Hinshaw, 1978).
In Bethlehem, for SATB, organ, and percussion (ECS, 1971).
In Sacred Manner, for SATB and piano (2008).
In This Day, for SATB and organ or piano (2010).
Invocation: Peace, for SSAA (ECS, 1988).
It Is Good to Give Thanks, for SATB and organ (Hinshaw, 1984).
Jesus, Whom Every Saint Adores, for SATB and percussion (1972).
Know That the Lord Is God, for SATB, trumpet, and organ (GIA, 2005).
Let the People Praise Thee, for SSAA and strings (1980).

Let Our Gladness Banish Sadness, for SSATB (2005).
The Little Cradle Rocks (from *Babe of Bethlehem*), for SSAA/S (Treble Clef, 2008).
Look unto Abraham, for SATB/S (GIA, 2005).
Love Is of God, for SATB and organ (Selah, 2000).
Magnificat, We Sing, for SATB and piano (2007).
Many in One, for SATB, violin, organ, or SA with keyboard (1987).
Meet and Right It Is to Sing, for SATB and organ (1981).
The Messaianic Call, for SATB and organ (1994).
Mind and Heart, for SATB and keyboard (1992).
Miss Masters' Proverb, for SSA (1994).
Most Glorious Lord of Life (from *An Easter Rejoicing*), for SATB (1972).
A Mountain Psalm, for SATB and keyboard (GIA, 2005).
My Feets Is Tired (from *A Sermon from the Mountain*), for SATB/A and keyboard (ECS, 1999).
Neither Spirit nor Bird, for SATB, flute, and drums (1994).
Now Glad of Heart, for SATB/B and organ (Lawson Gould, 1960).
O Gracious Power, for TTBB (Lawson Gould, 2000).
O Sing the Glories, for SATBB (GIA, 2005).
Offerings, for SATB (G. Schirmer, 2008).
Our Life Is Hid, for SATB and organ (Lawson Gould, 1987).
A Peace Canon, for one to five voices and piano (1991).
The Peacemakers, for SATB and organ (2002).
Praise God, for SATB, brass, and organ (1987).
Praise with Understanding, for SATB/SATB and brass (1980).
Pray for Peace, for SAATTB (1985).
Prayer, for SATB/SATB and optional brass (Lawson Gould, 1973).
Prayer (from *Hollering Sun*), for SATB (Lawson Gould, 1994).
A Prayer for Choirs, for unison or two-part chorus and bass (ECS, 1979).
Prayer of St. Francis, for SATB/SATB and echo chorus (Selah, 2008).
The Promised Land, for SATB, two trumpets, and brass quintet (GIA, 2005).
Psalm 136, for SATB/B (Lawson Gould, 1966).
Quiet (from *Hollering Sun*), for SATB (Lawson Gould, (1994).
Remembering Those Who Fly, for SATB, three trumpets, and three trombones (Lawson Gould, 1996).
Seasons and Times (from *An Easter Rejoicing*), for STB, harp, and percussion (1972).
Shrill Chanticleer, for SATB, organ, and percussion (ECS, 1971).
Sing and Make Melody, for SSAA (Treble Clef, 2004).
Sing for Joy, for SAB, keyboard, trumpet, and tambourine (2004).
Sky Family (from *Hollering Sun*), for SATB (Lawson Gould, 1994).
The Song of Simeon, for SATB, brass quartet, or keyboard (1979).
Sorrow and Gladness, for SSATB (Selah, 1998).
Speak Peace, for SATB (2010).
A Sun, a Shield, for SA, autoharp, and bass (ECS, 1979).
Sun, Rain, Wind, for SATB (ECS, 2008).

Sunday Rounds, for one to seven voices (Hinshaw, 1975).
Sweet Coming, for SATB and harp (2000).
Thou Shalt Call Thy Walls Salvation, for SATB/T (1967).
To the Trinity Be Praise, for two-part women's and men's voices (2001).
Together (from *Hollering Sun*), for SATB (Lawson Gould, 1994).
Trinitarian Blessings (from *Wren Songs*), for SATB (Hope, 1992).
The True Use of Music, for SATB, orchestra, or organ (1977).
A Universal Blessing, for two-part congregation and organ (2010).
Universal Praise, for SATB and brass (ECS, 1983).
"Unto Me" (from *An Easter Triptych*), for SATB and organ (Selah, 2007).
We Look Down Deep to Look Out Far, for SSATTB (2005).
We Sing of Peace, for SATB (2011).
The Wells of Salvation, for SATB (2011).
While He Is Alive (from *An Easter Triptych*), for SATB and organ (Selah, 2007).
Wilbur: Psalm, for SATB and cello (2011).
The Wine (from *Sacred Symphonies*), for SATB, flute, violin, cello, and organ (1984).
The Wings of Faith, for SATB and brass (1988).
Winter Solstice 2001, for SATB/SATB (2002).

SECULAR CHORAL COMPOSITIONS

All the Stars in the Sky, for one-, two-, or three-part chorus (Earthsongs, 2009).
Angels, Supposedly, for SA and keyboard (1975).
Away, Melancholy, for SSA/SSAA and tambourine (ECS, 1973).
Carmine Pu-Ursi, for SATB (1963).
Dickinson: Three Seas, for SSAA, piano or flute, bassoon, and harp (Treble Clef, 2000).
Earth Woman (from *Hollering Sun*), for SATB (Lawson Gould, 1994).
Dickinson: On "Nature," for SSAA (2005).
Escape at Bedtime, for SA and orchestra or piano (1992).
Fair Annet's Song, for SSA (Treble Clef, 1997).
A Fanfare for Gian-Carlo, for SA and brass (1986).
Games, for SSA and chamber orchestra or piano (Carl Fischer, 1976).
Give Thanks for Music, for SSA and piano (Treble Clef, 2005).
A Grace for Voices, for canon (1976).
Greeting to Spring, for TT/TTBB and percussion (2009).
Hellos and Goodbyes, choral rounds for SATB/S (Carl Fischer, 1975).
Honey, Pepper, Leaf-Green Limes, for SATB, flute, cello, guiro, two congas, and bomba (G. Schirmer, 2009).
Incantation, for SSA, cello, and piano (Treble Clef, 1997).
Invocation: Peace, for SSAA (Galaxy, 1988).
Madman's Song, for SA, clarinet, and piano (Treble Clef, 1997).
Many in One, for SATB, violin, and organ, or SA with keyboard (1987/1991).
Memories Flow, for three-part canons (Earthsongs, 2004).
A Midsummer Night's Dream: Fairy Songs, for two-part treble chorus, two recorders (Treble Clef, 1999).

Miss Masters' Proverbs, for SSA (1994).
Mystic Mooring, for SATB (1998).
Nameless Song, for SA, clarinet, and piano (Treble Clef, 1997).
Neither Spirit nor Bird, for SATB, flute, and drums (1994).
The Ocean, for unison and piano (1989).
A Peace Canon, for one to five voices and piano (1991).
Prayer, for SATB (Lawson Gould, 1994).
Quiet, for SATB (Lawson Gould, 1994).
Remembering Those Who Fly, for SATB and brass (Lawson Gould, 1996).
Singing Questions, for two-part treble and piano (Morningstar, 2003).
Sky Family, for SATB (Lawson Gould, 1994).
Three Settings of "Kedron," for SATB/TTB, youth choir, congregation/choir, and organ (1970).
Together (from *Hollering Sun*), for SATB (Lawson Gould, 1994).
Water Songs, for SA and piano (1990).
We Are the Music-Makers, for SATB (Hal Leonard, 2002).
The West Wind, for SATB (1945).
What Better Time, for SA and keyboard (Hal Leonard, 2002).
When We Played House, for SA and orchestra or piano (1991).

SONG CYCLES

Astrometaphysical: Four Songs to Robert Frost, for medium voice and piano (1968).
Echoes from the Hills, for soprano, flute, clarinet, horn, and strings, text by Emily Dickinson (1979).
A Gnasherie, for baritone and piano, text by Ogden Nash (1971).
Of Irlaunde, for baritone, flute, and piano, text by various Irish poets (1979).
Six Hymns to Dr. Watts, for SATB (ECS, 1977).
Songs for Eve, for SATB and string quartet, text by Archibald MacLeish (1975).
Songs of the Turtle, for soprano and string quartet, text taken from Taos Pueblo/N. Wood (1994).
Three Mountain Hymns, for soprano and piano, traditional texts (ECS, 1982).
Whole Earth Songs, for baritone or two-part treble chorus and piano, text by Parker (1992).

SONGS

"123 cheers for Dave Brubeck," for voice and piano (2010).
"Ad-Vancing," for solo, chorus, and piano (2006).
"The Bedtime Song" (arr. traditional), for medium voice and piano (1965).
"Coronation Day," for voice and piano (1997).
"Five Fragments," for baritone, SATB, and oboe (1969).
"The Gift to Be Simple" (arr. from "Shaker Song"), for medium voice and piano (1975).
"Hymns to Dr. Watts," for baritone with woodwind quartet (1966).
"I Will Arise" (arr. traditional), for SA and piano (ECS, 1982).
"Jenny Kissed Me," for medium voice and piano (1987).

"Love Is More Thicker," for mixed two-part voice and piano (1953).
"Mansions in the Sky" (arr. traditional), for voice and piano (Galaxy, 1982).
"O Thou, in Whose Presence" (arr. traditional), for voice and piano (Galaxy, 1982).
"An Occasional Cantata," for singers (1972).
"Singing Praise," for soprano, violin, and piano (1981).
"Three Lyrics," for tenor, clarinet, viola, and cello (1948).

HYMN TUNES

"Ach, Kinder, wollt ihr lieben" (arr. traditional), SATB (HWB, 1991).
"Ambivalence," for SATB (Hope, 1982).
"The Apple Tree," for unison and piano (HWB, 1989).
"As the Seed That Cleaves a Stone," for SATB (1997).
"Aweful Majesty," for SATB (HWB, 1991).
"Barbara Allen" (arr. traditional), for SATB (Augsburg, 1995).
"Beautiful Flower," for SATB (HWB, 1991).
"By the Babylonian Rivers" (Latvian "Kas Dziedaja"), for SATB (Augsburg, 1964).
"Coffey (Let All Creation)," for SATB (Hope, 1997).
"Consolator," for SATB (HWB, 1991).
"Creating God," for SATB (1984).
"Detroit" (arr. traditional), for SATB (HWB, 1991).
"Eternal Source," for SATB (1980).
"Give Thanks to God," for SATB (1980).
"Give to the Winds" (arr. "Divine Goodness"), for SATB (HWB, 1991).
"Go Silent Friend" (arr. "Londonderry Air"), for SATB (Lawson-Gould, 1968).
"God Moves in a Mysterious Way," for SATB (2000).
"God Sends Us the Spirit" (arr. traditional "Gonja"), for SATB (Hope, 1993).
"Grace to You and Peace," for three-part round (HWB, 1962)
"Holy Spirit, Truth Divine," for SATB (1966).
"Holy Trinity," for SATB (2007).
"The House of Faith," for SATB (1995).
"Hymn for Confirmation," for SATB (Hymn Society of America).
"I Cannot Dance, O Love," for SATB (HWB, 1991).
"I Shall Not Be Moved" (arr. traditional), for SATB (1990).
"In Beauty God Created Earth," for SATB (1981).
"Let All Creation," for congregation (1997).
"O Sanctissima," for SATB (HWB, 1991).
"O Waly, Waly" (arr. traditional), for SATB (HWB, 1991).
"One in Christ," for SATB (1983).
"Shout On, Pray On" (arr. traditional), for SATB (HWB, 1991).
"Star in the East" (arr. traditional), for SATB (HWB, 1991).
"Thanks Be to God," for SATB (1994).
"There Was a Maid," for SATB (New Hymnal for Colleges and Schools, 1989).
"This Joyful Eastertide," (arr. traditional), for SATB (Hope, 1968).

"Three Times Holy," for SATB (2007).
"West End: Holy Spirit, Truth Divine," for SATB (1966).
"What Wondrous Love Is This" (arr. traditional), for SATB (Mennonite Hymnal, 1970).

MUSIC COLLECTIONS (COMPOSED OR ARRANGED)

Come, Let Us Join, for SATB (Lawson Gould, 1966).
Eight American Mountain Hymns, for SATB (Lawson Gould, 1990).
Hymns and Carols, for SATB (Lawson Gould, 1965).
One, Two, Three Sing, vols. 1–2, for SAB and piano (Lawson Gould, 1955/1958).
The Riverside Sunday Book, songs and spirituals for young children, unison (1965).
A Season of Carols, for SATB (Lawson Gould, 1991).
Seven Carols for Christmas, for SATB and keyboard (Carl Fischer, 2006).
Shaw/Parker Book of Christmas Carols (1950s arr.), for SATB (Hal Leonard, 1991).
Shaw/Parker Easter Carol Collection (1951), (Hal Leonard, 1995).
Songs for Sunday, for SA and keyboard (Lawson Gould, 1966).
Vive l'Amour (1960s), for TTBB (Alfred, 2006).

INSTRUMENTAL WORKS (WITHOUT VOICE)

Cello Sonata, for cello and piano (1982).
Dances, for string quartet (1988).
Danny Boy (trad.), for flute (1993).
Double Concerto, for oboe, viola, and string orchestra (1980).
Double Dances, for organ (1970; Jaymar, 1992).
Four Hymn Preludes, for organ (1970).
Letters and Notes (varied composers), for piano (Lawson Gould, 1957).
Partita in A, for harpsichord (1978).
Scandinavian Dances, for piano (1988).
String Quartet in D (1988).
Suite for Piano (1964).
Sunday Music, for flute and guitar (1965).
Sweet Jubilation, for organ (1995).
A Windemere Suite, for piano (1992).

Kuandi Photo, Beijing

6

Chen Yi

Chen Yi was born into a musical family in Guangzhou, China, in 1953. Raised with a respect for European- and Russian-influenced classical art music, Chen learned piano and violin and spent years listening to her father's classical-music collection. Her knowledge and practice of classical music helped carry her through the events of the Chinese Cultural Revolution. During our conversation, this normally vivacious and enthusiastic woman softens her voice and drops in pitch as she describes the extraordinary efforts made to hide and preserve the music she loved in spite of the revolution's repressions. Her journey eventually led Chen to be among the first class of composers to enter the Central Conservatory of Music in Beijing when the Cultural Revolution came to an end.

When asked about the Chinese folk songs sung by farmers during the revolution, Chen reminds me that folk songs were outlawed because they are intimately tied to language and culture. Like Alice Parker and Gabriela Lena Frank, Chen recognizes that to reach the heart of music one must understand its culture. With knowledge of languages and cultural systems from both China and Europe, Chen seamlessly weaves the two in much of her music. Like Toshiko Akiyoshi, Chen's heritage is infused into her compositions through her choice of instruments, treatment of text, and aesthetic.

The first woman to earn a master's degree in composition from the Central Conservatory of Music, Chen went on to obtain a degree from New York's Columbia University. As composer-in-residence to the Women's Philharmonic, Chen then participated in outreach programs advocating for women in music. Being raised in China, she was not aware of the unequal treatment of men and women in music in the United States. Her exposure through the Women's Philharmonic to women's enthusiasm and support for one another was a profound experience for Chen. She explains, "From those education programs (and for me those are education programs), I learned about the history and vision. Responsibility." Today, she actively encourages and advocates for Asian women composers.

Chen currently holds the position of Cravens/Millsap/Missouri Distinguished Professor at the University of Missouri–Kansas City Conservatory of Music and Dance. She teaches that a composer should be able to write for diverse ensembles, and her own catalog includes works for orchestra, chamber, voice, and piano. During our conversation, her respect for the teacher-student relationship emerges as she discusses her mentors and her own teaching.

In addition to her residencies, awards, and commissions, Chen has served on advisory councils and boards of the American Composers Orchestra, International Alliance for Women in Music, Meet the Composer, and Chamber Music America. She founded the bilingual newsletter *Music from China* in 1991. Elected to the American Academy of Arts and Sciences in 2005, her numerous awards and fellowships include the Charles Ives Living Award from the American Academy of Arts and Letters, a Grammy Award for Chanticleer's album *Colors of Love,* the Lili Boulanger Award, New York University's Sorel Medal, the Chamber Music Society of Lincoln Center's Elise Stoeger Award, and four honorary doctorates. Chen's music continues to be commissioned by distinguished musicians and ensembles around the world and is published by Theodore Presser Company.

***

May 2010, at her home in Kansas City, Missouri

CHEN YI: Composers should write everything. If you look into history where composers have written everything in different media, then I think a composer is a general word that should include everything. And now you add multimedia. You add electronic music. You add experimental and theater, so I don't think there is a limitation.

JENNIFER KELLY: Is it important for any composer to know how to sing or understand the workings of the voice?

CY: Yes. It is a language, and you must study the instrumentation. When I teach instrumentation and orchestration, I include choral.

JK: Do you have a favorite medium you like to write for?

CY: Not me. I have written everything except for opera.

JK: Do you want to write opera someday?

CY: Yes, if I have time. No time, actually. You have to be very devoted. You also need concentration. The libretto is more important for me. I'm sensitive to libretto. If it doesn't work then you are wasting time.

JK: That brings up a good point. When you are working with choral music and text, what is your relationship to text? How do you find text?

CY: I read a lot of books, particularly Chinese ancient poem collections. I have a method to collect them. If I write a set of poems, I may have some examples, and then I should consider contrast, consider the meaning and styles. So that would be my point among my choral works. Most of them are sung in Chinese. I wrote my works and basically classify them into three different styles. One would be folk-song material, Chinese folk song. I even also have American folk song, Japanese folk song, Korean folk song. Folk-song arrangements would be one type of my choral work. I have written many choral works. At one point people even considered me as a choral composer.

JK: You have a lot of choral works, so I suppose in the choral world they might consider you a choral composer if they're unaware of your other music.

CY: Orchestra and band and chamber and choral. Those are the four types of music I write.

JK: You were saying within your choral compositions, you had three styles.

CY: One is arrangements in which I would maximally keep the original style, folk style and also singing style. Because folk music is closely related to language. So if the language is being sung, that should match the arrangement style and should match the vertical progression. I would use that kind of harmony according to their language and musical style. And sometimes I avoid using Western classical style of harmonic progression because that may not match a certain style of folk music. I want to follow their original style—and also sung in their own language. The second in my category would be something very much like folk style, also sung in Chinese, but may not be melodies taken from folk music.

JK: Not an arrangement. An original.

CY: Yes, but still in that style.

JK: Based on language. I imagine that European classical bel canto singing tradition, that open sound wouldn't be as successful with your music sung in Chinese because the bel canto sound is not based on Chinese language.

CY: When I worked for Chanticleer, they sang my work so seamlessly because they sing in early music style, which is straight tone and not with vibrato, and that matches my style. Except in *Chinese Myths Cantata.* That is a totally creative piece, not an arrangement, not any folk singing. Chanticleer learned not only to sing from heart, but they also dance on stage. They got training every day for two months to do this. My third category would be more abstract. And when I say there are three categories, it would also cover more of my instrumental works.

JK: All of your music? Not just choir?

CY: Yes. Because the third category, which is more abstract, sometimes you use the principle taken from Chinese ensemble music that might be rhythmic structure or the form. You have a whole piece of ensemble music in which you analyze the structure, and then you take the form to use. Or you took the pattern or design to use. Or you took the sound imagination or sound design into your melodic writing. Or you use reciting tune or translated them into melodic writing. Those kinds of techniques might mean something abstract but not directly into folk-song singing, or folk-song style of singing. So I classify them into three categories. Actually, I think Bartók did that. When I was in undergrad and master's program in China, my teacher, Professor Wu, taught me a lot of what Bartók was doing, his aesthetics and his method of creation. All his work is related to folk music. My teacher used to study in Moscow Conservatory, so he analyzed Bartók's string quartets and translated from Russian to Chinese, so I learned from him, Wu. When I went to Columbia University to study, my teacher, Professor Chou Wen-Chung, was the founder of the Center for U.S.–China Arts Exchange and also the associate dean of the School of the Arts at Columbia for more than a dozen years. He uses more abstract methods and styles to apply Chinese aesthetics into his composition. That influences me a lot, too, because of the way he treated Chinese culture in different aspects like calligraphy and painting, music, dancing, literature—all of this is translated into his music. The method that he used or the imagination he had. Those kinds of things influenced me. So all together as a combination, I got more influences from modern life often from teachers. Because you put a composer into a society, and you've got to learn a lot from where you have been living—from the people, styles, and cultures.

JK: Your work is a product of your whole life. You seem very interested in cultural context in your music. Are you always thinking, "Where is this coming from?" and, "How does this connect to culture?"

CY: Connect to culture and connect to society. That means people or history. The background and the people are totally into one. I think you can't separate them into any separate items. They are an organic whole.

JK: Do you consciously think about audience when you are composing?

CY: I do not know who the future audience is going to be when I compose. The people who come to commission me—I basically know their audience, but I don't know them particularly, and also every piece you finish flies away, you don't control it. You don't know who are the next performers. Also, they may take it to different locations to face different groups of people or media. Or many are broadcast. Like last year, National Public Radio, they listed the top ten CDs. They picked one CD of my chamber works, and you didn't know when they broadcast, and they could download from anywhere. So you can't predict, but you aim for a group of listeners.

JK: When you are composing and finishing a piece, is it easy to give it up to the performer or is that difficult?

CY: Not hard for me. First of all, all my works are commissioned works. I have to meet deadlines. My music should touch myself first, and then my music should touch the performers. They are very playable and performable. They must touch the performers in order for them to commit and transfer and present and express to the audience. If it works, the audience will be touched as well. So in that sense it shouldn't be hard. If I have these three steps, I can communicate with the audience through my music. That is ideal.

JK: What kind of relationship do you like to have with a conductor or performer after you give them the music?

CY: They always come back to ask me questions. Because every conductor came to me saying that they want to "speak in your language, speak for you. We want to express what is written in your style." So, I would sing back or tell details of a technique in order to make it more precise. Actually, my music is in the style with every detail written down. So if they follow the score, basically they will know. Now many other orchestras know everything from me. You don't need to tell them. They know because of maybe the repertoire they had performed, or they are connecting to these people or style.

JK: There are more Chinese or Chinese American composers around creating more repertoire.

CY: Exactly. And more American composers writing in Chinese style, too. Because after all of these being introduced, people could have interactions with each other. They also used this kind of technique as well. It became a kind of language. Now it's a real universal language. Universal language is not the old sense of music. Talking to everybody in the universal language. Now this language could include different styles of language, even only in music. So it's a very encouraging situation.

JK: Is the interaction between China and the United States starting to affect music in China?

CY: Yes. A lot of American musicians visited China in the last ten years, getting more and more school bands and school orchestras and school choirs. I mean thousands. I didn't calculate who has sung the Chinese folk-song arrangements. There are thousands of kids, high-school or college choirs that sing my works in China, some of my arrangements and compositions. I think they introduced my works to the Chinese [*laughs*]!

JK: So what is the reception in China to your music?

CY: They love it, and they learn it later. Because those works are commissioned by Americans. When Americans sing my works in Chinese, they are shocked. They give them a very warm welcome because they didn't have a decent opportunity to know those pieces, and now Americans are singing Chinese in Chinese style. Not many people knew, and not many people wrote for this medium. I think that is very good interaction. Like communication.

JK: Communication between European or American countries and China.

CY: Yes, because 90 percent of my orchestra works are commissioned by Americans or Europeans. Still, the Chinese know my orchestra works because the National Symphony has given three times whole-evening concerts of my orchestra works in Beijing. And many other local orchestras have done my works. They also won national competitions and produced a CD. Even the China National Center for the Performing Arts in Tiananmen Square commissioned me for a New Year's celebration orchestral work. The symphony in my hometown in the south also commissioned me.

JK: So they don't have a problem with the fact that you no longer live in China. You've lived in the United States for so many years, but they'll still commission you in China.

CY: I know the directors. They are still friends. They come to commission without asking where you are. They just commission the music.

JK: You talk a lot about connecting cultures. Is there a sense of responsibility you have as a Chinese and American composer wanting to connect the two cultures?

CY: Yes. Since 2006, the Chinese education minister appointed me as the visiting professor at my old conservatory in Beijing officially for a total of three months a year for three years. After three years, they kept me in the conservatory with the same title, invited by the conservatory, and in this case I help with many lectures, master classes, and many festivals like a consultant advisor. I brought in many Americans, including composers, professors in different instruments, conductors in different categories, chamber ensembles, and particularly new music ensembles. I'm responsible for introducing many new music ensembles that the Chinese didn't know.

JK: Are they accepting of new music?

CY: Yes. We have Beijing Modern Music Festival, the Musicacoustica-Beijing Festival, and we have the Central Conservatory Festival.

JK: As a composer today in the United States, do you think the U.S. is accepting of contemporary music?

CY: Certainly! It's totally advanced. Audiences in the States are, I should say, 100 percent understanding, open, accepting, and innovative. In this case, it is open to a thought, study, or to appreciate or observe.

JK: Would you extend that to say that we shouldn't be afraid to program new music in the States because audiences are ready to hear it?

CY: Yes. And also ready to learn from multicultural styles and products, inspirations. I think people are well educated. That word "educated" is not easy to reach. It has gone through so many decades of education to reach that point. Maybe in some areas we haven't reached that point yet. That's why we have to work harder.

JK: To educate children to grow up?

CY: For everybody. Because some older people might have never heard about such an idea or such a practice yet.

JK: How do we go about educating?

CY: Through education programs. Because education programs can touch different ages and levels and geographic levels.

JK: The world is getting smaller and smaller as communication between countries grows. Where does music play a role in that?

CY: I think music is a part of the foundation of a society and culture. It would have the influence in mind, which eventually became the power and resource of creation of the society. That is a part of that. I think it plays a very important role. Sometimes it is not visible or touchable—maybe not so obvious in front of you right away. Yet, it would play a role in the long term. If we don't educate our kids about the culture behind them from their ancestors, or they don't know what's going on in the living culture, then that is not good for their future creation. If one doesn't know history or culture, it will be dangerous to have this material creation. Material is certainly important, but it plays on the surface of the society. You need to dig deeply into the ground to the root to see how it builds later, and that would be more long-term.

JK: Is that one of the reasons you compose?

CY: I think this is a very important reason, because you carry the culture. We are writing the living culture. For my style now, I bring in deep Chinese cultural roots, and I introduce Asian culture to more audiences or students. They wouldn't feel like strangers or rejected. In another way, they would feel included and accepted. That would be really helpful for later creation. Because not only do you know everything well, you are a complete person who can predict, think, or look forward. Otherwise we would be kept in a narrow range. So maybe that was the motivation for me to work harder.

JK: When you are beginning a piece and ideas start to come to you, what's the first thing you hear? Is it melody? Rhythm?

CY: Usually a commission gives me the possible scope of a performing force first.

JK: All of the parameters and limitations and time. . . .

CY: All those things. Based on that condition I come up with an image, a so-called image that is abstract. Not a kind of a picture, but a kind of idea of a possibility. Sometimes it's related to what the organization wants. For example, my second violin concerto was written for the reopening of the Lady's Church in Dresden, because it was bombed by the British air force at the end of World War II. They rebuilt the church, and the British queen gave a golden cross on top, so I honored that reopening. The Chamber Music Society of Minnesota came to commission me for a chamber work for Yo-Yo Ma to remember World War II and call for the peace of the future. So I accepted. I learned from the history, and then I wrote my pieces. Most times, it's decided according to the performing force.

JK: Do you have input?

CY: Yes, I get to give ideas. Sometimes they come to you with certain resources available. You make up your mind. Most times they give you this orchestra and this band or this choir, which may be a girls' chorus. That is specific. Yet they will be flexible by telling you, "We have different levels and different groupings." When I come up with a suitable image, then the texture is what comes to my mind usually. I write down the basic idea and basic sounding from the image, and then I write a lot of adjectives.

JK: Adjectives in language, in words?

CY: Yes. I have a lot of these adjectives to inspire myself.

JK: Do you write these in Chinese language?

CY: Anything. Chinese, basically—or English. Whatever word or language that tells the direct feeling. Then I have the textures coming afterwards. You aim for certain instrumentation. So, this sound comes to your mind. After that, the structure is important. The structure also includes the beginning, ending, and basic sounding effect. All of these come. Also how to relate this and that. For example, language and music. How to construct this melody. Is it pure pitch-orientated in certain styles? Or reciting style, which has pitches written, yet they are not necessarily connected to diatonic or chromatic or whole tone or whatever scales? It will be different from existing scales or styles. It may be language-orientated, it could be pitch written. Yet it was not in singing style, it would be reciting style. Those are the possibilities. Even written for instruments, they could be in different styles and combinations as well. The texture would mean everything.

JK: When you're at the beginning of a piece, do you know where you're going?

CY: Most of the time when I write the first page, which is absolutely in draft form. Sometimes I have the idea of the whole structure first. I use the "golden section" a lot. The "golden mean."

JK: I use the golden mean in my rehearsals while conducting. It's very effective.

CY: I do that with plans and structures. Sometimes I calculate it into details. Sometimes I know in general the proportion. Some people analyze my works, and in their dissertations and theses they would pick different pieces into serious consideration of structure.

JK: In these dissertations and theses, do you discover things you didn't know about in your music?

CY: I did see things that I had not thought about, but I didn't reject because if they are very logical. . . . Sometimes they analyze with three possibilities, different constructing ways.

JK: You like to use very precise notation to guide the musicians, and yet it's still notation on a page. So how much freedom does a performer have?

CY: Sometimes I am not pleased when the tempo is totally different. For example, in the past, sometimes I didn't put the meter number on top, assuming the Chinese training, trained musicians, they are used to Russian or French style. And when they saw the musical term, they had that kind of a feeling.

JK: But when it comes to other orchestras that may not have the same training. . . .

CY: Exactly. Also, many musicians don't play the same repertoire of the musicians who you knew before, and they would have different interpretations.

JK: Does that make you be even more specific about what you want?

CY: Yes. Later I had to put everything in the beginning so I don't have to worry that much. Nowadays I hear recordings sent to me by different groups around the world, and I'm satisfied. Even though I don't know them at all, I'm really pleased with the outcome.

JK: What you're writing down is being understood.

CY: Exactly. Not even from the materials, the basic tempo, but also from the language and style.

JK: Do you read reviews?

CY: I like to read them and even some negative ones. It teaches me, because it shows you different aesthetics. And I read reviews of others. I read other compositions because I go to concerts a lot. Also I read other composers' music a lot, being on panels, being reviewers and evaluators. I use others' eyes and ears.

JK: I'm curious, when you combine instruments from two different cultures, how do you handle tuning?

CY: Now, the Chinese instruments are tuned in kind of a Western scale, although particular instruments have special tuning. Not until you really know the language itself, you cannot deal with the unisons or European classical harmonic progressions because that doesn't match the same system. So in my case, I avoid using that kind of unison or put those pitches in functional use.

JK: So the combinations are very important?

CY: Yes. That's why, when you hear my pieces written for so-called mixed ensembles with Chinese and Western instruments, you don't hear a kind of a Western harmonic progression. If you know the languages of both sides, then you know how to combine and how to avoid. The combination to pick the best possible combined form into your texture is important. I teach orchestration, which teaches me a lot, because when you teach orchestration you know what are the instrument's best possibilities to be used alone or combined with others. That "with others" is an important opening. It could be with Chinese instruments or with singers or with some others and so, when you think of different angles, it's a combination finally. It becomes a new product.

JK: You have absolute pitch. How do you handle perfect pitch when dealing with folk songs?

CY: That's easy, because many of the folk songs are sung. When the farmers sing, you immediately know the pitches.

JK: But they must have quartertones and bends.

CY: That's even easier with absolute pitch. Absolute pitch means any pitch. That means microtonal. That means sliding, and any kind of ornaments. And when you have that pitch in mind, you can notate them precisely. You don't skip anything when things are sung between keys. Absolute pitch doesn't mean any kind of a scale, it just means high and low relative in my case. Any noise as you sing any song. Because a song could be a noise, too, if it's not organized—the pitch is noise. A kind of a noise.

JK: Was there a defining moment when you knew you were a composer?

CY: Not really. I grew up as a classical-music violinist. Piano first. But piano was not my major. Violin was my major. My dad used to play a lot of records every day, and I grew up with this. He played the violin, not professionally. My mom plays the piano better than I do.

JK: Was it unusual to be a professional woman musician in China?

CY: In China there is not such discrimination in this field. If you say in countryside, it might be different, because women are not as important as men as labor for the family and the villages. They kept all these sons for their power and growing for the family. But in cities, for example, particularly after 1949, all women went out to work. They put kids in kindergartens to be taken care of collectively by teachers and not at home. So, generally, in the office working places, there is not much difference.

JK: So, when you came to the United States, was there a difference that you noticed about being a woman?

CY: When I first came, I didn't view it as strange at all, because New York is such an international city, and it's like Beijing. Then I started working as a resident composer in the Women's Philharmonic. The orchestra took my work to Washington, D.C., to play for the National Organization for Women. It was a huge hit. At the Kennedy Center. The whole audience was women! It was a whole women's event. It was striking, really. I went to the event, and it was so exciting. The first time I have seen so many women. This was so powerful. When the leader spoke on the stage, "We!" It was the first time I had a really strong education in this, and I started doing research, because I accepted many proposals from women around the world. I recommended many women composers to different organizations. I was responsible to write a lot of support letters and introductions. And then I reviewed hundreds of orchestra scores written by women composers. I also learned the history of how women were discriminated against and how women could stand up to fight for the right. I learned all this, and I played in many fund-raising concerts. We did research and told stories of older times. One hundred years ago, how women started composing and how women's position was suppressed in society and how and why we have to promote women composers and musicians. So our Women's Philharmonic not only promoted composers but also new music and also women performers and conductors. We invited several conductors a year for our reading session. We promoted them locally, nationally, and internationally and put their names out in order to let other officers know about those great younger women conductors, and then we promoted the musicians who are very good but were discriminated against by other professional orchestras. And from those education programs (and for me, those are education programs), I learned about the history and vision. Responsibility.

JK: So you feel as a woman composer you have a responsibility.

CY: To promote. Yes. I was in the position so I worked hard. Basically, I have promoted women composers since then until now. I have brought many names and their works. I recommended works to many other professional performing organizations.

JK: You became an advocate.

CY: Absolutely. I think that is my job.

JK: Still today?

CY: Yes, because after I started I cannot stop. I do not want to stop.

JK: Where would you like to see contemporary music go in the next twenty or fifty years?

CY: I think more multicultural and more deeply rooted in societies. Why do I say societies? Because they are multicultures, multifunctional, and different locations and different groups of people. Eventually they would be whole in the world. Still, I encourage them to do their own work well in their place. If you don't work hard enough as a person in your community, it's not going to work.

JK: So, you have to be a good citizen in your community, in your society, in your life, and that will help inform your music?

CY: Yes. That will help you get inspiration, and that will get more support from you to the societies and human beings. Get more positive feedback from you as a creative artist to benefit the culture and society. I think that is important. Not just being heard on the stage. It's important not only in the educational field, but also in the creation-artist field.

JK: I have learned that the more I understand about a composer, the better I can interpret her or his music. In that light, I would like to ask a few questions about your experience during the Cultural Revolution in China. It happened at such an influential time in your life as a teenager. How did you experience it?

CY: I was a farmer then, when I was fifteen and sixteen, because I was sent to the countryside. But it was not only me; it was the whole country. All students, high-school and middle students, were kicked out from the city. I was being sent to the countryside to work as a farmer, actually to be reeducated. It was particularly if you studied Western classical music and your mind was deeply polluted by capitalism thinking, thought, or ideas or tradition, so you should be reeducated. That was the brainwashing period of time. The hard labor work was pretty miserable. When I was fifteen, sometimes I would place all this mud, sand, stone, concrete into two baskets and use a pole to carry it to the top of a mountain more than twenty times a day. We got up at four o'clock in the morning to beat the sun. Our major job was to plant rice and vegetables. Helping farmers and being reeducated. You had to read all these political articles to be brainwashed. That kind of thing happened maybe everywhere in the country.

JK: You were there for two years. Did you have music?

CY: I brought my violin with me, located at the end of my bed. They didn't know, because it was hidden in the corner. I slept upper level. Too tall, they cannot see. Then, every night I slept with the violin, so I only slept in half of this small bed. In my spare time I would play. Only revolutionary songs were allowed to be played, and farmers could sing those tunes anyway, so when they recognized the tunes, they wouldn't stop me. And then I could play all the techniques along with the melodies. That's how I kept my fingers moving. I put all of these Paganini techniques underneath the melodies.

JK: Of the folk songs?

CY: Not folk songs. Folk songs were not allowed. I played the revolutionary songs. Folk songs were prohibited as well. You know why? Because, as I said, folk song is related closely to culture and daily life. Love songs are not allowed to be sung. Love songs are a kind of a pollution. To repeat the old tradition is pollution as well.

JK: So, as long as you played the revolutionary songs, they would let you play.

CY: Yes. Those were songs with Chairman Mao's sayings into music settings. Those were the songs. And I still remember all of his sayings through singing those songs. In these two years, hard labor dominated. But before I became a farmer, you remember, 1966, the whole country stopped. Ten years—no school. My mom borrowed books from her colleagues who had children a little bit older than we were. All these textbooks were sent to be burned already, but some were left. We learned those, continuing mathematics and geography and physics at home. My mom taught me Japanese and English. I still remember I was the one who copied those textbooks she borrowed, and that was the first time I learned how to type. My family, we hid all these things. Like a typewriter. I copied all these books. I typed them all. From 1966 to 1968 I did such things. We hung very thick curtains in the windows and hung a thin blanket between a hammer and the steel board of the piano. We read through my home library, my dad's collection of scores. We read through all of them on this piano. Nobody could hear it. I played through all of this, too, with the mute. The mute is metal. Heavy metal. Nobody could hear. When my brother played those concertos, I would play the piano parts of the orchestra for these two years. Because we escaped from the first wave of home search by the Red Guards. When they came the first time, the neighborhood said, "Don't touch this family. They're medical doctors who save many of our lives for the past several decades. They are model doctors."

JK: So you were saved from the first wave.

CY: Yes. So that's why we could keep all these scores at home and study secretly. We listened to these records, for how many hours a day I forget. Only six hours of sleeping. Otherwise, we'd play all these records. I can memorize all these records before they are broken. One day, the Red Guards came again. They were taken away. Everything broken. Destroyed all of this because the records became scratched and you could not listen to it. They are destroyed totally. Then I left the city to become a farmer the next day. In the countryside I played revolutionary songs. I used these scores as exercises, like inserts between phrases, because I memorized them already. I didn't need to read anything. Everything was taken away.

JK: So you found a way to keep the music.

CY: My mom told us to let them take anything and everything. Anything that can be bought is not a treasure. The treasure is in your brain. You learned them already. Those are the things I still could remember. I was fifteen and had already memorized these scores. But that's the way I kept my music fingers moving for the two years. I was fortunate. All my classmates stayed in the countryside for four or five years. I only spent two years because the revolutionary operas needed orchestra members.

JK: How did they know you could play and find you?

CY: Somebody from the Peking Opera Company noticed that there was a girl who used to win children's competitions by playing this violin, and then they searched. They found me; I was working in the field under the sun. It was an army officer who became the leader of the Peking Opera Company who drove the jeep to the countryside to pick me from the field. I was taken back to Guangzhou city. And when I arrived they said, "Play." That night was the time the army leaders would see the dress rehearsal of our show, and to say "yes" or "no." If it was a "yes," our whole company next year had a job.

JK: That was revolutionary-sanctioned opera, right?

CY: Yes, that was one of the model operas. I said, "Oh, no problem. It's sight-reading." They didn't have a good violinist because all the orchestra members from our symphony orchestras were sent to the countryside. They were considered worse because they were intellectuals. More polluted. They were not allowed to come back. That's why they took young students. I was a student. When I was seventeen, I became a concertmaster. That night we passed the audition, and we kept that job, and that is the Guangzhou Peking Opera. We had more than one hundred performances per year. It was a huge show with a fancy setting on stage. We had daily rehearsal full-time.

JK: Now that's a lot of music . . . was it a positive experience?

CY: Yes, it was. We were allowed to play Western music. We were the only people allowed to touch it, because it was for the purpose of playing revolutionary operas. You should be trained better. So we were allowed to accept all standard repertoire from Hong Kong. I could accept it if the accepting address was in the Peking Opera Orchestra, not at home, then we could take them.

JK: Because it helped training?

CY: Yeah. So I went though all standard repertoire. All concertos. All these studies. Everything. Every day we had practice time and rehearsal time and then rehearsal time with actors, and in the afternoon for two hours we had political study with groups from the orchestra. Three hours a show. And after the show you had to do self-criticism, if you played a wrong note or had a wrong entrance. Or, if you heard somebody make a mistake, you had to point it out. I was the concertmaster, so I pointed everything out. I was the point person to tell all these mistakes.

JK: Was that difficult to do? Not technically but personally?

CY: Personally, it's hard. Technically, it's the easiest part for me. Because these orchestra members asked me to be an assistant when they practiced their scales. So I know all instruments very well, because sometimes I was the one who helped them do such things like dictation of their cadenzas from a Russian trumpet concerto which they didn't have a score for. I helped orchestra members in practicing scales for every instrument.

JK: So you learned all the instruments?

CY: Yeah. Also, the Chinese instruments, I helped them to copy parts because they don't know Western notation better than me. I have to translate all this from Western notation to Chinese system for them to practice. Also they ask me to help and listen to their scales, to adjust the position of pitches on their instruments. I learned the structures of their instruments and their fingerings. Through the copying, I know all their marks and symbols of the fingerings.

JK: And you did that for eight years, yes?

CY: Yeah. I was a composer, too, because then they had to create some operas by their own company besides the ten models. I became a composer automatically, I guess.

JK: So it was during the Peking Opera troupe that you started formally composing.

CY: Exactly. We went to the armies to perform sometimes, and we didn't have time to change the stage setting. So we had to put out the violin group outside the curtains to play the revolutionary songs. I had to arrange them for the group to play to please the audience when they changed the staging for the show. So in that case I became a composer. Always wet ink. Sometimes, the whole orchestra members were in the room and fought for each page to copy their own parts. The next day was the performance. I did that for eight years.

JK: Wow. That's trial by fire.

CY: When the higher-education system reopened, they said to submit things. I went to the orchestra library, and the librarian said to take whatever I wanted.

JK: Do you still have that music?

CY: I submitted them to the conservatory when I was admitted.

JK: Is there anything you can take from the two years of reeducation and labor that you can put into your music today?

CY: Oh no! Nothing. That was totally not useful. But in that period of time, I got my view of my motherland, my view of society, and my view of people. . . . This was the first time I got in touch with farmers closely. I had never known any farmers when I grew up.

JK: Because you were an intellectual in the city.

CY: I figured out we spoke the same dialect. Everything. I knew a woman farmer, and she sang a lullaby to her kid. These were farmers who were not educated, but she could sing the lullaby. Pure sound. Like a beautiful melody. Like speaking actually, but straight tone, nontrained. After I went back to the city, she brought me plums during the harvest. We became friends.

JK: Are your parents still alive?

CY: My mom is still alive, ninety-one. In Beijing. We took her to Beijing.

JK: She must be very proud.

CY: Yes. Before my dad passed away, he was very proud, because all of us grew up already. My younger brother is the concertmaster of the China Philharmonic. And the orchestra toured the States three times, and he is also a professor and head of the Chamber Music Division of the Central Conservatory in Beijing. My sister, after leaving the conservatory, became a pianist in the army orchestra until she retired. Now she is a pianist in the China Philharmonic as well. She and my brother are colleagues now.

JK: Your experience as musicians during the Cultural Revolution is extraordinary. Is there a connection, a community, or is it something that happened in the past and is best left in the past?

CY: We are related closely. After the time of the Cultural Revolution, we were in conservatory. That was the first class of composers being admitted, my class of thirty-two composers. In 2008, we celebrated our thirtieth anniversary. We gave a concert in Europe with works composed by my classmates from the conservatory. I brought them into UMKC [University of Missouri–Kansas City] several of them different times. Carnegie Hall presented a concert of my classmates last year. Sometimes we meet at concerts and parties, and still I am a visiting professor back to Beijing, so I am very close to all others, because I teach all their students and brought some of them to UMKC. And all my classmates are high-ranked in China, department chairs, conservatory president and vice president. All of this became closely related.

JK: So you're not only an advocate for women composers, you're also an advocate for Asian composers.

CY: Yes, throughout all these years. Particularly Asian women composers. That is more specific.

JK: Now, you're still young and have lots and lots of music left, but are you at a point yet where you're beginning to think about legacy?

CY: I think all compositions are a learning process. I'm glad to see all the past compositions are being played throughout the world. They pick different pieces that I wrote to perform in different types of concerts. Orchestra, choral, band, chamber. Particularly chamber works on many albums and festivals and chamber series. I don't know about personal legacy. I only know about legacy for culture. Culture would be considered more important, because my music is part of my culture.

***

Works by Chen Yi

All works published by Theodore Presser Company unless otherwise noted.

ORCHESTRAL ENSEMBLES

The Ancient Chinese Beauty, for recorders and string orchestra (2008).
Ballad, Dance, and Fantasy, featuring cello (2003).
Ba Yin (the Eight Sounds), for saxophone quartet and string orchestra (2001).

Caramoor's Summer, for chamber orchestra (2003).
Celebration (2005).
Chinese Folk Dance Suite, featuring violin (2000).
Concerto for Reeds, for oboe, sheng, and chamber orchestra (2008).
Duo Ye, for chamber orchestra (1985).
Duo Ye, No. 2, for full orchestra (1987).
Eleanor's Gift, featuring cello (1998).
Fiddle Suite, for huqin and chamber orchestra or full orchestra (1997).
Fountains of KC (2011).
Ge Xu (Antiphony) (1994).
The Golden Flute Concerto, featuring flute (1997).
Jing Diao (2011).
The Linear (1994).
Momentum (1998).
Mount a Long Wind (2010).
Overture, for youth orchestra (2008).
Percussion Concerto (1998).
Piano Concerto (1992).
Prelude and Fugue (2009).
Prospect Overture (2008).
Rhyme of Fire (2008).
Romance and Dance, for two violins and string orchestra (1998).
Romance of Hsiao and Ch'in, for two violins and string orchestra (1995).
Shuo, for string orchestra (1994).
Si Ji (Four Seasons) (2005).
Spring in Dresden, featuring violin (2005).
Sprout, for string orchestra (1986).
Symphony "Humen 1839" (2009).
Symphony No. 1 (available from the composer, 1986).
Symphony No. 2 (1993).
Symphony No. 3 (2003).
Tu (2002).
Two Sets of Wind and Percussion Instruments (available from the composer, 1986).
Xian Shi, concerto for viola (1983).

CHINESE INSTRUMENTAL ORCHESTRAS AND ENSEMBLES

The Ancient Beauty, for dizi, erhu, pipa, zheng, and strings (2006).
Fiddle Suite, for huqin and Chinese traditional instrumental orchestra; adapted from *Fiddle Suite,* for huqin and orchestra (1997/2008).
Overture for Chinese Traditional Instrumental Orchestra (available from the composer, 1989).
Overture No. 2, for Chinese traditional instrumental orchestra (available from the composer, 1990).
Suite Quintet, for pipa, di, yangqin, sanxian, and erhu (available from the composer, 1991).

The Tide, for xun, yangqin, pipa, zheng, percussion, gaohu, and erhu (available from the composer, 1988).
Xie Zi, for two di, sheng, liuqin, zheng, and sanxian (available from the composer, 1985).

BAND/WIND ENSEMBLE

Dragon Rhyme (2010).
Spring Festival, for middle-school band (AMF Bandquest, 1999).
Suite from China West (2007).
Tu (2003).
UMKC Fanfare (2009).
Wind (2010).

CHAMBER ENSEMBLES

Ancient Dances Cheering, Longing, and Wondering, for pipa and percussion (2005).
. . . as like a raging fire . . ., for flute, clarinet, violin, cello, and piano (2002).
At the Kansas City Chinese New Year Concert, for string quartet (2002).
Blue Dragon Sword Dance, for string quartet (2002).
Burning, for string quartet (2002).
Chinese Ancient Dances, for clarinet and piano (2004).
Chinese Fables, for erhu, pipa, cello, and percussion (2002).
Dunhuang Fantasy Concerto, for organ and chamber wind ensemble (1999).
Feng, for woodwind quintet (1998).
Fiddle Suite, for huqin and string quartet or quintet (1997).
Fisherman Song, for violin and piano (1980).
From the Old Peking Folklore, for violin and piano (2009).
The Han Figurines, for violin, clarinet, tenor saxophone, double bass, piano, and percussion (2006).
Happy Rain on a Spring Night, for flute, clarinet, violin, cello, and piano (2004).
Joy of Reunion, for oboe, viola, cello, and double bass (available from the composer, 2001).
Near Distance, for flute, clarinet, percussion, piano, violin, and cello (1988).
Night Thoughts, for flute, cello, and piano (2004).
Ning, for violin, cello, and pipa (2001).
Pipa Rhyme, for pipa and fourteen players (available from the composer, 1993).
Qi, for flute, cello, piano, and percussion (1996–97).
Romance and Dance, for violin and piano (1999).
Romance of Hsiao and Ch'in, for cello and piano (1998).
Septet, for erhu, pipa, percussion, and saxophone quartet (2008).
Shuo, for string quartet (1994).
Song in Winter
  trio for harpsichord, di, and zheng (1993).
  quartet for flute, zheng, piano, and percussion (1994).
Sound of the Five, for cello and string quartet (1998).
Sparkle, for flute, clarinet, percussion, piano, violin, cello, and bass (1992).

Sprout, for string quartet (2009).
Suite for Cello and Chamber Winds (2004).
Three Bagatelles from China West (2006).
  flute and piano, or two flutes
  guanzi and sheng
Tibetan Tunes, for violin, cello, and piano (2007).
Tunes from My Home, for violin, cello, and piano (2007).
Woodwind Quintet, for woodwind quintet (1987).
Woodwind Quintet No. 3, for woodwind quintet (2008).
Wu Yu (2002).
  flute, clarinet/bass clarinet, bassoon, violin, cello, and percussion
  flute, oboe, clarinet, violin, viola, cello, and contrabass
Xian Shi, for viola, piano and percussion (1983).
Yangko, for violin and percussion (2005).

SOLO INSTRUMENTS

Ba Ban, for piano (1999).
Duo Ye, for piano (1984).
Guessing, for piano (1989).
Ji-Dong-Nuo, for piano (2005).
Jing Marimba, for marimba (2009).
Memory, for violin (2010).
Monologue (Impressions on the True Story of Ah Q), for B-flat clarinet (1993).
The Points, for pipa (1991).
Singing in the Mountain, for piano (2002).
Two Chinese Bagatelles, for piano (1985).
Variations on "Awariguli," for piano (1978).

CHORAL/VOCAL

Angel Island Passages, for children's chorus and string quartet (2010).
Arirang, Korean folk-song arrangement for choir (1994).
As in a Dream (1988).
  soprano, pipa, and zheng
  soprano, violin, and cello
Bright Moonlight, for mezzo and piano (2000).
The Bronze Taotie (from *From the Path of Beauty*), for SATB a cappella (2009).
Capriccio, for mixed choir, organ, and solo percussion (2001).
Chinese Mountain Songs, for women's choir (2001).
Chinese Myths Cantata, for male choir piano, strings, and Chinese instruments (1996).
Chinese Poems, for children's chorus in six levels (1999).
Distance Can't Keep Us Two Apart, for unaccompanied mixed choir (2011).
Early Spring, for mixed choir and chamber ensemble (2011).
From the Path of Beauty, for mixed choir and string quartet (2008).

A Horseherd's Mountain Song, for mixed chorus, a cappella (2003).
KC Capriccio, for wind ensemble and mixed chorus (2000).
Know You How Many Petals Falling, for mixed choir (2001).
Lament of the Twin Stars (arranged from Cantonese Music), for male choir (available from the composer, 1996).
Landscape, for mixed choir a cappella (2003).
Looking at the Sea, for women's choir (2006).
Meditation, for mezzo-soprano and piano (1999).
Sakura, Sakura, for men's chorus (1994).
A Set of Chinese Folk Songs (1994).
  children's SA(T) chorus and strings
  men's choir a cappella
  SATB and piano, vols. 1–3
Shady Grove, for SATB choir (2001).
Singin' in the Dark (Songs of the American Frontier), in collaboration with Alice Parker, for choir and orchestra (available from the composer, 1995).
A Single Bamboo Can Easily Bend, for mixed chorus, a cappella (2003).
Spring Dreams, for SATB chorus (1997).
Spring Rain, for SATB chorus (2010).
Tang Poems, cantata (1995).
  men's chorus a cappella
  SATB chorus and chamber orchestra
Three Poems from the Song Dynasty, for SATB choir (in preparation).
To the New Millennium, for soprano, mezzo-soprano, and mixed choir (2001).
Two Chinese Folk Songs, for mixed chorus (available from the composer, 2003).
The West Lake, for SATB a cappella (2003).
With Flowers Blooming, for women's choir (2010).
Written on a Rainy Night, for men's choir or SATB (1995).
Xuan, for mixed choir (2001).

COMPUTER GAME

Qin Tomb of the Middle Kingdom, original soundtrack, available from Warner Electronic Publishing (1995).

Michael Provost

7

Tania León

Tania León's connection to her birth country of Cuba is evident in her music. Born in Havana in 1943, her family has always been a great source of encouragement to her. Her formal music education began when she was four years old; her grandmother, noticing León's musical aptitude, insisted that the Peyrellade's Conservatorio de Música accept her as a student. León's awareness of global culture was cultivated at the conservatory. She explains that her school celebrated all composers, past and living, from distant countries and local Cuba, making traditional and contemporary sounds. This early influence of familial support, cultural fusion, and artistic acceptance gave León confidence to pursue her music on the world stage.

As we converse, León briefly recounts the challenge of her immigration from Cuba to the United States in her early twenties as a passenger in the Freedom Flights lottery program. Raised with the understanding that we are all from the same world culture, León connected immediately with the messages she heard from the U.S. civil rights movement upon her arrival in New York City in the mid-1960s. Although she struggled with the English language initially, she credits her music and the supportive Cuban population in New York for carrying her through difficult times.

León is an accomplished pianist. Like Jeanine Tesori, she was taught the musical skills of improvisation and transposition along with classical technique. Her skills prepared her for a life-changing moment when she was asked to play piano for a dance class in New York City. Although she and the dance teacher did not speak the same language, the music communication was clear. By happenstance, Arthur Mitchell heard León play that day, leading to an invitation to play for a new dance company. León recounts with joy the artistic education she received from some of the most prominent artists in New York while working at the newly established Dance Theatre of Harlem. Her musical education continued as a composer, conductor, and teacher.

Today, León's compositional catalog celebrates diversity of musical style and genre, consisting of works for orchestra, ballet, opera and theater, mixed genre, solo works, and smaller instrumental repertoire. Her work *To and Fro,* as performed by the Nodus Ensemble on their album *Sonidos Cubanos,* was nominated for a 2010 Latin Grammy for Best Classical Contemporary Composition. She was again nominated for a 2012 Latin Grammy for her work *Inura,* conducted by León and performed by Son Sonora Voices, Son Sonora Ensemble and DanceBrazil Percussion, on León's album *In Motion.*

Surrounded by musical fusion in Cuba and then the United States, León was prepared to develop her own language of melodic and rhythmic complexity. Often written for advanced musicians with technical skill and accomplished musicianship, her music develops out of both the language of the Americas and European influences. Her harmonies often combine European- and American-influenced sounds and compositional techniques with textural and rhythmic layers from her own heritage and experiences. Her work abounds with independent lines, rhythmic energy and motion, and unexpected percussive sounds. She recognizes that those unfamiliar with certain musical traditions may have challenges teaching or learning some of her work, and she encourages performers to seek out the whole before the parts. Equally respected as a conductor and a composer, León discusses in this interview how to approach her music effectively.

León finds her time divided between composing, conducting, and teaching. A professor at Brooklyn College since 1985, and the holder of three honorary doctorates, she was named Distinguished Professor of the City University of New

York in 2006. She is also in demand as a conductor, having gained early conducting experience as the first music director of the Dance Theatre of Harlem and providing musical direction for *The Wiz* on Broadway. León is a frequent guest conductor for the orchestras of Europe.

An advocate for local composers, new music, and one world culture, León instituted the Brooklyn Philharmonic Community Concert Series in 1978, and in 1994 she cofounded the Sonidos de las Américas Festivals with the American Composers Orchestra. From 1993 to 1997 she was new-music advisor to Kurt Masur and the New York Philharmonic, and in 2008, she served as the U.S. Artistic Ambassador of American Culture in Madrid. In 2010, León cofounded Composers Now, a citywide festival celebrating contemporary composers in New York City. In addition to owning many of her own titles, much of León's work is published through Peermusic.

Prepared for the opportunities that appeared throughout her life, and with a bravery and self-confidence gained through her family's encouragement and her schooling, León continues to make her mark as a composer and conductor.

***

July 2010, at her home in Nyack, New York

JENNIFER KELLY: Do you enjoy conducting your own works?

TANIA LEÓN: Yes. In my understanding, different music is like different languages. If someone doesn't know the language in my music, the translation might be with a thicker accent than the accent that I have already. So I like to conduct my pieces, so those that would listen to and play the music will be able to understand the work and its rhythms. The language. Once that happens, people have a beginning reference.

JK: When you are not conducting, what is the experience to sit in the audience and watch someone else conduct?

TL: Let's assume you conduct one of my pieces. You're going to do it with your ideas, and it's fine.

JK: As the composer, you accept that.

TL: I accept that, because what can I do? When we conduct Beethoven, we have been listening to Beethoven thousands of times. Even if we do our own interpretation, we know more or less how it goes. But specifically in cases of my music, which is so rhythmic, some of my music contains rhythms that people are not familiar with.

JK: Complex and polyrhythmia.

TL: Polyrhythmia, which is something that for me is a glass of water. I like to understand the essence of all of these different rhythms, or claves in different cultures, and then I create my own. If the person doesn't know the rhythmical syntax, or the flow of that rhythm, one might think it's like Bach, or think it's like Shostakovich or something like that, and it gives it another twist. And that's why it sounds sometimes much more complicated than it is. It's like when I do the polyrhythmia, I don't subdivide anything, and I tell the conductors don't subdivide, because then you break the flow. Musicians are very intelligent, and specifically if you repeat something, they understand all of a sudden where the groove is. So let the musician do it; trust the musician. Just give them the flow of how it goes, and the musician will get it.

JK: So we must make sure that we understand the language of the music. And the more we understand the language of your music, the simpler the process is going to be to come out with an accurate interpretation of the story.

TL: Yes. If you see me conducting my pieces, people say, "Oh, but it's easy!" You know, because I say "1, 2, 3, play! 1, 1, 1-2-3," you know? And then you are hearing all these [rhythm noises] happening.

JK: Don't subdivide, because it's really just 1, 1, 1-2-3.

TL: Exactly, because if you start with subdivision "1 and 2 and 3 and," you put the musicians on crutches. What they have in front of them is already subdivided; so don't try to subdivide on top of that.

JK: I'm remembering last year, I did your arrangement, *El Manisero,* with one of my choirs.

TL: Oh, you did!

JK: And I ended up teaching it both ways. First, I tried to subdivide, because they don't all read music, and so I did the slow subdivision. That worked to a certain extent, but it was frustrating for the students and for me. So I tried it the other way, one voice and one rhythm at a time. We would sing it back and forth and then layer it; we found the pulse, the flow, and then all of a sudden . . .

TL: It started to breathe!

JK: Yes! Everything was so much easier and more enjoyable for them and for me. All of a sudden, a complicated piece didn't seem as complicated.

TL: Exactly. It gets its own life, it starts breathing and pulsing, yes.

JK: So when a conductor picks up a score of Tania León, which can feel very contemporary and initially difficult, especially if they are not familiar with the rhythmic language, do you have any advice on how to better understand the language?

TL: Well, let me say this: basically, the pulse of my music, the heart of my music, sometimes evokes this region of the Americas, from top to bottom—from Canada to Chile, including the Caribbean. In other words, the roots of my music may come from everywhere. For example, you'll find jazz in my music. And it's not something that I am overtly saying, Well, this is going to be jazz. No, the thing is that I have been in the United States for more than forty years, so jazz is part of my experience. I have dealt with a lot of jazz players, jazz musicians, and I love jazz on top of that, so it creeps in there.

JK: What do your three sides, composer, conductor, and your education side, what do they each give to one another?

TL: Everything. It is all interrelated. If you as a conductor decided to compose tomorrow, you would find a way to simplify it for another conductor because you know what they are looking for. You would suggest to them how to do your music in such a way that the conductor will get it done without running into trouble.

JK: You mean in the notation?

TL: Yes, the notation and how it affects the beat or the pattern in the ear.

JK: So you consciously think about that when you're composing?

TL: When I'm composing, I think about how I am going to grid the material for a conductor precisely because I know the complexities that I can actually arrive to. And I know they may be complexities for other people, although not for me, because I'm used to it. So I have to put myself in their position. How am I going to make this in such a way that a conductor gets the idea, gets the results, without driving the conductor crazy?

JK: And as a conductor, what do you learn from the fact that you're a composer when you're up on the podium?

TL: As a conductor, I learn from everybody, because it's not only my work. There's nothing better than conducting someone else's pieces. Because you learn composition. You learn so much about composition. This is connecting to this now, oh I see, now what is important here, you know? You not only see sound; you see the whole technique of the whole thing. It's like seeing a building with x-rays: you see where the wires are, you see everything.

JK: Can one teach composition?

TL: I don't think so. You can teach a lot of theory, but you cannot develop a composer. A composer is there or not. I think you can teach the rules and give a lot of suggestions. I think one of the things in composition one has to do is to inspire the composer to find the key to his or her imagination.

JK: And how do we help them unlock that imagination?

TL: The inspiration could be actually finding out if these students are really, really drawn towards composition, to make this student in touch with all of the composers that preceded them. And I don't mean listen to the music, but get into their studies, study their scores. I am a big advocate of copying the entire score. By hand. If you want to learn technique, that is the most amazing way of learning technique. It makes you really see what is connecting with what, or how something is developed. I mean, we can teach lots of theory, but when you are going to compose and you're in front of that open page, blank page, I don't know what to tell you.

JK: Do you also compose by hand? Or do you use a computer?

TL: By hand, yes. I like the computer, but I don't like composing on the computer. Sometimes, it's like the computer has a mind, and it can overpower mine.

JK: When you're composing and the initial idea comes into your mind, what do you hear?

TL: It's different every time. When I hear something . . . for example, I always travel with a pad, and I jot down a lot of sketches. If you hear something in your mind, the best thing you can do is whatever is possible in that moment. If you can, grab what you hear and write it down, because when you revisit it, it's not the same.

JK: Are you someone that likes to figure out the architecture first and then go back and fill in, or do you start at the beginning and you don't know where it's going to go, and go to the end?

TL: Well, I have done both. Sometimes I have done the architecture, but I do not prefer it that way. I write a lot and have so many sketches. Later on, the sketches tell me what is the beginning and what is the end. I might have the beginning three times and then say, No, that's not the beginning. The form emerges from the process.

JK: So that seed, that initial idea converges with all of the sketches and tells you what else it's supposed to be.

TL: Yes, what I thought was the end might be the beginning, and what I thought was the beginning might be the end.

JK: How much freedom would a musician have to pick up one of your scores and play? Freedom of articulation, dynamics. . . .

TL: Well, I think that I put in the page as many details as possible. But if the musician gets to the point that those details become part of his or her language in interpretation, and can go even beyond what I've done, fine with me.

JK: What would you still like to write?

TL: I want to do another opera, but in Spanish. I love collaborations, and I love working with other people.

JK: I would like to ask about your history. I think it is important for performers and conductors to have an understanding about the composer as a human being. I believe the more we understand about their lives and what makes up their identity, the better we can understand their musical intentions and interpret their music. So, will you tell me how you got started in music?

TL: The person that is responsible for my life in music is that woman that you see over there in the picture, my grandmother.

JK: She was responsible for you starting to play the piano, yes?

TL: Right. This woman was ahead of her time. She was in Cuba training with the Alliance to be a nurse during World War II. She was like the umbrella over everybody in my family. My grandmother realized when I was four years old that I loved music. She would put on the radio, and I would go crazy. There was music! I would dance; I would sing exactly what was being played in the same key. So, she decided that I had something to do with music, and she brought me to the conservatory when I was four years old. They were not going to take me because I was so young, I did not even read and write. She insisted, so they took me.

JK: So how was it decided that you were going to play piano?

TL: I was so young. That's what they thought they could start me on, piano. And by age five, my grandfather bought a piano. They had to raise eight pesos a month for the piano, and it was not new, but it was a real piano. They all went to my first recital when I was five years old. When I finished playing, my grandmother gave me a bouquet of little roses. Those roses were pressed, and they are still with me.

JK: Your family was not wealthy, so when you talk about them sacrificing for your education, such as sending you to school, buying a piano. . . .

TL: They truly did sacrifice for my education. And I was the first-born, so my family was very interested in seeing or hearing melodies or listening to the music because I introduced new sounds into the house.

JK: How did you decide to leave all of your family and your homeland to go to the United States?

TL: I decided that when I was nine years old. I started saying that I would live in Paris, that I was going to travel and see the world. The first time I really wanted to leave I was seventeen. A family friend of mine with her daughter from the conservatory had left for Florida. They belonged to the Catholic church, and the church was giving applications for people that were in Cuba and wanted to leave as long as they had somebody to sponsor them. So, I asked them if they would sponsor me, and then I applied. I had to wait three years.

JK: So you worked and waited until your number came up! When you came to the United States, did you land in Florida?

TL: In Miami. Like all the Cubans, yes. I stayed there three days, and then I went to New York City, because I left Cuba in pursuit of education, and in pursuit of furthering my studies.

JK: To go deeper into music?

TL: Exactly. I wanted to end up at the French Conservatory, because I was in love with French music. My background included Debussy, Ravel. I studied many other composers, but I gravitated toward French composers. And so I thought that's what I was doing here, coming to the United States, getting some money together, because everybody knew that when one comes to the States, one has the opportunity to earn money. I thought I would be here one or two years, work, raise some money, and continue to France. But immigration told me once I arrived that I would have to stay for at least five years.

JK: That would be hard news to take, I would think.

TL: Yes, it was. So I had to stay here, I couldn't go anywhere. I was not permitted to travel anywhere, because I had no passport. And I decided I could not stay in

Miami and find a job that had nothing to do with music. So, I decided to continue to New York City.

JK: So many things were happening in New York City in the mid-sixties. How did you take it all in?

TL: Well, I am made up of many different things, beginning with my mentality and how I see life, and my experiences. My grandmother was a hybrid of two races, and my family is as hybrid as cheese. So I was fortunate to be in a family of different people, different cultures and races that had tremendous respect for their own cultures. They nurtured my thinking.

JK: And coming from such a mix of cultures, it's a respect for so many cultures whether or not they are part of your own.

TL: Exactly, so I never saw myself as this specific race, or specific anything, because I am a hybrid of all of these people. And these are the people that contributed to my education. So I wanted to contribute in this way. My grandmother, grandfather, mother, father—there is Spanish, Asian, African, Cuban, so many roots contributing to my education. They were all rooting for me. So I got here, and I realized what was going on. I arrived when Martin Luther King was publicly marching. And he was talking my talk, that we are all equal, integration, that school standards should be equal. That's how I grew up! I would go to the symphony, and everybody was in the symphony. So to arrive in the United States and to find what to me was so disparate, I just didn't understand why.

JK: Were you all alone in New York?

TL: Well, coming to New York was the best thing I did for myself by that point in my life. I was in the center of this incredible energy happening, and I saw for the first time, in a way, masses of people walking in the streets, and I started learning about the civil rights movement. I didn't understand anything at first. I was then taken in by two friends from Cuba, a married couple. I lived on their sofa for about three months. The Cuban community, everyone was helping each other. Sarita copied music, and that's how I met her in La Habana. Sarita and I found an organization called American Council for Émigrés in the Professions listed in the yellow pages. In fact, that organization gave me the first award I received in this country, 1971. That award is still up on my wall! They heard me play piano, so they offered to audition me in two weeks at the New York College of Music. I did the audition, and they gave me a scholarship on the spot. That was the beginning.

JK: How were you accepted by people at the college?

TL: While I was at the New York College of Music, they sent me to NYU [New York University] to learn English, because I did not speak any English, and I had to take academic courses in order to validate my music degrees. I was told that in this country, my degrees from Cuba did not mean anything. New York College tested my knowledge of music first. I passed almost everything that had to do with sight reading, and I transposed easily on the piano. They were surprised and asked how I knew these things. But at that time, I didn't yet know that the notes were called A, B, C; I know the *solfege* system, for me it was *do, re, mi, fa, sol. . . .*

JK: Different language.

TL: Yes, in a different language. So I took the tests, and I remember distinctly that one of the teachers said, "Go home and learn English, and then come back." It was really rough for me at that time, but I had to make this happen. I needed to earn money, so I got a job playing piano in a Spanish restaurant. I wrote to my grandmother about the news of my new job. To my surprise, my grandmother sent me a letter back asking why, with all of the years I spent at the conservatory, studying up to eight hours a day at the piano, why was I going to play in a restaurant where people were not even listening to me? [*Laughs*] So I quit that night.

JK: Her letter meant a great deal to you. What did you do after you quit?

TL: She was encouraging me to find my place. Well, things change; there is always a mystery. To me, life is a mystery, because sometimes things appear like magic as long as you are paying attention. Here is what I mean. So, while I was at NYU, I made friends with another pianist, Laura Wilson. One day, Laura got sick, and we were in the same class, so she said, "Tania, do me a favor. Could you go and play for me at this dance school? I cannot do it, and I do not want to lose the spot." I said, "Okay, what do I have to do?" She gave me the books—marches, waltzes, mazurkas, everything. "You listen to the beat that the teacher gives you, or she might say, 'I need a waltz,' whatever." Harlem School of the Arts, Dorothy Maynor. Okay, so I sat at the piano, the teacher came in, neither one of us spoke English, and we started. Between classes, it was my opportunity to really taste the piano. And while I was playing, a man passed by the studio, and I saw him in the mirror. I thought, Who is this guy? He looked and walked like a star! [*Laughs*] Later, he called me and explained that he had a project he wanted me to be a part of, and asked if I would like to be his pianist. I arrived to play, he had about four students there, and he started teaching. Laura lent me the piano books, but he said, "No books. You play, improvise."

JK: Which you learned how to do growing up, so that was easy for you. . . .

TL: Exactly. Arthur Mitchell. He said, "Follow me!" Then I found out that he was a premiere dancer of the New York City Ballet working with [George] Balanchine, the man for which Stravinsky wrote all of those scores that I studied. And then I met Balanchine and Jerome Robbins, and all these people started coming in to back up his project. And to train us. So Balanchine taught me all the choreography, the music with the choreography. He was a fantastic musician! We didn't have to speak English. So I started meeting all these people. The big stars of the community of color started coming in: Sidney Poitier, Leontyne Price, Harry Belafonte, Jessye Norman, Marian Anderson, Josephine Baker, and many others. Cicely Tyson gave all the dancers and musicians lessons about how to conduct ourselves on stage, how to move. Arthur taught me how to bow, everything. They took care of us.

JK: What an education.

TL: It was amazing! Balanchine himself would come and talk to us, teach us. Jerome Robbins taught me how to follow the choreography of his ballet *Afternoon of a Faun,* set to the music of Debussy. Debussy! So all of a sudden, I was there with French music and all these incredible people.

JK: So maybe New York wasn't so bad to be in!

TL: No! It was like miracles.

JK: One of the things I'm fascinated with is the notion of identity, and I don't mean a label of identity—to me, identity is everything that makes up a person. All of their experience.

TL: Yes, yes, absolutely.

JK: After reading about you, and now hearing you speak, I understand more about your music. Your music is every nuance of your experience, culture, and heritage. Your music is everything you grew up with and are connected to, and I better understand why you reject your music being put into a single category or classification. It is a hybrid of everything becoming its own entity.

TL: Yes that's my definition. Entity I created. In other words, you create your entity.

JK: So, in your music there's a little piece of this, and a little piece of that, and everything together, but then it becomes uniquely León music. It is your voice. Are you consciously aware of wanting to take from everything to mold it together?

TL: Well, I believe very much in the syncretic idea of everything—that's why I say that everything is interrelated. Syncretic, why? Because we call American music a hybrid of many things. All the music of the world, same story. Everybody says, "Oh, Cuban music!" But the Cuban music is a composite of influences of the Caribbean Amerindians, Spaniards, Africanos, Asians, people of French heritage that flew from Haiti every time that Haiti had a revolution, as Haiti is a French colony. In other words, you put all of that together in the soup—that created the music of Cuba.

JK: A giant mix of cultures creating a giant mix of art.

TL: Exactly. But we have to look back even earlier, because this music is already coming in to bear with all of the earlier heritages, like the French music already has its own mix. I always say that the Moors were in Spain for eight hundred years, so when you hear music from Spain, you hear the Arabs. So when I hear people talking negatively about immigration, I feel so bad. Because this is what we've been doing since day one of this planet, going from one place to the other. I happened to get here because the people that are my ancestors came to this continent from different parts of the world.

JK: You were just recently in a concert with a focus on immigrant composers, which brings up the question, Is there still a need in the twenty-first century for things like women-only concerts, or immigrant-only concerts, or Latin American–composer concerts? Is there still a need for that?

TL: I don't think so. What we need are for role models to be visible—Latin Americans, people of color. . . . Why do we still need to even categorize women composers? Because women composers might not be as active as they should be everywhere, or because their music is not included as much as it should be. Why do we still need concerts comprising composers of color? Because where are they? . . . Why do we still need concerts comprising composers of Latin America? One thing I can tell you is that when I studied in the conservatory, and I learned the music of Tchaikovsky, Liszt, Debussy, Satie, de Falla, nobody told me at that time, "This one comes from Spain, this one comes from Germany," you know? It was through the music. For example, when I learned Liszt's *Hungarian Dances,* I found out that Liszt was Hungarian. It became a conversation about culture. When I played the *Polonaise,* that's when I found out that Chopin was from Poland. Basically the label was "classical music," period. But they were from all these different countries, with different cultures, and each of their music sounded different. Role models we need. Role models we need to be visible.

JK: I would say that you are one who is very visible and works at making yourself visible, therefore becoming a role model for cultural connection.

TL: I understand what you are saying and yes, that is nice. But, on the other hand, I don't want to pursue being a token for the idea because it can get to the point where you are cosmetic. I want to be a creative entity. There may be someone who writes very complex music, and it ends up being not about the music but about the complexities of the music. This person may be known because he exists in the canon or in the pantheon of what we call composers. But that isn't what I mean about being visible. In reality, there are very few visible composers that look like me or talk like me, or come from the place I come from, or whatever, right? But I shouldn't be an exception. For example, El Sistema [the Venezuelan system of orchestral education and performance]. When you look at the members of the orchestras of El Sistema, they reflect the members of our society. The world of composition should reflect the same thing.

JK: There are clearly challenges to being a classical-music composer today: cuts in school funding, orchestras and choirs folding, grants being cut. So what does classical music or the composers and musicians in it need to do to ensure that there is still classical music one hundred years from now?

TL: Well, that is the interesting conversation that everyone has today, but what we call classical music is something we got used to over a couple of centuries ago. Carnegie Hall is going to celebrate its 120th anniversary. One of the composers that inaugurated it was Tchaikovsky. Dvorak premiered his *New World Symphony* at Carnegie Hall [in 1893, performed by the Philharmonic Society of New York]. Now, if we're going to talk about heritage, we have to thank those musicians that came from their own countries into the Americas, because they brought with them the music that they loved, their system of notation. They created the conservatories. All of this connects to immigration and came to be part of what we call the arts in this country. By nature, we love the arts! Otherwise why are we going into the caves trying to figure out the paintings? Why are we analyzing how they built the pyramids? Humans love to have an artistic expression. We hear stories about troupes traveling from town to town, dancing, playing music. And what is happening in Europe is happening in Asia. Musicians are traveling to central Africa to understand polyrhythmia. What I mean by all this is, art refines expressions, whether it's in music, painting, literature, sculpture, or architecture. Art is an integral part of being human. We have separated everything. That separation has made things really terrible. We called it classical music because we wanted to call it classical music. Fine. But we need to remember that it is really a refined and poetic expression of sound.

JK: You are saying that music is everywhere around the world, and it always has been and always will be, because we need artistic expression. Art doesn't stop.

TL: Art is art, and art is going to have a continuum whether you like it or not.

JK: So the more that we connect with one another, rather than concerning ourselves with defining and categorizing, then that art of refined and poetic expression of sound has a better possibility of continuing.

TL: Also exposure. I am a product of exposure. If my grandmother didn't take me to a conservatory, and if they didn't put me through the system and the rudiments of learning, maybe I would not be here. I was exposed to it, and then I would bring it home to practice and expose my family. For example, my mother and grandmother would hear a recording I made and point out a mistake. They never went to a conservatory, but their ears started to train because they were exposed to it. We have to acquire a taste for listening to something that is complicated. My mother doesn't have a note of understanding what I do at the piano, but she has acquired a taste for listening. Exposure. My point is that children should be given the opportunity to be creative from the very beginning. Creating something, anything, is about creativity. Because you don't know who is the next Beethoven or the next Frank Gehry. So, the more role models the better.

JK: When role models are visible, they promote wide exposure to the arts.

TL: Exactly. Young people need role models that look like them. How can you even think of a career in the art if it is totally deserted? And young people need exposure to women also. It is a joy to talk to you and be able to look in your eyes because you are also a conductor. Getting to know each other and forming those bonds and supporting one another.

JK: You had a very supportive environment, encouraged to study, exposure to the refined artistic expression of music.

TL: In my wildest imagination, I never thought that I was going to be a composer. As a pianist, I was in the conservatory where there were a few people that looked like me, and nobody ever made any kind of talk about the fact that my skin was darker. They talked only about the person that won the competitions, Tania León.

***

Works by Tania León

OPERA

Scourge of Hyacinths, libretto by León, based on a play by Wole Soyinka
Chamber opera (1994).
Full opera (1999).

BALLET

Belé (with Geoffrey Holder), for solo piano, percussion, and strings (Peermusic, 1981).
The Beloved (with Judith Hamilton), for flute, oboe, clarinet, bassoon, piano, cello, and bass (Peermusic, 1972).
Dougla (with Geoffrey Holder), for two flutes and percussion (Peermusic, 1974).
Haiku, for flute, bassoon, and five percussion (Peermusic, 1973).
Inura, for SATB voices, strings, and percussion (Peermusic, 2009).
Tones, for chamber orchestra and piano (Peermusic, 1970).

MIXED GENRE

Drummin', for chamber orchestra, large mixed ensemble, and percussion ensemble (Peermusic, 1997).
Duende, for baritone, three bata drums, four percussionists, and Latin percussionist (2003).
Samarkand, for speaker, SATB, children's chorus, alto flute, sax, two percussion, three bata drums, piano, and two cellos (2005).

ORCHESTRA

Ácana, featuring piano (Peermusic, 2008).
Batá (Peermusic, 1985, 1988).
Carabalí (Peermusic, 1991).
Concerto Criollo, featuring solo timpani and piano (Peermusic, 1980).
Desde . . . (Peermusic, 2001).
Didn't My Lord Deliver Daniel (arr. León), featuring baritone (2005).
Horizons (Peermusic, 1999).
Kabiosile, featuring piano (Peermusic, 1988).
Para Viola y Orquestra, featuring viola (Peermusic, 1994).
Seven Spirituals (arr. Ryan, orch. León), featuring baritone (1995).

WIND ENSEMBLE

Alegre (Hal Leonard, 2000).
Cumba Cumbakin (2010).

CHAMBER ENSEMBLE

A la Par, for piano and percussion (Peermusic, 1986).
Ajiaco, for electric guitar and piano (1992).
Alma, for flute and piano (in *Eight Visions: A New Anthology for Flute and Piano,* ed. Marya Martin [King of Prussia, Pa.: Theodore Presser, 2007]).
Arenas d'un Tiempo, for clarinet, cello, and piano (Peermusic, 1992).
Ascend, for brass ensemble and percussion (Peermusic, 1983).
Caracol, for violin, viola, cello, percussion, and piano (2000).
Crossings, for horn, four trumpet, four trombone, and tuba (1992).
Cuarteto No. 2, for string quartet (2011).
De Color, for violin and marimba (Peermusic, 1996–97).
De Memorias, for flute, oboe, clarinet, horn, and bassoon (Peermusic, 2000).
Elegia a Paul Robeson, for violin, cello, and piano (1987).
Entre nos, for clarinet, bassoon, and piano (Peermusic, 1998).
Escencia para cuarteto de cuerdas, for string quartet (Peermusic, 2009).
Fanfarria, for brass quintet and percussion (2000).
Hechizos, for chamber group (Peermusic, 1995).
Indígena, for chamber group (Peermusic, 1991).
Parajota Delaté (Peermusic).
  flute, clarinet, violin, cello, and piano (1988).
  flute, oboe, clarinet, bassoon, and piano (1990).
Permutation Seven, for flute, clarinet, trumpet, percussion, violin, and cello (Peermusic, 1981).
Pet's Suite, for flute and piano (Peermusic, 1980).
Raices (Tabla Raza), for flute, violin, voice, piano, bass, tabla solo, and percussion (2007).
Saóko, for brass quintet (Peermusic, 1997).
Satiné, for two pianos (2000).
sin normas ajenas, for chamber group (Peermusic, 1994).
Son Sonora, for flute and guitar (Peermusic, 1993).
Tau, for electric oboe, electric bass, and electronic keyboards (1995).
Tiempo en Clave, for violin and percussion (2008).
Toque, for clarinet, alto sax, piano, two percussionists, violin, and bass (2006).

INSTRUMENTAL SOLO

Abanico, for violin and interactive computer (2007).
Axon, for violin and interactive computer (2002).
Bailarín, for guitar (1998).
Four Pieces for Cello Solo (Peermusic, 1983).

Hebras d'Luz, for electric viola (2004).
Mistica, for piano (Hal Leonard, 2003).
Momentum, for piano (Peermusic, 1984).
¡Paisanos Semos! for guitar (Peermusic, 1984).
Para Noah, for piano (2006).
Rituál, for piano (Peermusic, 1987).
La Tina, for piano (2004).
Tumbao, for piano (2005).
Variación, for piano (2004).

VOCAL ENSEMBLE

Ancients, for two sopranos, flute, clarinet, percussion, viola, and cello (2008).
Batéy (with Michel Camilo), (Peermusic, 1989).
De-Orishas, for two sopranos, countertenor, two tenors, and bass (Peermusic, 1982).
Drume Negrita (Ernesto Grenet, arr. León), from "Two Cuban Songs," for twelve solo voices (Peermusic, 2002).
Estampas, for SATB chorus (2008).
Heart of Ours—A Piece, for tenor solo, men's chorus, flute, four trumpets, and percussion (1988).
El Manisero (Moises Simons, arr. León), from "Two Cuban Songs," for twelve solo voices (Peermusic, 2002).
May the Road Be Free, for children's chorus and percussion (1999).
Metisse, for SATB chorus and percussion (2006).
Namiac Poems, for voices and mixed ensemble (1975).
Rezos, for SATB choir (2001).
Rimas Tropicales, for treble chorus (2011).
A Row of Buttons, for SA choir (2002).
Sol de Doce, for twelve solo voices (Peermusic, 1997).
Spiritual Suite, for narrator, two sopranos, chorus, and amplified ensemble (1976).

VOCAL

At the Fountain of Mpindelela (2000).
Atwood Songs, for soprano and piano (2007).
Canto, song cycle for baritone, clarinet (B-flat and bass), marimba, cello, and piano (2001).
Ivo, Ivo, for soprano, clarinet, bass clarinet, viola, cello, and bass (Peermusic, 2000).
Journey, for high vocalist, flute, and harp (Peermusic, 1990).
Love after Love, for soprano and marimba (2002).
Oh Yemanja "Mother's Prayer" (from *Scourge of Hyacinths*), for voice, cello, and piano (Peermusic, 1994).
"Or like a . . . ," for baritone, cello, and percussion (1994).
Pueblo Mulato, for soprano, oboe, guitar, bass, percussion, and piano (Peermusic, 1987).
Reflections, for soprano, clarinet, tenor sax, piano, trumpet, string quintet, and percussion (2006).

Rimas Tropicales, for girls' chorus (2012).

Singin' Sepia, five songs on poems by Rita Dove, for soprano, clarinet, violin, and piano, four hands (Peermusic, 1996).

To and Fro, for vocalist and piano (Peermusic, 1990).

Turning, song cycle for soprano, piano, and cello (2000).

THEATER

The Golden Windows (text by Robert Wilson), a play in three acts, for flute (piccolo, alto), oboe/English horn, trumpet, percussion, harpsichord, piano, and strings (1982).

Maggie Magalita (text by Wendy Kesselman), incidental music for flute, clarinet, cello, percussion, piano, and guitar (Peermusic, 1980).

8

Hasu Patel

Hasu Patel's identity is shaped by her family, her experience growing up in northern India, and subsequent decades in the United States. Despite her early blossoming as a sitar player, Patel's life circumstances parallel those of many women composers around the world, and she is just now gaining the recognition she has earned. Privately, Patel has been composing ragas for years within the Indian system of music and improvisation. Publicly, she is just beginning and enters the field of formal composition with the fear that others may consider her entrance too late. Her musical expertise, creativity, perseverance, and dedication to her art are reasons enough why she should join the ranks of more established composers.

Hasu Patel represents not only those women who dream of emerging as respected composers but also those who have worked, unrecognized, to achieve that regard.

Patel was born in Baroda, India, in 1947, and through our conversation, she thoughtfully and honestly recounts her story. She began her musical studies at the age of three, and by age six she was learning to play the sitar. She had made her first public appearance by the age of ten, and at age twelve she was invited to teach a beginning-level sitar class. She trained under her gurus Professor Kikani Saheb and the sitar legend Ustad Vilayat Khan. Patel is the first woman to receive a music degree with a gold medal from the Maharaja Sayajirao University of Baroda, Faculty of Fine Arts. At the age of twenty-one, she won first prize in the State of Gujarat for the stringed-instrument competition held by All India Radio. Patel turned down the offer to teach at her university in India, immigrating instead with her husband and his work to a small town in western Pennsylvania. She describes how she was expecting to share her music with the people of the United States, but that plan did not come to fruition.

Raising two children, Patel eventually applied and was accepted to teach Indian music at nearby Carnegie Mellon University. Concurrently, her husband's job moved to Ohio, and Patel again turned down the offer to teach and chose to keep the family together in Ohio. Throughout the decades, Patel never gave up her music, playing in the early morning before waking the family to begin the day. She believes that music promotes healing if one is present and open to experience it. Today, with children grown and husband retired, Patel is learning to compose within the European notation system and fusing Indian ragas with European-influenced orchestral ensembles.

In recent years, Patel was invited to compose sitar concerti for Nan Washburn of the Canton Orchestra of Michigan and for Libi Lebel of the Doctors Orchestra of Houston. Like Meredith Monk, Patel realizes that music must be written in language spoken by the musicians. With this understanding, she composed her concerti in the Indian musical system and then had them translated into European notation for the orchestral players.

Patel founded the Sursangam School of North Indian Music, where students learn sitar, tabla, improvisation, and vocal style on a variety of instruments. Patel also teaches the classical music of India at the Conservatory of Music at Oberlin College. Today, she is known as one of the few world-class female artists performing classical music of India on sitar. She plays in a style known as *gayaki ang* (singing style), where the sitar replicates the fluidity and subtle nuances of the human voice. She seeks out playing opportunities with musicians from varied genres, including Pauline Oliveros, and has performed the Indian classical music known as Raga Sangeet at various universities, music and sound-healing conferences, and performing-art centers. Specific performance venues include

Woodstock's thirtieth-anniversary festival, the Chicago Asian Jazz Festival, the Rhineberger Chamber Hall of the Cleveland Orchestra, the Warner Concert Hall at the Conservatory of Music at Oberlin College, the International Congress of Women in Music in Beijing, and the Women in Music Festival at the Eastman School of Music.

As Patel works through the challenges of combining the Indian musical system with the European, her dream is to celebrate her culture and welcome the fusion of two traditional, yet radically different, musical art forms.

***

May 2009, at her son's home in Copley, Ohio

JENNIFER KELLY: When did you start listening to Western music?

HASU PATEL: About ten or fifteen years ago. I wanted to do a comparative study between classical Indian music and Western music, to incorporate amazing Western ideas into my own music. That helped me in composing my sitar concertos, where I used the harmonies and chords between the C and G and C and F, which occur naturally in Indian music all the time.

JK: To whom do you listen?

HP: For many years, I have been listening to Western classical music on National Public Radio in the early morning around 4:00 A.M. They give me knowledge every morning, and I am so grateful for them. When I began writing the concerto, I had no idea how the trumpet sounds. So I sat down and listened to CDs of all of the individual instruments—the piano, the trumpet, the flute, everything. And I have also attended many live orchestra performances. Also, I read their biographies for inspiration.

JK: Can you briefly describe the essence of Indian classical music?

HP: Yes. Music is the highest art of the Divine, because sound is free from all forms and thoughts. Indian classical music was evolved during Vedic period, which goes back thousands of years. It is offered to please the Divine. It is a language of soul. It is considered as a *sadhana*—devotion and spiritual practice. My music, my strength and training, is the music of North India, Hindustani music.

JK: You often speak of your guru. Is a guru a teacher?

HP: Both a guru and a teacher give you knowledge. The bond between guru and disciple is sacred and lasts a whole life and beyond. The blessings, wisdom, and inspiration stay with the disciple as long as he or she remains pure. My guru, the late legendary sitar maestro Ustad Vilayat Khan, said, "It is like two bodies and one soul"—truly a mystical relationship.

JK: Do you teach students yourself?

HP: Of course. It is my passion and vision to teach music to deserving students. Since 1996, I have taught classical music of India on sitar, tabla, and voice at Oberlin College in Ohio and at my Sursangam School of Music in Ohio. Inviting more foreign-music education, such as Chinese, Indian, and gamelan music, into the ethnomusicology curriculum is a good thing. The awareness of such music will give the students the broader outlook of world music. They can explore other music in their life, and they can come up with new ideas. Many of my students are performing Indian music on violin, double bass, viola, sitar, and tabla in different parts of the world. One of my students, Amie Weiss, developed improvisational skills on violin and was selected to workshop with Yo-Yo Ma Silk Road Project. Every week, I receive one or two emails from my past students. It is a wonderful enduring relationship.

JK: So tell me about composition. Westerners may have a difficult time understanding the difference in Indian music between improvisation and composition. Are they the same thing?

HP: First, it is important to understand the structure of the Indian music. The Indian music is based on *ragas* and *talas.* The *ragas* are the melodic form, with scientific and precise movements of notes, along with the unique use of specific subtle sounds known as *shrutis* (microtones), which invoke human moods. There are twenty *shrutis* (microtones) within the whole range of an octave. Also, each *raga* has a specific time to play, as the frequency of notes affect the body, mind, and soul. Each *raga* has sonant and consonant notes, which are played over and over again. *Ragas* are played in two stages. The first stage is known as *alap*—an improvisation that consists of innumerable combinations and permutations of notes within the permissible rules of *raga* structure. The second stage of the *raga* starts with the rhythmic composition, accompanied by a pair of drums known as *tabla.* There is always an improvisation embedded into the composition. Ninety percent of Indian Music is based on improvisation, with or without rhythm. The time of *ragas* and the microtones used in the *ragas* have not changed since their inception.

JK: The time and microtones used in *ragas* have not changed since their inception?

HP: No. For example, many centuries ago, a great musician named Miyan Tansen played a *raga* with oscillating flat third and flat sixth notes, which is the unique characteristic of that *raga.* Those nuances of the *raga* are still intact even today within the oral tradition. Very few musicians are capable of playing the right nuances. The tonic C remains constant throughout the performance of the *raga.* Each *raga* unfolds slowly, one note at a time, in ascending and descending order in the form of combinations and permutations of notes, as you open a petal of a flower. Once my guru told me, when I was learning improvisation, "Make a garland of the notes and present it to the Divine power."

JK: That's beautiful.

HP: I still dream about it like that, at this age also. Traditionally, there are three main stages of improvisation. In the first, there is a slow movement. In the second, various combinations and permutations of notes of rhythmic sounds are played, which are known as *jor.* The final stage, known as *jhala,* is played at a very high speed. All these three stages have no rhythmic boundaries and are not confined by rhythm. However, each combination will be played within the *raga* structure and aesthetic. The emotions of the musician unfold the mood of the *ragas.*

JK: Do you play the same *ragas* in different concerts?

HP: Performing the same *raga* in a different concert brings different moods of the *raga,* as my emotions may not be the same.

JK: Tell me about your learning to play Indian music.

HP: My father told everyone, "I am a physician, but I want my children to be more humble and to have compassion in their life, so they can serve the world." So, my musical journey started at the very young age of three, when I began training for vocal music. My sitar training started at the age of six and lasted until I was twenty years old. I practiced six to eight hours every day.

JK: Who instilled the commitment in you?

HP: Born in the culturally rich city of Baroda, India, it was my father who was instrumental in my life. In my early part of my life, he was the only audience who listened to my very horrible music in the beginning [*laughs*]. But he encouraged me to continue to play the sitar. I played and played. I always felt in my heart that I was born for this purpose. I have to do what I have to do. It's like a responsibility in my life. I have to continue and keep it alive. Today also, I have the same feeling. Nowadays, I still play two to three hours in the early morning. I crave to play my music every day, as it is part of my soul.

JK: Your playing often sounds as if somebody is singing.

HP: It is a humbling remark. I attribute the vocal aspect of my playing to my first guru, Professor Kikani Saheb, who was blind and taught me by singing and playing the sitar. In the middle stage of my life, my legendary guru, Ustad Vilayat Khan, who was the proponent of *gayaki ang* [vocal style], enhanced my vocal-style techniques. Above all, my life experiences and challenges influenced my unique playing of *gayaki ang* sitar.

JK: When did you come to the United States?

HP: I came to the United States in my early twenties.

JK: What was your experience coming into this completely different culture? Had you ever been here before?

HP: No, it was my first journey to the United States. First my husband arrived and studied full-time for a master's degree in engineering. Actually, I did not want to come to the United States, as I was offered a teaching position in my own university. Reluctantly, I joined him, hoping to make my music well known here in the new country. I was miserable, as there was no opportunity for my music in the small town of Beaver, Pennsylvania. The new lifestyle challenged me, but I continued to practice the sitar, totally depending on my memories, as there was no internet, and recordings were limited. I always felt that I have a responsibility to keep the music alive.

JK: And where did the responsibility come from?

HP: My inner voice tells me that I have a responsibility to keep the music alive.

JK: Did you have children yet?

HP: Yes, a daughter and a son.

JK: And you worked as systems analyst, is that right?

HP: Even though I had degrees from India, I did not find any opportunity. So I said, "What do I do?" I felt like I had to do something with higher education to work. I did not want to sit in the house, so I decided to study further. I wanted to raise my children, so they could have a better life. I could not find any opportunities in the master's programs of music, so I decided to pursue the master's degree in accounting and financial-information systems. My son was only three years old, and it was a challenge to study full-time with the responsibility of running the house. Upon receiving the degree [from Cleveland State University], I worked as a systems analyst.

JK: Did you ever think about teaching music?

HP: Yes, while I was in Beaver, Pennsylvania, I talked to the professor at Carnegie Mellon University, who managed to interview with me and later invited me to perform, which led to the opportunity to teach classical music of India. I still have the newspaper article: "Indian Musician Joins Carnegie Mellon." I still have that. But my husband decided to change a job, so we moved to Ohio. It was a setback for me. Do you know what my father said to me, many years ago? "When you play sitar, and you are in a time of sorrow and challenge, you can close the door, play quietly, and take your stress out." I closed my door and practiced alone, every day. I would get up three-thirty in the early morning, which is considered as *Brahman* [auspicious] time for the music *sadhana* [spiritual practice]. At four o'clock, I would start playing very softly, so nobody would get up in the morning. I put my fingers on the strings to stay connected with my music. I am not complaining. It was a good thing that happened to me. I worked for my music.

JK: What kind of connection do you feel you have today in the United States?

HP: It's a good one. My goal is to teach, perform, and compose the music of India. I am so fortunate to bring an awareness of the music of India in United States, the land of opportunities. When I began teaching, I started to teach music with one student. Today I have many, and they are all playing the music of India in various places around the world. Through my music, I am connected to many colleges and universities, music festivals, music and sound-healing conferences, yoga centers, and schools. My affiliations with the Ohio Arts Council, Arts Midwest, and IAWM [International Alliance for Women in Music] have given me the opportunities to travel to China, Canada, India, and around the United States. I have met many musicians with whom I share music. My sitar concerts at the Asian Jazz Festival in Chicago and Woodstock's Thirtieth Anniversary Concert were significant events. My historically unique achievements were to compose the sitar concertos for the Western orchestras at Houston, Texas, and Canton, Michigan. This was the first time in the history of Indian music that any woman composer had ever composed a purely classical Indian music to be played by Western musicians to its entirety.

JK: How long were you a systems analyst? How long did you have that life?

HP: Twenty miserable years.

JK: Twenty years you got up at three-thirty in the morning?

HP: Yes. I still get up, because if I do not play then, my life will be choked. I want my music to reach to the higher level.

JK: How long ago did you quit your job as a systems analyst?

HP: Five years ago. The company gave me an early retirement package, and it was the best that happened to me. At the same time, my son finished medical school, so I did not worry about finance or anything.

JK: Not being allowed to follow your passion in music because of so many obstacles sounds painful. Many people would have given it up.

HP: That's why I say the inner voice tells me every single day, "Get up and do it." Pain is always there. Pain is what creates the beautiful music. Since my childhood, I have had a great desire to become a successful musician, playing sitar as my main instrument. I worked tirelessly to learn as much as possible in the thirteen or fifteen years of my training period. By the age of twenty, I did receive a music degree with many accolades, medals, and recognition as a professional sitar player. I also studied for the other bread-earning degrees, as this was my father's wishes. But I ended up marrying into a nonmusical family. As Indian society tends to be conservative and was clinging to old-fashioned values at that time, it was not an easy environment to be a woman musician. It is my culture where a person suffers in silence for no fault of her. My life took an opposite turn, and all came to a halt. I was denied this lifestyle, and I was socially rejected. Most of the hurdles came from social injustices and from adjusting to family members' unjustified demands. I could not find time and place for my music and started feeling abnormal pain as I saw my music was slipping away. I was too young to bear the separation from my musical world, and I hid my books in my suitcase and read when no one was around. I sang the *ragas* in my mind so I would not forget them.

A few years later, I came to the United States to join my husband. The fate followed me all along. I was again denied this lifestyle and could not play publicly for more than two decades. In the midst of this, I had a great responsibility to raise my two children. I wanted them to be humble and have higher education.

After more than twenty years, I began to play publicly and teach the music. It was greeted with so much opposition, but I started teaching at the college and at my home. I became a member of a few musical organizations. This gave me the opportunities to meet women musicians and gain some confidence. I have a long way to reach to my dream, and my path is lighted. My new homeland, the United States, gave me a new life in pursuing my musical dream.

I remember my father's words: "To be a one in a million, to make a path and let others follow you." All along, my inner voice always was calling me to get up and not to give up. I started practicing, teaching, and performing with full determination. I decided to dedicate the rest of my life to serve the music. The path of music is divine, and, of course, life is a journey. Sometimes, I think that my pain did not go in vain. Today, my strength is the blessings of divine power through my guru. My inspiration comes from my children and my students, and my aspiration from my audience. My pain added humility in my life and led me to surrender to the supreme divine power unconditionally. And, as Hindus believe in karma theory, I have accepted this life. I truly feel *blessed* that I have been able to play for divine power. Such a faith helps the one who is helpless.

JK: So, at this stage in your life, what are your goals?

HP: I have a few goals. My passion is to teach the music of India to deserving students; to perform sitar concerts and conduct music workshops at various schools, colleges, universities and yoga centers throughout the world; to compose and perform many sitar concertos for the Western orchestras; and to compile and publish a book on *ragas* in the Indian music and Western music-score system. Also, to record these compositions in the form of CD and DVD. This can help anyone to learn music of India in a pure form. My biggest worry is that I'm not young. I want to do this before I'm gone.

JK: So you are creating a record in written form and audio form, so that, after you have passed on, the music will still be passed along, and others can play it.

HP: Yes. It is my vision and a lifelong dream to preserve this divine music of ancient India. I want to play with so many orchestras. This is no ordinary music. I brought the score for you to see and the recording of one of the performances, so we could listen and you feel about it and what you feel as a musician. The recording is just to listen, not to record. The musicians are in the union group. It should be free when you play! [*Laughs*] I don't want to be confined by anybody else. This whole life, in the confinement, I remain unconfined. And I want to play everywhere in the world. Before my body fades, I want to do that. The maestro plays, and the orchestra plays, but I am planning such different music than anybody because my whole lifestyle, the fabric of my life and my emotions and my knowledge, is about *raga*. It's combining and creating new music.

JK: You're creating a legacy.

HP: I hope I can leave a legacy. I've been planning for the past thirty years.

JK: Why did you decide to write a concerto?

HP: It was my lifelong dream, and it came true when the conductor Nan Washburn of the Canton Orchestra of Michigan called and asked me to perform sitar music with a Western orchestra. She mentioned that she will find the music. For days, I was mulling over the ideas to play my own composed music. With sheer determination, I asked Nan to let me compose and perform a sitar concerto for her orchestra. She agreed and said that we all will take the challenge. Surprisingly, I received a call from the conductor Libi Lebel of Doctors Orchestra of Houston, Texas, to compose another sitar concerto for her orchestra. It was truly a challenge.

JK: How did you begin your first sitar concerto?

HP: The dichotomy between the structure of Western and Indian classical music is a big challenge when an Indian musician like me tries to compose for Western symphony orchestras. It was necessary for me to teach Indian notation, *raga* theory, the usage of microtones, and the complex rhythm system to the Western musicians. However, I began my journey with no clear vision.

JK: Was there a lot of communication between you and Nan Washburn before rehearsals?

HP: There was a lot of communications with phone calls and emails. I personally delivered the score to Nan at a coffee house in Sandusky, Ohio. We both checked the scores and listened to the computer-generated music. She was very happy with my work. Even today we are in contact and exchange our musical news.

JK: What was your process for writing your sitar concerti?

HP: During the initial planning period, I listened to the solo recordings of Western instruments. I began to understand the distinct sounds and colors of each instrument. I was also aware of the tempered scale, chords, and modulations where Indian music does not allow these elements. The tonic C remains constant throughout the performance, and accidental harmonies, such as C and G and C and F, always occur in Indian music. Once I became fully absorbed into the process, I composed for each instrument in sequence, every day for at least five hours uninterrupted, for two weeks for each concerto. The hardest part was to find a musician who could transpose into Western score acceptable to the nuances of Indian music. This took more time and effort than anticipated, maybe over two months.

JK: Do you read Western notation?

HP: At the time, I did not. I talked to [the musician who would translate the score into Western notation] about Indian music first, about the notes and how it goes, the flat notes, the signs, my pauses, and everything. Then I sang the whole concerto piece by piece for him. And I went over every nuance with my notes, because I didn't know Western score. He always told me, "How can you understand these small nuances?" I said, "My ear will tell me." That's how he put it together. Today I read some Western notation, but I learned from my Western student, and I am still a novice.

JK: A *raga* is never played the same way twice. So I am wondering how it worked with the concerto, because Western classical musicians usually need to have music in front of them. They play it more or less the same way every time. It is written into traditional composition. And since Indian music is a different kind of composition, which is highly improvisatory, how did you do that? How did you combine the two?

HP: Usually, *ragas* are played differently each time they are improvised. The orchestral musicians played the music from the score, which was a very small part of the improvisational music. With the understanding of Indian music and the *raga* structure, they can learn to improvise and play the same *raga* differently.

JK: Did the orchestra play microtones?

HP: To an extent, yes.

JK: How did your musical translator notate that?

HP: In the beginning, the musician who transposed the music was unable to understand the process. I sang all the notes and sat with him to put "slurs" around the notes, which replicated the microtones.

JK: And you had only two rehearsals for each performance?

HP: The orchestra was practicing the concerto several weeks before the rehearsals. We had two rehearsals where I had the opportunity to finesse the performance.

JK: How was the concerto received by the [Canton] orchestra?

HASU'S SON, MEHOOL: I think they really enjoyed it, because it was different for them. During the rehearsals, it was evident that they weren't sure; I mean, they knew the beats and the notes, but they didn't know how to put it in the right microtones. Also, the end is very fast in Indian music, and it was a challenge for them to keep the tempo. We discovered all that during the rehearsals. So I think the rehearsals were very challenging, but they got the hang of it. Also during rehearsal, when she was playing her solo [on the floor], they would all stand up and look, because they were all sitting in chairs. So they were gathering around, moving close enough to figure out what was going on. I think it was a challenge for Western and Eastern alike. The conductor was very complimentary of this collaborative music.

JK: What else do you want to compose?

HP: I hope to compose, play, and record more sitar concertos in *ragas* for Western symphony orchestras and unknown *ragas* on sitar.

JK: You must be disciplined to have kept up with the music as a player every morning, and then all of the work you have done in the past five years to begin presenting your compositions to your audiences.

HP: My father was the most disciplined person in the family. He would wake me up at five o'clock in the morning for my sitar practice, then three to four miles of morning walk, yoga asanas, breakfast, and school homework. It was a ritual in our home every day. This discipline was extended to my siblings. The childhood disciplined life helped me in achieving my musical dream. I have continued the early-morning musical practice even today.

JK: What, in your opinion, can we do as a people to keep music alive in the futures of our children?

HP: Parents and teachers should train and supervise the disciplined life to their children, filled with regular physical exercises, music lessons, different art forms, regular homework, watching selected educational shows and less violent TV shows. Many parents do not follow the disciplines, which leads to the erratic minds in the young generation. We as musicians have a moral duty to keep this music alive through the teaching, composing, performing, and practicing. Pure music is eternal.

JK: So can you learn all of these things through music?

HP: Of course. Music will bring the humility and discipline that will help mankind.

JK: Well, one of the things that I find challenging here in this country is that music education is not valued very much, and it's getting to be less and less.

HP: Yes, it is true not only in United States or in India but everywhere in the world. Nonclassical music is more popular and lucrative. Classical music everywhere has always had a limited audience. Even great musicians have died in poverty.

JK: And what about girls? You were telling that women musicians in India are not valued.

HP: This is true everywhere in the world. Anywhere you go, women musicians have a hard time, as the society thinks that a woman should be married, have a husband, clean the house, raise the kids, and that way life should be over. We are born as women, but we are musicians.

JK: Do you think we have a responsibility to help young girls in music?

HP: Any girl who has talent and aptitude towards the classical music should be encouraged to pursue her dream. To bring that sleeping giant, the talent in their mind, to wake up and arise from the fear. They can be very powerful.

JK: So is there a place today for all-women recordings, festivals, and concerts?

HP: Yes, there is a limited opportunity. This will give women the opportunity to showcase their talents. It will also help them to support each other. We always have a blend of both the men and women musicians. Both are different as they are unique in their own creations.

JK: What is different?

HP: Women musicians have tenderness in their compositions where men musicians have power, which shows the ego of the men.

JK: Would you mind if you were referred to as a "woman composer"? Or, given that you have lived in this country for so many years, perhaps "American composer"?

HP: Woman composer is fine. However, "American woman composer of Indian music" would be more accurate. Know exactly who you are.

JK: Do they accept you a master sitar player in India?

HP: [*Laughs*] You want to know the truth? First, they see me in a very skeptical way. They say, "She is a woman musician, so what she going to play?" or, "She is an Indian musician and living in America, so what is her caliber?" During my performance, sometimes the *tabla* player tries to overpower me. When I play very intricate rhythmic patterns and *jhala,* the final fast movement of rhythmic composition, that time he knows exactly who I am. Usually, the real musician will always respect other musicians. My guru always advised me, "When you go on the stage, the audience does not think that you are young, old, sick, upset, or any other excuses. They want the best performance of you."

JK: Tell me about your connection with the Woodstock Thirtieth Anniversary Concert.

HP: In 1969, Pandit Ravi Shankar performed sitar music at the Woodstock Music Festival. He brought an awareness of Indian music into the Western world. He became a world-renowned musician. In 1999, I received an email from Jeryl Abramson of Yasger's Farm inviting me to perform sitar music at the Woodstock Thirtieth Reunion Music Festival. I felt that the history is repeating after thirty years. My son asked me not to go, as he has heard of some strange incidences. I said, "I have to go, because it will make history—a female sitar player who played there, and it was *me*!" There were thousands of people at Yasger's Farm. People were so respectful of my music. They were so quiet, all relaxed, and it was a big honor to me. I brought a difference in the music as a female sitar player in the world.

JK: You describe yourself as a composer, a performer, and an educator, so how do you embody each of those descriptions?

HP: Traditionally, 90 percent of Indian music is improvisational. From the very beginning of my training, I was taught to compose various compositions, abiding by the complex structure of *ragas.* Also during the training, I had to perform every month before the faculty. And also I was asked to teach the beginner-level sitar classes when I was only twelve years. To me, all this training and these experiences helped me to become a better musician.

JK: Tell me about your inspirations. You said your family was a big inspiration for you.

HP: My father built my character and instilled love for music. My mother supported my music and inspired me all the time. My children always attend my major sitar concerts around the world and support me unconditionally.

JK: Are live music concerts equally as important as recording?

HP: Live music concerts are much better than the recordings because, when you see it live, you can see the performers' expressions, how they play, and how they interact with each other.

JK: Do you ever throw anything away, or do you keep it?

HP: I always try to preserve my compositions and recordings. But I hardly ever listen to my own recordings. I'm a critic of my own: "I should have done it that way," or, "I should have done it this way." I don't throw things away, but I always like to enhance the way I did it. I never listen. Once it's gone, it's gone. I pick up the same *raga* and same melody, same notes again, and something new comes out. I don't worry about anything. But I don't throw away.

JK: So when you perform your sitar concerto, how much freedom do the conductors have to interpret the music with the ensemble?

HP: This collaboration was really an uncharted territory. I think that they did not question me, as this was such a new and developing concept. They were concerned with learning the nuances, microtones, and the rhythm system of Indian music.

JK: What do you wish to communicate with this piece? Do you have a message?

HP: I have two messages. First, Indian music is so pure and rich, and, because of the use of microtones, it can be played on any string instrument. Second, one has to surrender the ego, which brings out the emotions. Humility prevails in the Indian music.

JK: As a conductor, please understand that putting aside ego is a little difficult for us because, as Western conductors, we have to have an ego. We're taught that if we don't have some sense of an ego, we don't have control, strength. Especially as a woman.

HP: Try one time to conduct the orchestra without ego and see the outcome of performance. To be humble is not a sign of weakness. By humbleness, one can receive tremendous strength from the Divine and respect from the fellow musicians as well as audiences. You know I am humble, but I am not weak. When I play my music, no one can tell me what not to do. I was a conductor here, too. I listened to make sure everyone played right. When they play wrong, I get up and tell them this is the way you should play. I will show you. Same thing what you are doing. I even tame the *tabla* players when I sit with my eye gesture.

JK: What can an audience bring with them when they come to listen to your music? How can we be prepared?

HP: When you come as my audience, I want you to be empty. Do not expect anything. Do not expect anything from yourself. Sit, relax, close your eyes, surrender your ego, and just listen. Every nuance, note, *raga* I play will give you the inner vision of yourself.

JK: Now what about performing the same composition again?

HP: It will not come out exactly the same. Western musicians will play the same written score, where I do not have any written score and will play the spontaneous improvisation, which will make the difference in the performance. Do you think it's a good idea to play like this?

JK: Yes, I do. We keep talking about globalization, and I think it is a wonderful example of a positive aspect of globalization without becoming completely homogeneous—still retaining one's identity and yet being able to share that identity with others around the world. I think this is a lovely example of that. You are very interested in legacy. What do you want to make sure we've learned from you and your music before you pass on?

HP: One should understand the great musical heritage of ancient India. One should know *raga* theory, structure of *raga,* the moods, the time, the microtones, and complex rhythm system. Over thousands of years, this great legacy was handed down to worthy musicians through oral traditions taught to students through guru-disciple relationship.

JK: I understand that. It's part of culture.

HP: Yes, it is a part of my great Vedic culture. And then, because I don't want to lose my identity, my musical identity, I want to do some collaboration in a way that there is a fine line. Myself and another musician from another genre should stay within our limits but always combine that melody in such a form that we both come out as a nice blend of collaboration. No matter who is my audience, when I play, that note must wake you and tell you something. Wake up, accept it, and get out of your rut and make something new. A beautiful bright future is waiting for you. You cannot just stop what you are doing. Keep going, keep going. There's a torch burning there.

***

Works by Hasu Patel

RAGAS

Bhairavi
Charukauns

Darbari Kanada
Kaushik Ranjani
Kirwani
Lalit with Komal Dhaivata
Malkauns
Parameshwari
Poorbi Kalyan
Sahana
Todi
Yaman Kalyan

CONCERTOS

Mangal Dhwani, "Auspicious Sound," for sitar and chamber orchestra based on the raga *Bageswari* (2008).

Swara Managalam, "Musical Notes Are Auspicious," for sitar and chamber orchestra based on the raga *Yaman Kalyan* (2008).

9

Pauline Oliveros

Pauline Oliveros's creative process accepts that everyone is part of the composition. Widely considered one of the most influential composers of the twentieth century, she encourages deep listening, being open to what comes, and she has spent a lifetime actively creating communities of participation so that anyone can be part of the music-making experience. Born in 1932, Oliveros is a composer, performer, author, and philosopher known around the world as an explorer of and experimenter with sound. Raised in Houston, she grew up listening to radio broadcasts from the Metropolitan Opera, New York Philharmonic, and the NBC Orchestra. During our conversation, she mentions her mother as one of her earliest influences on her own creative thought and sense of play, her introduction to the accordion, and the possibilities of improvisation and experimentation.

After three years at the University of Houston, Oliveros left for San Francisco to study further in composition. After graduating from San Francisco State College in 1957, she and her schoolmates Terry Riley and Loren Rush began experimenting with free improvisations. She explains that, while the conventional music circles of the 1950s were not exploring music in this manner, the jazz world was exploring the breadth of improvisatory sounds. During the mid-1960s, Oliveros served as the first director of the Tape Music Center at Mills College in Oakland, California, later renamed the Center for Contemporary Music.

While Oliveros is highly regarded as an experimentalist and early pioneer of connecting music to technology, she considers one of her greatest musical breakthroughs to be the creation of her *Sonic Meditations* in 1974. A series of improvisation experiences with directions written in English as opposed to scored notation, *Sonic Meditations* was composed in such a way that participation is not reserved for those who read conventional musical language. Oliveros encourages participants to listen deeply to themselves and the sounds of their environment, creating community as a path toward healing.

Oliveros has been an active scholar for decades, publishing many uncollected articles, conference presentations, and two book collections: *The Roots of the Moment* and *Software for People.* She has taught her philosophy of listening and creation by example as a professor of music and the director of the Center for Music Experiment at the University of California at San Diego, and she currently teaches as Distinguished Research Professor of Music at Rensselaer Polytechnic Institute in upstate New York. She also serves as the Darius Milhaud Composer in Residence at Mills College via telepresence teaching. During our conversation, Oliveros describes her nontraditional style of teaching, creating "improvatory" experiences (contrasting with the goals of a conservatory). Her students over the years are numerous, whether in a classroom, a performance space, or simply through a listening ear, aware and accepting of alternative creation. For instance, even though neither Pamela Z, nor Beth Anderson, nor even Svjetlana Bukvich were direct students of Oliveros, they all mention her during their interviews, and the influence of Oliveros's work can be heard in their music.

Concerned more with the present and the future than with the past and continuing to challenge standard practice, Oliveros's current research focuses on the collaborative development and distribution of the Adaptive Use Musical Instruments (AUMI) software interface, which enables people with severe mobility limitations to create music. During our conversation, she explains the significance of AUMI, continuing her leadership as one of the most innovative thinkers in music. Oliveros is also the founder and executive director of the Deep Listening Institute. The institute's Web site explains how Oliveros "pioneered the concept of

Deep Listening, her practice based upon principles of improvisation, electronic music, ritual, teaching and meditation, designed to inspire both trained and untrained musicians to practice the art of listening and responding to environmental conditions in solo and ensemble situations."[1]

Oliveros has been awarded three honorary doctorates, the Beethoven Prize from the City of Bonn, the Gaudeaumus Prize, and the John Cage Award; she was honored with Pauline Oliveros Day in Houston on March 3, 1984. She is also the recipient of the William Schuman Award from Columbia University for lifetime achievement, resulting in a thirty-year retrospective performed in 2010.

***

June 2010, via Skype

JENNIFER KELLY: I'd like to ask about people's evaluation of music. There is so much music out there today, and we seem to be encouraged, almost taught, to listen passively. Is that dangerous to the younger generation?

PAULINE OLIVEROS: I think it was dangerous to the older generation, because I think what is left out is the understanding that everyone is involved in the composition. Listen, it's not a one-way street. That's my thought.

JK: Is it that people stop thinking about what's really going on around them and end up being passive participators rather than active participators?

PO: Yes, I think that happens to some people. Some people are intimidated for their whole lives. And I think it is very important to create beauty and create a place of sharing.

JK: When you first began turning around the paradigm of exploring what was music, who tended to be the most receptive?

PO: It was radical; musicians were not used to that. Nonmusicians were the most receptive.

JK: So much of your music is community-oriented—wanting to create a sense of community.

PO: Yes, that's the intention.

JK: So what communities are you wanting to explore, promote, or integrate?

PO: Instantaneous ones. Across abilities.

JK: Over your long and varied career, the communities have changed and merged with one another. How have the changing communities affected your creation of music?

PO: I listen. The through line is the beginning of belonging and sharing with one another, whatever it is.

JK: When I explore your music, it is clear there is more than what is on the page or in the recording. I connect it with something larger, and I wonder how much of that is conscious for you, and how much of that is a happenstance of the creation itself.

PO: There's a lot of consciousness involved in terms of how we direct our attention. It's about intention. It's about listening. There's a difference between hearing and listening. Hearing is simply the wave forms going into the ears and being transformed to electrical energy that is transmitted to the brain. When the sound goes to the audio cortex, then listening takes place, but not before. Some mistakenly feel that using hearing and listening are equivalent, and they're not. One has to build experience. One has to add experiences before listening can actually take place.

JK: So is it up to the individual to consciously pay attention to what he or she is hearing, as though saying to themselves, "I am going to listen as opposed to simply hear"?

PO: Yes! It's about collective attention to wave forms.

JK: And how can we as teachers, and as performers, how can we teach to listen?

PO: I think we have to model listening. Then, there can be a transmission that takes place to others. That is the performer or the conductor's job: to model the listening process for the ensemble and for yourself.

JK: I am curious about your creative compositional process. What elements can one bring to the table to participate actively and consciously in the creative process?

PO: First of all, willingness is needed. A willingness to be open to possibilities. Drop judgment and analysis of everything that comes from verbal consciousness. Be open to sensation and feeling.

JK: So in your mind's ear, when an idea first comes to you, do you hear something first, or do you feel something first?

PO: Yes, any and all of the above. It isn't just one way.

JK: You've been doing this for such a long time. How do you keep the curiosity alive—or keep it from becoming routine where you know what to expect?

PO: I don't expect. I am open to that which I don't know. Let it be there. This is the way to keep your brain alive.

JK: Are there times when the idea simply doesn't come?

PO: Patience and stillness, quietness is important. Sometimes I may have something that I need to do, and I have a deadline. Conferences, et cetera. Ideas may not present themselves in any one particular way. I usually meet my deadlines. Patience is a big part of it.

JK: You grew up as twentieth-century technology evolved—the recording, the computer. How does your relationship with technology continue to evolve?

PO: Well, right now, I just got back from a conference in London. The title of this conference was Music Technology: Solutions to Challenges. The interface between music, engineering, special needs, and neuroscience. This was the first conference of its kind. And I have been working for three years now in creating software for people with special needs, so this work is extraordinarily rewarding. Our musical improvisation software [Adaptive Use Musical Instruments] from the Deep Listening Institute is online to download for free, and people have been sending me back data on how they use it. It's a software interface that allows for the people with the least possibility to participate in improvisation.

JK: How does it work? Using the computer to help the mind create the sounds?

PO: No, it's not like that. This software is unique; you can download it yourself from DeepListening.org. I have a friend who is an occupational therapist, and we have been having conversations for many years. She is always talking to me about how she would like to have better technology to better work with the students there at the school for students with special needs. There is a range of abilities. . . . Instead of saying "disability," we say "ability." Everyone has ability. I asked her to give me three students who have the least possibility, and I organized a team to work on the software which would allow them to make sound. So the first three students to participate used wheelchairs, had no speech, and the only voluntary controlled movement they had was moving their heads. These three students attended sessions with their therapist to see what they did and how they did it, and we immediately saw that digital technology could enable something much more extensive. Because they were using switches to turn things on and off, and they used switches with their head. So, one of my senior students at RPI [Rensselaer Polytechnic Institute] where I teach did a prototype so that you could sit a student down in front of a computer screen showing a vertical line. It was possible to put a virtual marker on the nose, and then, as they turned their head and went past the vertical line, they could make a sound. Then also there was a virtual keyboard on the screen, and you could move along the keyboard and play notes. So the very first time they encountered this interface, they had no problem at all making sound.

JK: What a fantastic leap toward therapy.

PO: Well, the leap was towards making music! Now, it's three years later, and I just came from this conference and presented this information for the first time. It was very well received, and we are very excited about it. My friend Leaf [Miller] created a drum class for the whole school. So this is really a beautiful development of community, to have all of the students in the school very excited about drumming and using the software. We had an event about six weeks ago here, we gave a concert, and the concert was called Play the Drum. And all the students came down with their therapists, aides, and so on, and Leaf had a way of having them all coordinate with the beat; the beat was, "Play the drum. Play the drum. Everybody play the drum." She could ask them to play the sticks so they could hear the software; the students that were playing the software interface kept circulating in and out according to their stamina. They couldn't do any of the movement like this, but they could use the software, and it was really remarkable, the feeling, the excitement, the joy that everyone felt. It was really a very special kind of benchmark after working all this time with them.

JK: Wonderful. And in addition to the work it would do with a single individual and a community, it also helps move us toward a sense of equality as a whole.

PO: That's exactly right. That's where my primary interest lies. Because these are the most marginalized people in the world. After you start this kind of work, there is no going back. It is absolutely amazing.

JK: To watch the growth, to see it in somebody's eyes.

PO: That's right. You feel it. It is palpable.

JK: With regard to equality, I'd like to ask about one of your earlier essays on the contribution of women as composers. This was an essay of forty years ago, when you hypothesized that the emergence of women in male-dominated fields meant a move towards the inclusion of intuition as a complementary mode of creativity, and that women's emergence was a significant evolutionary development towards synthesis or wholeness. My question is, forty years later, have we moved towards a cultural development of synthesis between the analytical activity and the intuitive?

PO: It's happening. Because more and more women are being present, in making music, composing, or creating, and we're doing it differently. Some of them are not—some women are simply replicating what has gone before—but the ones who are not are creating new pathways. They are establishing new neuronal pathways.

JK: When you say "replicating what has gone before," do you mean using traditional training?

PO: Yeah, traditional classical training. A codified way of making music.

JK: So simply by the emergence of women in this field and going toward the experimental and the explorative side of creation—that alone means that there is a directional shift towards that synthesis of wholeness, in everybody.

PO: I think so. It doesn't mean that it's happened completely, but it's on the way.

JK: How will we know if we ever get there?

PO: We'll feel it [*laughs*].

JK: Does your concept of intersecting the analytical activity and the intuitive as the creator of music apply to the audience's reception of the experience?

PO: Absolutely.

JK: So ideally, everyone would be equal in the whole, whether they are part of the creation or not.

PO: That's the way I think, yes. And I think one of the problems that I run into is that people who are not musicians, let's say scientists or other professions, may be really far out in their exploration in their field, yet, when it comes to music, they were educated by music-appreciation courses. So they don't have any feeling for new music. They are more or less disparaging of any kind of new music.

JK: And when they do experience that music, they are reading a textbook of whomever determined what should be in that textbook, and then listening to music without actually participating.

PO: Absolutely—without feeling and without sensation.

JK: In the same essay, you also pose five questions of study which would explore various comparisons between men and women and their composition, creativity, et cetera. Do you think that, in order to begin even asking those questions, we need to have a general acceptance of certain labels, such as "woman composer"?

PO: [*Sigh*] Well, do we have to accept that?

JK: I don't mean to accept it in a pejorative sense. I ask whether we need to acknowledge it. For example, do I need to acknowledge that I am a female conductor in order to begin an exploration or comparison of how I tell a story through conducting as opposed to how a male conductor may tell his story through conducting?

PO: Well, first of all, I think we need some study of the work that goes on in the brain—the brain and in the body as well. (I don't want to reduce us to just heads.) Neurons are all over the body, not just in the brain. There are neurons in the heart. And the heart and brain communicate nonverbally, because the heart doesn't have verbal communication. Those are the kinds of needed studies, explorations, and knowledge. And it is fascinating. I mean, because we have the technology now that can possibly answer some of these questions. It doesn't mean everything—consciousness, for example, is still a mystery. We have consciousness. And then consciousness itself is not defined. It teaches us about listening.

JK: In your work today, how are you moving toward a balance of the analytical and the intuitive?

PO: Analytical listening, well . . . this means that your attention is focused in a narrow and exclusive way. If you use global attention, then it is more open, more fuzzy than exclusive. Attention to the point.

JK: So would that be more of the intuitive reception, the fuzziness?

PO: Receptive, meaning being open to everything. I mean, look around. You can't walk around being open to everything all the time. It could be dangerous. You need a balance of exclusive and inclusive attention wherever you go. You need inclusive attention to detect what's going on in the environment. If your attention is exclusively focused, then you miss what's going on in the environment. If all of your energy and all of your attention is focused exclusively—and I've seen people in that state, and they don't know what's going on around them. A bear could be in back of you, and you wouldn't know it [*laughs*].

JK: So we need both as participators, whether as an audience member, creator, participant, anything. The idea is to be both, which then promotes wholeness, which promotes community, which promotes healing.

PO: You're right.

JK: Was there a defining moment in your life when you realized you were a composer, a creator?

PO: I was sixteen years old when I knew I wanted to be a composer. I was listening, and my mind was filled with sound. Not necessarily musical sound, but sound. Not necessarily recognized as music. So I already decided by that time, that's what I wanted to do.

JK: Now by that point, you were still being traditionally, classically trained as a musician, correct?

PO: Yes, I suppose you could say that.

JK: But you were also exploring with other sounds.

PO: Oh yeah!

JK: So when you knew that you wanted to be a composer at the young age of sixteen years old, even though your formal training was traditional, did you already know at that point that you wanted to go to a more exploratory or experimental side?

PO: All I knew was that I wanted to create music. That's what I knew. I didn't know what it was going to be. Because if you're creative, you don't know [*laughs*].

JK: Now, at some point you made a conscious decision to break with traditional music notation and the preconceived style of composition that you were trained with and grew up with. Why did you decide to break with that traditional musical notation?

PO: Well, because I wasn't able to express what I wanted to express using the conventional system of staff, notes, and so on. It didn't fit. It was too confining at that point, expressing myself.

JK: Was it difficult to go against your initial musical training, especially when you were so young?

PO: Well, I think it happened rather organically. Nobody was telling me I couldn't do that.

JK: So your family supported the fact that you wanted to be an artist, and you wanted to be a nontraditional artist?

PO: Well, by the time I was really getting into more experimental work, I had already left home. I left when I was twenty years old. I was still writing notes on a conventional staff. And about 1960 I began to start to break down that notation.

JK: Along those same lines, I find that the word "improvisation" means different things to different people. What does improvisation mean for you and your work?

PO: It doesn't mean jazz necessarily, because that's codified, depending on whether you are doing traditional jazz or free jazz. Around 1957, when I started to do group improvisation with Terry Riley and Loren Rush, we were doing improvisation together from our Music Center when nobody else was doing that. Around the same time, Ornette Colman and Cecil Taylor were moving away from traditional jazz. So there was something in the air.

JK: True. Today, I have found that some composers consider contemporary music a single-listening art form. There may not be many venues in which to perform, or there often isn't great support for new music, and therefore, when they receive a commission for a new piece, it is frequently considered a single listening. Or a single experience.

PO: Well, that is certainly true of a lot of my improvisations. It is part of the spectrum. I have some pieces that have received hundreds of performances. I have some pieces that haven't even been performed. Very few of those, but I'm sure we could find some.

JK: Can a composer be concerned with what an audience understands or does not understand?

PO: One of the things that helps an audience to understand something is to experience it. There are many things that I might hear for the first time. And after I've heard it more than once, I hear more things and understand more. This is how we build a community of listeners who take the time to find or to think. A lot of people don't understand folk music and give a huge amount of attention to those that are familiar because there are certain feelings that can be revisited. But I think children need to be free to experience exploration and to experience how it feels to find something. And when we hear it again, it becomes part of our neurology.

JK: How would you like an audience member or a participant to remember your music as they leave the auditorium or the experience?

PO: Well, I don't care [*laughs*]. Because the experience is different for each person. How will I know what's it been like?

JK: Can you tell when a piece is making an impact?

PO: There's a feeling.

JK: Who is sitting in the audiences today?

PO: Lots of young people, for me [*laughs*]. They are exposed to many people. They find me. They can go on the internet and find all kinds of things.

JK: So, what can traditional classical music learn from composers such as yourself, where young people are finding your music and experiencing it?

PO: Put your music up on the Web, for heaven's sake. Make it accessible.

JK: You are having a lot of retrospective concerts in the past few years.

PO: Yes, we just had a big one at Columbia University. It was a wonderful evening. There was a full house with friends from all over the place, from many different places and different times. The performance was very special. I had old friends and new friends playing—it was a very happy moment.

JK: Your music seems to be about the physical experience; it is about the whole body. So nowadays, when there are people creating virtual ensembles through the computer, can it still achieve the same sense of physicality and community of feeling?

PO: Well, I've experienced that, yes. Since 2002, part of my research in my seminar at RPI is working on distance performance. I have a seminar which is called Experimental Telepresence. We've done many performances now with distance ensembles, sometimes as many as four sites all at once, including ours. And it's not exactly, like you are saying, about being in the same place, because it's also something new. There's something additional going on here. So you have the physicality of your own group and your own site, but then you have the addition of other sites so that you have to be willing to stretch, feeling what's going on at the other sites. And it means you've got to listen.

JK: Beyond hearing, you've got to listen.

PO: Right. Go beyond. So I find that very interesting.

JK: That takes us into a realm of creativity. How do you think about creativity?

PO: I am interested for people to realize their own creativity.

JK: So how can we as teachers help to foster creativity in our students?

PO: Make it possible. Make a safe place for it to happen. If you're going to pounce on everybody and pounce on what they do, then it's not safe anymore.

JK: So, what kind of music education or training do you think would be most beneficial to emerging composers?

PO: I wrote an article called "Quantum Improvisation: The Cybernetic Presence," where I propose an "improvatory" music which would complement the conservatory. Conservatory is and will remain concerned with conserving standard practice. "Improvatory" is completely opposite and would be involved with improvisation and opening to new things.

JK: I would imagine that your students of a much younger generation are in support of this idea of improvisation and creating music based on listening.

PO: Yes, more and more.

JK: That's interesting, because often times, when we speak to teachers, they say that as the years go by, the students are becoming less and less engaged. And yet I am hearing you say that students are more and more interested in listening and improvisation.

PO: Yes, they are [*laughs*]. In my seminar, I have an improvisation group seeded in my seminar called Tintinabulate. It has a range of participants, from freshman to post-doc. And they come in, and we work two hours of the seminar to just improvise. And as time goes on, people suggest different things or even compose things for Tintinabulate. One of my Ph.D. candidates wrote a piece for the RPI orchestra and Tintinabulate, and the RPI orchestra is used to playing traditional music, but they really loved playing this piece. And it sounded good. It was played in the RPI orchestra spring concert in our Experimental Media and Performing Arts Center.

JK: So how can a student prepare to be in one of your seminars on improvisation, or even as a member of this ensemble?

PO: I had a freshman who wanted to come into the course because he heard about it and wanted to try it. It's a graduate seminar, and I said, "Sure, come in, and see how you like it, and, if you like it, hang out with us, and enroll in the course." And he agreed, and he was very excited. And it turns out he is a good contribution to the seminar and Tintinabulate. And the older students started working with him, so you see the community of Tintinabulate works there as well. So I stay out of the way and let it happen.

JK: Again, you are making a safe place for them to explore.

PO: That's right. So they can try whatever they want to try.

JK: So what does teaching give to your creative side when you compose?

PO: For me, it's always creative. I don't go into the seminar with a hard and fast series. I go in and look at who's there, what they want to do, and then I try to make it possible for them to do what they want to do. So my teaching is definitely different. It isn't about something that I've got to let them know. And so, if you watch me teach, you might think I'm not doing anything. They already know how to do something.

JK: Your music is often classified as avant-garde. How do you experience avant-garde?

PO: [*Sigh*] Yeah. Avant-garde is such an old category. People still use it, and that's okay; they can still use it. But, really, is classifying my music as avant-garde about the music or not?

JK: Do you prefer exploration, experiment?

PO: I don't know. I make music, and there it is, you can experience. And, if you want to know about it, you need to listen to it more. But if you try to classify and want to know about it too soon, you're not going to get it.

JK: You have so many decades of work, of real exploration. You've been vetted among musicians, audiences, and critics, but you are also human. Do you still have the occasional moment of nervousness or self-doubt?

PO: [Long pause] I'm trying to think if I do, I'm not sure [*laughs*].

JK: What a great place to be! How do you balance the work and nonwork parts of your life, or do you not differentiate the two?

PO: I don't think there's that much difference between the two. Because I always enjoy what I do, so I am usually engaged in some way. I'm always doing something.

JK: With regard to critics, is there a responsibility that critics have to review new music?

PO: Well, I'm not sure if critics have as much cachet as they used to. After all, the newspapers are diminishing. I think there are good journalists, and there are journalists who aren't as interesting. Most of the time, a good journalist is going to have something interesting to say. I used to think it was better to be reviewed than not. It gives you PR.

JK: There's no such thing as bad press.

PO: Right [*laughs*].

JK: In the creation of experimental music, when critics were and are frequently not quite as prepared to critique experimental music, how was it to be part of those initial reviews?

PO: Well, I was spoiled. Because in San Francisco in the sixties, when I was involved in the San Francisco Tape Music Center, my *Variations for Sextet* was one of the first pieces to be reviewed. There was Alfred Frankenstein [at the *San Francisco Chronicle*], who was a wonderful reviewer. It was still about developing in a developing field. He reviewed us very interestingly. He covered [Ruth Crawford] Seeger in Chicago in the thirties, so he was interested in modernist music in the thirties. And he moved to San Francisco, and he came to our Tape Music concerts and reviewed them, as did Alexander Freed, who was with the *Examiner* at the time. It was a remarkable confluence; it really was. So we got a lot of really interesting reviews. We weren't always pleased with them, but they were constructive and thoughtful. So we were very lucky. They were an understanding audience to our work.

JK: You bring up an interesting point when you mention Seeger. Growing up in Houston, when and where were you initially introduced to living contemporary music?

PO: When I went to the University of Houston. I had a composition teacher playing Schoenberg or Berg. And people came to town. Leonard Bernstein conducted the Israeli Philharmonic. Stan Kenton came to town with his band. So there were different aspects of music that I was exposed to, but it wasn't until I got to San Francisco in 1952 that I began to experience a broader range.

JK: Is that when you realized that there were other people like you who were interested in experiencing all sounds?

PO: It took a while. It was when I was in college at San Francisco State College, and I learned more, and there were colleagues like Terry [Riley] and Loren [Rush], you know. And then I met Ramon [Sender] soon after that, and we were similarly interested in this new electronic music.

JK: When did you become consciously aware of being a woman in your musical career?

PO: Oh, when in search of a teacher, some prospective composition teacher said, "What do you want to do that for? Women don't do that."

JK: I bet they're ruing the day now [*both laugh*]. What does it mean to be called a woman composer today in the twenty-first century?

PO: Well, I think it's kind of stupid.

JK: It doesn't mean anything anymore?

PO: Well, I don't know. It means something to some people. The canon is all male. It must mean something to them.

JK: Do you concern yourself with the canon?

PO: Yes, I like all music.

JK: Does it bother you that the canon is still traditionally classified and tends to have dead white male composers in it?

PO: No, I don't mind that. I think that's fine. It's just that I would like additional broadening of what traditional ensembles do, and I think that's happening in the younger ensembles. Like ICE, the International Contemporary Ensemble.

JK: Is there still a gender barrier?

PO: Well, I think that male bonding continues.

JK: Through technology?

PO: Yes, and they always bond through music, and in college. If you look, it's there. You still see mostly all-male jazz ensembles.

JK: So how did you end up in electronics, given the male bonding through technology and music?

PO: Well, I think that I had bonded with my colleagues, Ramon [Sender] and Morton Subotnick. They were different. I didn't feel excluded. I had a lot to learn, but everybody did.

JK: So it wasn't that you had a lot to learn as a woman, you simply had a lot to learn as a young person and as a new person in electronics?

PO: That's right. Absolutely.

JK: Was there ever a sense that you had something to prove?

PO: Always I had trepidation that I knew enough, that I could learn enough, and I'm still there. I'm still trying to learn everything I can possibly learn.

JK: It keeps you young.

PO: That's right! [*Laughs*] Well, it keeps the newborn neurons that the brain creates daily from dying.

JK: If you were starting out in the twenty-first century as a composer today, how would your path in music be different?

PO: Well, I would certainly be a computer programmer. I would know several programming languages.

JK: Is that the advice you would say to a young woman interested in composition?

PO: Learn computer language.

JK: Is there still a place or a need for women-only concerts and festivals and recordings?

PO: Well, is there still a place for men-only concerts?

JK: I think there's a place for it. I don't think there's a need for it.

PO: [*Laughs*] I think from time to time it is a good idea.

JK: I heard someone say recently that there was a need for women-only concerts; however, we shouldn't advertise the fact that it's a woman-only concert. Just do it.

PO: That's right! Just do it! That's good.

JK: What is woman's place in the commercial publishing house or in the textbook?

PO: There are so many interesting women who are doing extraordinary work, I think there should be much more representation [in the textbooks]. Definitely. There should be much more inclusion. You find that in Kyle Gann's work.

JK: I am also fascinated with a trend in your writing on alternative space. We need alternative space to have the freedom to explore and experiment.

PO: That's what I mean when I say we have to create a safe space.

JK: So that alternative space could happen anywhere; it doesn't necessarily mean the recital hall?

PO: No, not at all. Alternative spaces are in lofts and garages . . . wherever you can find a space.

JK: Is that where new music thrives today—in all of those alternative spaces?

PO: Yes, it does. I went to a concert last night in New York in a place called the White Box. It's mostly a gallery, but a lot of really interesting new music is being played there right now.

JK: Where do you think composition is taking us?

PO: Oh, now there's so much composition and so many different things that I don't think I can answer that.

JK: Well, that itself is a good trend, when there are so many different kinds. Two hundred years ago it wouldn't be recognized as such.

PO: That's right. That's wonderful, to have a big variety.

JK: Now as an artist, you've managed to have a career lasting over fifty years. When times were tough, how did you continue? What got you through it?

PO: Making music! It's the only thing I wanted to do.

JK: Is there a sense of responsibility or pressure that comes with being Pauline Oliveros?

PO: [*Laughs*] I don't know if there is or not. I just do what I do and am who I am on a day-to-day basis. I don't worry about that.

JK: There are a lot of composers who credit you as one of the factors that made it possible for them to exist in music. On whose shoulders do you stand?

PO: My mother's. She was not only a piano teacher, as she certainly was for more than seventy-five years, but she also was an improviser, and she played for modern dance classes at the YWCA in the forties. At that time, you were supposed to take ballet.

JK: So you really did have an early influence in modern music and improvisation and experimentation.

PO: Yes. From my mother. That modern dance class was very key in bringing out her creativity, too, which was rooted in humor. It was fun. Some of the pieces she wrote, she improvised very quirky little pieces. It came out of playfulness. She was always playful until the very end.

JK: We're already reading about you in the textbooks, but a hundred years from now, when we read about you in the textbooks and you are no longer here, what do you see as your role in music?

PO: Well, I think it is facilitating creativity—making it possible for others.

JK: And perhaps a whole new role for you in the textbooks will be your work with this new software, helping, as you mention, the most marginalized members of our society experience sound creation and improvisation. When you look back through all the memories of an amazingly creative existence, what makes you feel really good about your creation and pleased that you were there to be a part of it?

PO: I'm glad that I wrote *Sonic Meditations.* That was a real breakthrough for me. That was a real radical departure for me from what I had been doing.

JK: I use those in one of my courses, Women in Music. After we experience several of them, I have my students make up their own and have them teach them to the rest of the class. It's hard for them at first to become engaged, but, as soon as they start creating their own, all of a sudden they become much more open to the experience.

PO: That's right. I do that too. I do that with my students at school.

JK: What's a typical day for you?

PO: There is no typical day [*laughs*].

JK: You seem to have an uncanny sense of place and time, where you connect very much with the now, the present, but you also seem to connect with the future. I don't find that many people can do that. Perhaps it's being open to it?

PO: Yes, it certainly is being open to it. Everything is looking forward—that's what I want to do.

JK: In what way do you hope to continue the evolution of your music?

PO: Well, I just keep going and see what happens.

***

Works by Pauline Oliveros

MUSIC FOR THEATER, FILM, DANCE, AND MULTIMEDIA

4H Club, film score (1958).
Aga, for voice, concertina, whistle conch, trumpet, electronics, and digital delay (1984).
Antigone's Dream, with choreographer Paula Josa Jones (1999).
AOK, for accordion, violins, chorus, conductor, audience, and tape-delay system (1969).
Art in Woodcut, film score (1963).
The Bath, for dancers and tape-delay system (1966).
Before the Music Ends, for tape and dancer (1965).
Big Room, for solo trombone and Expanded Instrument System (Deep Listening, 2003).

Candelaio, music for the San Francisco Mime Troupe (1965).
Cat o' Nine Tails, theater music (1965).
The Chronicles of Hell, music for the San Francisco Mime Troupe (1965).
Circuitry for Percussion and Light (1967).
Cock a Doodle Dandy, theater music (1958).
Covenant, film score (1965).
Crow's Nest (the Tuning Meditation), installation with film and dance (1979).
Double Basses at Twenty Paces, for two basses, their seconds, and a referee with slides and tape (Smith, 1968).
Drifting Depths, soundtrack (Deep Listening, 2008).
DroniPhonia for six iPhones and multi-instrumentalists (Deep Listening, 2009).
The Dying Alchemist Preview, for trumpet, violin, percussion, narrator, and slides (1969).
Epigraphs in the Time of AIDS, for accordion, trombone, keyboard, long string instrument, and Expanded Instrument System (Deep Listening, 1994).
Events, film score (1969).
Evidence for Competing Bimolecular and Termolecular Mechanisms in the Hydrochlorination of Cyclohexine, theater piece for specialized and unspecialized performers (1968).
The Exception and the Rule, music for the San Francisco Mime Troupe (1965).
The Eyes of Taxes Are upon You, soundtrack (Deep Listening, 2008).
Festival House, for orchestra chorus, mimes, films, and projections (1968).
Fifteen for an Ensemble of Performers, for instruments, singers, actors, and dancers (1964).
Fifteen for Four Dancers (1964).
Five for Trumpet and Dancer (1964).
Fwyynghn, theater collaboration (1980).
George Washington Slept Here Too, for amplified violin, film, projections, players, and two-channel tape (1965).
Ghostdance, with choreographer Paula Josa Jones (1996).
Hallo, for electronically modified piano, two tape-delay systems, violins, voice, actor, light projections, and dancers (1966).
The Heart of Tones, for solo trombone and electronics (Deep Listening, 1999).
Hommage a Serafina (1994).
The Indefinite Integral of Psi Star Psi d Tau = One, for mixed media (1969).
Inside Outside Space, for chamber orchestra, vocalist, and Expanded Instrument System (Deep Listening, 1992).
Io and Her and the Trouble with Him, an opera (Deep Listening, 2001).
The Library of Maps: An Opera in Many Parts (Deep Listening, 2002).
The Library of Maps IV: The Map of the Heart, the Map of Stones, and the Map of Unruly Threads (2008).
Light Piece for David Tudor, for electronically modified piano, lights, film, and four-channel tape (1965).
The Lightning Box, for Accordion, Voice, Keyboard, Marimba, and Expanded Instrument System (Deep Listening, 1990).
Lion's Eye, for Javanese gamelan and sampler (1985).

Live Electronic Piece for Merce Cunningham's Dance (1969).
Lulu, theater music (1962).
Lunar Opera: Deep Listening for Tunes (Deep Listening, 2000).
Lysistrata, theater music with tape and electronics (1968).
MMM, a Lullaby for Daisy Pauline, for audience (1980).
Maquilopolis, film score (2005).
Night Jar, for viola d'amore, tape, film, and mime (1968).
Njinga the Queen King: The Return of a Warrior, musical theater (Deep Listening, 1993).
The Noh Project II, for June Watanabe Dance Company (2004).
Oracle Bones, for spoken word, accordion, koto, and electronics (Deep Listening, 2009).
Participle Dangling in Honor of Gertrude Stein, for mobile, film, and two-channel tape (1966).
Paulina! film soundtrack (1997).
Please Don't Shoot the Piano Player, He Is Doing the Best He Can, for mixed media (1969).
Postcard Theater, mixed media for solo performer (1972).
Primordial/Lift, for accordion, cello, electric cello, harmonium, violin, sampler, and oscillator (Deep Listening, 1998).
Red Shifts, for trombone, oscillators, and noise (Deep Listening, 2000).
Seven Passages, for dancer, mobile, and two-channel tape (1963).
Sonic Images, for narrator and audience (1972).
Sound Geometries, for chamber orchestra and Expanded Instrument System (Deep Listening, 2003).
Sound Light Migrations, for accordion, Expanded Instrument System, and light (2009).
Spirit Light, for solo accordion and Expanded Instrument System (Deep Listening, 2003).
Stacked Deck, theater music (1980).
A Theater Piece, for fifteen actors, film, projections, players, and two-channel tape (1965).
Theater Piece for Trombone Player, with hoses and tape (1966).
Theater of Substitution, for solo performer (1975).
Theater of Substitutions: Blind/Dumb/Director (1977).
Tom Sawyer, theater music (1958).
To Valerie Solanas and Marilyn Monroe in Recognition of Their Despair, for orchestra, chorus, organ, electronics, and lights (1970).
Traveling Companions, for three percussionists and three dancers (Deep Listening, 1980).
Twenty-two Cuts from the Red Horse, theater music (1976).
Valentine, for four card players with amplification (1968).
View from the Bridge, theater music (1958).
Walter's Finest Hours, for Susan Marshall Dance Company (1992).
What to Do, mixed media for two or more performers (1972).
The Wheel of Fortune, for clarinet, slides, monologue, and costumes (1969).

MEDITATION OR OPEN ENSEMBLE

Anarchy Waltz, for any number of performers (1980).
Angels and Demons, for any number of performers (1980).

Beyond the Mysterious Silence: Approaches and Departures—Appearances and Disappearances, for an ensemble and singers (Deep Listening, 1995).
Bonn Feier, an intermedia piece for indeterminate numbers of performers (Smith, 1977).
California 99, collaboration (1969).
Carol Plantamura, for one voice and twenty instruments (1979).
CCCC, for instruments (1992).
A Ceremony of Sounds, for audience participation (1974).
Cheap Commissions, for composer and individuals (1976).
Crow Two—A Ceremonial Opera, for specialized and nonspecialized performers (1974).
Deep Listening Pieces, for voices and instruments, some including audience (1971–90).
Dissolving Your Earplugs, for classically trained musicians (Deep Listening, 2006).
Dream Gates, for solo or ensemble (1989).
Ear Rings, for any ensemble (Deep Listening, 1995).
Earth Ears: A Sonic Ritual, for any ensemble (Deep Listening, 1982–85).
Gone with the Wind, for assorted ensemble (1980).
The Heart of Tones, for ensemble (Deep Listening, 1999).
"I Hear a Boy Singing . . ." (1968).
Illegal Harmony, for two players (Deep Listening, 1992).
Inner/Outer Matrix, for mixed ensemble (Deep Listening, 2007).
Inside Outside Space, for accordion and electronics; for instruments and voice (1992).
Lake CHARGOGGAGOGGMANCHAUGGAGOGGCHAUBUNABUNBAGAUGG, for any number of performers (1981).
Link, for specialized and nonspecialized performers (1970).
Monkey, for children's ensemble (1981).
Music for Stacked Deck, for mixed ensemble (Deep Listening, 1979).
A New Indigo Peace, for piano and audience (2008).
Olas, Sobre las Olas, for any ensemble (Deep Listening, 2010).
One Hundred Meeting Places, for flexible orchestra (Deep Listening, 2006).
Pebble Music, for mixed ensemble (Deep Listening, 1992).
Phantom Fathom (II) from the Theater of the Ancient Trumpeters: A Ceremonial Participation Evening, for any number of performers (1972).
Portraits, unique score computer generated for each performer encouraging creative interaction with the material, for soloist or any ensemble (Deep Listening, 1988).
Queens of Space, for mixed ensemble (1991).
Rattlesnake Mountain, for accordion (1982).
Rock Piece, for any number of performers (1979).
Sonic Meditations I–XII, for musicians of all ages and skill levels to help them learn how to listen to and produce sound naturally (Smith, 1971).
Sonic Meditations XIII–XXV, for specialized and nonspecialized musicians (Smith, 1973).
Sound Fishes, for solo or ensemble (Deep Listening, 1992).
To Those in the Grey Northwestern Rainforests, for unspecified ensemble (1976).
Unnatural Acts between Consenting Adults (1975).
The Well and the Gentle, for ensemble (1983).

Why Don't You Write a Short Piece, for solo performer or group (1970).
The Witness, for soloist and an imaginary partner or ensemble of up to one hundred (Deep Listening, 1980).
The Yellow River Map, ceremonial mediation for a large group (1977).

ELECTRONIC

50-50 1 Heads, 50-50 2 Tails (1967–70).
5,000 Miles, for two-channel tape (1966).
I, II, III, IV, V of IV, and III, pieces for two-channel tape (1966).
Accordion, for amplified accordion with tape-delay system and eight channels (1966).
Alien Bog, for two-channel tape (1967).
Angel Fix (1966).
Another Big Mother (1966).
Apple Box, for amplified apple box and small objects (1964).
Apple Box Double (1965).
Apple Box Orchestra, for amplified apple box, mallets, and small sound producers (1964).
Beautiful Soop, for two-channel tape (1967).
The Beauty of Sorrow, for accordion and delay system (1988).
Big Slow Bog (1967).
Boone Bog (1967).
Bog Bog, for two-channel tape (1967).
Bog Road with Bird Call Patch, for two-channel tape (1967).
Before the Music Ends, for two-channel tape (1965).
Big Mother Is Watching You, for two-channel tape (1966).
Bottoms Up 1 (1966).
Bye Bye Butterfly, for two-channel tape (1965).
The C(s) for ONCE, for trumpets, flutes, voices, organ, and three tape recorders (1966).
Contendors, for tape (1990).
Continuing Variations, for accordion and Expanded Instrument System (2000).
Crone Music, for accordion and Expanded Instrument System (1990).
Cyber Talk (2011).
The Day I Disconnected the Erase Head and Forgot to Reconnect It, two-channel tape (1966).
Dear John: A Canon on the Name of Cage (1986).
Ear Piece, for tape of randomly selected citizens of Köln located in different environments (1998).
Engineers Delight, for piccolo, seven conductors (not electronic) for amplification of program sources, four turntables, and modulation (1967).
Fed Back 1 and 2 (1966).
The Flaming Indian, for tape recorder and microphone (1971).
The Heart of Tones, mixed realities version for trombones, voices, and Avatar orchestra (2008).
In Memoriam Nikola Tesla, Cosmic Engineer, for live electronics (1969).
Jar Piece, for two-channel tape (1966).
Lion's Tale (1989).

Listen Edgemar, sound installation (2004).
Listening for Life, for tape (1991).
A Little Noise in the System (1967).
Mercury Retrograde, for instruments and electronics (2011).
Mewsack (1967).
Mills Bog (1967).
Mind Bog (1967).
Mnemonics (multiple sets), mixed media (1964–66).
Murphy Mixup, for Princeton Laptop Orchestra (Deep Listening, 2006).
Music for Expo '70, for multichannel tape (1970).
Music for Stacked Deck, for four players (1979).
Nite (1966).
NO MO, for two-channel tape (1966).
Poem of Change, for text, World War II sounds, accordion, voice (1990).
Red Horse Headache (1967–70).
Ringing the Mods 1 Heads, Ringing the Mods 2 Tails (1966).
Rock Symphony, for live electronics and tape-delay system (1965).
Seven Passages for Elizabeth Harris, for two-channel tape (1964).
The Seventh Mansion: From the Interior Castle, for amplified accordion and effects (1983).
Some Sound Observations, for two-channel tape (1968).
Something Else (1966).
Sound Geometrics, for chamber orchestra and Expanded Instrument System (2002).
a sound signum (1997).
Sudophonia, for sudophone orchestra (Deep Listening, 2009).
Team and Desecrations Improvisation (1966).
Three Pieces I, II, III (1966).
Time Perspectives, for four-channel tape (1961).
Ultra Sonic Studies in Real Time, for two-channel tape (1966).
Waking the Noise Intoners (Intonarumori), sixteen players (Deep Listening, 2009).
Winter Light, for tape, mobile, figure (1965).

INSTRUMENTAL

1,000 Acres, for string quartet (1961).
18 Children's Pieces for Accordion (1959).
70 Chords for Terry: A Meditation on String Theory (Deep Listening, 2005).
Aeolian Partitions, for flute, clarinet, cello, and piano (1969).
All Fours for the Drum Bum, for drum set (1990).
Blue Heron, for piano and string bass (Deep Listening, 2006).
Breaking Boundaries, for piano solo or ensemble (Deep Listening, 1996).
Concert Piece for Accordion (1956).
Double X, for quartet or octet of instruments (1979).
Duo for Bandoneon and Accordion with Possible Mynah Bird Obligato, Seesaw Version (1965).
Elephant Call, for solo trumpet (1975).

Essay for Piano (1954).
A Fluting Moment (2008).
Four Meditations for Orchestra (Deep Listening, 1997).
Fugue for Piano (1953).
Gathering Together, for one piano eight hands (Deep Listening 1984).
The Gender of Now: There but Not There, for trombone and piano (Deep Listening, 2005).
Grand Improvisation, for accordion, oboe, bass, and synthesizer (1990).
Horn Etudes, for French horn (1959).
I've Got You under My Skin, for solo percussionist and Bat Man (1965).
. . . *Jam,* for accordion ensemble (1980).
Letting Go, for accordion solo/ensemble (1984).
Link, for specialized and nonspecialized performers (1970).
Magnetic Trails, for violin and piano (Deep Listening, 2008).
mirrorrorrim, for saxophone and piano (Deep Listening, 1994).
Mother's Day, for two concertinas (1981).
Norwegian Wood, for piano (1990).
Ode to a Morbid Marble, for piano (1951).
One Hundred Meeting Places: In Memory of Ron George, for violin, cello, and percussion (Deep Listening, 2006).
Outline for Flute, Percussion, and String Bass (1963).
Outline for Septet, for accordion, trombone, trumpet, double bass, piano, and two percussionists (1963).
Out of the Dark, for string orchestra (Deep Listening, 1998).
Pauline's Solo, for accordion (Deep Listening, 1992).
Pieces of Eight, for flute, oboe, French horn, contrabassoon, bass clarinet, trumpet, trombone, clarinet, and conductor (1964).
Portrait of Malcolm, for violin (1998).
Portrait of Quintet of the Americas, for flute, oboe, English horn, clarinet, and bass clarinet (1987).
Portraits for Brass Quintet (1989).
Prelude and Fugue, for string quartet (1953).
Quantum Flirts and Fits, for solo accordion (Deep Listening, 2003).
Quintessential, for string quartet (Deep Listening, 1999).
Quintuplets Play Pen—Homage to Ruth Crawford Seeger, for solo piano (2001).
The Roots of the Moment (1988).
Saxual Orientation, for saxophone quartet (Deep Listening, 1997).
Serenade for Viola and Bassoon (1956).
Shape Shifting, for accordion (1994).
Sister Dreams, for solo percussionist (2001).
Six for New Time, for four electric guitars and two percussion (Deep Listening, 1999).
Skin, for accordion (1991).
Song for Horn and Harp and Dance Band (1952).
Song for Piano (1952).

(Spiral) Mandala, for bass drum with four players, four clarinets, eight tuned glasses, and solo chanter (Smith, 1978).
Stay the Same to Change . . . and Change to Stay the Same, for accordion duo (1993).
St. George and the Dragon, for accordion (1991).
String-utopia, for cello and violin (2005).
Tara's Room, for accordion (1988).
Tashi Gomang, for orchestra (1981).
Tasting the Blaze, for percussion, electronics, trombone, cello, clarinet, four accordions, and gagaku orchestra (1985).
Thirteen Changes, for violin (Deep Listening, 1986).
Tree/Peace, for violin, cello, and piano (Smith, 1984).
Trio for Accordion, Trumpet, and String Bass (Smith, 1961).
Trio for Clarinet, Horn, and Bassoon (1955).
Trio for Flute, Piano, and Page Turner (Smith, 1961).
Undertone, for violin and piano (1951).
Variations for Sextet, for flute, clarinet, trumpet, horn, cello, and piano (Smith, 1960).
Vigil, for piano (2002).
Waking the Heart, for accordion solo/ensemble (1984).
The Wanderer, for twenty-two accordions and percussion (Deep Listening 1983).
What If, for accordion (1991).
The Wheel of Time, for string quartet and tape (Smith, 1984).
Wings of Dove, for double wind quintet and two pianos (Deep Listening, 1983).
A Woman Sees How the World Goes with No Eyes, for accordion (1989).

VOICE(S)

The Chicken Who Learned to Fly, for voice, narrator, and synthesizer (1985).
Drama of the Five Families, for narrator, soloist, and chorus (1984).
Dream Horse Spiel, for voices and sound effects (1989).
Elemental Gallop, for flute, piano, cello, and voice (Deep Listening, 2000).
For the Memory of Christine, for percussion and voices (Deep Listening, 2006).
The Future of Anonymity, for accordion and voice (1991).
Horse Sings from a Cloud, for accordion and voice (1977).
In Memoriam Mr. Whitney, for accordion and voices (1991).
In Memory of the Future, for solo voice (1992).
King Kong Sing Along, for chorus (1977).
The Klickitat Ride, for chorus and/or instruments and caller (1979).
Legend, for chorus, amplified accordion, and percussion (1985).
Meditation on the Points of the Compass, for chorus, percussion, and audience (1970).
Metalorgy, for pipes and voice (1992).
Midnight Operas, for chorus (1992).
Music for T'ai Chi, for accordion, two cellos, and three voices (1970).
A New Indigo Peace, for piano and chorus (Deep Listening, 2008).
The New Sound Meditation (1989).

O Ha Ah, for mixed chorus (1968).
Oh Sister Whose Name Is Goddess, for voice and digital delay (1984).
Open Circuits (1984).
The Pathways of the Grandmothers, for accordion and voice (1976).
Phantom, for instruments and voice (1992).
The Ready Made Boomerang, for instruments and voice (1992).
Reflections on the Persian Gulf, for accordion and voice (1991).
El Relicario de los Animales, for twenty instruments and singer (1979).
Rose Moon, for chorus and marathon runners (Smith, 1977).
Rose Mountain Slow Runner, for voice and accordion (1975).
Seven-up, for voice (1992).
Song of the Ancestors, for voice, shell trumpet, and didjeridu (1984).
Sound Patterns, for mixed chorus (1961).
Sound Patterns and Tropes, for chorus and percussion (Deep Listening, 2001).
The Space of Spirit, for vocalists, organ, and carillon (Deep Listening, 1999).
*SY*YdY=1,* for readers, celli, bassoons, amplified heartbeat, and shakuhachi (1969).
Talking Bottles and Bones, for voice, effects, and digital delay (1984).
Three Songs for Soprano and Piano (1957).
Three Songs for Soprano and Horn (1957).
Time Piece (1992).
Tower Ring, for gong, chorus, mixed instruments, and the Ann Hamilton Tower (Deep Listening, 2011).
Uncensored Sound, for accordion, trombone, voice, and keyboard (1991).
Urban Echo: Circle Told, for chorus and dance (Deep Listening, 2008).
The Wandering: a Love Song, voice and digital delay (1983).
The Wheel of Life, for vocal ensemble (1978).
Willowbrook Generations and Reflections, for mixed winds, brass, and voices (twenty or more) or chorus alone (Smith, 1976).
Wind Horse, for chorus (Deep Listening, 1990).

Massimo Agus

10

Meredith Monk

Born in 1942 in New York, Meredith Monk is an artist who has been defying categorization for decades. Often labeled a performance artist, she prefers the term "composer," because the core of her interdisciplinary art is born out of the music. Inspired as a young artist by the ability of Jean Cocteau to combine many art forms, Monk began her own integrated artistic training through her early introduction as a child to Dalcroze Eurhythmics. She credits her family with exposing her to the "powerful, plaintive, and very honest" singing of women like Peggy Seeger, Jean Ritchie, and Cynthia Gooding. While a student at Sarah Lawrence College, she was trained in the vocal traditions of European lieder and opera as well as in dance and theater. Monk's realization that she could treat her voice with the same flexibility as her body was a crucial breakthrough, and soon she began to develop her own vocal vocabulary through experimentation with what have come to be known as extended vocal techniques. Monk's catalog of works includes composition, interdisciplinary stage pieces, site-specific works, films, and installations. Always forward-thinking and risk-taking, Monk continues to cultivate like-minded followers of all ages. During our discussion, she expounds on audience, creativity, and art as a living being.

In 1968, Monk founded the House in New York City, known today as the House Foundation for the Arts, a company dedicated to interdisciplinary performance. Drawn toward collaboration, she founded Meredith Monk and Vocal Ensemble ten years later. This interview, like those with composers preceding it, demonstrates the credit Monk gives her collaborators, respecting their knowledge and dedication. In addition to her many awards for creativity, sustained achievement, stage works, and music, Monk received the MacArthur "Genius" Award in 1995. A holder of five honorary doctorates, Doris Duke Artist, and Musical America's 2012 Composer of the Year, Monk was also inducted into the American Academy of Arts and Sciences and named a U.S. Artists Fellow in 2006.

Particularly illuminating in our conversation is Monk's discussion of creative process. Like Pauline Oliveros, Monk's art is born out of listening. She explains that, as she accepts the fear of beginning with nothing and remains open to what comes, the music reveals itself. Turning off the self-judgmental mind, as in meditation, Monk is "totally at one with the material." Both as creator and interpreter, she is adept at using the vocabulary of a given artist because she works within many artistic languages. Compositionally, Monk rarely uses texts, instead favoring nonsensical syllables and vocal-sound exploration. During our conversation, she says that the possibilities of new opera excited her early on, while the accepted norms of the traditional genre were frustrating. The interdisciplinarity of opera intrigues Monk most, and she premiered *ATLAS: An Opera in Three Parts* in 1991. Although she is well-known in part for her site-specific work and interdisciplinary performance involving a visual element, she remains aware of the lack of visual elements when creating an aural recording. Consequently, she will rewrite a work when necessary to enable it to stand on its own in recording. This conscious reediting is reflected in her works list, which follows the interview.

Monk's vocal-sound exploration exists on several recordings, including *Book of Days* (the soundtrack to her 1988 feature-length film), *ATLAS: An Opera in Three Parts*, *mercy*, and *impermanence*. Desiring still to connect generations of performers and audiences and pass her work on, Monk began producing a few scores for publication by Boosey and Hawkes. Like many composers in this book whose music does not necessarily fall within traditional publishing language—she continues to teach much of her music through oral/aural means—Monk discusses facing the challenge to put her work on paper to be published. She meets that challenge as she has always met creative obstacles, with the acceptance of doubt toward self-renewal, reflection, and reaffirmation of what is important.

When Monk first developed and performed *Education of the Girlchild* in 1972, about the transformation of an old woman into a young girl, she was not yet thirty years old, imagining the feelings of being elderly. As she performs *Girlchild* today with seasoned wisdom and experience, Monk continues to renew, reflect, and reaffirm what is important to her.

***

December 2010, via Skype

JENNIFER KELLY: There are so many artists today that credit you as one of the people who made it possible for them to exist, and I'm curious, on whose shoulders do you stand?

MEREDITH MONK: Oh my goodness. Where to begin? Jean Cocteau was somebody who was very inspiring to me when I was a young artist as an example of a person who combined forms. Then, as far as music is concerned, I got my voice from my mother and my grandfather. I'm very grateful that I inherited their vocal ability and that they exposed me to a lot of music in my childhood. Women like Peggy Seeger, Jean Ritchie, Cynthia Gooding—those women were doing a very powerful, plaintive, and very honest kind of singing. That kind of honesty is something I've always tried for as a singer. And two teachers at Sarah Lawrence were very important to me: Bessie Schönberg, the director of theater and dance; and Ruth Lloyd, my music teacher. I think that Bessie knew right away that I was going to be singing, and having some of that movement background was very helpful for me. Movement was very hard for me. I had a lot of physical limitations with my eyes and my body, so it was very challenging. And, because of my limitations, I had to find a very idiosyncratic way of moving. I was quite successful at finding a vocabulary that was built on my own body. Maybe the limitations worked to my advantage in that situation. When I really started working with my voice, I had a revelation that I could use that same methodology with my voice. I asked myself, "How do I actually find the material based on my own vocal instrument?" Ruth Lloyd, a remarkable pianist and organist, taught me composition and music history. She opened up the whole world of music to me. She and Bessie both saw who I was. I think as human beings, if we're seen, anything is possible. They saw my spirit and encouraged me to find my own way.

JK: While doing the research for this interview, I was struck by a brief essay that you wrote for "Ages of the Avant-Garde" in the *Performing Arts Journal.* You were talking about reviving the solo *Education of the Girlchild,* which you first performed in 1972. Since the time the article was written [in 1992], you've performed that piece again in 1993, 2008, and then again in 2010. So, forty years since the solo's inception, how has your perspective changed in the performance of it?

MM: Well, I'm amazed that at the age of twenty-eight I was thinking about what it would be to have an eighty-year-old voice in an eighty-year-old body. You know, it's so strange, because at that time I actually embodied the young woman in that piece. And it was almost my fantasy of my future as a middle-aged woman and as an old woman. And now I am closer to the time between the middle-aged woman and the old woman, so now it's like the piece is more a reverie of my past as well as the past of the character. Performing it is just so deep for me now.

JK: Well, it's very intense.

MM: And particularly the old woman, "Ooh, my back." So I feel like in 2008 it was much more about getting the structure into my body and voice. It was more about really getting the vocabulary back. But in spring 2010 in Paris—and we also did it about a month ago in Tennessee—I feel that I'm at another level. I'm so deep into this transformational aspect of the piece.

JK: Do you use the same movements, performing the exact same piece but with a different perspective?

MM: Yeah, pretty much. I have room, particularly in my solo, to play a little bit. I went back to a well-documented performance videotape from 1973, and I just stuck with that. So, in a way, in 2008, it was a way of being very, very precise. Getting the mechanics and the structure, and really getting the form totally secure in my voice and body. And now, because of working so hard on the form, the piece is able to speak through me. Because it really is about transformation in front of your eyes.

JK: Do you envision yourself continuing to perform it, five, ten years from now?

MM: Hard to say.

JK: I remember reading that you said you always knew you were not going to be an interpreter of music. Was there a defining moment when you realized you were a creator?

MM: I think when I was in my teens, you know, I think it was some impulse that I had. I always loved to make things; I had a creative urge, I guess you would say. I'm sure that I didn't know how it was going to manifest at the time, but I had a glimpse of it. And then, when I was at Sarah Lawrence, I was in the voice department singing lieder and also opera workshop singing roles. Somehow, I knew that it just wasn't quite right. I knew that I had to make my own world.

JK: Your connection, the kinesthetic connection between music and the body, is so apparent.

MM: I was studying Dalcroze [Eurhythmics] with Lola Rohm when I was three years old. Lately, I've been doing research on Dalcroze, and the more I read about him, the more I think this guy was incredible! Solfege, rhythmic training, and improvisation. I don't know how you could do better than that. So, to everybody I know that has children and asks me about music lessons, I just say, please start your kids with Dalcroze. It's the best beginning for any child.

JK: I agree. It is an amazing path to creativity and kinesthetic connection between the mind and the body. You don't necessarily have to go into music or dance, but just to open up the acceptance of the present.

MM: Exactly. Lola Rohm was very important to me.

JK: With regard to creativity, what can we as teachers, conductors, and performers do to help teach and foster creativity in others?

MM: Well, I would even take it back one step and then go on to creativity. Even as interpreters, I think the Western European tradition has separated one function from the other. Now, these are singers over here, these are dancers over here, and these are instrumentalists over here, and these are actors over here. And it has this philosophical basis that the universe is finite and we have to connect to a system that is also fixed, like a geometric system, and we fit our bodies and voices into that system. For example, with singing, I always think why is everybody, on some level, supposed to sound alike? I guess the answer is to be able to blend and from top to bottom every note of your voice is supposed to be one seamless sound. It's all those systems that we as human beings are supposed to fit into. And there's a problem there, because the body and the voice, and humanity and nature, got split into a dualistic kind of a system. That's where I think the problem began. In other words, the metaphor before that was alchemy. So as soon as the Renaissance came in and then, after that, the Enlightenment, it became "man over nature." There's the problem right there, and it manifests in all these ways. So I think that one thing you could say to your singers is that the voice and the body are one; there is no separation. In other words, it's not just that you're going to have to make this pear-shaped tone—you're going to have to sit on your sound. The body and the voice are one. It's forward motion as you're moving through. You also have to stay empty enough to let this music come through you. That's really what it's about. It's about listening with every cell of your body, so the music can come through you.

JK: What about the evaluation of music? It seems as though nowadays we're almost taught to listen passively because music is everywhere, all the time. And a lot of it is not necessarily designed to really say anything. So, if we're encouraged in that passive experiential way, how can we teach or encourage the present experience, even in listening?

MM: Exactly. And by extension, this creativity is in a way the same process as performing, because it really is about listening, and listening to actually what the world of sound that you're creating wants. Our practice as artists, both as creators and interpreters, is to get out of the way of what is actually coming through. So, as an interpreter, you try to leave your channels open, so the music actually comes through you. When you're performing, it's probably the closest thing to meditation that there is, because you're totally in the moment. The way that I've experienced it when I've felt that happening was when the evaluation part of my mind is actually not active at all. That judgmental, "Oh that's terrible, that's flat, that's sharp" part of the mind is not there. I'm totally at one with the material.

JK: So that is the ultimate goal?

MM: That is the ultimate goal. Your consciousness is very pinpointed, focused. Simultaneously, you're absolutely open and deeply relaxed—you know from inside, a very deep relaxation. I don't mean not having any energy; I'm talking of the deepest level of relaxation, open to what's going on in the moment. So it's got a pinpoint awareness and a completely spacious aspect simultaneously. It's the same thing when you're performing with other people. My ensemble works so much on listening with every ounce of our beings. For instance, in some pieces, like the last section of *Dolmen Music,* even how the cuing happens within that section has to do with spacious awareness. I'm listening with all my heart and my body and my being to what's going on, and then the cuing is like an instinctive thing. That can only happen from listening. And also with *Dolmen Music,* the intonation is really challenging. And what we've all found out about intonation is that when you're really listening and have that quality of listening, you're making adjustments all the time. I'm talking about performing—that experience of listening and performing with other people, and being in tune emotionally, in tune spiritually. I mean, there's nothing like that! That is about as good as life can get. You're pulling for the other people; you're hearing them as much as you're hearing yourself. There's nothing like that. So how can we as teachers convey that listening to an iPod will never be as good as that? Never. It will never be, there's no way. I think that the only thing you can do as a teacher and a conductor is to just turn people on. I guess that all we can do as teachers is to expose people to something that they don't know.

JK: Being that it's fairly common to basically "turn off" to help oneself get through the day, if you turn off once, then it becomes easier to turn off a second and then a third time. But if, within a performance, even for a song, you can get one person in the audience to "turn on," to be present in the moment, then perhaps they'll get used to that experience.

MM: Exactly—that's what we're trying to do. We're also turning them on to themselves. We're turning them on to memories or emotions or the feeling of being alive and the magic of being in the moment, and the presence and the vulnerability. If we're in front of a screen all the time, we are in danger of losing those aspects and moments of ourselves. That's actually all we have are moments. I mean, are you going to think about your iPod when you're on your deathbed? But it's not easy to stay present when all this information is coming in. I have a sense of compassion for young people now, because when I was coming up, I was the only person that I knew doing work like this. It was quite painful; it was very lonely. The jazz musicians knew what I was doing vocally, and they gave me a lot of support. But I wouldn't say that the general culture was ready to hear some of my vocal language of sound. I just knew that I found what I was looking for, and that this was my path, so it wouldn't have stopped me. I knew I had somehow uncovered something that was universal and timeless and human. And now you can hear everything, anything that's coming in, twenty-four hours a day, everything that's ever been done, every singer that's ever sung. How do you find your individual voice through the clamor? I have a sadness about it. I just talked with two composers, and they said, "Well, you guys pushed aside all the boundaries of the forms. You already went through everything. And now we don't know, what are we supposed to do? So we just combine everything that exists into something else." And I said, "Well, don't you think there's only one of you in the universe, and that the idea is to find what you and only you can do?" There's always more to find. How can you say that we've pushed the boundaries of music? I feel like there's always more to find.

JK: You bring up a good point. You've been performing and creating for almost fifty years now. When you begin to create something today, is it a comfortable, easy beginning? Or have you really used every idea you can think of already?

MM: It's completely terrifying. It's like being at the edge of a cliff every time. I ask myself every time, Why am I putting myself through this voluntarily? But it's more like having the fear and then saying, "Well, it's daily work, it's daily discipline. I'll just take it step by step, a little at a time." Then, at a certain point, and it happens every time, a question comes up. And once you have the question, that's the key. The thing that keeps me going and being alive is curiosity. The beginning process is very, very hard, but I think there is also the joy of actually sensing that a question will come eventually. And that question is the key to the world that you are uncovering, that may already exist. And then you're listening for what are the principles of that world. The moment that interest starts coming in, the fear goes, and curiosity is aroused. That's very, very exciting. And then you feel part of the universe. You feel part of the creative impulse of the universe.

JK: Is it part of an answer to the question?

MM: I'm not sure it's an answer. I'm not sure that it's ever an answer. I don't think that any of us ever have answers. For example, the last piece I composed, a commission for St. Louis Symphony, my question ended up being, How would I make a piece that has orchestra, chorus, and vocal soloists, where the orchestra is sometimes the chorus, and the chorus is sometimes the orchestra, and the soloists are also instruments in the orchestra, and the orchestra is sometimes solo instruments? So how do I do that? That was the question. And then *Weave* came out. And it was a miracle!

JK: It must be a great sense of encouragement for young people when you speak about this. It's sort of a validation, saying it's okay to have fear, or it's okay to have some kind of self-doubt at the beginning, I'm going to power through it.

MM: Absolutely. I think doubt is very important. And as painful as doubt is, doubt is also good because it is what makes you renew yourself. It's then that you reflect and reaffirm what is important to you. I have learned to be patient during those periods because something fresh always comes out of them. It's a matter of how you think about your work. There are some people that make work more like products. It's pretty much cut out of the same fabric, every piece, more like a product-oriented way of thinking about music. I can't do that. I don't want to do that to music. My way of thinking about things is that, in every piece that you do, you start as much as possible from nothing. And one's sensibility as a being is going to be there anyway, so you don't have to be afraid of that. For instance, I don't think that my work is eclectic; you always know that it comes from a particular inner center. It's a way of thinking process more than product.

JK: So dealing with process, when an idea first comes to you, or that question first comes to you, do you first hear a sound, see an image, feel a movement—what is it?

MM: Every piece is different. So, for example, the thing that was worrying me about *Weave* was, I didn't really have an image, or I didn't even really at the beginning have an idea. And it's interesting because the older I get, the more I trust that. I remember that John Cage used to say, "You can have too many ideas." When I was a young artist I had lots of ideas. And when you're a young artist, you think you have to put every idea that you have into a piece as you do it. As you get older you realize, no, this piece wants this, this is the world of this particular piece. The last piece I did with my ensemble was called *Songs of Ascension.* I was intrigued by this idea of songs of ascent, of the tradition of going up, rising to make music that was a form of worship. And then I started to think also about, in the Buddhist tradition, the circumambulation, and then also in the American Indian tradition, the earth going down. So that dimensional thing about music was my concept.

JK: Do you start at the beginning?

MM: Again, each piece is very different. For example, with *Weave* I was only working on musical material; that's all I had. And within that, I had to trust that the material was going to lead me to the overall form of the piece. Whereas with *Songs of Ascension* it was pretty abstract, but I had a point of departure, and then, as new material came up, I knew whether it was part of the piece or not. So you see, that's two very different ways of working.

JK: Your work is also very precise, so how do you balance the precision with the role of improvisation or just organic growth?

MM: That's what I work very hard on, the combination of discipline and freedom. Some of the forms are so intricate, there can be no leeway at all. And then within some sections we can play. But it's still, again, within a precise and rigorous parameter. There's room for play, particularly with people that I've been working with so long who know what those parameters are. So people say it sounds like we're improvising, but actually we're not.

JK: In the creation of a piece, how do you know when it is finished? Or is it ever finished?

MM: I always ask painters that. I ask, "How do you know that one more stroke is not going to ruin it?" You were very sensitive to ask before about the organic growth. And that is true about live performance and a way of working that is not score-oriented. With *Weave,* because it's for orchestra and people have to read it off the page, when I want to make a change, I have to go back to the score and say, "You know, I'd like to try a little oboe line there." But with my ensemble, where it is a living form, we are making discoveries as we go along, and that is actually the beauty of live performance. And then sometimes after many, many years, there are little modifications that I'm not even that aware of, but it obviously has grown. When we record, I sometimes go back to the absolute original because I realize the piece has naturally grown, but we have to remember the original principles.

JK: Right. I find that with this book. Every time I do an interview, I have to remind myself of the original goals, the principles, and work from there.

MM: You have to, because otherwise life takes over, but that's also the nature of writing and performing. It's a living being. The first time a piece is performed, it's like an infant, but that, again, is why I find the orchestral world very hard. The piece comes out kicking and screaming, and then you get two performances, and it never has a chance to evolve into what it wants and even become an adolescent.

JK: Well, you bring up a very good point with regard to being a contemporary composer or creator. What if the audience only experiences the piece once? Can the composer be concerned with what the audience understands if they don't get multiple listenings?

MM: I always have a hard time with the word "understands," as far as music is concerned. I think "understanding" is the wrong part of the brain. I think more "perceived" would be what I would say. You know, when someone says, "I don't understand," I just say, "Well, there really is nothing to understand." It means that the narrator in your mind is trying to analyze what you're hearing instead of hearing it.

JK: So, whatever the individual's experience is . . . is.

MM: Yeah. To me, the beauty of live performance is direct experience. It's not pointing out to yourself what your experience is, and it's not verbalizing your experience, because then you're not in the experience. So to me, the beauty of music and the beauty of live performance is that you transcend what we call the discursive mind. And you're actually in the absolute experience of the moment. That's the beauty of it. That's why we do it.

JK: And what if the audience experiences the piece only once?

MM: What is so wonderful about music is that each person can have her or his own images. I don't have to provide the imagistic level. Each person can have her own unique experience, his own images, or her own memories. If an audience was just going to have a one-time experience, what I would hope for would be that they are open enough to actually experience it. At the same time, I'm very aware of what you're saying—that if you hear something more than once, there are so many layers to it, again, something quite intricate. You hook in on a different dimension every time you hear it. I try to make work that isn't just skimming the surface of something, that on multiple listenings you would be able to hear something more in there. Sometimes people think my work is very simple, and it's not. It's deceptively simple-seeming on the surface, but it's actually complex, and so you can go down, down, down into it, hopefully, and you'll have a different experience. So that's the sad thing about the one-time experience. Not only for the piece for its own growth, but also for the audience.

JK: I really understand how important it is for you with live music; we happen to share that belief. You have multimedia pieces. So how do you translate some of your works into recording, which gives someone the opportunity for multiple listenings, but you don't have the same kind of layers, necessarily?

MM: Well, what I usually do is rewrite for recording, because I'm very aware that the images are not there. And so my forms are much richer and more dense and usually more compressed. For *mercy,* I didn't originally have a clarinet in there, but I wrote a clarinet part for the recording and was so happy with it that every time we performed it again, I included the clarinet. I am very aware of that. What I have wanted for my albums is for the music to stand by itself.

JK: *Impermanence* includes text. And because you rarely work with text, whenever I do hear text in your music I think it is particularly meaningful, particularly poignant. What was it about *impermanence* that made you decide you needed text?

MM: Well, I'll tell you the history of *last song.* I started working on it at the MacDowell Colony in November 2001. We were in shock, because of September

11, and we were all up at MacDowell wondering what we were doing as artists. It was quite hard to work. I was reading a wonderful book by James Hillman called *A Force of Character.* And there was this one chapter where he does a meditation on the word "last" and how we use the word "last" in our culture. And that litany of words used in the song was in his book. I usually use words in an abstract way, often lists of words, repetitive, so it becomes a kind of mantra or litany. Then in 2002 my partner died, and I was grieving, really grieving, and in 2003 I was supposed to go on tour with Bang on a Can All-Stars. I was supposed to make a new piece, and it was a hard time to be thinking about creating. But somehow I thought to myself I didn't finish that "last" song, and I think I'll just work on it. Simultaneously, I got an email from a woman who is the head of an organization in England called Rosetta Life. It's an organization that goes to hospices all over England, sending artists to work with people who are in the dying process to help them create art. They asked me to write music for a play using their stories, but I said I'd love to make a whole piece about impermanence, because that's all I'm thinking about night and day. I felt that a piece about the transience and ephemerality of life needed to have the grounding of words, and yet in an abstract way. So that's why I used *last song.* And then in my partner Mieke's notebook, I found some writing which I eventually called *between song,* "between the paint and the wood, between the rug and the floor, between the lipstick and the lips." She was such a metaphysical, highly evolved person, I thought I just have to try to write a song with some of this. The words are mostly sung on one note, so you get that kind of mantra, chantlike use of words. It becomes more of an invocation rather than an illustration of text.

JK: So *impermanence* came out of this project working with Rosetta Life, September 11, and then your partner Mieke passing away—the connection of all of that happening at the same time. That's a lot of insight into the work.

MM: Yeah, it happened in about a two-year period, because in 2001 I was in MacDowell, she died in 2002, and then 2003 was when I made contact with Rosetta Life. I went to London and did a workshop with these people in the dying processes in hospices all over England. And they would tell me about their experiences. Since they were coming from different hospices, they were also sharing their experiences with each other. We laughed a lot. And then I played *last song,* and one person said, "At first, it felt too close to my experience, and then once I let go, I could listen to it all night." So, it was special. My feeling in that part of the process of making the piece was, How could I do something that's worthy of these people?

JK: Where do you think new music can really thrive today? Is it in the universities, in the concert halls, the small clubs, in the out-of-the-way places? Where does it thrive?

MM: Everywhere. I just feel that the sky's the limit, however we can get out there, wherever and whenever. From Carnegie Hall to Le Poisson Rouge.

JK: That's a very positive outlook on new music.

MM: I think a lot of very good things are happening in music.

JK: Who is in the audience today? Who's listening?

MM: All the way up and down the range of ages, which I think is very hopeful and positive. Also, I'm hoping that young people use me as a prototype of the possibility of following what they know is right for themselves; that they have a dream and aren't afraid to follow it, no matter what the world is saying. I think that people are longing for that. And I think that may be a reason why they are coming: to have an example, not just going to school to learn what kind of job they're going to get. I know I'm saying this from the point of view of someone who is . . . I mean, I'm not out on the street. But I'm struggling. I'm still struggling, but that's a kind of commitment that you make. I guess the question becomes, Is the freedom worth it?

JK: It's all for the love of what you do.

MM: Yes. But why are we not helping our young people follow their dreams?

JK: Have you always had a broad audience?

MM: Pretty much. I've been lucky enough that in the early days there was basically a built-in audience of the downtown world. I've never had a problem having an audience, and they've stuck with me. I've always been less interested in a lot of hype, but I have been interested in word of mouth. So I think there have been audiences that have followed me over the years, and that's been great.

JK: And today, you continue to have young people in the audience. It sounds like, whatever you're doing, the traditional, classical, art-music world can really learn something from it.

MM: I think the traditional music world is disappointing and has been backward as far as art forms have gone. I think visual arts are usually ahead, partly because in art school they learn that interpreter and creator are the same thing. In the music world, there is the interpreter branch and the creator branch. And interpreters are not taught that a life of interpretation is a life of creativity. With a great interpreter, you actually see them creating on stage. They're always finding. That's what a great performer is—they're always finding in the material what's there, more, more, uncovering, uncovering. That's creation, and that's honorable. And I love the classical-music tradition—Bartók, Stravinsky, Mompou, Satie. I think part of what it is to be able to play Bach, Beethoven, that repertoire, you have to work six hours a day to just have the chops to be able to play these things. You become a creature of the rehearsal room. It's like being a surgeon. It's so much pressure just to achieve the technical, technocratic world that we're living in. I was so excited about performing in the opera world because everything I've done that combines forms, I've always thought of as opera. Opera has such capacity to have all those mediums woven together. After I did *ATLAS,* I was getting *Opera News,* and I was so excited. But after a while I just got sick of it. I'm not putting traditional operas down, but let's jump to the twenty-first century. Let's even jump to the twentieth century.

JK: What kind of concerts do you enjoy attending?

MM: What young composers are doing, and what's going on in new music. It's very exciting.

JK: There are committed folks that want to make sure your music continues. What are you doing now in terms of preserving the music so that your legacy continues on a hundred years from now?

MM: Well, we're working so hard on the scores. And it takes years. *Panda Chant* is a minute and a half long, and it took two years to do that score. I do have the recordings.

JK: Fifty or a hundred years from now, would you appreciate an homage recording, re-creations of your work, or would that be false?

MM: I don't know. Why would anyone do an imitation of Billie Holiday? But as a composer, with some of the ensemble work, first my ensemble and then a younger group like the M6, people who have worked with me directly, would know the music in their bones and would know how to bring it to life. Maybe that generation would pass it on; that's more the oral tradition. I'm really struggling with this right now. I'm really working hard to get some of this music scored out. One supplementary idea is that on my Web site there would be a recorded demonstration of the techniques so that, when you would see it on the page, you'd be able to hear it. I'm trying to pass the music on because I want people to have the joy of performing it.

JK: You're talking again about connection. It goes back to the essay we discussed earlier, "Ages of the Avant-Garde," where you talk so much about combining generations. Whether it is combining generations of women or ages of people, again it's about that connection.

MM: I want to pass on this joy, the way that, from time immemorial, people have passed from one generation to the next what they learned and their insights. You want to pass it on, so people can have that insight themselves and then have that experience. That's what the impulse is.

JK: Is there some sense of responsibility that comes with being Meredith Monk?

MM: Responsibility. Well, I mean, I do feel very responsible; I have a wonderful group of people that have worked with me for many years, some people for thirty-eight years, and I have tried to keep that group together. That is a very strong responsibility for me. It's an ensemble that's worked for years and years, and they know this language backwards and forwards, so some part of my responsibility and struggle is keeping this group together. I also feel a kind of responsibility to keep going. You know, while I'm still alive, to keep on creating. That's a responsibility to myself, because it has always been my biggest wish to be working until I die.

JK: I've always been impressed by the way you continually credit your ensemble. You talk about the individual people and what they bring to the ensemble or to individual pieces. You don't always hear people do that.

MM: I just think it's so important.

JK: So, when somebody new is brought in, does it become a completely new ensemble?

MM: Definitely a shift of energy, and I write differently. I'm really writing for the particular voices that are there.

JK: Duke Ellington did the same thing. Is there any one thing that you could point to within your work of which you are the most proud?

MM: Oh gosh, that's a hard question. I would say the thing I'm proudest of is that I just kept going over the years, even with my fears and doubts, the ups and downs. Sometimes I think that, as a young artist, I didn't take care of myself that well, but I feel that somehow underlying everything, I've had a deep belief in the worthiness of art and its healing power, and that I've kept working no matter what. That would be what I'm most proud of.

JK: How would you like your music to continue to evolve from here?

MM: I would like to keep finding new sound worlds. I'd like to keep myself open. Working more with instrumentalists and hearing the beauty of instruments as singers in a way, I'd like to keep enriching that. You know, I think as an older person you do refine. You get more elegant; that's a natural evolution. But I think never to forget the rawness of life.

JK: I'm curious what your thoughts are about the theorists and musicologists and the categorizations and all of that, that delve into your music and describe it. How comfortable is that for you?

MM: I actually feel like there hasn't been very much serious writing about my music. And I always feel very sad about it. I feel it's always put in terms of, "She's a multimedia 'blahdiblah.'" Since I was in my thirties, the center in my work has been music, so I really appreciate serious writing about it.

JK: So you welcome it then?

MM: I do.

***

Works by Meredith Monk

OPERA/MUSICAL THEATER/SITE-SPECIFIC WORKS

16 Millimeter Earrings, solo incorporating film and original music (1966).

Acts from Under and Above (collaboration with Lanny Harrison), for three performers (1986).

American Archeology No. 1: Roosevelt Island, for seventy performers (1994).

Anthology and Small Scroll, for nine performers (1974).
Ascension Variations, for 130 performers (2009).
ATLAS: An Opera in Three Parts, for twenty-nine performers (1991).
Blueprint
for twelveperformers (1967).
2: Overload, for five performers (1967).
3, for three performers (1968).
4, for two performers (1968).
5, for eight performers (1968).
A Celebration Service, for thirteen performers (1996).
Chacon (collaboration with Ping Chong), for twenty-five performers (1975).
Co-op, for thirty performers (1968).
Education of the Girlchild: an opera solo (1972).
(part I), for thirteen performers (1973).
Revisited, for four performers (2010).
Evanescence, choreography for Donald Ashwander's *Particular People* (1993).
Facing North, for solo voice and instrument (Boosey and Hawkes, 1990).
The Games (collaboration with Ping Chong), for sixteen performers (1983).
The Impermanence Project, for eight performers (2004).
Jewish Storyteller/Dance/Dream, for chorus (Boosey and Hawkes, 2009).
Juice: A Theater Cantata in Three Installments, for eighty-five performers (1969).
Magic Frequencies, for eight performers (1998).
mercy, for eight performers (2001).
Music Concert with Film, for eight performers (1981).
Needle-Brain Lloyd and the Systems Kid: A Live Movie, for 150 performers (1970).
Overload, for five performers (1967).
The Plateau Series, for eight performers (1978).
The Politics of Quiet: A Music Theater Oratorio, for twelve performers (1996).
Quarry: An Opera, for forty performers (1976).
A Raw Recital, for voice and electric organ (1970).
Recent Ruins: An Opera, for fourteen performers, incorporating the Monk film *Ellis Island* (1979).
The Ringing Place, for twelve performers (1987).
Songs of Ascension, for twelve performers (2008).
Specimen Days: A Civil War Opera, for fifteen performers (1981).
Street Corner Pierrot, choreography for Donald Ashwander's *Particular People* (1993).
Tour: Dedicated to Dinosaurs, for sixty-five performers (1969).
2: Barbershop, for sixty-five performers (1969).
3: Lounge, for fifty performers (1969).
4: Organ, for sixty performers (1970).
5: Glass, for fifty performers (1970).
6: Gym, for twelve performers (1970).
7: Factory, for fifteen performers (1970).
8: Castle (1971).

The Travelogue Series: Paris/Venice-Milan/Chacon (collaboration with Ping Chong), thirty performers (1976).
Turtle Dreams, for seven performers (1983).
Turtle Dreams (Cabaret), for seven performers (1984).
Vessel: An Opera Epic, for seventy-five performers (1971).
Vessel: An Opera Epic (Berlin version, revival), for eighty performers (1980).
Volcano Songs (1994).

FILM/VIDEO

16 Millimeter Earrings, silent, black-and-white and color film, 16 mm, 7 min., directed by Monk (1966).
16 Millimeter Earrings, color, sound, 16 mm, 25 min., dir., prod., photography Robert Withers (1980).
24 Hours of Faces (Parts 1 and 2), silent, color film, $\frac{3}{4}$-inch, $\frac{1}{2}$-inch videotape (1994).
Ballbearing, silent, color film, 16 mm, 6.5 and 13 min., play continuously forward and backward (1968).
Book of Days, black-and-white and color film, sound, 35 mm; 1-inch, $\frac{3}{4}$-inch, and $\frac{1}{2}$-inch videotape, (1988).
Children, silent, black-and-white film, 16mm, 9 min. (1967).
Ellis Island, silent, black-and-white film, 16 mm, 7 min. (1979).
Ellis Island, color and black-and-white film, sound, 35 mm, 28 min. [also videotape], prod. and dir. Bob Rosen (1981).
Girlchild Diary, film for Dance Theater Workshop (2012).
Humboldt's Current, silent, black-and-white, 16 mm and super-8, 5 min.; incorporated into Ping Chong's *Humboldt's Current* (1977).
Mermaid Adventures, silent, color film, 16 mm, 10 min., projected during *Turtle Dreams (Cabaret),* (1984).
Mountain, silent, color film, 16 mm, 10 min. (1971).
Paris (collaboration with Ping Chong), videotape, 26 min., prod. and dir. Mark Lowry and Kathryn Escher (1982).
Quarry, silent, black-and-white film, 16 mm, 5 min. (projected in *Quarry*), (1975).
Quarry, color documentary film of the opera, sound, 16 mm, 86 min. (1978).
Raven, Parlor, Cat Breath, Graveyard Pavane, music for Ellen Fisher's *Dreams within Dreams: The Life of Edgar Allan Poe,* (1988).
Turtle Dreams (Waltz), color film sound, video, 27 min., dir. Ping Chong (1984).

COMPOSITION

16 Millimeter Earrings, for voice, guitar, and tapes (1966).
Acts from Under and Above Ellis Island, for two pianos (1986).
American Archeology No. 1: Roosevelt Island, for nine voices, organ, bass, medieval drum, and shawm (1994).
Ancestor Shout (collaboration with David Behrman), for voice and electronics (2001).
And Sarah Knew, for five performers (1962).

Anthology and Small Scroll, for voice, piano, and soprano recorder (1975).
Arm's Length (sound collage), for six performers (1964).
Astronaut Anthem, for chorus (Boosey and Hawkes, 1983).
ATLAS: An Opera in Three Parts, for eighteen voices, two keyboards, clarinet, bass clarinet, sheng, bamboo, sax, string quartet, French horn, percussion, and shawm (1991).
Basket Rondo, for six voices (2007).
The Beach, solo (1965).
Biography, for solo voice and piano (1973).
Blackboard, solo (1965).
Blueprint: Overload/Blueprint (2), for voice with echoplex and tape (1967).
Book of Days, for twenty-five voices, synthesizer, and piano (1985).
Book of Days (chamber version), for seven voices and synthesizer (1985).
Boys 1; Boys 2; Boys 3, for four voices (2001).
Break (tape collage), solo (1964).
Candy Bullets and Moon (collaboration with Don Preston), for voice, electric organ, electric bass, and drums (1967).
Cartoon, for seven performers (1965).
Cat Song, for solo voice (1988).
Cello Study No. 1, for solo cello and voice (1999).
Chacon, for twenty-five voices, piano, and percussion (1974).
City Songs, for two voices and two keyboards (1984).
Clarinet Study No. 1, for solo clarinet (1999).
Cowell Suite, solo (1964).
Custom Made (1993).
 Steppe Music, solo piano
 Volcano Songs, for two voices
 St. Petersburg Waltz, for two voices and piano
 New York Requiem, for solo voice and piano (Boosey and Hawkes, 1993).
Den-Kai and Krikiki Chants, for four voices (1995).
Diploid, for two performers (1964).
Dolmen Music, for six voices, cello, and percussion (1979).
Double Fiesta, for voice and two pianos (1986).
Duet Behavior, for two voices (1987).
Duet with Cat's Scream and Locomotive, tape collage, for two performers (1966).
Dying Swan with Sunglasses, for solo voice with echoplex and tape (1967).
Earth Seen from Above (from *ATLAS*), for SATB divisi (Boosey and Hawkes, 1991).
Eclipse Variations, for four voices, Esraj, and sampler (2000).
Education of the Girlchild: An Opera (Part II), for six voices, electric organ, and piano (1973).
Ellis Island, for two pianos (1981; available alone, or in *Piano Album,* Boosey and Hawkes, 2007).
Engine Steps, tape collage (1983).
Fayum Music, for voice, hammered dulcimer, and double ocarina (1989).

Folkdance, for piano (1996; available alone, or in *Piano Album*, Boosey and Hawkes, 2007).
The Games, for sixteen voices, synthesizer, keyboards, Flemish bagpipes, Chinese horn, and Rauschpfeife (1983).
Goodbye/St. Mark's Window, solo (1967).
Graduation Song, for sixteen voices (1984).
I Don't Know, for voice and piano (1986).
impermanence (part 1), for eight voices, piano, keyboard, marimba, vibraphone, percussion, violin, winds, and bicycle wheel (2004).
impermanence (part 2), for eight voices, piano, keyboard, marimba, vibraphone, percussion, violin, winds, and bicycle wheel (2006).
impermanence, for six vocalists and three instrumentalists (Boosey and Hawkes, 2004).
Juice: A Theater Cantata in Three Installments, for eighty-five performers (1969).
Last Song, for solo voice and piano (2003).
Light Songs, for solo voice (1989).
Little Breath Motor (collaboration with David Behrman), for voice and electronics (2001).
Magic Frequencies, for six voices, percussion, two keyboards, theremin, and violin (1998).
Merce Cunningham Events (musical accompaniment)
No. 118 (1975).
No. 148 (1975).
No. 189 (1977).
No. 215 and No. 216 (1978).
Micki Suite, for four voices (2000).
Needle-Brain Lloyd and the Systems Kid: A Live Movie, for 150 performers, electric organ, guitar, and flute (1970).
Night, for eight voices and chamber ensemble (1996) (Boosey and Hawkes, 2005).
Nightfall, for sixteen voices (1995).
Our Lady of Late, for voice and wine glass (1973).
Panda Chant I, for four voices (1984).
Panda Chant II, for chorus (1984), (Boosey and Hawkes, 2007).
Paris, for solo piano (1973; available alone, or in *Piano Album,* Boosey and Hawkes, 2007).
Parlour Games, for two pianos (1988).
Phantom Waltz, for two pianos (1990; available alone, or in *Piano Album,* Boosey and Hawkes, 2007).
Piano Album, contains *Railroad "Travel Song," Paris, Window in 7's, St. Petersburg Waltz, Ellis Island, Folkdance, Phantom Waltz* (Boosey and Hawkes, 2007).
Plainsong for Bill's Bojo, for electric organ (1970).
Plateau Series, for five voices and tape (1977).
The Politics of Quiet, for ten voices, two keyboards, French horn, violin, and bowed psaltry (1996).
Portable, for two performers (1966).
Possible Sky, for voices and orchestra (Boosey and Hawkes, 2003).
Processional, for voice and piano (1988).
Quarry: An Opera, for thirty-eight voices, two pump organs, two soprano recorders, and tape (1976).

Radar, for two performers (1965).
Raven, for solo piano (1989).
Realm Variations, for six voices and mixed ensemble (Boosey and Hawkes, 2012).
Recent Ruins, for fourteen voices, tape, and cello (1979).
Refractive Voices (collaboration with David Behrman), for voice, electronics, and viola (2001).
Relâche (Eric Satie; collaboration with Dick Higgins), for six performers (1965).
Resonance, solo (1963).
The Ringing Place, for nine voices (1987).
Road Songs, music and choreography for *True Stories,* dir. David Byrne (1985).
Roots (collaboration with Donald Ashwander), for two performers (1974).
Scared Song, for voice, synthesizer, and piano (1986).
Small Scroll, for voice, piano, and soprano recorder (1975).
Songs from the Hill, for unaccompanied solo voice (1976).
Songs of Ascension, for eight voices, string quartet, woodwinds, percussion, shrutis, and chorus (Boosey and Hawkes, 2008).
Specimen Days, for fourteen voices, piano, and two electric organs (1981).
St. Petersburg Waltz, solo piano version (1994; available alone, or in *Piano Album,* Boosey and Hawkes, 2007).
String, for unaccompanied solo voice (1986).
Stringsongs, for string quartet (Boosey and Hawkes, 2005).
Tablet, for four voices, piano four-hands, two soprano recorders (1976).
Three Heavens and Hells, for four voices (Boosey and Hawkes, 1992).
Three Heavens and Hells (choral version), for forty-four voices (Boosey and Hawkes, 2007).
Timestop, for five performers (1964).
Title: Title, for two performers (1969).
Tokyo Cha-Cha, for six voices and two electric organs (1983).
Troubadour Songs (medieval French music), for three performers (1963).
Trumpet Study No. 1, solo trumpet (1999).
Turtle Dreams (Waltz), for four voices and two electric organs (Boosey and Hawkes, 1980).
Two Men Walking, for three voices and electric organs (1983).
Untidal: Movement Period, for five performers (1969).
Venice/Milan, for fifteen voices, piano four-hands (1976).
Vessel: An Opera Epic, for seventy-five performers (1971).
Vibrato, for four performers (1963).
View No. 1 (music for Ping Chong's *AM/AM*), for piano, synthesizer, and voice (1982).
View No. 2, for voice and synthesizer (1982).
Volcano Songs (Duet), solo voice with taped voices and piano (1994).
Weave, for two voices, chamber orchestra, and chorus (Boosey and Hawkes, 2010).
Wedding March, for vocal ensemble (2012).
Window in 7's (for Nurit), for solo piano (1986; available alone, or in *Piano Album,* Boosey and Hawkes, 2007).
Window Song (music for Ping Chong's Nosferatu), (1985).

INSTALLATION/EXHIBIT

Archeology of an Artist, art installation (1996).
Archeology of an Artist 2, art installation (2004).
Eclipse Variations, sound installation (2002).
Show People: Downtown Directors and the Play of Time (2002).
Shrines (1999).
Silver Lake with Dolmen Music "Soundings" (1981).
Vocal Gestures, art installation (2005).

Michael Benabib

11

Svjetlana Bukvich

Svjetlana Bukvich was born in 1967 in Sarajevo, in the former Yugoslavia. A composer, producer, performer, and teacher of electro-acoustic and multimedia works, Bukvich describes her influences as a hybrid of culture, inspiration, and art. Her music is the result of an amalgamation of her experiences before the Bosnian War, her immigration to the United States during the war, and her subsequent time in the United States. She studied piano performance in Edinburgh and earned two bachelor's degrees in composition and musicology from the Sarajevo University's Music Academy before the war. During our conversation, she describes how the Bosnian War interrupted her "blissful youth" and how music helped her cope with the aftermath of leaving her family in Sarajevo as she immigrated to the United States.

Inspired by such composers as Meredith Monk, Pauline Oliveros, and Steve Reich, she already knew that she wanted to participate in their approach to experimental work in the United States. Three months into the Bosnian War in 1992, Bukvich received a scholarship to study at Rensselaer Polytechnic Institute (RPI) in upstate New York. With her bags packed, she took her scholarship letter to a bus evacuating people out of Sarajevo. The graciousness of a bus driver allowed her to board, and she left for America. Bukvich soon earned a Master of Fine Arts in Integrated Electronic Arts from RPI, the first multimedia program of its kind.

Already immersed in the sounds of her own musical languages, Bukvich had not worked with computers or electronics prior to attending RPI. Today, her electro-acoustic and multimedia performances embrace technology, using live and soundtracked electronic processing combined with her classical European training. Nevertheless, she begins our conversation by mentioning the irrelevance of discussing technology. Articulating her compositional philosophy, Bukvich alludes to music perception as a product of one's experience with organized sound and how it is voiced through one's original musical language. She thoughtfully expresses her views on sound, energy, and developmental language based on pitch and timbre by connecting her own hybrid musical sounds with her experience as a mother raising a young child.

Like several other composers in this book, Bukvich explores the alternative performance spaces of New York City. She seeks out the collaboration of solidly trained musicians who demonstrate an openness to new music, improvisation, or experimental work. As a composer, she writes for film, animation, dance, electro-acoustic ensembles, and instrumentalists in the new-music world. For Bukvich, intention is the essence of her music. As she discusses her creative process, she explores issues surrounding intention and understanding. I first encountered Bukvich's music in 2008 at the Congress of the International Alliance for Women in Music in Beijing. The audience was enveloped in her work *Before and After the Tekke* for electronics, keyboard, voice, and amplified violin. *Tekke* was also awarded first prize in the International Chamber Music Festival in Sarajevo.

Bukvich lives in New York City as a composer, performer, producer, teacher, and mother. Like Alice Parker, Hasu Patel, and Pauline Oliveros, she expresses strong opinions on the education of youth, the creation of excitement with sound energy, ways to inspire creativity, and means to connect with the world around us.

***

January 2010, at her home in New York City

SVJETLANA BUKVICH: I feel like talking about technology is becoming irrelevant because, in the end, it's still the sensation of experiencing sound and energy. It's about how we put it together. There are so many toys and tools, and they keep upgrading. You could be wrapped in that whole rat race, make it part of your consciousness all the time, and I refuse that. I want to use what I use well. I want to master something. I tell my students, "You don't have to tell me the latest thing you've used because I can tell you if it's used well in context." This conversation distinguishes between compositional skills and production skills.

JENNIFER KELLY: But aren't you in the business of keeping up with the latest technology?

SB: I thought I had to do that when I was in my early thirties. I don't feel that way anymore. I feel powerful in what I do, and if I need something to produce the sound I want, I go get it. But it isn't a big deal anymore. I think it has to do with how I grew up, actually, because I wasn't born into technology.

JK: You are a fairly young composer. When did you begin using technology?

SB: I started using computers when I was twenty-five and came [to the United States]. Back home [in Sarajevo], there were studios with technology, and I worked with someone who produced a children's record I made. I would tell him, "Okay, this is what I want. I want this repeated four times. . . ." So I would track, but I didn't know how to track. No, I personally started using computers when I came [to the United States].

JK: How did you feel when you realized all of the tools available in the computer toolbox?

SB: My mind exploded. And by the way, to me, the multimedia was much more interesting in the 1990s when I was doing an MFA [at Rensselaer Polytechnic Institute] in Integrated Electronic Arts, which was combining multimedia performance with electronic composition and analog video. It also kept me sane, because I had just come out of a war situation back home, and it kept me from continuing to be glued to CNN for months. I would just go into the studio, stay up all night, read manuals, and get inspired. I was deeply engaged.

JK: It sounds like a very powerful distraction, or even escape.

SB: Well, I think if CNN didn't exist, I would still have been completely overwhelmed and intrigued by it all, and I still would have loved it. I also think I had a kind of survival instinct and, later, survivor's guilt. How do I say this? It implemented itself in times of trauma and stress, as if extra adrenaline was pumped into my system. I think it gave me strength and desire to dive into that work deeply. A combination of things.

JK: You call yourself a hybrid. What do you mean?

SB: Well, I am one foot trained in German/Russian school of pianism, composition tools and theory, and history. One foot I am in musicology and ethnomusicology, which I have a degree in as well and which had a strong department at the music academy back home. And I am one foot in writing my own songs and things that inspire me musically. Hmm, how many feet is that? [*Laughs*] From very early on back home, I was working with bands as a vocalist and working with children in theater and TV. All these things were about to come to fruition, and then the war started. It was a very specific sociopolitical situation for a composer like myself, because it clearly stopped a stream of events, musically speaking, as well as gave me an insight—the tools and the strength—of how to survive that. So what I became after that, I think, is a result of a pretty unique journey and a pretty unique string of events. Looking back, I am so very grateful for going through everything, and I am grateful that I had exposure to different religions, which dictated the cultural nuance of my fairly socialist youth. Even though we didn't practice religion in my family, my grandmother was a Croat from the North on my mom's side, my mom's dad was a Muslim from Sarajevo, and my dad's parents were Orthodox Christians from Herzegovina. When the war started, I was utterly confused and just desperate because I could not really take sides fully, and as a musician that wasn't my job. All these things were thrown in my lap, all these big world events. And I just wanted to do music. There was a lot to figure out and sort out.

JK: Did the music help you sort things out, or did it remain separate for you?

SB: It didn't remain separate. I had a need to prove in my late twenties, when I first came [to the United States], that I didn't come from this savage country. I come from Europe. My friends were great people who were worldly and great artists, and it seems very silly, but I had to do that. My work was very dark and about all these different cultural aspects of where I came from. I tried to put them all together to show how all these things coexist and that it was possible for them to coexist in people peacefully. But it was me. I had to let them coexist in me. Today I still have elements of sound and musical experiences from where I come from. How can I not? You hear sounds when you're five months old and even before you were born. It's all part of how you understand pitch. And it is liberating, because musical content for a purely musical purpose is the first reason these elements coexist. There is no politics in it anymore for me, which is very nice.

JK: That's quite a process you've gone through.

SB: I'm an idealist anyway, and I don't really want to spend too much time dwelling on all the political problems, because I am very compassionate and it disturbs me deeply. I would just be annihilated. My mom said to me, "If you had stayed back home when the war took off, you would have lost your mind."

JK: Did you leave as soon as it began?

SB: I left three months into it. I could see it from my window; that's how I knew about it—processed it as an abstraction, really. The roads were already locked in traffic. The telephone lines were cut down. The shelling had started. There was no electricity already, and parts of the city were burning, and people were going down to their basements to hide. But I had received a full scholarship to go study at Rensselaer Polytechnic Institute in Troy, New York. There were buses that were evacuating foreign citizens, cellists, ballet dancers, and politicians. It was all happening by chance. I asked the bus driver to let me on that bus because of my scholarship. I looked into his eyes and said, "You have the power to make this a reality or not."

JK: So without even knowing it, he was a big influence on your life and even on your music. He let you on the bus.

SB: Yeah. I don't even know his name, but if he hadn't let me on the bus, I wouldn't be here today. That's how it works sometimes.

JK: Do you still have family there?

SB: Yes, my mom is still there. She comes quite often to visit. And I go there now. I love going there. Just to recharge my poetic batteries big-time [*laughs*]. I was there in October, actually, when they gave me first prize at a chamber-music festival for *Before and After the Tekke*. I was very surprised that I won, actually, because the piece was the only electro-acoustic work. All of the other submissions were acoustic. The judges were from Slovenia, Croatia, Bosnia, Herzegovina, and Serbia, and for them to recognize that piece was very interesting to me. First of all, it was my first time applying to a competition like that since I left. And second, there is a lot of mediocre music being written there right now. After the war, there was a rise of national passions about the identity of the music of that region, with the borrowing of folk elements and quotations from the wealth of extraordinary ethnic music we have there. But it fails when it is translated into an acoustic situation with Western instruments (which is how they had it at the festival). That's why I say I was surprised that they chose that composition. I don't use quotation in my work, and I made up the intonation, and so on. But I would say that it had the intonation that is similar to the kind of pitch relationships I heard as a child and that the rhythms were similar kinds of rhythms I heard in folk music growing up.

JK: And yet uniquely your own.

SB: Yes, it wasn't about putting down an exact rhythm that I heard. But the phrasing, the melodicism, and a certain joy in that piece had to do with where I'm from. Also, working with the violin timbre and equating that with the synthesizer in the intonation that I assigned to it gave me total pleasure. Timbre is really important in my processes. So, I locked into it and found what I was trying to say.

JK: Tell me about your intonation and pitch relationships.

SB: I have learned through study and my own experiences that it takes maybe two years early on for pitch relationships to be fully established. For example, if you hear a lot of children's songs with perfect fifths, it is most likely that, when you're five and ten years old, it will become part of your vocabulary. Being part of your vocabulary means that, whenever you hear a perfect fifth, you know you've heard it before, you attach a certain emotive recognition to it. If you're in another part of the world listening to different pitch relationships for the first two years, then that vocabulary develops. It would be easier to learn many different languages than to completely change the syntax that was formed early on in one's life. So one of the areas that interests me in my work is how we could possibly be fluent in different pitch "ecosystems" without having to spend ten years in a particular culture. I personally would love to be completely fluent in these very different systems, like Indian *ragas* versus European music versus Native American. I want to be fully invested, to be able to experience and participate in any system. It's not about quotation; it's about going inside. If there was a computer program for this, I'd run to it.

JK: How did you come up with the pitch relationship in *Before and After the Tekke*? Is it microtonal?

SB: I came up with the melody, and when I tried to play it on the keyboard, it didn't work. I felt the melody so deeply that I had to find ways to manifest it. This was all in the early nineties, and at that time I was changing user tuning. I was just learning all of this technology, and things were very exciting. I would change, change, change, and change until it clicked, until contextually what I was hearing in my head was what I was playing. So if you want to call that microtonal, you can, but it really has nothing to do with the mathematical process of saying, "Well, now I am going to take the scale and divide everything by such and such."

JK: Did you grow up with what some might call "microtonal" music?

SB: It was all around. It was in the mountains and in ethnomusicological research and fieldwork, and the old traditions in the villages were definitely not well-tempered. Not so much in the city where I lived. I grew up listening to Led Zeppelin, Pink Floyd, Kate Bush, and whatever my sister, who was a hippie, was listening to at the time. I was young in the sixties and seventies. The British scene was big back home, and then the eighties hit with a different sound. I was very much growing up in my urban world. But, if you lived in the city, it was a matter of driving thirty minutes up into the mountains and changing your world completely. And I loved that. I could go ride horses saddle-less in cornfields, then thirty minutes later I'm downtown in my leather pants doing whatever else. Down at the coast, the Dalmatian Coast, they had beautiful music. . . . And in

Macedonia. The music came from everything people have been doing for centuries, both sacred and secular. It was ritualistic, too, for the various parts of life like funerals and weddings. It was that kind of experience growing up.

JK: There are many people who have difficulty adapting to so many completely different parts of culture. And yet you seem to thrive on it, given your experiences growing up.

SB: It was easy and much fun. Mind you, geography has something to do with it. I have a theory that the kind of landscape one is looking at and the kind of altitude one is on and the kind of air one breathes all has to do with how the mentality of a people is formed. For me, looking at the exquisite landscape with pristine water and breathing fully is how I remember my time in the mountains. There is an old saying that Sarajevan women are beautiful because they always drink good water [*laughs*]. I was just having a great time in my blissful youth. And that's why, when the war hit, I was completely unprepared. It hit me hard, and I had to go through it to grow up, I think. And then becoming a mom deepened the growing. I like to try to remember nowadays when my brain gets into these habitual ways of thinking. . . . Calling back some of those blissful states of mind helps me to have a more balanced existence these days. So I was exposed to a lot, but I cannot possibly write as villagers in Sarajevo or in Herzegovina, because I live here now. I've spent twenty years in new music, and I'm a producer. I even use my voice in a different way. So I don't think I'm really influenced by folk music today. It was an organic process, and now I'm here.

JK: You mentioned earlier that what you compose is about the "now," and, as we study music to perform, we need to understand the historical context about the composer, geography, and culture of the times in which the piece was made in order to get a true understanding of the music itself. Am I understanding that correctly?

SB: Absolutely. When I go to concerts today, it seems immediately clear to me whether the musicians have an understanding about what they're playing. And it has nothing to do with technique or phrasing or whether it's rhythmically accurate. It is the layer of knowing where the music is coming from and who are the people it was associated with when it was made. I think many performances these days lack that understanding.

JK: So with your music, how do you know if or when the players have a real understanding to then make an impact in performance?

SB: Well, I don't let it be played by just anybody. I like to be engaged with people who are performing my music. I like to be on stage with them whenever possible. Sometimes logistical issues make it difficult, but the collaboration comes naturally to me. It wasn't a conscious decision. It just seemed like, what other way is there? And as I am a hybrid, I'm not really fully into any one genre.

I produce a lot of my own sound, and therefore I have the freedom to find people to perform it and the freedom to inject myself into the performance because I provide most of the electronic stuff. So I rarely have a situation where a trio takes my music somewhere and has no real connection to me. I'm also not that kind of composer with tons of work out there that is constantly being performed. I would go insane if that were the case! If I had that output, I wouldn't really know how to wrap my mind around it. Perhaps it's a vestige of my growing up where enjoyment of life is praised and elevated to almost an art form. I like to have my clan around me for that.

JK: When you are commissioned to write a piece, do you ever write it and simply hand it off when you are finished? Let it go?

SB: No. I hand it off, and then we are in the process together of bringing it into the other dimension. How can it be about dots on paper? One of the reasons why I became a producer as well as a composer is that I saw the need for me to be part of the process of how the music forms sonically. The ultimate product, if you wish. I want to have an informed conversation with people in that process. I create, and I also control the mixing, et cetera. If you think about the work of people who produce and are creating with the studio, that is their instrument as much as they do work with acoustic instruments or electronic instruments, like keyboards or any number of the interactive gadgets we can get today. For me it's all one experience. It's one sound.

JK: I heard *Before and After the Tekke* for electronics and violin at ICWM [International Congress on Women in Music] in Beijing. I felt the reverberation among the audience, so the performance itself truly made an impact. Could you feel that it was really working for the audience at the time you were playing?

SB: Yes. It has to do with whether I'm making an impact on myself. If I can communicate in that moment about what the piece is, like suspending time for myself, then my audience will also know that. So we come to this conversation about what sound energy is. The whole body is involved. It isn't solely a cerebral process. It is more about your every cell being there, and, if you're lucky to experience those moments on stage as a performer, then anybody in the room will experience something. I can't tell you how it is going to manifest for them, but something is going to be communicated. That is the joy and the mystery of doing this work, because it really becomes about that which we cannot describe completely. We don't have the vocabulary.

JK: Whose work inspired you to go in this direction?

SB: Meredith Monk, Steve Reich, and Pauline Oliveros were definitely people who made such a difference to me that I felt I wanted to be in America doing work. I saw Meredith Monk's *Book of Days* when I was fourteen on some obscure TV channel in Sarajevo. I immediately knew that I wanted to be near people like that. Whatever that meant at fourteen, I don't know [*laughs*]. This is not to say that their music influenced my writing that much. It's more about the joy that I get knowing that there are people who do such work. And again, my whole body is involved when I experience that.

JK: What are you trying to communicate in a piece like *Before and After the Tekke*?

SB: If I'm lucky enough to have an audience want to come through the door and be inside the piece, which probably happens within the first ten seconds, then it becomes a world I've built for them to experience. *Tekke* is about a spiritual journey from being young and living in an urban environment and then coming to a faster environment, which would be New York. And then, in all that busy traveling, finding a place of repose and quiet, femininity, reflection, and reconnecting with my roots. Now, I can't pretend to think that an audience would experience all of that.

JK: Well, it's a sharing.

SB: Yes, it's a sharing and being informed by the journey we were on.

JK: Do you commonly use elements of improvisation in your work?

SB: Not commonly, up to this point. But that is changing. Back home in Sarajevo, my schooling and my work was with academia mostly. The rock bands of the eighties weren't big improvisers, and the jazz scene was almost nonexistent back home. So, when I played with musicians there, it was mostly nonimprovised. I started to open up more toward improvisation here because of my experiences with a jazz guitarist and violinists. Based on how they are processing the music energetically, I will give them more freedom as we go through the piece. I don't think I will ever be fully an improviser, because I need to be aware of the subtleties of energy, but I can see myself opening to more elements of it.

JK: I can understand how communicative trusts would build as more musicians you work with understand your musical intentions.

SB: Intention is the biggest word! [*Laughs*] There is intention in everything one does as a producer, as a writer, and if that intention isn't communicated effectively, then somebody's confused in the process. If I'm still fortunate enough to work with these musicians, then I will probably have an album where I would use some of my own made-up intonations for those emotional spaces that I cannot otherwise reach, and have them be the conduits for it. That could be achieved with voice and analog synths, as well as Vipers [specialized violins], even though they are fretted instruments.

JK: Do you use notation?

SB: Yes, instrumentalists' parts are notated. After it sinks in, I ask them to internalize it and learn it by heart. Then we talk about intentions and phrasing. Some things can sound completely different with the slightest change in pressure, dynamics, and the rhythmic accuracy or inaccuracy, which is what gives it uniqueness sometimes. But most of the time with this hybrid kind of work, I find that notation is a suggestion of organizational points in space and time. And even with all the Italian words we know, the core needs to be communicated from the composer. As a performer, I'm always interested if I can find out what the composer has to say. It's a goal of mine, and it helps a great deal. Quite frankly, I don't comprehend why more new music isn't being performed, given the fact that living composers are here and available. Why aren't performers working with them in a more intimate and organic way? Because it's possible—we're here!

JK: What do you want from those of us sitting in the audience?

SB: That would depend on the type of event you're attending. If it's an immersive environment where you are being called to engage with multiple senses, then you must come with an open mind, or it will be to your detriment. But there are situations where you would simply come to listen and be still. And that's all right. There are other situations when you come to use your body fully. All of these are little aspects of what it means to be in the musical world that exists today. Music pushes the envelope, so you can go clubbing or hear Rachmaninoff or one of my favorites, Scriabin. I want us—creators and creative listeners—to bring all these experiences a little closer so that there doesn't have to be a separation of what's tolerable or allowed or expected.

JK: Where does the composition lie? For instance, you said that you hand a piece of paper with notes on to the musicians, but that is only the beginning, because they need to internalize it and experience it. So at what point does the composition exist in your music?

SB: Wherever one decides as a creator. For instance, if I'm creating a listening experience that is going to end up on the stereo on playback, then I create it with that mindset. If I'm inviting you to a live show, I'm putting you in a different environment, so the rules will be slightly different.

JK: Again, it is about intention.

SB: Yes! The composition lies in the feeling, which is being fulfilled by intention. The sound world revolves around that feeling. Actually, everything we do is influenced by our feelings. If I can manifest a feeling that I know is true in my heart, then I am successful. How I construct it and the compositional tools I choose to use is all a matter of going back and forth between conscious and subconscious. But it all comes from the inside, from creating and accessing a feeling. I take that feeling I had in mind when I first look at the blank page or set of tracks. And once that engagement starts happening, then it goes like crazy. Sort of like saying: When you hear it, it will talk back to you. Then I can really put something together fast. If nothing is inspiring, if the sound isn't pulling me in, if the composition isn't talking to me and telling me what I need to do next.

. . . I don't actually know how I would do what I do if I had to put on some kind of a hat and just do it from some learned practice in my life.

JK: It's almost as if you have to unlearn some practical things to be open to the engagement.

SB: It's so amazing to look at all the things we have to unlearn. But it's good that we have something to unlearn, because if we had nothing to unlearn, we'd be completely oblivious to different processes.

JK: Despite the unlearning, how do you think the knowledge that you've gained has aided your creations? Was it about giving you the tools?

SB: All the knowledge I've gained in music and all the historical books that I've read, music or otherwise, all of that gives me a sense of where I am in the world. But it doesn't help a lot in my music. I think that music has the ability to access places of feelings that other art forms for me do not access. This I didn't find in history. When I hear a sensational piece of music, I'm invited to go for a ride, and it suspends time. My mind, my cells—everything learns. But it doesn't help me in my work. It is not about, "Oh, I'd like to make something like that!" Because what do I know about the feeling process that the composer was going through? I can only trust or seek the truth within my own world. That's the only thing I really have. And as we know, everything is in the eyes of the beholder. This is a highly subjective reality we live in, highly subjective. And I'd like to have people step into my shoes and have me step into theirs a little bit. But it all has to do with accessing feelings. If they synchronize, it opens up a portal where you can really come close to a person. I believe the world could be a better place if more of those nonseparation experiences existed. That also inspires me in my work.

JK: Can you take me through your creative process a bit? When you first have the blank tracks or the blank page, how do you get started?

SB: Well, actually, I'm never really confronted by a blank page per se, because I write little. I know my music by heart, so there's always something coming through or sounds or timbres, timbres that stay with me. So if there is a commission, or there is a general idea of what I'm expected to write, then I can bring to my mind the kinds of timbres I feel would justify the feeling that is associated with that theme, and that's a portal to me. And that I can easily summon up because it's something that I either used or have, or it's just knowing your tool well. Sometimes I might make a mistake and discover something that could take me to other places. So it's about remembering, and it's about searching, searching, searching for the portal. Once I'm in, then I can compose the piece. It's about figuring out the sound and what the energy is going to be. And the rhythm writes itself.

JK: Do you write one track at a time? Or do you hear it all and write it all at the same time?

SB: It's both. Sometimes working intensely on one track with such detail is almost painful. Other times, it's about three or four tracks working together, and you get the gist of the sound you are looking for and then craft it on a vertical and horizontal plane. Then it's about mixing in the different planes, different dimensions of sounds. It's not only about the stereo left and right, but it's about the depth of field or sound mass that you're working with. To me, I feel like an alchemist mixing, and it's one of my favorite things to do because you can bring a piece of music's essence forth in many different ways with the kind of tools we have now. And that again has to do with finding a sound, adjusting to the initial feeling. Sometimes, things might change two-thirds into the piece. The world that has revealed itself becomes another portal, and you realize there is so much more you can do with it. So, the process starts for me from remembering and from sounds that work for me.

JK: How do you know when it's finished?

SB: I know when it's finished when I don't have anything else to say on the subject.

JK: That makes sense. Do you ever allow yourself to throw anything away?

SB: Well, since I don't write a whole lot, I'm usually happy with things, and it's rare for me to cut out five minutes of music and throw it away. Because I've sculpted those five minutes for a long time, there is something there that is informative in it and can help me. Or, if nothing else, it's a teaching tool for the kind of energy that I'm trying to project later. So I don't throw away much. And as I get older, I've honed this ability to cut with a sword so that the landscape can become clearer.

JK: Self-edit as you go?

SB: Yes, and clarity is of utmost importance to me. If I'm not sure what this thing is communicating to me, how can I expect an audience member to be sure? So yeah, the editing is cutting up little things here and there to get the melody right.

JK: What can we do to ready our children to be excited in sound? Like your son, Jade, how can he learn to be excited in sound?

SB: Well, he already is excited. I think it's the preservation of the mystery of it that children naturally take to well. It's finding the excitement and adventure in things they hear and looking at what they're hearing from different angles and then have them be invited to insert themselves into that matrix and see where it would take them. At the same time, based on the system they're growing up into, it's very useful to have some structured learning around pitch relationships to give them the confidence of being. It's like a vocabulary that you're confident with, so if they need to sing in minor six, they can do it, it's not a big deal. Playing an instrument is also part of that. Basically, have music not be forced, but have it be something that makes them feel vital and full and excited in life. Music has value.

JK: How do you impart on a young person that music has value?

SB: Well, you could jam all the concerts in the world on them, but it's the level of engagement and then the various ways of teaching the children and allowing the children to be musical with the experience that has lasting effect. I believe that all children are musical, and they need to be given an opportunity to exercise that.

JK: Active participation.

SB: Yes. That which you do more of, you probably get better at. It's the nature of things. I teach a class at [New York University] called Software Production, where students come with laptops. I teach them how to use some stuff, but most importantly I think I teach them a little bit of how and why they're doing what they're doing. And then I had a class where we did breathing. Deep-breathing techniques with all of us in a circle, and they were all game, which was great. So we fell into silence, did the breathing, and then I said, "Go mix now. Go see how you're feeling about how you're hearing." And it was a very nice break from the traditional sitting and doing things on the computer. You come back to it fresh in a way.

JK: Were you happy with the results?

SB: I was really happy with the results and the fact that they were so open to it. And it's all guys in the class, too, which is another dimension. Teaching production and technology is still male-dominated, even in this country. But it's an exciting place to be. Like, I'm the only woman in the room, and I'm teaching these guys how to produce their music [*laughs*]. Teaching that it's okay to imagine and have big ideas and that it's not just going to be about turning the knobs. And then I invite them to share and give constructive feedback. I bring them my own work in progress that nobody else has heard. And I share that, and I say, "See, I want you to help with this, and what do you think?" So by the time we reach the final weeks, they are like gold to each other because they feel safe to give each other constructive criticism.

JK: Are you currently the only woman in the music-technology faculty?

SB: No, but I think I am one of the few producer-type women. And it's odd because when I was eighteen and wanting to record and produce my own records, I would have to do background vocals in order to trade with the guys to let me in and show me a few things. And looking back, perhaps I just didn't see it like that. Historically and culturally, it was difficult at the time for a woman to produce inside the power circles. There just wasn't anything like that. They were singing, maybe writing or composing a little bit, maybe writing lyrics.

JK: But you found a way through barter system to be able to have your own control over it.

SB: Yes, exactly. The reason I am mentioning this is that essentially things haven't changed, some twenty years later. The moral of the story is that, if you want something, you will find a way.

JK: As a composer-producer, a teacher of music, and a mother, what kind of music education do you see as relevant?

SB: A lot of people talk about life-changing experiences with sound. To me, sound is food. In the value of societal goods, food is needed, water is needed, air is needed, and music is needed. The life-changing experience with music can propel a person to want to be with sound from that day forward. How many times have you heard an important figure who has contributed significantly to the nature of sound talk about that particular moment when they were six or ten, and they went to an opera house or a jazz concert for the first time? They talk about what that meant for their development. If musical events can have that kind of power, what would happen if more people had those life-changing experiences in education?

JK: What was your first moment of recognizing music as powerful?

SB: My sister taught me [Beethoven's] *Für Elise,* two hands, when I was six years old. And I distinctly remember loving the experience of emanating sounds from both of my hands and what they conjured up together.

JK: I find that image fascinating. Especially because that is so much about what you do: you create with your hands all of these layered tracks and complex sounds, and they come into one. It's the same experience, but done in a more knowledgeable and sophisticated way.

SB: Good observation. Also connecting that experience of emanating sound with your body outward into the world. Education seems to isolate different art forms. When a child is very young, I believe there is synergy between sound, movement, and moving image, and that is the experience of life from when we first pop out. But the early education doesn't really address that. There's something very gestural about life early on and the interconnectedness that allows for that expression. And then later we can deepen this. It is a great opportunity.

JK: How do you integrate the producer side of you, the composer side of you, and the performer side of you? Is it easy to put on that different hat and switch back and forth, yet remain in control?

SB: It's very easy, because one part informs the other. But it isn't about enjoying the control for the sake of control. It is about a cry to preserve authenticity. It is about a struggle to have that voice come out without it being changed by any economical or societal forces. Finding my producer's voice was like a missing key between the composer and the performer. The sound can be complete. It is a relatively new way of working for me, and it takes years to mature in production skills, so my hope is that, in the next decade, I will finally fully be able to reap the benefits of that effort.

JK: Some would call you an American success story.

SB: Well, what is success? Here we need to put it in the context of an immigrant who had a certain set of hurdles or obstacles to overcome in order to function in society. I feel good about the fact that I put myself on my two feet and created a life in music and with music and with family and that I'm relatively sane. I think if you see me in that light, then I will accept the compliment. As a self-made person, I think the conversation around success has value for other people coming from my part of the world, younger women in particular. What we leave behind us is more valuable than how big we are in our life right now. It's all relative, anyway.

***

Works by Svjetlana Bukvich

ELECTRONICS/MULTIMEDIA

Back to the Heart-Planet, for mixed chorus, electronics, electric bass, and drum set (2012).
Before and After the Tekke, for amplified violin, electronics, and voice, animated paintings by Jessica Lee (2006).
Dream Matrix, for French horns, electronics, voice, and video projection (2000).
Ex Libris, music for a short film directed by Marc Millhone, for viola, electronics, and voice (2004).
Fruits of Eden, music for a short film directed by Sasa Savic, for electric violin/Viper and electronics (2010).
Hope and 01, for voice and electronic percussion (1993).
If Swallows Came Back . . . , for one-channel video with electronics and voice (1994).
Lullaby, for electronics, voice, and video projection (1995).
Over Water over Stone, for cello, electronics, and voice (2008).
Proud, additional orchestral music for a film directed by Mary Pat Kelly (2005).
Remember What We Have, for electronics and voice (1999).
Rozdenstvo Tvoje, for electronics and voice (2007).
Sabih's Dream, for amplified violin and cello, electric viola, minimoog, electronics, and voice (2011).
Secret, for electric violins/Vipers, electronics, and voice (2009).
Six Letters, for electronics, voice, dancer, and video projection (1997).
Standing Alone, for electronics, voice, and two-channel video (1995).
Three Reconstructions . . . , sound installation for electronics and voice, architectural drawings by Lebbeus Wood (1993).
Thunderhead . . . , electronic sound for two-channel video installation, videography by Roberto Bocci (1993).
Unlimited Potential, music for a short film directed by Fay Ann Lee, for retuned piano and electronics (2003).

theVoyage, with Rick Nichols, multimedia theater production and soundtrack CD for electronics, voice, dancers, and video projection (1998).
You Move Me, for electric guitar, alto flute, electronics, and voice (2008).

INSTRUMENTAL

Bosanska Sonata (Bosnian Sonata), for piano (1990).
Gudacki Kvartet (String Quartet), (1990).
Kraljica od Sabe (The Queen of Sheba), for piano (1989).
Plave Sume (Blue Woods), for orchestra (1991).
Vila Raviojla, for amplified chamber ensemble with altered tuning, flute, piccolo, string quartet, and electric bass guitar (1994).

VOICE

D.U.H. "Djeciji Umjetnicki Hor," for youth choir and rock band (1992).
Iz Vise Razloga (For Several Reasons), for soprano (1989).
Life Is What You Make of It, songs and stories by Alzheimer's patients (2001).
Stand-Up to Saddam, for piano, soprano, and tenor (2002).

Donald Swearingen

12

Pamela Z

Pamela Z is a multimedia artist who fuses varied components into her work: voice, live electronic processing, body movement, sampling technology, found objects, and video. A composer-performer, Z works in alternative performance spaces that celebrate artistic community. Our conversation took place in the lobby of 3-Legged Dog, an experimental media and theater space in New York City. Born in 1956 and raised in Colorado, Z had limited access to much of the new music being produced in the 1960s and 1970s in metropolitan areas like New York City and San Francisco. While in college at the University of Colorado at Boulder, she found that her classical vocal education conflicted with her outside interests of singing in folk clubs and playing alternative music on the radio as a disc jockey.

During our conversation, Z explains her struggle to find intersections between these two musical worlds.

Z was introduced to electronic fusion while attending a concert of Jaco Pastorius using digital delay. The effect on Z was so profound that she turned her musical direction toward the experimental, multimedia work she makes today. She fell in love with timbres and textures and opened her ears to listen in less conventional ways. During our conversation, Z discusses the freedom she felt by making that turn and the musical permission granted by minimalist composers. Combining visual and aural worlds, she goes on to discuss the difference between artistic development of these two worlds and acceptance of both. Continuing her studies in Japan, Z studied Butoh with Kazuo and Yoshito Ohno, Japanese language at Kanda Gaigo College, and Noh at Kita Ryu with Richard Emmert.

Z is more interested in process than product, and she explores subjects to inspire thought in an audience. During our interview, she discusses how access to technology has affected art and the "blurry lines" between experimental work and mainstream. Technology allows her to play with an audience, experiment with reaction, and progress through her own artistic creation. At the same time, she explores ideas on the avant-garde, alternative performance, and popular culture. Z's thoughts on using experiment in the creative process lead to insights about improvisation. Her multimedia art demands that she be comfortable in various artistic languages to collaborate with other performing artists. Like Meredith Monk and Hasu Patel, Z's process varies depending on whether she is working alone as composer-performer or working within the musical language of a given collaborator.

As an African American female artist of nontraditional and multimedia music, Z is often approached about identity by groups who claim her as a member. Her responses regarding the chosen and unchosen aspects of her identity are sensitive and humorous.

In addition to her performance compositions, Z has a growing body of intermedia gallery works that employ multichannel sound and video installations. Known for blending various sounds and techniques, Z's art includes digital looping, processing her voice in real time, experimenting with extended vocal techniques, operatic bel canto training, and integrating found objects, text, and sampled *concrète* sounds. Z currently lives in San Francisco, frequently traveling to New York City and various artist residencies around the country.

***

July 2010, at 3-Legged Dog theater space in New York City

JENNIFER KELLY: I'm really interested in how you became involved with experimental performance. At what point in your background or training did you realize that the kind of exploration that you enjoy and create could be found in a whole community of artists and alternative spaces?

PAMELA Z: I was a music major in college, and also a singer-songwriter paying my way through college by playing in clubs. I had voice teachers saying, "Oh, you shouldn't sing that kind of music," while people in the pop-music world were telling me, "Oh, your voice sounds too trained" [*laughs*]. I guess there were basically two things that kicked me into gear with the experimental-music world. First, I did a radio program shortly after I got out of college. I was very interested in the avant-garde, and my radio program was very much about experimental music and about erasing the boundaries between all the different genres of experimental music, from very academic stuff to punk rock. This was the seventies and early eighties, and so I was listening to all of this experimental music and getting my "new music" education more through doing radio programming than I ever got at school. I was in Colorado, majoring in voice at Boulder, and at that time there were only a few professors that I knew of on the faculty with an interest in new music. If I had been in California at Mills College, then I might have been studying with Robert Ashley, Steve Reich, and Pauline Oliveros, but I was at the University of Colorado at Boulder. As it turns out, Richard Toensing had a program with a basement computer lab at that time, but I knew nothing about it! Today there are a lot of contemporary-music and new-media people on the faculty at CU, and there's an amazing music-technology program and computer-music lab there that is so prominent that even an undergrad voice major buried in as heavy a course load as I was would not be able to miss it, but at that time I had no idea.

JK: Were you still in Boulder when you were doing the radio program?

PZ: Yeah, KGNU Boulder, public radio, and I was playing people like Laurie Anderson, and interspersing [Edgard] Varése with the Sex Pistols on the same show. I kind of woke up to the fact that the music that I was really interested in was not the music that I was actively singing. I was singing these very conventional songs or opera arias and having a hard time because I was loving all this different music, but it was difficult to find intersections.

JK: Finding intersections between the conventional music and new music?

PZ: Yeah, in the conventional music world, everything has to be kept so separate. And then I realized people who do experimental music combine all these things. They write operas, but they have electronic music in them. So that was one thing that sort of woke me up to experimental music. And I was still playing guitar. I was playing a twelve-string guitar and also a hollow-body electric, but the most unusual things I was playing was covering the Talking Heads [*laughs*]. And then singing opera arias. I wanted to do more experimental music, but I was having a hard time finding my voice in that way. Then, I went to this concert where bassist Jaco Pastorius played a solo using a digital delay and making loops of his bass.

This would have been 1981 or 1982; nobody in any kind of mainstream situation was doing it yet. [Artists such as Pauline Oliveros were already using nondigital tape delays outside of mainstream music.] I thought, Wow, if I could do that with my voice, that would be very interesting. So, I went to a music store and described what he was using. They told me it was digital delay. I bought one, took it home, and stayed up all night playing with it. That was an enormous break for me, because what I really needed to do was to have new tools, so I could get out of my old habits and learn. I felt like I found my voice as an artist.

JK: So you introduced yourself to technology.

PZ: This was before personal computers had really taken off with the general public. It was much more common to find people doing computer music in academic settings, where they had access to computer music programs like the Tape Music Center at Mills, CCRMA [the Center for Computer Research in Music and Acoustics] at Stanford, or CRCA [the Center for Research in Computing and the Arts] at the University of California–San Diego, for example. My first forays into electronics involved commercially available hardware devices. So I started using a rack-mountable digital-delay unit. And immediately I had to have more of them. I bought a rack, and I had a stack of them, and I was doing all these pieces. I felt like Philip Glass and Steve Reich and all of these minimalist composers gave me permission to play with repetition and to work with minimal structures and processes where things develop slowly over time. Working with these machines really taught me to listen in a whole different way. My whole composing method that I'm still pretty steeped in these days was sort of born out of that.

JK: I read your article, "Tool Is a Tool," where you talk about how tools affect the work.

PZ: When I find a tool, and I start struggling with it, I often discover sounds and methods and all kinds of things that I wouldn't have come up with without having this obstacle of something new to wrangle and figure out. Everyone works differently. There are some people who become virtuosic on one instrument, devoting their entire life to that, and that's how they deepen themselves as an artist. But for me, every once in a while, popping something fresh into my arsenal of tools makes me find things. I really fell in love with textures and timbres playing with that and exploring that really deeply.

JK: So, do you have a favorite, latest tool?

PZ: My work has gotten very visual, and I've started working a lot with video. There is a program called Isadora, and it's not so much Isadora itself, but this idea of making compositions where the audio and the video are tied together somehow. And I'm manipulating it with my voice. It's really challenging for me, because I'm finding that I'm almost more interested in creating the piece as a whole, including the visual elements, than I am in composing the music. For example, my recent work *Baggage Allowance* was a hybrid sound-and-media installation piece. Multimedia. I spent the whole first several months of the piece just making objects. I spent the next several months making video, and then finally there was music, because I was so absorbed in the whole picture. I do think that it's the visual art world that's sort of forcing my hand that way sonically, because I get so involved in it, and the music becomes a bed for that.

JK: Well, it's very integrated. In *Baggage Allowance* you have three components, right?

PZ: Yes. The first component was a gallery installation, because the first ideas that came to me for this piece were sculptural, not sonic at all. So some of the pieces are just visual and don't have any sound. The exhibition was at the Krannert Art Museum in Illinois [at the University of Illinois at Urbana-Champaign] for four months. It had seven media works, including a piece called "Weeping Steamer Trunk" that was an antique trunk with sound and video embedded in the drawers. And another one called "Bag X-Ray" that looked like an x-ray machine—you know, with a conveyor belt. I had to do a lot of Isadora programming for that one. People put their bag on the belt, and it goes into an enclosure where a camera grabs an image of the bag and displays it so that it looks like an x-ray image, but with surprise objects superimposed on it like a pistol, a pair of scissors, or even a live monkey. The second component was a large-scale multimedia performance work that I performed live with voice and electronics and multiple channels of interactive projected video. I did the performance premiere at Theater Artaud in San Francisco, and its New York premiere is happening at The Kitchen. The third component is the Web portal, actual online art work found at baggageallowance.tv. I want to include a Web version of the steamer-trunk installation so that people can actually click on it to open the drawers, hear the stories, and deposit their own stories.

JK: Is there a particular thing you're trying to say with this piece?

PZ: I'm never trying to say a particular thing with a piece. I feel like it would be boring if I tried to build a whole piece to get some idea across. To me that's like an advertising jingle. It's like they want to sell a product, so let's write a song and give it some interesting images and try to sell this. I'm the other way around. This is an interesting subject to me, so I want to explore it with this piece. And I want to raise questions about it, and get people thinking about their version of the stories.

JK: Start a dialogue.

PZ: Yes, it's more like that for me. There are stories I like to tell, but if the piece could be boiled down to a finite number of stories that I could tell, then it seems limited. People are always finding things in my work that I didn't realize were there. And I love to hear what people find. I learn from the audience what's in the piece. That's when the piece is really the best, when the audience tells me.

JK: When you are first creating a piece, do you think about audience and audience communication while you're actually creating?

PZ: I try not to compose for the audience. I really compose for me. I try to make things that I like, because one's work finds one's audience. But I do always feel like a piece isn't really finished until it's been presented to an audience, especially the performance works, because I am a live performer, and so, like it or not, my reaction and behavior on stage is really partially imposed by the audience and their reactions and energy. So I find that I learn about the work when it's done in front of people.

JK: Because the audience doesn't always react the same way.

PZ: Yeah!

JK: In performance art, can a composer, can an artist be concerned about what an audience does or does not understand?

PZ: Yeah, I think they can be, because that's one of the layers of the work. I think really good works have multiple layers, even if it's very simple work. For example, I use a lot of technology in my work, and for years I've always used some kind of gesture-controlled instrument. So I can do gestures, and it will trigger sound, or change the video, or whatever. And it's important to me, when I'm using those instruments, that the audience can tell that it is my hand gesture that's making the something happen. But if the work is really good, it's okay that they don't. There's still something there for them to enjoy or grasp without that knowledge, but it certainly adds another layer to it. Usually, if I do something that's technologically complex, and it's more of a concert as opposed to a theatrical show, I'll talk to the audience and explain to them what's actually going on. For instance, when I use the BodySynth,[1] which allows me to use physical gestures to control sound, I often will explain it to people. And today, everybody's got their Wiimotes,[2] so even people who aren't into experimental music are becoming used to everything being interactive. For a long time I've been looping my voice; I sing a phrase, it gets caught in the digital delay, you hear it come back and loop, I add another phrase to it, the loop gets more dense. In the early days, people often thought I was singing to a background tape. "How could she harmonize with herself in real time?" Nowadays they just know it's looping.

JK: Given that people today are a bit more sophisticated and savvy with technology, how does that affect your composition and your art? Do you take it further? Are you trying to challenge them?

PZ: When I first became involved in doing experimental music, I think in those days a big part of it to me was doing something that was cutting-edge or doing something that was . . . odd. But I think that as artists mature, they realize that cutting-edge is a side effect of the depth of the art. It's not about trying to be cutting-edge. People who are avant-garde or cutting-edge aren't there because they said, "I want to be on the avant-garde." It's because they were forward-thinking and had ideas that other people hadn't had before.

JK: And other people called them avant-garde.

PZ: Yes. When you're making new work, eventually you get to the point where you want it to be about how powerful the work is. Now, there will be innovative things in it, and there's a certain cachet to being innovative, especially if it becomes expected of you. And to a certain extent, there's always a part of one trying to satisfy that. But I do think that I'm much more interested in making sure that the work is interesting. In fact, I think it's fun to do something that's way more low-tech than it seems. For example, one time I had battery-powered Christmas-tree lights in my hair, and I plugged them into a fader device that I put in my lap. I sat in a chair, and I sang this little song. Every note I sang, I would punctuate it by fading the lights up. If I sang really loudly, I would fade them up louder, bigger, brighter, and if it was quiet, I would fade it down, on and off. My hands were in my lap, and I was just doing it with the fader. I wasn't trying to trick the audience, but I just knew that because of my reputation and because of what's possible today, that they would probably assume that it was some pitch-to-MIDI controller, and my voice is controlling the lights, like the thing that I do with video. But I was actually just doing it with my hand on a fader device. Why bother to write some really complicated program when I could just push this fader in my lap, you know? *[Laughs]*

JK: What role does improvisation play in your work?

PZ: I used to tell people that I wasn't much of an improviser because I used to compose all my works before I got on the stage. I think the necessity to improvise came when I started wanting to collaborate with other people. And sometimes the easiest way to collaborate with other people is to improvise, because it saves you having to compose something specially for it and have lots and lots of rehearsal and preparation. If people are good listeners and good improvisers, you can get great improvised duets and trios. Actually, in my opinion, all music is improvised. It's just that when composers that don't improvise in front of the audience do it, they do it in their studio and maybe at the piano. They're improvising—"Oh, that sounds good"—and then they write it down. Or some people do it in their head, and then they write it down. But even these really stodgy, by-the-book, "We only believe that a composer is somebody who makes black marks on pieces of paper" kind of people—at some point, improvisation is involved, whether they're doing it on an instrument or they're doing it in their head. So I feel that whether it's called "improv" or not is based on when it happens—whether it happens in front of the audience or not. Actually,

I realized that all of my composing is done by improvising. Not only that, I'm kind of a first-take kind of gal. Usually, if I just start playing around, it's a good thing that I have tape rolling, because I'll do something and say, "Oh, that's perfect," and then I'll try to reproduce it, and I'll realize that the first time I did it was right, and I don't even want to change it.

JK: Is that how you typically work? Do you record everything that you play?

PZ: I try to record whenever I'm working on something. I compose a couple of different ways. One is by doing stuff live just in my studio, using the same tools I use on stage, improvising, and when I come up with something I like, hopefully I've recorded it, and then I learn it. I hone it, but it's the basic textures, colors, and even sometimes the patterns or the form in the work. Sometimes it comes all at once to me. The other way that I compose is I get commissions to make sound-works for choreographers, or filmmakers, or theater, where they want a recorded sound design or composition.

JK: And in those cases, are you a part of the performance?

PZ: I usually don't perform the work live. I give them a recording as the end product. So I will sit down and actually build little pieces of things. I sculpt the whole thing in Pro Tools.[3] That's usually how I work when I'm composing that way. I may sing little fragments, or record sounds of found objects, and then I will take them into Pro Tools, where I have these little discrete short regions and some longer regions, and then I just start treating it like I was a sculptor—putting these pieces into the tracks, and layering and building a structure in the computer. Often I will end up building something in Pro Tools for a recorded project, and I wonder what it'd be like if I perform this live, so I learn a way to do it live.

JK: Traditional notation?

PZ: Yes, when I'm composing for groups like Ethel or Bang on a Can All-Stars. I've probably had about ten commissions for chamber ensembles where I've actually had to produce a score. The other times when I've produced written scores were when I had theater pieces where I included other musicians, not just me, and so I needed to write parts for them.

JK: What happens when you give a recording for a commission with film or dance?

PZ: Often, it is for choreographers, and it's usually collaborative. I'll show up at a rehearsal with some of the music, and they'll give more direction: "This is good, but can you make this part a little longer . . . ?" And then, when the whole thing is done, I create a CD to give to them and their sound engineer.

JK: Sounds similar to composing for a film.

PZ: If somebody takes it on tour, maybe they'll retool the piece down the line. A couple of times they've called me back and said, "We're doing such-and-such again, but we need this, or we've now changed, or we've tightened up this section." With video or filmmakers, they'll give me the video file, and then I can open that in Pro Tools and actually cut and compose to the video.

JK: It's really interesting hearing you talk, because you seem very visual—for instance, when you're talking about building, sculpting, and layering a piece. It seems a natural evolution that your music would go into the visual realm, and you would add visual components to it.

PZ: Yeah, it's interesting, because for years I've been using Pro Tools. When you visually see a Pro Tools project by somebody like me, it's all these little bits, and they're stacked up, and you can actually visually see the piece. You can see the texture or the density in the tracks just by looking at this Pro Tools document. Yes, it is very visual.

JK: Well, it makes sense that your art would be interdisciplinary.

PZ: I think for a long time I've done interdisciplinary work. I remember we used to use the word "multimedia," and I remember when "multimedia" was stolen from the art world.

JK: By whom?

PZ: By the computer industry. Basically, by the technology world. When people used to talk about multimedia productions or multimedia work, it meant many different media. It would include visuals and sound, and it might include dance or film or acting, and all these different things were mixed together in one piece. And then at a certain point, right around the time of the dot-com boom, "multimedia" came to mean anything done on a computer. So it went from meaning many different media to one medium—if it's on the computer, it's multimedia. People thought, if they just did a PowerPoint presentation, that it was multimedia. And so, at first, I think artists resisted and continued to keep using it the same way, and eventually people stopped using the word to mean what it originally meant. But, I still say I do multimedia performance work.

JK: Other artists will know what you mean.

PZ: Yes, other artists will know what I mean. Most people just think that it means computers are involved. What I do mean is that you're projecting image, you're moving on the stage, there are props involved, text being spoken, singing, gesture. . . . I'm combining many different media.

JK: Who is sitting in the audience today for experimental work with technology?

PZ: In the early days of that work, technology was kind of an elitist thing. It was only people who were in universities. I think experimental work got so tied up with technology in recent decades. Average people didn't feel that they needed to have a computer, and now everybody needs a computer. There has always been an avant-garde, people that did something really interesting, and then way down the line the mainstream world would catch up with it. Then, people would begin inserting it in advertising and into products, and people would think it was really cool. By that time, the artists were over it and had moved on to something else. It always took a couple of decades, and then it took a couple of years, and now it's like no time at all. It's like people in the avant-garde world do something, and then the next minute a DJ does it, and then that person has a Levi's contract, and it's in every Levi's ad, and there's this weird blurry line between experimental work and mainstream. For example, not too long ago, it became the style for advertisements to look so confusing that you didn't know what they were advertising. Layered text and symbols, rough, torn edges, and some weird high-tech thing "glommed" on. It was meaningless. Artists who made that kind of art—it came from somewhere for them. At first, it was a little disturbing as an artist, because we feel like we have our own little world. It's not that we don't want them to "get us," and it does give people an inroad for someone that may not have been originally interested in a certain kind of work, but they've been exposed to it at this really vapid, surface level.

JK: Because they are exposed to it, perhaps they'll pay more attention to the real artists that are creating the experimental art.

PZ: Yes, but . . . I remember the day that I said to someone, "I create electronic music," and they said, "Oh yeah, my friends do that." They do? And then I realized they thought that I was a DJ or doing techno. The problem is that there is one algorithm that becomes popular, and then it's in every pop song, like right now the thing is Auto-Tune.[4] They're taking Auto-Tune technology and setting it totally quantized, so fluid singing sounds robotic. In our world, we don't want to do it because we've already done it. In their world, they think it works, so everybody does it all the time.

JK: Is there a sense of backlash in the artist world against the technology that's gone so commercial in the pop world?

PZ: There may be for some people, but I don't think that connection is close enough to what I'm doing. There's nothing the pop world is doing that I have to stop doing. I mean, they're processing their voices, but they're processing them in a different way than I'm processing mine. Something that is interesting to me about the pop world is that there has always been some kind of iconic, forward-thinking person in that world who is more creative and more of an artist, but they're so firmly in the pop world. These days, it's Lady Gaga. I don't know too much about her, but she seems to be a real performance artist. She has all this artifice that she dons when she does performances—crazy costumes, really over-the-top stuff, and then weird actions and events that happen on stage, and it's very interesting. But what always frustrates me is how she can be so forward-thinking about that, but then the music is not interesting. There's nothing wrong with being really commercial in the pop world. But if they can get really out there with everything else they're doing, why can't they get out there with the music? They can't get past these formulas.

JK: Well, it is true that experimental music is not as commercial. It's harder to make a living if you're going to be completely in the experimental world.

PZ: It's not that I'm expecting them to do experimental music, because obviously they're pop musicians. But if she's able to do a pop-music show and then throw a completely new twist on her presentation as a performer, why can't she throw a new twist on the music, too? Something that will stand out not just because she's wearing a crazy feather costume, but also because she's doing something very different sonically. There are people who can manage that in the pop world—lean toward the experimental, but they still have hits, like Björk.

JK: Björk found a way to walk that line.

PZ: But she manages to do really different things and still sells out huge venues. She's much better-known in the popular music world than somebody like Diamanda Galás or Laurie Anderson. I always used to think of Laurie Anderson as sort of the pop star of the avant-garde because of *O Superman.*

JK: That's a thoughtful commentary on Lady Gaga, and I agree there is an aspect of her that really is performance art.

PZ: Yeah, and I'm glad she's doing it. But if she likes to break the mold, why doesn't she try to break the mold musically, you know? I think that the hardest thing for people is to be adventurous sonically.

JK: Is it a lack of music education, or is it a fear to explore?

PZ: If you have an abstract painting on the wall, and if you really don't want to look at that painting, you can turn your back, and you don't have to look at it. But if there is abstract music being played, you can't shut your ears off. And I think that music plays an incredibly important role in almost everyone's life. Everyone has music that is important to them, and they all have very strong opinions about what they like. They have much stronger opinions about their musical taste than they do about their taste in visual art. Most people do not want to be challenged by music. They'd rather be challenged by a book, or by a play—not music. They want music to be comfortable.

JK: So with all the saturation, does it tend to devalue the technology or devalue the art?

PZ: Sometimes I worry about that. There's a lot of mediocre stuff out there, now that everybody has the tools to do it. And sometimes I worry that it will lower the cachet of what we do. Like, what we do used to be kind of special.

JK: And now everybody with a computer has GarageBand.

PZ: Exactly, but then I have to remind myself that what's good is going to be good, and what's interesting is going to be interesting, and the rest is going to be boring, and that's always been the way it is. It is changing people's attitudes about the availability of things. Nobody is buying CDs anymore, but you just go with the flow.

JK: So as someone who is a creator of music and art, how do you sustain yourself financially? If you can't put out something that other people can purchase . . .

PZ: One of the reasons why I'm sort of mourning that CDs seem to be disappearing pretty quickly is that I've really been bad about releasing my work. I've got pieces on several compilation CDs, and I have one solo CD that I released on the Starkland label. I'm such a busy performer that I don't get the time. Even if I have it recorded, I still have to put it together and master and finish it. What if I don't get around to doing another CD before CDs completely disappear? So that's a little frustrating. But the reality of it is that if you ask most musicians, you do not make most of your money from selling product. You give half of it away, like business cards. It's a way of getting gigs, or you trade them with other musicians. Most of my money comes from playing gigs, the actual artist's fee for performing, and from commissions. For big projects, I write grants. Also residencies, where you give a concert and give workshops with the students.

JK: I want to go back to your entrance into technology. You kind of found it yourself at a time when it was still very, very new, as far as the masses go. What was your experience being a woman when you first started working with technology?

PZ: Even when I first started doing it, it never occurred to me that I shouldn't be doing it. In Colorado, none of the clubs had sound systems, and all the artists had to bring their own. So I used to haul these speaker columns and set them up, and I had my mixing board, and I'd have to patch all the cables and set my microphones up, and then I added this rack of digital delays, and I was patching it all together, and I didn't have any colleagues when I first started doing that. I was the only name in town, the only person doing it. And people would come up to me afterwards, generally men, and they would say, "So, who set all this up for you?" [*Laughs*] The other thing that was really funny is that, when I first moved to San Francisco, I was teaching sound and performance workshops. I would have guys in my class, and there was always this weird thing where they didn't think that a woman should know more about technical stuff than they did. It was this awkward thing where they had to learn from me, but they also had to pretend that they already knew everything [*laughs*]. But I got used to it.

JK: Has it changed?

PZ: It's much better now. It used to be that if I were on a compilation, I would be the only woman on it. And then somebody would want to put out a compilation of women composers, or women in electronic music. There were all these women's compilations, and people would say, "I don't like this ghettoized women's thing." But it already was that way. Like all of the other compilations are men's; they just don't say that. They were men's compilations, so it's like the only way for women to be on one was to have one that's all women.

JK: Are compilations such as those still necessary?

PZ: I'd rather be represented in the general populace instead of seen in the scene as a female artist—like a token. For example, there was a new-music marathon that happened every year in San Francisco. There was a handful of us that had been on every year, and the coordinator was trying to mix it up a little bit, so he asked us if we wouldn't mind if we weren't on the festival itself, but instead have a benefit concert the week before with us "elder statespeople," the stars. We said, "Great!" Without him even trying, it just happened that all of the composers that he'd chosen for that benefit were women, except for one. Four of us were women, and one guy. So he said, "Oh, let's call it 'Ladies blahblah.'" Why? You didn't deliberately pick us because we were women; you picked us because we were good composers. No! We don't want you to call it that. We don't even want you to call attention to it. See if anybody even notices. To me, it showed the progress in our community, that many of the prominent composers who had been on the new-music festival every year turned out to be mostly women. The real progress is made when it is part of the whole and not just some little subculture or some special flavor. Like women are a special flavor of people, like there are people, and then there are female people. On the other hand, I know there are some people who really are interested in studying the feminine culture.

JK: Well, as a woman composer, do you think there's a feminine voice?

PZ: The more interesting question to me is, Is there something special about male music? Because no one ever asks it from that angle. No one ever says, "Well, what is male music like?" For instance, Eric Singer with all his robots. It's probably no surprise that Eric Singer is a guy, that the person who's famous for doing the robots is a guy and not a girl.

JK: It's a setup expectation.

PZ: Yes, it's a setup expectation. They don't say, "Is there something really special or different about this work because it was done by a man?" They say, "Is there something special and different about a work because it was done by a woman?" Now the fact is, there's something special and different about everybody, because of all of the things that make us up vary from one person to another.

JK: Gender is only a little tiny piece. So performance art, like modern visual art, tends to have a plethora of interpretations surrounding the work. What do you think about musicologists coming in and analyzing it?

PZ: Well, I think it's funny that people get it wrong a lot of times when they try to say what artists are meaning by their work, but then maybe it spurs on some interesting conversations or thoughts about it.

JK: There was a particular musicologist who wrote an article about you, George Lewis. He was speculating on the relationship between technology and African Americans: the embrace of technology, the expectation, and the possible renouncement because it is not part of the "traditional" music. Do you ever think about that?

PZ: I've been asked to think about it constantly. It's just another. . . . When we were having the conversation about the whole woman thing, ghettoizing of the women, having compilations of women, that goes in the same subject to me as this whole person-of-color conversation. Which is always a term that I've hated, because everyone has color. "Person of color" or "African American" or whatever—those things have always been double-edged swords for me. In a way, it offers me yet another community, another angle. I feel like, in a way, my life has really been enriched because I am embraced by all these different communities. I'm very thankful that I've been able get a lot of gigs and play a lot of festivals, because I can fall into so many different pots: electronic music, new opera, vocalist, composer-performers, women composers, composers of color, African American composers, female composers of color, artists who use technology, multidisciplinary artists. My work falls into so many different places, and people make festivals and conferences about these things, and I get invited.

JK: So by subcategorizing you . . .

PZ: I should be feeling lucky because I was somehow able to be appropriate for all of these different categories because I fit into so many of them. But some of them I fit into by choice, because I chose to work with voice, I chose to work with technology, I chose to work with experimental music. I didn't choose to be a woman. I didn't choose to be African American. And I also tend not to make very many choices about my work that involve those things. But I fully acknowledge that prominent aspects about oneself have an effect on whatever one does.

JK: Whether it is conscious or unconscious.

PZ: But it's a matter of whether it's a conscious choice. The stereotypical effect of what those choices would be is not necessarily what those effects really are. And I realized something. It took me a very long time to understand, growing up, some of the reasons why African Americans make certain choices, or do certain kinds of things, or are good at certain things, or pick certain things; a lot of those reasons are cultural. So if you were not raised in what's thought of as "typical" African American culture. . . . I've gone through a lifetime of everyone trying to paint me with one brush, and I've gotten it more from a side of the people who consider me a part of their community. It doesn't happen as much as it used to, but more often than not, it's African Americans approaching me: "Why aren't you making work about your culture?" or, "I curate for an African American museum, and I want you to make a piece for our new exhibition called 'I Do It for My People.' Can you make something to fit that?" And I'm like, "I don't know. How about you let me make whatever piece I'll make, and if you feel that I've done it for my people, you can put it in the show"[*laughs*].

JK: Quite honestly, it seems like a lot of pressure. Are you supposed to represent all black women?

PZ: My favorite comment was Denzel Washington being interviewed on some talk show, and the interviewer said something along the lines of, "Does the black community think such and such . . . ?" And Denzel said, "I don't know. The black community doesn't meet at my house on Wednesday nights" [*laughs*]. I've gone through all kinds of different phases and varying degrees of being down with people wanting to focus on issues of race and culture and somehow contextualize me that way. And the way I look at it today is that there's absolutely nothing wrong with it. As a matter of fact, there's something very important about people making work that focuses on issues of race, or issues of culture, or issues of gender. There are some people whose work does that, and there are some people whose work doesn't do that. As a rule, my work doesn't do that, at least not in very surface kinds of ways.

JK: My last question: how did you choose your name?

PZ: For a couple of years I really wanted to change my name, but I didn't know to what, and then you have to train everybody to use the new name. And then I moved to the Bay Area and thought, if I'm ever going to change my name, this is the time to do it. So I chose it for completely aesthetic reasons. At the time I was really finding my own as an experimental artist, and I wanted a name that somehow reflected that. In my mind, having this single-letter last name was good in that way. It was either going to be a letter or a number. I could have been Pamela 13, I almost was! [*Laughs*] Then, I wanted to choose a letter that has a sound to it that's almost like a word. So that it feels sonically. . . . *Z* is a voiced consonant; it has "zzzzzz." It has voice in it, and it's the last letter of the alphabet. I liked the sound of it.

***

Works by Pamela Z

CHAMBER AND VOCAL WORKS

Badagada, for solo voice and electronics (1988).
Bone Music, for solo voice, found percussion, and electronics (1992).
Correspondence (joint commission with 77Hz), for voice and electronics (1995).
Dr. Melfi, for solo voice and string quartet (2007).
Ethel Dreams of Temporal Disturbances, for string quartet and tape (2005).
Four Movements for Violoncello and Delays (2003).
In Tymes of Olde (from *Parts of Speech*), for solo voice and electronics (1991).
Layers (joint commission with Lukas Ligeti), for voice and electronics (1997).
Mona Lisa (with Laetitia Sonami, Donald Swearingen, and Visual Brains), (1996).
The Muni Section (from *Metrodaemonium*), for solo voice and electronics (1995).
Nihongo de Hanasoo (from *Gaijin*), for voice, electronics, and video (1999).
Notice of Baggage Inspection, for solo piano with tape (2007).
Parts of Speech, for solo voice and electronics (1995).

Persistence, for acoustic chamber group, voice, and electronics (2001).
Pianobend, for solo voice and electronics (1994).
Pop Titles 'You' (from *Parts of Speech*), for solo voice and electronics (1986).
Shifting Conditions in the Southland, for acoustic chamber group, voice, and electronics (1998).
The Schmetterling, for acoustic chamber group, voice, and electronics (1998).
Syrinx/Birdvoice (from *Voci*), for solo voice, electronics, and sampled birdsong (2003).
Twenty Answers, for acoustic chamber group, voice, and electronics (2008).
Typewriter (from *Correspondence*), for solo voice and electronics (1995).
Unaccompanied Melody with Minor Ninths and Octaves, for solo soprano (1989).

INSTALLATIONS AND SOUND WORKS

Baggage Allowance, media installation with objects, video, and sound (2010).
De-Star Spangled Banner, four-channel surround-sound installation (2008).
Declaratives in the First Person, six-channel sound installation (2005).
Forensic Art, performance/installation with video, voice, and processing (2002).
Just Dust, six-channel site-specific sound installation (2004).
Lift, 5.1 surround-sound installation (2005).
Metal/Vox/Water, two-channel video installation with amplified metal (2001).
Parts of Speech, four-channel sound installation with cloth-bound books (1998).
Sonic Gestures, multichannel video and sound installation (2007).
Syrinx, four-channel and eight-channel surround-sound installation (2004).
Timepiece Triptych, surround-sound installation (2008).
Trying to Reach You, New American Radio (1989).

LARGE-SCALE, COLLABORATIVE PERFORMANCE WORKS

Baggage Allowance, for solo performer, voice, electronics, and multiple channels of video, created and performed by Pamela Z, lighting design and visual direction by Elaine Buckholtz (2010).
Gaijin, for four performers, voice, electronics, dancers, and two channels of video, composed and directed by Pamela Z, video by Jeanne Finley and John Muse, lighting design by Elaine Buckholtz, set design by Lauren Elder (2001).
Metal/Vox/Water, for solo performer, voice, electronics, one channel of video, and amplified metal, composed by Pamela Z, video by Pamela Z, Jeanne Finley, and John Muse, lighting design by Elaine Buckholtz (2005).
Parts of Speech, for solo performer, voice, electronics, multi-image still projections, and video, created by Pamela Z, multi-image projections by Larry Ackerman, video by Please Louise Productions, lighting design by Joey Williams, set design by Lauren Elder (1998).
The Pendulum, for solo performer, voice, electronics, and three channels of video, created and performed by Pamela Z, lighting design by Stephen Seigel (2008).
Voci (Voices), for solo performer, voice, electronics, and three channels of video, composed and performed by Pamela Z, video by Jeanne Finley and John Muse, lighting and set design by Elaine Buckholtz (2003).

Wunderkabinet, for two performers, voice and electronics, cello and electronics, and multiple channels of video, composed and performed by Pamela Z and Matthew Brubeck, video by Christina McPhee, lighting design by Elaine Buckholtz (2005).

DANCE SCORES

The Ballad of PollyAnn (2008).
Batman, No Robin (1996).
Copra Dock Dances (1999).
The Economics of Place (2001).
Hashi (Bridge) (1999).
How to Be a Citizen (2003).
Mission Wall Dances (2002).
Outdoors in Oakland (1992).
The Quivering Mass (1996).
Waving Not Drowning (2009).
Z Songs (1990).

FILM AND VIDEO SCORES

Diese Jugend, Elena-María Bey (1984).
Language Lessons, Jeanne Finley and John Muse (2002).
Lover/Other, Barbara Hammer (2005).
O Night without Objects, Jeanne Finley and John Muse (1997).
San Francisco Arts All Over the Map, Searchlight Films (1993).
Tender Fictions, Barbara Hammer (1995).

13

Toshiko Akiyoshi

Born in 1929, Toshiko Akiyoshi came to the United States from Tokyo in 1956 as a young woman who played jazz piano. Akiyoshi is considered a pioneer in many respects, including her use of timbral color in big-band composition, leading her own band playing her own music, and incorporating her Japanese heritage and sometimes Japanese instruments into her charts. Her expanded use of color and fronting a jazz orchestra with her compositions influenced later composers such as Maria Schneider, whose interview follows. Akiyoshi's albums have received fourteen Grammy Award nominations; her discography is large and respected; her piano playing is still in demand; and her compositions and arrangements are played by big bands, orchestras, and schools all over the world.

Despite these accolades, Akiyoshi has never been awarded a Grammy. Most of her recordings were published in Japan, and her 1996 autobiography, *Life with Jazz,* in its fifth printing in Japanese, has yet to be printed in English. She explains during our interview that her husband Lew Tabackin describes her as "demographically challenged." Akiyoshi does not dwell on the obstacles she faced as a young Japanese woman playing jazz in the mid-century United States, early questions about her authenticity, or suspicions that her husband was responsible for her music. Akiyoshi would rather remember her experiences on the bandstand, writing for her families of big-band musicians, practicing piano almost every day of her life, and being grateful for the opportunity of arriving in America at such a golden time for jazz.

Akiyoshi's music grows out of a hybrid of cultures. Inspired by Duke Ellington's celebration of African American heritage in his music, Akiyoshi fused Japanese Noh drama and traditional instruments with contemporary jazz, creating a sound all her own. As in her music, Akiyoshi's Japanese roots emerge in her speech. Although our conversation is edited for clarity, her authentic linguistic profile is preserved.

Like Chen Yi, Tania León, Hilary Tann, and Svjetlana Bukvich, Akiyoshi came to the United States in part to further her college education and musical studies. Her journey is famous among bebop jazz musicians: born in Manchuria, Akiyoshi began playing piano at age six and moved with her family back to Japan after they lost their assets during World War II. Without a piano at home, Akiyoshi continued her playing in dance halls during the Occupation, learning American jazz from records and musician soldiers on the bandstand. Eventually, she formed her own trio and began developing a reputation as a competent jazz pianist. The famed musician Oscar Peterson heard Akiyoshi play, which led to her first recording, *Toshiko's Piano,* and an invitation to study at the Berklee School of Music in Boston. After three years in Boston, Akiyoshi moved to New York at the height of bebop jazz. Her piano skills and ambition allowed her to play with nearly every great jazz artist of the mid-twentieth century. For this reason, she credits the bandstand for much of her education.

After a brief earlier marriage and the birth of her daughter, Akiyoshi met and married the saxophonist/flutist Tabackin and moved to Los Angeles in 1972. Together, they formed a big band in Los Angeles, playing Akiyoshi's own composed and arranged charts, with Akiyoshi as bandleader. During the ten years they lived on the West Coast, the Toshiko Akiyoshi Jazz Orchestra featuring Lew Tabackin became known as one of the most innovative big bands in jazz. It quickly developed a reputation for sophisticated sound and complex timbral colors with emphasis on vertical harmonies and a woodwind section provided by Los Angeles studio musicians who doubled and sometimes tripled on different instruments. In 1976, *Stereo Review* named *Long Yellow Road* the best jazz album of the year; Akiyoshi and her band continued to be recognized for years in *DownBeat* magazine's Critics Poll and Readers Poll. Akiyoshi and Tabackin returned to New York in 1982, reforming the big band on the East Coast. In 2003, she officially retired her big band, and they played their final concert at *Birdland* in New York City, where they had a weekly gig for years. Akiyoshi still tours as a pianist with her own trio or quartet, often including her husband, whom she credits with encouraging her to continue even in challenging times.

Just beginning to accept being called a pioneer, Akiyoshi recognizes that she has come a long way from being questioned about her authenticity to being named a National Endowment for the Arts Jazz Master in 2007.

***

July 2009, at her home in New York City

JENNIFER KELLY: Is it fair to say that a lot of your education took place on the bandstand?

TOSHIKO AKIYOSHI: Yes, playing with other musicians. That's the best school. When somebody else hands down to you their knowledge, it's almost like learning how to swim [*laughs*]. My main influence is Bud Powell—not only on piano but the way his rhythm conception is a little bit different from others, and his punctuation is in different places from most people. And I think that has stayed with me a long time. My main writing comes from my experience playing with other people. I came in at a very good time. I came [to the United States] in 1956, when the music wasn't quite so "productionized" like today. There were many clubs all over the country. A big band could stay in one place like the Storyville Club for a week, sometimes even two weeks at one time. People like Max Roach and Miles [Davis] had their own arrangements, and if you knew the tune, you could sit in [and play]. I probably listened to every record they ever made up to 1956. So they would let me sit in, and I learned a lot from playing with them. That's my asset, and that's my source of my writing. Dizzy Gillespie would say things like, "It's not *what* you play but *where* you play it." Today, you have a group and the presentation with your group. I only know of one or two groups today that will let you sit in [to play]. Today, young players may have no opportunity to hear some old player, not just to play together, but maybe they talk about their experience—what they think is appropriate and what they learn and pass on to the next generation. Those things, I think, are very important. For the past twenty years or so, real, active, and professional musicians would teach school. And then some retire, and some die, and so on. Now it's more that teachers are teachers. They know a lot—harmonic structure, what have you—but they are not players. In my case, I think I'm very fortunate that I came at a very good time. It was fifty-three years ago, so everything was very open. I came at a very good time, and I learned a lot from my predecessors.

JK: Did you learn a lot of the American standards while you were still in Japan?

TA: When I was in Japan, I started playing in 1946, and there was nothing available. The thing that got me interested in playing jazz was a Japanese jazz-record collector.

JK: A record collector?

TA: Yes. Many jazz fans in those days were the so-called elite. And when they were in college, they were interested in collecting records. This was one of the persons who had a record collection. He invited me over to his home, and he played Teddy Wilson. That's what got me interested. I wanted to play just like that. Teddy Wilson was a very clean player. His runs are so beautifully put in place. It's almost like everything is the same-sized pearls strings. So that's what got me interested, but nothing was available. Basically, he had a record. Later, I was hired by the band that was playing at the American officer's club, where they had gramophones—but they were electric, not by hand. They used to have American—it's called a V-disc, the LP's pioneer. In other words, it was plastic, and if you drop it, it won't break. It was twelve inches, and I think the name was Victory disc, but it was called V-disc.[1] They had quite a lot of different groups. That's something I could listen to in the daytime because we only played in the evening, and I would learn the music from that record. Then later, 1952 or so, I had my own group, and I used to have American professional players who were drafted and stationed in Japan, and they would sit in, and I would learn from them. Just the simple things, like a tune! You have to learn from them because, like I said before, nothing was available. So I used to learn the tune from them and also got used to playing it. I was young, and consequently I was a little bit arrogant, so when they came sitting in, I played a really fast tempo, and if they can't play it, it would get them off [the stage] [*laughs*]. So those were the times when I was learning tunes and getting used to the language and jazz language. So it's now maybe 1953 in Japan, and I had the opportunity to play for Norman Granz, a jazz musician, and Oscar Peterson noticed my playing. With his suggestion, I had my first recording. I was twenty-three years old. And about that time, I started going to jazz coffee shops. They had American records, and you could go there and listen to them. Coffee cost about fifty yen. That was a very important place for somebody like myself to learn the tune, get used to the tune, and also learn the American players.

JK: Your first group in Japan, were you playing jazz? I know there wasn't much available, and you were learning about the tunes and the jazz language. . . .

TA: Yes. I started to play piano when I was seven years old. And needless to say, it was classical. When [World War II] ended, my family lost all assets, so I didn't have anything. My family couldn't afford to furnish me a piano. So I got a job in dance halls, so I could play piano. That was the beginning of the story. If the war hadn't ended, I would have probably played classical music. But things worked out the way they worked out.

JK: Do you see any of your classical technique or knowledge come into your jazz playing?

TA: Yeah, some people have a problem—they are classical players—and they want to know how to play jazz. But I feel, if you can't really feel the rhythm, which is so different from classical, I don't really think you're going to be a jazz player. Not too long ago, I heard a women's jazz pianist competition, four finalists. They all play very good piano, but they can't swing. They play great Latin beat. Really great. But they can't play four beat. They can play a fast tempo, yes, because fast tempo you can get away with it. The sense of swing is more difficult when it becomes slow. Playing slow swing is more difficult. So I think the music is shifting. It has become much more European now than it was. I have that feeling probably because school has a lot to do with it. They say, "Jazz went to the academy" [*laughs*]. It's become more academic music because it is away from how jazz was born and what it's about. Jazz has always been about a life. Different people, different life, but I always believed that jazz was something to do with life. The entire academy world, which is mainly the European music world, has quite a lot of influence today. Some of the writing I hear today sounds very European. Jazz is always organic music, anyway. And to me, jazz is not for everyone—either the people who are playing and the listener as well. Not everybody can play jazz. Somehow you have to identify it with yourself. Like in the old days, people said black people can swing, and white people cannot. That's nonsense. I know black musicians who can't swing if their life depended on it. It's purely an individual thing. There are some things you are born with. There are other things that you have to "woodshed" a lot; you have to work at it. But if you don't have anything to begin with, even if you work at it, it's not going to work. So not everybody can be a jazz player, which I think is okay, because the world doesn't need that many jazz players anyway. Also, listening to jazz, you need a sophisticated ear. Like getting to know a person. It's the same thing—you have to have patience. You need to get to know the person. When I would listen to a record in Japan, I thought some players sounded really good. And when I came here and listened in person, it disappointed me. And vice versa. There's a certain thing about live performance with the air and atmosphere.

JK: Do you prefer playing live or recorded music?

TA: I like live better, because the studio is so unnatural to me. I have a problem with studios [*laughs*]. I keep repeating takes, and it always ends up that the first one is the best one, but you don't really want to accept that, so you keep trying it over again. If you have this much time in the studio, you spend it all hoping that you'll do better. But in most cases, the first take is the best. I don't calculate the solo. I take a lot of chances, and sometimes I don't make it. But that's okay. I get a certain excitement from live music.

JK: How do you know when your music is right? When it's working?

TA: Well, I consider myself the first audience, the first listener. Because I'm the writer. It has to be right for my ear, and I would like to say that I have good judgment. If it's not right, I fix it.

JK: You still perform live, yes?

TA: Yes.

JK: But not with the big band?

TA: Well, the big band wasn't my idea to begin with. Actually, I was in New York, and I was barely paying the rent, even though I would get jobs playing for the festivals or very high-profile concerts. But if you get that once a year, you can't live on that, so I was barely surviving. Anyway, most of the songs have lyrics. I would like to be able to improvise to express that. So many times I hear a tune and, when the improvisation comes, it has nothing to do with the tune. That's okay, but I would like to be able to play what that tune was meant to be. It came to the point where I wanted to express myself in the jazz language about different things. Like, I'm very interested in social issues, and I may want to express myself about an issue in the jazz language. And then I started thinking that I like to have a little color, more color, which means more instruments. At the same time, I had my own concert in 1967, at Town Hall. I had a solo, trio, and then I wrote a big-band track. I liked writing. You can always change writing. Improvising, most of the time you don't do a perfect job. Most of the time you say, "Why did I do that?" But the writing, if you don't like it, you can always change it. But I didn't have the economic resources to have a big band. Then Lew [Tabackin] and I met, and we married in 1969. His job required us to move to Los Angeles in the summer of 1972. Los Angeles had very little jazz opportunities, but Lew found out that the union had a rehearsal room you could rent for fifty cents for two hours and forty-five minutes. So he came back and said, "I'll get musicians together, and I know you have tunes. Play your music. Do something." That's how it started. I mostly went to writing, and consequently the time I spent practicing piano decreased every day. Also, the jazz band is all jazz players—otherwise it wouldn't be a jazz band. And a jazz musician's happiest time is playing a solo. So to play with a big band is a second choice for a musician. And if I played a solo, I will have taken someone else's solo spot. So I say I will give it to somebody else, and so on. I don't know if you ever noticed or not, but there are very few piano solos in my big-band music.

JK: I did notice.

TA: And the more I wrote, the more I became a slow writer. It took longer than the one before. I was actually getting very depressed, and I said to Lew that I didn't think I was talented enough to write because the more I write, the slower I get. And he said, "That's the way it's supposed to be. Because you're not competing with other people's music. You're competing with the one you've already written, the work that you've finished. You're competing with that." So I said, "Okay, in that case, I don't have to be depressed." I thought I was the slowest writer on the earth, but I understand Gil Evans was also a slow writer. The band disbanded in 2003. I thought, I had a band for thirty years, and that's fine. I have no regrets, actually.

JK: I wish I could have been at the last Birdland concert.

TA: People lined up! They never lined up for our Monday night! In all the seven years, never! So Lew said we should say, "This is the last concert," about thirty-four times [*laughs*]. We did the last [formal] concert at Carnegie Hall in October 2003, but we kept Birdland to the end of the year. That's the first time I saw people lining up, and I said, "Wow." So it was good.

JK: Tell me about your band.

TA: The band that we had was rather unique because it was started in Los Angeles with studio-work-oriented musicians. And because of that, all saxophone players doubled [on flute and clarinet], so there was a woodwind section involved. Even today, there is no woodwind section in any large jazz ensemble. The point is not because I wanted to have a woodwind section, but they were there, so I utilized it. It was a two-way street, because it made it more like my trademark. Bebop is basically virtuoso music, a lot of notes. Even today, I think that is the most technically difficult music. The college had a competition conference, and a teacher asked Lew, "Why is her music is so damn difficult?" And Lew said, "Well, difficult today, easy tomorrow." And that's what it is. There's a way to write, and I think, if you're a real pro, you write probably 70 percent of the musicians' capability. And whatever I have written was nothing new, all done before. All jazz was done before by somebody—Dizzy Gillespie or Charlie Parker or somebody. I never created anything. I just utilize in a different way. So I know it can be done. Whether they can do it or not, that's another question. That's their problem. By doing it, they become a better player. Everything unnecessarily feels difficult because it's the first time we hear it. Once you hear it, you have something to go by, so it's not that hard. Everything is the growing process. I learned a lot from being with musicians who can do certain things. I would say, "Oh, that's nice. Maybe I can use that." I learned by doing that, so it's a two-way street.

JK: Are West Coast and East Coast jazz still different?

TA: The globe became very small, and communication is much smaller, so I'm not sure if you can categorize that today. To me, I hear music built on an American jazz tradition, or I hear a lot of infusion of European influence. That's what I hear. In the old days, like in the early fifties, there was quite a distinct difference between East Coast and West Coast jazz. I used to think it was because of the weather [*laughs*]. Because on the West Coast in Los Angeles, the weather is nice; all you need is two different sets of clothes, and that's it. Here [in New York] the weather is sometimes very cold and up and down, and sometimes that affects people, the way they think. At the same time, New York is the center for musicians who are trying to get recognition as a player. Now in Los Angeles, they are trying to get into the studio, so they can have a better life economically. And Los Angeles had a very distinctive sense of swing. Everything is sort of a little bit mellowed down. There's a certain harshness that's here [in New York], which some people might call "cutting-edge."

JK: When you moved from Los Angeles back to New York City, did your music change?

TA: I don't think it changed, because it didn't change when I moved from New York to Los Angeles. The only thing different in Los Angeles was writing with the woodwind section.

JK: How would you describe your music?

TA: My music is based in hard bebop. Then I try to build something on the top. Some is obvious, some is not. If I use a Japanese instrument, that's obvious. The concept of jazz big-band music is basically concerto music. It is a vehicle for the solo player. I don't particularly go nuts over "nothing but ensemble" with no solo. It's okay, I guess. You can call that jazz too, probably. But what makes a band so exciting is the solo player. The solo player and the writing are like a horse and jockey where both have to be great. So there is a relationship between writer and solo player. I always consider the concerto tradition at the very beginning. The classical concerto pieces, they are always a little slow in the middle, little *cadenza* in the middle, and the big one comes last, the long *cadenza*. So I said, "Why can't I do that?" So I wrote *Tales of a Courtesan* for the flute as a ballad. It has the middle part that has a little *cadenza*, and the very end of it has a long *cadenza*. I tried to put in some Japanese elements, because it wasn't there before in jazz. Everybody knows this part of jazz is from Europe, and this part is from Africa, and it is born in this country; but there was no Japanese, so I thought that would be my job to do that.

JK: Fifty or a hundred years from now, what would you like people to think about Akiyoshi music?

TA: I hope my music contains the universal human nature. It's in the music that people can feel. What's good about instrumental music is that it's not like a lyric. Lyric designates. Instrumental music is so abstract. If I may exaggerate, ten people listen to the same music, and ten people feel ten different ways. That's the good thing about music. I hope my music contains something beyond time, which appeals to human nature. I don't really think that since the Stone Age human nature has really changed that much. Intellect might have changed but not the nature. That's what I'm trying to play, too.

JK: How do you write differently for fast tunes or slow ballads?

TA: Fast tune is basically not storytelling music. Basically, it's purely instrumental. A ballad is a story. I believe that a jazz ballad is about life. Of course, my life experience is different from someone else, so it comes out differently. But, to me, a ballad is telling some story. *Tales of a Courtesan* is a ballad about the courtesan. I was commissioned to write a tune from a small village in Japan, *Four Seasons.* The winter song is a ballad, just waiting, because it's a very cold place, and it is just waiting to become spring so that they can start working—they can pollinate the apple flower and start planting things, and so on. In 2000 I was asked to play that solo at a concert. After we finished the concert, a woman came up to me who spent a lot of time in the northern part of Japan, and she said, "That tune . . . I could see the icicle on the house." In other words, if you write something, the music has to contain that, so the listener can receive that. So the ballad usually is about the story. I had a hard time writing ballads because when you are a pianist, you develop a sense of harmony. I had no problem with rhythm because that was something natural to me. But the melody, I could not come up with a melody. So I worked really hard at it. The first time we played in New York I think could have been 1978 (we had a live recording with the L.A. band). At that time, the *New Yorker* magazine's writer wrote a review that talked about the beautiful melody. And it reminded me of the time I said to Bill Evans, "Boy, your harmonic senses are so great." And he said, "Thank you, but that was my poorest point, so I had to work very hard at it." So when I go to clinic, I always mention, if you hang in there and work very hard, you'll come up with something. So don't give up.

JK: I'd like to ask you some questions about the early days. When you first started your band back in Japan, were you immediately accepted as a player and leader?

TA: I was the highest-paid sideman in Japan. In those days, it was all dance halls. And I just wasn't satisfied with playing dance halls. So I decided to form my own group in 1951. This was the Occupation times. There was a service club where you could play jazz, and I formed my first quartet. So to some degree, when I formed my own group, I already had a certain reputation as a pianist. At that time, the most popular jazz group was called Six Joes, and they had a pianist who was an American soldier in the air force. Because he was a soldier, sometimes he couldn't get a pass, and they hired me. He paid me 9,500 yen, which was quite a lot in those days. My quartet, when we worked, the whole performance fee was five thousand yen. And he paid me 9,500 when I subbed. In other words, I had high respect from people, but that doesn't mean I had a lot of work. I never had commercial success because I never played commercial music. I think it's the same thing with the [big] band. The band wasn't commercial enough. I wish the musicians had more jobs because, when you don't have commercial appeal for certain music, you have fewer jobs. But what we did have was high profile. More so than other bands. But we never played for dances. We didn't have that kind of chart.

JK: You arrived in the United States in the 1950s, a young Japanese woman in her twenties. Were you immediately accepted as a player?

TA: Oh yes, because I made that record in 1953. Basically, that record brought me to Boston. The school was looking for something to advertise the school, and I was it. That's how I got the full scholarship. I came in 1956—January—and played in Newport [Jazz Festival] that summer, and every year after I usually did some kind of festival. Then, when I had the big band in Los Angeles, people really started paying notice.

JK: Was being a woman in jazz ever an issue for you? Jazz itself is still a very male-dominated profession.

TA: I never even thought about it. I never thought, *I am a woman.* And in Japan, I was better than anybody else because I was practicing more than anybody else. When I was in Japan, there would be ten jobs and nine musicians. The musicians don't have to work hard. Here, if you don't work hard, you don't get the telephone call. So that's the difference. But I was working hard because I wanted to get better. And I knew I could get better. I think it has a lot to do with society. I think in the old days in society, men think you can't hire women because if you're traveling with a bus, you need to have a different dressing room, a different blah, blah, blah, what have you. The society today is much more accepting; young men are different from older-generation men. They're already looking at a young woman more like a colleague or a buddy. They probably didn't have that kind of camaraderie in the older generation, I think that does have a lot to do with it. At the same time, if you're conscious about it, then you're going to feel that way. If you're not conscious about it, you don't. Sometimes it depends on you.

JK: And leading the big band? This was your first large band, yes?

TA: I always had a trio or quartet at the most. I knew them well, but when you have sixteen of them, you don't really know them. And they didn't really know my work, most of them. So from the very beginning I had to be very careful that the music was right. There was no place where they questioned and said, "What is this?"

JK: The writing has to be great to begin with.

TA: Everything, yes. And I had to say to myself, "Myself, I am the only one that goes to different jazz clubs with my own name. No one does that." You know, I say [authoritatively] "Myself!" [*laughs].* So the first time I had to be very careful that the music was right. No loose ends. Everything. And if somebody asks a question, I know the answer. "How come this one has the same changes, but you have a different note?" I said, "Because it feels differently. That's why I write different notes." There are so many ways to harmonize. They all have a different face. It took about six months or so to gain their confidence. I can understand it. I am barely five feet [tall], and here comes this Japanese woman saying, "I'm a jazz player" [*laughs*]. They say, "Really?" But one thing about musicians: if you can deliver, they respect you. If you can't deliver, they don't respect you. They take face value. That's what I've learned. If you can do it, fine, and if you cannot, *sayonara.*

JK: Coming back to New York when you basically had to start all over again with a new band . . .

TA: Not start all over, because there were ten years with the L.A. band. We had recordings. By that time, maybe four or five came out. And the music had a certain reputation by this time. So when we moved here [to New York], musicians wanted to belong to the organization. So that's the difference. The ones who paid the most dues was the L.A. band. They started with zero. Never having seen me before, no music was like that, and there were "too many notes." They had to work hard, really hard. But the New York band, they already had ten years of my track record, so it wasn't that difficult. They wanted to be in the organization.

JK: Was it hard to leave Los Angeles?

TA: Yes, it was very difficult. Lew wanted to leave, which I don't blame him. When it became busy, he quit The Tonight Show Band, and at that time, there was no reason for him to stay in Los Angeles. There was nothing there. Suppose you have one club job for a weekend in Boston. If you're here, you can drive up there and do it. You cannot do that from L.A. Economically, it isn't feasible. So it was too hard, and he wanted to get back to New York, and so that's what happened. It was hard for me, because for ten years with the band, we became more like a family. But the New York band was then together twenty years. Some people were there from the very beginning and stayed twenty years. Ultimately, the last one was the best one. That was a good band. We have two live recordings with the New York band. With live recording, you make one mistake, and that's it. But they never make a mistake. It was a good band.

JK: I was surprised to hear that you didn't consider yourself a pioneer.

TA: Yeah, I didn't, but I guess I am. People say I am a pioneer. But I was never tied up with the fact that I am a woman or a man. More than that, my case was that I didn't fit the profile, so I got some resistance from some media. I was never picked up by a record company. Concord really respected me, so I have a couple of records with Concord. I would be stupid and naïve to not acknowledge that I don't fit the profile, just because I am Asian, Japanese, and so on. That's the fact. If I didn't recognize that, I would be naïve. But, for me, it's only temporary things. At the end of this year I will be eighty years old. Life is too short to worry about things like that. The band played only my music. Even Duke [Ellington], he had a standard tune in the very beginning. So if you start thinking about that as a pioneer, then it may be so. I think it's very important to have one writer because a band should have an attitude. One great thing about [Count] Basie, he didn't write, but he knew what worked for the band.

JK: What is jazz to you?

TA: I think jazz to me is like Duke Ellington said, "Don't mean a thing if it ain't got that swing." Now, "swing" means different things to different people.

JK: What does it mean to you?

TA: For swing, it's like a swing. The slower it is, the more deliberate, you can really feel it. For example, bebop. When bebop came out, some of the critics said the musicians don't swing. But it is very fast. The fast is more like a drive instead of swing. You have to have room for swing, but with a fast tempo there is no swing, like a bebop tune. So you could say it's more like a drive. But I think there is a certain reason for drive. Classical music, they don't have that. The drive, that's probably why they call it "hard bebop." The medium tempo has to have swing. Medium tempo without swing is like a beer without hops. It's not good to me. Gil Evans is the one who opened Pandora's box. Because before that, European writers couldn't identify with American jazz writers because they couldn't swing—they didn't have it in their blood, so to speak. In that, Gil Evans is a very important figure because he was a bridge to the European writer. But now, American writers are influenced by European writers. It's losing a certain dynamic, I think. Certain things seem to be a thing of the past.

JK: So where can one find jazz today?

TA: I think you can hear it just about any place. It depends on who is playing it. I'm not talking about the band; that's a different thing. But the individual player. New York has many small jazz clubs that do hire young people. Also they have a jam session. They have had that for a long time. It's small, and they have it all day long. Those places, young players, they actually are well-informed about early bebop tunes. So when they play, some play pretty well. So you can't really say jazz is dead.

JK: Do you still compose?

TA: Yes and no. I have a commission piece I have to finish. A couple of things. Also, next year I'm gathering my old band and going to China. And I'd like to have Chinese instruments. Once, we had Chinese koto player. We went to school, and I had some string players, and they put the bow on the inside of the strings, not outside. And every country has drums. I would like to utilize those to do something together.

JK: Who are some of your heroes?

TA: I think, spiritually, of course Duke Ellington, because Duke Ellington was very proud of his race, so a lot of his composition is based on his race. Sometimes somebody has to point it out, otherwise I don't think about it, like *Harlem Suite* or *Black, Brown, and Beige.* So that's what triggered me actually to look into my [Japanese] tradition, which is so different from other American jazz. So spiritually, Duke is my hero. My actual hero, where I learned a lot of technical aspects? I could name them all, but probably Bud Powell, Max [Roach]; I mean, these are people that I played with. Miles [Davis] asked me, "Why do all piano people play way up there? Why don't they play low?" He said, "Are you nervous?" I said, "Yes." He said, "Don't be. I was nervous. I felt the same way when I played with Bird [Charlie Parker]." I learned a lot from the players. I was in the [Charles] Mingus group for about ten months or so, and of course I learned a lot from that, too. Mostly, my influences are all my predecessors that I had encounters with.

JK: It was written in a paper a long time ago that, if you were to list your priorities, you'd say, musician first, woman second, member of society third. Where are you today?

TA: I think it's the other way around. I think I am a member of society first, then I am a woman, and I just happen to be a jazz musician. Aside from that, my priority is human relationships, because I learned a lot from my bitter experiences. When I was young, I used to think I am a musician; that was when I was a student in Japan. And I just happened to be a woman. I never even thought about being a member in society. I learned a lot about things from my experiences. So I have come to the conclusion that the most important thing is human relationships. I don't put my career before my marriage. Everybody knows Lew is ten years younger than I am. Consequently, he started late. I came at a very good time. The old jazz clubs were all over the place, and they would hire me and hire everybody else. I had my time, and I learned a lot from people, and I did myself. Lew didn't have that. When he came out, jazz clubs were gone; just a few existed. So I don't put my career before marriage. I think the main thing for me is to make better conditions or surroundings musically for him to be. Anything I can do, I do. Which is unfortunately not that much [*laughs*].

JK: Well, he's obviously been a great influence on you and your music.

TA: He's a very good and very wise person, very helpful to me in many ways, very supportive. As far as the music is concerned, I'm not quite sure, though, because he has his own, and I have my own. At the very beginning, the first recording, *Long Yellow Road,* was Grammy-nominated. There was a radio station in Los

Angeles, and the man asked Lew, "Are you sure you're not helping her?" and Lew says, "I don't even know what she's writing until she finishes and brings it to the band for rehearsal." Leonard Feather was a good friend of ours, and, because he is a critic, they sent a press release with the LP, and Leonard showed it to me. It said Lew did all the arrangements! And the purpose of the press release was to sell the whole recording!

JK: That sounds very frustrating. Today, you must know that everyone in jazz knows of your work.

TA: We started the band in 1972, and in 1974 we played in Monterey [Jazz Festival]. Some paper said, "I question her authenticity." So in 2007, I received the Jazz Master Award from NEA [National Endowment for the Arts], and you have to make a little speech. So I mentioned this and that and said that I came a long way from being written about and people questioning my authenticity to this highest honor. But things like that happen. Lew has always said that I am demographically challenged [*laughs*]. It seems to me that I am a pioneer. I never saw it that way before, but now it seems that way. When a person is the first to do this or that, like [African American baseball player] Jackie Robinson got a lot of heat, I'm sure. It comes with it. America has the saying, "If you can't stand the heat, stay out of the kitchen." We [in Japan] have a saying: "Stick out, and the nail will be beaten." You know? Stick out and they will beat you! [*Laughs*] Those things come with it, so I have to take everything together. It all worked out okay in the end, I think.

***

Works by Toshiko Akiyoshi

COMPOSITIONS FOR BIG BAND/JAZZ ORCHESTRA

A-10-205932 (also called *Alien Registration Card*), (1977).
After Mr. Teng (also called *Alcazar*), (Kendor Music, 1980).
American Ballad (1974).
Autumn Sea (1980).
Between Me and Myself (1954).
Blue Dream (1984).
Celebration of Duke's Birth (1999).
Chasing after Love (1978).
Children in the Temple Ground (1974).
Children of the Universe (1991).
China Remembered (1996).
Dance of the Gremlins (1996).

Deracinated Flower (1977).
Desert Lady (1994).
Double Exposure (1970).
Drum Conference (2008).
Duke for the Ages (1999).
Elusive Dream (1978).
Epilogue: Hope (2008).
Eulogy (1999).
Fading Beauty (1984).
Fantasy (with Lew Tabackin), (1994).
Farewell to Mingus (1980).
Feast in Milano (1982).
The First Night (1974).
Fool (1970).
Four Seasons of Morita Village (1996).
 Harvest Shuffle
 Norito
 Pollination
 Repose
Glass Ceiling (1998).
Hangin' Loose (1977).
Happy Hoofer (1984).
Harlequin Tears (1994).
Henpecked Old Man (1974).
Hiroko's Delight (1994).
Hiroshima: Rising from the Abyss (2001).
 Futility-Tragedy I
 Futility-Tragedy II
 Survivor Tales I
 Survivor Tales II
 Survivor Tales III
 Hope
How Do You Get to Carnegie Hall (1992).
I Ain't Gonna Ask No More (Kendor Music, 1976).
I Know Who Loves You (1992).
Interlude (Kendor Music, 1976).
Jamming at Carnegie Hall (1984).
Jazz Club (Opener) (1998).
Kogun (1974).
Kourakan (1992).
Lady Liberty (2004).
Lazy Day (1978).
Let Freedom Swing (2008).

Liberty Suite (1986).
Long Yellow Road (Kendor Music, 1974).
March of the Tadpoles (1977).
Memory (1974).
Minamata (suite), (1976).
  Peaceful Village
  Prosperity and Consequence
  Epilogue
Mobil (Kendor Music, 1977).
Monopoly Game (1998).
My Elegy (also called *Toshiko's Elegy*), (1958).
My Teacher, Mr. Yang (2010).
Notorious Tourist from the East (Kendor Music, 1974).
Opus No. Zero (1974).
Quadrille, Anyone? (1974).
Relaxing at Zell am See (1982).
Remembering Bud (1982).
Retro Zone (1996).
Road Time Shuffle (1976).
Salted Gingko Nuts (1978).
Shades of Yellow (1980).
Silhouette (1958).
Since Perry (1974).
Soliloquy (Kendor Music, 1976).
Song for the Harvest (Kendor Music, 1980).
Son of Road Time (Kendor Music, 1978).
State of the Unison (1998).
Strive for Jive (1976).
Studio J (1976).
Suite for Koto and Jazz Orchestra (1998).
  Caribbean Dream
  Kyoto Paradox
  Urban Rhapsody
Sumie (Newport Music Co., 1976).
Tales of a Courtesan (Oirantan) (1976).
Ten Gallon Shuffle (1984).
Time Stream (1978).
Toshiko's Elegy (also called *My Elegy*), (1958).
Transience (Kendor Music, 1976).
Tuning Up (Kendor Music, 1973).
Two Faces of a Nation (1982).
Unrequited Love (1986).
Uptown Stroll (1993).

The Village (1976).
Warning! Success May Be Hazardous to Your Health (1976).
Wishing Peace (2001).
Yellow Is Mellow (Kendor Music, 1977).
Your Beauty Is a Song of Love (1992).

COMPOSITIONS FOR JAZZ COMBO

52nd Street Theme (2004).
After Mr. Teng (also called *Alcazar*), (1978).
American Ballad (1978).
Autumn Sea (1990).
Between Me and Myself (1957).
Blue Dream (1980).
Blues for Father (with Mariano), (1960).
Blues for Toshiko (1957).
Central Park West (2004).
Chasing after Love (2006).
Chic Lady (1980).
Children in the Temple Ground (arr. traditional), (1965).
Deracinated Flower (1996).
Drum Conference (2006).
Elusive Dream (1994).
Endless Journey (2004).
Eulogy (2008).
Euphoria (1971).
Farewell to Mingus (1996).
Feast in Milano (2006).
First Night (1968).
Five Spot after Dark (2004).
Going Home (1963).
Grooving in Yokohama (1999).
Hakone Twilight (1961).
Hangin' Loose (1978).
Harlequin Tears (1993).
Hiroshima Bushi (2004).
Homework (1956).
Hope (2006).
I Ain't Gonna Ask No More (1987).
I Got It Bad and That Ain't So Good (2000).
I Ken Pien Tan (arr. traditional), (1965).
I Know Who Loves You (1987).
Improvisation in Five (2000).
Interlude (1987).

Jammin' at Carnegie Hall (1996).
Kogun (1996).
Kyōshū "Nostalgia" (1956).
Kyoto Paradox (1999).
Lady Liberty (1991).
Last Minute Blues (1980).
Lazy Days (1993).
Let's Roll in Sake (1968).
Long Yellow Road (1960).
Lullaby for You (1965).
Manhattan Address (1956).
Mari To Tonosama (1999).
Memory (1978).
Night Waltz (1994).
Notorious Tourist from the East (1978).
Old Pals (1961).
Opus No. Zero (1968).
Pea, Bee, and Lee (1956).
Phrygian Waterfall (1968).
Pollination (1995).
Prayer (1999).
Prosperity (1984).
Quadrille, Anyone? (1994).
Remembering Bud (1990).
Repose (1999).
Saikai (arr. traditional), (1963).
Salute to Shorty (1956).
Skating in Central Park (2004).
Soliloquy (1978).
Song of the Farm (1960).
Solidado (1953).
State of Being (1970).
Studio J (1957).
Sumi-e (1971).
Sunday Afternoon (1956).
Ten Ten (2000).
The Third Movement (1958).
Time Stream (1984).
Toshiko's Blues (1953).
Toshiko's Elegy (1960).
Tosh's Fantasy (1957).
  Down a Mountain
  Phrygian Waterfall

Running Stream

Tsurusaki Odori (1999).

Tuppen Och Honan (1965).

Tuttie Flutie (1980).

United Notions (1958).

The Village (1970).

Warning! Success May Be Hazardous to Your Health (1978).

Watasu No Biethovin (1961).

RECORDED ARRANGEMENTS FOR LARGE ENSEMBLE

Air (Bach), for trumpet, trombone, tuba, cello, percussion, and rhythm section (1995).

Amapola (LaCalle/Roldan/Gamse), for trumpet, trombone, tuba, cello, percussion, and rhythm section (1995).

Bebop (Gillespie), for big band (1994).

A Bit Byas'd (Tabackin), for big band (1981).

Broken Dreams (Tabackin), for big band (1994).

Day Dream (Ellington/LaTouche/Strayhorn), for big band (1999).

I Let a Song Go out of My Heart (Ellington/Nomo/Redmond/Mills), for big band (1999).

Kangding Qingge (traditional), for big band (2010).

Kisarazu Jinku (traditional), for big band (1961).

Lament for Sonny (Tabackin), for big band (1981).

Land of Peace (Feather), for big band (1964).

Let the Tape Roll/"Lew's Theme" (Tabackin), for big band (1981).

La Mucura (trad.), for big band (1993).

Once I Loved (Jobim), for trumpet, trombone, tuba, cello, percussion, and rhythm section (1995).

One Note Samba (Jobim), for trumpet, trombone, tuba, cello, percussion, and rhythm section (1995).

Pollination (Jobim), for trumpet, trombone, tuba, cello, percussion, and rhythm section (1995).

Prelude to a Kiss (Ellington/Mills/Gordon), for big band (1999).

Santa Barbara (Mariano), for big band (1964).

The Shout (Mariano), for big band (1964).

Star Eyes (Raye/DePaul), for trumpet, trombone, tuba, cello, percussion, and rhythm section (1995).

Tanuki's Night Out (Tabackin), for big band (1981).

Tico Tico (Abreu/Drake/Oliveira), for trumpet, trombone, tuba, cello, percussion, and rhythm section (1995).

Unrequited Love (Tabackin), for big band (2004).

Walkin' (Carpenter), for big band (1964).

Yet Another Tear (Tabackin), for big band (1981).

Lourdes Delgado

14

Maria Schneider

Maria Schneider is known today mostly for her big-band compositions and for leading her own ensemble, the Maria Schneider Orchestra (also known as the Maria Schneider Jazz Orchestra). Like Toshiko Akiyoshi, Schneider's band focuses on Schneider's compositions, to which she adds color by incorporating instruments uncommon to the jazz orchestra, such as the accordion. Schneider differs from Akiyoshi in that her music does not often use the standard jazz forms and may be through-composed or sound programmatic. Nevertheless, she is fine with being called a jazz composer: "It's the best way to describe what I do. Non-jazz musicians could never play music for my band, so therefore it's jazz." At the same time, she recognizes that the boundaries between jazz, classical, Brazilian, flamenco, and other styles of music are becoming increasingly more blended, and Schneider's own music blurs genres. Continuing to write for her jazz orchestra while accepting new commissions from classical ensembles, she takes much of her inspiration from flying, motion, and dance, and her conducting reflects the fluidity of her works.

Born in 1960 in Windom, Minnesota, Schneider was introduced to piano, jazz, and composition at an early age. Disenchanted by traditional composition in college, she was encouraged by a university professor to write for the college big band. She recounts with awe attending a concert in Minnesota by the Toshiko Akiyoshi Jazz Orchestra and being enthralled that any person could play her own jazz music in an auditorium and front her own band. Schneider later became the first recipient of the Gil Evans Scholarship established by the trumpeter Herb Alpert in 1993, and she went on to work with Evans as a copyist.

Although the influence of Gil Evans can be heard in Schneider's music, the Maria Schneider Orchestra has developed a unique sound, as they play mostly her own compositions, often inspired by real-life images or experiences. She and her orchestra released their first recording, *Evanescence,* in 1994. She writes for the specific players in the ensemble, and, although each work is a distinct composition, improvisation plays a large role in her music, as she considers the instrumental solos played in real time to be the unknown compositional element.

With the same humility evinced by Jennifer Higdon and Shulamit Ran, Schneider speaks with great respect about the members of her ensemble, valuing them as the musicians who breathe life into her work. She explains that her music is left intentionally vulnerable, allowing the musicians to contribute their part in ways that defy notation. To date, Schneider and her jazz orchestra have received nine Grammy nominations, resulting in two Grammy Awards—one for the recording *Concert in the Garden* (the first record to win a Grammy with internet-only sales), and the other for her composition *Cerulean Skies.* Two of her albums, *Concert in the Garden* and *Sky Blue,* were named Jazz Album of the Year by both the Jazz Journalists Association and *DownBeat* magazine Critics Poll.

To address the challenge of expenses required to produce an album of big-band music, Schneider collaborated with her friend and business partner Brian Camelio to develop the innovative ArtistShare Web site. ArtistShare is a brilliant, informal, and changing consortium of individuals who can directly commission, fund, and support a piece of an artist's work. In exchange for varying contributions, a patron receives access to the creative process, inside looks into rehearsals, extra information on the work, and honorable mention. Schneider has commissioned and recorded complete albums using ArtistShare to help pay her large big bands.

A life-changing event for Schneider came when she was confronted with breast cancer. Through that experience, she discovered that her true calling, her place of center and peace, was to compose. During our conversation, Schneider shares that journey in a particularly honest and personal manner.

Today, Schneider is broadening her compositional output, accepting commissions from the Saint Paul Chamber Orchestra to write a piece featuring the soprano Dawn Upshaw, and other crossover classical commissions. In addition to expanding her compositional output, the Maria Schneider Orchestra is an active guest at festivals and in famed clubs, and she receives invitations to lead workshop clinics around the world.

***

July 2009, at her home in New York City

JENNIFER KELLY: You describe your music as a time-orientated art. What do you mean by that?

MARIA SCHNEIDER: You have to carry someone's attention through time to have your work even be witnessed, to be taken in. A painting isn't like that. Architecture is not like that. Even a book and poetry, they deal with time in a different way. It's a sequence of things, but you're not really taking somebody through a fixed amount of time in the speed that you intend to. So my first interest in composing is, How do you grab somebody's attention? And in what manner do you grab somebody's attention? Do you entice them, seduce them, whisper? Do you scare them, shock them? Once you have them there, how do you take them through the piece? My feeling is that everything in the piece has to happen in an inevitable sense. You want people to feel that they trust in where you're going to take them. That means that you're going to surprise them in a way that makes them excited. They're going to want to find out how you're going to resolve the piece, because they trust that things will resolve somehow. I can't stand when I listen to music and I feel like the composer drops ideas or throws certain things in. At a certain point, I don't want to be vulnerable to it because I lose interest. Why am I going to put the effort in to take this journey when there's no conscious journey created? It's almost like someone was going to take you on a tour, and then you got there and found out they were winging it. They're saying, "Well, we could go here." And you're thinking, "I could do this on my own." That's what I mean by time-oriented art.

JK: It seems like you really want the audience to get something out of the music, have a good time, enjoy. Do you want them to come away with the same sort of feelings or inspirations that inspired you to compose the piece, or let them take it wherever they want to go?

MS: There's a very interesting book called *The Art Spirit,* by Robert Henri. He was an art teacher at the Ashcan School, a New York school of artists in the early 1900s. It's taken from his lectures, and everything is so analogous to music. What he talks about is that when an artist—I'm paraphrasing, but it's exactly how I feel—when you go into your inner place, where you're finding your music, the music is like a trace or a footprint of that place that you go to. I need time and attention and energy to get to that place—to not be distracted. Once you're inside that world, you actually feel expansive. Whatever you're creating becomes a trace of that experience. If you, with great care, try to create a sound representation of where you're going, then somebody else can take that in. They go to that place too, but in their own personal way. Because I really think that part of the reason it feels so good when you go there is that it's not lonely. It's a universal place. It's the spiritual ocean that we all go to and find ourselves, but we also find each other there. That's why music communicates so strongly to other people, because it's so universally personal. I have this piece called *The Pretty Road,* and it's very personal, very specific. But there was a girl in Brazil that said to me, "It reminds me of a road going into a place we have outside of Rio." Okay, first of all, Windom [Minnesota] and Rio could not be more opposite. And she wrote Portuguese words to the whole thing called "Estrada Bela," which means "pretty road." She totally related to the whole thing. And I think everybody does if they have a place to go back to that they love.

JK: Can you take me through your creative compositional process? What do you do first?

MS: I can't really take you through the process, but I can sort of tell you what I experience. I sit down, and I'm just trying to find something that I like.

JK: So you don't wait for a commission. You just say, "Okay, today I'm going to write."

MS: Yes. I mean, a commission helps. A deadline always helps! But just sitting down, sometimes it happens. For instance, I'm working on something now where the musical idea came to me when I was working in this disgusting laundry room in the basement of this building. I heard this tune, came up, played it, and wrote it down. But most often it comes from fooling around at the piano, and if I happen upon something, I say, "What would happen if I went here and there?" And just trying to find something that touches me. It's almost just like someone touching your body. You're looking for a place that hurts. You're looking for a place that feels good. I'm poking around for something. What I enjoy the most is when the idea, as I'm playing it, is carrying me. All of a sudden I find myself daydreaming about something that happened in my life which that musical thing conjures up. It's as if it wants to come out and be manifested. I think a lot of times it's an internal healing process for me. I think that I've used music. I think a lot of people use music, and they don't realize it. I realize it afterwards. It's sort of alchemy for me—

turning things that maybe weren't always so great into something really beautiful. I think of all the music I love now, if I think of what attracts me, it's all the music that is coming out of pretty deep human suffering that is channeled into beauty or, through alchemy, becomes beautiful. Blues music is like that. Flamenco music is like that. A lot of Brazilian music is like that. Cultures with a lot of hardship have been the source of a lot of very powerful music.

JK: Are you listening for something? When you listen to music that you enjoy, what is it that you listen for?

MS: Nothing specific; just something that moves me. But usually that thing is beautiful harmonic movement together with beautiful melody. How can you really appreciate a melody without knowing the harmony? Even the most unmusically conscious person, when they sing a melody, they are imagining all the harmony in their head. To me, harmony is so important because it can make or break a melody. And that's probably the most important thing. Some people say, "Well, rhythm is the most important." All of the elements work together. It's just like in a relationship with a person, you can't say, "Well, my relationship is great because we laugh." Well, it's great that you laugh, but. . . . It's all these different aspects that make up a beautiful relationship. It's humor, it's a common sort of spirituality, it's respect, and it's intellectual connection. And then somehow, how you communicate and pass through all these different things you just can't separate out. You can't separate out music like that. So I will tell you this: music has to move me. I'm not looking to be impressed. I don't listen to music and analyze it. I get really tired of jazz in a big hurry because in jazz, people are feeling pressure to do more or be something different, and their idea of being something different is more complex rhythm, more complex harmony, more notes, faster speeds, more people playing at once, or longer solos. Everything becomes more, more, more, but it's really less, less, less. There are people who can do that and have a lot to say, but most people don't have anything to say, because going over that is "noodling," so it's like the same old format, and it's just chattering at you. I get really frustrated with that. And in the classical world, too: so much music is trying to impress you by being more modern and more complex. I just want someone to come up with a beautiful melody that's sung in a heartfelt way—a sophisticated harmony that can be simple, but touch me, make me feel something. Otherwise, what is the point?

JK: I love listening to the way that you craft the harmonic structure behind a soloist. You must take a long time with that.

MS: I do. The solos are really hard, because for a lot of my music, the soloist is not playing over what the opening material was. Generally, I'm not writing in traditional song form. Sometimes I write solo sections that continue the harmonic development of the piece. They're carrying the piece to some other place, and it's very hard to know, to compose that, when the biggest element of that isn't composed yet. There's a big unknown factor, and that's what the soloist is going to play. And trying to figure out what's the proper length of time and how is the rhythm section going to build this. And it's one thing if you write it open, like it's a section that repeats and is going to build. It's another thing if I'm tailoring it. I hand sew every chord and note and orchestration. Nothing repeats, and that's why it's so hard to play. That's the type of architecture I like. [Antoni] Gaudi—where the whole building feels like a body that's breathing. It's not just a box that they built on the street.

JK: What role does improvisation play in your music?

MS: I always felt it strongly, but I felt it even stronger recently when I did my first piece that wasn't jazz—my first classical orchestra piece. I did a piece for Saint Paul Chamber Orchestra with Dawn Upshaw. She's amazing, and I'm going to do another thing for her. I told her I want to include some kind of improvisation, finding ways in which her part can breathe depending on who's playing with her and what they're doing. We played the first piece for three nights, and I conducted, which was a little scary. We'd finish at the end of the night, and yeah, that was good, but I felt lonely as the composer and the conductor because, although they enjoyed it, it almost felt like they were trying to play the music well for me.

JK: But you don't feel that way when you conduct a band?

MS: Never with my band. After a performance, everybody's talking about each other's performance and discussing what amazing things happened that never happened before. I can see everybody enjoying it. Somebody will be playing, and I watch the faces in the band and see them appreciating what the other is playing. So I feel like I'm the host of the party, and I've invited the right people to the right place with great food and great music, and I can just watch everybody have an amazing time and enjoy each other. It's like my music is going out there, and it's not quite finished; it's not quite complete. It needs them to breathe life into it and have personality, and each of them is going to put something in that I'm not capable of, so I leave it kind of vulnerable, and it becomes more than me through these incredible players. I think if classical composers got to experience what I experience conducting their orchestra, they would cry. I'm a people person, so I love connecting with people, and I love the intimacy—so my music is creative intimacy. To leave your music vulnerable, that's what I love.

JK: You said that it was scary when you were conducting the orchestra—not the band but the orchestra. How was that experience compared to what the band gives back to you? How was that different?

MS: First of all, it's the sensation. Okay, conducting the orchestra is different because there's no rhythm section and the sensibility of time is different. With my band, if I give a downbeat, they are right there. The orchestra is behind, and I was constantly fighting that. And then somebody pointed out to me that what I was doing to try to get them to be with me is actually working against me. So what's not instinctive to me I had to learn to do. They just react differently, and they needed everything conducted exactly the same every single time. With my band, I'm a little conscious that I don't always want to be the same. I probably do things the same but try to just feel what's in the moment and look for what will be able to make it a little different from night to night for my own part.

JK: How did you end up choosing the big band as the medium to write for?

MS: Oh, it's more like it chose me. Because in college I started out as a theory major, and then I added composition to it. The classical-composition thing really wore thin on me. Back then, if your music wasn't super atonal, serial, or whatever, it was just considered completely useless. And I loved tonality. Luckily, a composition teacher heard that I was really into jazz and said, "Why don't you go listen to the big band rehearse?"

JK: At the college?

MS: Yes, and they didn't even have a jazz program. He said, "You should write for them." So I did. I started watching the rehearsals, and a student in the group gave me some lessons, and I just started studying on my own. I got books and scores and just started doing it. And then I decided to go on to graduate school, and what did they have there? Big bands. So I wrote for big bands. Later, I moved to New York and wrote something for the Mel Lewis big band. By that time, I had kind of amassed a certain amount of music. So when we started the band, my boyfriend—who became my husband, John Fedchock—he had been in the Woody Herman Band. So we just started another big band out of practicality, but I have to say, there were a lot of times that I was wishing my band had something, a different kind of instrumentation. But then, by that point, the band had started playing, and people started hearing it in Europe and invited me to play with their big bands, so I got so molded in the cement of instrumentation because of the practicality. What's funny is, everybody was saying to me, "You're doing the most impractical thing. You'll never make a living doing big-band music." But actually there are big bands all over the planet. I am doing the big-band instrumentation because it is something where I can make a living. If I had a really odd instrumentation and everybody had to put together a unique group for it, I wouldn't work nearly as much. So, like any limitation, they can be your greatest creative resource. So I think my whole way of orchestration has been in search of stretching the big band to not sound like a big band.

JK: You've added the accordion. How did you come up with that?

MS: The first time it occurred to me that I would love to write for accordion was when I was working in Slovenia. There was an alto sax player in this group of violin, accordion, alto, and bass. It was really beautiful. And then I was writing this piece called *Concert in the Garden,* and it needed something. We were rehearsing in a room at Hunter College with an organ, and I started playing the melody on a break, asking out loud, "Why can't it sound like that?" Ingrid Jensen was eating her lunch not far from me and said, "Man, you should call Gary. That sounds like accordion." Gary Versace came over and showed me things about the accordion, and I've used it ever since. It really gives a different color to the band. And an accordion can play a long time up high, softly, purely, forever and ever. So it just gives a top end to the orchestra that is very delicate and beautiful.

JK: Since you like the different color palettes, did you enjoy the process of writing for another orchestra, like Saint Paul, with different colors?

MS: Yes. It's funny, because I thought the composition of that piece would be the hard part and the orchestration would be the easy part. It turned out that the composition came more easily; there was something liberating about having words. The words that I had were amazing. I picked this poetry that was phenomenal. It was English translations of Brazilian poetry by Carlos Drummond de Andrade. The words pulled the music out of me. It gave me the rhythm and the sentiment—everything. Then it came time to orchestrate, and I was just terrified, because it was such a different animal from what I'd been dealing with. So I put together a rehearsal in New York. First I had a string quartet play the string parts to figure out bowings and the lines and make sure everything works. Then we put together basically the whole orchestra and gave it a dry run. And so I could go and fix everything that I was misjudging. I always have rehearsals and revise.

JK: What's the name of the piece?

MS: It's called *Carlos Drummond de Andrade's Stories,* because the poems are like little stories. It was fun to have the drama element off of me. I could get into somebody else's dramatic landscape through the poetry, adding my perspective to it. It's one of my favorite things of mine that I've written. I'm so hard on myself when I'm writing, but if I create something in the end I love, I say it. If I say something sucks, it's because I really think it sucks, and if I like something, I'm very willing to say it's good.

JK: Do you give yourself permission to throw music away?

MS: Oh, yes. I wrote a particular piece once that is not going to see the light of day again [*laughs*]. Next week, we're going to do new commissions through ArtistShare on my Web site.

JK: Tell me about ArtistShare.

MS: It's just been the greatest thing for me, artistically and business-wise. Brian Camelio is a really good friend of mine. I was doing my records through the usual record company like almost everybody did, and the records were getting more and more expensive. And I wasn't getting my money back. The first record I made for thirty thousand dollars, and they bought it for ten thousand. And even though I was selling twenty thousand records, I didn't make my full twenty thousand dollars back. It seems you should make your money back, right?

JK: I would hope so.

MS: The second record they paid for. But I never made any more, even though it sold well. The third record was getting too expensive, and they said they couldn't budget it. I'm not going to make a record and cut the quality, so I put in a third of it in exchange for a third of the royalties. Well, the statement came, and I saw that I was in recoupment. I wasn't getting my money simultaneously to them, even though I had sold the first ten thousand. Then I started investigating. And what I realized is that the record company isn't making that much money, and they don't begin paying royalties until much later. So Brian and I got to talking. At the same time, all this stuff was in the news about how file sharing was destroying the music business. One day Brian said to me, "What's the one thing that nobody can file share?" And he came up with this idea to start this Web-based thing where I would share the whole creative process with fans in front of making the record. And then people would come on board and preorder and witness the process through the site, and we'd have people at different levels of participation. There's no longer a distributor and record store. Now, the second half of that is that if the record doesn't do well, I'm taking the hit. So it puts the pressure on. My last record was $170,000. I was taking out some loans to do that. I got a lot of the money up front, but not all of it. But I managed to pay for it, and now I'm able to make much of my living through that site. It's amazing.

JK: So having your creative process so open for anybody who's willing to support it to see, has that affected your writing?

MS: Well, it's a little scary to do it. But I did do it. And I sort of like it. I like the idea that if somebody commissions me, that's just the kick in the butt I need. Just knowing that this person is waiting makes me want to create something really beautiful, so that, when they hear it, they say, "Oh my god, I commissioned that." And if it's a piece that I play and then I decide I don't like it and we're not going to perform it, I'll do another one and make sure they get something that I am happy with and proud to play. I respond really well to trying to make everyone happy. It's one of my faults in my life, but it's a great motivator for me, because it's my nature. So if I put that pressure on myself that people bought this thing up front and people have expectations, I hate it, but I thrive under that situation. Isn't that crazy?

JK: I think it's important for people to realize it's not just easy. I think it helps with the appreciation of the process.

MS: I think it's important, too. When I teach, I'm like that. I often have students come up to me crying. Almost every clinic, I have somebody come up to me crying, saying, "I feel so relieved right now." And I know a lot of musicians that will go into a clinic, and they want to give everybody the impression that they just pee music, you know? And it's just a lie almost every time. And I think it's unfair to give people that impression. As if to say, "I have some golden thing that you don't have." I think most people have a difficult time. Not always, but most everybody goes through their periods of insecurities.

JK: Well, now you've already been vetted with players and audiences and critics. Do you still have the occasional "freakout moment"?

MS: Oh, I always freak out. Yeah, the "freakout moment" is when I'm writing. Oh yeah.

JK: How do you get past it?

MS: I just have to get in and get in that place. It's like stepping into ice-cold water. You step in, and then all of a sudden it feels good. But it's so painful when you first get in. I've had visualizations of walking by that chair [where I compose] and kind of walking around it and not even wanting to get near it because it's just scary. And it's weird that it's scary, because it also is my biggest place of comfort. I can tell you a story about that. I had a real turnaround for myself, because sometimes I wondered if I was a real composer or if I was somebody who just worked hard. And I've always had this crisis when I have commissions. "I can't write. I'm not good enough." So I had this big commission for Lincoln Center a few years back, with the premiere at the end of January. It was getting towards the end of December, and I was really distracted because I had found a lump on my breast. And my best friend was dying of breast cancer at the same time. My first rehearsal was going to be on January 17, and on January 3, I found out I had breast cancer. I had huge amounts of music I hadn't written. And I was terrified to write this piece anyway. So I suddenly felt like, "Well, I have a good excuse not to do this." I was so freaked out over the whole breast-cancer thing because I saw nothing but black with that disease. And I was such a wreck—my fingers—I felt like I had pins in my fingers. My stress level was so high that my fingers were tingling constantly. I just felt like I was plugged into a wall with electricity, and I just couldn't stop it. So one night I said to myself, "Okay, I'm just going to call the [Wynton] Marsalis people and tell them I'm bailing, and I'll play, but I can't write this piece, and they can have the money back. I don't care. I'll do a concert, but I just can't do this. They're going to have to understand." And it was weird. Once I gave myself permission to not do it, I sat down and was looking at my sketches, and I started playing what I had been writing. All of a sudden, I just started getting into it. And I had this visualization of myself being a submarine that was on the surface of the water, and the water was tossing me around, and all of a sudden I got in the music, and I went down, and I could see the funeral. I could see the dying. I could *see* all the worst-case scenarios, but I wasn't *feeling* them, so I felt safe. When I was writing, I was in this area where I couldn't be touched. I wasn't stressed. I was in a place I could deal, a place separate from myself. And the music just started coming. The tingling in my fingers stopped. And I realized then that the only way I'm going to be able to deal with this is through writing this piece. So I just told my friends that I didn't want to talk on the phone, I just had to write, and trust me, it's the best thing for me now. I had until my scheduled surgery, a lumpectomy, on the fourteenth. So, I got the piece to the copyist the night of the thirteenth, did the surgery the next day, and three days later was in a lot of pain, but went to that rehearsal and rehearsed it, and we did the piece. I wrote what I think is one of my strongest works. It is on *Concert in the Garden,* the last piece, called *Bulería, Soleá y Rumba.*

JK: Did they ever know?

MS: The band? Oh, yes. Everybody in the band knew. But what I discovered through it was that I am a composer. I realized that I am a composer because the place that I have to go to get the music is my center. That was the most pure and calm place for me. And talking to you earlier, when I was talking about the trace, the footprint that music and art leaves, I'm not a religious person, but I am a person who thinks a lot about the spiritual realm. My feeling after that experience was that the creative place is sort of the center. To me, it's sort of the God kind of place where we're all kind of one. And that's why music speaks so powerfully, because you're touching that, and the trace that you have is not just your life but also something that we all recognize as being our source. I think it changed my music a lot. After that, I cared a lot less about whether my music was impressive.

JK: How are you now?

MS: I'm fine. I found a Chinese doctor, and I do everything holistically now. I'm really lucky. But I also—I made those two records, *Concert in the Garden* and *Sky Blue.* I did my strongest work in that period. My Chinese doctor is a Taoist priest, too. I gave him my CD. I thought he might like to listen to it, and he said, "This is like your immortality, right?" And I think I did see it that way. It was like, I have to put as much out there because I don't know if something could happen. When I would write, I used to think, if somebody told me I was going to die, I would be relieved because I just wouldn't have this pressure on me anymore. And then suddenly, when I found out I had something that could make me die, I was like, I want to write more music! It's this desperation. I told myself I would never forget this lesson, but I do forget it at times. Why should I be avoiding writing? Maria, don't you remember that that's your gift?

JK: That's quite a catharsis, going through all that and coming out the other side. And yet still being so young. You have so many years left of music.

MS: Yeah, hopefully. My friend with cancer, she died. I wrote *Sky Blue* for her.

JK: It's a beautiful piece.

MS: Thanks. She was a beautiful person.

JK: So, given all that you went through and where you are now, and you're no longer thinking, "I'm going to impress everybody," where would you like your music to go?

MS: I go through a hard time every time I finish a record. It's like a field and farming—this idea of changing the crops and then having a couple years of grazing with the manure and letting it just kind of refill. I guess I'm grazing and shitting right now [*laughs*]. I don't know what's next. I get so scared that there's nothing next, that maybe I wrote my greatest thing and I can't get past it. I think it's what I go, through, because I've been really lucky with my music critically. I've had very few bad reviews, except for this one guy who wrote a blog that was just frightening. It was in Montreal. This guy came to the gig and was talking about how my hair was "steely," my body was stiff, and he looked into the audience and there were all these women with "steely" blonde hair dressed like me, and he was so repulsed, and the band "schlumped" across the stage. It was the most sexist, racist, appalling, slandering, monstrously sick thing I have ever read in my life. I really haven't had anybody say anything bad, but boy, when they do, they really go at it.

JK: From my perspective, you're not done yet, and I don't think you've done your best work yet.

MS: I hope not. When I did the piece for Dawn Upshaw, I was originally so scared of it. I heard that and thought there is so much more I can do. It just started. My biggest fault is my fear and wasting time being scared or coming up with an idea and spending two weeks playing it, going, "Is that any good?" And then in the end, I end up using it. How much music would I have written if I just didn't worry about whether it was good and just move on? Just do it.

JK: That's very powerful. And the fact that you're aware of it is also pretty huge.

MS: Yeah, I guess. I did a thing on my Web site, all my procrastination techniques when I was working on *Cerulean Skies*. That was the piece that won a Grammy for Best Instrumental Composition. I was a wreck writing that thing. We did pictures of me cleaning the toilet [*laughs*]. I organized my underwear drawer. I never ever do that unless I'm supposed to be writing. Suddenly, pedicures become very important.

JK: You have a great sense of humor and not taking yourself so seriously. I want to change gears if I could. I know that you don't like to deal with the gender issue, and I respect that. I also remember you saying that the time you are most aware of gender is when people keep asking you about it.

MS: Right. Because I don't think of it on my own.

JK: I hear you. But when I was doing this research, I read an article from the 1990s in *Time Out* magazine which said that the photographer originally asked to photograph you in the bathtub. To which you replied, "Would you photograph Copland in the bathtub?" Then the article went on to talk about your eyes.

MS: Did you see the picture they used? They were doing all these pictures, and then my phone rang, and they were all talking, and I was lying on the bed talking on my phone in the other room. And I put my head back, and they took a picture of me on my bed with the phone in my hand.

JK: Okay, so as a woman in music myself, that would have affected me. How was that for you?

MS: I have to say, the guy in Montreal finally got to me. And I felt really angry at him about it. Because I felt like, "Wait a minute, I've enjoyed my naiveté for so long. Don't you take that away from me." But then I realized that this guy is sick. So, luckily, my core has never been from a place of weakness. I mean, I do have some ideas about gender. I think I was lucky that my first piano teacher was a woman. She was extraordinary. She was a classical and jazz pianist from Chicago.

JK: So you had a woman introduce you to jazz?

MS: Yeah, and she was an amazing woman. And there were also very good artists in the [Windom] community. My sister Kate was an artist, and her mentor was a woman. The theater director in my school was a woman, and she was very good, and my other sister became an actress for quite a few years, largely inspired by her. So even though the records I had were Vladimir Horowitz and Rubenstein, and all the composers were men, my practical experience in the world of the people that I connected with in the arts, and that were very confident and with no apologies, they were women. At the same time, my father. . . . There were three girls in my family. I was the third. My father was a very "masculine" man—hunter, fisherman. So at age eight I shot my first duck. I was constantly out hunting with my dad and all these men. And I was in this world of men, and I was really comfortable. And they really were very respectful to me. It wasn't like, "Oh, little Pinkie. She's weak." No, man, it was, "Get the dogs and shoot that gun" [*laughs*]. So I took in the world in a different way. I was kind of protected, in a way. At the same time, I think the biggest challenge in being a woman is with the nature of being a woman and the messages that we're given.

JK: From society?

MS: From society. Because I see myself with my friends. My best friend has two kids, a little boy and a little girl. I find myself looking at Charlotte and saying,

"Oh, that's so cute! I love those little shorts you have on and that little top." To the little boy I'll say, "Oh, Evan, what are you making? Oh, that's so cool, I love what you're building!" I would never say to Evan, "Oh, I love your little shorts," or, "What a cute little top." It's all about what he's creating. Society teaches us that. I know what it is to feel the pressure of feeling I'm not valued by society unless I look pretty, unless my hair is nice, unless I have my make-up right or my figure is nice. And this guy in Montreal finally admitted it, because he got so lambasted in the comments for his blog.

JK: I'm glad he read the reactions.

MS: Oh, yes. He finally said, "I'm not a musician. I just decided to go to this concert on a whim. This isn't really a review." So clearly, in the world out there, you would never, and that's what a lot of people wrote in, you would never say how Ethan Iverson is dressed or how Ron Carter dressed. So I know both sides, and I struggle, and I think it's a big distraction for women, this whole thing that it's important how you look. I think that's actually what holds a lot of women up at a young age. That's what I see as being a big gender problem.

JK: I think it's fascinating what you're talking about, because I'm a conductor, and people do ask, "What are you going to wear on stage?" I don't want it to be important, but at the same time, I like being a woman. I don't try to hide my curly hair or my figure.

MS: You can't separate the fact that you're a conductor from the fact that you're a woman. Women are beautiful. So why not try to look beautiful and do your work and be smart? I mean, that's my attitude. I'm not going to dress down or anything. I like looking pretty if I can. God knows, you know, maybe I only have a few years left of it [*laughs*]. So I've got to use what I have. I love to see a woman conduct.

JK: Do you think that translates into music? I remember reading that you were nervous about something, and [the trombonist] Bob Brookmeyer said, "You know what? What's beautiful about you is that you're you. And you're a woman, and the femininity is going to be there." Do you think that's true?

MS: Yes, it is. I think in the beginning, if you listen to my early music, I was much more aggressive, and I think I was really trying to prove my power, that I had power. I think my music has become much more willing to be . . . pretty. Just, like, stereotypically pretty. Well, that's what I hear these days. What can I say? And I don't feel apologetic for it. And I don't feel like I have to prove that I can write muscle. Because I can write muscle, and I just don't want to. Not now. It's not my thing. It might be in a week. So I think Bob helped me that way a little bit to realize that it's not a liability. It's actually something different. It's such a wonderful perspective.

JK: There's so much emotion in your music, so much movement. I listen to it, and I feel like I'm lifted constantly.

MS: That's good, because I like the idea of music lifting or feeling like you're flying or dropping.

JK: Did you ever study dance?

MS: Yes, I did when I was young. And I figure skated. And my father was a pilot, and he flew. His plane was right behind our house. I loved being in the air. I still do my best thinking in the air, looking out of a plane window. I feel like I'm outside of myself and the world when I'm flying. So I think I like my music to feel like that.

JK: Another aspect of your music that I notice is your use of color. How do you relate to color?

MS: Well, more than color, I think I relate to it more in texture. Sculpture. Like ephemeral sculpture. The colors I see more as materials, like bright colors are a Harmon mute or something metallic, literally metallic, and other lighter textures are more gauzy. I think of my pieces more like ephemeral sound sculptures.

JK: Are you comfortable with the label "jazz composer"?

MS: I am, I suppose, because it's the best way to describe what I do. Non-jazz musicians could never play music for my band, so therefore it's jazz. But I think that the boundaries between jazz and classical and things like Brazilian and flamenco, it's just getting more and more blended. The piece that I wrote for Saint Paul [Chamber Orchestra] sounds very much like me. I thought, I'm just going to try to figure out what my language is and find the way that I can build my rhythm into the writing and in the orchestra. And I don't know if somebody would listen to that and say it sounds like jazz. I don't know what they would say. The orchestra told me it was something very unique and different from anything they've done.

JK: When did you first think there was a possibility of fronting your own band, playing your music?

MS: When I was at the University of Minnesota, and I was just starting to write for big bands, Toshiko Akiyoshi came through with her L.A. band. They played at Orchestra Hall in Minneapolis, which is mostly a classical venue, and I saw her conducting. She's fun to watch conducting. I thought she was amazing, and the music was so expressive, and it was definitely concert music. And I remember thinking, Wow, maybe I can do that. And it wasn't that she was a woman. It was jazz being played in a concert hall. It made me realize that there was a possibility. It was the first time I saw anybody doing that—fronting a band, conducting their music, playing a concert hall. I asked the guy I was studying with, "Do you think I could do that?" And my confidence was so low that if he had said to me, "Not really. I don't think you started early enough." I would have been like, "Yeah, you're probably right." But instead he said, "Yeah, sure. Why not?"

JK: I hope he knows that. As a teacher myself, I hope that he knows that what he said was the right thing in that moment, and look at you now. That's fabulous.

MS: I'll have to tell him. I don't know if I ever told him that.

***

Works by Maria Schneider

Unless otherwise noted, works are available through MSF Music, on Maria Schneider's Web site (www.mariaschneider.com), sponsored by ArtistShare.

COMPOSITIONS FOR BIG BAND/JAZZ ORCHESTRA

Aires de Lando, add accordion and cajons, and featuring clarinet (2006).
Allegresse, add optional percussion, featuring trumpet and tenor sax (2000).
Anthem, add solo valve trombone (2002).
Bird Count, blues (Kendor Studio Writers Series, 2006).
Bulería, Soleá y Rumba, add cajons and rumbas, featuring tenor sax, flugelhorn, and voice (2004).
Cerulean Skies, add voice, featuring accordion and sax (2006).
City Sunrise, featuring trumpet (Kendor Konvertibles, 2004).
Concert in the Garden, add voice, featuring piano and accordion (2004)
Coot Stew, featuring piano, baritone sax, and muted trumpet (1990).
Dance You Monster to My Soft Song, featuring guitar and trumpet (1994).
Dissolution, featuring soprano sax (2000).
El Viento, featuring guitar, trombone, and trumpet (1994).
Evanescence, featuring tenor and trumpet (1994).
Green Piece, featuring tenor sax and piano (1994).
Gumba Blue (1994).
Gush, featuring soprano sax (1994).
Hang Gliding, optional percussion, featuring flugelhorn and tenor sax (2000).
In a Pinch, featuring tenor sax and trumpet (Kendor Studio Writers Series, 1991).
Journey Home, add cajon, featuring alto sax and trombone or guitar (2000).
Last Season, featuring flugelhorn and soprano sax (1994).
Lately, featuring trombone and piano or bass (1987).
Lembrança (2010).
Mountain Aire (1992).
My Lament, featuring tenor sax (optional vocal arrangement by Paris Rutherford/lyrics by David Castle), (1994).
Nimbus, add accordion, featuring alto sax (2010).

Nocturne, optional piccolo and trumpets, featuring piano (2000).
Out of the Hush, collaboration with David Castle (2007).
Prairie Dance, featuring alto sax (1989).
The "Pretty" Road, add accordion and voice, featuring trumpets and electronics (2006).
Recapitulation (2004).
Rich's Piece, featuring tenor sax (2007).
Salina, featuring trumpet (Kendor Konvertibles, 2008).
Samba Solstice (1988).
Scenes from Childhood (1995).
  Bombshelter Beast, featuring baritone sax and guitar
  Coming About, optional percussion, featuring piano and sax
  Night Watchmen, featuring flugelhorn and tenor sax
Sea of Tranquility, featuring baritone sax (2000).
Sky Blue, featuring soprano sax (2004).
Smooth Talk, featuring tenor sax (Kendor Archive Editions, 1989).
Some Circles, featuring tenor sax (1994).
Swing Street, featuring tenor sax and piano (1990).
This 'n' That, featuring alto sax and muted trumpet (1991).
Thompson Fields, add accordion, featuring guitar and piano (2010).
Three Romances, suite for big band (2004).
  Choro Dançado, add percussion
  Dança Ilusória, featuring piano and trombone
  Pas de Deux, featuring soprano sax and flugelhorn
Tork's Café, featuring tenor sax and trombone (2001).
Waltz for Toots, featuring bass and soprano sax (1995).
Waxwing, featuring flugelhorn (1993).
The Willow, featuring baritone sax (1989).
Willow Lake (2000).
Wyrgly, featuring tenor sax, trombone, and guitar (1994).

CHAMBER MUSIC

Carlos Drummond de Andrade Stories, for soprano and chamber orchestra (2008).
Finding Flight, for studio orchestra (2004).
String Quartet No. 1 (2010).
Tranquilidade, for studio orchestra (2004).
Winter Morning Walks, soprano, chamber orchestra, and rhythm section; lyrics by Ted Kooser (2011).
  Perfectly Still This Solstice Morning
  I Saw a Dust Devil This Morning
  All Night, in Gusty Winds
  How Important It Must Be
  My Wife and I Walk the Cold Road
  Our Finch Feeder

Spring, the Sky Rippled with Geese
Walking by Flashlight
When I Switched On a Light

COMPOSITIONS FOR JAZZ COMBO/SONGS

"Alchemy," lyrics by Nora York
"Among the Clouds"
"The Blasphemy," lyrics by Nora York
"Cry to the Stars," lyric version of "My Lament," lyrics by David Castle
"Divided by Two," for brass, rhythm section, and sax
"Free Fall"
"The Grail," lyrics by Nora York
"The Green Song," lyrics by David Castle
"Now and Then"
"Only Toots," lyrics by David Castle
"Returning"
"Song for a Willow," lyric version of "The Willow," lyrics by David Castle
"Two Becoming One"

Young Lee

15

Augusta Read Thomas

The composer and professor Augusta Read Thomas treats her scores with a meticulous hand. When composing, she is always thinking about the conductors and performers who will interpret them. Thomas is drawn to the details of notation, explaining, "My scores are highly nuanced, certainly detailed, every note having a dynamic, articulation and/or adjective. The notation explains exactly what I heard." Unlike composers such as Alice Parker or even Gabriela Lena Frank, Thomas believes that all the information one needs is provided in the score, and she prides herself on crafting such a detailed score that few questions are left unanswered.

Thomas's catalog includes music for varied ensembles, although she emphasizes orchestral composition. Championed early in her career by the Chicago Symphony Orchestra as composer-in-residence from 1997–2006, she has numerous large orchestral works to her name. Certainly able to compose for any level of ensemble, Thomas is like Shulamit Ran in the sense that her music tends to be self-selected by more technically proficient musicians. She admires the young students emerging from conservatories with the technique to play any repertoire, and she cuts, crafts, and constantly reedits to create a composition perfectly suited for those technically proficient players. Thomas's concern for specific detail does not negate her acceptance of varied interpretations. During our conversation, she recounts an experience she had in the audience during the premiere of one of her works when the tempo was slowed beyond her initial level of comfort. Eventually, the conductor's choice taught Thomas something new about her own composition.

Thomas believes in the power of listening to understand a composer's output, compositional choice, and musical development. A self-proclaimed "voracious listener," she extends this importance of listening to all aspects of her career: she includes large listening assignments in her teaching; she listens extensively to a commissioning body's representative recordings; and she laments past concerts where no lasting record exists. Sharing Hilary Tann's desire to be present for all recordings, Thomas points out, "If recordings do not exist, there is much less work. . . . Composers depend heavily on past recordings to be offered future employment."

Born in 1964, Thomas has composed actively since her twenties and is already thinking about the legacy of her music and the legacy of compositional art. Composing in the large forms approximately every ten years, she wants to leave a developing chronicle of her compositional voice. She appreciates the need for an audience to hear more than a single work of a composer to gain any real insight into her or his work, and she supports festivals of just one or a few composers, exposing an audience to their depth and breadth. Thomas has consistently volunteered her time to serve on artistic organizational boards and to program festival concerts as an advocate for "musical excellence," expressing great hope for the future of her profession. Although her compositional style contrasts starkly with that of composers such as Alice Parker, Maria Schneider, or Tann, they all share a desire to leave a recorded output and involve themselves directly in recording their works.

Currently a professor of composition at the University of Chicago, Thomas has also taught at Eastman and Northwestern. In addition to her longtime residency with the Chicago Symphony Orchestra under the direction of Daniel Barenboim, she was also the Music Alive composer-in-residence with the New Haven

Symphony 2009–11, as part of the national residency program for the League of American Orchestras and Meet the Composer. Her works have been commissioned and performed by a number of high-profile orchestras and ensembles around the United States and in Europe. She curated the Festival of Contemporary Music at Tanglewood in 2009 and founded and curated the Music Now Series at the Chicago Symphony during her residency. The recipient of numerous awards and accolades, she was inducted into the American Academy of Arts and Letters in 2007, and her work *Astral Canticle* was one of two finalists for the Pulitzer Prize in Music in 2007. Her works are published through G. Schirmer.

***

June 2010, at her former home in Becket, Massachusetts

JENNIFER KELLY: Being so busy, how do you balance the work and nonwork parts of your life?

AUGUSTA READ THOMAS: They're the same. I can't separate my life from my life. It's all the identical integrated, holistic existence.

JK: You must love what you do.

ART: I do. It's fun! It's hard—very hard. But, for instance, if we have family coming for a picnic, I'm not going to be at the piano. I'm going to be laughing, cooking, and eating. That could seem like I'm outside of or away from the music, but I'm not. I'm going to be thinking about music, carrying it in my ears.

JK: Your husband [Bernard Rands] is also a well-respected composer. Do the two of you have a sense of competition among composers?

ART: I don't feel competitive with anybody in the world.

JK: That's a nice place to be. Have you always felt that way?

ART: Well, I'm competitive with myself. Like all artists, I want to improve and make my pieces better—more refined, more elegant, more nuanced. To satisfy my own ears is demanding enough. I don't think the arts are competitive in the purest sense. Monteverdi was fabulous, Mahler was spectacular, Ella Fitzgerald was a genius. They're all A+ superstars, none of whom does anything similar to another. History has shown us that there are a lot of brilliant ways to make and shape sounds. Vision, craft, and excellence are key. Both Bernard and I want to create elegant pieces while hoping to be in good health with physical strength to compose.

JK: When you sit on the boards, judge a competition, or program festivals—when you look at new music—how do you choose what is programmed?

ART: There's a side of me that's a twenty-first-century musicologist because I listen to lots of current music and tend to know about what's being written. James

Levine asked me to curate the Festival of Contemporary Music at Tanglewood for the summer of 2009; I founded and curated for nine years the Music Now Series at the Chicago Symphony. I listen daily, always seeking excellence, asking: Is the piece superlative on its *own* terms? The sounds could be of any style, syntax, language, duration, or genre. I ask myself: Is it excellent at what *it* set out to achieve and mean? I like to put great music on concert menus where diverse compositions start talking to one another such that there are far-reaching, interesting shifts from voice to voice. Concert programs should be like wonderful, delightfully arranged menus. In the process of looking for excellent compositions, often one will find a score with a magnificent opening section, but then it falls short of itself; or another score that worked up into something superior, but it took forever to get there; or a score where the ending didn't work, or was way too long for its ideas, or was far too compressed, or didn't breathe musically. Then you come across a composition with stunning proportions, beautiful harmony, gorgeous notes, extremely creative hearing and thinking, plus a striking individual voice. A blockbuster! You know it when you hear it! Additionally, if we're going to do a deep listen into the works of a composer, we've got to really listen not just to one piece. Any serious composer, when being reviewed, deserves to have ten pieces heard. We need to hear different genres as well as different eras from that composer. When we listen to Mahler, Stravinsky, Bach, or Mozart, we listen across their lives and genres. Too often with contemporary composers, an audience member will, sadly, hear only one short piece.

JK: When you are creating those menus for the programs, is there a sense of responsibility of being a programmer to be egalitarian about it? To make sure that certain new composers are represented, living composers, women composers, and other underrepresented composers? Is that part of the decision process?

ART: My first criterion is excellence, second is diversity of sounds (appetizing menus), and third is egalitarian balance.

JK: You were saying that when an audience hears a piece by a living composer, that may be the only chance that they get to hear not only that piece but also that composer.

ART: Right. A person might hear one piece, and then five years later they'll hear another piece by the same composer, but they can't remember the first one! Three years later they'll hear another piece, but alas, it's hard to string those memories all together in one's inner ear. Among the things composers enjoy are residencies when people invite us to visit, and they perform many of our compositions on a "portrait" concert at which there's a body of work being shared—it's alive, it's out there, being played, breathing, evolving.

JK: As a living composer, do you compose with the thought that this piece may be the only time an audience member hears you?

ART: No. When I'm composing I'm just humbly seeking beautiful, integral sounds for my ears. I'm the first and most analytical, questioning, deeply listening audience member.

JK: Some people consciously want to make sure it's accessible to the audience member.

ART: There are a lot of things in life that contain mystery, such as religion, death, nature, the stars, the cosmos, trees, poetry. . . . Likewise, music can be mysterious and does not need to be instantly accessible. If a composer has a voice and is writing music which has a richness about it (if it isn't just "surfacey" but rather truly has some nourishing protein in it), such as Bach, Mahler, Debussy, or Stravinsky, and so forth, then there exists a genuine artistic fortitude. All great composers' works require multiple hearings; that's why we keep coming back to their music for centuries. The music is lavish, life-affirming, and teaches deeply about the universe—thus we revisit it and crave it often. No problem if someone says, "Gusty, I think I liked your premiere. It was sparkling, colorful, and I loved the rhythms but . . . I don't understand it all. . . ." That's okay! Hopefully, they can hear it again someday, because fertile music has to withstand multiple hearings. Some music is instantly accessible, but alas, the second time we hear it it's over quickly if in fact there's no meaningful, personal, imaginatively nourishing, original content.

JK: How do you know when a piece of yours is making an impact?

ART: One of the things that was characteristic of my career—I hate that word, *career*; my *life*—is that I wrote a piece, somebody heard it, and they commissioned another piece. Then somebody heard those two scores and commissioned a third work, perhaps even as much as twenty-five years later. My life evolves as people are playing the music, hearing the music, and then commissioning another composition. I feel blessed indeed.

JK: Your catalog is quite diverse. Is that part of what keeps the curiosity alive?

ART: It is. Every composition is a new adventure. If anyone listened to the one hundred pieces published by G. Schirmer, it would be obvious that they're all tailor-made, vivid journeys. For *Absolute Ocean,* I listened to fifteen recordings of the soprano for months before I wrote it. Composing for a wide variety of genres and custom-making distinct pieces is my deep-rooted passion.

JK: That leads me to ask, what would be your ideal relationship between you and a performer or conductor of your pieces? Are you very hands-on and want to be there, or do you give your piece and then back off?

ART: I can go either way—I am very flexible. I try hard to be sensitive to how they wish to collaborate. My scores are highly nuanced, certainly detailed, every note having a dynamic, articulation, and/or adjective. The notation explains exactly what I heard, and players are often saying, "These are the most articulate scores. I have no questions. Thank you." I kind of pride myself a tiny bit on such comments from virtuosic musicians. To give you an example, if I were rehearsing with a musician, I might say, "This should be majestic, or play here with a lightness of touch. . . ." So why not write that down on the manuscript? I feel responsible to present a commissioner with a lucid, nuanced artwork, not an amorphous blob. Proofreading carefully is essential.

JK: So, on the continuum of one side being everything you'd ever want to know is in the score, and on the other side the score is only the beginning, you're way over on the first side.

ART: Way over there. Yes, I guess I'm a type triple A [*laughs*]. It's not vague for me. The players are awesome—very technically equipped. They come out of Juilliard, Eastman, Northwestern, et cetera, and can play the entire repertoire. If I want the crescendo on the second beat, then I should put it there. They'll play it, and they can also feel why the crescendo had to be right there—same with articulations and other nuances. It's akin to a beautifully punctuated poem, where you know exactly what the poet wanted and meant. I like my music to be sculpted, skillfully punctuated, and clean.

JK: Does that equate to the performer not having much interpretive freedom?

ART: Well, no. I see it differently. I present artists with an eloquent, fluent poem, and then with their sublime expertise, musicianship, years of training, they take the sounds to a higher level. At least we start our journey together with a persuasive text and with their technical instrumental brilliance. Subsequently, performers can spin and weave their inspired magic and make the music theirs—'tis not mine anymore.

JK: Can a conductor ever pull something out of a piece of music that you didn't know was in it?

ART: Yes, definitely! One instance where this often comes up is with tempos. Christoph Eschenbach has premiered many of my works, and I remember he took exceedingly slow tempos in one of the movements from *Chanting to Paradise* for chorus, solo soprano, and orchestra. I thought the whole thing was going to grind to a halt and was a nervous wreck. There are big, rich chords, and Christoph wanted the chorus to be holding them in the air, like floating sunshine, just hanging in the resonant concert hall. My thinking was that the harmonic rhythm was stagnant because, although the chords were plush, when you slow it down that much . . . ? And when he came off stage, he said, "I love that—hear the space!" The next night I listened to it through his ears and thought, "It really does work well at his tempo." It worked because of the manner in which he conducted the 180 choral members as if virtually not breathing. Christoph generously taught me something. Whether I changed the tempo marking for those twenty bars of the piece is neither here nor there; rather, it's that it taught me something for my next pieces, for which I remain forever in his debt. Ditto with all the musicians with whom I have had the luxury and privilege to work closely. My favorite thing in life is working closely with performing musicians, as they have been among my most vital teachers. I love to hear their critique and advice and am never defensive. When they will tell me exactly what they think, I consider it a huge gift they are granting.

JK: Since we're dealing with certain details like articulation, dynamics, and tempo, let's talk a little bit about creative process. You mentioned the piano earlier. Do you compose at the piano?

ART: I do use the piano daily, but I don't compose *at* it. In Chicago, I will play for two hours in the morning, writing chords, notes, tunes, rhythms—generally creating a force field of musical materials. Then I move to my drafting tables, in a different room, to compose on manuscript.

JK: When an idea first comes to you, what do you hear?

ART: It's different for every piece, as well as for every section of each composition. Some pieces start with a motive, others start with a chain link of chords, or with a color, or with a capricious rhythm. Never the same twice! The beginning of my ballet *Terpsichore's Dream* is dancelike, with motivic materials built for *pizzicati* and two harps. Then there is a long section with lush chords that span five octaves, hanging in the sonic space, through which threads a long, lyrical, high trombone solo accented by bells and cymbals. There's another section where it's fast, punchy, and jazzy. Each section is uniquely composed. In short, I try to invent a force field of plentiful, flexible materials, always transform and sculpt those materials, hopefully, creating sounds that are vivid, alive, and imaginatively moving.

JK: At what point does architecture come into it?

ART: Right at the beginning.

JK: So you know the form or the architecture before you start?

ART: Well, genre and duration are prescribed. When I know the musical materials, I draw lots of formal maps. I feel that for my music (and this does not apply to how anyone else should compose!), the form should be the reaction to the objects calling it into being. The opposite of what I describe casually as ice-cube trays, where all of the formal "phrases" are predefined. The formal, block, ice-cube-like sections are prearranged, and one pours the material into them. I'm doing the opposite by, to continue the silly metaphor, letting the water settle where it naturally settles; that's then the form. The form is a response to the objects calling it into being, not unlike a jazz improvisation. Added to this method, then, I'm constantly editing down to only the essentials. Cut, cut, cut, so that before anyone hears my music, I have tightened the form countless times, taking my organic field of ice, fashioning and sculpting it.

JK: I think one of the hardest things for any creator to learn is how to self-edit. Where did you learn it?

ART: From twenty-five years of wanting to create concise music. Even a tiny cut makes clarity. Removing ten seconds makes a world of difference. I constantly ask my performers, just out of curiosity, if they think the music needs a short cut of a few bars here or there.

JK: I know that you read a lot of poetry. Your compositional process sounds like you are crafting a poem. Everything is very deliberate.

ART: Crazy as this sounds, I think of my compositions as poems on fire—very precise, yet with a lot of spontaneous life and human spirit. [Gerard Manley] Hopkins's poems are burning off the page they're so hot, imaginative, creative, and full of explosively gorgeous images and words. Ditto with Emily Dickinson. Every word is like a little bomb—beautiful words in elegantly crafted, blazing juxtapositions. Here are two poets whose works are vastly inspiring for their content, sounds, and concision. Yes! Definitely a corollary!

JK: So when you're writing for chorus or for voice, what's the relationship you like to have with text?

ART: I have to love the meaning of the words as well as the sounds of the words.

JK: The way you verbally speak them?

ART: Yes. If the poem is one and my music is one, it shouldn't add up to two because, in that scenario, the poem didn't need my music, and my music didn't honor the poem. One plus one has to add up to something like twenty-seven—to multiply, transform, and turn into another object. Also, vis-à-vis the sounds of the words themselves, I'm very aware of the physiology of a singer.

JK: So you're consciously thinking about this when you choose the text?

ART: I sing all my pieces; thus I am aware of a singer's lungs, tongue, cheeks, and throat. I'm really thinking about what they are physically doing to make this exact vowel sound right here on this pitch. So when looking for poems to set, yes, I'm already thinking about vocal mechanics.

JK: Do you feel a responsibility to use the entirety of the poem?

ART: Yes, generally.

JK: Was there a defining moment that you realized you were a composer?

ART: Gradually, over twenty years, I started to find composition more interesting than playing. I thought it might be more fun to make everything up out of thin air rather than sit and play my one part. So steadily, composing evolved and bloomed from a childhood filled with singing, playing, and writing. My childhood was akin to a big, musical river morphing into a composer as a deep result of twenty years practicing, performing, and singing.

JK: Did you have mentors that helped bring you along?

ART: Yes, I did. Many! One of the high-school teachers noticed how much I was composing. Consequently, the school had an outside composer, Marilyn Ziffrin, come to campus to teach me. It was amazing. When I went to college I had many wonderful mentor teachers, Alan Stout being especially fantastic. I still consider him my teacher, even though I haven't had a lesson in over twenty-five years. The other teachers I've had, not to sound preposterous, include Byrd, Bach, Mozart, Ravel, Debussy, Stravinsky, Berio, Takemitsu, Boulez, Knussen, among many others, including countless jazz artists and numerous performing musicians.

JK: So you really studied their works.

ART: Yeah, I did. Mahler. Mingus. Art Tatum. Schumann. There's a lot to learn. You don't have to sit with a composer, nor show them your own music seeking their comments, in order to be taught directly from them. Music by others is a mammoth, lifelong inspiration to me.

JK: You bring up a good point. How does one teach composition?

ART: It depends on the student, but the way my private lessons were structured at Eastman and at Northwestern was with a third of the lesson as an exercise, not necessarily to go into a piece (make three chords that progress, or make three chords that don't progress, or take this rhythm and transform it eleven times—i.e., tiny crossword-puzzle assignments.) A third of the lesson was repertoire study and listening (in-depth listening assignments for which students had to write what they liked, didn't like, and what they learned from the music). This was something I learned to include in lessons from my close friend Chris Rouse. The remaining time on the music they composed of their original composition.

JK: As someone who has spent many years teaching the next generation of composers, what has become important to you to pass on to them?

ART: In addition to the craft, repertoire, and creative work structured into my lessons, it is fundamentally my passion to inspire them to be 100 percent honest, pure, soul-searching, and iconoclastically who *they* are as artists—to be *them* to the max. Furthermore, they need to recognize, from my teaching of the great repertoire, that spending a lifetime creating new sounds and forms out of thin air each day, for eighty years, takes the determination of a rock-solid, purposeful, visionary soul. Teaching is a natural extension of my creative process and of my avid enthusiasm for and curiosity about the music of other cultures and artists, so it is also my hope to pass along to my student colleagues the simple and humble model of my sheer daily enthusiasm for and delight about all kinds of music. I want them to love music. I need them to love music for me to be effective as a mentor.

JK: What skills did you need beyond your formal training to prepare you for a life as a composer?

ART: Oy! [*Laughs*] Let's see . . . in any random order . . . time management, compartmentalizing various duties into certain sections of a given day, citizenship at large, stopping everything in one's inner ear plus creative life to try to help a student in some small way, acting like a travel agent, disciplined diet when traveling, working on very little sleep, catching a 6:00 A.M. flight from O'Hare, which means arriving at the airport at 4:30 A.M., chairing boards, responding to requests for CDs and scores in a timely fashion, delivering preconcert lectures, delivering onstage lectures just before a world premiere, participating in interviews and radio shows, hiring someone to build a Web site, chairing faculty searches, programming the music of my colleagues, advocating for the music of my colleagues, administrating engravers' schedules, getting to FedEx fifty-five seconds before the cutoff time, all while being a devoted family member to my siblings, taking charge and care of a mother with Alzheimer's for a decade. . . .

JK: Wow. There is clearly a lot to do that has nothing to do with the music itself. What does classical music have to do to make sure it's still viable fifty years from now?

ART: Classical music is viable because the repertoire is excellent and performers are awe-inspiring. What Beethoven made changed the universe—same with Mozart, Mahler, Brahms, Debussy, Ella, Miles, Coltrane, Tatum, Evans, et cetera. The early Stravinsky ballets are unbelievable and among the greatest constructs of civilization. The *Goldberg Variations*—transcendent! Glen Gould plays Bach beyond gorgeously!

JK: Do you think people just find them?

ART: There are infinite amounts of great music, as well as musicians who have the technique to perform it exquisitely. I don't think the problem is on the performance or creative side, nor people fundamentally needing and loving music. People want to play and hear [Stravinsky's] *Rite of Spring.* It's fun! With all of that positive energy . . . I get up every morning for the past thirty years and compose. We have to be optimists that people will seek and find all kinds of music.

JK: Who is sitting in the audiences today?

ART: It depends. For a chamber-music event it's one group; for an orchestra event it's a different group of people. If it's a solo violin recital, it's again a different audience. Choruses usually have yet again a different set of devoted audience members. I don't feel that I'm going from hall to hall, city to city, encountering the same "generic audience."

JK: So does it come down to programming?

ART: It takes time to get to know great music, to study it and inform oneself about its contexts. These days, people don't have a lot of time; furthermore, they can do hundreds of other things, such as watch videos, movies, and sports. Who is going to sit down and listen to a forty-five minute symphony when they could watch the New England Patriots, play ping-pong, or go swimming? It's a devoted type of person who wants to read all of James Joyce. Who has read the complete Emily Dickinson. If people can get to the music, they'll like it. Part of the problem with classical art music, especially in the large genres, is disseminating recordings. It's a tricky thing; for instance, I never received recordings of four of my Chicago Symphony Orchestra world premieres. Heartbreaking!

JK: That would be hard. All the work you put into it.

ART: And all the work they put into it. There's no document—whatever it was evaporated instantly into thin air, unless G. Schirmer can inspire another orchestra to play the composition. Unless we can sort out how to get new music recorded and circulated, it's going to be problematical because, as I said earlier, most of the work composers receive is due to people hearing recordings of their music. Patrons don't commission just because they like us. They carefully listen to previous works; hence composers depend heavily on past recordings to be offered future employment.

JK: Was there a point when you realized that you were a woman in this compositional career?

ART: Sometimes people refer to me as a woman composer. I remember the *New York Times* wrote a very long time ago about me as "the young woman composer." They used "woman," but I don't have the word "female" or "woman" on my Web site, resumé, nor biography. I'm a composer. Yes.

JK: Do you think there's still a need nowadays for things like women-only concerts, festivals, and CDs?

ART: What we need is excellent work by whoever wrote it—male, female, gay, bisexual, transgender, old, young, green, blue, or purple. I teach, program, and listen based on artistic excellence and grace.

JK: Where would you like to see classical art music go fifty or a hundred years from now?

ART: I would like to see it well funded. It takes a lot to write a quartet. It takes a lot to perform a quartet. It takes a lot to present a quartet.

JK: It does take a lot. And more so for contemporary music.

ART: Exactly. Sports stars making twenty million dollars a year and bankers paying themselves million-dollar annual bonuses when compared to a string quartet that asks for an extra hour of rehearsal space and they're told no is truly crazy. If the arts are going to survive, we all have to support them. I have never been an "each man for himself"-type person. Rather, it interests me to be part of an international team of musicians working together to continually elevate and fund the arts for all.

JK: Reading your biography, you consistently are part of a board or are volunteering here or there. Not only are you an artist-creator, but also you're an artist who is a citizen of art to perpetuate the art.

ART: I'm trying to be, yes. Endeavoring every day to spread positive ripples.

JK: Why is it important to you to spend so much time in volunteer positions, and what do you hope to affect?

ART: There are many close mentors in my life who are sublime artist-citizen-leaders in the profession. Far too many to list in this interview. Though, for your reference, a very short list would include John Harbison, Oliver Knussen, Steven Stucky, Pierre Boulez, Shulamit Ran, Ed Harsh, Fran Richard, James Kendrick, Daniel Barenboim, Yehudi Wyner, Cliff Colnot, Gunther Schuller, Ed Yim, David Robertson, David Rakowski, Martin Bresnick, Tony Fogg, David Felder, Claire Chase, Frank Oteri, Jesse Rosen, David Skidmore, Aaron Kernis, Gil Rose, . . . and the list goes on, on, and on. I could spend this whole interview just listing some very small portion of the rest of these superstars! Citizenship is important, because our art form at large immensely needs numerous mentors and leaders creating broad and creative contexts in which we can all work together to further music's flexible, diverse capacity and innate power. So yes, for this reason, I consider it a huge honor to try, in some tiny way, to serve, hoping to make a modest effort to affect, for the better, with energy and love, our huge and vibrant profession. All composers throughout history have needed the strong backing of great leaders, colleagues, and musicians who have depth, soul, excellence, vision, and who think, program, and perform with expertise and sparkle. Without such complete backing, composition is an impossible endeavor for a culture to improve.

JK: Many people would love to commission a composer but don't know the first thing about what's a fair price or how to go about it. Some of it would be the responsibility of the composer in marketing so that the conductors know where to find the composers and the composers know where to find the people that are looking to have commissions.

ART: Yes! True! The history of music is a history of private individuals who took the leap of faith to commission a new piece. Due to such vision and generosity, humanity has a treasure trove of masterpieces.

JK: Is there a piece you'd love to write, and you're just waiting for the right commission to come along?

ART: I'd like to compose another cello concerto. . . . I have an early one, titled *Ritual Incantations* from 1999, of which I'm proud, though I am yearning to create another. I'd also like to compose a piece for a hot big band. Every ten years I want to continue to do a substantial piano work. In 1989 I composed *Concerto for Orchestra,* and then seventeen years later I created *Helios Choros.* Accordingly, in five to eight years, I'd like to share another extended orchestral vision.

JK: It sounds like even in your mid-forties you're already thinking about legacy.

ART: The difference between early Stravinsky and mid-period Stravinsky is fascinating. Early Beethoven/late Beethoven. Early Mozart/late Mozart. I'm an avid listener, and I find it remarkable how artists transform.

JK: You are somebody who has been well vetted by musicians and critics, and certainly a publisher is championing your work. Are there ever periods of self-doubt in your writing?

ART: I am very grateful for G. Schirmer's support. Every moment of my life has a yin and yang of complete self-doubt balanced, interconnected, and interdependent with utter hope. As if 100 percent full of self-doubt and 100 percent full of hope. They flip back and forth. I ask, "Can this chord or motive be improved? It's got to be more integrated. How can I refine it? Oh my goodness, this is weak. Oh my goodness, it's good." Back and forth . . . I torture myself daily! My core needs to design and shape things, so even in periods of doubt I still invent something. The best way I might put it: I exert endless self-criticism, but the creative river runs very deep inside of me, so I don't have "freakouts." I am too entrenched in artistic journeys, every day trying to fill silence with a graceful, personal sound.

***

Works by Augusta Read Thomas

All works published by G. Schirmer unless otherwise noted.

ORCHESTRAL ENSEMBLES (SEE ALSO CHORAL/VOCAL)

Astral Canticle, double concerto featuring flute and violin (2005).
Aurora, featuring piano (2000).
Canticle Weaving: Trombone Concerto No. 2, featuring trombone (2003).
Cello Concerto No. 3: "Legend of the Phoenix" (2013).
Ceremonial (1999).
Credences of Summer (2005).
Dream Threads: A Ballet, for youth orchestra and ballet (2007).
Galaxy Dances (2004).
Helios Choros: A Ballet, a triptych for orchestra (2006–7).
Helios Choros I
Helios Choros II
Helios Choros III
Jubilee, for orchestra (2010).
Light of the First Evening, for orchestra with single strings (2002).
Meditation: Trombone Concerto, featuring trombone (1990).
Of Paradise and Light (2010).
Orbital Beacons: Concerto for Orchestra (1998).
Prayer and Celebration (2006).
Prayer Bells (2001).
Radiant Circles (2010).

Ritual Incantations, for cello and chamber orchestra (1999).
Shakin (2004).
Silver Chants the Litanies, horn concerto, in memoriam Luciano Berio featuring horn (2004).
Spirit Musings, for violin and chamber orchestra (1997).
Tangle (2003).
Terpsichore's Dream, a ballet for chamber orchestra (2007).
Trainwork (2002).
Vigil: A Cello Concerto, featuring cello (1990).
Violin Concerto No. 3, Juggler in Paradise, featuring violin (2008).
Words for the Sea (1995).

BAND

Dancing Galaxy (2004).
magneticfireflies, for high-school band (2001).
Ring, Flourish, Blaze! fanfare for sixteen winds and brass (2000).

CHAMBER MUSIC

Angel Tears and Earth Prayers, for trumpet, flute, oboe, clarinet, and organ (2006).
Cantos for Slava, for cello or viola and piano (2007).
Capricious Angels, for flute, oboe, clarinet, horn, violins, and viola (2009).
Carillon Sky, for solo violin and small ensemble (2005).
Chant, for cello or viola or alto saxophone and piano (1991).
. . . a circle around the sun . . . , for piano trio (2000).
Dancing Helix Rituals, for violin, clarinet, and piano (2006).
Eagle at Sunrise, for string quartet (2001).
Fête, for six trumpets and three trombones (2010).
Fugitive Star, for string quartet (2000).
Invocations, for string quartet (2000).
Jeu d'Esprit, for paired instruments (C trumpets, F horns, soprano saxophones, oboes, B♭ clarinets, or piccolos), (2010).
Lake Reflecting Stars with Moonrise, for saxophone and cello (2008).
Mansueto Tribute, "double helix," for two violins (2011).
Memory: Swells, for guitar duo (2005).
Moon Jig, for violin, cello, and piano (2005).
Murmurs in the Mists of Memory, for eleven solo strings (2001).
Of Paradise and Light, for cello ensemble (2010).
Passion Prayers, for solo cello, flute, clarinet, violin, piano, harp, and percussion (1999).
Pilgrim Soul, for English horn and two violins (2011).
Resounding Earth, for percussion quartet and bells (2012).
Rise Chanting, for string quartet (2002).
Rumi Settings, for violin and cello or viola (2001).
Scat, for flute, oboe, violin, viola, cello, and harpsichord (2007).

Scherzi Musical, for horn, trumpet, and trombone (2007).
Silent Moon, for violin and viola (2006).
Squeeze, for saxophone, alto saxophone, and tenor saxophone (2007).
Sun Threads, for violin, viola, and cello (2002).
Toft Serenade, for viola or violin and piano (2006).

INSTRUMENTAL SOLO

Around Midnight Variation, for piano (available from the composer, 2001).
Aspen Starry Night Prayer Chords, for piano (2001).
Ballade: Weaving Skyward, for piano (2008).
Bells Ring Summer, for cello (2000).
Caprice, for violin (2005).
D(i)agon(als), for clarinet (2005).
Dream Catcher, for viola or violin (2008).
Eurythmy Etude, for piano (2007).
Euterpe's Caprice, for flute (2008).
Incantation, for solo violin or viola (1995, 2002).
Love Twitters, for piano (2006).
Pulsar, for violin or viola (2002, 2006).
Rush, for solo violin or viola (2004).
Silhouettes, for marimba (2004).
Six Piano Etudes, for piano (2006).
Spring Song, for cello (1995).
Traces, for piano (2005).

CHORAL/VOCAL

Absolute Ocean, for solo soprano, harp obbligato, and orchestra (2008).
Alleluia, for SATB chorus (available from the composer, 1996).
among dawn flowers, for soprano and piano (2001).
Bubble: rainbow, for soprano, flute, oboe, percussion, piano, violin, and cello (2003).
Chanting to Paradise, for solo soprano, SATB chorus, and orchestra (2002).
Daylight Divine, for solo soprano, children's/women's chorus, and chamber orchestra (2001).
Earth Echoes, for mezzo-soprano, baritone, and chamber orchestra (2012).
Final Soliloquy of the Interior Paramour, small ensemble, mezzo-soprano, and counter tenor (2004).
Flash, for SATB chorus and orchestra (2011).
Floating Temples, for SATB chorus and orchestra (2011).
Four Basho Settings, for SSAA youth chorus (2002).
Fruit of My Spirit, for SATB chorus (2004).
Gathering Paradise, for solo soprano and orchestra (2004).
In My Sky at Twilight: Songs of Passion and Love, for soprano and large chamber ensemble (2002).

Juggler of the Day, for female chorus (2007).
Love Songs, for SATB chorus (1997).
Midsummer Blaze (Alleluia), for SATB a cappella (1993).
Prairie Sketches I: Diamonds on Orchid Velvet, for soprano and ensemble (2004).
Psalm 91: Verse 11, for SATB a cappella (1996).
Purple Syllables, for SATB a cappella (2004).
The Rewaking, for SATB or TTBB a cappella (2005).
Ring Out, Wild Bells, to the Wild Sky, for solo soprano, SATB chorus, and orchestra (2000).
Roses, for SATB a cappella (2008).
The Rub of Love, SATB a cappella (1995).
Song in Sorrow, for solo soprano, SATB chorus, and orchestra (2000).
Sunlight Echoes, for SATB chorus and orchestra (2002).
Sun Songs—Three Micro-Operas, for mezzo-soprano and percussion (2004).
To the Rain, for SSA a cappella (2003).
Two E. E. Cummings Songs, for SSAA a cappella (2008).

Lawrence White

16

Hilary Tann

In 1947, when Hilary Tann was born, the coal mines were still open in South Wales. The landscape was green, yellow, and brown, the mountaintops bare, and the sky close. Born and raised in the town of Ferndale, high up in the enclosed valley of Rhondda Fach, Tann makes music that is inspired by the natural world around her. In fact, much of her varied musical catalog can be illustrated as the composing out of images and landscapes. Tann began writing music at age six because she had a waltz-like melody in her head, and she wanted to remember it. She became a cellist in the Glamorgan Youth Orchestra as well as the National Youth Orchestra of Wales and later attended the University of Wales in Cardiff to study music. Like Chen Yi, Tania León, Svjetlana Bukvich, and Toshiko Akiyoshi, Tann came to the United States in part to further her college education and musical studies. Leaving Cardiff as the first woman to graduate with a first-class honors degree in composition, she went on to become the third woman to graduate with a Ph.D. in composition from Princeton University.

Remaining in the United States, Tann joined the editorial staff of *Perspectives of New Music* and became an active member on many executive committees for the International League of Women Composers (ILWC) from 1982 to 1995. During our conversation, she discusses the active role she played in the organizational merging that created the International Alliance for Women in Music and explains how the merger resulted in a sense of community for women composers with less competitiveness than before.

Tann lives in the southern foothills of New York's Adirondack Mountains and is the John Howard Payne Professor of Music at Union College. In addition to her worldwide commissions for orchestral, chamber, solo, and vocal/choral works, she is recorded on a number of albums and was the 2011 composer-in-residence for the Eastman Women in Music Festival.

Further understanding about Tann as a composer can be drawn from her experience as a Welsh immigrant to America who found her way back to Wales via Japan. While living and working in the United States, she developed a deep interest in the traditional music of Japan that led her to study the *shakuhachi,* an ancient Japanese vertical bamboo flute. Tann was entranced by its clear lines and varied textures. To further her study and continue developing her unique voice, Tann traveled to Japan in 1990 to teach at Kansai University. Her studies in Japan further influenced her understanding of silence, stillness, and image. Tann believes "the bone, sinew, and vein" of her work constitute a world music, a synthesis of Welsh heritage, Japanese influence and study, and time spent in the United States.

Throughout our conversation, the thoughtful, soft-spoken composer discusses how her life in composition taught her to balance musical creativity with the practical matters surrounding the business of composing. Like many composers in this book, Tann's sense of the practical derives from the experience of being a working composer for decades, in particular her adaptation to changes in the publishing business. No longer a house composer for Oxford University Press (as Oxford changed formats), Tann articulates the benefits and challenges of being both composer and professor.

Image is significant to Hilary Tann, beginning with the images she surrounds herself with to inspire composition, the seed that begins a work, and even the metaphors she crafts as she speaks. Throughout our conversation, I was struck by her vibrant imagistic references to the gilding on a medieval portrait; to musical pieces being conceived, brought to term, and then birthed; to curved climaxes; and to the still pond of a listener's ear as the pebble of music grows into a ripple.

Like Libby Larsen, Laura Karpman, and Mary Jane Leach, Tann is consciously aware of the influence of technology on composition. She believes that the playing field has been leveled for women in the United States because of access to technology, and she refers to today's "audience of one" for recorded music in digital formats. She continues our discussion by explaining changes in publishing and the declining need in the United States for women's-only concerts and recordings. Tann stresses the need for a national understanding of the "extraordinary benefits for supporting the arts" in the United States. She explains compellingly that an investment in music is an investment in peace.

***

October 2009, at her home in Schuylerville, New York

HILARY TANN: When I met Shulamit Ran in Louisville, she was so open and friendly. There was no feeling of competitiveness—which is interesting, because in the early days I felt that there was some competitiveness among women composers. People would angle to be ahead because there were only a small number of performances, and you had to kind of fight for a place at the table. People now have realized the table for contemporary music is so small anyway, the best thing you can do is to get everyone out there, ourselves and others. It's a rising tide. . . .

JENNIFER KELLY: How did the competitiveness change?

HT: I was an assistant editor of *Perspectives of New Music* when I joined the International League of Women Composers in the early eighties and therefore got involved with the International Congress of Women in Music [ICWM], which is the annual organization. I also knew about, but was not a member of, American Women Composers [AWC]. When we had three groups, there was some friction, because funding for one might mean no funding for another. So we were quite literally competing for the same funds as we tried to get this movement under way. I was coordinator of the Executive Committee of the ILWC as we gradually dissolved the ILWC into the ICWM and AWC, and I was the person who suggested the word "alliance" because we wanted to act together: the International Alliance for Women in Music [IAWM].

JK: You chose the word "for" consciously?

HT: Yes, because we didn't want "of." For instance, Aaron Cohen is the person that compiled the *International Encyclopedia of Women Composers* because his wife was a composer. Now, did we want him *not* to be part of the movement? So anyone, male or female, could join. There was a meeting in Alaska in 1993 when we in the ILWC and ICWM decided that there should be one group. I think people now . . . the women are working together.

JK: Are you happy with the evolution of collaboration and success of contemporary music composers?

HT: That's a huge question. One thing that immediately occurs to me is that Jennifer Higdon does not have a publisher. She chooses not to have a publisher, and she and her partner do a lot of her publishing. Again, women would be fighting to be *the* woman published by whatever press, but when you take the press out of it. . . . Once self-publishing becomes acceptable, the idea of being selected the highest of the high by some outside organization is no longer operative. It's been a great leveler to have methods of self-promotion available and not looked down upon. It is no longer a question of me knocking at the door someplace, saying, "Please would you make a CD of my music?" It is instead the case, "Better get my act together. Better get my grant proposal in." And lo and behold, these things happen. It's a lovely thing when I get a letter in the mail saying, "Has *Arachne* been recorded? If not, I want to do it." And then I don't have to look for any funds. It's just being done out there.

JK: I really enjoyed your CD *Songs of the Cotton Grass.*

HT: Thank you. Violist/violinist Matthew Jones came to visit me to rehearse *The Cresset Stone.* He was sitting in this room and asked if I had any more music. "Well, yes, I have this and this." And I played him recordings of what then became the other pieces on the CD. It's wonderful when it happens the old-fashioned way. But I am seeing online that a whole lot of people are making their own promotional CDs and videos that others can access. I am a part of ClassicsOnline, but it still feels odd. For example, my piece *Shakkei* was performed in Bangkok and is now available on YouTube, and I find out that for $1.59, you can download the first movement. The idea that you have a dollar value for an individual audience member . . . [*laughs*]. What's happened is, the whole concert apparatus has been short-circuited. Normally, when I think of an audience member paying for a ticket, I think of the hall and heating the hall and the caretaker and the person who put together the posters and the grant writer and also the musicians and the orchestra. My relation with the audience member is that both the audience member and I have benefited from the work of huge numbers of people, and we are grateful for them so we can have this date. Whereas now, any person across the globe can go to ClassicsOnline and for $1.59 can download the performance and enjoy it. They can play it all day. We're not in the business of who is going to be played in Carnegie Hall, or who is going to be played by the New York Philharmonic. The people that download the piece will probably not have read a newspaper critic. It feels like the Velvet Revolution in that all the structure of diplomacy falls apart when you can have Western rock concerts in Poland, and the next thing you know, the government has been overthrown. So I feel that many of the ladders that we used to scramble to climb don't exist anymore, because we're not dealing with that kind of pyramid structure. I'm dealing one on one—ClassicsOnline, you put your $1.59

down, and you get my work. Only the first movement, mind you! Not even the second. You get one movement. I'd like you to have both [*laughs*]. I'll sell you the second movement . . . cheap! You get one, but you don't have the other? The criteria are so different.

JK: Going through that evolution yourself, does that affect the way you compose? Do you think about that entire process when you're writing a piece?

HT: I was a house composer with Oxford University Press [OUP-USA] for seventeen years, from 1989 to 2006. It was wonderful, because all my music got published. All I had to think about was composing. OUP-USA is no more as I knew it, and now that Oxford-UK has changed its system to publish on demand through Goodmusic Publishing, I have to do other things for the posterity of my music. The National Library of Wales has an arrangement with me whereby they will archive all my music. Everything that's published by OUP-UK is there already. They're getting the American works, and they want all the haiku books as well, and articles that I have written, and also old recordings and all the handwritten manuscripts.

JK: They want to be your archival place of everything connected to you.

HT: Yes, absolutely everything. It's a wonderful thing.

JK: That's legacy.

HT: Yes, but notice I started pursuing that. To be more exact, I asked a Welsh friend, Rhian Davis, about it. I had a lot of commissions and performances in Wales last year. She then talked with the archiving people at the National Library of Wales, and they said yes. I had thought that because Oxford had been around for a long time and was likely to be around for a long time, being one of the Oxford house composers meant that I didn't have to worry about the archival aspect of composing. There are really four aspects to publishing: archiving, printing, commissioning, and promotion. So, the National Library of Wales is going to archive my work. And the printing is going to be on demand for the most part. There just won't be so many scores in libraries. With respect to publishing, I established my own music company, Rowanberry Music, a few years ago, because then I get 100 percent of the royalties. Now, if someone wants to perform a recent piece, I send off a PDF, which is just one click . . . and at some point I'm going to have to say, "Can I have the parts back after the performance, please?" I still yearn for the days when I didn't have to fuss with all this. Trying to do all the business-of-composing stuff and hold down a full-time job at the same time is very difficult.

JK: Has all of this affected the business end of composition in any positive way?

HT: I can now speak to the audience members that actually want to hear Hilary music. What's happening with the commissions is that people who already know my music are coming back and saying, "We want more of this." It's not that I'm a woman composer, and we need a woman in the concert. It's not that I'm a

Welsh composer. What technology is doing is enabling us to target our audiences, which is a different concept. So the audience that will target my music is probably not the audience that is going to want a different-sounding composer's music. There's a sort of a bright cosmopolitan audience for some music, whereas my music is going to sound like something pretty coming out of the boondocks. One of the best things that was ever said to me was, "I listen to your music as though I'm in a landscape. Listening to your music is like being in a landscape." Perfect. That's it. Say no more. So targeting is happening.

JK: Now is that creating more work for you, or simply more efficient work for you?

HT: The oboist and composer Patricia Morehead once introduced me as, "This is Hilary Tann. She writes beautiful music." And my immediate reaction was, "I don't write *beautiful* music. I went to Princeton! I am a contemporary composer!" And I'm glad I didn't say that out loud. I said to the monkeys in my mind, "Quiet. It's not a bad thing to be thought of as someone who writes beautiful music." So I now feel that I'm beginning to have my own particular audience. It's what novelists want to know—who reads the novel? I'm beginning to know that. The commissions are happening on a one-on-one basis, which is interesting, because when I write for someone, I still write Hilary music and put it out there to see what the international society thinks about it, and that's that. With respect to promotion, for the first time in my life I have engaged someone to deal with the promotion side of things. It's on a percentage basis, which means he sees to the contracts. I just wrote a piece for the Lunar Saxophone Quartet in London. He saw to the contract, he made sure I got the fees, and he put the fees in my bank. Perfect. The dialogue can happen outside of the composer. He calls himself "composer-manager." So I have a composer-manager, and that's a new model. So far, it's working. The only problem is having to teach at the same time, but the rest of it is working. After losing Oxford-USA, which is what it felt like to me, I felt that maybe I was lost. I thought I would slither down some slope. I'd been taken care of so well. Now I've discovered that there is life after the big press. In fact, my composer-manager is David Wordsworth—who used to be the head of repertoire-promotion at OUP-UK.

JK: What does this modern process of commission, publication, and promotion mean for composers today?

HT: I think technology has leveled the playing field, so the question of whom you know still matters, but it doesn't matter as much. We women are now on the same playing field as the men. We're all facing the same economic and societal problems. With respect to the competitiveness, we know that there are more of us, so that's good.

JK: Are you aware of one another?

HT: We are aware of one another, which is essential. It's very important for people in countries where women's music is not performed to know that there are other places in the world where women's music *is* performed. It is essential. Now people can go online. They can join the IAWM. A lot of the IAWM email list is, "I have a performance in Los Angeles. I'd like to see you there." So we all know there are performances.

JK: Do you think there is still a need for women's-only concerts, CDs, et cetera?

HT: I think in some countries it may be a need. I don't think it's a need in the United States. No, I don't think it's a need anymore. Years ago, we didn't know that the other women composers existed. I think what the Women's Philharmonic did in San Francisco was absolutely essential. There was a great need, but the great need began to be met in the 1970s, and we're now in the second decade of the twenty-first century.

JK: That's a very positive step. I've noticed that when you discuss contemporary music, you often mention jazz and world music as a separate category.

HT: I put them in separate categories for the sake of the grant organizations. In other words, this particular grant needs to have a world-music aspect, educational outreach; this other grant needs to have a jazz-music aspect. The old idea of being given time to write for your fine string quartet for a small audience is gone.

JK: So it's almost being dictated to us by the institutional organizations that are funding it.

HT: But it's also excluding. I don't have a jazz bone in my body. I do have many world-music bones, and in fact world music, I would say, is the bone, is the sinew, is the vein of my music. I have a lot of rhythmic things from Indian music, but I'm not using tabla. I'm not using Indian instruments or aesthetic. My aesthetic side would be more Japanese, like my oboe concerto, *Shakkei.* It's not Japanese enough to be called "world music," but I think it transcends what it means to be world music because it is a genuine synthesis. I can't say, "Well, I think I'll use a little Japanese music," because unless the audience hears some plicky-plicky pentatonic stuff, it's not going to be recognized as such. We're still working our way through that. And I hope we never work our way all the way through it, because that's like having all the colors of Play-Doh merge into a gray-brown ball. I don't want that to happen. I want Japanese music to remain Japanese music and Indian music to remain Indian music.

JK: Will you explain how you consider *Shakkei* a work of world music, of synthesis?

HT: You've seen the cover of the score, with the twin images of the rock garden and stroll garden, and you know the two movements are based on this contrast. How do I have the words? We don't have these kinds of words in English. For example, in English, silence is a void, and it's so weird this Halloween time, when people are thinking emptiness and darkness as scary. Whereas in Japanese music, there is the concept of substantive silence. I interviewed [Toru] Takemitsu, and he talked about *ma* as the entire universe. *Ma* is the mother of the universe. We are a small part of the universe. And so asking an orchestra to create a universe within a piece, the universe of a piece, using substantive silence in a piece is an extraordinary adventure. *That* kind of synthesis. I wouldn't have been willing to carve out so many *emptinesses* without having this background. It's not that I'm using one of the Japanese scales, although there's a little of it because, once you pile up fifths, you're going to end up in a pentatonic realm, and, once you reflect those fifths, you will end up toward the Japanese scales, but you're coming at it from a depth. It's like Sanskrit being the base language for so many others. The weight of the fifths *predates* pentatonicism. I consider that I have as much access to it as those who developed the instrument in China that became the shakuhachi in Japan. So we're talking about a deep structure fed through the East that I came to know in Japan and that now I'm using in Western orchestral music. What a strange thing. But I think it's there.

JK: Do you want the conductor, the performers, to be aware, or the audience to be aware, of this inspiration and connection?

HT: I would actually like them to see the two different inspirational photographs. I would like to give them a hint that what they may be thinking is accurate.

JK: The audience as well?

HT: Yes, but the program note says it. In the rock garden, the first movement, gradually the soloist's line begins to be heard/seen better and better by the rest of the orchestra. I need them to hear that. And then the other movement of the diptych doesn't really go places. It shimmers in place, which is what trees do. They don't lumber across the landscape like vegetative dinosaurs, but they respond, they move. I am working on a piece right now for the community women's orchestra in Oakland, California, called *Reibo.* "Rei" is the bell, and "bo" is yearning. The title means "yearning for the bell." But the bell is an instrument of meditation. Sometimes the shakuhachi is considered an empty bell, and my piece has to do with reverberation. You strike something, and then what happens? I'm in the "then what happens?" stage. What do I want to do? I know how to make people excited. Not a problem; I have that skill. But now I want to get my climaxes . . . want to do a feminine thing? I want my climaxes to be curves [*laughs*]. I want to go over and come down and then lead on. I have an analysis of a piece, a long shakuhachi piece called *Futaiken Reibo.* One of the first things I say is, "The event memory becomes enclosed within the event itself." So I'm trying to write motives and phrases that do that and then to create the whole flow of the thing. That's what I have in mind. That's what I want to do.

JK: Small curves within larger curves within larger curves.

HT: Layers. And these curves are asymmetrical curves; otherwise they would sit. Like lapping the shore of my audience's consciousness.

JK: Where does contemporary music thrive? Is it at the concert hall, festival, schools, and composition classrooms?

HT: In certain people's iPods. That's an audience of one.

JK: So does contemporary music thrive?

HT: I think of Sarah Bob in Boston, who runs a contemporary-music series in an art gallery. I suspect she has about fifty people at each of her concerts. The kinds of music that she programs are everything. She could have jazz or some world-music aspect. She could have classic contemporary, which is what I would be, and these are all responding to colors and textures on the wall by artists. I think we're in a terrific new time of synthesis. Watch out for the gray-brown ball! I don't want to go there. A concert hell for me is the *Egmont Overture* followed by the *Emperor* [concerto] and *Eroica*—a whole evening of E-flat, and I am completely dead. Bad programming. A famous Australian composer was featured on a particular concert. Because he's from Australia, they had two minutes of didgeridoo at the beginning of the concert, at which point that concert was labeled a "world music" concert and got funding as such. It's wrong to present three Beethoven E-flat pieces like we don't have any ears. Please give me a C-sharp. And it's wrong to diminish the idea of world music and the concert that follows. So I think composers are seeking a kaleidoscopic shift that's taking place across the globe. I think of new venues like Sarah Bob's art gallery series of concerts, the online concerts that take place. I love the idea of different sorts of concerts. Just like I'm very happy you don't want to read a lot of [Gerard Manley] Hopkins. You read one poem. So I would like people to be able to pick up a piece of mine and pay the $1.59 and have it in their own environment with their own cat on their lap or drink in their hand or in a meditative place or wherever they are. I would like an audience member to be able to hear a piece of mine at the right time for that person. That's what I would like. I do not need three thousand people increasing their circulation in the same place.

JK: It is clear that there could be more funding for the arts, but why do you think it has lost so much importance in the United States?

HT: It hasn't realized the extraordinary benefits for supporting the arts in so many domains. If the arts are supported, then the idea of community at large is enhanced. It's very easy for the United States to see that athletic teams contribute to the core, the definition, of towns and cities and so on. Sports are part of how we define ourselves. Imagine for an instant if the amount of resources that are put toward sports in America (and somewhere male competitive sports is what I'm really thinking about) got put into the arts. Support of the arts isn't simply a matter of the box-office take from some Madonna event in a large city. It's the way the arts can define smaller communities. It's the way that the arts can get people to be wider thinkers, wider viewers, and wider listeners. We need to listen to what people around the world are saying, seeing. We need to see what they are writing and painting. So an investment in music is an investment in peace, and there's no greater calling. That is the level I think we should be talking about funding for the arts.

JK: Real human communication.

HT: Imagine how big a football team or an orchestra is. Imagine how many people get to talk and communicate with one another within sixty, seventy, or ninety of the students in your choirs. Imagine your students in college belonging to these organizations and not being part of frat parties and the rest. There is an amount of consciousness raising needed in American society. Music should not be seen as elitist. That is the worst problem, because it allows the prices to go way up and allows the venues to be exclusive. The venues should be *in*clusive. The prices should be such that your average person can go to a movie *or* go to a concert. The benefits are innumerable and would take a whole other book. Some countries understand the importance of this. When you think of the new countries like Estonia, then you see what the musicians have done. You see how musicians have brought their countries to the fore. We are backward in that we think of classical music as the province of the elite. This is not the case. It's bad for music that it's seen to be the case, and it's bad for the population as a whole.

JK: What advice would you give to a young woman with some skills who says she would like to go into composition?

HT: Oh, sure, do it! But do it wisely. If you want to go into composition, know that most composers have day jobs. There are some women who have husbands or partners who help financially. I know another composer with family wealth. We go back to Virginia Woolf and five hundred pounds a year, right? *A Room of One's Own.* So the room-of-one's-own syndrome is going to affect women artists across the board—composers, painters, poets, sculptors, and dancers. You have to find your way of getting five hundred guineas. One way is to teach. As a composer, I find teaching a problem. I am a good teacher, and I've now taught forty years or so, but when you're teaching, you're always being confined. You're saying, "It *is* like this." When you're composing, you're saying, "It *might be* like that." As a composer, I'm looking for all sorts of possibilities. What I want to have is a way of hearing a minor third where you take the obvious and make it incandescent. Whereas, when I'm teaching, I define intervals as a minor third or major third. I'm holding things in. So teaching is giving the information from the mountain or the tablet to the students. When I'm composing, I just want to be walking, and I don't need to know what the end is. I need to know the direction I'm going, but I don't need to be listening to the present so hard. That is part of the reason I am a haiku poet, because being a haiku poet keeps you at the "aha!" moment. It preserves the "aha!" moment, which is the moment I need when I'm composing. So I've chosen to have a day job that has given me June, July, and August. And when you look at my work, I've done the big pieces during the summers, I've done the chamber pieces during the December break, and I write solo works in the spring break. It's very clear what the pattern is. So a young person is going to need something to keep her going. But go for it, and bring your whole self to it.

JK: When did you find your musical voice?

HT: It took me to my composition *Llef*, 1988. It took me until this piece to accept my Welsh heritage. I would say that *Llef* is when I finally broke into my own language.

JK: Finding Hilary music.

HT: Yes, and that's where I've stayed, pretty much. I see that in the opening of my piece *Shakkei*—the rock of the fourths and fifths, being willing to stay there with a strong interval and then let the leaves and the streams flow around these intervals. But it took me a long time of trying to prove that I had the craft in different ways. How would I encourage a young person? What I'm going to say is discipline, craft, and commitment. Discipline—you get up in the morning and write. Whenever you have your writing time, you need to sit down and *do it.* You can't talk about being a composer. You have to do the composing. Because if you're sitting around talking about being a composer, you're thinking about the glitz, and the glitz is not even the gilding on a medieval portrait [*laughs*]. It is such a small part of what it is to be a composer. And then the craft of it—no one has time to rehearse. You have to know how to notate things simply, clearly, and accurately. That is just a given. You must not go out of range. You must not keep your altos stuck in that same minor third for three minutes—they'll hate you, bad for the voices and bad for the choir. You have to know your ranges and your trills. There's just a lot to know. I mean, you have to know this. I started writing when I was six, but after fifty some years, I still worry about which is the better to use—are we going to get the A off the D string or the A off the A string? You're always working on the craft side. And then the commitment side says you get up and work; I guess it's the Zen side of it. You have to learn how to deal with the monkeys in your mind. But if you have the discipline, and if you have the craft, and the Zen of it, for heaven's sakes, go *do* it. And do it in whatever language your particular music happens in—that's the commitment part of it.

JK: You discussed craft. I know that you're also a conductor. What does your conducting side give to your compositional side?

HT: Everyone who composes for orchestra must conduct.

JK: Why?

HT: I have a piece, *As Ferns.* It was part of my Ph.D. thesis, and I wrote it as quarter-note triplets in a slow tempo. I rewrote the whole piece in 1990, where the triplet quarter became the beat in three-four because I had started studying conducting seriously. When you're a composer, you need to know what a sense of beat is and what the conductor can do and what the conductor shouldn't be expected to do. A conductor can make a space for the musician to do something. But you can't make manifest all those dotted things. You can't expect the conductor to do that for the whole orchestra the whole time. And composers need to know what it's like to be only able to glance at a page.

JK: And then eyes are up.

HT: And then eyes are up. We composers get so used to this zoom on the computer. [As a conductor,] you get used to the whole visual sense of the score. I can remember writing the score for *From Afar,* which is a big triple-wind piece. I had an architect's board, which I would prop up so that I could work on the score. I was doing it by hand. I ended up with all these red marks on my midriff because of the physical sense of leaning over to write the whole score. That's a physical sense. We don't really do that anymore, because on the computer we see bits of the score, and then when we see the whole thing we can't even read it because it's too small on the screen. Composers need to know what it's like to lay the whole score out—the *physicality* of reading from a score. To my mind, an orchestral score has to be written boldly. What composers need to know is how unwieldy an orchestra is—getting an orchestra to feel the phrase together, the stress of the rhythms. The physicality of conducting has to do with making gestures that people can respond to. Imagine writing your music with that sense of gesture. I would say it is absolutely essential for anyone who is going to write music, classical music, to conduct. Absolutely essential.

JK: How does composition affect your conducting?

HT: It tends to make me a wordy conductor—not necessarily a good thing.

JK: You mean verbally.

HT: Yes, because I want to tell the audience what's going on. I want to tell them, "Hold all the bees in the bottle, and now let them out!" I try to keep my words to a minimum, but because I'm a composer, the idea of just doing it with a stick—no! They need to know, "Hey, did you hear that?" I tend to get up there and explain a lot, because that's what I see and that's what I'm trying to get the orchestra to do. While coaching chamber music, I am not willing to say, "Play it quieter." But what I will say is, "The 'emerging from the fog' marking means that we need to be in the fog first; therefore, play it quieter." In other words, I'm always giving a reason.

JK: Do you enjoy conducting your own works?

HT: No, because I can't hear it. I enjoy *rehearsing* my own work. But as a composer, I just want that moment at the end of the piece when everything comes together. That's why the iPod version of the piece is okay by me.

JK: What kind of relationship do you ideally like to have with either a conductor or performer of one of your works?

HT: I like to know they like the work. I have a feeling that, if they like it, then it works. But I'm interested to hear it. So for me, until it works *coming back to me,* it is not birthed. For example, I was to write a large orchestra-and-choir piece. And I conceived it. So the seed idea was planted and ready to go. Two things happened that circumstantially delayed the piece. So suddenly I have conceived a piece, but I wasn't allowed to bring it to term at all. And it's still there. I have this piece. I have it, and I hope to be able to continue the process at some point. But unlike a painter, I can't just paint the thing. I have to have a performance.

JK: Well, that makes sense, because it's an art that exists in time.

HT: As long as we're both trying to make music. I think of it as a process and a group activity. It's like a relay race, and I happen to have the baton for the first stretch. That's it. Then I hand it over, and we have to be a team. I hope that I run my part of the race well enough that the performer is able to take it over. The last part of creation takes place in the mind of the listener. If the listener is worried about the car in the parking lot or having dreams about the guy in the row next to her, or if he doesn't like modern music and is just waiting for Beethoven in the second half, the piece hasn't worked.

JK: So the listener has the responsibility to be part of the team as well.

HT: Yes. The listener has a responsibility. Absolutely. That's why the iPod means the listener has chosen to listen. That's hugely important to me. You've chosen to listen to my piece.

JK: So what can a listener bring to a concert of Hilary Tann music?

HT: A mind like a still pond, so that the piece can fall in and ripple into the shape of that particular pond.

JK: That's a lovely image. One hundred years from now, what would you like to make sure that the performers or conductors know about Hilary music?

HT: That the notation is accurate. Here on my desk is a grant application for me to attend the rehearsal and recording of a piece I've just finished. The justification [for this grant] is that I'm at the stage in my recording career when it is important for me to be present during the premiere recording. It is an archival process and the beginning of the long-term performance history of the work. So one hundred years from now, I've to have had input into the first recorded performance, because I have to know that my notation works. One of the reasons I want to do this recording is that this piece is actually supposed to be in *alla breve.* [The publisher] decided there wasn't such a thing as *alla breve* anymore. There would be only $^4/_4$. I can't believe it. I wanted *alla breve.* So, even though it must be in $^4/_4$, I'm only going to write "half note equals. . . ."

JK: A conductor will see that and know what you want.

HT: Right. That's part of just trying to get these things accurately marked. It's really important. One problem with the kind of life I lead is that there would inevitably be inaccuracies in the music. I don't have an editor anymore, which means I don't have another person to look at the work, and that is a problem. And, of course, I'm teaching Monday through Thursday, and then Friday morning I do the plants and the shopping and call my mother, and I do the bills or whatever. So I can start to get into stuff Friday night. Saturday I have. Sunday I have church in the morning, and then we start with the work week again. It ends up that there's this lurching from one thing to another, which is really difficult. So there are pieces where I would like to . . . I don't need to rewrite anything, but I need to make sure things are just plain right.

JK: So you are taking responsibility for a hundred years from now by making sure that your scores are accurate the way that you want them and being as present as possible in the recording process so that there is both oral and written record of exactly what you want.

HT: Yes, as much as possible. I know what I want to say musically. I just need to make sure that I've said it well enough. So, the posterity question. . . . What would I like conductors to know a hundred years from now? I would like them to have an accurate score with accurate parts and referential recordings. I'd also like someone to know how deep some of the music is—that if you *think* there's something there, it's probably there. I'd like the conductors to know that I was a serious, intelligent, honest, thoughtful, believing worker. Everything is intentional. I don't play. I don't go for quick effects.

JK: Development.

HT: Development, yes. If I am successful, it will come through. I'd like them to know that I took the work as a high calling. I think that would be a fair assessment.

JK: Audiences: have you given thought to how you want them to remember your work a month later?

HT: Like being in a landscape. I'd like them to feel that they were safe with me, and I wouldn't suddenly throw some dense cluster into the middle of the texture, and I wasn't going to refer to the Holocaust unexpectedly. What I'd like them to remember is that during my performance they were safe and had thoughts and were free to think, free to respond and bring the music into their own experience, however they wanted.

JK: What kind of continued evolution would you still like in your music?

HT: I just want to get better at what I do.

JK: The craft.

HT: Yes, I just want to be better. Even in *Shakkei*. Did I have to make all those time changes? I think I did, but could I write . . . I want to be as invisible as possible, and I want my performers to feel that they are really great, that I've shown them off beautifully. That's what I would like.

JK: What do you do when you get stuck? How do you go past it?

HT: I look and see when the deadline is. I can't afford to be stuck. I don't have the luxury. I just have to work through it. Whenever I'm stuck, the calendar is there. And next to it is a Celtic boar, meaning "do it!"

***

Works by Hilary Tann

ORCHESTRAL ENSEMBLES (SEE ALSO CHORAL/VOCAL)

Adirondack Night, with narrator (Oxford University Press [OUP], 1996).
Anecdote (Soliloquy for Solo Cello and Orchestra) (OUP, 2005).
As Ferns, for string orchestra (OUP, 1992).
Fanfare for a River (OUP, 2001).
From Afar (OUP, 2001).
From the Feather to the Mountain (OUP, 2005).
The Grey Tide and the Green (OUP, 2001).
Here, the Cliffs (Rhapsody for Solo Violin and Orchestra) (OUP, 1997).
High Rock Spring (Rowanberry Music, 2008).
In the First, Spinning Place (Concerto for Solo Alto Saxophone and Orchestra), featuring alto saxophone (OUP, 1999).
The Open Field (In Memoriam Tiananmen Square) (OUP, 1995).
Reibo (Rowanberry Music, 2010).
Sarsen (OUP, 2002).
Shakkei, for oboe (or flute or soprano sax) and small orchestra (Rowanberry Music, 2007).
Through the Echoing Timber (OUP, 1996).
Toward Dusk, for piccolo, flute, and string orchestra (OUP, 2002).
The Walls of Morlais Castle, for string orchestra (Rowanberry Music, 2009).
Water's Edge, for string orchestra (OUP, 1994).
With the Heather and the Small Birds (OUP, 1994).

CHAMBER MUSIC

Duo, for oboe and viola (OUP, 1992).
From the Song of Amergin, for flute, viola, and harp (OUP, 1998).
Gardens of Anna Maria Luisa de Medici, for flute, cello, and piano (OUP, 2005).
In the First, Spinning Place, for alto sax and piano (originally, concerto with orchestra), (OUP, 2010).
Llef, for flute and cello (originally for shakuhachi and cello), (OUP, 1995).
Nothing Forgotten, for violin, cello, and piano (OUP, 2000).
Of Erthe and Air, for flute/piccolo, clarinet or saxophone trio, and percussion (OUP, 1995).

On Ear and Ear . . ., for piano and viola (Rowanberry Music, 2011).
Shoji, for flute and oboe (Rowanberry Music, 2010).
. . . Slate, Blue-Gray, for violin, cello, and piano (Rowanberry Music, 2012).
Some of the Silence, for saxophone quartet (OUP, 2011).
The Walls of Morlais Castle, for oboe, viola, and cello (OUP, 2001).
Water's Edge, for piano duet (OUP, 1994).
Winter Sun, Summer Rain, for flute, clarinet, viola, cello, and celesta (OUP, 1992).

INSTRUMENTAL SOLO

The Cresset Stone
  cello (Rowanberry Music, 2004).
  viola (OUP, 2002).
  violin (OUP, 1995).
Doppelganger, for piano (OUP, 1993).
First Watch, for carillon (OUP, 2003).
In the First, Spinning Place, for piano or alto saxophone (OUP, 2009).
Kilvert's Hills, for bassoon or horn (Rowanberry Music, 2006).
Light from the Cliffs, for piano (Rowanberry Music, 2005).
Like Lightnings, for oboe (OUP, 2005).
Look Little Low Heavens, for trumpet (OUP, 1994).
Pinnae Ventorum, for organ (OUP, 2005).
A Sad Pavan Forbidden Mourning, for guitar (OUP, 2002).
Windhover, for soprano saxophone or flute (OUP, 1993).

CHORAL/VOCAL

Arachne, for soprano and crotale (OUP, 2002).
Between Sunsets, for soprano and piano (Rowanberry Music, 2011).
Children of Grace, for SATB and organ (Rowanberry Music, 2006).
Contemplations 8, 9, for SSA (Rowanberry Music, 2011).
Contemplations 21, 22, for SSA (Brichtmark Music, 2007).
Exultet Terra, for SATB antiphonal choirs and double-reed quintet (Rowanberry Music, 2011).
A Girl's Song to Her Mother, for soprano and oboe (OUP, 2003).
The Moor, for SA chorus (OUP, 1999).
Mother and Son, for soprano, E♭ clarinet, viola, and cello or soprano with string trio (OUP, 2000).
Paradise, for SAATBB (Rowanberry Music, 2008).
Psalm 104 (Praise, My Soul) (OUP, 2002).
  for SATB and chamber orchestra
  for SATB, two trumpets in C, and organ
Psalm 86 (Incline Thine Ear), for SATB, organ, and optional trumpet (Rowanberry Music, 2006).
Psalm 136 (Luminaria Magna), for SATB and organ (OUP, 2003).

Songs of the Cotton Grass, for soprano and oboe (OUP, 2009).
Sound Dawn, for TTBB, and piano (OUP, 1983).
That Jewel-Spirit . . . (Brichtmark, 2007).
  for SSA, flute, and piano
  for SSA, flute, and string orchestra
Wales, Our Land (Cymru, ein gwald), for SATB, flute, and optional piano (OUP, 2004).
Wellspring, for SSA (Brichtmark Music, 2007).
Wings of the Grasses, for soprano and oboe (OUP, 2004).

Ann Marsden

17

Libby Larsen

Libby Larsen's musical inspirations derive from our dynamically changing American culture, as she asks herself when she sits down to write, "What is music itself today, to me?" Born in 1950, Larsen has spent most of her life in Minneapolis. Her work is filled with performance directions drawn from common language, such as "Bring it!" designed to encourage conversation among performers. Larsen's more than four decades of work depict the changing American culture and vernacular, and she hopes that depiction will facilitate a deeper understanding and performance of the music.

Larsen has long recognized the cultural impact of technology. Her critically acclaimed opera *Frankenstein* (1990) was a multimedia work combining live vocalists and instrumentalists with video and audio technology, and she has created numerous other works involving electronics throughout the years. Our conversation includes a lengthy dialogue about how technology is influencing the creation and the listener's expectation of the musical art form. A freelance composer who accepts a small number of students at a time, Larsen has witnessed the declining ability in young people to hear acoustic sound. She explains that in addition to acquiring the necessary compositional skills, young composers today need integrated listening skills for acoustic and electronic sounds.

Equally comfortable in the instrumental and vocal worlds, Larsen acknowledges significant differences between the two. Our conversation includes a discussion of choral versus instrumental publication, performers, and audience. Well-known for her vocal and choral music, Larsen has great respect for text and poet. She recognizes the rhythmic influence of American culture and language, and consequently she writes with a rhythmic focus representing natural speech. Like Alice Parker's, Larsen's music for voice emphasizes the natural fluidity of language.

Forty years of freelance composing teaches one about the importance of balancing craft with an understanding of the business of composition. Larsen plans for the fat and famine of her art. Her Web site has been shaped by her grasp of evolving performer expectations, making it possible for performers and conductors to have access to music and information whenever they need it. A prolific composer with over three hundred works for varied mediums, Larsen is conscious of her legacy, working hard to leave a "boulevard" of work for future generations to discover. At the same time, she acknowledges frankly the vicissitudes of the composing world, evident in both the changing "It-girls" of composition and the anxiety that emerges unexpectedly despite her years of success.

Many composers, including Jennifer Higdon, credit Larsen with helping to eradicate the glass ceiling for women composers. Larsen would much rather discuss her work than her gender, yet she recognizes the changes over the years for women composers. In her own experience, the lack of female role models in music while she was growing up encouraged her to seek out various other women artists, resulting in her numerous settings of women poets. Larsen has received copious awards, including a Lifetime Achievement Award from the American Academy of Arts and Letters, the 2010 George Peabody Medal, the Eugene McDermott Award in the Arts from the Massachusetts Institute of Technology, and a 1994 Grammy Award for producing the CD *The Art of Arleen Augér.* Larsen's song cycle *Sonnets from the Portuguese* (1989), based on poetry by Elizabeth

Barrett Browning, is featured on that same CD. In 2003–4, she held the Harissios Papamarkou Chair in Education and Technology at the Library of Congress Kluge Center. Her work is published through Oxford, ECS, and Libby Larsen Publishing.

***

May 2010, at her home in Minneapolis

JENNIFER KELLY: You have been composing professionally for about forty years. How has your creative experience changed over time?

LIBBY LARSEN: I moved from horizontal time to vertical time in the creative process when my daughter was born. It took me about a year to learn how to create in vertical time. Vertical time means, while it appears to be scraps of time on the surface of daily life, it actually is not. That's only clock time. So instead of luxuriating in the hours of consideration, if I had twenty minutes, I went deep, so that the twenty minutes could have felt like twelve hours.

JK: I can understand the need to do that with a new baby.

LL: Yes, so what has changed radically is my ability to focus on an idea as it is becoming. Focus fast. Feel it, see it, work with it, and work deeply with it. Editing quickly. Considering with laser-like focus, rather than asking should I, shouldn't I, would this, could this? That whole process speeds up rapidly when you work vertically.

JK: How old is your daughter now?

LL: Twenty-four.

JK: Since she grew up, do you find that you still work that way or still want to work that way?

LL: Oh, absolutely. It's the romantic notion that you need guarded solitude in order to develop the big idea well. That now seems, to me, to be a completely Victorian notion.

JK: Well, our society is multitasking and moving faster everywhere.

LL: Yeah. And the key is not to multitask. I think it's becoming clearer in our culture that, as you're multitasking, you're not actually doing anything deeply. So the key is, when vertical time presents itself, simply go there. Cast off everything else and go there, even if it's for a minute or two minutes. I can't put this any other way. If you actually focus and work in vertical time, you just don't exist in the time plane that we've constructed to civilize our lives.

JK: I would imagine that it would also help one manage better in our current state of crazy making.

LL: Although the more crazy it gets, the more centered I am. I do know how to go in and come out. At first it was very awkward. It was right before notational programs and file sharing, 1986 to 1992. When I was first doing it, I wrote two operas and a piano concerto. Looking at the scores, I can see where my daughter Winnie was crawling all over my rug while I was writing things out.

JK: You bring up the issue of technology. As a composer, what is your relationship with technology?

LL: I've kept up with plugged-in computer technology as it's been developing, which is a ridiculously short amount of time that we've had it. I was trained in the traditional skills, and now I'm part of, like it or not, the beginnings of the next two hundred years—whatever that is. So I have an interesting perspective on it. I think we're going to be very impoverished musically. Because the computer requires input by fields, and it's binomial.

JK: Moves in fields. Do you mean programs like Finale, layer upon layer?

LL: Yes. It's also binomial, and music is not. Music is spherical and multidimensional. And the computer is such a meager replacement for the brain. Only speed and calculation. Anything else you can do on the computer, the brain does infinitely better.

JK: So, given the fact that as a contemporary composer you understand that you must use this tool, how do you get to the depth and all the spheres? How do you combat the tool?

LL: Well, I don't use it to compose. If I did use it to compose, I would be composing computer music. Music that the computer-instrument can create. I do use it to construct sound and to add sound to acoustic sound—to morph sounds together. And I'm developing a character for my next opera to be performed with computer. So I'm treating it as a companion instrument, an instrument to morph. In this particular opera I will be able to use it for what it does very well. And what it does well, it does *very* well. What it doesn't do is acoustic music. It's just terrible at it. It will not get better because of the quality of sound. It is produced sound, which is compressed and put through the worst speakers imaginable to man, and, as long as it is a mass-marketing tool, the sound will not get better.

JK: Can you speculate where American composed music might go?

LL: I think there will continue to be a great deal more of "at-home" composing. Journey of the self through composing will become much more commonplace.

JK: Perhaps there would be more composers.

LL: Many, many more. Which then changes the notion of what is a composer. That's why I know we're at the end of the last era. The *über*-genius "knows"—that's a romantic notion.

JK: So how does it feel to be in the midst of that change—a conscious and active participant prior to the change, being in it, and coming into the next?

LL: I am letting go quite a bit. I am thrilled by the change, so what I'm doing more of is articulating to people what I see. Talking to composers who are in faculty departments. Talking about what composition looks like in a department.

JK: For example, what would you propose for a composition department?

LL: I think a good composition department now needs to understand that, if the composer they produce is going to be a viable member of the community at large, you have to do both technology and acoustic. They have to be integrated, as they do in all performing arts. Right now, there are no microphone-technique classes in conservatories; it's crazy. There's no studio-technique classes.

JK: You know where you find those things? Community colleges.

LL: Yeah, you do. Community colleges, community music schools, and Berklee [School of Music]. You want composers and performers and conductors to be as fluent as possible in the techniques of music making in the world in which they live.

JK: Otherwise, we'll have fewer and fewer trained, educated students doing this, because they won't go to the schools.

LL: They won't. They will not go to the schools. So that means we need to take a very careful look at the reasons we teach what we teach. For example, it was assumed consensus that the ear knows the acoustic sound. That was assumed prior to the recent influx of technology, but now it's not so clear. Performance practice and tradition are going to be very different within twenty years. We really need to define the masters in a world of music that has been excluded from the academy, the masters of a music that has been informing us as a culture.

JK: Now, would that be creating a new canon? Or is "canon" an antiquated word anyway?

LL: The easiest, laziest thing to do would be to develop a parallel canon. I've been researching this, and my idea of the canon is that it's created from the Victor Red Seal records that went out with the gramophone in the early 1900s while we were building music education and turning concerts into an industry. Henry Edward Krehbeil, Walter Damrosch, and Frances Elliott Clark—the three of them worked for RCA and put together their box of records. The canon was built around that finite set of Victor Red Seal records and the few men who decided what pieces would be on them. It created defining articulations.

JK: A few people who had so much power that still holds.

LL: Yeah. It was the first mass marketing all over the country of a hierarchy like that. Orchestra. Opera. Choral master works. Solo piano. Today, we have multitudes of music available in individual customized time and place, which is the exact opposite of a hundred years ago. So, if that's the case, it seems to me that we need to examine the best of our educational tools, how we prepare to be great musicians and how we prepare the mind to receive music, be curious about it, reproduce it, research it, integrate it into other parts of our lives. I think we probably need to change the whole assumption of what a musician is when they're done matriculating with us. They would be much more creative, deeply spontaneous, broader thinkers.

JK: Which leads to the question, can we teach evaluation in music?

LL: Yes, we can, but we need to teach listening skills, how to actually listen to music itself. There are books that do this, but they are so outdated. Talking about music really becomes a very important part of an education about music.

JK: As a conductor, I want to know what composers think, because it changes how I re-create and interpret the music.

LL: Well, I've been thinking about what is essential in music, and it seems to me there are only four things: pitch, motion, architecture, and emotional connection. I decided that humanism was so important in every piece I write. I ask myself each day that I'm writing, "What is music itself today, to me?" And it changes every day. I think about how is the world moving, pitching, shaping itself, and connecting emotionally to itself. For instance, I've never been particularly beholden to pitch as the most important compositional parameter. I think pitch actually was more important in another culture. Our language is rhythmic. It's not a pitched language. It's a rhythmic language.

JK: How do you know when a piece of yours is making or will make an impact?

LL: I can just feel it. I can't say how it's going to touch them, because listening is unique. It's really sensing the energy of what's going on and working that way. For example, there is a tonal thing that I've been dealing with and thinking hard about. The twelve equal tones that are given to us by the piano are useful only to a certain point. A direct pitch, a piano-tuned pitch almost feels antique. I never liked piano in the first place, because I was trained in Gregorian chant, and so singing to a piano has always been rather hideous to me. And I'm at a crossroads, because I don't want to write piano choral music right now. I want to write choral music with CDs, with other sound, with speakers—to do what the computer was meant to do. And I want to write mixed-sound pieces.

JK: As a conductor who does a lot of choir, I look forward to that. Choral music seems to be very accepting of newly composed music. It's always about what's hip and who's new. But I find that much of the new music being written for choir uses old techniques, as if the two possible sound aesthetics are either common practice period or cluster chords. I crave choral music finely crafted, meaningful, and interesting for the singers using mixed media or alternative sounds. There is some, but not very much.

LL: I find that many of the conductors don't know the techniques. I'd like to see choral ensembles evolve so that my and others' music can evolve and be heard. And that is my new horizon. The young composers will do it, but they don't know how to compose yet. They're just beginning, babies, like I was forty years ago, just trying to put the piece together.

JK: What about instrumental music? Can you use those techniques?

LL: Oh, yes, much more so in instrumental music. Instrumentalists are much more curious about how to do electro-acoustic pieces, so there's a great deal of electro-acoustic chamber music, which is a body of repertoire being developed, much of it very fine. Personally, in instrumental music, I'm interested in working with the very best performers possible and giving them pieces that challenge them.

JK: In a 2005 interview with me, you described contemporary music as a single-listening art form because it is newly composed, and one doesn't know if there will be a recording or a second performance for those listeners. Do you still hold to that view, or have your views changed?

LL: My views have changed a little bit. Probably in the concert hall, it is still a single listening art form, but, because of file sharing and iTunes and YouTube, I would say no. It's available to millions. It's a question of finding it now. The finding it is quite a different journey.

JK: So, going back to how things have changed for you over the past forty years, what about the business end of things? Marketing, finding the commissions, et cetera.

LL: That's changed quite radically. The technology and expectations changed, and now people will email me and say they need to hear a piece, and they can't find it on my Web site. So I'm putting everything up on my Web site. Whole pieces. It could be that that might be the only time the person will listen to the piece. So the question becomes, Am I putting the piece up for sale or for listening?

JK: So which is it?

LL: Listening. The concert hall now is YouTube and the Internet, or the iPod. I can't control the listening, but I can protect the taking of the music to be used in other ways. I would like people to listen. That is a new concert hall. I don't know that composers need to walk out on stage and take a bow. What I need is communication with people of curious minds that want to listen to music.

JK: Do you have the same needs with choral music?

LL: Different with choral music, I have to say. What I need with choral music is communication with the whole community. All levels, ages, styles. Oversight organizations try to treat choral music as if it was instrumental music, and it is not. It's fundamentally different. It's a community of voices that come together, breathe together, and receive their energy from each other and the people who are there. Ever it has been, and ever it will be.

JK: Sounds like you hold a lot of reverence for it.

LL: I do. It's a completely different animal. For me, the choral experience is a gathering of people coming together to keep time through breathing, which is the most primal experience we have. I care about words. I care about the nature of the bard—the chorus as bard. We count on certain choral sounds, such as the St. Olaf sound or the Zielinski sound, but they are all in service of the community. The community of the words, the people, the singers, the hearers.

JK: I agree with you. I don't particularly enjoy listening to a lot of recorded choral music, but I really enjoy going to live choral concerts, as long as they're telling me a story. If I go to a live concert where the goal seems to be to sound like a perfect recording, I'm bored instantly.

LL: Me too. Completely bored. I just think, You're not here to sing to us. You're making nice sound, and I hear the words, but you're not singing. You sing the soul, the breath. I think choral music is in for a big heyday here, because it's human.

JK: And one of your responses as a composer to that sense of community and upcoming heyday is thinking about new directions, such as adding mixed sounds.

LL: I want to develop my own sound. I'm not really fond of a lot of the choral music that is around today. It feels like warm, wet washcloths to me. There is beauty, but so often it doesn't matter what the words are. I think the human voice is just dying to express itself. Plus, there's the other cultural fact that it's very hard for people to hear music today that doesn't have text. Very difficult to find music that doesn't have text.

JK: And to get young students interested in it.

LL: Everything is texted. So now you have generations who aren't actually practicing listening to music itself. They're listening to texted tonality.

JK: I know you've always revered the poet and revered the text itself, but, with this understanding of the cultural changes, does that change your relationship with text or change how you compose with text?

LL: I'm digging much deeper. Digging to understand what word—if I can only get one word through this particular composition, what is it? Why? Actually, I am about to start a blog on my Web site about composing, so I can reveal process. I'm involving people in the whole process. Now, if they come to me wanting a composition, I say, "Good, let's get busy." It's not going to be about me giving you a composition. It's going to be us talking about it and thinking about it.

JK: From its inception. Are you in a place where you can choose between commissions?

LL: No. I don't think any of us are. There are usually two or three composers for about five years that can pick and choose, but that seems to be the nature of it. New "It-girls." Give it another ten years, and it will be somebody else. So I am not currently in a place where I can pick and choose.

JK: Was there a defining moment when you realized you were a composer?

LL: Yeah, I was in a class in college. It was an undergraduate theory class—I can't even remember what we were studying, but we had to write a piece for an assignment. I sat there, and the piece just arrived whole in my head. *Circular Rondo* for treble, wind, and guitar. And right then I knew I must be a composer. Not that I love to do it, just that I am it.

JK: What is the importance of composer mentoring?

LL: I think it's very, very important. You can't teach composition, but you can guide it. I only take three students at a time because there are techniques you can use for getting pitch going and hearing rhythm in a different way, analyzing scores, doing things to free up the subconscious that holds up the music in the brain of a composer. And so teaching, from my perspective, is to learn the person pretty well. Help the student where you can, and direct the student to others in places where you can't help them.

JK: So you have to let go of ego. You have to say, "This is where I can help a student, and this is where I can't."

LL: Absolutely. Letting go of ego is tremendously important. As a composer, you need to think that everyone wants to hear what you put on paper, but then, the more you let go of it, the better the music is. I find the same thing with teaching. Let go because you want your students to be really good. And in my case, I don't want them to sound like me. I feel like if they do, I'm doing something wrong.

JK: You want them to find their own voice. You obviously care about this, so why didn't you go into a university teaching position in composition?

LL: I'm too restless. Another reason is that I have to write music.

JK: And that would take away from writing music.

LL: Enormously. And I'm prolific, so that would be frustrating. Another reason was gender battles. I was considering teaching. I was about to get my doctorate, and I was looking around to see the lay of the land. It was 1978. I'd already been on many committees at the university, and I knew that wherever I went, I would be on every gender-issue committee on campus.

JK: Because you happened to be the woman.

LL: Yes, so I would be spending lots of time articulating the role of women to a generation that didn't want to hear it. I thought to myself that we just had to let these guys change. It's going to change, but this whole generation is going to have to retire.

JK: That was 1978. So has that happened?

LL: It's 2010. It's much better. Although what I didn't count on was technology. With the introduction of technology as an entry tool and a pool of composers, there are fewer women composers. It's pretty drastic, actually. They're not studying.

JK: So is it because technology is still sort of considered a boys' club?

LL: Yeah, that's part of it. Another part of it is that there are many other roads open to women: doctor, lawyer, physicist, marine biologist. There's a different playing field than there was previously. Where are the American women studying composition?

JK: There are more role models for women to see other women actively working in a host of fields.

LL: Yes, there are.

JK: Who were your role models?

LL: Thea Musgrave, Pauline Oliveros—I found them on my own later. I knew about Vivian Fine, Ursula Mamlock. In grad school I started looking for models, and they were hard to find. So I started to find writers. Literary writers. I started looking for women who were communicating through any art form.

JK: That voice.

LL: Yeah, articulating themselves through an art form. Not so many in composition. I met Thea Musgrave right away, which was very helpful. We're still friends. And I've known Pauline Oliveros for many, many years. I never met Vivian Fine and Ursula Mamlock; I only knew about them.

JK: Today, I think the world is smaller. This may sound like a stereotype, but it's almost as if living women composers all know each other. Do you?

LL: We mostly do, and it's really nice.

JK: Do you think that is one of the roles of women's-only concerts, to meet each other?

LL: Yes, I would say. I met Ellen Zwillich on a National Endowment panel where we were the only women. And Joan Tower, I think we got to know each other through some women's concerts. Victoria Bond I met through the Meet the Composer program. Jennifer Higdon I don't really know—we just met each other around and about. She's younger, and I think it's through seminars and meetings. We find each other.

JK: Is there some kind of sisterhood, where if you're on a panel of a bunch of people and there's one other woman over there, you make sure to meet her?

LL: That's interesting. I don't think it's anything planned, but we do. I also notice that when there are a couple of us on a panel, we go out of our way without anybody asking to give everyone a chance to talk. Very supportive. There will always be some composers who are not that way. And you just think, "Wow, you're missing out. Don't do this."

JK: Because it's a community, which is interesting, because it seems to me that composition is a very isolating experience. So you've got to find your community somewhere.

LL: Yeah, you do. It can be very isolating. You have to know how to love solitude and not confuse it with loneliness. And so you find your community wherever you can. And with women in particular, I think we have a special, warm place in our hearts.

JK: If you were beginning your compositional path now at the beginning of the twenty-first century, how do you think your path as a woman in the career of composition would be different?

LL: I'd grow up with a broader skill set, so there would be a broader range of opportunities to make pieces. I might not have to travel the way I've had to travel, because technology makes it possible to not travel and still be places, so I would think that the appearance would become more of a rare coin.

JK: Is there still a need in the twenty-first century for women-only concerts, festivals, books?

LL: Yeah, I do think so. There's not yet a critical mass of information available. We really need a critical mass, so we need as much activity as we can get. How it's presented is important. There is still women's history month. And black history month. We're getting there. But it's still going to take another generation to make it.

JK: What can I do as conductor, teacher, and scholar to help it change?

LL: Contribute to the critical mass. As conductor, you could be doing women's music on every single concert. It's always there. This is what I'm doing myself as a scholar: I'm checking my own assumptions. By assumptions, I mean the way that I phrase references that first come out of my mouth. I'm still saying "Bach and Beethoven." What's the matter with me? Why am I not adding women? So what I'm working on now is the way I articulate myself. If I change my points of reference, people will, too, because they'll hear us, because we're leaders.

JK: It seems like we can affect an entire generation quickly by doing that.

LL: We can by changing our own referential language. And just do it without any hoopla. For instance, I talk about the twentieth century as music of the 1900s as a way of positioning the now. I think we, because we're the leaders, need to reshape our own referential language and practice the inclusion of works we think need to be included, without hoopla.

JK: Just be equal.

LL: Just be equal. Recordings and publishing, that's another question, because those industries are in such trouble.

JK: Is that in part because people are going into self-publishing?

LL: Yes. It's also because a lot of publishing houses are going to five-year profit margins. A piece needs to make a fairly substantial profit within five years of the music's publishing date. But of course that's not how any pieces work, except disposable choral music and piano music. A piece like my *Rodeo Queen of Heaven* may become part of the repertoire, but it's going to take between ten and fifteen years.

JK: I notice you are doing some self-publishing now.

LL: I am doing some self-publishing, specifically of my instrumental music. Because the teachers have to teach the students the pieces, and then the students have to become teachers, and it needs time to become part of its own repertoire. I'm not with Oxford anymore, but I don't want to self-publish choral music, so I'm going to approach a publishing house for those.

JK: What are the advantages and disadvantages of working with a particular house and then self-publishing?

LL: With a house, the advantages are market and distribution. So with choral music it makes perfect sense to use a publishing house, because I need to compose, and I really want to be represented by someone at the choral conferences. The choral publishing houses do it so much better than I could do it or want to do it. The downside is just money, because with choral music you get 10 percent of a sale, and the publishing house owns it. They get 90 percent, and you get 10 percent, and they own the work. If you publish it yourself, you get 100 percent, but you have to market it yourself. You have to print it and service all the clients. You have to advertise and show up. You have to do business, and business in the choral world is quite different than business in the instrumental world.

JK: Shifting gears. . . . As someone who has composed through the evolution of what some call "feminist musicology," what do you think has been its role, and does it still have a place today?

LL: Well, I admire feminist musicology because it has successfully created a conversation about music that allows, asks, and invites anyone who cares to be part of the perspective to look at music in a very different way than it's been looked at.

JK: Whether or not everyone agrees, it inspires thinking and questioning.

LL: Whether or not they agree. The thinking and questioning that feminist musicology has brought to the front is really useful because it's brought all kinds of active energy into the dialogue in whatever way that you see it, and that I think is brilliant. I also find it ironic that feminist musicology has used a very patriarchic, hierarchical system to establish itself as a discipline by accepting the monastic academic system and the dialectic—the whole notion of the dialectic.

JK: Of choosing where feminist musicologists present their information?

LL: Yes.

JK: Does use of the word "canon" assume a patriarchal hierarchy?

LL: It is already assuming a patriarchal hierarchy and assuming an either/or situation. It's just so incredibly patriarchal.

JK: So by discussing it, we're already subcategorizing it. And yet by discussing it, we're offering dialogue and opportunity for people to think and talk about it.

LL: Yes, so I admire it, but I also find it quite ironic. Does it have a place? Sure, it has a place, because it continues to create dialogue. Does it give us insight into gender and music? I don't think so. Not music itself—meaning pitch, motion, architecture, and emotional connection. Yet it has caused many people to focus on music that maybe would have not focused on it in any analytical way. Does it still have a place? Yes, because the dialogue goes on. If it polarizes, though—if it ever says it "must be" or "is,"—then the dialogue is over.

JK: How do you balance the work and nonwork parts of your life? Because you made some choices, some priorities, like having a family.

LL: Yeah, that's why I'm so clear about vertical time. Something else, too, is that I had to work through part of my domestic assumption of power. Such as who does what and how I really felt about it. If something is really important to me, then I have to take that on. If it's not really important, then I'm going to compose. I had to wash away all the fifties and sixties, those kinds of role things. But also give up some things. Vertical time comes really fast. You'll see. It just does.

JK: When describing your *Love Songs: Five Songs on Texts by Women Poets,* you said when I interviewed you last that you were talking about the holding on and letting go that comes with mature love. Is that holding on and letting go a common thread for you among your text-based music?

LL: I hadn't thought about it, but yes. And also acoustic music in the face of a technological future. If I can't be part of the technological future, I let go of the professional. Continue to write music but let go of the profession.

JK: So you choose to adapt, change with it, and bend.

LL: Yeah, and either love the changes as they go, or let go. I guess it's because I learned music by learning Gregorian chant, which has long since been let go of. Just being embodied is a process of being and letting go. Just like every breath is a letting go. I'm not trying to tell anybody anything about it. I'm just trying to communicate about it.

JK: Certainly. What kind of relationship do you like to have with a conductor or performer?

LL: It's happiest when I respect as fully as I can the talents of the conductor and performer and they respect as fully as they can my talents as composer, what I bring to them, and we both respect the piece more than we respect each other. So that we really look at the piece, really dig in. That's when it's happiest. Some people say it's really collaborative, and I find that a relief to the old notion of the romantic composer, where it's perfect on the page and nobody gets to deviate. It can't be perfect on the page, because every hall is different and every instrument is different. The most fun I get to have is when we can really dig in and figure out what the piece is. When we respect each other and we respect the music more.

JK: Some say everything a performer wants to know is on the page, and others say the page is only the beginning. Where are you on that continuum?

LL: It depends on what measure, what gesture, and what beat [*laughs*]. I'd say I move back and forth on the continuum, as do the performers. They have the same continuum with how they approach the piece. But my job has to be to get it pretty much on the page.

JK: Are you at a point in your life where you've started to think about legacy?

LL: A little bit. I am doing a lot more proofreading to make sure that everything is as I want it or, if there are mistakes, that it's up on the Web site. Every piece has an errata page. All my materials are very well organized. I always wanted to leave a legacy of at least forty years of constant public work, of working in public with integrity. And I don't want to leave just a path; I want to leave a boulevard. Because I do think that in terms of women composers, and now I think it would be in terms of concert composers—that as music itself changes, people will always be digging around to find what was. So I'm leaving as many droppings as I can! [*Laughs*] I'm really upset that young women don't seem to be showing up to learn the craft. And it appears cyclic to me, so I'm worried that it's going to be a long time before there's another wave. And then people will start saying, "Wait, who was around? What was going on?" So I want to make sure that we're found. I want to make sure that if there's opportunity for a rebirth in my work that it can be found.

JK: As someone who's been well vetted on the stage, do you still have the occasional "freakout" moment?

LL: I still have a bad dream. In some unnamed, fairly large auditorium that's sort of sage green and birch, I'm sitting there and getting ready to listen to the piece, and before it even starts people start streaming out of the hall. There is also a manifestation, a silly side of that dream. I'm backstage, and I don't know why, but I'm dressed in a *La Traviata* gorgeous gown, and I have to sing, and I'm not trained as a singer, but it's my turn to go out on stage, so I go out and play jazz bassoon [*laughs*].

JK: Who is sitting in the audiences today for contemporary music?

LL: Very complicated question. It depends on where the concert is. For choral concerts, everybody is in the audience, because it's the nature of the community. New pieces of orchestra, it's just the orchestra audience. I'm talking about America, because I haven't been in Europe at a contemporary concert in quite a while. I think clubs have the best, most interesting audiences now. Kids who tend to be very young, really going after learning how they want to listen. They often have an interdisciplinary appreciation, so they get bigger connections.

JK: How do you make it work financially as a freelance composer? Balance everything forever?

LL: Yes [*laughs*]. It's cash flow. You have to be very careful about how you allot the money that's in, because in times of fat you can't assume that it's going to last. Save like crazy. And then try to get enough to have a cash flow so that I can keep steady work going. For instance, it's always down in August just because the kind of music I write tends to go with the academic season; the classical-music season is sort of the academic season. It's just very careful money management.

JK: You've composed so much music. How do you keep the curiosity alive in it?

LL: By listening to people talk. I'm never not curious. The language, our language—it is so fluid. It continues to evolve every day in new and different ways. It's just fascinating to listen.

JK: You can definitely see examples of your language connection in your vernacular performance directions. I remember talking with you about that. You were saying that it changes over time depending on the nature of a culture. What's happening now?

LL: What's happening now? To me, rapid hip hop sounds so antique now. And I've learned to analyze and take what I can from it, but our language now has gotten much more inflected lately. It's more slighted, curved, and hooked.

JK: Do you work every day?

LL: I do, yes, in vertical time. Quiet in the morning for a half hour. And I run maybe four or five times a week with friends. We don't talk about music. I spend the rest of the time thinking. I love to think.

JK: I'd like to ask about your role as a composer in American music. Perhaps you will be known as a composer of cultural reference reflecting a culture that constantly changes.

LL: Well, if the way I am perceived is to stay vigilant and current with how the culture articulates itself, then that could very well be it. I do know that I consider rational techniques in service to instinct. You have to know all those techniques, but it's in service to instinct, which is human. It's not an encampment. I'm not waving any banners. I'm just writing music. And instincts change.

JK: What are you most proud of at this point in your life?

LL: In my working life, I think I'm most proud of being consistently productive with integrity, purpose, and being. That I am most proud of. In my personal life, I'm just proud of having a well-rounded life. I wanted to live a well-rounded life, and I'm living a well-rounded life. And it feels like I'm not hurting anybody, and I feel good about that. The other thing that went through my mind is that I won't be quiet. I just won't be quiet. A lot of my friends would say that. My parents kept trying to make me be quiet.

JK: We need loud people. People with voices.

LL: People who will walk into a room and say something doesn't smell right. I just won't be quiet.

***

Works by Libby Larsen

OPERA

Barnum's Bird, chamber choral opera in two acts, libretto by Bridget Carpenter (Oxford University Press [OUP], 2000).

Clair de Lune, two-act chamber opera, libretto by Patricia Hampl (ECS, 1984).

Dreaming Blue, opera in one act for child actor, SATB soloists, children's chorus, rhythm chorus, and drumming group (OUP, 2002).

Eric Hermannson's Soul, full-length opera with orchestra, libretto by Rader-Shieber (OUP, 1998).

Every Man Jack, chamber opera based on the life of Jack London, libretto by Philip Littell (Libby Larsen Publishing, 2006).

Frankenstein: The Modern Prometheus, full-length music drama (ECS, 1990).

Moon Door, full-evening performance with slides, tapes, and costumes (ECS, 1976,1980).

Mrs. Dalloway, full-length music drama in two acts, libretto by Bonnie Grice (ECS, 1993).
Picnic, opera in three acts, based on the play by Willian Inge, libretto by David Holley (Libby Larsen Publishing, 2009).
The Silver Fox, one-act opera for the young, libretto by John Olive (ECS, 1979).
A Wrinkle in Time, one-act opera, libretto by Walter Green (ECS, 1991).

ORCHESTRAL ENSEMBLES

All Around Sound, for orchestra and cued CD (Libby Larsen Publishing, 1999).
Ancient Places (Libby Larsen Publishing, 2008).
The Atmosphere as a Fluid System, for flute solo, percussion, and string orchestra (OUP, 1992).
Bach 358 (Libby Larsen Publishing, 2008).
Blue Fiddler (OUP, 1996).
A Brandenburg for the New Millennium, for trumpet, marimba, electric guitar, amplified harpsichord, and string orchestra (Libby Larsen Publishing, 2002).
Collage: Boogie (ECS, 1988).
Concerto: Cold, Silent Snow, for flute, harp, and chamber orchestra (ECS, 1989).
Concerto for Trumpet and Orchestra, featuring C trumpet (ECS, 1988).
Deep Summer Music (ECS, 1982).
Evening in the Palace of Reason, for string orchestra and string quartet (Libby Larsen Publishing, 2008).
Fanfare: Sizzle (OUP, 2001).
Fanfare, Strum, for orchestra, no strings (OUP, 1996).
Marimba Concerto: After Hampton, featuring marimba (ECS, 1992).
The Moabit Sonnets, for two sopranos, tenor, bass, and chamber orchestra (Libby Larsen Publishing, 2011).
Overture for the End of a Century (OUP, 1994).
Overture: Parachute Dancing (ECS, 1983).
Piano Concerto: Since Armstrong (ECS, 1992).
Pinions, for violin and chamber orchestra (ECS, 1981).
Ring of Fire (OUP, 1995).
Roll Out the Thunder (OUP, 1997).
Solo Symphony (Symphony No. 5) (OUP, 1999).
Song Concerto, for saxophone (alto and soprano) and chamber orchestra (Libby Larsen Publishing, 2005).
A Spell on Me That Holy Hour: Overture to Tsvetaeva (OUP, 1997).
Still Life with Violin, featuring violin (OUP, 2000).
String Symphony (Symphony No. 4), for string orchestra (OUP, 1999).
Symphony: Forward (Libby Larsen Publishing, 2011).
Symphony No. 3: Lyric (ECS, 1992).
Symphony: Water Music (Symphony No. 1), (ECS, 1985).
Tambourines! (ECS, 1991).

Weaver's Song and Jig, for chamber orchestra and string band (ECS, 1978).
What the Monster Saw, for orchestra and optional slides, adapted from *Frankenstein* (ECS, 1987).

BAND/WIND ENSEMBLE

Brass Flight, for brass choir (OUP, 1996).
Concert Dances, for concert band (OUP, 1996).
Cri de Coeur, for solo euphonium and wind ensemble (Potenza Music, 2009).
Grand Rondo, for concert band (ECS, 1988).
Hambone, for concert band (BandQuest: American Composers Forum, 1999).
Holy Roller, arranged by Boyd, for solo saxophone and wind ensemble (OUP, 1997).
An Introduction to the Moon, for symphonic wind ensemble, tuned water glasses, recorded voice, and eight collaborative improvisations (OUP, 2005).
River Fanfare, for brass band (Libby Larsen Publishing, 2004).
Short Symphony, for concert band (OUP, 1996).
Strut, for concert band (OUP, 2003).
Sun Song, for concert band (ECS, 1991).
Ursa, for tuba and wind ensemble (Libby Larsen Publishing, 2010).
Within the Circles of Our Lives, for soprano, baritone, and wind ensemble (ECS, 2007).

ORCHESTRA WITH CHORAL/VOCAL

Canticle of Mary, for SSA chorus and chamber orchestra (also four-hand piano version), (OUP, 1994).
Coming Forth into Day (Symphony No. 2), for soprano, baritone, SATB, and full orchestra (ECS, 1986).
Encircling Skies, for double choir, full orchestra, full wind ensemble, three marimbas, three pianos, and samples (Libby Larsen Publishing, 2009).
I It Am: The Shewings of Julian of Norwich, for soprano, countertenor, baritone solos, SATB divisi, and chamber orchestra (OUP, 2003).
In a Winter Garden, for soprano, tenor, SATB, and chamber orchestra (ECS, 1982).
Notes Slipped under the Door, for soprano, solo flute, and orchestra (OUP, 2001).
Praise One, for SATB, SATB chorus favori, and orchestra (OUP, (2004).
Raspberry Island Dreaming, for mezzo-soprano and orchestra (Libby Larsen Publishing, 2002).
Sacred Vows, for tenor, baritone, narrator, SATB chorus, and full orchestra (Libby Larsen Publishing, 2009).
Song: Dances to the Light, for SA, Orff instruments, and full orchestra (or piano), (OUP, 1994).
Songs from Letters, for soprano and chamber ensemble (also piano version), (OUP, 1989).
Songs of Light and Love, for soprano and chamber ensemble (OUP, 1988).
Sonnets from the Portuguese, for soprano and chamber ensemble (also piano version), (OUP, 1991).

This Unbearable Stillness: Songs from the Balcony (orchestral version), for soprano, percussion, celeste, and string orchestra (Libby Larsen Publishing, 2008).
Three Summer Scenes, for SATB, optional youth chorus, and full orchestra (ECS, 1988).

CHORAL

Alaska Spring, for SATB and string quartet (Libby Larsen Publishing, 2011).
All Shall Be Well, SA, sop, sop recorder, triangle, and keyboard (ECS, 1979).
Alleluia, for SATB (ECS, 1992).
And Sparrows Everywhere, for SATB and piano (ECS, 1985).
The Ballerina and the Clown, for SSA and harp (OUP, 2002).
The Blackbird, for TTBB chorus and piano (Libby Larsen Publishing, 2007).
A Book of Spells, for SSAA and piano (Libby Larsen Publishing, 2009).
By a Departing Light, for SATB (Libby Larsen Publishing, 1999).
Canticle of Mary, for SSA and four-hand piano (also chamber orchestra version), (OUP, 1994).
Canticle of Mary, for SSAAA, finger cymbals, synthesizer, and organ (ECS, 1987).
Celebration Mass: Catholic Edition, for congregation, SATB, and organ (Libby Larsen Publishing, 2011).
Celebration Mass: Lutheran Edition, for congregation, SATB, organ, optional handbells, optional brass quartet/quintet, and optional timpani/percussion (Libby Larsen Publishing, 2010).
Chain of Hope (writings re: Frederick Douglass), for SATB, baritone, actress, and piano (Libby Larsen Publishing, 2010).
A Choral Welcome, for SATB divisi and keyboard or orchestra (Libby Larsen Publishing, 1994).
Clair de Lune, for TTBB and tenor solo (ECS, 1985).
Clair de Lune in Blue, for SATB jazz choir and piano (ECS, 1986).
Come before Winter, for SATB, baritone solo, and orchestra or piano (Libby Larsen Publishing, 2003).
Concord Fragments, for SSAA choir, oboe, clarinet, and piano (Libby Larsen Publishing, 2010).
A Creeley Collection, for SATB, flute, percussion, and piano (ECS, 1984).
Crowding North, for SATB, guitar, flute, oboe, bassoon, and string quartet (Libby Larsen Publishing, 2007).
Cry Peace, for SATB divisi (Libby Larsen Publishing, 2004).
Dance Set, for SATB, clarinet, cello, percussion, and piano (ECS, 1980).
The Day of Pentecost, for SATB, brass, and organ (Libby Larsen Publishing, 2012).
Day Song, for SSA (OUP, 1999).
Deck the Halls, for TTBB, five soloists, piano, and handbells (Libby Larsen Publishing, 1992).
Density of Light, for SATB Choir, treble choir, and brass (Libby Larsen Publishing, 1998).
Double Joy, anthem for SATB divisi, handbells, and organ (ECS, 1982).
Eagle Poem, for SATB and four-hand piano (ECS, 1992).

Eine Kleine Snailmusik, for SA and contrabass (OUP, 2005).

Eleanor Roosevelt, for soprano (two), mezzo-soprano, speaker, SATB chorus, clarinet, violoncello, piano, and percussion played by chorus (OUP, 1996).

Everyone Sang, for SATB, harp, and percussion (ECS, 1983).

Falling, for SATB, SATB quartet, SAT trio, trumpet, piano, and percussion (Libby Larsen Publishing, 2001).

Fanfare and Alleluia, for SATB, brass, handbells, chimes, and organ (OUP, 1995).

Flee We to Our Lord, for SATB (OUP, 2003).

Four Meditations for Mechthild of Magdeburg, for SATB, organ, and handbells (Libby Larsen Publishing, 2007).

Free, Fearless, and Female, for SSAA and marimba (Libby Larsen Publishing, 2009).

A Garden Wall, for unison choir, keyboard, Orff instruments, two adults, five children with speaking roles, and congregational singing (ECS, 1987).

Giving Thanks, for SSAA and string quartet (Libby Larsen Publishing, 2005).

God as Ribbon of Light, for SATB and organ (ECS, 1993).

God So Loved the World, for SATB (OUP, 2005).

How It Thrills Us, for SATB (ECS, 1990).

How-To Songs, for SSA (children's) chorus (Libby Larsen Publishing, 2000).

I Am a Little Church, for SATB and organ (OUP, 1991).

I Arise Today, for SATB and organ (OUP, 1995).

I Dream of Peace, for SATB chorus and percussion, with texts by children of former Yugoslavia (Libby Larsen Publishing, 2005).

I Find My Feet Have Further Goals, for SATB (OUP, 1997).

I Just Lightning, for SSAA and percussion (OUP, 1994).

I Lift My Eyes to the Hills, for SATB, handbells, and organ (Libby Larsen Publishing, 2007).

I Love the Lord, for SATB and organ (ECS).

I Will Sing and Raise a Psalm, for SATB and organ (OUP, 1995).

If I Can Stop One Heart from Breaking, for SSA, woodwind quintet, percussion, and strings (OUP, 2001).

If Music Be the Food of Love, for SATB and piano (Libby Larsen Publishing, 2011).

Invitation to Music, for SATB and string quintet or string orchestra or piano (OUP, 1995).

Is Go, Our Endless Day, for SATB (OUP, 1999).

Jack's Valentine, for SSAA (OUP, 2001).

Jesus, Jesus Rest Your Head, for three- or two-part chorus, solo voice, and piano (OUP, 2004).

Little Notes on a Simple Staff, for SATB and piano (ECS, 1992).

Lord, Before This Fleeting Season, for SATB (OUP, 2000).

Love Songs, for SATB and piano, based on love poems by American women poets (OUP, 1997).

A Lover's Journey, for six-voice male a cappella group (Libby Larsen Publishing, 2000).

May Sky, for SATB divisi (OUP, 2002).

Mind You, Now, for SSAA and string quartet (Libby Larsen Publishing, 2009).

Missa Gaia: Mass for the Earth, for soprano solo, SATB choir, optional SSA choir, oboe, strings, and four-hand piano (ECS, 1992).

Mother, Sister, Blessed Holy (from *Missa Gaia),* for SATB and four-hand piano (ECS, 1992).
Natus est Emmanuel, for SSSAAA (OUP 2004).
The Nothing That Is, for SATB, baritone solo, three speaking voices, and chamber ensemble (OUP, 2000).
Novum Gaudium, for SATB (Libby Larsen Publishing, 2007).
Now I Become Myself, for soprano solo and TTBB (ECS, 1992).
O Magnum Mysterium, for SATB chorus and prerecorded seven-track solo voice, with sitar, vibraphone, bells, and laptop computer plus speakers (Libby Larsen Publishing, 2011).
Of Music, for SSAA and four-hand piano (Libby Larsen Publishing, 2006).
Peace, Perfect Peace, for SATB (ECS, 1985).
Pied Beauty (Glory Be to God, from *Missa Gaia),* for SATB and four-hand piano (ECS, 1992).
Psalm 121, for SSSAAA (OUP, 2000).
Reasons for Loving the Harmonica, for SATB and piano (OUP, 1997).
Refuge, for SSAA (ECS, 1988).
Ringeltanze, for SATB, handbells, and string orchestra (ECS, 1983).
Ring the Bells, for SSA chorus (children) and piano (OUP, 1998).
A Salute to Louis Armstrong (from *Seven Ghosts),* for SATB divisi and piano (OUP, 1995).
The Settling Years, for SATB and woodwind quintet or piano (ECS, 1988).
Seven Ghosts, for soprano solo, SATB, brass quintet, piano, and percussion (OUP, 1995).
The Shepherds and the Angels, for SATB chorus, soprano and baritone soloists, organ, and brass ensemble (OUP, 2004).
A Simple Gloria, for SATB (Libby Larsen Publishing, 2007).
So Blessedly It Sprung, for SATB, oboe, viola, and harp (OUP, 1996).
Songs of Youth and Pleasure, for SATB (ECS, 1986).
Stepping Westward, for SSA, handbells, oboe, and marimba (ECS, 1998).
The Summer Day, for SSAA and string quartet (Libby Larsen Publishing, 2005).
Sweet and Sour Nursery Rhymes, for SATB and French horn (OUP, 1998).
To a Long Loved One, for SATB and string quartet (Libby Larsen Publishing, 1999).
Today, This Spring, for SA and piano (OUP 1995).
To Sing, for SSA chorus and piano (Hal Leonard, 2008).
Touch the Air Softly, for SSAA (Libby Larsen Publishing, 2000).
We Celebrate, for SATB and piano or organ (ECS, 1985).
Welcome Yule, for TTBB and strings (ECS, 1984).
Western Songs, for SATB (OUP, 2005).
Whitman's America, for SATB (Libby Larsen Publishing, 2007).
Who Cannot Weep, Come Learn of Me, for mezzo-soprano, tenor, and SSA (ECS, 1985).
The Witches Trio, for SSAA (OUP, 2000).
The Womanly Song of God, for SSAA divisi (OUP, 2003).
A Young Nun Singing, for SAA (OUP, 2003).

VOCAL

The Ant and the Grasshopper, for soprano and piano (Libby Larsen Publishing, 1998).

The Apple's Song, for baritone or mezzo-soprano and piano (Libby Larsen Publishing, 2001).
Before Winter, for baritone solo and organ (ECS, 1982).
Beloved, Thou Hast Brought Me Many Flowers, for mezzo-soprano, cello, and piano (OUP, 1994).
Center Field Girl, for soprano and piano (Libby Larsen Publishing, 2007).
Chanting to Paradise, for soprano and piano (Libby Larsen Publishing, 1997).
Cowboy Songs, for soprano and piano (ECS, 1979).
De Toda la Eternidad, for soprano, wind ensemble, or piano (Libby Larsen Publishing, 2003, 2005).
Donal Oge, for soprano and piano (Libby Larsen Publishing, 2011).
Far in a Western Brookland, for tenor and piano (Libby Larsen Publishing, 2008).
Fern Hill, for tenor (Libby Larsen Publishing, 2004).
Forget-Me-Not, for soprano, tenor, and piano (Libby Larsen Publishing, 2008).
Hell's Belles, for mezzo-soprano and handbell choir (Libby Larsen Publishing, 2001).
How Lovely Are Thy Holy Groves (from *Missa Gaia*), for soprano solo and piano (ECS, 1992).
I Cried unto God, for tenor and piano (Libby Larsen Publishing, 2011).
I Love You through the Daytimes, for baritone and piano (Libby Larsen Publishing, 2003).
Jazz at the Intergalactic Nightclub, for tenor and piano (Libby Larsen Publishing, 2001).
Late in the Day, for soprano and piano (Libby Larsen Publishing, 1998).
Lord, Make Me an Instrument, for tenor and piano (Libby Larsen Publishing, 1997).
Love after 1950, for mezzo-soprano and piano (OUP, 2000).
Lullay of the Nativity, for high voice (Libby Larsen Publishing, 2012).
Margaret Songs, for soprano and piano (OUP, 1996).
Mary Cassatt, for mezzo-soprano, trombone, orchestra, and slides (OUP, 1994).
Me (Brenda Ueland), for soprano and piano (OUP, 1987).
My Antonia, for high voice and piano (OUP, 2000).
My Candle Burns, for high voice and piano (Libby Larsen Publishing, 2012).
Perineo, for baritone and piano (ECS, 1993).
A Pig in the House, for tenor and piano (Libby Larsen Publishing, 2004).
A Quiet Song, for baritone voice and piano (Libby Larsen Publishing, 2007).
Raspberry Island Dreaming, for mezzo-soprano and piano (originally orchestra), (Libby Larsen Publishing, 2002).
Righty, 1966, for soprano, flute, and piano (Libby Larsen Publishing, 2007).
Saints without Tears, for soprano, flute, and bassoon (Libby Larsen Publishing, 1976).
Selected Poems of Rainer Maria Rilke, for soprano, flute, guitar, and harp (Libby Larsen Publishing, 2005).
Sifting through the Ruins, for mezzo-soprano, viola, and piano (Libby Larsen Publishing, 2005).
Song, for soprano (Libby Larsen Publishing, 2009).
Songs from Letters, for soprano and piano (also chamber version), (OUP, 1989).
Sonnets from the Portuguese, soprano and piano (also chamber version), (OUP, 1991).

Stone Soup, for three medium voices, narrator, and piano (Libby Larsen Publishing, 2011).
The Strange Case of Dr. H. H. Holmes, for baritone and prepared piano (Libby Larsen Publishing, 2010).
Take, for soprano and piano (Libby Larsen Publishing, 2006).
This Unbearable Stillness: Songs from the Balcony, for soprano and string quartet (OUP, 2003).
Three Love Songs, for baritone and piano (Libby Larsen Publishing, 2011).
Three Rilke Songs, for high voice and guitar (Libby Larsen Publishing, 1980).
Try Me, Good King: Last Words of the Wives of Henry VIII, for soprano and piano (OUP, 2000).
Turn, Turn, for baritone and piano (Libby Larsen Publishing, 2011).
A Verse Record of My Peonies, for tenor, tape, and percussion (Libby Larsen Publishing, 1980).
When I Am an Old Woman, for soprano and piano (ECS, 1990).
Within the Circles of Our Lives, for soprano, baritone, and wind ensemble (ECS, 2007).

INSTRUMENTAL

The Adventures of Wonderboy: Issue One, for bass, sampler, narrator, cartoons, and strings (Libby Larsen Publishing, 1992).
And Another Thing, for saxophone quartet (Libby Larsen Publishing, 2012).
Argyle Sketches, for guitar (Libby Larsen Publishing).
Aspects of Glory, for organ (ECS, 1990).
The Astonishing Flight of the Gump, for flute, oboe, bassoon, and piano (Libby Larsen Publishing, 1987).
The Atmosphere as a Fluid System (chamber orchestra version), for flute and chamber orchestra (OUP, 2001).
Aubade, for flute (ECS, 1982).
Barn Dances, for flute, clarinet, and piano (OUP, 2001).
Bee Navigation, for clarinet (OUP, 2004).
Bid Call, for alto saxophone and violoncello or viola (OUP, 2003).
Black Birds, Red Hills, for clarinet, viola, and piano (OUP, 1987,1996).
Black Roller, for flute, oboe, clarinet, bassoon, piano, violin, viola (featured), and cello (ECS, 1981).
Blessed Be the Tie That Binds, for organ (OUP, 1996).
Blue Piece for Violin and Piano (Libby Larsen Publishing, 2010).
Blue Third Pieces, for flute or clarinet and guitar (OUP, 1996).
Blue Windows, for woodwind quintet and piano (Libby Larsen Publishing, 2005)
Blues in Six, for clarinet and piano (Libby Larsen Publishing, 1992).
Brass Flight, for brass choir (OUP, 1996).
Brazen Overture, for brass quintet (Libby Larsen Publishing, 2000).
Bronze Veils, for trombone and two percussion (ECS, 1979).
Cajun Set, for guitar and string trio (Libby Larsen Publishing, 1980).
Circular Rondo, Canti Breve, for oboe and guitar (ECS, 1974).

Concert Piece for Bassoon and Piano (Libby Larsen Publishing, 2008).
Concert Piece for Tuba and Piano (OUP, 1995).
Concertino for Tenor Steel Drum and Chamber Ensemble (Libby Larsen Publishing, 2004).
Corker, for clarinet and percussion (ECS, 1977).
Dancing Solo, for clarinet (OUP, 1994).
Double String Quartet (Libby Larsen Publishing, 2008).
Downwind of Roses in Maine, for flute, B♭ clarinet, and mallet percussion (Libby Larsen Publishing, 2009).
Engelberg: Trio for Brass and Organ, for trumpet, horn in F, trombone, and organ (Libby Larsen Publishing, 2006).
Fanfare for a Learned Man, for brass quintet (Libby Larsen Publishing, 2005).
Fanfare for Humanity, for brass ensemble (Libby Larsen Publishing, 2003).
Fanfare for the Women, for trumpet (OUP, 1994).
Fantasy on Slane, for organ and flute (ECS, 1989).
Firebrand, for flute/piccolo, violin, cello, and piano (OUP, 2003).
For Two, for four-hand piano (Libby Larsen Publishing, 2004).
Four on the Floor, for violin, cello, bass, and piano (OUP, 1983).
Gavel Patter, for four-hand piano (Libby Larsen Publishing, 2004).
He Arose: Fanfare for Easter, for organ, two trumpets, two trombones, and optional French horn (Libby Larsen Publishing, 2007).
Holy Roller, for saxophone and piano (OUP, 1997).
Impromptu, for flute, clarinet, and bassoon (Libby Larsen Publishing, 1998).
In Such a Night, for two violas and recorded voice (Libby Larsen Publishing, 2010).
Jazz Variations for Solo Bassoon (ECS, 1977).
Juba, for cello and piano (Libby Larsen Publishing, 1986).
Kathleen, as She Was, for oboe and harpsichord (ECS, 1989).
Licorice Stick, for clarinet and piano (Libby Larsen Publishing, 2002).
Like Blind Men Tapping in the Dark, for one marimba and two performers (Libby Larsen Publishing, 2010).
Mephisto Rag, for piano (OUP, 2000).
Neon Angel, for violin, cello, clarinet (or saxophone), flute, piano, percussion, and cued CD (Libby Larsen Publishing, 2000).
Now I Pull Silver, for amplified flute and prepared CD (Libby Larsen Publishing, 2005).
On a Day of Bells, for organ (OUP, 2002).
Pealing Fire, for carillon (Libby Larsen Publishing, 2004).
Penta Metrics, for piano solo (OUP, 2004).
Piano Suite, for solo piano (Libby Larsen Publishing, 1976).
Pocket Sonata, for oboe, alto saxophone, violin, cello, marimba/vibraphone, and piano (Libby Larsen Publishing, 2003).
Prelude on Veni Creator Spiritus, for organ (OUP, 1997).
Quartet: She Wrote, for string quartet (Libby Larsen Publishing, 2008).
Ricochet, for marimba I and II (Libby Larsen Publishing, 2008).
Ricochet (Piano), for solo piano (Libby Larsen Publishing, 2008).

Ridge-Runner, for trumpet and percussion (Libby Larsen Publishing, 2012).
Rodeo Queen of Heaven, for clarinet, violin, cello, and piano (Libby Larsen Publishing, 2010).
Sarabande: In Profane Style, for guitar (Libby Larsen Publishing, 1979).
Schoenberg, Schenker, and Schillinger, for flute, oboe, viola, cello, and keyboard (OUP, 1991).
Scudding, for cello (Libby Larsen Publishing, 1980).
Seventy-nine Fossil Gestures, for piano duo (Libby Larsen Publishing, 2011).
Slang, for clarinet, violin, and piano (OUP, 1994).
Slow Structures, for flute, cello, and piano (Libby Larsen Publishing, 2005).
Sonata in One Movement on Kalenda Maya, for organ (ECS, 1983).
Song without Words, for clarinet and piano (ECS, 1986).
String Quartet: Schoenberg, Schenker, and Schillinger (OUP, 1991).
Tango, for guitar (Libby Larsen Publishing, 1978).
Theme and Deviations, for harp, (Libby Larsen Publishing, 1973).
Three for the Road, for violin, cello, and piano (Libby Larsen Publishing, 2000).
Three Pieces for Treble Wind and Guitar (Libby Larsen Publishing, 1974).
Trio for Violin, Cello, and Piano (OUP, 2001).
Trio in Four Movements, for flute, viola, and harp (Libby Larsen Publishing, 2005).
Up Where the Air Gets Thin (Libby Larsen Publishing, 1985).
Viola Sonata, for viola and piano (OUP 2001).
Wait a Minute, for saxophone quartet (Libby Larsen Publishing, 2004).
With Love and Hisses, for double woodwind quintet (optional accompaniment to the silent Laurel and Hardy film *Love and Hisses*), (ECS, 1985).
Xibalba, for bassoon and percussion (OUP, 1990).
Yellow Jersey, for B♭ clarinet duet (OUP, 2004).

Nora Kroll-Rosenbaum

18

Laura Karpman

Born in 1959 in Los Angeles, Laura Karpman first established herself in concert music with degrees from the University of Michigan and Juilliard, studying with Milton Babbitt. She was among the first composers selected as a Sundance Institute Film Scoring Fellow (at the recommendation of the forward-thinking Babbitt). Attending the Sundance Institute was a life-changing event for Karpman, introducing her to the possibilities of computers in music production. She remarks, "I saw computers and music work together, and I flipped. I thought that this was the future of music . . . and I wanted to be involved in an aspect of music production where technology was supported." Equally important to Karpman was her introduction at Sundance to the late Shirley Walker, a celebrated film composer, who was a great source of encouragement. During our conversation, Karpman discusses the significance of these experiences and her introduction to the field of commercial music.

Commissioned by such organizations as Carnegie Hall and the Los Angeles Opera, Karpman's body of work is diverse, including music for concert hall, film, documentary, television, and video games. She has been awarded four Emmys and a Game Audio Network Guild award, along with an additional seven Emmy nominations and an Annie nomination. Karpman's frequent collaborations in the visual arts extend to several mediums. Her score setting of the Langston Hughes text *Ask Your Mama* featured the operatic soprano Jessye Norman, the hip-hop group the Roots, and George Manahan conducting the Orchestra of St. Luke's for its premiere at Carnegie Hall in 2009. Karpman's current activity includes the *110 Project,* a commissioned work with a Web component from the Los Angeles Opera in recognition of the city's first freeway. Like Libby Larsen, Karpman discusses the influence of technology on music and the concert world's need to be aware of audiences' changing demands. She expounds on her own use of technology and remarks that the "Digital Revolution makes the Industrial Revolution look like child's play."

In contrast to many of today's composers of video-game music, such as Winifred Phillips, Karpman's game music reflects her film and concert works, employing sophisticated orchestration, compositional arcs, and solid understanding of an orchestral ensemble. Describing her own work as "dense," Karpman finds inspiration studying romantic and mid-twentieth-century composers. For instance, she approached her work for the game *EverQuest II* as a grand orchestration exercise and studied the scores of Shostakovich, Smetana, Schubert, and Lutoslawski. In the end, *EverQuest II* included nearly one hundred minutes of orchestral music. Like many media composers, Karpman often conducts her own work for film and video games. Ever flexible, however, she usually hands over the baton for her concert music.

As a contrast to some of the more traditional concert composers in this book, Karpman describes her flexibility in collaboration and uses of critique to make revisions as a media composer. Her creative process is enhanced by having had to learn to interpret critique from commercial producers, who are usually unfamiliar with musical composition. Consequently, her approach to composing concert music is similarly affected, as she welcomes varied interpretations, allowing the work to breathe. Like Phillips or Deborah Lurie, Karpman wears different musical and business hats comfortably, writing several minutes of music per day if necessary and working on several projects at one time. One of the few successful women composers of media music, Karpman holds strong opinions about the changing role for women in the industry. She honors her mentors and is excited about continued developments in new music, its effects in popular culture, and the possibilities of collaborative mediums.

***

April 2010, at her home in Playa del Rey, California

JENNIFER KELLY: As I was doing research for this book, I found there was a multitude of composers for concert music but hardly any women for theater or film music. Why do you think that might be the case?

LAURA KARPMAN: Sexism. In film music, the statistics are gruesome for women directors, and I think they're even more gruesome for women composers. As with all fields, women must be at the top in order for younger people to see that this career path is even a vague possibility. Not many women have broken through to the top tier in film music. There are still a lot of misconceptions as to what women can and cannot do. I have composed music for a lot of science-fiction projects and done some video games, but I think those domains are perceived as being *so* male that it's very, very hard for women to break in. I didn't experience as much overt sexism in network-television movies, because I think there is more of an expectation that a woman can write "that kind" of music. Certain fields in Hollywood have traditionally been more open to women—women have always worked as editors, and, though editors are an incredibly important part of the process, they are still in the service of the male director. We may see some changes in the near future. Katherine Bigelow won an Oscar [Best Director in 2010 for *The Hurt Locker*], and that was wonderful. Debbie Lurie is breaking through and doing some big films. The more women that break through, the more the floodgates will open. Women must teach in film-scoring institutions and must teach composition to younger students. Girls and young women must see that other women compose and that composition is a possibility for them. It's about being open and brave and talking about some of these issues even if they are difficult.

JK: When you were coming into the business, whom did you look to in terms of other women?

LK: I had a really remarkable and life-changing experience. I have a doctorate from Juilliard, and I was hoping to become a professor, and then Milton Babbitt nominated me to attend the Sundance Institute in 1987.

JK: You were originally planning to be a professor and composer of traditional concert music?

LK: That's right. Then I went out to Sundance in 1987, and I saw computers and music work together, and I flipped. I thought that this was the future of music, and I wanted to be involved in this. I wanted to be involved in an aspect of music production where technology was supported. At that point in 1987, that support was in commercial music and not in concert music. There at Sundance was Shirley Walker, not as an advisor, but as the wife of an advisor, John Walker.

JK: Was she already a successful film composer?

LK: Yes, she certainly was. I didn't know her work, simply because at that point I didn't know that much about film music, much less female film composers. At that point in my life, I wasn't aware of sexism. I was like a lot of young women then and perhaps now, in that I didn't think about it; it wasn't part of my reality. I felt that everything was possible for women. But at Sundance, there was a conversation that really stunned me. Later, an agent who was there came up to me and said, "Why didn't you ask any questions?" And I said, "Because it was so exclusionary. I just figured there was no room for me."

JK: Why did you feel it was so exclusionary?

LK: The way that they were talking about the movie business in this lecture—there wasn't a woman in sight in terms of the language of inclusion. I had grown up in a household without sexism. Babbitt, my teacher, was not sexist. There were things that always came up, but I just didn't pay much attention to them. There at Sundance, we were supposed to conduct our own cues, and I did not consider myself a conductor. I felt I wasn't qualified to do that, even though, in retrospect, I had the musical training to do so, just not the confidence. Shirley said, "You know, you really should do this." She was a terrific conductor and worked with me on her own time. I conducted the cue, and Shirley gave me the confidence to do so.

JK: Was it that Walker was a mentor in film composing, or simply that she was a woman in a business that you never thought about pursuing?

LK: She just spent time with me and gave me this tremendous support and confidence. Remember, she was there as the wife of an advisor, not as an advisor. I was back at Sundance as an advisor myself nearly twenty years after I was there as a fellow and thought so much about her then. Shirley died so ridiculously prematurely. She was the one who carved the path for everybody. Period. And did so with such courage. She did not do *women's work* in terms of the style of music she wrote. She wrote very "muscular" music, and I use that term very purposely. She scored a lot of action films, a traditionally male domain. She was fierce.

JK: So how would you describe the importance of composer mentoring? Can one teach composition?

LK: I've never really taught composition, but I've certainly had mentees. You can teach people how to think about music; that's what Milton Babbitt did for me. He taught me how to approach music in a way that I had never approached it before. Our lessons were filled with examining my work in the conceptual stage, as well as doing a lot of analysis of other works and developing a compositional philosophy. I think mentors are hugely important and, in fact, utterly necessary for the serious study of composition.

JK: Do you find yourself actively trying to encourage other women?

LK: I do. Whenever I look to hire someone, I really try to look to women. When I talk to classes, sometimes I'll spend extra time with women after class and discuss some of the things they may encounter. I think there needs to be more of a feminist consciousness in Hollywood, and people need to come out of the closet and talk about the fact that it's simply harder for women. There are even fewer people of color in this business than women at this point. It's a problem, and we need to be out loud about it, trudging ahead and working on it. The fact that there are so few women working means that fewer doors are open because we're still such a novelty.

JK: You'd rather talk about being a woman so everyone can be aware of it?

LK: I am a woman composer. I don't think that limits me in any way. I have no problem being a very vocal feminist, and I encourage other people to do so.

JK: Do you think there is still a need for all-women concerts, CDs, books such as this, et cetera?

LK: Sure I do. I believe in affirmative action, and I believe anything that can be done to help anyone should be done. If it helps get your music out there, and people hear it and people are inspired, great. If at a certain point it becomes useless or irrelevant, it won't happen anymore, because it won't need to happen.

JK: You brought up technology. . . .

LK: I think all composers who want to work in film music at this point have to be versed in technology. Period. The way the business has moved you have to be able to create "synth mockups" of music for directors. It's not a luxury; it's a necessity. I love technology. I embrace it and use it in all of my work, concert and film. I love to record music. I love playing with sound. I think it's a really exciting twenty-first-century way to think about music, so it is an essential part of my musical arsenal.

JK: Were you already technologically savvy when you went to Sundance?

LK: No, I had never touched a computer. It turned my life around. After Sundance, I got a DX 7 and a Mac Plus, and I started messing with it. The first time I heard a composition played back by the computer, I wept. To be able to work with actual sound instead of me hashing it out at the piano before a performance, and really be able to work on tempi, lengths, durations, it's just an unbelievable tool. And that's not even talking about recording and manipulating timbre, altering sounds, seeing what you can do in the recording studio and concert hall, and using all the tools we have now. That was the beginning of musical digital technology, and it was just unbelievable. I loved it from the day we met.

JK: How much of your work on the computer stays on the computer, or is the goal to bring it to live musicians to record? Where's the balance?

LK: In film music, it just depends on budget. I'm working on a documentary right now, *The Naked Option,* a beautiful story about Nigerian women who rise up against Shell and Chevron criminally polluting their environment. For that, I'm doing a sampling from tracks of the women chanting and singing, so I'm altering that and adding new voices to it. I'm also starting another project where we'll record a small orchestra. So it depends on the budget. For my concert music, I've been playing with live music plus technology, like in a recent premiere of *Ask Your Mama,* written for Jessye Norman, the Roots, and Orchestra of St. Luke's. I prerecorded Miss Norman, and I sampled from an archival recording of Langston Hughes, who actually participates in the piece itself, and I took a lot of other pieces of audio and processed them. Two onstage laptops triggered all this. That's a way that my work in recording, processing, and sound production can come to the concert stage.

JK: You are someone who wears many hats for many different mediums. Is your creative process the same for each medium?

LK: It's basically the same, but different projects require different things. For example, for a score for a Moliere play for L.A. Theatre Works, the director wanted a "period" score, but I couldn't go out and hire an early music ensemble, so I sat there, and I pulled out scores of Rameau and Couperin, and I played *at* them and created my own music from it. *The Naked Option* documentary is about finding a concept to develop—in this case, sampling from the production track of the women themselves.

JK: So you find the concept, some theme, for each project that is going to carry you through, and you stay true to that.

LK: Exactly. For *Taken,* a twenty-hour miniseries for Steven Spielberg, the idea was to draw heavily from traditional American music, so we found American tunes and developed some of those as themes. The idea for a PBS series, *Craft in America,* is to take traditional American music and turn it on its ear, creating a theme for each craftsperson related to what they're doing or where they're from and making it all very new. The idea in *Ask Your Mama* was to create this massive work where I would follow the musical directions that Langston Hughes indicated in the poem.

JK: So you have to find the seed first.

LK: Yes, you have to find the seed first.

JK: When you get stuck, how do you get unstuck?

LK: I take a walk on the beach. I have a lot of ideas, so I don't tend to get stuck. When I am under a tremendous amount of pressure, I'll pull out scores. For example, when I was working on *EverQuest II,* a massive multiplayer video game,

I decided to make the whole project a huge orchestration exercise. I pulled out the scores of midcentury masters like Shostakovich, Britten, and Lutoslawski and decided to find something in each piece to spark me. It was an extensive job with one hundred minutes of orchestral music.

JK: With video games, do you compose from beginning to end, or is it a series of cues as in film?

LK: For that particular video game I had no timings, so if I wanted to write a piece that was six minutes long, I could! Those are real compositions. That score was more like writing concert music than commercial music.

JK: I'm fascinated with video-game music. In the concert world, it's just beginning to be legitimized, and I'm not sure if many in the concert-music world realize that video-game concerts are selling out.

LK: Yeah, they are selling out! I've had my video-game music played by a lot of orchestras worldwide. I was part of Video Games Live with an audience of eleven thousand at the Hollywood Bowl. It was fantastic. Video games are great compositional venues. I composed the score to a PS3 launch title called *Untold Legends*. It really turned out to be an antiwar requiem with a Middle Scots text, and I'm extremely proud of it. There is a lot of opportunity in video games, but that's *really* a boys' club.

JK: A boys' club, why?

LK: Most of the people who play them are men, at this point. That's going to really change.

JK: What can the traditional classical world learn from video-game music and the way it is getting marketed, played, and concertized?

LK: I think they can learn that young people do listen to orchestral music. It's delivered to them in ways that are unusual, ways that don't occur to most classical organizations. I think that, fundamentally, all entertainment is changing. The users want to be involved in it. They want to make their own entertainment, they want to author it, and they want it available to them when they want it.

JK: Tell me about the *110 Project* with the Los Angeles Opera.

LK: We want to do a live performance of it, but the times are tough right now, certainly for opera. So, I want it to premiere on the Web.

JK: It's about the 110 freeway in Los Angeles?

LK: Yes. I was asked to write a piece on the 110 freeway—I'm a second-generation native Angelino, and I love this city, so I leapt at the chance. The piece is evolving into a real history of Los Angeles told through the eyes and the sounds of the 110 freeway. There are living, breathing librettists, the author and Los Angeles historian M. G. Lord and lyricist Shannon Halwes. There's also a lot of text from the *California Eagle*, which is the African American newspaper from mid-twentieth-century L.A. It was an important paper that ran counter to the

Hearsts [*Herald Examiner*] and the Chandlers [*Los Angeles Times*] and told the truth about race in Los Angeles. I'd like to premiere it on the Web, followed by a performance. I really want to use the Web so that people can experience this piece in their own way and in their own time. If you want to find out about Abraham Frankenstein (the composer of the state song of California), the Zoot Suit Riots, or the internment of Japanese Americans, you can take a moment, exit the opera, and do your research! If you're sitting in an opera house, that is not a possibility. This is how to be an artist in a recession.

JK: Going back to film. When composing for film, is the music supposed to be in the foreground, or is it supposed to give context to the visual without the audience ever really being aware of the music?

LK: Both. I think it depends on what you're doing and where it's sitting in the film. Sometimes music comes to the fore, and it's the most important thing. And sometimes it needs to recede in the background and be extremely subtle. I'm not a minimalist composer. My music is dense. When I get hired to do projects, I get hired because people want that. I don't get hired when people want super-simple music. That's just not my thing.

JK: Can you work on more than one thing at a time?

LK: Oh, yes, and I always do [*laughs*]. I have to.

JK: What about the business aspect of your career? You've been in this business for a long time. You're successful at it, and you've been vetted. Is it still up to you to deal with marketing and self-promotion, or do others do that for you?

LK: Yes [*laughs*]. I have a wonderful film agent, whom I like very much. I also have a great agent and publicist for concert music. And I also do stuff myself. So I think "yes" is the answer to all things.

JK: When you compose for media music, such as film or video games, is it intended to be only for that specific project, or do you want the music to live on its own outside of the original purpose?

LK: It depends on the project. Often, when you work on a film, you don't own the copyright. The studio owns the copyright. If it is a small independent film or documentary, I will often own it. When you're working on a film, your first job is to service the film. The same thing goes for video games. With film, there are timings you have to achieve, so if in forty-nine seconds or three and a half minutes or seven minutes you're doing something that can live on its own, great.

JK: And do you conduct your own musical cues?

LK: I do most often conduct my own music. A lot of people don't conduct their own music and prefer to be in the booth. I like to be out there because I can communicate with the musicians, be flexible, and move quickly.

JK: With a composition such as *Ask Your Mama,* what kind of relationship do you like to have with the performer or conductor who will present it?

LK: Everyone is different. With Marin [Alsop], you have to wait until she is ready for your comments. That's her style. She holds you back, and you don't say a word until she's ready to hear what you have to say. George Manahan is different. He wants input as the rehearsal progresses. *Ask Your Mama* has so much going in it. His job is not only to interpret the music, but also to keep people who are not used to performing with orchestras in the right place at the right time. I like my music to breathe, and both Marin and George are great interpreters who come in and bring so much to the process.

JK: So you're open to somebody's interpretation of your music.

LK: Well, yes. Take Jessye Norman—a truly great artist. She's so fine and so outrageous in what she does. Every decision she makes and every choice she makes is so fearless and bold and astonishing. You get out of her way and let her do her thing because it's better than anything you could have conceived of.

JK: I find it somewhat surprising that you are able to give up control and be as flexible as you are.

LK: I think that comes from working in commercial music. You have to be flexible, because you could be on a scoring stage, and the producer who would have heard the music five times and approved everything suddenly hates a cue, or the studio can say, "You know, I don't like that. You have to change it." It has to do with working in a business where you're sitting with nonmusicians who love their films. They've worked with them longer than you have, and they will tell you what they think. Sometimes they'll stumble around to figure out what doesn't work for them, and it's my job to interpret that and to continue to keep the musical level high and implement their musical notes.

JK: It's probably what makes you very good and lasting in this business. You're willing to not take it personally, and you can let it go. You adapt to change.

LK: Let me clarify that. It's not about letting it go, but making it better. You need to use the criticism to improve the work, whether it is a cue for a film score or a piece of concert music. That's the trick—interpreting that criticism in a way that improves the music.

JK: When you're working on a film, are you the last element that comes into the film?

LK: Often I am. It depends. Many directors say they want to start thinking about music in the script stage, and some really fine professional scripts I've read have music all over it. So sometimes they'll want to start talking to a composer at that point.

JK: How much time do you typically have for a project?

LK: It totally depends, again. I wrote an Emmy-nominated score—forty minutes of music—in three days once.

JK: With such limited time, do you start from scratch, or do you have a library of ideas to pull from because you don't throw anything away?

LK: I start from scratch. You just get your skill level up so you can do that. I have tricks, things that work for me. Or sometimes you listen to a "temp dub" that may inspire you. I tend to write quickly and work quickly. I take on a lot of work, and I've just gotten very fast. The miniseries *Taken* was twenty hours of film consisting of ten two-hour movies, and I had to learn to write very quickly. So I do.

JK: Do you ever wish that you had found a professorship to teach composition and write concert music?

LK: Certainly that idea of consistent work is appealing to me, but I've managed to get by, and I love the freedom of not having it, too. I enjoy teaching part-time at UCLA. I have tremendous respect for academics, and there's always that wistfulness when I walk onto a campus and see people that are engaged in serious, rigorous intellectual thought. But I've had a wonderful run of it, and I enjoy my life.

JK: Do you enjoy teaching?

LK: I love teaching.

JK: Does it affect your composition?

LK: Yeah, I think it does, mostly because I'm not teaching musicians. I'm teaching graduate film directors. It certainly affects the way I look and listen to films, and it's made me sharper. I listen to new things, think about the way sound works in film, and I think about who is making the right choices and who's not. I think about all this technology that I've espoused as this fabulous tool, which it is. But it's also diminished the art of film scoring in many ways. A lot of people don't get the education they used to. When you listen to Bernard Hermann and Max Steiner and Elmer Bernstein and all those composers of another age, the music was so intense, so different than it is now. There are a lot of wonderful composers working now, and there is also a diminution of excellence in some ways. And there is a tremendous amount of music being generated now. It's not like it was in those days, when there was only film. Now we have film, television, cable, webisodes, and video games. A lot of content that needs music.

JK: If a young woman came up to you and said, "I'm thinking about going into composition," what would you say?

LK: Well, if you're thinking about it, you're probably not going to do it [*laughs*]. The more relevant question is, "I'm desperate to do this, how do I break in?" And I guess the funny thing is that we're all always breaking in. I certainly feel like I'm always breaking in. I've had dazzling kinds of things happen, but I've worked really, really hard, and I continue to work hard all the time. Things have not fallen into my lap. People ask, "How does it happen?" You just work hard and keep loving music.

JK: Can I assume that part of the business side of commercial music is being a people person, because you are dealing with people so often?

LK: I think you've got to understand that getting along with people is super important and that you've got to respect what people have to say about you. You have to respect other people's opinions, and I do. And I enjoy collaborating. I think it makes me a better composer.

JK: How do you balance out the work and nonwork parts of your life, because it sounds like you work all the time?

LK: I'm working on that [*laughs*]. Yeah, I don't balance it well. I'm really trying, but I have to push myself not to work. That's a discipline, too. I believe in resting. I like it, but I have to push myself to do it.

JK: So what does Babbitt think of the commercial side of your music?

LK: He loves it. He's very intrigued by all that.

JK: You also worked with Nadia Boulanger? You must have been very young.

LK: I was very young, and she was very old. I went to study with her at the Conservatoire Américain at Fontainebleau when I was nineteen. Louise Talma was there and really took me under her wing. I had another fabulous female mentor, Elaine Barkin, with whom I studied in high school and summers home from college. I took classes from her at UCLA and then studied with her privately. She sent me to study with Milton. We have spoken about mentorship, and I was lucky to encounter these women who composed. You see men, men, men, and when you meet women making music, it makes you think there's a possibility of a career.

JK: Was there a defining moment when you knew you were a composer?

LK: No. My mother decided I was going to be a composer when she was pregnant with me. She was a painter and always thought music was the highest art. I started writing when I was a little girl, and that was just always what I was going to do.

JK: So you were always very encouraged by your family?

LK: *Very* encouraged by my family. My mother is gone, but my dad is still with us, and he is a great man and a great supporter of mine. In fact, when I first finished *Ask Your Mama,* the first person I played the MIDI mockup for was my dad.

JK: How did you work with the Langston Hughes text for *Ask Your Mama*?

LK: *Ask Your Mama* is great piece of literature—the poem is in all capitals, and this, I believe, has kept people away from looking inside the text. It's [Edvard Munch's] *The Scream.* The text in the right-hand margins is all in italics, and these are all poetic musical directions from Hughes . . . its brilliant. And the rhythms and music are not only in these directions; they are in the text itself. For instance, there's one section of text where you feel "chucka-chucka," and it's about trains, here the Freedom Train of Harriet Tubman. So that's a traditional shuffle beat. It doesn't pop out of the text, but if you look at it, you feel it. Working on *Ask Your Mama* was like mining for gold. It was all there, and it was this thick, thick modernist text. It reminded me a lot of Milton Babbitt's writing, because there are these dense, long sentences. You need to get into it and hear the way that he speaks and listen to it in order to understand what he means. Same thing with Hughes.

JK: Are you recording *Ask Your Mama* on CD to be sold?

LK: Yes, we're looking at a lot of things with that, including recording to CD, which is of course an old-fashioned model at this point.

JK: That is a very good point. So as technologically savvy as you are, what do you do? How does a composer get her or his music out there nowadays?

LK: Every way. I want to make a film out of *Ask Your Mama.* I think it deserves to be a film. In terms of the *110 Project,* we're going to record it as part of the performance, which is why I'm also interested in the Web aspect of it.

JK: Is YouTube a useful tool?

LK: I haven't put too much stuff on YouTube, because you have all these restrictions. I'm really enjoying blogging about the *110 Opera* in *L.A. Magazine* and putting music up, showing people the creative process.

JK: When you do that, do you have to worry about rights?

LK: Yes and no. There is very, very different scholarship in terms of fair use. And every lawyer will say something different about it. It's risk assessment. A lot of people are making art this way. The question is, are you making money off of it? There are many issues in the notion of fair use—this is something I grapple with all the time. I make a good part of my living from royalties, so trust me, I believe in them. In some ways, I think these laws are an impediment to creativity, but they also protect the artist, so it's very confusing, and I don't have the answer.

JK: What would you like an audience to remember about your music once they leave the auditorium or movie theater?

LK: There are different kinds of music that I create that serve different purposes. I love the immediacy of film music. You just do it, and it's done. It exists as part of these projects forever, but I like the lack of preciousness. On the other hand, *Ask Your Mama* is an important work. Langston Hughes deals with some of the most difficult issues of race that still very much exist in this country. Do I want people to think about that? I do. I felt really happy when I received some comments, especially from Hughes's biographer, saying that my work realized Hughes's vision. With my concert music in particular, I'm really interested in social issues, and I want to write music that feels significant. I'm hugely interested in music that can serve as a vehicle for social change. I actually have written a lot of political commercials. That music is not deeply complex, but I've participated in getting candidates that I believed in get elected. That feels really good. I was able to use the things I've learned about drama and melody to bring out a candidate's character and further my political goals.

JK: Being successful and long-lasting in this business for years is not easy. How do you do it? How do you make it work?

LK: I work really hard. I'm really good at what I do, and I'm getting better all the time, and I listen. I listen to what people have to say, and I listen *into* it. I'm also a curious person, and I don't resist change—I embrace it. In my career, things have changed so radically in the last twenty years. Everything has changed. The Digital Revolution makes the Industrial Revolution look like child's play, and I love it. The iPad comes out, and I think, "Can I use it?" I'm not interested in reading a book on it yet, but I might be interested in using it as a controller for Pro Tools. That's an interesting use.

JK: That leads me to ask, where do you think contemporary music thrives today? Is it in the movies, documentaries, universities, or clubs?

LK: Oh, everywhere, and everybody is crossing over and doing different and interesting things. Seeing the collaboration in *Ask Your Mama* between the Roots and Jessye Norman was really exciting. Watching artists from totally different musical backgrounds coming together to make this great work of Langston Hughes come alive was astonishing. There is certainly more music pluralism now than when I started out. If you were interested in scoring films, you needed to live in L.A., and you needed to choose between film music and concert music. I think those lines have blurred, and it's more acceptable to do it all.

JK: Given all the changes and blurry lines, where would you like to see American music go?

LK: I think of the symphonic culture and what's going on now with classical music as symphonies fold—this makes me incredibly sad. Everybody is in trouble. Classical music, for some reason, is not communicating to young people as it should. Video-game music does, because gamers are emotionally connected to these games, but, here again, they *are* listening to orchestral music. The music I've written for video games is hugely complex. There's nothing simple-minded about that music. We do have to think about what a community needs and wants and then how to deliver that. For instance, the way we're receiving our entertainment is changing, and I think that we should be able to adapt. If people are receiving their entertainment on the Web, what does that mean for classical music? People in television and movies spend a lot of time thinking about these questions, and they come up with answers, and that's why commercial entities are able to adapt to these technological changes. That's not to say that we shouldn't go to Disney Hall and hear Beethoven, because we should. But we need to think about other things, too.

JK: We're at the beginning of the twenty-first century now. Where are women in all of this?

LK: So much has changed. We grew up with one set of rules. For instance, I went recently to get a physical, and I went to a female doctor in my father's practice. I remember when my father hired her years ago, it was a big deal. I remember thinking, "A woman doctor, how weird is that?" Where is women's place today?

It's obviously everywhere. I think things are changing slowly. I'm gay, and my niece and nephew don't think the first thing about it, so with their generation homophobia will be gone. Sexism will change too. I think it is important for women to speak out about what they encounter out there in the workplace. And people need to have a consciousness that it is good to hire women, even if it may feel uncomfortable. The race between Hillary Clinton and Barack Obama was huge for this country. Not just for the obvious reasons, but because people were really talking about racism and sexism.

JK: Where do you see your place in American music?

LK: I'm happy to have a place. One of the reasons I was drawn to commercial music was because I liked the practicality and the "dailyness" of it, that sense of making music daily.

JK: You have to like the process.

LK: Yeah, and so I don't think about posterity. I'm proud I've written a significant work like *Ask Your Mama,* but mostly I feel really proud of having this open discussion about race with so many people and with myself.

JK: Has anyone pointed out that you are a white woman setting a significant Langston Hughes text?

LK: Of course. And I asked myself that tough question: "Can I write this music? Or should I?" I asked Arnold Rampersad, Hughes's biographer, this question before I started writing the piece. He told me that Langston collaborated with a lot of different people, white and black. I had to learn a lot, and I had a lot of angels who helped me, but I also had to look hard about what it is to be a white American in this country and what it is to benefit in some ways from this terrible thing we've done to one part of our population for so many years.

JK: What are you most proud of in your work?

LK: I like the fact that I work all the time. I would like to think that ultimately what I've learned from commercial music and recording and working with people and collaborating and all of these skills I've had to attain—that I'm bringing it all to concert music, like *Ask Your Mama.* I think it helps having a business sense when you approach these kinds of pieces. Understanding what's practical and empathizing with people at Carnegie Hall who are trying so hard to put this together. I've had to produce my own scores, so I get what it takes. Most composers who work in commercial music have a heavy hand in producing their music. I'm glad that I've been able to work, and that you're here, so obviously I've developed a reputation, one of the very few women who have. I think that's a real achievement.

JK: What's a typical day for Laura Karpman?

LK: Well, what happened today? I finished a revision on a cue for the Moliere play; I worked on music for a documentary, where I sang and worked with my own voice on that; I got a new job, which is exciting; I had my gear break down thirty-five times and had to reboot; I sent an email to the mayor of Los Angeles hoping to engage him in the *110 Project*; and I sent an email to the head of jazz at Lincoln Center [in New York], who is interested in doing something with *Ask Your Mama.* So that's what I did before you came. I've got two students who are coming over tonight after you leave, and we're trying to develop a curriculum at UCLA that encompasses many departments. And downstairs we're reediting a film about Milton that I've codirected.

JK: That's a big day.

LK: That's a big day. But I still watched my soap opera for fifteen minutes. How's that for feminism!

***

Works by Laura Karpman

CONCERT MUSIC/MULTIMEDIA

About Joshua, for harp, viola, and flute (2003).
Ask Your Mama, for soprano, jazz vocalists, spoken word, orchestra, and electronics (2009).
Bibliotheque, for saxophone and piano (1979).
Butter My Tongue, for women's choir (2000).
Capriccio for Alto Saxophone and Piano (1981).
Caprices for String Trio (1990).
Common Tone, for electric viola solo and digital accompaniment (2004).
Conversations for Piano Four Hands (2004).
Different Lanes, for string quartet and electronics (2012).
Duets, Trios, Quintets, concerto for flute, oboe, clarinet, and bassoon (1986).
Escape, for chamber opera (1997).
For Viola and Piano (1984).
Greetings from L.A., for synthesizers (1989).
Heebie Jeebies, for mixed chorus (2006).
Hidden World of Girls, for orchestra (2012).
Invariably Paganini, for two pianos (1988).
Love Is Not All, for soprano with piano (1999).
Matisse and Jazz, for soprano, saxophone, piano, and percussion (1987).
Music for Violin Alone (1985).
Now All Set, for saxophones, trumpet, trombone, bass, drums, vibes, piano, and samples (2011).
One Ten, an opera for soloists, orchestra, and Web component (2009).
Out of Bounds, for jazz ensemble (2011).
Plucky, for string orchestra (2009).

Plum Sugar, for orchestra (2000).
Portrait of Jaco: A Fantasy Based on Themes of Jaco Pastorius, for violin, viola, cello, double bass, and piano (1989).
Portraits for Orchestra (2012).
Rounds for Viola and Piano (2000).
Saxmaniac, for alto saxophone (1987).
Scat, concerto for bassoon and orchestra (2005).
Six Etudes for Piano (1983).
Six Forms for Five Brass, for brass quintet (1979).
Six of One, Half a Dozen of Another, for youth orchestra (1987).
Song Pictures, for wind synthesizer and soprano (1989).
Stanzas for Music, for voice and chamber ensemble (1985).
String Quartet (1987).
Switching Stations, for chamber orchestra (1990).
Take 4, for saxophone quartet (2008).
Take Six, for brass quintet (1986).
Theme and Variations, for piano and chamber orchestra (1983).
Three Arias from Rapunzel, for soprano, mezzo, baritone, and choral ensemble (1980).
Transitive Property of Equality, for orchestra and electronics (2005).
Untitled Work for Solo Cello (1998).
Waxing Nostalgic, for viola, guitar, and samples; based on Charles Lumis's wax-cylinder recordings (2011).

MUSIC FOR THEATER

American Songbook: Tonya Pinkins (underscore), Jazz at Lincoln Center (2005).
Antony and Cleopatra (underscore), A Noise Within (2012).
As You Like It (songs and underscore), A Noise Within (1996).
Caroling (musical), A Noise Within (2004).
The Cherry Orchard (underscore), Georgia Shakespeare Festival (2005).
A Christmas Carol (underscore), A Noise Within (1996).
Comedy of Errors (songs and underscore), Georgia Shakespeare Festival (1998).
Dear Brutus (underscore), A Noise Within (2007).
Electra (underscore), A Noise Within (2004).
Henry IV, Part 1 (underscore), A Noise Within (2008).
The Homecoming (underscore), A Noise Within (2004).
The Imaginary Cuckold (underscore), L.A. Theatre Works (2010).
Merchant of Venice (underscore), Georgia Shakespeare Festival (2008).
The Misanthrope (underscore), A Noise Within (2000).
The Miser (songs and underscore), Georgia Shakespeare Festival (1998).
Much Ado about Nothing (songs and underscore), A Noise Within (1998).
Othello (songs and underscore), A Noise Within (2005).
Pericles (underscore), The Old Globe (2007).
Phaedra (underscore), A Noise Within (2005).

School for Husbands (underscore), L.A. Theatre Works (2010).
School for Wives (underscore), A Noise Within (2005).
Stephen Sondheim's Seventy-fifth Birthday (underscore), New Amsterdam Theater (2005).
Taming of the Shrew (underscore), A Noise Within (1999).
Tartuffe (underscore), National Theatre Conservatory (2010).
The Tempest (songs and underscore), Georgia Shakespeare Festival (1997).
The Tempest (underscore), A Noise Within (2007).
Twelfth Night (songs and underscore), Georgia Shakespeare Festival (1999).
A Wilde Holiday (musical), A Noise Within (2001–3).
A Woman (Two-Channel Video) (underscore), Aspect Ratio Theatricals (2009).

TELEVISION/MADE-FOR-TELEVISION FILM

Abandoned and Deceived (ABC, 1995).
Based on an Untrue Story (Fox, 1993).
Blue Rodeo (CBS, 1996).
The Broken Cord (ABC, 1992).
Brotherhood of Murder (Showtime, 1999).
Carrie (NBC/MGM Television, 2002).
A Child Lost Forever: The Jerry Sherwood Story (NBC, 1992).
Dash and Lilly (ABC, 1999).
Doing Time on Maple Drive (ABC, 1992).
Emma's Wish (CBS, 1998).
Fathers and Sons (Mockingbird Pictures/Showtime Independent Films, 2005).
Frankie and Hazel (Showtime, 2000).
If Someone Had Known (NBC, 1995).
In Justice (twelve episodes), (ABC/Touchstone, 2006).
Innocent (TNT, 2011).
A Labor of Love (Lifetime, 1998).
Last Man Standing (Sony/Lifetime, 2011).
Love Lessons (CBS, 2000).
Man in the Chair (IFC, 2007).
Masters of Science Fiction (ABC/Industry Entertainment, 2007).
  Jerry Was a Man
  Little Brother
  The Awakening
  Moment of Truth (NBC, 1994).
  A Mother's Deception
  Broken Pledges
  To Walk Again
More Than Meets the Eye: The Joan Brock Story (Lifetime, 2003).
A Mother's Revenge (ABC, 1993).
The Moving of Sophia Myles (CBS, 2000).
My Brother's Wife (ABC, 1989).

Odyssey 5 (nineteen episodes), (Columbia TriStar/Showtime, 2003).
One Night Stand-Up (All Out Films, 2008).
The Princess and the Marine (NBC, 2001).
A Promise to Carolyn (CBS, 1996).
Reversible Errors (CBS, 2004).
Run the Wild Fields (Showtime, 2000).
Scared Silent (Lifetime, 2002).
Shameful Secrets (ABC, 1993).
Sins of the Mother (Lifetime, 2010).
The Sitter (Fox, 1991).
A Stranger to Love (CBS, 1996).
Surviving Gilligan's Island (CBS, 2001).
Taken (ten episodes), (DreamWorks, 2002).
What If God Were the Sun? (Lifetime/Fox, 2007).
WIOU (CBS, 1990).
Within These Walls (Lifetime, 2001).
A Woman of Independent Means (NBC, 1995).

FILM

Ace Ventura: Pet Detective Jr., dir. David Mickey Evans (Morgan Creek Productions, 2009).
American Slices (short), dir. Shannon Halwes (2000).
The Annihilation of Fish, dir. Charles Burnett (Regent Entertainment, 1999).
The Break Up, dir. Paul Marcus (Miramax, 1998).
Center Stage: Turn It Up, dir. Steven Jacobson (Sony Pictures, 2008).
Fish Don't Blink, dir. Chuck DeBus (MGM, 2002).
Girl Play, dir. Lee Friedlander (Goff-Kellam Productions, 2004).
Hurricane Party (short), dir. A. P. Gonzalez (2006).
The Last Run, dir. Jonathan Seagal (New Line Cinema, 2004).
Lover's Knot, dir. Peter Shaner (Cabin Fever Entertainment, 1996).
A Monkey's Tale (short), dir. Eric Goldberg (Dedica Group and the People's Republic of China, 2006).
Nothing Special, dir. Angela Garcia Combs (Yellow Wallpaper Productions, 2010).
Out at the Wedding, dir. Lee Friedlander (Paramount, 2007).
Restless, dir. Jule Gilfillan (Celestial Pictures, 1998).
The Sandlot 2, dir. David Mickey Evans (20th Century Fox, 2005).
The Tournament, dir. Scott Mann (Weinstein Company, 2009).

DOCUMENTARY

American Masters: Carol Burnett, dir. Kyra Thompson (PBS, 2007).
Black Tide, dir. Michael Tobias (Discovery Channel, 1990).
The Butch Factor, dir. Christopher Hines (Logo, 2009).
A Century of Women, dir. Barbara Koppel (TNT, 1994).
Classic Stand-Up Comedy of Television (Museum of Television and Radio, 1996).

Climb against the Odds, dir. Karen Carlson (PBS, 1999).
Craft in America (PBS)
  Community, dir. Hilary Birmingham (2009).
  Landscape, dir. Daniel Seeger (2009).
  Memory, dir. Nigel Noble (2009).
  Origins, dir. Nigel Noble (2009).
  Process, dir. Daniel Seeger (2009).
  Family, dir. Carol Sauvion (2011).
  Messages, dir. Carol Sauvion (2011).
The Daring Project, dir. Becky Smith (Waterloo Films, 2008).
Egypt: Beyond the Pyramids, dir. David DeVries (History Channel, 2001).
Egypt: Land of the Gods, dir. Joshua Alper (History Channel, 2002).
Extraordinary Moms (Red Om Films/OWN Network, 2011).
Indiana Jones and the Temple of the Forbidden Eye (Zaloom/Mayfield Productions, 1995).
In Pursuit of the Shroud, dir. Reuben Aaronson (ABC/Kane Productions, 1998).
Journey into Amazonia (Icon Films, 1999).
The Living Edens (twenty-four episodes), prod. Alex Gregory (PBS, 1997–2003).
The Los Angeles History Project: Chinatown, dir. Arthur Barron (PBS/KCET, 1990).
The Los Angeles History Project: Hollywood Strike, dir. Arthur Barron (PBS/KCET, 1990).
Mysteries of the Bible, dir. Reuben Aaronson (ABC/Kane Productions, 2003).
The Naked Option, dir. Candace Schermerhorn (2011).
Nature: A Conversation with Koko (PBS, 1999).
Rita Hayworth: Dancing into the Dream, dir. Frank Martin (HBO, 1990).
Sex, Censorship, and the Silver Screen (Showtime, 2007).
  Censored
  Forward into the Past
  The Temptations of Eve
Something Ventured (Miralan Productions/Zeitgeist Films, 2011).
The Wonderful World of Disney: Forty Years of Television Magic, dir. Frank Martin (Zaloom/Mayfield Productions, 1994).
Turmoil and Triumph, dir. David Devries (PBS, 2010).
Undersea Edens (six episodes), dir. Nate Scripture (Smithsonian Channel, 2009).
Voice of Disney (Walt Disney, 1992–96).
Whiz Kid, dir. Tom Shepard (Sandbar Pictures/Naked Eye Productions, 2009).
World of Discovery (ABC)
  Earthquakes: The Terrifying Truth, prod. Alex Gregory (1994).
  What Really Happened to Adolf Hitler, dir. Alex Gregory (1994).
  Powers of Russian Psychics, prod. Alex Gregory (1996)
  Touched by a Dolphin, prod. Jim McQuillan (1996).

POLITICAL COMMERCIALS/OTHER MEDIA

Lois Capps, DCC 2000, Diane Feinstein, Dick Gephardt, Jane Harmon, Harry Reid, Chuck Schumer

VIDEO GAMES

Everquest: The Buried Sea (Sony Online Entertainment, 2007).
Everquest: Depths of Darkhollow (Sony Online Entertainment, 2005).
Everquest: Prophecy of Ro (Sony Online Entertainment, 2006).
Everquest: The Serpent's Spine (Sony Online Entertainment, 2006).
Everquest II (Sony Online Entertainment, 2004).
Everquest II: Desert of Flames (Sony Online Entertainment, 2005).
Everquest II: The Fallen Dynasty (Sony Online Entertainment, 2006).
Everquest II: Kingdom of the Sky (Sony Online Entertainment, 2005).
Everquest II: The Splitpaw Saga (Sony Online Entertainment, 2005).
Field Commander (Sony Online Entertainment, 2006).
Kinect Disneyland Adventures (Microsoft/Frontier, 2011).
Kung Fu Panda 2 (THQ/Griptonite, 2011).
Untold Legends: Brotherhood of the Blade (Sony Online Entertainment, 2005).
Untold Legends: Dark Kingdom (Sony Online Entertainment, 2006).

19

Winifred Phillips

Winifred Phillips is a media composer who lives and works in Los Angeles. From 1996 to 2005, she composed the music for *Radio Tales,* a series of dramatic programs airing on National Public Radio affiliate stations and SiriusXM Book Radio. Through *Radio Tales,* she met her working partner, the producer Winnie Waldron. Together they have won four Gracie Awards from the Foundation of American Women in Radio and Television and continue to work as a team on most of Phillips's projects.

Today, Phillips works predominately as a composer of video-game music, and she is known in part for composing for games attached to feature films. As one of the leading composers in this particular niche, she explains that while both game and film may be released concurrently, their music is written separately and may differ completely in sound. Phillips and Waldron have nearly a dozen game credits to their names, including *Shrek the Third, The Da Vinci Code,* and *Charlie and the Chocolate Factory.* The Hollywood Music in Media Awards chose Phillips's work in *Legend of the Guardians: The Owls of Ga'Hoole* as Best Original Song–Video Game in 2010. That same song was also nominated for an International Film Music Critics Association Award. The Hollywood Music in Media Awards nominated her work in *LittleBigPlanet 2: Toy Story* for Best Song in a Video Game, while the game itself was celebrated with several audio- and music-award nominations within the gaming community. In addition to games attached to feature films, Phillips's credits include music for games as diverse as *SimAnimals, Spore Hero, God of War,* and *The Maw.* She creates work through her own studio and production company, Generations Productions.

The video-game genre shares the mystique of popular culture, and Phillips herself is evasive about her origins, adding to that mystique. She prefers not to provide date of birth or information about her education and path to composition. Indeed, current "scholarship" on video games is found almost exclusively in trade magazines and blogs, at a few focused conferences, in the Entertainment Software Association, and through the Independent Game Developers Association. Technology changes quickly in game development and consequently in game music as well, so that information is often out of date by the time it is printed. The few books that exist to date on the topic are mostly outside of academia; they focus on the controversial history of game development and sociology of players, with brief information on producers, developers, and composers. Despite the rapid growth of this multi-billion-dollar industry, academia is just beginning to recognize game music as a viable genre for composition.

The unique demands on a media composer are apparent in Phillips's interview. She explains how the competitive composer audition, the requirements of a specific development team, their creative process, and the degree of collaboration within the larger team all vary by game. She may be the sole composer or one of many on a single project. As Deborah Lurie mentions in her interview regarding film music, the common denominator for game-music composition is that a composer first meet the needs of the game. Game music, in another similarity to film music, includes much collaboration. Phillips explains that the process is fluid in that a game composer must adapt to new ideas and technological developments and must prepare for score revision based upon critique by nonmusician game developers. Composers for game music may be brought in during early stages of game development and given broad information to work with. For instance, specific features of the game may or may not be available to composers: visuals for them to see; sporadic gameplay for them to experience; or specific timings determined for each compositional piece. Making game music is rapid work;

Phillips describes the profession as having a "seat-of-your-pants feel." To remain competitive, she must be aware of the latest technological composition tools, developments in the varied game platforms, and the progression of interactivity among sound, music, and game development. When the game accompanies a commercial film, Phillips has the added challenge of pleasing the film producers and the film's audience while not duplicating the film's original music. And, as with writing for commercial film, game composers do not often own their music. They have no control over the game's release date, soundtrack development or release date, or even soundtrack accessibility. Like Laura Karpman and Lurie, Phillips's career as a media composer is an example of the blurring lines of musical genre in the twenty-first century and the influence of popular culture on composed music.

***

2011–12, over email

JENNIFER KELLY: Looking at your projects and awards, you are obviously well respected in your field. What makes you a sought-after video-game composer?

WINIFRED PHILLIPS: I try to always listen to what the developer and the publisher want. I try to be sensitive to the needs of the game and the aspirations of the development team. I work very hard to be reliable, consistent, and professional. I have a good deal of experience and enough projects under my belt so that I can compose under difficult conditions and create music with a broad range of styles and techniques. Plus, I'm working with a fantastic music producer, Winnie Waldron, so my clients know that they have an extra set of expert ears monitoring the music-creation process and a strong advocate for story and pacing. Also, we've won a number of awards, including the Hollywood Music in Media Award for our work on the *Legend of the Guardians* game and the Interactive Achievement Award for our work on *God of War.* That reassures our clients that we're committed to always producing high-quality work.

JK: Was there a defining moment when you knew you were a composer?

WP: It was after I'd finished the music for the pilot program of the *Radio Tales* series. The series adapted classic works of fiction for the radio, using narration, sound effects, and full musical scores. The series was my first gig as a working composer, and the pilot program was an adaptation of Edgar Allan Poe's *Masque of the Red Death.* I've done a ton of projects since then, and sometimes it can be tough to call to mind what some of those projects sounded like, but I still can remember all the themes I wrote for *Masque of the Red Death.* I remember the waltz I wrote for Prince Prospero, the theme I wrote for the plague, the music for the multicolored chambers where the prince held his masquerade ball. If there was really a defining moment for me when I knew I was a full-fledged composer, it was when I'd finished the score for *Masque.* It was also a special project because it was the first time Winnie and I worked together. She produced the series and also served as the script editor and on-air host of each program. We now have a long-term working relationship, with Winnie serving as my music producer on all my projects, overseeing my work at all stages of production.

JK: What role does video-game music play in the game itself?

WP: That depends on the game. Video games have as many stylistic genres as any other dramatic medium, so the role of music varies just as widely. Plus, the developers and publishers in the video-game industry all have different concepts of the role that music should play. I can bring to mind at least two of my game projects in which music served an integral role in the gameplay. In *God of War,* I wrote the "Siren's Song," which formed the basis of a puzzle as the player was tasked with following the sound of the Siren's voice as it wove a melody across the desert. For another project, *SimAnimals,* I was asked to create a different musical motif for each type of animal that would enter the large simulation area, and that musical motif would serve as a notice that the playing field had changed and that action was required. It was an interesting challenge, and I enjoy creating music that takes an active role in the gameplay dynamic. I try to approach each project with an open mind regarding what role my music will be asked to play in the overall game experience.

JK: Does the music help to determine plot?

WP: Game designers and writers collaborate on plot, and the role of the game composer is to serve their vision. Winnie's experience as a script editor gives her a very strong appreciation of the story structure, and her focus is always on making sure that my music serves the story and helps the player understand what's going on.

JK: Given your prominence as a video-game composer, do you still audition for some projects, much like a well-known actor may still audition for a part? What is involved in the audition process?

WP: Sometimes I'm asked to compose for a project without having to audition, and sometimes I am invited to participate in a competitive audition process. I landed *The Da Vinci Code* video game after a fiercely competitive audition involving a large pool of composers. I was chosen for that project by the game's developer, Collective Studios. However, for the *Legend of the Guardians: The Owls of Ga'Hoole* video game, I auditioned alongside a select handful of other composers, and the director of the film, Zack Snyder, made the final decision. The audition process tends to vary, dependent on the working methods of the developer and publisher involved and the possible involvement of third parties, such as the director of an associated film.

JK: Take me through your creative process.

WP: In my experience, writing music for video games has a very seat-of-your-pants feeling to it. Every game developer is different, and each one will make different requests of me. Some will have radically different working methods from each other. For some projects, I'm given the entire list of music assets that the whole game will need and the instruction to essentially "go forth and compose," with no restrictions except for the final deadline. That kind of project gives me the luxury to get mentally ready, to research, to gather materials, organize my time, and begin composition with a sense of being thoroughly prepared. For other projects, the game itself is in such a state of flux that the developers have very little idea of what music they'll need for their game, and their requests for music come to me in spurts with short deadlines. I'll quickly compose a small group of pieces and submit them and then wait for the team to implement that music and see how it works with the game. Then, after some time passes, another request for music will be sent to me, and sometimes that second request is so different from the first one that it seems obvious that the game itself went through some very big changes. That kind of project requires me to be as flexible as possible, which I think is a good trait for any person working in the arts. You certainly can't get stale when you never know what your next gig will be like.

JK: I understand that the game graphics are produced often at the same time as the music. As the composer, are you involved in the graphics or directional ideas?

WP: The graphics and game direction are the creative purview of the developer and publisher. My role is to provide music that enhances their vision. It's particularly interesting when the game is based on a film that is set to be released concurrently with the game because the graphics and direction are strongly influenced by the style of the film. For example, for the *Charlie and the Chocolate Factory* video game, the art style followed the zany direction that Tim Burton chose for his film, and so I wrote music to enhance that weird, colorful, and whimsical world that Tim Burton had created. Tim Burton personally approved each track of music that I wrote for the game, which was very gratifying. There was a great synergy between the film and the game, and I found that to be a very exciting environment in which to work.

JK: What information are you provided with to begin composing for a game?

WP: I usually request as much information as possible. I like to have a copy of the design document, which is the creative bible for the overall development process. I like to see concept art, which gives me an idea of the aesthetic that the developer and publisher are aspiring to reach. If possible, I like to receive "builds" of the game, which are playable versions of the game during development. Sometimes that isn't possible, though. It is always helpful to be able to consult video captures of gameplay and cinematics, so that I can get a feel for the game's pacing and atmosphere. For instance, for the *Speed Racer* video game, I was given a "previsualization" video that [directors, writers, and producers] the Wachowskis had created to demonstrate to the movie studio what their plans were for their film. The previz film showed a race sequence in rough CGI [computer-generated imagery], with just some placeholder sounds, but it gave a great sense of what the kinetics of the races would be like, and it was very inspiring!

JK: What kind of research is necessary to compose for a game?

WP: That depends on the nature of the game. For *God of War,* I did some historical research, as well as some reading of ancient Greek myths. I also read the play *Medea* by Euripides because the publisher of *God of War* was using a quote from the play in the game's early P.R. efforts, so I thought I'd delve into the play a bit. The quote was, "Whom the gods would destroy, they first make mad." Reading the whole play turned out to be very helpful, as it explores the concept of vengeance, which is an important theme in *God of War.* I did a lot of that kind of research for *The Da Vinci Code* because the story is so focused on religious and historical iconography. And for every project I also do music research. I try to learn as much as possible about the styles, techniques, and instrumentation that I'm planning on exploring and developing in an upcoming project.

JK: How do you consider elements such as melody, rhythm, and form in your compositions?

WP: I think all of these things are integral parts in the working method of the modern composer. Each project calls upon me to consider these elements differently. For instance, I'll be thinking about melody, rhythm, and form differently if I'm writing big-band jazz for *LittleBigPlanet 2,* as opposed to a postminimalist orchestral work for *SimAnimals.* The *Shrek the Third* video game called for a very impressionist symphonic style at times, and the *Speed Racer* game required a blend of techno and funk. I reconsider my own personal relationship with melody, rhythm, and form each time I start a new project.

JK: Composed video-game music is a new medium, less than three decades old. Many people may equate it with movie music for a basic understanding. How are the disciplines different? For example, composing for film requires lots of directorial input, script, often watching the dailies, and cue-to-cue directorial approval. Is this a similar experience composing for a game?

WP: Sometimes. I've worked with development teams that were very proactive and hands-on, involving lots of communication and many musical iterations before final tracks were approved. When working with these kinds of teams, the process feels similar to what you just described. However, there are also teams that have worked with me before and trust me to understand their needs and deliver music that will fit in with their design. For those projects, my communication with the team involves requests for art and video assets, design documents, and discussion of overall style. For one of my video-game projects, *The Maw,* the development team handed over the music creation to my music producer and myself, trusting us to develop the style, asset list, and implementation plan on our own. That was very exciting for us, and a tremendous opportunity to be innovative and experiment with interactive techniques and stylistic choices. There is an enormous wealth of variety when discussing the day-to-day working methods for each project, which keeps things very interesting.

JK: When composing, do you consider the music living outside of the specific project for which it was originally intended (such as a standalone recording or live performance), and must you compose with that in mind?

WP: My first responsibility is to the needs of the game, and I concentrate solely on those needs while the game is in development. After the project is completed, I will begin preparations for the release of a soundtrack album if one will be released. I've had four soundtracks released for my projects—*God of War, Sim-Animals, Spore Hero,* and *Legend of the Guardians: The Owls of Ga'Hoole.* The soundtrack-preparation process involves mixing and mastering the material to the specifications of a soundtrack album, as well as putting the pieces into an order that feels satisfying to the listener. I give these considerations a great deal of time and effort, but only after the actual game project is complete. My responsibility is first and foremost to deliver the best music possible for the game.

JK: In what ways did your musical education and training prepare you for video-game composition?

WP: While a music education is invaluable in giving a student the knowledge necessary to create quality music, I don't believe that any music education can prepare an aspiring composer for the demands of video-game composition. Thankfully, I had a lot of preparation in my earliest professional work, most specifically for the *Radio Tales* drama series on National Public Radio. For that series, I had to create music for nonvisual media, in which my compositions were required to create the mental pictures that were necessary to involve the listener in the stories being told. In that project, the demands on the musical component were greater than they would be in film and television. Games also place greater demands on the musical component. The music is often more dominant in the experience, with interactive requirements, and sometimes incorporating functionality designed to assist the player (either in providing an aural mechanic to problem solving or furnishing audio clues that help the player advance). From my experiences writing music for radio, I was used to rising above the call of traditional composition for media, so I was more comfortable with the process than I would have been otherwise.

JK: What can teachers do to help foster creativity and imagination so needed as a composer?

WP: I learned by listening to great works of music, and I think that's the best way to inspire young minds. If teachers can instill in their students the ability to truly *hear* great music, then that will be an endless source of creativity and inspiration. I can compare it to the training of a chef. Before she can create a fantastic dish, she has to train her palate to enhance its sensitivity, so that when she takes a bite of something, she can recognize all its spices and sauces, appreciate the labor and techniques that are involved. For the aspiring composer, training the ears involves the same kind of process. Listening to great works should become an active experience, and after enough exposure, the young aspiring composer should be able to identify the techniques and elements that have combined to create the sound she is hearing. That's the most important skill to have. Music is a living language. As years go by, music changes and evolves, but we always have the ability to "taste" it, to appreciate its complexity and learn from it, and that's the most important ability we have.

JK: How can a person prepare to be a game composer? In other words, what kinds of skills, whether in music or outside of music, does a future game composer need to learn (computer classes, business, graphics, et cetera)?

WP: Computer proficiency is a must. Pencil and staff paper won't get a composer very far in the modern industry. We're expected to be able to produce finished-quality recordings that can be incorporated immediately into the games we've been hired to score. A game composer has to be especially savvy when it comes to technology, because we are asked to create music that interacts with the choices of the game player, and that entails specific technical requirements for music composition and delivery. It's best to embrace the hi-tech nature of the work and adapt to suit those needs. The music I compose is sometimes written to loop several times, so I have to create a musical structure that will feel satisfying and logical as it goes around the loop and returns to the place where it began. Sometimes the music must be written to be interactive. In that case, I may be writing pieces of music that can be broken into segments to be shuffled and reordered according to what's going on in the game. In other situations, musical interactivity can involve writing pieces in audio "layers" that can be added and subtracted to the whole. That way the music can become more complex or can be simplified and reduced to a quieter state. As per the other skills you mention (business, graphics), they can be as helpful to a game composer as to any other professional, but they can be especially crucial if you're working as an independent contractor (rather than a salaried in-house composer). The job of a contractor involves the constant pursuit of employment, so we have to be able to sell ourselves. It is helpful to have a comfortable public-speaking technique, a user-friendly Web site, and an effective writing style for pitch materials and correspondence. I've also found it helpful to be competent with computer-graphics software. While our own creative field is fundamentally aural (rather than visual), many of the people with whom we work are strongly visual people, so it can sometimes be important to appeal to them on that level.

JK: Your projects are created and marketed through your own company, Generations Productions. How do you balance your time between project creation and the necessary business, promotion, and marketing that comes with them?

WP: I evaluate my priorities on a case-by-case basis and address the needs that are most pressing at that moment, whether they be creative or business-related. When I am in the middle of a project, the deadlines of that project override all other concerns. Sometimes the timing of my project deadlines allows me to squeeze in P.R. tasks (such as lending promotional support to a previous project that has been recently released). This isn't always the case, though. P.R. can be a huge time-sink, so it is frequently impossible to pursue it fully, and sometimes public relations has to be either deferred or foregone altogether. Business can't be foregone, however, and neither can marketing. The main activity of a business is to keep the organization financially strong. Financial issues aren't the most romantic aspects of the job, but they make it possible to keep working, so they can never be ignored or delayed. Likewise, marketing yourself to prospective clients in the game industry is a virtually ceaseless endeavor, because today's efforts translate into tomorrow's jobs.

JK: Technology has changed radically in the past five years. How has it affected your compositional style, and in what way has it changed the business of composition?

WP: Technology changes tremendously fast, so I wouldn't say that my compositional style has been affected by only the past five years of technological growth. I'd say it's been also affected by the past five months, and the past five weeks, and the past five days. It's ever-changing. One of the big truths I've learned in my career is the incredible importance of keeping up with the tech advances that are constantly changing and mutating the tools used by media composers. It's important to stay in touch with technological developments, constantly assessing them for applicability, judging the sonic improvements and the user-interface adjustments, weighing the incremental advances against the costs, the disruption in workflow, and the learning curve that would be involved. It's a constant process. In this day and age, a media composer has to be a one-stop shop, so we have to have the best tools possible.

JK: What equipment and/or software do you use to write your music?

WP: At present I'm using six computers in my recording studio. One of them is a dedicated DSP PC running T.C. Electronics System 6000. Four of them are focused on sound-library hosting via Native Instruments Kontakt, and the last one is my Pro Tools DAW (which also hosts sound libraries via plugins). However, I'm in the planning stages of another of the many studio upgrades that I have to go through on a regular basis. It is likely that by the time this book is published, my studio will be dramatically different than it is now. As media composers, we're all required to remain technologically agile.

JK: As video games continue to change (changing demographics, gaming platforms), can you speculate how the music will change with it?

WP: Recently, there was a surge in excitement about broadening demographics for video games, introducing a whole new audience that would be hungry for games with more user-friendly interfaces and an overall gentler experience. But the market for these sorts of games has proven to be extremely tough, especially for third-party developers. Some companies who were concentrating solely on those types of gaming experiences are now moving back to products for the more traditional, hardcore demographic, or leaving the console-development space entirely in favor of bite-sized casual games available solely on the internet. The Playstation Move and Microsoft Kinect are signs that the trend of motion-control is here to stay, and the Wii continues to enjoy success, but with the volatility of the current environment, I couldn't speculate about what sorts of games will be developed in the coming years, and which among them will succeed. The type of music required by video games is wholly dependent on the types of games being made, and lately it can be very dangerous to make guesses about what the market will bear.

JK: Do you ever compose for acoustic instruments (whether video games or not) and/or compose for other genres of composition?

WP: Regarding genres of media composition other than video games, I have written music for television, and my compositions have appeared in many television programs. Of course, I have also written music for the radio. Regarding your acoustic question, I am very enthusiastic about writing choral music for any medium. I find it endlessly inspiring to write for the human voice, and I've written choral music extensively for many of my projects, including television, radio, and video games.

JK: As I was doing research for this book, I found it quite interesting that I could find a multitude of female composers for traditional concert music, but very few women composers of commercial mediums such as film, television, and video games. Why do you think that is?

WP: I only know my own experiences as a successful female media composer, so I have no idea why more women haven't taken the same path, and I don't have a point of reference for speculation. I'd love to see more women as media composers, and it's very strange that there aren't more. It would probably benefit the creative energy of the medium if more women were contributing music to it.

JK: In a previous interview, you mentioned quality-of-life issues for women involved in video-game music, and that improvements in working conditions may invite more women to join in. What quality-of-life issues and working-condition improvements would invite more women?

WP: I was referring to quality-of-life issues for all women in the industry, not just women working in the music field. At the time, there was an active controversy brewing regarding the harsh working conditions at one particular video-game publisher, which has since rectified the situation somewhat. Nevertheless, the industry as a whole is difficult because of the very long hours and the intense crunch periods. The issue becomes a bit simpler for an independent contractor, such as a composer who is contracted from job to job. Certainly there are periods of intense work, crunch times in which the job takes over your life. However, as a contractor you have a little bit of flexibility in terms of how you schedule your time.

JK: I have noticed that video-game music is just beginning to be given some "legitimate" status in the world of academia and concert music as seen through scoring classes at universities and concert programming. As a composer, is this accepted "legitimacy" important to you?

WP: I think it is great that the music has attracted this attention, and I'm always happy to hear about the concerts and the university programs for the education of game composers. I think that this sort of legitimacy is a good thing for the field of game music as a whole. I also find great satisfaction in the legitimacy afforded me by the approval of people I admire. For instance, when I was working on the *Shrek the Third* video game, the film's composer, Harry Gregson-Williams, commented that he thought I had "chops." When I was auditioning for the *Legend of the Guardians* video game, the film's director, Zack Snyder, said that he thought my music had the right "gravitas" for the project. This kind of affirmation is very gratifying.

JK: Video games are on the rise in popularity, and so is game music, whereas many contend that classical music is on the decline. Is there something that traditional classical music can learn from game music and the gaming industry?

WP: I think that there is more that can be shared across the two communities. As video-game music begins to be appreciated in the form of soundtrack albums, more people are realizing that music for video games can be as intellectually stimulating as music written for concert halls. The problem involves the setting, not the actual music. While game music is slowly infiltrating concert halls in the form of Video Games Live and the Play! Video Game Symphony concerts, I think that it would be great if "classical" music would infiltrate video games in the same manner. I think video-game music might benefit from the creative infusion of modern composers who are now composing music in the classical style. The music of video games created in Japan often incorporates a decidedly classical feel, and that music is voraciously consumed and appreciated by an avid community of fans. In past projects I have composed music in a number of classical forms. For example, in *The Da Vinci Code,* I had the opportunity to compose a number of liturgical pieces for choir, including a complex motet. For my last project, *LittleBigPlanet 2,* I wrote a lengthy fugato section. I think our communities can benefit from collaboration, and I think we can energize each other.

JK: How do you feel about those live video-game performances, and how do you see your place in productions such as those?

WP: I think the Video Games Live and the Play! Video Game Symphony concerts are a lot of fun and a great way to energize fans. These kinds of concerts are happening all across the spectrum of music for media. Not just for video games. For film, there are the London Symphony Orchestra Film Music Concerts and [the International Film Music Conference] in Úbeda, Spain. For television, you can go to television-music concerts by the Golden State Pops or attend any of the numerous composer-specific performances. You can hear trailer music in concert at the Trailer Music Live! concert tour. I think this trend will continue and grow. My focus is on composition at this point, but sometime in the future I would be happy to hear my music included in a live concert, when I have the time available to prepare my music for live-concert performance.

JK: Can your notated music be found for others to perform? For instance, I am a conductor who would be interested in performing some of your work. . . .

WP: Thank you for being interested in performing my work! That's very flattering. Unfortunately, I haven't had the opportunity to release any of the music in notated form, since I've been working on back-to-back projects for many years now. Someday in the future I may have the time and opportunity to make the music available for performance.

***

Works by Winifred Phillips

VIDEO GAMES

Charlie and the Chocolate Factory (2KGames, 2005).
The Da Vinci Code (2KGames, 2006).
God of War (multiple composers), (Sony Computer Entertainment America, 2005).
Legend of the Guardians: The Owls of Ga'Hoole (Warner Bros. Interactive Entertainment, 2010).
LittleBigPlanet 2 (multiple composers), (Sony Computer Entertainment Europe, 2011).
LittleBigPlanet 2: Toy Story (DLC), (Sony Computer Entertainment Europe, 2011).
The Maw (Microsoft Game Studios, 2009).
Shrek the Third (multiple composers), (Activision, 2007).
SimAnimals (Electronic Arts, 2009).
Speed Racer (Warner Bros. Interactive Entertainment, 2008).
Spore Hero (Electronic Arts, 2009).

RADIO

Radio Tales series (sixty-six episodes), prod. Winnie Waldron (1996–2005).

MUSIC LICENSED FOR TELEVISION AND FILM

$100 Makeover (Screaming Flea Productions/A&E, 2010).
The Academy (Fox Reality, 2008).
America's Most Wanted (Twentieth Century Fox Television, 2008).
Baseball's Seasons (MLB Network, 2008).
Beretta Wild and Raw (Outdoor Channel, 2010).
Bonde Söker Fru (Farmer Seeks Wife), (Meter Film and Television/TV4, 2011).
Caught on Camera: Bold, Brazen, and Bizarre (MSNBC, 2011).
Chris Moyles's Quiz Night (ITV Studios, 2010).
Coverage of the Olympics in Beijing (CBC Television, 2008).
The Daily Show with Jon Stewart (Comedy Central, 2008).
Dateline: Behind the Badge (NBC News, 2010).
Dateline: The Mystery in Rock Hill (NBC News, 2010).
The Door (ITV Studios, 2010).
La Facture (Télévision de Radio-Canada, 2008).
Fairy Jobmother (A&E, 2010).
Fashion File (CBC Television, 2008, 2009).
Fetch with Ruff Ruffman (WGBH/PBS, 2008).
Fifteenth Annual Critics Choice Movie Awards (Bob Bain Productions/VH1, 2010).
Hoarders (Screaming Flea Productions/A&E, 2010).
Ice Loves Coco (E! Entertainment, 2011).
Kirstie Alley's Big Life (A&E, 2010).
The Nate Berkus Show (Harpo Productions, 2010, 2011).
On-Air Promos Fall (CBS, 2008).
Plain Jane (Fly on the Wall Entertainment, 2010).
Santa Files with John Sergeant (ITV Productions, 2010).
Sell This House (A&E, 2010).
The Solomon Treasures/Decoding Bible Relics (TV6/National Geographic, 2008).
Storm Stories (Weather Channel/Towers Productions, 2007, 2009, 2010).
Taken: The Elizabeth Smart Story (MSNBC, 2010).
Violent Memories (DMM Films, 2007).
Weird, True, and Freaky (Animal Planet, 2008).
Workaholics (Comedy Partners/Comedy Central, 2011).
You're Cut Off (VH1/Fly on the Wall Entertainment, 2010, 2011).

Danika Singfield

20

Deborah Lurie

Deborah Lurie is a collaborator at heart. Born in 1974, this composer of commercial media, known for her feature films, was named one of the top young composers to watch by the *Hollywood Reporter.* She was born with perfect pitch as well as the rare condition synesthesia, which allows her to identify every note by seeing a specific, corresponding color in her mind's eye. Her career path was defined when her high-school drama teacher gave her the opportunity to write her first score, adding music to the school's production of Shakespeare's *A Midsummer Night's Dream.* Immediately after this collaborative experience, she enrolled as a film-scoring student at the University of Southern California.

A fan of all "good music" no matter the genre, Lurie has always been interested in what the people in the United States are talking about at any given moment. While at USC, her compositional path was influenced by another teacher, Morten Lauridsen. A singer in the choir, Lurie sang many of Lauridsen's new works now considered mainstays in the choral world. She learned that a beautiful melody could make a real impact, and she decided she would rather write meaningful music for the moment than be concerned whether a work was considered "important." Since then, Lurie has composed and orchestrated for feature films and produced, arranged, and collaborated on music for live stage productions and popular genres.

Lurie can always be found working, and she launched her career from the bottom up. Graduating from USC in 1997, she began her professional career by scoring the short cult film *George Lucas in Love.* Her rare musical and visual gifts gave her the reputation of someone who could find musical flaws in a studio recording session, and during our interview she describes being brought in on projects to "fix" problems. Lurie's desire to mentor emerging composers stems from her own experience wishing she had looked to mentors early in her career. As she explains, "Had I made friends with some people who were further ahead in their careers, I may have felt a lot less scared and lost all the time." Eventually, she began working alongside such noted composers as John Ottman and Danny Elfman, writing additional music on their scores and orchestrating for ensemble. Her many film-score credits include *An Unfinished Life, Dear John, Imaginary Heroes, Footloose* (2011), and the Tim Burton–produced animated feature *9*. She has arranged, orchestrated, and/or composed additional music for film projects including *The Dictator, Wanted, Spiderman 3, Charlie and the Chocolate Factory* (2005), *Alice in Wonderland* (2010), and *Men in Black 3*. Her first self-described "concert-hall music," *String Quartet No. 1 in Green,* was debuted in 2012 by the Ives Quartet.

More comfortable with the word "collaborator" than "composer," Lurie recognizes that having a trusted team is essential in her career. The creation of a movie score involves being able to interpret highly detailed notes, read the mind of a producer and director when finding that first musical sound, accept and adapt to criticism from nonmusician movie makers, and weave the given visual elements of a project with her newly created musical elements, and sometimes added songs from popular culture. She explains, "The biggest challenge is to find that same exact story that the director is telling. . . . Once it becomes a back-and-forth collaboration, it becomes fun. Well, *fun* is a strong word [*laughs*]."

Like Laura Karpman, Jeanine Tesori, and Winifred Phillips, media composers who wear many hats to create a career, Lurie accepts that a sense of business savvy is necessary. Large-budget feature films can be the product of hundreds of people, and Lurie does not necessarily own the music she writes for these collaborative projects. She has developed a working knowledge of the marketing, promotion, business, and even the law surrounding her field. Also, like the other media composers represented in this book, Lurie does not seem terribly interested in whether a piece could stand alone without the visual medium for which it was written. Lurie writes knowing that her music serves the film as a whole, and she expresses the great compliment when one hears her music and remembers the movie.

***

April 2010, at her home in Studio City, California

DEBORAH LURIE: The word "composer" still feels like a funny word sometimes, because I'm such a collaborator at heart.

JENNIFER KELLY: Many composers discuss the compositional process as an isolating experience. I thought film composing would be different because there are so many different people involved on a project. Is it still an isolating experience?

DL: I'm finding that the bigger the movie is, the more interactive it is. The higher-budget projects can have a bigger team to get things done. But also, the more people there are, the more everybody is nitpicking at you [*laughs*].

JK: The music is a product of your work, thoughts, and ideas, and yet you still have the director and producer saying, "Do this. Don't do that." Is that a hard balance to maintain?

DL: I feel like it is what I was born to do. I was not born to write concert music. I mean, I might write some at some point. But, the way I see it, I'm basically a fanatic about movie making, and I happen to be the music person on it. The rush of scrambling to get this great thing put together is what I'm about—fulfilling the musical vision of the director and often a team of producers. It can be very hard to please everybody, but all in all, I enjoy the process.

JK: Sometimes you work on projects with a very hands-on, involved composer, such as Danny Elfman. What would be your role on those projects?

DL: Basically, in the modern process of filmmaking, there is a lot of tweaking of the picture. There are often countless rounds of new edits, new experiments, trying a bunch of musical alternatives. Now that it's all digital, they have the power to change things until the last moment. That has made composers' workloads get bigger than they used to be, as the music has to keep up with the film changes. I've had the amazing opportunity to write some additional music on a number of his scores. The larger movies with a zillion picture and schedule changes, that can be unrealistic for one person, so it's been a thrill to be part of such big, amazing movies.

JK: If you're collaborating with someone who is much more prominent, do you get credit in the film, or are you a ghostwriter like some literary writers?

DL: For the most part, I've been really fortunate. Sometimes the credit is "additional music," which actually reflects the truth. In the past five or six years, when everything has been going right, I've never felt like anyone's dirty little secret. Unfair ghostwriting situations go on in the industry, I'm sure, but I've been lucky to work with great people with nothing to hide.

JK: For some, this would be a dream business. How did you break in?

DL: I was definitely someone with no connections and no preconceived understanding of how the business worked. And my approach was that I basically said yes to everything for the sake of experience. I made every mistake in the book, but, in retrospect, I really got to do some exciting things. I was able to get jobs composing, producing, and arranging music largely because I was probably the only person crazy enough to put up with the insanity of these projects and get paid next to nothing. Sometimes, I would get into the situation where I had created something I was really proud of, and then somebody else got the glory. In retrospect, the only regret that I have is feeling bad about that stuff. I realized that, if the wiser, older self could do it again, I would. I know how to do so many different things, and I experienced so much. I'm in my thirties, yet, in work years, I feel like I'm eighty. Every day was an emotional rollercoaster. I was essentially young and naïve and scared. So I met some of the toughest people you'd ever meet. Saying that I've paid my dues is a massive understatement.

JK: It is somewhat comforting to hear that the phrase "it's all in who you know" isn't necessarily true. You worked hard and really did it from scratch.

DL: Yeah, maybe I would have done just as well or better by spending more time networking. But what I spent all my time doing—all my time—is writing, producing, and arranging music. I had no time to schmooze because I was working on music day and night. I think it's the work I did that led to good jobs, not a winning smile or a flashy business card.

JK: And your hard work has led to a house with your studio attached. That must be such a pleasure.

DL: I had my studio builder put in a giant window and high ceilings, both of which are not necessarily smart, acoustically speaking, but I wanted to be able to see the back yard, and I needed high ceilings because they make me feel calm. I don't care what it does to the sound. I'm realizing that it's so important to feel good and feel happy and optimistic. It took me a long time to realize that.

JK: Was there a defining moment when you knew you were a composer?

DL: Yes. It was in high school, and I got to be the assistant director of *A Midsummer Night's Dream*. Jim Shelby, the drama director at my high school, was my hero, and he asked me to write the score for the production. The previous year, I had taken a music-theory class, and for my final composition project I created a scene from *Romeo and Juliet* with actors and all. Mr. Shelby must've gone to the concert or heard about my slightly overly ambitious final project. So he handed me some music software, and it was really the first time I had seen any of this stuff. When that show opened and I had written this music that became part of a very magical production of *A Midsummer Night's Dream,* it changed my entire life. I had applied "early decision" to a liberal-arts school, and it was this huge, "Wait, stop everything!" And I was on a plane to USC [University of Southern California] within a few days. Everything changed. I had no idea I was going to be a musician until then.

JK: You grew up with the combined aural and visual senses of synesthesia. Can you describe that a little for me?

DL: I didn't understand that I had synesthesia until I realized that everyone else wasn't seeing those colors when they heard particular musical notes. Basically, I have perfect pitch, but I identify the note I'm hearing from the color it evokes. For instance, every time I hear a C, I see red. Synesthesia could also apply to people that combine other senses, i.e., someone can taste words. It is basically the fusion of two or more senses.

JK: If you're hearing a composed work, is it almost like seeing a painting in your head?

DL: Yeah, in tonal music like classical music of centuries past, with Mozart and Beethoven, the tonic key is the overwhelming color, but everything I hear is visual.

JK: And when it's atonal music?

DL: If it's truly atonal music, such as the twelve-tone music of Schoenberg, containing a deliberate system to avoid a tonic key, I tend to hear the pitches as individual colors, but it's not a particularly colorful experience overall. Music definitely doesn't need to follow the tonal system to be colorful to me, but my vision of a piece of music is definitely based on, say, the weight of a tonic key or root.

JK: I understand that you rely on sound for composition, but do you also find that you rely on the colors that you associate with the music that you create?

DL: Definitely. I never really think about it until years later, but the keys I choose are absolutely the colors I associate with the movie. I've done a fair number of teen comedies, and I'll pick bright keys. To me, F is orange and fiery, and so I'll pick keys like that. On a movie like *Imaginary Heroes,* or something else really intense, I'll pick a key like B because that's like a bluish gray. Actually, I should probably listen to those again and make sure it's true. Often there are other defining reasons for a choice of key, but color and mood is a big influence for me in choosing.

JK: And you grew up in musical theater, so you always had some kind of visual combined with music.

DL: Yeah, so many film composers grow up being movie-music fans, and I feel like an outsider because I saw *Star Wars* and *Superman,* but I wasn't a movie-music nut. I did modern dance starting from a really young age, so it's always been the coming together of the visual and aural. I participated in musical theater productions throughout my childhood, and my most profound understanding of music came from those experiences.

JK: When you are writing music for something that has a visual component like film or theater, what's the balance between the visual element and the music?

DL: The way I see it, if the music draws attention to itself, it's not really doing its job. It's really about the storytelling. I don't really separate the two, but to think the music is any more important than any other aspect of a film, in my opinion, is a dangerous place to go.

JK: You mentioned the word "storytelling." As a film composer, do you have the luxury of telling a story from beginning to end, or is it basically cue to cue with no real thread through it?

DL: It depends on the filmmakers. If they allow you to follow your heart and really do your thing without them picking on everything, then it feels like telling a story.

JK: I think of the animated feature film *9*. That seemed a story.

DL: Yeah, talk about stories. Ultimately, once I won the filmmakers over and convinced them that I had a good idea and knew what I was doing, they did allow me to tell a story and go on a musical journey. There were other situations, especially in modern filmmaking that's done on computers—everything is so changeable at all times that it can become very scene-by-scene. To me, that's really unfortunate. I don't think too many films benefit from feeling like a series of scenes. And I think that's directly related to how much the filmmakers are letting the composer do their thing, or micromanaging.

JK: As a young woman in her mid-thirties, how do you convince the filmmakers that you have a good idea and they can trust you with all of their money and effort and time? How do you do that?

DL: [The movie] *9* was the most dramatic example of that so far in my career. As it was a collaboration with Danny Elfman, gaining the trust of the filmmakers in my own right was a bit of a challenge. There's a long story here, but in a nutshell, it felt like a big triumph, and I ended up having an incredible experience.

JK: Is the music the last thing created in the movie, or is it part of the whole creation from the beginning?

DL: It's generally speaking quite late, often the last thing. When you see trailers in the theater for a movie that comes out in a few months, generally speaking they haven't even scored the music yet, so they're using music from another movie to advertise it. It's even more dramatic with the work that I've been doing because the majority of my opportunities as I got my foot in the door were solving some sort of crisis in the eleventh hour when they ran out of money and ran out of time. I basically developed a reputation for being able to come in and fix it and do what they want. Make it all better.

JK: So you work fast?

DL: Well, it's very necessary, especially in that context.

JK: Some concert composers describe writing only a few minutes of music per month.

DL: In my job, that's the norm per day [*laughs*].

JK: What do you mean by solving a crisis in the eleventh hour or coming in and fixing something to make it all better?

DL: At the very beginning of my career, I helped other composers out by sitting in the recording booth and calling out any wrong notes I heard. That was considered kind of a special ability of mine to say. For example, "I'm hearing an E-flat in the third trombone, and it should be E-natural." The music then was often still written by hand then rather than by computer, so there was more room for human error and therefore more mistakes in the music. The "fixing" jobs grew to become rescoring situations, whether it be just a few scenes or even an entire film. Sometimes the film would get changed dramatically after the composer had already scored, so I would come in to write new music that was appropriate for the new version of the film, replacing the music that had originally been written by another composer. For example, sometimes at the last minute, the filmmakers would decide that the love-story aspect of a film was not romantic enough, so I would come in and rewrite just those spots while making it blend with the rest of the existing score as not to sound like a patch-up job. A few times, I've "fixed" scores (and one stage musical) by dramatically rearranging the music of another composer. One might call some of that work "ghostwriting," but that tends to be a more negative term than I generally choose to use. Basically, I developed a reputation of solving musical problems on film scores, whatever those problems may be.

JK: And you're working on several projects at a time, or do you get one at a time?

DL: That can be a sensitive subject. But yes, there can be some overlap of project schedules. Movies rarely stay on the same schedule that they first had in mind, so you have to be flexible and not freak out when a couple of things hit at the same time.

JK: Or you might be scoring one and orchestrating another. What's the difference between scoring and orchestrating?

DL: To score a film, at least in my world, is to compose, record, and produce the musical underscore of a film. It can often be used as a term for the actual recording dates of the scoring sessions. For example, someone might say, "We score on August 15," meaning that's the first recording date, though the composing has begun weeks or months in advance. In modern film scoring, orchestration is one of the preparation steps that takes place between the composing and the recording. I think the most common use of the word "orchestration" in film music means taking a composer's shorthand and putting it literally into music that's going to be performed by live musicians. Composers that I've worked with, including myself, Danny Elfman, and John Ottman, the "sketch" is incredibly detailed, so orchestrating is often not a hugely subjective task.

JK: So the real skill is being able to understand all of the shorthand and know exactly what they want.

DL: Exactly. It's all about relationships and trust and experience. When you're working with someone for the first time, you just hope you get lucky with someone who can read your mind.

JK: When I was researching composers, it was difficult to find women film composers. How is your experience as a woman in this field?

DL: I've never really experienced any prejudice. At least, I don't think I have. I've always sort of been oblivious to the fact that I was part of a minority group in being a woman film composer. I guess I owe that to my parents for raising me to not even consider the idea that different professions are for different genders.

JK: So as long as you can do it, you get the job.

DL: Yes. I've always felt like I've had an absolute equal shot. I don't know if it's actually true, but it's what I choose to believe—and so far, so good, right?

JK: Did school really prepare you for the career that you are now having?

DL: No [*laughs*]. I did my undergraduate at USC and combined it with the film-scoring program. I had a great academic music education. I loved my teachers, and I loved what I learned at USC. But as for making it in the business and knowing how to handle oneself, I didn't learn anything. I think the program might be stronger in that department now.

JK: So how'd you learn it?

DL: By making every mistake you could possibly imagine. I was so passionate about every project that came my way. I did just an incredible amount of stuff for very little in return, but I also got a foot in the door based on my ability to transcribe music easily. The first *X-Files* movie was looking for somebody who could transcribe an entire orchestral score from a stereo audiotape, and I was recommended by word of mouth. That movie led to other projects. Back in those days [*laughs*], the majority of the score was hand written, so there could be human error in the scoring stage. So some composers liked to have me in the booth telling them if there was a wrong note or something, which was essentially like a spelling error. They don't need that anymore so much, because computers are keeping things more error-proof. I sort of got in with that particular skill, but I also pursued so many other things.

JK: Speaking of technology, did you always compose with a computer?

DL: I remember exactly when it was, what movie it was, when I found out that it is just not possible to be a pencil-and-paper person. I finally got this movie I really wanted, called *Imaginary Heroes.* John Ottman wrote the theme, and I ended up writing the score. I found out I had three weeks to do the whole thing. I always assumed you had a couple of months. And then I ended up getting another movie at the same time. Be careful what you wish for! I learned overnight I couldn't do pencil and paper anymore. I had to use computers, because the director needs to hear mockups, and they need to hear the demos. There would be no time to write it and then have it put into the computer, and that's a fact of life. So it was like learning another language. But I tend to just hold the mouse and click. I'm basically doing the pencil-and-paper equivalent on the computer.

JK: You do a lot with live orchestras. Is that a sound choice that you make, or a musician choice?

DL: It's both. I have always valued acoustic music. It was always so important to me whether it was a wise financial decision or not. I love the sounds the synthesizer can make, but I really don't like imitating acoustic instruments with synthesizers. It also has to do with interacting. In the short films I got right out of college, people were playing for pizza or whatever I could offer them. And I'm still like that today.

JK: Is it more of a rarity to have live musicians today?

DL: Yeah. Right out of school I was working writing additional music for a Disney cartoon. We were recording with a live group every week, and it was the most incredible boot camp for me. A show like that today would never have a live ensemble. Some TV shows still have it. I love the music in *Family Guy.* Not to mention all the J. J. Abrams stuff like *Lost.* And then on that topic, nobody scores in L.A. anymore. They go out of town to go to the cheaper places or to avoid the back-end payments. I definitely grew up in this industry at a time when everybody was saying everything was going to hell in a handbasket. It's similar to the gender issues. If you believe that, then you'll find that it's true.

JK: What do you mean by back-end payments?

DL: When scoring in Los Angeles, the musicians are generally working under a union agreement in which they are entitled to participate in a small percentage of the profits of the film. More specifically, recording musicians in L.A. earn health and pension benefits (if they work enough to qualify) and receive royalties that are based on the profit of the films on which they record. Other popular recording cities (London, Prague, and Seattle, among many others) do not have a system set up involving royalties for the recording musicians. The scoring work done in those cities is a "buyout" situation in which the musicians are paid up front for their work, and that's it. So, to avoid paying royalties to musicians, movie companies more and more often go to these other cities to record. Los Angeles has some of the best musicians in the world, and it is such a joy to record here, but unfortunately, to some extent, it's considered kind of a treat these days, given those "buyout" alternatives. I always do everything I can to try to persuade filmmakers to record in L.A., but obviously the decision is not usually in my hands.

JK: Where would you like to see the film-music industry go twenty, fifty years from now?

DL: I hope that all the tinkering around that's going on with film and with music, the filmmakers trying a million different things and recutting their film and therefore recutting the music, I hope that it basically hits a wall. Trying to capture somebody's complete thought is actually a lot more valuable. That is one of the reasons that music of the past is so good. Some say people don't write good music anymore. No, they are just keeping up with a very different situation. I hope it would go back in style to let people do their thing.

JK: Is there a favorite era of music that you like that connects with your music?

DL: I've always been obsessed with the Renaissance, and all of my music has sort of a Palestrina-type sensibility. I think it's because I had such a great experience in choral music when I was in high school. I'd love to do something that actually uses that.

JK: Are you still able to go to the movies and enjoy it, or do you start analyzing everything when you're listening?

DL: I have to admit, going to the movies is not as relaxing as it used to be. I do listen to more music. I never overload on music.

JK: Whom do you listen to?

DL: It could be anything from Stravinsky to Nine Inch Nails. That's not really a fair comparison; those things are both *rockin'*! I love classical music, jazz, rock, pop, country, musical theater—as long as it's good music. I listen to a lot of current rock and pop radio. I've always been really interested in what the entire country or the entire world is hooked on that week and why. From a sociological perspective I find it absolutely fascinating. And I work as an arranger on a lot of rock records, so it doesn't hurt for me to be aware of what's going on.

JK: Do you conduct your own music on films?

DL: I don't usually conduct for my film music. On one of the earlier movies, I decided to conduct. By the time we did the first cue, I decided I hated this. It was the worst feeling. I love being around a conductor that loves to conduct, and I like to be working with the director in the booth. There are a lot of advantages to not conducting.

JK: When you're in the booth, what kind of relationship do you like to have with a conductor who is working with your score?

DL: We're talking through the session, but I'm not micromanaging. If I'm working with a talented conductor, there's no need to. And I do most things to a click track, and things are pretty specific with articulation. Plus, the players in this town know what you what. There's a shorthand there, certainly, which I love.

JK: Do you get to choose your conductors and players?

DL: Generally speaking, yes, and that's a really heated, complicated political thing just because there's so many great players and not enough spots. It's competitive, and to be oddly in a place of power over this one thing is very strange.

JK: As a film composer, you have more control than I thought you did. That's a nice place to be because, although you have the filmmakers telling you what they want and don't want, you still have a lot of control over the music.

DL: Yes, I feel like I have a lot of control about how the music is produced, who I'm working with on my music team, how I'm going to do it, where I'm going to do it. I often have a lot of say. The music itself—that's where it's . . . collaborative.

JK: So how do you handle that? You must be very flexible and have a thick skin for somebody to say, "This doesn't work at all. Take that out," or, "We need more of this."

DL: Absolutely. You wouldn't believe the kind of music that gets thrown out of things. I learned that also from working alongside Danny Elfman. I would sit there in the back of his room while he was playing back a cue and listen to the music. It would be magnificent and move me to tears. And then the filmmakers might say, "Well, we changed the scene, so this doesn't exist anymore," or, "Actually, we decided to put a song here." So I've had big examples that have helped me adjust. You can't be precious about anything, and you have to know the music is just there to support the film. It will end up being something; you just don't know what. The biggest challenge is to find that same exact story that the director is telling. Sometimes it's so scary to play that first cue for the director, because you might be revealing that you have no understanding of what he or she is doing, or you might be dead-on. Once it becomes a back-and-forth collaboration, it becomes fun. Well, *fun* is a strong word [*laughs*].

JK: When you're writing for something like film, do you think about it possibly lasting outside of the film? Letting it stand on its own?

DL: I feel that causes trouble to think that way. Will it make a good soundtrack or good driving music? Are people going to buy it on iTunes? Basically, questioning the use of the music or the value of the music outside the realm of the actual film would never be helpful, at least to me. It actually touches on a subject, which is why I came to film music in the first place as opposed to a concert hall. I loved academic music. I was really good at it, and I understood it. I had a great time in school, and I would have loved to get graduate degrees and write it all. But what I really didn't like was the speculation about what music was important, which pieces of music were important. I felt like all of these young composers were talking about their music as if they died two hundred years ago. There was a lot of speculation and a lot of talk about the music that made me feel uncomfortable. So some of the culture surrounding the activity wasn't for me. Film music was very much for the moment. It was being written quickly. It was exactly where all these people were at that particular moment, and if it lasted forever, great. But that's not what you're trying to do. You're trying to tell that story. And I feel like in history, it seems like Mozart and all these great composers, Bach, they all were doing a similar thing to film music. They had some boss who wasn't particularly musical, and they were cranking this stuff out. So I got very turned off by sitting around deciding whether you're important. I like doing and not talking about doing. And I don't spend a lot of time listening to anything I've done before. I'm always moving forward, and that's what it seems like with some of my mentors, like Danny Elfman. He's not basking in the glory of his past works. He's forever curious about new things.

JK: So is there anything the concert world can learn from the film-music industry?

DL: Just because something is simple or has sort of been done before in one way or another, it doesn't make it bad. There's no shame in a beautiful, little, lyrical, simple tune. I think just having equal reverence for every genre of music that ever existed, from country tunes to concertos, evens out the playing field, so some things are not worthier than others. And I think that's starting to happen.

JK: The lines are definitely getting blurrier as we move further into the twenty-first century. I find a lot of composers don't want to be categorized. From your perspective, what trend is current in composed music?

DL: I'm not really in touch with the modern concert-music scene, but somehow I think people might be starting to embrace beauty and emotion again. There's less of a separation between genres and different cultures now, so influence from just about anything is fair game, if that makes sense. My composition teacher at USC was also the head of the department at the time, Skip [Morten] Lauridsen. At the time, he was writing the simple songs, *Les Chanson de Roses.* That had a very profound impact on me and the people around me. Within the academic environment, the majority of composers were writing very cerebral pieces, more interesting intellectually than emotionally. And suddenly the head of the department writes essentially a set of pop tunes. I was in choir at the time, and we were the first ensemble to sing his *O Magnum Mysterium.* Those Lauridsen harmonies are still in all my film music, and that was an exciting place to be.

JK: You've already been talking to me about certain mentors. It sounds like the composer-mentor relationship is valuable to you.

DL: I started looking to mentors much later than I wish I had. Even when I was working with different film composers, I wasn't asking them about their experiences. I wasn't talking to them. I was just doing music. I think, had I made friends with some people who were further ahead in their careers, I may have felt a lot less scared and lost all the time. And now I spend a huge amount of my energy trying to properly mentor the people in my life. For example, my assistant is a composer, and I take it so seriously what happens to him and what decisions he makes. I'm trying to do better for people. I didn't have anyone looking out for me at all, like making sure I got a credit on a movie. It is so nice now to have agents and a lawyer, so a lot of that stuff gets taken care of. Yes, I would definitely advise young composers to try to seek out mentors.

JK: So do you have to work on things like self-promotion, or are you now able to give that up to your agent and manager?

DL: It's a bit of a Catch-22 situation. You can't get an agent without having credits, and you can't have credits without an agent. I do have a great agent now, but I definitely feel a sense of responsibility, just as a freelance worker. I think anybody who works for themselves should be trying to do everything they can to find good work.

JK: I talk to some classical composers who tell me how iTunes has changed a lot for them, and now there's an audience of one in an iPod as opposed to writing only for the concert hall. As a film composer, how does the internet, YouTube, and iTunes enter into your work?

DL: I think something can become an internet phenomenon, and that's just another way you can explode into the public consciousness. People can now email me directly with comments about the scores, so it's all really interesting. I am definitely not trying to make money off of selling music. I have scores up on iTunes, but I don't even ask the business people in my life about the income from that. I just assume there won't be much.

JK: Do you find that, to do your business, just to actively do your job, you need to know all about licensing and copyright? Is that part of your job?

DL: Because I've chosen to go into so many aspects of music, I have had to learn everything the hard way. As a result, I've become somewhat interested in law. It's just part of something you have to know.

JK: When someone says, "I need you to write music for *this,*" how do you find the inspiration? Do you watch it over and over until something clicks, or do you have to find outside inspiration?

DL: I watch it just once or twice before I go off and think about it intensely. I like to write based on my memory of it. Writing the rest of the entire score is easier than coming up with that first thing, that little theme or that tone of what the music is going to be like. It's exhilarating, but it's also very torturous.

JK: What do you hear first?

DL: It absolutely depends, but a lot of times it is a melody that I want to come up with. I still love melodic themes and try to find filmmakers that value that so I can explore melodic themes.

JK: I'm sure, with all you do, there are times you get stuck for an idea. How do you get yourself unstuck?

DL: Oh, boy. Well, one of the ways that I find myself getting stuck is when everyone starts chiming in, all the different authority figures, and they say, "No, don't play that. Don't do that." Then I become like a scared animal, like I don't know what I can do. Or it could be a panic that I don't have the idea that I want early on in the project. But they're both handled by walking and just somehow letting go. Saying, "It's okay." Oftentimes, a friend will call me and be really helpful, another composer friend who says, "Who cares? You could get fired tomorrow. It just doesn't matter that much." And that's when the good music always comes.

JK: It sounds like you have a really good support system.

DL: Yeah, definitely. But that's been a journey of its own, growing to love it. Because I used to feel very tortured by it. I think a lot of people doing creative things have this sense of agony and torture. As I'm trying to find balance in my life, another part of it is realizing how cool this job is and even the music itself, how I really do care, and I really do like it. I've always had some sort of trouble with that, and now it's all coming together so that it feels like a real privilege to have this job.

JK: What would you like audiences to remember as they leave the movie theater?

DL: The biggest compliment in the whole world would be if somebody heard the musical theme and they remembered the movie.

***

Works by Deborah Lurie

FILM

9, dir. Shane Acker (Focus Features, 2009).
The Best Man in Grass Creek, dir. John Newcombe (Lovestruck Pictures, 1999).
The Betrayed, dir. Amanda Gusack (MGM, 2008).
Bubble Boy (additional music), dir. Blair Hayes (Bandeira Entertainment/Touchstone, 2001).
Dance Flick (additional music), dir. Damien Dante Wayans (Paramount/MTV Films, 2009).
Dear John, dir. Lasse Hallström (Screen Gems, 2010).
Deep Sea 3D IMAX (additional music), dir. Howard Hall (Warner Bros./IMAX, 2006).
The Dictator (additional music), dir. Larry Charles (Paramount, 2012).
Dreamgirls (additional music), dir. Bill Condon (DreamWorks/Paramount, 2006).
Drop Dead Sexy, dir. Michael Philip (Arrival Pictures, 2005).
Evil Hill (short), dir. Ryan Schifrin (1999).
Footloose, dir. Craig Brewer (Spyglass Entertainment/Paramount, 2011).
Fun Size, dir. Josh Schwartz (Paramount, 2012).
George Lucas in Love (short), dir. Joe Nussbaum (Quality Filmed Entertainment, 1999).
Gilroy (short), (independent, 2002).
Hercules (additional music for TV series), dir. Phil Weinstein (Disney, 1998).
Imaginary Heroes, dir. Dan Harris (ApolloProMedia, 2004).
Justin Bieber: Never Say Never, dir. Jon Chu (AEG Live, 2011).
Katy Perry: Part of Me (documentary), dir. Dan Cutforth, Jane Lipsitz (Insurge Pictures/Imagine Entertainment, 2012).

The Little Traitor, dir. Lynn Roth (Evanstone Films/Panther Productions, 2009).
More Than a Game (documentary, additional music), dir. Kristopher Belman (Harvey Mason Media, 2008).
Mozart and the Whale, dir. Petter Naess (Big City Pictures, 2005).
My Baby's Daddy, dir. Cheryl Dunye (Miramax, 2004).
My Name Is Modesty: A Modesty Blaise Adventure, dir. Scott Spiegel (2003).
One for the Money, dir. Julie Anne Robinson (Lakeshore Entertainment/Sidney Kimmel Entertainment, 2012).
Prom, dir. Joe Nussbaum (Rickshaw Productions/Walt Disney, 2011).
The Promise (short), dir. Matthew Barry (independent, 1997).
Safe Haven, dir. Lasse Hallström (Nicholas Sparks/Relativity Media/Temple Hill Entertainment, 2013).
Sleepover, dir. Joe Nussbaum (MGM, 2004).
Spider-Man 3 (additional music), dir. Sam Raimi (Columbia Pictures/Marvel, 2007).
Spring Breakdown, dir. Ryan Shiraki (Code Entertainment, 2008).
Surfacing (short), (independent, 2002).
Sydney White, dir. Joe Nussbaum (Morgan Creek Productions, 2007).
An Unfinished Life, dir. Lasse Hallström (Miramax, 2005).
View from the Top (additional music), dir. Bruno Barreto (Miramax, 2003).
Wanted (additional music), dir. Timur Bekmembatov (Universal/Spyglass Entertainment, 2008).
Whirlygirl, dir. Jim Wilson (All the Way Round/Tig Productions, 2006).
The Year without a Santa Claus, dir. Ron Underwood (Warner Bros. Television, 2006).

ORCHESTRATION/ARRANGING

Alice in Wonderland (score by Danny Elfman), dir. Tim Burton (Walt Disney, 2010).
Charlie and the Chocolate Factory (score by Danny Elfman), dir. Tim Burton (Warner Bros, 2005).
Charlotte's Web (score by Danny Elfman), dir. Gary Winick (Paramount, 2006).
Crazy in Alabama (score by Mark Snow), dir. Antonio Banderas (Green Moon Prod/TriStar Pictures, 1999).
The Day Lincoln Was Shot (score by Mark Snow), dir. John Gray (Robert Greenwald Productions, 1998).
Halloween H2o (score by John Ottman), dir. Steve Miner (Dimension Films, 1998).
Hellboy 2 (score by Danny Elfman), dir. Guillermo del Toro (Universal Pictures, 2008).
Men in Black 3 (score by Danny Elfman), dir. Barry Sonnenfeld (Sony Pictures, 2012).
Urban Legends: Final Cut (score by John Ottman), dir. John Ottman (Original Film/Phoenix Pictures, 2000).
X2: X-Men United (score by John Ottman), dir. Bryan Singer (Twentieth Century Fox/Marvel, 2003).
The X Files: I Want to Believe (score by Mark Snow), dir. Chris Carter (Twentieth Century Fox, 2008).

CHAMBER MUSIC/ORCHESTRA

String Quartet No. 1 in Green (2012).
A Symphony of Hope: The Haiti Project (multiple composers), (2011).

STRING ARRANGER

90210 Soundtrack, All-American Rejects (2009).
All I Ever Wanted, Kelly Clarkson (2009).
Breaking Dawn soundtrack, "A Thousand Years," Christina Perri (2011).
Daughtry, Daughtry (2006).
Disconnected, The Buzzhorn (2002).
Dreamgirls soundtrack (2006).
Every Man for Himself, Hoobastank (2006).
Fame Soundtrack, Finale, "Hold Your Dream" (2009).
For Your Entertainment, Adam Lambert (2009).
Full Circle, Creed (2009).
Gather Up, Peter Bradley Adams (2006).
Go Mad, Caleb Kane (2006).
Halestorm, Halestorm (2009).
Just Like You, Allison Iraheta (2009).
Katy Perry—MTV Unplugged, "Thinking of You" (2009).
Leave This Town, Daughtry (2009).
Live at La Cigale DVD, Hoobastank (2006).
Lonely Road, The Red Jumpsuit Apparatus (2009).
Move Along, All-American Rejects (2005).
One-X, Three Days Grace (2006).
The Paramour Sessions, Papa Roach (2006).
The Reason, Hoobastank (2003).
Revelations, Third Day (2008).
Scars and Souvenirs, Theory of a Deadman (2008).
Sisters of the Red Death, Vendetta Red (2005).
Skeletons, Hawthorne Heights (2010).
Stronger, Kelly Clarkson (2011).
Time of My Life, 3 Doors Down (2011).
Tug of War, Gabriel Mann (2002).
Unstable, Adema (2003).
What Do You Got, Bon Jovi (2010).
When the World Comes Down, All-American Rejects (2008).
Year of the Spider, Cold (2003).
You and I, Paul Freeman (2008).

21

Jeanine Tesori

Jeanine Tesori, like Deborah Lurie, considers herself both a composer and a collaborator. Most known for her music in live stage productions, Tesori's celebrated scores include *Shrek the Musical, Caroline or Change, Thoroughly Modern Millie, Twelfth Night,* and *Violet.* During our conversation, Tesori openly discusses motherhood and the choices she continues to face as an active composer and a mother. Born in 1961 to parents in the medical profession and growing up on Long Island, Tesori was raised in a household enriched by science and music. She began her young-adult life intending to enroll in medical school but was introduced to musical theater as a possible career when she worked summers as an accompanist for the Stagedoor Manor Performing Arts Camp. After graduating from Barnard, Tesori spent several years in New York as a pianist, arranger, and conductor of musical theater on and off Broadway.

Tesori was prepared for this career shift thanks to a progressive piano teacher who taught her early on that "music is music"—that musical style does not automatically determine worthiness. Tesori learned classical technique and transposed music on the keyboard as common practice, a skill whose value became apparent when it helped her become a marketable accompanist and arranger in her early days on the theater scene. Like other commercial or media composers, such as Laura Karpman, Lurie, and Winifred Phillips, Tesori has always participated in various projects of music making. For instance, in addition to composing, she worked as associate conductor for such shows as *The Secret Garden* and *The Who's Tommy* and wrote arrangements for dance numbers in several shows, including the 1995 revival of *How to Succeed in Business without Really Trying.*

Tesori embraces challenges, having decided early in her career that she would stop talking about writing music and actually write it. She left a flourishing career as an accompanist and arranger, bought the rights to a story, and wrote her first full musical, *Violet,* in collaboration with Brian Crawley. Produced off-Broadway in 1997, *Violet* was nominated for seven Drama Desk Awards, including Outstanding New Musical. It won the Drama Critics' Circle Award for Best Musical, the Lucille Lortel Award for Outstanding Musical, and an Obie special citation for Tesori's music. Discussing the business of her profession, Tesori explains how she balances commercial works such as *Shrek* with less commercial projects such as *Twelfth Night* and *Caroline, or Change,* the latter a collaboration with the playwright Tony Kushner. Her work with Kushner continues; they premiered a new one-act opera, *A Blizzard on Marblehead Neck,* for the Glimmerglass Festival and work toward an outstanding commission from the Metropolitan Opera.

Tesori thrives in the collaborative process and considers each new partnership a "marriage" of styles, working lives, working habits, and conversations. She explains that composition is an isolating process, and so she loves the interaction of working with others. At the same time, she describes the enormity of the collaborative process that brings any musical to fruition. This process has earned Tesori several Tony Award nominations for her scores *Shrek, Millie, Caroline,* and *Twelfth Night.* In fact, *Caroline* opened before the end of *Millie's* run, making Tesori the first woman composer to have two new musicals running concurrently on Broadway. She has composed for other media, including music for the films *Show Business: The Road to Broadway, Nights in Rodanthe, Wrestling with Angels* (the 2006 documentary about Tony Kushner), and *Shrek the Third,* as well as writing new songs for several animated Disney videos. Tesori's current projects include a collaboration with the playwright Lisa Kron to bring Alison Bechdel's graphic novel *Fun Home* to the stage.

***

July 2010, at her home in New York City

JENNIFER KELLY: How did you transition from a pre-med student in college to a life in musical theater?

JEANINE TESORI: Music was a given in our family. I had started playing the piano by ear when I was quite young, and then I began formal lessons at five or six. Music had been a part of my life forever and a part of my sisters' lives. Also, my dad was a doctor, and my mother was a nurse. His office was in our home, so we all knew words like "hemostat" immediately. A couple of us may have gone into the sciences somewhat blindly, without realizing the relationship between music and science. Halfway through college, I began questioning my chosen science path. But I didn't even realize there was an industry of Broadway.

JK: Were you in Manhattan?

JT: Long Island. There's a big music scene at Barnard and Columbia, and we frequently went downtown to listen to music. I rediscovered a love for it, but it didn't occur to me that I could make it a career. I picked up a booklet at the Barnard career center that said the Stagedoor Manor [Performing Arts Camp] needed music directors and pianists. I auditioned, got a job, met Jack Romano, and that was it. Everything changed.

JK: When you went in to audition, did you think yet that you could have a career in music?

JT: Oh, no, not at all. I was floundering like any person is at that point. I didn't know what I was going to do. I *did* know that I could play. A brilliant teacher [Richard Benda] taught me a very natural method, so I could play by ear and transpose. Those skills were commodities in those days. So I fell right into it.

JK: It sounds like Stagedoor Manor was quite a turning point for you.

JT: It wasn't until I began working at Stagedoor and finding out about the theater that I realized this is absolutely what I was going to do. There was no question about it. It was instantaneous.

JK: Later, didn't you take a year off from everything because you were afraid you were going to turn into one of the "shoulda-woulda" people?

JT: I felt restricted. I didn't feel like playing the piano was the end goal for me, even though I loved it. I still love it. But I felt like playing the piano was in service of something else. And my mentor [Buryl Red], who is a very dear friend and partner, said, "You know, there's talking about writing, and then there's actually writing. And those two things are quite different." A lot of people talk about it, but very few actually do it because it's boring. It's tedious and lonely, and you become filled with doubt. It takes courage to really put it on the line, as opposed to talking about how you would write it better. So if you really want to do it, go do it.

JK: If you knew how hard it was, how boring and tedious, and filled with doubt it was going to be. . . .

JT: I decided it was better to know than to regret later. Then I could at least say, "I tried that." I wanted to see where I had the talent. Am I going be the greatest pianist? Absolutely not. I'm really good, but I can't compete on that level. And I don't want to compete on that level, because it's not what I do well. Done. Next. I also know that I'm not a great lyricist. I'll study it to effectively discuss what should happen in the story, but I can't actually do it. I think there is wisdom in knowing where your talents lie and where you are completely average.

JK: So, you found the thing that you do really well.

JT: Yes. I think I found what I want to do really well. And I want to master it. I really, really want to master it.

JK: Did Stagedoor initially open some doors to help you break into the business?

JT: Stagedoor gave me the idea of going into the business. After that, I got myself into all of the doors. I would go anywhere; I was incredibly tenacious because I really wanted it.

JK: You basically said yes to everything?

JT: I said yes to things that were really worthwhile. I said, "I need what you have. I can file for you; you don't have to pay me. I'm willing to do whatever it is, so I can just listen?" I apprenticed, I assisted, I played everywhere, I constantly studied, and I always went to live concerts. I learned that from my father—the power of seeking what you need to improve, as opposed to just perpetuating what you already know. That mentality is part of medicine because it's the never-ending quest of new techniques.

JK: For you, is it still a never-ending quest?

JT: The variables in a show are endless, which is why a great team can sometimes put on a bad show. Tiny decisions become huge decisions because there are so many people working on any given show. Does a song fit here? Does this character sing it? Is it a duet? Is it in this key? Does the score sound like the costumes look? It's much easier to steer a sunfish than a tanker. And a show is a tanker—it really is! Those musicals are big. But to work well, they have to feel like the committee is small enough to talk with one another. Like a startup business, where everyone has their desk and you lean around and tell each other ideas. The beauty is in the communication. Sometimes, when companies get really fancy, they can't talk to one another anymore, because there are too many hoops to go through to communicate. I think a musical can suffer from that as well.

JK: It's interesting to hear you emphasize communication, because I have found that a lot of composers, especially of traditional concert music, describe it as an isolating process. But you're talking about active communication and collaboration.

JT: There's enough isolation involved because the writing is about you and your choices, but the whole reason I went into it was for the conversation. I thrive on that. The isolation comes with the territory, but that constant dialogue of, "What are we doing, and why are we doing it, and should we do it this way?" It's all an expression hopefully emanating from the same center.

JK: How was your experience collaborating with Tony Kushner?

JT: Oh, he's so dear to me. My collaboration with him was life-changing. He raised the bar so high; I didn't realize the bar could be that high in musical theater. I learned so much from him, and we affected each other, which was nice. I discovered early on how we were going to collaborate. For instance, I can't compete with his brain—very few people can. But the playground was very level when it came to the project at hand, and when it came to the repertoire. I know musicals really well, and the ones that I don't know, I try to learn. I've musically directed so many of them, and I was playing in the pit for so long that I know musicals from the mailroom up. I know how they work and how to put them together. That knowledge and experience has come to benefit me greatly. And [Tony's] ear is so musical. He is generous and smart and challenging, so it's a great marriage [of collaboration].

JK: In a collaborative process, what comes first? Lyrics, music. . . .

JT: It changes all the time. That's kind of like saying, "How do you have a conversation? Who starts it?"

JK: It is just part of the collaboration.

JT: Exactly. It just starts. I like the idea of how music sits—how a lyric sits on my music, and going back and forth. The shadings compared to the beats of what the actor is doing, or what we think the actor is doing. It's a very, very back-and-forth process. We spend hours and hours of time alone, just sitting in silence and contemplating all of the choices. But the real fun of it is talking about the possibilities, which are endless.

JK: And are you thinking about the visual aspect as well? The set, and how it's going to be performed on stage?

JT: Oh, definitely. I work very visually and think about where they might be standing in a scene, how they might do this or that. I want to know how it exists in three dimensions as opposed to in my brain, on a flat, so I often graph a show.

JK: Continuing with the process of putting a show together, once you think you've got an idea for a story, what comes next?

JT: I can only speak to my career, but it's like saying, "How do you raise a kid?" It depends on the kid. Some kids need braces, some are easy, and you hear parents say, "This one gave me no trouble," or, "This one didn't learn to speak until he was six!" And each child has a DNA and a completely different take on the world. That is, to me, what a show is. It has a completely different musical fingerprint. I think part of the fun and part of the challenge is to know that you're new to it; no matter how many musicals you've done, you're new to this show. This show has not yet been written. It's the humbling part of it. And as much expertise as you feel you might have, this is new. So you start with new eyes. Every single show that I've done has started differently. I gave up saying, "This is how we're going to start." We just start. If my collaborator has never written a musical, we start by going to see musicals and building a vocabulary. If I'm working with someone who's tremendously experienced, we might begin outlining. We always start with dinner and coffee because . . . it's a marriage. You have to find out where your skills are in terms of communication, what your families are like, where you're going to work, the structure. It's all about providing the structure that will free you to get the work done.

JK: While you compose, do you consider the music living on after the show closes? Do you write with that in mind?

JT: No, I write to finish the show. Once it goes out, I write another show. And the rights of the book merge. They begin separately, but there's a point after the show where they become inextricably tied. One cannot be performed without the other. It's very rare that someone would perform only the lyrics to something, because the idea is that one begot the other. The beauty is the thing that ties it together, holds it together.

JK: When you're writing a show, do you think about which song will be the hook or the showstopper or the belt number to use in marketing?

JT: It's not the same business as when Jule Styne wrote "People" [for *Funny Girl*], knowing that would come out as the popular number in the show. It's not part of the pop dialogue or part of that culture anymore. Today, it's a specialty culture. I can compare what happened in show business to medicine with the intense study of the elbow and elbow doctors. It got very specific. Songs depend on the range and the character. I think about them as what the songs need to activate, what they need to do. Sometimes, they need to simply activate what I call "idiot space" in a piece where people need to just listen. *Caroline, or Change* is a hard listen because it doesn't have a lot of "idiot space." That show just keeps going, behaving like a play that happens to be set to music. As George Wolfe said, "Musicals are about rhythm and inevitability." You have to feel what their individual rhythm is. Feel whether the meal is balanced. Balance and inevitability make you glad when something starts. In that moment you feel that it can't be any other way.

JK: I know you feel strongly about the back and forth of collaboration. So, what kind of relationship do you like to have when you give it up to a conductor? Or do you conduct your own scores?

JT: I never conduct the theater scores. I conduct the film scores, and I'm going to conduct the upcoming opera. For shows, I like being the music director at first, because I like to work back and forth. I don't have to write the music out right away, so I can take time to feel how it lives and make sure that it's an easier notation. I think the point where you give it to someone else is when you have to step back and listen. And that's hard. A lot of people like conducting, because they like to participate. Sitting there and watching someone else's process, having them make mistakes, gritting your teeth. . . . It takes a lot of control, and I don't think a lot of writers are really known for their impulse control.

JK: When a director says something isn't working or asks for cuts, is that an easy experience?

JT: Generally, yes. I rewrite very easily. I cut really easily. If I don't think it's working out, it goes. There's no discussion. I'm not attached to it. Besides, you always have it for possible use later. You can pull it for another show, or use it elsewhere. I do feel reluctant if I don't feel it's being staged correctly, and the writing is having to change because someone else has not delivered.

JK: I know you are working on an opera project for the the Metropolitan Opera. Do you have to go into a different vein when writing for opera as opposed to musical theater?

JT: I think music is music. I've studied classical music my whole life. The beauty of what my early teacher taught me when I was five was that music is music. There's no judgment. Whether it is a television theme or Shostakovich or the Talking Heads, there's validity and nobility in much of it. Don't judge it. It's like a language. Is French better than Italian? It's just a different language, so play it.

JK: Are you ever a part of the textual writing?

JT: I have always been a part of that. In *Caroline, or Change,* we worked closely on structure and dramaturgy. Over the years, I've learned a ton about dramaturgy. You have to understand dramaturgy, because it's about where things should go and the impact of taking something out or moving it. Understanding dramaturgy makes you a better writer, and it's better to be in on it as opposed to just receiving or waiting for something. It's just not how I work.

JK: There seem to be fewer live theaters around. Is there still opportunity to take shows out to the smaller cities?

JT: First of all, people don't want to go out on the road today. It's a very hard life. The road used to be a natural. Mary Martin would run a show for three years and then hit the road. But that isn't what happens anymore. It's changed. When Moss Hart was working on musicals, you could travel a show for a year working with the audience as a scene partner and respond in kind by rewriting. There would be time. Today, there are fewer out-of-town performances. Part of the difficulty is that you lose a show in tech. I mean that in tech, a show gets pulled apart like taffy, and then you mush it back together, and it's just a mess at first. Then it starts back with intention, and there's usually one performance when it clicks in. So you can't really see the show until it unifies and behaves as itself.

JK: With so much money riding on a show nowadays and little time to really work it out, it seems like a lot of pressure.

JT: It's hard. I write pretty quickly. I can turn a song around quickly, but making changes in musicals takes days. Everything has multiple parts. You make a change, then you have to teach the change, then put the change in the pit, then it has to be orchestrated, and then it has to be cued, and then it's just eleven steps.

JK: How much of your life is spent on marketing, promotion, and the details of business?

JT: I don't market anything; I don't promote anything. But the business end is a huge amount, huge. I know quite a lot about secondary markets, because the way I was trained to actually make a living in this business is in passive income. It means taking some very nonglamorous jobs because those jobs are the ones that will return to you, enabling you to have a family or work on projects really important to you. I learned that early on.

JK: That's not the kind of thing you learned in school. Was that on-the-job training?

JT: Yes, and asking a lot of basic questions, such as, "How do you live?"

JK: You wear a lot of hats.

JT: I do wear a lot of hats. You have to. I think the more hats you wear—as long as you don't get chafing—the better you are at what you do. You understand another view when you stand in a different position. You learn what is going to be hard to do, and you work on making it easier.

JK: I imagine it also helps you sustain in this business.

JT: I'm quite happy doing four or five different things. I used to dance, and I write a lot of dance music. I'm happy as a clam to watch dance for a couple of months, study it, and then note new music. And [New York] is chock-filled with people making music, so that's also endless. You can participate, or you can just sit and watch. That's what I love about this city. I've lived here now for thirty-one years.

JK: There is clearly a lot that goes on in the making of music that has nothing to do with music. How much of your time is spent actually composing?

JT: Well, it used to be different. I'm a parent. When we had Sisi [her daughter Siena], I wanted to make sure that people still saw me as a writer. You have to be willing to insist that people see you that way. I've learned with her that writing did not wait for this magic time. You go in, you say, "I'm going to write for five hours," then dammit you close the door and you write. Even if you just write crap, it's the only way for it to get done. That discipline I have in spades. That's never been the issue. I think it's more about making sure that there's time for everything else.

JK: So how do you balance the work and nonwork parts of your life?

JT: You have no idea! I think that there are times when I just run into the ground. It's really about using your time well. I don't watch television, so that is found time for me. When Sisi is doing homework, we often work side by side. Time is finite, and once it's gone, you're done. I try to keep that lightly in mind when it comes to deadlines, because I can do nothing without a deadline.

JK: Have you found support in this business being a mom?

JT: Oh, I wouldn't do it if I weren't supported. I said once, "I have an eight-month-old. She's got to come with me." And the reply was, "Well, why wouldn't she?"

Door open! When Sisi was six months old, she came to her first orchestra rehearsal. She started traveling with me at ten months for *Twelfth Night.* When I did six or seven Disney projects, Sisi came out with me [to Los Angeles], and we'd sit together with the animators. The contracts broke new ground. Making sure I had a car with four doors for the car seat. Saying, "No, I need another plane ticket," and, "No, I'm not paying for a babysitter," and, "No, I can't meet a babysitter out there," and, "No more traveling after preschool." Asking myself how to keep this continuity and not make her feel like she's the second. All of those concerns come into it, because you are trying to build a career and take care of your child. Sometimes I feel in charge of it, and sometimes I feel swamped. And it's different to be the mom than a dad or to be in the mother role in a same-sex couple. It simply is not the same, but this is who I am. A lot of actors have to pretend that they are not parents. But for me, if a project doesn't work with being a mom, then I'm not there. It takes a little bit of stealing from yourself. For instance, I just got an offer to go to Australia for six months. Sisi is in seventh grade now, so I'm just not going to do it. It's a huge amount of money, and I'm just not doing it. It's a no brainer. There's no regret. It's just what it is.

JK: Priorities.

JT: Yes. And talents. Sisi has lived in London because of it, she's lived all over the States, and she's seen so many wonderful and appropriate-for-her-age kinds of things. I made sure everyone knew I was a mom also, so we can change the climate and incorporate the idea that kids are not always excluded. It isn't that I want children at a cocktail party, but they are little people! I think sometimes in America we want to pretend that these mothers don't have kids. And they do. You know, Sisi and I recently wrote our first song together. I never write music with anybody, so that was a first. I'd never even considered somebody saying, "Why doesn't it go this way?" I didn't know what it was going to be like, and it was so much fun. Working with my daughter Sisi was the first time I ever wrote music with somebody.

JK: What I hear you saying throughout our conversation is, Learn as much as you can about everything, and do what you do really well. Then, more specifically, choose what you are going to do that will give you the most benefit for whatever choices you are making, either to have a family or be able to travel or work the next project, or what have you.

JT: Well, I would put it this way: Your twenties are your second adolescence, and you say yes to a lot of things. For me, the thirties were about focusing and taking it seriously. Not just dreaming about it but doing it and failing a lot, which I think is very unpopular but very necessary. And it is also very humiliating, because it's very public, what we do. I think the forties are simplifying. Sometimes saying, "I don't have to do that." What does it mean to develop ideas as opposed to invent ideas? Look what Bach did in the first measure, and how he spun it all from there. And listen. I'm quite clear about what I want to do well and where I want to go. Find a way to get it done, find funding, work and get yourself funded, and then take six months off and do it.

JK: So now that you're in your late forties, how would you like your music to evolve from here?

JT: I'm trying to take more chances and not give a shit, which is difficult. I'd like to free myself up, not edit or do any self-imposing. I think a second adulthood. I see in the patterns of a lot of my great women friends, especially, that there is a freedom. The show I'm working on now is definitely down new roads. I'm very scared. I'm really good when I've been down that road once. But at first, I think, "I don't know this road!"

JK: It's interesting. You say a lot of your women friends are finding a sort of second adulthood. I guess it's true: some say forty is the new twenty, and fifty is the new thirty.

JT: And sexuality is not used as currency in the same way any longer. I think you wear it differently. That's what I see happening. My passion for teaching has become important to me, trying to pass on what other people have passed on to me. It's a lot of time, but I think it's important. I love teaching.

JK: What aspect do you teach?

JT: One of things I do when I teach is have people discuss what they've seen, discuss what they'd like to see, discuss what they think went wrong. They can't use blanket general words, and it isn't about being right; it is about expressing and effectively communicating your thoughts. Tony Kushner is brilliant at it. He was on the debate team. So I teach a lot of master classes with different themes, such as performance through the eyes of a writer: how you write, how you create a performance. I think a lot of people in musical theater forget that it's called *musical* theater. They don't analyze or look at a piece like they would a piece of classical music. Some musicals are beautifully designed, and you can study it in that way. Others, not so much.

JK: Can you see that level of study or analysis in a performance?

JT: Oh, definitely. When you watch them conduct, you know when they know the piece. They have a point of view. They have feelings about how this piece was made. They almost have the writer's hand when they conduct it.

JK: Tell me about the educational series you did years ago.

JT: Yes, that was a long time ago. I did tons of them. I learned a great deal from that experience. We went to Nashville, and I worked thousands of hours with the symphony. It was a great learning. We did everything from gospel to opera, original to front porch.

JK: Did that experience contribute to your composition?

JT: I think everything contributes. Being a part of those educational series specifically helped my ear training. I was twenty-four when I first started, and I would conduct. After we would finish, I would often sit there at the podium and say nothing. Or I'd say that every cue was very nice, very good. I didn't know how to respond to sound. It taught me that sound can be molded, sculpted.

JK: How important is mentoring to you?

JT: For me it's crucial, because I went into this quite late. I wasn't a music major until I was nineteen. I think it's only recently, the past two or three years, that I've felt like I no longer have to catch up. I was plagued for a long time with the mentality that I've missed a lot or don't know as much as everybody else. I think I tended to be in overdrive, because I felt like I had to catch up to so many people around me.

JK: You've had many successes and work steadily. Are you out of that place now?

JT: I hope so! [*Laughs*] Until I think, "Oh my God, I have so much to learn!" It just feels endless. I quit the piano and music altogether from age thirteen to nineteen. Those six years—crucial. But for me it was the best thing I ever did, because I came back to it on my own terms.

JK: Who were some of your early mentors?

JT: Jack Romano, who ran Stagedoor Manor. And my piano teacher, Richard Benda, because of his attitude and his acceptance of music. We used to play everything in the circle of fifths, and he taught without judgment. It never occurred to me that not everybody played everything in four different keys. That was an incredible gift he taught me. I met my business partner, Buryl Red, when I was twenty-four, and we've been partners more than twenty years. I would not be in this position if it were not for him.

JK: I'd like to ask about a few specific shows. How was your experience with *Thoroughly Modern Millie*?

JT: That was the show that established me. When I wrote *Violet,* I was just too young. There were some solutions that were beyond me, and I was guessing so much of the time. I didn't have enough writing behind me. By the time I got to *Millie,* I was starting to understand the rhythm. The second act of *Millie* is really great. You learn by doing, and I've learned since *Millie* too. Once it's going, you can't say, "Oh, that intro is too slow!" It's too late [*laughs*].

JK: In 2004, you collaborated with Tony Kushner on *Caroline, or Change.* Was it a risk to take on such a noncommercial project?

JT: I don't think so, because I had done *Violet* and *Millie. Violet* is about a girl with a scar on her face who goes on a bus to Tulsa. It's not going to bring them in, you know? I did it because I felt that show so much. I needed to do it. I flew down and paid everything I saved for those rights. I put it on the line for that show. And then, when *Millie* came along, it was really about craft. I'd also done *Twelfth Night,* which is really out there, with all these exotic instruments. And I'd done a lot of dance, like the gospel, brassy arrangements with Ted Spurling on the revival of *How to Succeed in Business without Really Trying.* Things started lining up, and people began to ask, "Who is this chick?"

JK: When you wrote *Shrek the Musical,* it was already a successful movie. What kind of pressure was it to take on that project and write all new music?

JT: That was horrific. Shrek is a brand. I took it because I love William Steig, and I love the movie, and I thought it would be fun. Also, I always have to do something that's commercial and something that's not, and I really wanted to work with a movie studio to see what it was like. I had already worked with Disney on numerous projects, and it was fantastic. And *Shrek* was really fun. The version that we put together for the tour is absolutely great. We put numerous changes in, basically rewriting a third of it. I remember saying at the last run-through that I really appreciated having another go at it. That run-through, that is the show that I can stand by. It was the greatest feeling.

JK: How do you know when a piece is going to make an impact?

JT: I have no idea, no clue, until the lights go up.

JK: Do you think about audience when you write?

JT: Oh, yes. I think that a final scene partner is the audience coming in. Like it or not, that's the final stage. The audience will tell you if it's moving or funny. That's the agreement with an audience. It's terrifying, but there they are. Watching a new piece in front of an audience is a fascinating process, especially an audience with a piece they have heard nothing about. There's no reference point for them. That's what I loved about *Caroline, or Change.* Nobody knew anything about it. It was great. They didn't know how to say the title, they didn't know what the title meant, they didn't know who I was. They just came in and sat. I want to do that again.

JK: It sounds frightening.

JT: That's much less frightening to me than adapting something, where people already have an expected set of responses when they sit down, like *Shrek.* With *Shrek,* they had a complete reference point. I'll take the other, any day!

JK: It's fascinating to hear you talk about this, because you could be describing classical music. Audiences sit down often with a set of expectations in their heads about classical music. Once they hear the contemporary or new side of their expected classical music, they stop and think or question.

JT: Absolutely. That is also because of the repetition of repertoire; it almost feels like ownership. Similar to how a movie studio owns the music for a film. They didn't really write it, but it feels like they wrote it, and they are the legal author.

JK: Where would you like to see musical theater go?

JT: I would like to see it written about intelligently. There are certain reviewers, two or three, who really can write. Unfortunately, very few people who are writing about the theater know about music, and it's frustrating. It really is a shame, because a lot of people who write about theater miss the whole element of how things come together.

JK: You are obviously passionate about writing for projects that collaborate with a visual component, whether for musical theater, dance, film, opera. . . . Have you ever thought about writing something that is only for absolute music?

JT: No. No interest.

JK: You love what you do.

JT: Yes.

JK: What's it like being in New York today?

JT: It's such a hard question. New York today . . . it's safer. And the risk in its safety is that the city is somehow reduced. That is really hard. I'm glad it's safer because of the people I love, but I'm sorry it's safer because the "smashing" was the excitement. And I miss that. It was absolutely so thrilling. New York in 1980, 1981, was a dangerous place. The art was dangerous, and there was this audacity to have bad taste. I miss that, too. You can't really have that taste anymore. There's no bad taste in the theater anymore.

JK: I'm going to quote something I read: "Tesori, the first woman composer in history that has two original musicals running concurrently on Broadway." Do you mind the press pointing out that you are a "woman composer"? Or does it matter?

JT: I think it's factual.

JK: In the field of musical theater, you really are one of a very few.

JT: It's true that the few of us are often the only woman in the room besides the assistant choreographer or maybe a lyricist. I know some people really do mind being pointed out as a woman composer, but I don't care. Actually, I'm glad they're writing about it, because somebody may recognize it the more a light is shone on it. The only way that I knew it was even possible as a woman was that I saw somebody doing it. I saw Linda Twine conducting Lena Horne on Broadway, and I'd never seen a woman on stage doing theater like that. That experience actually seared into my memory. It was so important. If you don't see it, how are you going to know you can do it? I was nineteen.

JK: That was the age you switched your focus from medicine to music.

JT: I was just beginning to see shows, and I thought, What is she doing? Who is that? I had the chance to really know her well later.

JK: As you've been in this business about twenty-five years now, have you seen the place for women in musical theater grow?

JT: Yes. Certainly in conducting, orchestrating—a woman finally won a Tony for orchestration [Sarah Travis in 2006 for *Sweeney Todd*]. There are female composers in the ranks coming up, and there are a lot of women producing here in theater. It's great.

***

Works by Jeanine Tesori

MUSIC FOR THEATER

A Blizzard on Marblehead Neck, lyrics by Tony Kushner (2011).
Caroline, or Change, lyrics by Tony Kushner (2004).
A Free Man of Color, lyrics by John Guare (2010).
Mother Courage and Her Children, New York Shakespeare Festival (2006).
Shrek the Musical, lyrics by David Lindsay-Abaire (2008).
Thoroughly Modern Millie, lyrics by Dick Scanlan (2002).
Twelfth Night, William Shakespeare (1998).
Violet, written with Brian Crawley (1997).

MUSIC FOR THEATER—ARRANGEMENTS

Dream (dance arr.), music by varied artists, lyrics by Johnny Mercer (1997).
How to Succeed in Business without Really Trying revival (dance arr.), music and lyrics by Frank Loesser (1995).
The Secret Garden (dance arr.), music by Lucy Simon, lyrics by Marsha Norman (1991).
The Sound of Music revival (incidental music, dance arr.), music by Richard Rodgers, lyrics by Oscar Hammerstein II (1998).
Swing! music and lyrics by varied artists (1999).

FILM/VIDEO/DOCUMENTARY

The Emperor's New Groove 2: Kronk's New Groove (select songs), (Walt Disney, 2005).
Every Day, dir. Richard Levine (Ambush Entertainment, 2010).
Lilo and Stitch II (select songs), (Walt Disney, 2005).
The Little Mermaid: Ariel's Beginning (select songs), (Walt Disney, 2008).
Mulan II (select songs), (Walt Disney, 2004).
P.O.V. Wrestling with Angels: Playwright Tony Kushner, dir. Freida Lee Mock (PBS, 2006).
Nights in Rodanthe, dir. George C. Wolfe (Warner Bros. Pictures, 2008).
ShowBusiness: The Road to Broadway (score and arrangements), dir. Dori Berinstein (Dramatic Forces, 2007).
Shrek the Third (select songs), dir. Chris Miller and Raman Hui (DreamWorks, 2007)
Winds of Change (ABC, 1994).

Elliotte Rusty Harold

22

Beth Anderson

As the founder and producer of Women's Work, an annual concert series in New York City featuring women composers, Beth Anderson openly discusses what it means for her to be a woman composer in the twenty-first century. Born in Lexington, Kentucky, in 1950, Anderson recalls how her compositional influences began when she was a young teenager and her piano teacher, Helen Lipscomb, showed her how to take two different musical ideas and put them together into a short composition. At the University of California at Davis and Mills College in the late 1960s and early 1970s, Anderson's influential teachers also included John Cage, Terry Riley, Robert Ashley, and Larry Austin.

In 1973, Anderson became coeditor and publisher of the avant-garde musical and literary magazine *EAR*. With the help of a National Endowment for the Arts grant, she moved to New York in 1975 to pursue a career in music. In addition to composing, she taught at the College of New Rochelle for eight years and played piano for dance classes at the Martha Graham and Alvin Ailey dance schools. As it had for Tania León, playing for dance classes greatly influenced Anderson's compositional development. Her skills grew rapidly, and she developed a sense of humor in her music.

John Cage also influenced Anderson's early works, and she became an explorer of technology. Her text-sound pieces are rhythmic, layered collages of poetry and text, involving her careful analysis of words, individual letters, and equations combined with her use of tape. Examples of her early works include the multimedia piece, *She Wrote* (written for her thesis at Mills College and taken from *Q.E.D.* by Gertrude Stein), her oratorio, *Joan* (about Joan of Arc), and what Anderson calls her mother-father pieces, *Ode* and *Torero.* Like bookends, *Ode* and *Torero* use her father's rhythmic work as an auctioneer along with her mother's thoughts and voice on tape. Reading Cage's writing collection *Silence* opened Anderson's mind to new music and to ideas about chance. So strong was Cage's influence that, when Cage asked why anyone should write music, Anderson stopped writing it. After working through that period, Anderson, thankfully, continued to compose.

Anderson's compositional style began to change in the early 1980s, and she documented her thought process in an essay significant to her own development, "Beauty Is Revolution."[1] In this essay, Anderson, herself sometimes termed an electronics-based, experimental, post-Cagean composer, begins to question the notion of beauty and determines that expressing one's own definition of beauty is revolutionary in itself. Going back to her Kentucky roots, Anderson then began writing "swales." As she explains on her Web site and in various notes for swale performances, "A swale is a meadow or a marsh where there is nourishment and moisture and, therefore, a rich diversity of plant life."[2] (Also of note is the large "crazy quilt" of patchworked swatches made by her grandmother on view in Anderson's living room.) Often described today as a neoromantic composer, Anderson uses "swale" as a musical term, and her work since 1984, beginning with *Pennyroyal Swale,* has been assembled from pieces of newly composed music reminiscent of diverse marsh plant life and quilt swatches. Anderson has composed numerous critically acclaimed works for chamber ensemble, orchestra, and string quartet, as well as music for the stage, multimedia, electronics, text-sound works, pieces for solo instruments and tape, band, dance ensemble, and voice.

With her characteristically dry humor, Anderson responds smiling to the question of whether she still thinks, as she said in the past, that being a woman composer was a heroic struggle: "Sure, against all odds! With the wind flowing in your hair and the tattered flag in the background, absolutely! It's a great fight."

***

March 2009, at her home in Brooklyn

JENNIFER KELLY: In your 1981 article "Beauty Is Revolution," you wrote, "I once believed that the concept of the music was much more important than the sound, that the politics of the notation is more important than the time limits of the rehearsals and therefore more important than the sound of the performance." And then later in the article you say, "It's a very liberating feeling to come back to my childhood definition of composition. Beauty is enough." Tell me a little bit more about that. Today, is beauty still enough?

BETH ANDERSON: I don't just write down the music and leave it alone. I futz with it all the time. It's like if you were making a crazy quilt [patchwork swatches]. You wouldn't take the swatches that were left over from making the dresses and just sew them up in the shapes they were in. You would actually cut them up more and make them interesting to you. So I write swatches of music, and then I cut them up or don't and put them back together in ways that I think are beautiful. I don't think that it's really necessary to make the next big thing. I'm not looking for a new black box, a new electronic gadget that will make some weird noise that I can record for forty-five minutes and call that my new piece and that people will see as a movement forward in technology or pushing Schoenberg's envelope into the logical, historic . . . I don't care about that anymore. I think that's . . . "goofalicious." I think the musicologists will take care of what the history of music is. And the theorists, obviously, seem to me to be behind the composers when they were writing, trying to explain what they had written. So I think I'll let them do that, too [*laughs*].

JK: You wrote in a different article that you write music for the listeners, but not necessarily music that sells. I find your recent music to be lyrical, beautiful, and melodic, and to me that is part of what sells. So I'm curious, what do you see as something that sells today as opposed to what you compose?

BA: Well, the problem about selling anything is that you have to get it past a lot of people that are in between you and the actual listeners. So certain record companies that still put out new music may have a point of view that John Adams is "the thing." And John Adams is great, but there is other music, and their view precludes them including other kinds of things. They either think of themselves as too avant-garde or too traditional. I mean, the only advertising you ever hear about really for CDs, at least me, is for Yo-Yo Ma and Cecilia Bartoli, both of whom are wonderful, but there's so much more in the universe. And you also have to get past the players, because sometimes players will initiate recordings, and they have to be excited by it in some way, and often players want to play something that is thorny or difficult. If they're into any new music, they don't want to play Beethoven. They don't want to play anything that requires the same skills as Beethoven. They want to do stuff inside the piano or things that have electronics.

JK: Still today?

BA: Yeah, still today. Things that they see as cutting edge, which to me are historic, are things from the late sixties and early seventies, and everyone runs around saying everything is derivative [*laughs*]. You just have to be patient and hopeful that somebody will find it and like it.

JK: Does new music still thrive in New York City?

BA: Thrive? I mean, it needs health care! [*Laughs*] If they are mortgaging the Chagalls at the Metropolitan, what chance do American women composers have? It's really small, very small.

JK: So whose responsibility is it? Is it up to the marketers or to the players to be adventurous and play everything that's out there? Or is it up to the composers to make sure and write it to put it out there? Or to consumers, what we purchase and support?

BA: I think it's a great conglomeration. I mean, certainly, if the composer gets too depressed and doesn't write anything, there's nothing to sell, nothing to push, nothing to do. But a lot of composers wrote a very small amount of duration music and yet have still had a major impact.

JK: Looking at your music specifically, how do you think Kentucky influences your music? For instance, *Pennyroyal Swale*: how is Kentucky in *Pennyroyal Swale*?

BA: I guess I'm sort of sentimental with Kentucky. It's a beautiful, beautiful place. *Pennyroyal Swale* starts with what I think of as a fiddle-tune style. Some musicologist wrote about it and said that it was a tune from *Carmen,* and even if it is, even if the gypsy thing that Bizet was ripping off to put in *Carmen* is somehow related to the Irish fiddle tune that I was fantasizing, I certainly wasn't trying to create anything like *Carmen* [*laughs*].

JK: I heard Irish folk music. I find it interesting that it was named after a healing herb, and I'm wondering if there is any connection there for you.

BA: I was looking for something that had "Roy" in the name because of Mr. James Roy, who used to run the concert music at BMI. He was just the sweetest southern gentleman. He was so kind to me. I didn't have any friends when I moved to New York, and I just would dress up and go to BMI and say hello to Mr. Roy.

And he'd talk to me like I was a serious person and not some twenty-five-year-old nut from Kentucky via California [*laughs*]. He was good to a lot of women composers. There was a piece in *The Sacred Harp* that he really loved, and he encouraged me to get the book and hang out with it and play through things. I'm sure that had some influence on that piece.

JK: If there is a piece you want to write, do you wait until you're inspired, if it's not on a commission, or are you constantly reading poetry or looking at pictures, et cetera?

BA: I read a lot of poetry, because I'm always sort of on the lookout, but I don't write constantly. Some people get up every day and write, but I don't. I go through periods where I write a lot, and then I don't. I love to look at pictures, and I think that a lot of women do try to translate the painting into music somehow. That never works for me. It's usually more of an improvisatory thing at the piano and then finding something in it I like. When I worked with dancers a lot, I would use some of that energy. If I wanted to write something slow, I would think about what their center floor was like, or if I wanted to write something fast, that sense of getting across the floor and getting into the air.

JK: How long did you play piano for dancers?

BA: Twenty years. When I was at school, to get my little scholarship they said, "Go across the street and play for dance classes." And I had never improvised in my life. I had no clue. So, I went over there, and they sat me down, and I think Judith Rosen was already there, and she said something like, "The two simplest things to do are play either all white keys or all black keys. And you're on." And blessedly, it did come. I did think of something to do. White-key modes were a really nice suggestion, and pentatonic [black keys] was a really nice suggestion. And then you begin to branch out from there, and I understood how to follow them. I love to play for teachers that love what I do. I've since discovered that Limón influenced people like me a lot. And I used to play for [Martha] Graham. I was not so well suited for Graham, but I worked for them well enough because I had a sort of kinesthetic sense of how to support them in doing what they were doing. But my music isn't tortured enough to go exactly with all the contractions and pain, the drama that she was doing.

JK: Going back to Kentucky for a moment, your grandmother also seems a source of inspiration for you—her natural gifts.

BA: She had a lot of gifts. I think she was a visual artist, and she was a quilter. And she had great pitch and musical memory. She could play anything by ear. I mean anything. She loved to listen to the opera. She went to church and would come home and play the hymns. She could go to the movies and come home and make the dress. She didn't use cookbooks. She just adored me, and I loved her.

JK: It sounds like she was a composer herself, in a way. And her patchwork quilts are made of swatches, just like your music.

BA: It's true. I have always had a real urge to make collages, even when I layered music. My final piece for my master's was *She Wrote,* which is really layers of the same thing. You have the Gertrude Stein letter within *Q.E.D.* that's spoken in multiphonics, and then it's decoded over and over again using different versions of the code. And it's played over each other, and then it's spoken onto the tape just straight, so that you've got the three people on stage and then this tape, but they're all doing the same thing. They're all doing this tiny letter, and to me that was a process of showing the letter in layers, like sedimentary rock.

JK: You bring up technology. Is it true that technology taught you about silence, layering, and sequence of events?

BA: Yes, because when I was in the studio and couldn't do anything, that was pretty silent [*laughs*]. And then you think of things to do with what you've got. You'll write for four flutes if you have four friends that are flutists. If you have studio time, it seems like a good idea to put something together. Read the text, and then play over top of it. And then you start to think, What else could you do? Well, you could use the speed control that's sitting over here and play around in the studio and make things. And if I had continued to have access to it, I'd have probably continued to make electro-acoustic music, but I lost that availability, so I wrote for what I had.

JK: You describe it like it's collage. You've got a piece of this and a piece of that, and you can put these together. Even through your musical evolution, that really does seem to be where you're centered and where your heart is. Didn't you actually stop writing for a while?

BA: Oh, for sure. I figured [John] Cage said there was music all around you, you just have to listen to it; you don't need to write anything. And so clearly what you need to do is keep the dead guys' music alive. So I was busy practicing six hours a day playing my Beethoven and Liszt on the piano. And then, when I was twenty-three, I started writing again and wrote a whole bunch of stuff. After I came to New York, I just kept writing. I love New York! This seemed like the center of the universe to me. In New York, so many people care so violently about aesthetics. They care about how the dance is made, how the poetry is written, how the music is, how things are played. They're wildly opinioned and noisy about it, and they're interested. The problem in New York is, sometimes you have these great players, but they don't practice because they have rent to pay [*laughs*]. They have to move along. One and a half rehearsals, and you're on the stage—next!

JK: Jill Johnston at the *Village Voice* was someone you admired in New York, yes?

BA: Yes, she was a big critic for the *Village Voice* and general maniacal character. I admired her so much. She was descriptive. That's one of the things I liked about her as well as Tom Johnston. The *Voice* had descriptive critics, and generally speaking, if they didn't like something, they didn't write about it. They were trying to tell you about something that you had probably missed. That was a different view than the [*New York*] *Times*. The *Times* put it up as the next new thing or put it down as bad. And you had this feeling that, when the *Times* says something, God is speaking. They don't really have to describe it to you. They just say no or yes.

JK: I want to talk a little bit about your early musical influences, like your father. And I put him under musical influences because of your piece called *Ode*.

BA: All of the "text-sound music" is absolutely related to my childhood experiences listening to him be an auctioneer. It's a fast-talking thing. It's a rhythmic thing. It moves. I enjoyed that. I never learned to do it, but I thought it was fun because it's a way of playing with words, and I was certainly interested in that. They're just trying to keep you listening to some pattern so that you'll foolishly make another bid [*laughs*]. The speaker in *Ode* was a tobacco auctioneer that was his friend, Spec Edwards.

JK: He was so lyrical to me, so singsong. Your dad was the same way?

BA: Yeah.

JK: I'm also fascinated by the *Torero* piece with your mom and placing the two pieces together.

BA: Absolutely. They're like two vases on each side of the fireplace. They're the mother-father piece.

JK: Those were your mother's words, right?

BA: Yes. Every time it's been performed, whoever does that half (because there are instructions) discusses their most dramatic event or relationship in their life. The first time I went to Europe, the only thing anyone had heard of mine was this piece, and they were of course in shock because, by the time I got there, I wasn't doing that kind of music anymore. They were shocked that I hadn't kept on with it.

JK: What about Pauline Oliveros? What kind of an influence has she had on you?

BA: When I went to look for a teacher, when I went west in 1968, I was hitching, and I got a ride past San Diego, where she was at the time. I was just letting chance decide where I went. I might have studied with Pauline instead of Richard Swift and John Cage, but I didn't. She was definitely on my mind because she was the only woman composer in this country that I knew about because she was on the flip side of Steve Reich's *Come Out*.

JK: What was your reaction the first time you realized that it was a woman composer on the flip side of Steve Reich?

BA: "Yaay!" It's the same way I feel whenever I go to a museum and I walk up to a painting and it's by a woman artist. "Thank you!" That's why I love the National Museum of Women and the Arts in Washington, D.C. It's one of the greatest places on earth, because they're all by women. That's where I discovered Remedios Varo, one of my favorite artists of all time. Anyway, once I began to read about Pauline Oliveros, I discovered that she had all these women composition students. And then I started to see that there were many women composers, but it was all completely hidden. I had not seen it. It was never mentioned. Elisabeth Jacquet de La Guerre did not show up in my universe until at least 1976. Never heard about any of these people in school. You didn't even hear about Hildegard. Nothing. So there's been a vast lot of scholarship since then.

JK: That brings me to another question. What do you think music education can do for the progression of American art music in the future?

BA: They have to hear it young. And they can't just hear it in a, "Listen to this, kid. This is serious," kind of way. They've got to somehow see it as part of their heritage. They've got to play William Grant Still for the black kids so that they see that black composers wrote this, and they've got to play some women so that girls can see that it's humanly possible for women to write, and they have to have living composers in schools so that everybody doesn't think Beethoven was the last composer. Dead guys. Dead white guys from Europe. That just so doesn't work. But the way schools seem to be going, they don't even have Beethoven, so it's hard to get Tania León in there. We just need more arts in the schools. All kinds of arts. For example, I was not much of an athlete in school, but today there are so many more athletics for women. If they had yoga or some kind of running program where they understood people were starting out, it would have made such a big difference to my whole physical life. But that wasn't there. For music, certainly opera isn't there now. So people don't even get the chance to reject it. They've never heard of it.

JK: If I'm hearing you correctly, you're saying that one must be experienced with something in order to have any kind of reaction to it, whether it's acceptance or rejection.

BA: Yeah, I don't think you just wake up at age fifty-two and say, "Hmm, I think I'll go to the Metropolitan opera tonight. I have an urge to hear Verdi" [*laughs*]. I do think the opera broadcasts that the Met is doing are really good for the country. I just wish there was more of it. I taught voice at the College of New Rochelle for a campus that was in East Harlem, and everybody that came to the class was thinking about singing pop songs. But I was thinking seventeenth-century Italian art songs and maybe a little *Abide with Me* or something [*laughs*]. So I brought a most wonderful black soprano to sing art music for them, and they were so amazed that she would sing this way. And they asked her, "How did you get into this?" Well, she had heard it at home from her family when she was little, and she just totally responded. She wanted to be that noise. She wanted to make that sound. And they were amazed. I think they got more out of just hearing her sing than all my pushing to try and get them to sing Italian songs that they couldn't get very interested in. They could now see that it was something they could theoretically do. It wasn't some crazy thing that was being forced on them by this white chick from God knows where.

JK: After your work with electro-acoustic and harking back to your article "Beauty Is Revolution," your music came full-circle back to acoustic instruments. You've described acoustic instruments as having a "human quality."

BA: They sing, they vibrate, and they have little errors to them that make them more interesting. If you just have a sine wave or something, it is what it is. But if you have a violin playing, you have a whole universe of thought in there. It's much more personal and of course unpredictable, and that's kind of exciting.

JK: Are there drawbacks?

BA: Well, sure, because the women composers that have worked just with electronics have the problem of electronics, but the solution is that they have complete control, and they don't have to talk the player into playing it. They can make the work, control the performance of it, and put it on a CD, so people in Japan can hear it.

JK: Composer becomes performer.

BA: Yes, and producer of final product. Because with acoustics, I can write the music, and then I could get somebody to play it, and then I can talk to a record company about maybe putting it out. But then there is the record producer/editor person that's changing the sound quality and the performer changing the tempo or whatever it is they want to change. So there are a lot of people between me and the final sound.

JK: You are a composer who chooses not to write exhaustive performance indications. So what innate qualities from the musicians are you expecting when they perform your music?

BA: I was always taught when you play the flute, when you're playing a low note, it is softer. So, when you are low, you are softer, and when you are high, you are louder, and you make it gracefully come down. And phrases are like sentences. They start off, and they get bigger, and then they finish off. I expect things like that.

JK: You do mark tempos. Is there equal musical freedom with regard to tempo as in the momentum of a sentence? For instance, if I'm speaking a sentence, I'll start off, and then I might have a little more momentum in the middle of it, and then, when I finally come down for the cadence, I may relax. Is that a freedom that a string player would have in the midst of a phrase?

BA: I don't think so. And the problem with a lot of my swales is that the players have a tendency to want to go from section to section and soften the end of the section and lift their bow and breathe and then start off into the next section.

But what I want is like a real collage, where the ticket is against the red, which is against the button, so that it really rams right into it.

JK: Abrupt transitions.

BA: Yeah, otherwise they're separate. They don't touch. They create edges of silence around things, and I don't like that. I want it to actually run into each other.

JK: I love your use of strings. You write beautiful melodies. Even when they're short, they are always beautiful, which is perhaps one reason Kyle Gann may have compared you to Schubert and Fauré because of your singing melodies.

BA: I'm influenced by folk music. And I think that was their fountain as well.

JK: When you compose your string quartets, like *March Swale,* what else should the players know about you as a composer to better interpret that piece, such as knowing that you want abrupt transitions between sections?

BA: I tried to give really thorough instructions with how to play that, how to make that racket. I was thinking some kind of calliope in the wind in the beginning. And it's a big party, so it would be useful if they heard some rock and roll and some Spanish pop music.

JK: So you'd like them to do some background research on the music that's embedded in the piece in order to better understand the piece itself.

BA: Yeah, and to have fun with it. Otherwise you're just playing notes with rhythms. You should have some knowledge of where it comes from. For instance, if it says "hymnlike," and you've never heard a hymn, you're not going to think of what to do with that, even if you do play softly and in tune. There's a bit of a different feeling if you know what a hymn is.

JK: What about vibrato?

BA: I like it, generally speaking. I like a warm feeling.

JK: Dynamics are quite subjective. For you, what is *forte*?

BA: I was just at a rehearsal last night having this discussion. You cannot cover the singer. If she sings a sort of *mezzo-piano* kind of *forte,* then you have to play *pianissimo* under her, and you have to generate a sense of *forte*-ness with your rhythm or your physical bearing. You can't do it in amplitude, because you cannot cover her. You have to see the main thing about the piece. If it's instrumental, who has got the tune? If you don't have it, then you maybe need to be under a little bit. It's all relative, like common sense to me. There is a lot of minimalism music out there. Starts loud, stays loud, and that's the way it is, and it's a beautiful kind of square thing, but my music really isn't that. *Pianissimo* is hard to get, because you still want some intensity and intention there.

JK: Do you ever compose at a computer?

BA: I actually get better results at the piano. I think the computer makes it too easy to make certain choices and repetitions. And you get all bogged down in the notation of it, because you're putting it directly in. And once you get it in, and it's perfect, it's harder to say, "Oh, I don't like that!" Because it's perfect. It's in there exactly. It's much harder than if you're at the piano with a pencil and you just put a mark through it and say, "Nix that." Or you put brackets around it and use it later. It's easier to actually cut things up at the piano.

JK: Looking into the future, say another fifty years from now, when the next two or three generations look at your music . . .

BA: God willing, they will.

JK: Is there anything else you want to make sure they know about your music and your creative process or how you want them to approach it if you're not here to tell them?

BA: I think what I ultimately want is people to spend time with it, to not need cues, to actually know where they are in the piece. And the only way to do that is to practice separately and then together if it's a group. And to try to make something beautiful, meaningful, fun.

JK: To understand how they individually fit into this story and how it's all put together.

BA: Yeah, and how it's all made with love. You want the love to come back to the music somehow. The energy is expended on both the creation and re-creation of it.

JK: Are you interested in having composition students?

BA: If you teach anything, you get a lot from it as well as giving something out, and younger people have so much energy and fire to make something. But I think composition is a really hard thing to teach. I learned a lot more from listening to stuff and orchestration books. Actually, it's really peculiar what I didn't learn. And I know that it's partially the time that I went to school, because the avant-garde was big, so you weren't getting the craftiness that you might have gotten in central Germany in 1830. The best I got was Bob Ashley telling me, "Yes Beth. You can be a composer." Which was tremendously important at the time.

JK: What does it mean to be a woman composer today?

BA: To me, it means that it's hard. It's not as easy as the young ones believe it is. They don't understand that there was a time when people did not know there were women composers, and they think that the reason they have not been performed on The [BBC] Proms is because they are young, but it's actually not. It's because, so far, they haven't much chance of getting on there. May it change tomorrow? I fervently hope. But I don't see that happening, because we made a lot of noise about this in the early seventies, and before that they made a lot of noise about it in the twenties—women chaining themselves to fences and trying to get the vote and putting together women's bands and orchestras. Today, all the women string quartets dress up really sexy, and they look great, and they play great. But there were all these wonderful women in white glittery dresses in the twenties and thirties doing these things, and they sort of get forgotten.

JK: Do you think there's still a place for women-only CDs, women-only concerts and series, such as Women's Work?

BA: Absolutely. I think it's important because if you want to hear a work, that's a way to hear it quickly. Because if you go to ten concerts in New York, you'll be lucky if you hear one or two pieces by women.

JK: Which brings us back to what you were saying about music education. You have to be exposed to it when you're young. Where do you stand on being identified as a woman composer?

BA: I think it's only logical. It's who I am. I'm an American woman composer.

JK: There are a lot of women who really don't like those labels.

BA: Yes, there certainly are. They're irked by it. They don't want to be "ghettoized" by this. They want to be simply a composer, and I would agree. In the best of all possible worlds, that would be true. And in the best of all possible worlds there'd be women and men in concerts in equal amounts. No, we're not there.

JK: How do you think that women can fit into the future of American concert music?

BA: Well, we have to have more women making more money generally—to support it and be educated in music first of all, including investors, backers. And we have to have more women conductors and more women concertmistresses and more everything. The tentacles have to spread out all over the place, and then hopefully they'll pull music in as the last thing over the line. There have been many women novel writers and many women painters, but women composers have had a tremendous problem, because they don't get to the people as easily. They have too much interference. In any university I've ever been associated with, the music department was always the most conservative spot. The philosophy department was far out and freaky. The art department was wild. The English department was curious and multi-interested. But music, it's still Bach, Beethoven.

JK: You once said that being a woman composer is a "heroic struggle." Do you still believe that?

BA: Sure, against all odds! With the wind flowing in your hair and the tattered flag in the background, absolutely! It's a great fight.

***

Works by Beth Anderson

All works available through the composer unless otherwise noted.

MUSIC FOR THEATER, DANCE, FILM, AND MULTIMEDIA

Avon, theater music for medium voice and piano (1990).

Elizabeth Rex; or, The Well-Bred Mother Goes to Camp, musical, for eight voices, piano, bass, and drums (1983).

The Fat Opera, musical, for four voices, piano, and drums (1991).

Good-Bye Bridget Bardot; or, Hello Charlotte Moorman, for cello, tape, and cloth wrapper (1974).
Hallophone, environment, for two saxophones, steel guitar, voice, tapes, slides, and dancers (1973).
He Said, for two clarinets and tape, and optional video (1975).
Joan, oratorio, for soloists and orchestra (1974).
Manos Inquietas (Parts 1, 2, and 3 for Dance), for piano (1982).
The Messiah Is Come, human sculpture, for internal and external sound sources, tape, bass, flute, voices, speakers, piano, percussion, slides, collaboration with the sculptor Paul Cotton, revised as *The Bridegroom Is Hear* (1974).
Morning View and Maiden Spring, for speaker, tape, speaker, slides, and lights (1978).
Music for Myself, for voice, piano, vibraphone, mirrors, and light (1973).
Nirvana Manor, musical, for twenty voices, piano, bass, and percussion (1981).
Qoheleth, operetta for contralto, tenor, string quartet, harpsichord, and percussion, libretto by Royce Dendler (1998).
Peachy Keen-O, for voices, electric guitar, organ, vibraphone, membranophones and metalophones, dancers, peach light, and tape (1973).
Queen Christina, opera, for three voices, chamber orchestra, tape/film/slides, and audience participation; libretto by Beth Anderson (1973).
Quilt Music (for choreography by Daniel McCusker) for piano (1983).
Recital Piece, for piano, tape, and theatrics (1973).
Remembering the Women: "The Seneca Falls Follies," theater music for female chorus and piano (2003).
Riot Rot, radio opera, text-sound, and rock band (1983).
She Wrote, for voice, two violins, and tape (1974).
Soap Tuning, for two to four speaking voices (1976).
Skaters' Suite, for soprano, violin, cello, bass, and tape, for Diane Jacobwitz Dancers (1979).
They Did It, for piano and tape (1976).
Tower of Power, for church organ and four-channel tape (1973).
Tulip Clause, for tenor, eight instruments, and tape (1973).
Valid for Life, for two pianos and percussion; or two large strung things (1973).
Whatever Bernhardt Goetz, play by Stephen Paul Miller (1985).
World Honeymoon, film score (1980).
Zen Piece, for two speaking voices and props (1976).

ORCHESTRA

July Swale, for string quartet or string orchestra (2001).
Minnesota Swale, for chamber orchestra (1993).
Mourning Dove Swale (dedicated to those who died 9/11/01), for string orchestra (2001).
Piano Concerto, for piano, string orchestra, and percussion (1997).
Revel, for chamber orchestra (1984).
Revelation, for chamber orchestra (1981).
Three Swales, for string orchestra (2000).
  Kentucky Swale, for string orchestra

Blue Bell Swale, for string orchestra
March Swale, for string orchestra

BAND

Suite for Winds and Percussion (1981).
Overture for Band (1981).

CHAMBER MUSIC/SOLO INSTRUMENT

April Swale, for viola and harpsichord (2001).
Archaic Tale, for violin and piano (2010).
August Swale, flute, oboe, bassoon (or cello), horn, violin, and viola (1992).
woodwind quintet (2003).
Belgian Tango
violin and piano (1984).
piano (2000).
violin, accordion, and piano (2000).
Brass Swale, for brass quartet or quintet (1988).
Comment, for flute (2003).
Dr. Blood's Mermaid Lullaby, for flute or oboe or violin or cello and piano (1980).
Cleveland Swale, for two double basses and piano (London: Recital Music, 2001).
The Eighth Ancestor, for flute, violin, cello, and piano; or baroque flute, alto recorder, cello, and harpsichord (Joshua Corp./General Music, 1979).
Flute Swale, for flute (1996).
Full Circle, for piano (1985).
Ghent Swale, for bass and piano, (1999).
Guitar Swale, for two guitars (1993).
I Am Uh Am I, for string quartet (1973).
January Swale, for string quartet (1995).
Jasmine Swale, for violin, viola, and cello (2005).
July Swale, for string quartet or string orchestra (2001).
June Swale, for string quartet (2001).
Kummi Dance, for violin and piano (2011).
Little Trio, for flute, viola, and guitar (1984).
Lullaby of the Eighth Ancestor, for flute or violin and piano (Joshua Corp./General Music, 1979).
Manos Inquietas, Part I, II, III, for piano (1982).
March Swale, for string quartet (2000).
May Swale, for bass or viola or bass flute (London: Recital Music, 1995).
Music for Charlemagne Palestine, for string quartet (1973).
Net Work, for piano (1984).
New Mexico Swale, for flute, violin, viola, cello, and percussion (1995).
Pennyroyal Swale, for string quartet (1985).
Preparation for the Dominant: Outrunning the Inevitable, for flute, violin, and ocarina (1979).

The Preying Mantis and the Bluebird, for flute or violin, and harp or piano (Joshua Corp./General Music, 1979).
Promised Church Beautiful River, for trombone and tape (1977).
Revel, for chamber orchestra; or electric violin, sax, bass clarinet, trumpet, trombone, bass, piano, and percussion (1984).
Rhode Island Swale, for piano or harpsichord (1996).
Rosemary Swale, for string quartet (1986).
Saturday-Sunday Swale, for brass quintet (1991).
September Swale (Antes/Bella Musica, 1996).
  mandolin and guitar
  piano or harpsichord
  violin and piano
Shakuhachi Run, for flute or shakuhachi with optional hand drum (1981).
Skaters' Suite (Joshua Corp./General Music, 1979).
  violin, flute, cello, piano
  flute, oboe, cello, piano
  Baroque flute, alto recorder, cello, harpsichord
  violin, cello, string bass, mezzo
Taking Sides, for piano (1984).
Tales Nos. 1, 2, 3, for violin and piano (2000).
Toledo Swale, for two violins and soprano sax or flute (2001)
Trio: Dream in D, for flute or violin, cello, and piano (1980).
Wallonian Waltz, for piano (1986).
Water-Strider Courrente, for flute, clarinet, drum set, piano, small organ, and double bass (1979).

CHORAL/VOCAL

Alleluia, for two tenors (or tenor and mezzo-soprano) and two trumpets (1978).
The Angel, for soprano, string quartet, and harp (1988).
Angel Songs, three songs for voice and piano (2011).
Animal Songs, seven songs for voice and piano (2004).
Avon, four songs for voice and piano (1990).
Beauty Runs Faster, for voice and piano (1978).
Cat Songs, six songs for voice and piano or bass (2000).
Dark Songs, three songs for soprano, alto, and piano (2004).
A Day, for voice and piano (1967).
Dream Song, for chorus (2009).
Dreaming Fields, three-song cycle for mezzo-soprano and piano (1987).
The Good Christmas Cat (2000).
  voice and piano
  chorus and harp or piano
Harlem Songs, four songs for baritone, bass, with or without piano (1999).
He Says He's Got, for voice and piano or guitar (1977).
If You Have a Thought in Your Head, round (1978; in Sol Weber's *Rounds Galore!* 1994).

In Six, for mezzo-soprano and piano (1979).
In the Company of Women, for chorus with or without piano or organ (2000).
Incline Thine Ear to Me, for voices and any instruments (1975).
Junk Love, for voice and piano (1981).
Knots, for mezzo-soprano and piano (1981).
The Land of Counterpane, for voice and piano (1991).
The Little Tree (2000).
  voice and harp or piano
  female chorus with or without piano
Lullaby, for voice with or without piano (1997–98).
Magnificat, for chorus and organ or piano (1998).
May We Ever Mindful Be, for chorus and piano (2000).
My Laughing Child, round (1992; in Sol Weber's *Rounds Galore!* 1994).
My Private Beach, for voice, two flutes, two oboes, soprano sax, alto sax, tenor sax, and piano (1981).
Night Song, for soprano, viola, and piano (2005).
The Only One I Want, for voice and piano (1978).
Paranoia, for voice and two flutes (or piano), (1968).
A Postcard, for voice and piano (1967).
Precious Memories, for SSSAAT, (1996/2003).
Sam the Same, for voice and piano (2006).
Swimmers on the Shore, for baritone and piano (2004).
Time Stands Still, for voice and piano (1978).
Twinkle Tonight, for mezzo-soprano and piano (1979).
A Way Back Home, for voice and piano (1990).
We Thank Thee, for chorus and piano (2003).
Who Is This Jesus? for voice and harp or piano; or female chorus with or without piano (2000).
Winter Solstice, for soprano and piano (2005).
What the Heart of the Young Man Said to the Psalmist, for voice and piano (2011).
Womanrite, for voice and piano (1973).
Wynken, Blynken, and Nod (1987).
  mezzo-soprano and piano
  chorus

ELECTRONIC AND TEXT-SOUND WORKS (SEE ALSO CHAMBER MUSIC AND MULTIMEDIA)

6.76 Kentucky Poem, text-sound piece (1976).
Black/White, text-sound piece, multiple speaking voices (1976).
Country Time, text-sound piece, speaking voice, percussion, with or without taped bird calls (1981).
Crackers and Checkers, text-sound piece (1977).
German Swale, tape (1990).

He's Not Afraid of Marrying Me, text-sound piece (1976).
I Can't Stand It, text-sound and percussion (1976).
I Wish I Were Single Again, text-sound piece (1977).
If I Were a Poet, text-sound piece (1975).
Jackson Mac Low, text-sound piece, speaking voice (1977).
Joan, fifteen-track tape, based on material from the oratorio *Joan* (1977).
John Cage, text-sound piece (1979).
Killdeer and Chickory, text-sound piece, voice, and percussion (2005).
Kitchy Kitchin, text-sound and percussion (1979).
Let It, text-sound piece (1976).
Nongovernmental Process, text-sound piece, speaking voice (1976).
Ocean Motion Mildew Mind, text-sound and percussion (1979).
Ode, text-sound piece (1975).
The People Rumble Louder, text-sound piece, voice and electronics or solo speaking voice (1975).
Pe-Yo-Te, text-sound piece (1976).
Poem to Michael, John, and Alison, text-sound piece, speaking voice (1975).
Sally's Success, text-sound piece, speaking voice and piano (1979).
Six Stories in Series, text-sound piece, speaking voice and piano (1979).
Thus Spake Johnston, tape, voice of Jill Johnston (1973).
Torero Piece, text-sound piece, two speaking voices (1973).
Tulip Clause and Buchla Bird Hiss down the Road of Life, tape (1973).
Twelve Bar Blues, text-sound piece (1976).
Yes Sir Ree, text-sound and percussion (1978).

23

Janika Vandervelde

Janika Vandervelde truly enjoys teaching composition to her students at Perpich Center for Arts Education, a statewide, innovative arts high school with a composition-based music program. During our conversation, Vandervelde discusses the importance of teaching the creative process through composition, as opposed to using the standard levels of theory and analysis. She explains, "This is the sort of thing my students are hungry for. Not theory for its own sake, but theory as applied to the craft of composition. And not composition that others engage in, but composition they themselves engage in." She continues to have success with the composition curriculum she designed using music technology, *Music by Kids for Kids,* through the American Composers Forum.

Vandervelde's name was first made famous as the composer of *Genesis II* for piano trio, the subject of a chapter in the musicologist Susan McClary's 1991 groundbreaking book *Feminine Endings: Music, Gender, and Sexuality.* I was particularly interested in Vandervelde's take on her participation in McClary's work and in her compositional path since the book came out. Born in Wisconsin in 1955, Vandervelde attended the University of Minnesota, where she worked with Eric Stokes and Dominick Argento. The path to discover her voice as a composer and a woman began when Houston Symphony and Rice University hosted a conference, "Current Trends in Contemporary Women Composers: Post-Feminism," featuring composers like Libby Larsen, Joan Tower, and Meredith Monk. As an emerging composer, Vandervelde was invited to join the conference with a new piece. During our conversation, she describes the significance of her participation in this event, where she was exposed to new ideas and a worldview that included reflections about gender.

Vandervelde's music is reflective of her interest in world cultures and social issues, as represented in numerous languages for her text settings and in her work with organizations such as the Women's International League for Peace and Freedom (WILPF). A collaborator at heart, she seeks out events supporting her shared ideals with the goal of bringing artistic communities together for awareness of a common cause. A composer of over ninety works, mostly published through her own Hothouse Press, Vandervelde's catalog is varied, with an emphasis on choral music. She has written works for such noted choirs as Chanticleer, Minnesota Chorale, Dale Warland Singers, and Oregon Repertory Singers. She also composes works for stage and multimedia, including the score to *Adventures of the Black Dot,* an innovative and well-received choral storybook about actively creating music.

During our conversation about the teaching of composition, Vandervelde stands out as one of only a few composers in this book who believe it can actually be taught. She recounts specific moments that contributed to the development of her compositional voice and explains the importance of encouraging a thoughtful creative process. As the population of senior adults continues to grow, Vandervelde is also excited to share with them the possibilities of creative thought while hoping to affect brain plasticity, explaining, "As you get older, it's really important to exercise that all-important organ, your brain. I think that when people reach an age at which they're no longer in the workforce, it's the perfect time for them to immerse themselves in creative work and rediscover the pleasures of self-expression."

***

May 2010, at her home in St. Paul, Minnesota

JENNIFER KELLY: Do you consider the audience when you compose?

JANIKA VANDERVELDE: I think about the occasion for which a piece has been commissioned. For instance, if I'm asked to do something for a festival in a small town in Wisconsin, that piece might end up being quite different from a piece I'm writing for a professional choir in New York City. They're different audiences. Audience members in different communities come with different expectations, and I try to make adjustments accordingly.

JK: So you expect a piece of yours to be heard differently depending upon where it's played?

JV: Definitely, because everybody's experiences of music are different. That's one of the things that, as a teacher of composition, I talk about right away. I have an exercise in which I compose something on the spot, in front of the class, writing it out without hearing it at all. Then I play it for the first time while everyone listens. I'll say, "Okay, now, what needs to be fixed? How would you begin to craft this into your own composition?" Everyone has a different response. One person thinks it's too chaotic and wants to simplify it, while someone else thinks the chaos is exciting. People come to music with different ears. That's my first lesson as a composition pedagogue—my first lesson to the teachers, the facilitators of the compositional process. The teacher needs to respect everyone's personal tastes—how they're hearing at any given moment in time.

JK: What about the performer or conductor presenting the work to the audience? Can everything they need to know about the piece be found on the page?

JV: I hope that everything is on the page. The composer isn't always going to be there, so it's all about effective communication through the page. That's part of the craft you have to master as a composer, and it's the part that improves with age and experience. I believe there are three aspects to the creative process. I call them the Three V's: Vision, Voice, and Virtuosity. Vision is really a synthesis of all your life experiences and passions, which are channeled into the act of creation. Voice is expressing that vision in a distinctive way, with a particular attitude and a corresponding stylistic signature. Virtuosity is effectiveness of communication, which is all about putting everything on the page that goes to the performer.

JK: As a composer, how has technology entered into your music?

JV: Technology is my primary tool. I'm a technology geek. My approach is often to generate music out of an architectural plan, then mold it and shape it almost like sculpture—whittling away at it. Sometimes I move and shift things around, building pieces up through the tools technology provides, then fine-tuning the result until I'm satisfied. Technology makes it possible to generate pieces rather quickly. It used to be that, in creating music, notation took the most time. Before computer notation, the composer's vision often went directly from the brain to the page. What takes the most time now is the creative process itself, because technology makes it possible to work in a nonsequential way.

JK: Take me through your creative process. What do you do first?

JV: Every piece is different, but usually there's a long period at the beginning, filled with the tension of having to start the piece. It's the gestation period. There is a buildup of tension, like something that's pressing to birth. It builds until the only possible course of action is to start writing, because the stress involved in not starting is greater. I usually try to set up an architectural plan for the whole piece in advance, then begin filling in the details. I'm very interested in the shapes of the containers that hold the sound. They inspire me to fill them in. If I set up the architecture ahead of time, it lets me see the whole piece from above. Then I begin to set the architecture in motion from within. The music blooms inside this container.

JK: We performed your *Cançao de Embalar* at Lafayette. It is an accessible piece that was built so well, it was easy to teach quickly.

JV: That's a good example of what I'm talking about—a very simple snapshot of architecture. Design elegance.

JK: Do you compose on a computer?

JV: Yes, I use a computer connected to a small electronic keyboard. My studio used to fill a whole room. I was tied to the space. But everything changed with laptops. Five years ago, I went to Australia and carried my studio in a backpack. It was so wonderful! I could go anywhere and work on my music. I didn't even need an electrical outlet if the battery was charged.

JK: So technology is freeing.

JV: Yes, the portability is a terrific thing. But it's also freeing in terms of the process itself. The gift of the computer is that you can start with a whole piece and then morph it. You can move things around, see what the result is, and choose to go back. You just push the back button until it's restored. This means you can experiment to your heart's content, trying out ideas. My students love that. It's what exercising creativity is all about. Their inner ears aren't particularly well developed yet. And not all of us have the genius of Bach in terms of an inner ear, so we experiment and try things out, exercising the patterns of invention. That's why, when I'm teaching workshops, whether with students or teachers, I take away their headphones. I want them to see intellectually and create patterns in the music, generating large chunks of material as quickly as possible. Then I let them put the headphones back on. The result is that they produce things they never would have created had they used their headphones to begin with because, as soon as they engage their ears, they quickly get stuck on minute details—on individual notes and rhythms. I'm trying to get them to generate larger sections of music using design principles. This is phase one—a blueprint for creativity, a vision for the piece. Then, as phase two kicks in, they work the material through their ears. That's when the sifting and sorting of their compositional process and artistic taste takes over. By the end of the day, students have created a whole piece, and a piece they never expected to write. They've been stretched. The technology lets them take the score and performance home on a CD and say, "I did this."

JK: Tell me more about teaching composition.

JV: In 2006, I developed a composition curriculum for the American Composers Forum and Make Music, Inc. It's called *Music by Kids for Kids*; the subtitle is *Blueprints for Creativity.* It grew out of my experience teaching at the Perpich Center for Arts Education, a statewide residential arts high school in Minnesota. I became very interested in composition pedagogy, because I'm convinced that everyone can and should learn to read and write music in the same way that everyone can and should learn to read and write words. There's something in the experience that elevates us. Music, as a means of creative self-expression, should be an everyday activity at all stages of life. In fact, I'm going to explore that with some senior adults later this year. We're doing a project to promote brain plasticity. As you get older, it's really important to exercise that all-important organ, your brain. I think that when people reach an age at which they're no longer in the workforce, it's the perfect time for them to immerse themselves in creative work and rediscover the pleasures of self-expression. At Perpich, all the music students engage in compositional activities every day. It's part of their routine.

JK: Teaching is obviously very important to you.

JV: It is. I have a strong desire to help others experience what it's like to write a piece of music and then perform it themselves or hear it performed by others.

JK: So what does teaching do for your compositional side?

JV: I don't know whether I can articulate that. My students—young composers, juniors and seniors in high school—are at the cutting edge of culture. I make it my business to know what they're listening to and how they're listening. I suppose I absorb the musical culture that surrounds me in any given year through osmosis. Over time, this gets integrated into my personal tastes, but even so, my students will never hear music the way I do, and I will never hear music like them.

JK: They don't hear the way you do because of their youth?

JV: In a sense, yes, because they came of age in a different world, with different sounds. Their influences over time are very different than mine, and that's what dictates their personal tastes and the choices they make when putting their music together.

JK: So does teaching young students help connect you to what is cutting-edge or help you open your mind to possible sounds and combinations?

JV: I hope we are open to each other's sounds and combinations. The students are teaching me to hear the way they hear, through their musical prism, and I'm teaching them to hear the way I hear, through mine. It's a shared experience. I teach a course called Trends in Music, where I often begin with the eighties—my own coming-of-age music. For instance, I'll bring in a documentary about Meredith Monk. The students love her! They tend to like anything that they find new and different. I do a "lecture" where I don't talk at all. I just play [Steve Reich's] *Music for 18 Musicians,* which lasts the duration of our class period. I'll put the CD on fairly loud, so it saturates their whole experience. I even dim the lights and then turn on an overhead projector, where I write notes about the music, guiding them through the listening experience. Afterwards, they're speechless. Most have never heard classic minimalism, the kind that changes your perception of time and opens up new visions for how music can be constructed. Later, I turn the course over to them. They get to present reports about their influences, and I get to learn about all the things that are going on today, from their perspective.

JK: Your compositional catalog contains instrumental music, but I notice that your repertoire includes more choral works.

JV: Over the last dozen years I've shifted more into choral. In 1998 I was awarded a Meet the Composer New Residencies Grant, which puts a composer in residence with several organizations for three years. In my case it was a full-time position with three organizations, including the Minnesota Chorale. That's when I became involved with conductor Kathy Romey. Also, [Minneapolis/St. Paul] is a choral center, due largely to its Scandinavian and German heritage. The area has spawned many choral composers, conductors, and singing groups. As these groups discovered I was writing choral music, I started getting more choral commissions. Then Earthsongs [publishing company] in Corvallis, Oregon, published several of my pieces, and I started getting commissions from outside the region.

JK: So do you mind the label "choral composer"?

JV: I don't mind the label, but I've worked in almost every medium. I had a period where I wrote quite a few orchestral pieces for young audiences; before that, I did a lot of musical theater; before that, chamber music. I'm currently very interested in electro-acoustic music and collaborations across disciplines.

JK: It helps to stretch the opportunities for performance. How much time, as a living composer, do you spend on the business side of things, such as promotion, publicity, and application processes, as opposed to the music itself?

JV: Well, it goes in spurts, depending on when I need to generate more work opportunities. But that said, I do very little self-promotion.

JK: Do you work with a manager or an agent?

JV: No, I don't.

JK: What is the process to find a commission?

JV: Well, when I do have to scarf up a commission, it's usually a submission-based opportunity, where you have to put together your catalog, your work samples, your artist statement, a statement about what you might do if you receive the commission, and sometimes there's an application fee. Then you ship everything off and wait. I spend a little time every year writing grants and applying for various opportunities. Teaching has been a stable source of income, but I like to have a steady stream of new commissions and performances to keep my career going. I've done a little promotion of my choral music, because there is a market out there for it. It does pay off in the long run, but it also takes up a lot of time—time away from the creative work.

JK: You're very easy to find at Earthsongs.

JV: Earthsongs does a nice distribution worldwide, and because of that I've gotten some commissions from people outside my network.

JK: So working through another publisher is helpful because it helps with publicity, marketing, and distribution. Why did you decide to create your own publishing house, Hothouse Press, as well?

JV: It's mainly because of the extra royalties it generates and wanting to have more control.

JK: If you were just starting out today as a composer, like one of your students, how would your path be different?

JV: Today there are more composers than ever and fewer opportunities. When I started out, one of the first pieces I wrote was for the Saint Paul Chamber Orchestra. That could never happen today, because the Saint Paul Chamber Orchestra only commissions a few pieces a year from composers in the top tier. The marketplace is very different. The stakes are higher. It's hard to break in, and it's even harder to sustain a career. We're in a period of fusion and constant change. I see boundaries dissolving between score-based composition and improvisation, between acoustic and electronic music, between genres. I see young composers today having to do a lot of different things to make ends meet, including gigs, teaching, residencies, grants and fellowships, self-publishing, Web sites, social networking, and even commercial work. It's exhausting just thinking about it. But to be a dedicated concert composer, living only on commissions and performances—I'm not sure that career exists anymore.

JK: Do you believe there should be a sense of responsibility for the academic institutions to stay open to all forms of composition?

JV: Academic institutions, by their very nature, tend to focus on the past, but some are changing. Music education is coming around to the idea that it needs to train music educators in composition pedagogy. After all, composition is a major part of our national standards in music education. Increasingly, music-education majors are being trained to use music technology in the classroom. At Perpich, all music students compose—both individually and in small groups. They write for themselves, for their peers, for the choir, even for professional ensembles we hire to do residencies; they write music for the dance, for video and film, for the theater and various interdisciplinary projects; their active engagement in the creative process saturates our curriculum. All our arts teachers have become facilitators of creativity and are very good at it. Students love being empowered in this way. I notice a big difference when the choir kids are rehearsing music by their peers, people they know personally, who might even be in the room. They sit up, pay attention, and work twice as hard. Their experience comes to center on the living, breathing music of our time, written by living, breathing young people.

JK: What I hear you saying is that the ensembles have a responsibility, too. It isn't just the teachers of composition or teachers of theory and harmony courses. It's our programming of ensembles.

JV: It's true. Ensembles value the practice of making music. They have a responsibility to teach current practice. Yet student composers as well as music education majors spend an exorbitant amount of time taking theory 1, theory 2, theory 3, et cetera, when they could be taking composition 1, 2, and 3—instrumental, choral, orchestral—learning about the creative process and getting a practical dose of theory at the same time. This is the sort of thing my students are hungry for. Not theory for its own sake, but theory as applied to the craft of composition. And not composition that others engage in, but composition they themselves engage in. Theory for effective communication through music, expressed in scores and through improvisation.

JK: Not necessarily just score-based composition.

JV: That's true, because most music being produced and performed today is not score-based. Students love making music with their friends, collaboratively building pieces out of improvisation, or arranging their favorite hit song, as opposed to sitting in front of a music stand and counting rests while the conductor waves a baton in front of them.

JK: As a composer in today's world, where arts programs are continually being cut, how do you stay positive? How do you stay in the space of creation in order to keep going with it all?

JV: Well, I've been quite fortunate. Minnesota is a great state in which to be a composer. I've never really had to struggle for that next opportunity. I've always had just the right amount of work to look forward to. My life feels relatively well balanced. There are composers that have commissions stacked up fifteen or more deep, but that would burn me out. I recently had cause to look back over my whole career, and it was interesting to see how it's gone along like a very steady stream—four or five new pieces a year. The part-time teaching position has kept me constantly infused with both variety and creativity, because students today are so amazing. Every year, their work seems to rise to new levels. At the same time, I've learned to be a better facilitator. For instance, this year my fall composition class wrote string quartets. As the facilitator, I generated the blueprint. The blueprint for the quartets was designed to include, at a later stage, a choral component, based on some Renga poems. Our choir and a student quartet performed all the pieces in a cycle that lasted thirty minutes. Then later, the dance department choreographed all the quartets, performing them as a set with live music, so the composers got a lot of performances out of it. Between my own work and the work I facilitate, I've been blessed with plenty of opportunities to grow and develop as both a composer and an artist-educator.

JK: What kind of relationship do you ideally like to have with another conductor of your works?

JV: I like to be able to spend plenty of time in rehearsals, participating in the process. One highlight in this regard was when David Willcocks was coming to Wisconsin every summer for a week-long choral festival. Because the festival was located near my hometown, he would occasionally include one of my choral works on the program. I would go for the whole week just to sit and watch him rehearse. He could work magic. Watching him and hearing what he was able to do with the singers was such a rewarding experience.

JK: The whole process of it. How much freedom does a performer have in interpretation of your music? Do you want to be asked about meaning and interpretation in one of your works?

JV: Yes, I do like to be asked, but most of the time my work is pretty straightforward. My notation is very detailed, sometimes to a fault. I usually find that the end result is very close to my internal perception of the music.

JK: You've honed your craft. When you first started thinking about composition, did you model any composers?

JV: I did a little composing in high school, but I didn't know any composers. I had no living role models. When I went to the University of Wisconsin–Eau Claire, there really wasn't an undergraduate composition program at that time, but there was a composer in the department: Michael Cunningham. I showed him one of my pieces, and the first thing he said was, "You must listen to a lot of Hindemith." I said, "What? Who?" I grew up in a really small town in Wisconsin. I didn't know anything about the wider world of music, especially contemporary music. For example, I had an old vinyl recording of piano concertos, where one side was Prokofiev and the other Bartók. I didn't find out until I was in graduate school that the labels were reversed, so for years I thought I was listening to Bartók when in fact it was Prokofiev. In high school, neoclassicism intrigued me. It was the most exotic music I had ever heard. I tried to emulate some of the harmonies by stacking fourths and fifths and began writing a piece for piano and horn that was full of quartal harmony. When my composition teacher said I sounded like Hindemith, I went to the library and checked out every Hindemith recording I could find. For several years, I studied composition privately with Michael Cunningham. Then, in my senior year, I had a pivotal moment. I petitioned the music department to let me make a complete shift in focus, switching from a piano recital to a composition recital. I was the first person there to do this, and now UW–Eau Claire has a thriving undergraduate composition program. The composition recital was a turning point. It gave me the confidence to apply to graduate school. I'd found my true passion.

JK: Wow. Being allowed that freedom to go where your passion really lay changed your life's direction.

JV: If that hadn't happened, I don't know where I'd be today. As it was, I went on to the University of Minnesota, where I received a teaching assistantship. I taught undergraduate theory and ear training and got to study with composers like Dominick Argento and Eric Stokes.

JK: Is that when you became aware of other women composers?

JV: There weren't any women composers on the faculty at that time, but I met Susan McClary, a musicologist shaped by feminist theory. She was a pivotal presence in my thinking. Around that same time, the Houston Symphony and Rice University hosted a conference titled "Current Trends in Contemporary Women Composers: Post-Feminism," featuring composers like Libby Larsen, Joan La Barbara, Joan Tower, and Meredith Monk. One of the composers dropped out at the last minute, and I was asked to fill in with the piece I'd just written for the Saint Paul Chamber Orchestra. The conference was one of my first experiences with the gender-in-music issue. I went to Houston totally naïve. I had just started my work with McClary at that point, and it was before I wrote *Genesis II.* So there I was, sitting around a table with women composers who were grappling with postfeminism. I heard composers like Libby and Joan—composers I really looked up to—talking about gender and music. It changed the direction of my life and work.

JK: How?

JV: A lot of interesting things all happened at the same time. Some of the composers at the conference were really upset about the way we were being treated. The whole idea of having a concert featuring only women was controversial. The orchestra players were grumpy and disrespectful. There was even a point in rehearsal where one of the percussionists was seen throwing wads of paper around and goofing off. It opened up to me that world of prejudice. Yet, in the face of it all, I knew I had been given a great opportunity. I was there only because I was a woman and because there was a movement afoot to focus on contemporary women composers.

JK: Did that experience affect your composition?

JV: When I came back from the conference, I was determined that I was going to find my own voice. When the concert in Houston was reviewed, the critic said, "Vandervelde is skilled at imitating other composers' styles." Yet the point of the conference was to showcase women composers who had their own distinctive style, recognizable and identifiable. In my training, I had been taught how to emulate every imaginable style and technique. Trained in Western European classical music, I had learned to play, and more importantly to hear, a vast repertoire. We studied the techniques associated with each style—those of Bach, Mozart, Beethoven, Chopin, Debussy, Schoenberg. They were all men of a certain tradition. I began to ask where my own voice was in all of this, and eventually I revolted. I finally came of age in terms of my own expression. Once your ear has been trained to hear in a certain way, it's very hard to switch it off. That's why I think it might be beneficial to help composers develop their own theories, their own voices, their own styles, sooner rather than later. That doesn't mean that theory should go out the window altogether, but if you start with composition and then learn the historical theory later, you are starting with the current practice and then branching out from there. After Houston, I began thinking about my own personal style. I drew diagrams and made a list of components I wanted to include. The result was the *Genesis* series of compositions. That's when Susan McClary came on the scene and helped me with the process of finding and understanding my own voice.

JK: What was your reaction to McClary's article ["Getting Down off the Beanstalk: The Presence of a Woman's Voice in Janika Vandervelde's *Genesis II*"] when it first came out?

JV: When the first draft of it was published, it contained some things that needed to be toned down. In fact, neither of us had given final consent for its publication, yet somehow it managed to mysteriously appear in print. I don't know if you've ever seen that version, but it created an uproar in certain circles. *Jack [and the Beanstalk]*, after all, was written for young children. The article discussed the fairy tale in terms of the Oedipus complex, sometimes in graphic detail. Certainly not appropriate for kindergarteners. When the essay was reprinted in book form, some of these more controversial parts were taken out.

JK: It was pretty groundbreaking. How did you feel about the analysis of your work?

JV: I love Susan's analysis of those two pieces in the book. The *Genesis* series came into existence as a reaction against a certain type of training—the training that had produced *Jack*. Susan's analysis unlocks the mechanics of the two styles and their gender associations in great detail. We are all products of our time. My abrupt change in compositional style was the result of my experience at the conference in Houston, filtered through Susan's mentoring in feminist theory. I was ready for a new style to emerge—a style that captured who I was and what I believed in. Suddenly everything crystallized.

JK: Do you think there is still a need today for women-only conferences, concerts, recordings, and festivals?

JV: I haven't seen a whole concert featuring women in a long time—really, since the Bay Area Women's Philharmonic folded—but I don't think the need has completely passed. Just the other day I was looking at the Barlow Prize, a hefty commission to create a major new work in a specific genre, which changes from year to year. I looked over their published list of past winners and was surprised to discover that they're almost all men. Less than 10 percent seem to have gone to women. I heard Lucy Lippard, the feminist art critic who now lives off the grid in Arizona, speak at a water-rights conference at the University of Minnesota. She said that young women today don't think there are these issues anymore. I've worked with so many young women who are coming of age, and it's true that they don't have a focused interest in matters of equality, unless they're gay. Most abhor conflict. I think we have to be mindful that around the world, women are still grossly underrepresented and mistreated in all sorts of ways. Women in this country have made some strides since the 1980s and are certainly on more of an equal footing, but matters are still far from perfect and may even have begun to slip. Women still aren't being promoted to top positions in most areas and suffer from discrimination in pay. At least in the U.S., we're allowed to protest and file lawsuits. In many other countries around the world, women's voices are still completely suppressed.

JK: So perhaps our focus might be better served looking at women's standing in other countries.

JV: The world has become small and congested. How can we help in those places that need assistance? Artists have always found ways to help. For instance, I have just been part of an enormous collaboration that included some amazing women from WILPF—the Women's International League for Peace and Freedom. WILPF has taken up the cause of global water rights because women are often the ones who have to carry water long distances in dangerous areas. WILPF's project—Women and Water Rights: Rivers of Regeneration—brought attention to these issues. They organized an international art exhibit and conference. I worked with them to coordinate an Education Day, which was called *Water Dance*. It involved a lot of school choirs. Choral music is perfectly suited for social-justice projects because it involves communities of people working together, singing a common song.

JK: Choir has text.

JV: And there's text. For the *Water Dance* project, the student composers set to music a series of little poems tracing the water cycle. The concert was really intended to be a celebration of water. I organized a mass choir of about two hundred singers—high-school choirs and the University Women's Choir—along with dancers, drummers, and a professional new-music ensemble called Zeitgeist. A group of fourteen student composers wrote almost all the music—instrumental and choral—creating scores and parts. The entire piece lasted about an hour, but there was also a forty-five-minute preshow consisting of video poems related to the topic. Poets, songwriters, and videographers worked together to create the video poems. The dancers made banners with sayings like, "Water Is a Basic Human Right!" A parade of banners started the main performance. Then, at the end, the dancers came down from the stage and handed off their banners to audience members—students from middle schools in the Ramsey County Watershed District. Going down into the audience was like passing the baton. Each school was doing its own special project related to water issues.

JK: How would you like to see your music evolve?

JV: I think I would like to continue moving in the direction of collaborations, especially collaborations across disciplines. They're invigorating. I'm really looking forward to spending a good deal of the summer working on a new project with choreographer Deborah Jinza Thayer. I'm also just starting to work on a new chamber piece with poet Eva Hooker and recently finished setting a children's story by scratch artist Brian Pinkney.

JK: Is there a piece you would point to that you are the most proud of?

JV: It's usually the piece I'm working on at the moment. I think that's largely because every piece is about its time. Every piece is a crystallization of all the things that are important to you at that juncture in your life. I'd like to say I take pride in everything I do.

JK: In that light, it must be fascinating to go back and listen to pieces a couple of decades old and see where you were.

JV: You'd think so, but I don't really like doing that. I'm not all that comfortable exploring the past. Music, for me, is about the present. I remember when my mother was dying—she loved my music—and for almost a week I sat in her hospice-care center playing all the music she loved. I was told that hearing was one of the last things to go. For that week, there was no place I would rather have been. But now it's over, and I never want to return to that place.

JK: What a beautiful way to say goodbye.

JV: My mother was always very supportive of my composing career. And even though she died more than a year ago, she seems to keep popping up in mysterious ways. For instance, about ten years ago I wrote a piece on commission for the inauguration of a new organ by Dan Jaeckel, a Minnesota builder. It's actually a choral piece that features the organ in a prominent way. The text is by Walt Whitman, and the commissioners had approved it in advance. When the score was finished, I shipped it off and waited to hear back, but didn't, for almost a year. It turned out that the commissioners had a problem with the text. They wanted me to change it—change Whitman! They were concerned about the symbolism of the organ, which, in the poem, is God's own instrument—Creation itself. I didn't know how to make the changes they were seeking without sacrificing Whitman, so the piece wasn't performed. I tried over the course of the following decade to get a performance somewhere else, but every time the piece got close to being realized, something weird would happen. It was as if the piece was jinxed. Finally, I decided to give up, putting it away for good. Then, the summer after my mother died, the music festival near my hometown in Wisconsin wanted to honor her with a special dedication and asked me to send them a piece. This was the old Willcocks festival with a new conductor. I sent *Medicine Woman,* with a text by Wisconsin's first poet laureate, Ellen Kort, which I thought was perfect for the occasion. But the conductor looked it over and said, "This really isn't quite the right piece. Do you have anything with organ?" I was stunned. I did indeed have a piece—the Whitman. I was really nervous about resurrecting it. I couldn't bear the thought of it being rejected again, this time for my mother's memorial. But I pulled it out, stuck it in an envelope, and sent it off with no explanation.

JK: And they dedicated it to your mom?

JV: They did. So at the concert I got up and addressed the audience, telling them the whole story. It was as if the piece had been saved for that very moment. The sudden realization that it was a premiere so energized the choir that they gave the performance of their lives. The Whitman text is an excerpt from his "Proud Music of the Storm." There's an allusion to this storm in the music, at the very end of the piece, where for almost thirty seconds the organ builds up a rainbow effect from low to high, using the pitches in the overtone series. At just that moment in the performance, a little storm blew in outside the church, and there was a gentle roll of thunder that seemed to engage in a duet with the organ, right on cue. You can hear it on the recording. Everyone was smiling and looking around. And then a shard of light came through the stained-glass window of the church, casting an eerie, orange glow. There were gasps of awe coming from the audience. It was as if my mother had found a way to insert herself into the premiere of "her" piece, which, by the way, is titled *Tutti for Earth and Heaven.*

JK: Wow. That's a beautiful story. This was just last year?

JV: Last summer [2009]. And I have to tell you that my participation in the *Water Dance* project was born, just as mysteriously, from within my mother's hospice-care center. A few days before she died, I received an email from an acquaintance—Terry Hawthorne from WILPF. Terri was hoping I would get involved in a water-rights project. Despite my sad circumstances, something instantly called me to that project, as if my involvement were preordained. So when I got back to the Twin Cities in February 2009, I began attending monthly planning meetings. At first, there were so many people and organizations involved in the planning that I couldn't see a role for myself. Every month, different groups of people would show up. But art works in mysterious ways, and soon a core group of grassroots movers and shakers had ignited a flame. I was among them. Then, as everything was coming to fruition, there was yet another strange coincidence involving a storm and a rainbow. On the first Wednesday of each month, at exactly one o'clock, the Twin Cities' civil defense sirens are tested. These are the sirens used to warn of approaching tornados. The *Water Dance* performance was scheduled for noon on a Wednesday—March 3, 2010. The forty-five-minute preshow started around 11:20—a bit late. Near the end of *Water Dance,* following the storm section, there was a brief pause before the instrumental transition that leads into the final rainbow section. In that brief, not more than five-second gap, we could hear the sound of the storm siren—a faint, ghostly wail—coming from somewhere outside the hall. It was so perfectly timed that most people thought it was part of the music. The musicians of Zeitgeist looked over at me with barely suppressed glee. I knew they were thinking about my teacher Eric Stokes, a composer and environmentalist who was killed tragically in a car crash. Eric had taught many of us how to be arts activists through his own music. But I was thinking about my mom, and what had happened the previous summer during the rainbow section of *Tutti for Earth and Heaven.* The memory still gives me goosebumps.

***

Works by Janika Vandervelde

All works self-published by Hothouse Press unless otherwise noted.

CHORAL

All the Great Ships, for SATB (2008).
All Things Resounding, for twelve voices (2007).
Alleluia, for SATB and harp (2003).
Ave Maria, for SATB, tenor, cello, and piano (2001).
Beijing Cai Hong, for SATB, soprano, violin, pipa, and narrator (1998).
Birds of Oz, for SATB divisi (2003).
Cancioncilla del primer deseo, for SATB and Latin percussion (2004).
Cançoes de Embalar, for SATB (Earthsongs, 2000).

Come, Ye Weary, for SATB and piano or handbells (1983).
Dance Ablaze! for SSA and percussion (Earthsongs, 2001).
Earthbeat, for SSA and percussion (2001).
The Gathering, for SATB or SSA, violin, piano, or harp (2002).
Hilariter, for SATB and handbells (Boosey and Hawkes, 1994).
In a Thousand Tongues, for SATB and piano (2005).
It's Alive Now, for SATB or SSA and percussion (1999).
Kindling Humanity's Heart, for SATB and organ (2004).
Kyla Vuotti, for SATB (Earthsongs, 2002).
Little Boy Lost, Little Boy Found, for SAB and piano (1979).
Mar, for SATB (2005).
Medicine Woman, for SATB, Native American flute, percussion, and piano bows (2005).
The Mystic Trumpeter, for SATB, trumpet (1986).
New Face, for SSA (2000).
O Factura Dei, for SATB, electric bass, and percussion (2002).
O Viridissima Virga, for SATB, percussion (Earthsongs, 1992).
Positive Women: Susan, for SSA, violin, and narrator (Earthsongs, 1992).
Sing Me a Home, for SATB and percussion (2007).
Slip Away, for children's choir and Orff ensemble (2006).
The Spacious Firmament, for SATB, violin, and electronic score (2003).
Three Psalms, for SATB (1978).
Three Songs of the Spirit, for SATB, percussion, bass clarinet, and piano (1998).
Villages of the Earth, for SATB and percussion (Earthsongs, 2004).
Villancico, for SATB and percussion (2004).
Wataridori, for SATB and oboe (1997).
Water of Life, for SATB, string quartet, two oboes, and two pianos (2010).

CHORUS WITH ORCHESTRA

Ancient Echoes across the Stara Planina, for SSAA and orchestra (1994).
Polyhymnia, for SATB and orchestra (1992).

ORCHESTRA

Cafés of Melbourne, for accordion and chamber orchestra (1997).
Clockwork Concerto, for viola and chamber orchestra (1987).
The Dreamweaver, a Chinese folk tale with narrator and visuals (1996).
The Farthest Shore, for narrator and chamber orchestra (1981).
Journey to the End of the Shaking Lands, with two actors (1988).
Metaphors, featuring handbells (1980).
Mythos (1991).
Pacific Transit, a pipa concerto (1998).
Testaments, for chamber orchestra (1979).
Womanhood Shines the Seasons, for soprano and chamber orchestra (1981).

STAGE AND MULTIMEDIA

Adventures of the Black Dot, a choral storybook for Minnesota Chorale and youth choir (2001).
The Bacchae, incidental music for the Guthrie Theater (1985).
Cosmos, an All-Person's Guide to the Orchestra and Space Adventure, with narrator and video animation (1999).
Cycle One: The Politicians, for the New Music Theatre Ensemble (1985).
Diana Takes a Swim, an electronic work for Deborah Jinza Thayer (2011).
Hildegard, a video-performance opera for the Southern Theater (1989).
Love Song to the Plains, a ballet for the Whispers of America Chamber Dance Ensemble (1982).
Seven Sevens, an opera for the New Music Theatre Ensemble (1993).
Sound Environments I–V, recorded on CD (1988).
A Time of Hands, an interdisciplinary performance piece for Corn Palace Productions (1997).
Water Dance, an hour-long choral ballet tracing the hydrologic cycle; this includes music written by high-school students under Vandervelde's direction (2010).
Why Do My Eyes Refuse to See? an interdisciplinary performance piece for the Minnesota Center for Arts Education and Women's International League for Peace and Freedom (2000).

VOCAL

The Bee and the Soul, for three sopranos, clarinet, sax, trumpet, violin, cello, and piano (2011).
Crystal Light, for voice and CD (1988).
God's Grandeur, for baritone and piano (1988).
Henry's Fate, for tenor, clarinet, cello, piano, and percussion (1983).
I Am the One, for tenor and piano (1998).
In Celebration, for soprano and piano (1988).
Item de Virginibus, for soprano and CD (1989).
The Prayer of Manitonquat, for soprano, violin, and guitar (1996).
Skyborn, for soprano and piano (1985).
Skyros, for baritone, flute, clarinet, violin, piano, and percussion (1982).

CHAMBER MUSIC/SOLO INSTRUMENT

Aeolian Palindrome Clockwork, for saxophone and CD (1989).
Birthday Music for N.D.B., for piano (1980).
Chi, for two pianos (1983).
Clockwork Concerto, for viola and CD (1991).
Clockwork Rhapsody, for piano (1985).
Dabhar, for three cellos (1988).
Four Miniatures, for piano trio (1981).

Genesis I
  oboe and piano (1983).
  oboe and CD (1991).
Genesis II, for piano trio (1983).
Genesis III, for flute, viola, and harp (1984).
Genesis IV, for clarinet, violin, and piano (1987).
Genesis V, for guitar quartet (1988).
Genesis VI, for string trio (1988).
Genesis VII (1989).
  soprano sax, two percussion, piano
  soprano sax and CD
Getting Your Z's or Not, for clarinet, piano, and two percussion (2008).
The Greenfly
  percussion ensemble and jazz vibraphone (1987).
  vibraphone and CD (1991).
HaChZaRaH, for organ and violin (2008).
Hilariteri, for violin and organ (Minneapolis: Augsburg Press, 2010).
Jack and the Beanstalk, for eight instruments and narrator (1984).
Klucevsek's Web, for accordion (1994).
Labyrinth, for organ (2009),
Max Found Two Sticks, for eight instruments and narrator (2010).
Monapacataca, for string quartet (2004).
Petric's Web, for accordion (2005).
Physis, for horn and piano (1978).
Saxworks, for saxophone quartet (1986).
Two Clockworks, for double woodwind quintet (1985).
Viriditas, for violin and synthesizer (1988).
Voxworks, for SATB (1986).

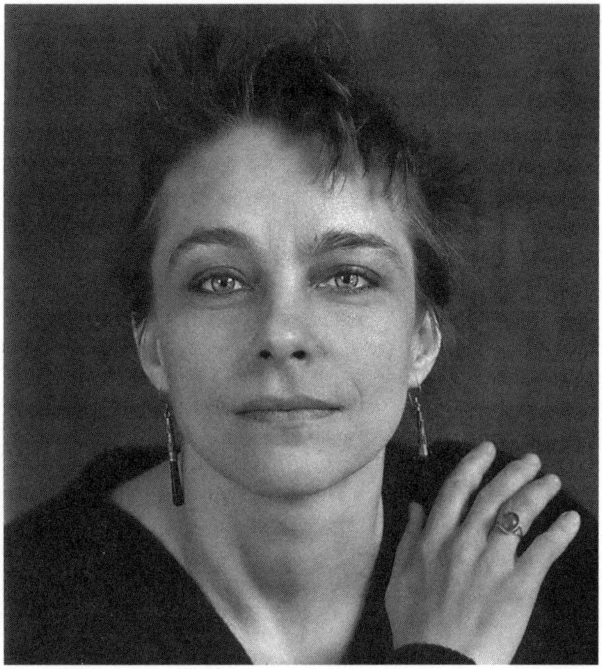

Marion Ettlinger

24

Mary Jane Leach

Mary Jane Leach's music has evolved from instrumental music for multiples of the same instrument to an embrace of technology and on into music for vocal ensemble. Today, her compositional output varies, yet she focuses on advanced music for multiple voices as commissions dictate. Like Libby Larsen, Leach foresaw decades ago the technological shift in our culture and recognized its power within music. Leach's early electro-acoustic works demonstrate this understanding. She has always embraced the exploration of acoustics and sound, seeking the fundamental pitch as well as created partials. Like Svjetlana Bukvich, each piece of Leach's music has its own system based on the tuning of that particular piece. Not tuned to a piano or other instrument, Leach's vocal music is based on tuning to the fundamental pitch of the work, while the surrounding partials are tuned to that fundamental. When working with technology, Leach completely controls the created partials achieved by tuning to the fundamental pitch; with live vocalists, the listening and tuning must emerge from the ensemble and the physical placement of singers within the space. In other words, all of the pitches played for both instrumental and vocal music must be tuned to the fundamental pitch of the piece.

Leach was born in 1949 in Vermont and earned degrees from the University of Vermont and Columbia. An early member of the Downtown Ensemble and an active participant in New York's new music scene in the 1970s and 1980s, Leach laments many of the changes made since then to clean up Manhattan. Her awards and commissions include a grant from the Foundation for Contemporary Performance Arts, established by Jasper Johns and John Cage to support innovative artists in the performing arts.

Leach's early works scored for multiples of the same instrument include *4BC,* for four bass clarinets, and *Feu de Joie,* for eight bassoons. Out of necessity, she began exploring technology to add multiple instruments and virtuosic lines to her sound. In light of that exploration, her friend and colleague Dora Ohrenstein suggested that she might have better access to musicians whose instrument was their voice. A trained vocalist herself, Leach thus began exploring writing for multiple voices. Beginning in 1985 with *Green Mountain Madrigal,* Leach has composed increasingly for vocal ensemble and created numerous works aimed toward advanced women's ensembles. In addition to vocal-ensemble works and electro-acoustic repertoire, Leach's catalog includes works for solo, chamber pieces, and a recent single-movement piano concerto.

Despite Leach's description of how she became a "choral composer," I specifically do not use the word "choir" to describe her vocal music, because she approaches neither her music nor her treatment of text in the same manner as most composers of choral music. Leach's music for multiple voices is more concerned with the aforementioned treatment of sound, developing partials and tuning to the fundamental. During our conversation, she explains her relationship to sound and how she acoustically composes some of the electronic effects of panning and layering. Leach is interested in the combination of tones at exact intervals and beats and how those combined tones interact with the acoustics of a space. When she adds instruments to the voices, as in *O Magna Vasti Creta,* they are usually intertwined with equal importance, neither as foreground nor background. Leach also has an appreciation for early music and the celebration of women within early texts, specifically the story of Ariadne, for which tale she composed a series of works and made a collected CD. Ariadne is also the name of her self-publishing company.

Leach moved away from Manhattan when the New York scene changed, and she is currently a freelance composer living in a small town in upstate New York. Her Web site includes a picture of an old brick church "with good acoustics" that she purchased to use as her home and an occasional place for concert performance. Like Hilary Tann, she credits technology in part for her ability to stay connected and expand her fan base. A business-savvy individual, like many composers in this book, Leach recognizes that if one's music is to be found, one must make it easily accessible. Through digital social networking and a comprehensive Web site, Leach has enjoyed strong support in Europe through grants and performances and also composed a single-movement piano concerto for an Italian orchestra thanks, in part, to Facebook.

***

November 2009, at her home in Valley Falls, New York

JENNIFER KELLY: Were you looking for an old brick church to live in?

MARY JANE LEACH: Are you kidding? You could never find a place like this if you were looking! [*Laughs*] I was living in New York City, and I was getting really tired of it because the arts are being forced out, and the work that is being done is all safe now. It's become provincial in a weird kind of way. Everyone comes and performs their safe pieces, because no one can afford to lose money on these things. So artistically, it was becoming stifling and also sterile, to make it safe for the tourists. All the interesting, quirky places are disappearing. So I felt like I was making a lot of compromises. And I was in my favorite pastry shop near Columbia University reading the college paper and saw a house for sale in this area and realized that geographically, this area is pretty conveniently located, because it's equidistant between Montreal, New York, and Boston. The church is basically in good condition, and it's huge. And it has really nice acoustics.

JK: Have you tried to manipulate the acoustics here?

MJL: They're fine the way they are. I'm also a singer, and when one vocalizes in a place with good acoustics, you start supporting the sound better. You actually start sounding better and singing better because you can hear exactly what's happening.

JK: And there's more direct vibration coming back to you.

MJL: I usually am sitting at the piano and singing towards the short wall. It's counterintuitive to a lot of people, but that's why we all sound good in the shower, because the walls are right there for the sound to bounce off of. For example, I was performing the amplified piece *4BC,* and the sound person and I realized that all the upper partials were missing. So he turned the speakers to the wall. It worked. As a singer, if there's a situation where you're losing all those highs, you just turn so that you can bounce off of a wall somewhere—unless you only want the fundamentals.

JK: How would you define physicality of sound?

MJL: That it actually has a presence. Sound is vibration. The most physical it ever got was when I was making a recording with an alto flutist, *Trio for Duo,* where much of it was about sound phenomena in a very limited range. We were playing one of the main notes, which happened to be the resonant frequency of the room. It was the spookiest feeling, because every time I hit that note, it was as if the air had turned to Jell-O. Another early piece I had done, *Note Passing Note,* had tones coming out of two speakers, and then I would sing and create beats and move the sound around. And sound is different in different places. That's what I mean about the physicality of it. There really is a presence to it.

JK: When you compose, do you write for the space where the piece is going to be performed, or do you look for a space that is going to present that piece well?

MJL: A little bit of both. The trouble with doing it for a specific space is that it limits the number of performances. I had a piece, *Pipe Dreams,* that I did in Cologne on an organ with two sets of pipes that could be played separately. It also had a stop that could play a ninth. So, of course, I had to play a second and have two ninths, and it would start beating at a certain point, which changed depending on the weather. I try to have that kind of awareness that a specific room can be different on different days. But the trick is to find a room that it will work in. One other piece that was sung in a church in Cologne didn't work at all. The singers hadn't really thought about the space it was going to be performed in, and after about a measure it was just mush. All the dissonant notes fell out.

JK: Do you have a favorite space, or does it all depend?

MJL: I really like rooms that are cylindrical and have great acoustics, like old cisterns. Places that reinforce a lot of partials. The trick is to find ways to reinforce things without getting too mushy.

JK: When you discuss partials, are you tapping into the presence of the overtone series, or are you accessing other phantom notes or interference tones?

MJL: Yes, the interference tones. Especially with voice, because voice has formants instead of overtones anyway, so you just can't sit there adding frequencies, and that result will be the note that you hear. It's a lot more complicated.

JK: Do you leave a lot of it up to chance, or do you know what to expect?

MJL: I know what's going to happen. When I first started out, I was doing a lot of multitracking studies. Then computers came out, and you could do MIDI playbacks. Now you have more of a choice of instruments that would have the characteristics of the real instruments you are writing for. And I do a lot of studies. What does it sound like when you have eight oboes playing in unison? What happens if you start panning them differently? What happens when one is playing a different octave? I can do a lot of it pretty intuitively now, but when I was starting out, I did a lot of work figuring out precisely what would happen.

JK: It seems the reverberation and partials are so key to the overall performance. How does it translate to recording?

MJL: I don't know; it just happens.

JK: So you're satisfied with recordings you can get—it doesn't necessarily have to be a live performance?

MJL: Right. Tuning can be an issue. We did the recording of my piece for bassoon, *Feu de Joie,* which is six taped bassoons and live bassoon. With multitracking, tuning to the wrong note can throw things off. So I wanted to record all the low notes that the piece revolved around first. The bassoonist said, "I can't do that. I'll just blow my lip out." So we tuned to the octave, and that made things slightly out of tune. So we redid it and retuned it to the lowest note. Kyle Gann got it wrong in his book, *American Music in the Twentieth Century,* when he wrote that I achieved the effects because everything was played slightly out of tune. The point is that everything is played precisely in tune using tempered tuning, not just intonation or other tunings.

JK: You bring up a question. Spending time both in the States and in Europe, do you tune to A440?

MJL: The frequency doesn't make much difference. It's about tuning with the fundamental, how they all go together. Working with the women singers in the New York Treble Singers, a number of them have perfect pitch, but they have slightly different alignment, so we would have to decide which singer to tune to. So, you could be tuning to A448 or anything else. You adjust.

JK: Has anyone ever told you about the physical vibrations with one of your pieces affecting somebody with perfect pitch?

MJL: No, but I've had people come up to me after concerts saying they saw people physically moved by the vibrations. More of a cathartic or spiritual kind of experience.

JK: Do you concern yourself with the fact that, as a contemporary composer, an audience may have only one listening of a work?

MJL: I'm very aware of it, and a performance can affect everybody's perception of your writing. It really depends on the performers and the space.

JK: So the performance itself is really critical.

MJL: Yeah, and things have changed a lot with the internet and so much streaming.

JK: You have a very accessible Web site. We can get a sense of you and your music just from the Web site, and I think that's very necessary for living composers.

MJL: When I was researching composers for a multiples project, there were certain things that I was looking for, and it always bugged me if it was hard to find certain compositions or information. There's certain information you want to be readily available, so that's how I built my own Web site. For instance, pieces are listed chronologically, alphabetically, and by genre. You want it to be easy to find information. Some people have these really lovely multimedia sites, but it's not clear. Unless you're only going to visit that site one time, having this beautiful opening with music and animation and stuff is pointless. You have to think, Is someone going to want to sit while it plays out? So, thanks for the compliment, because I did work a lot on that.

It's also made life so much easier, because you don't have to run to the post office all the time. There are notes on every piece. There are bios and score samples. I go the extra mile. For singers, there's the range of the voices. I try to put as much information on there as possible, because that's what I would want. I put in what I would want to find.

JK: It seems like you have a strong business sense, too.

MJL: Maybe more practical sense. It isn't generating money [*laughs*], but it is generating interest or information. I had always thought that if I had written my earlier pieces for eight guitars as opposed to eight voices, I would have had a totally different career, because then I would have been hip. I was about to do a concert at BACA Downtown [Downtown Cultural Center of the Brooklyn Arts Council], and I was going to do all this multitrack vocal music. A singer friend of mine, Dora Ohrenstein, said, "You know, you could get eight singers and do it all live." And I thought, Wow. That's how I became a choral composer. Totally by accident.

JK: I notice you frequently use the soprano voice.

MJL: That's because I wrote for myself, and I have a very high voice. And I kept saying, "Well, this is the last piece like this I'm going to do." But it was just practical. Then you have two pieces for all sopranos, but that's not enough for a concert, so I kept writing more. Now I have pieces for sopranos and altos, and I have some for mixed chorus, too. Unfortunately, for me, the pieces are a little more difficult than your average choir can perform.

JK: They have to be comfortable with dissonance, and be very comfortably independent with intervals, tuning, and listening.

MJL: Yeah, they're easy to get lost in. You have to be a really secure singer. *Ariel's Song* is an antiphonal piece. There are patterns of sound going clockwise, counterclockwise, and diagonally. In the right configuration, which is a rectangular shape with the audience in the middle, the singers can hear how the patterns move through the space. The separation makes it easier to hear.

JK: That brings up another point. What kind of relationship do you like to have with a performer or conductor?

MJL: As a composer, you don't want to be so rigid that you're excluding any possibilities of things that work better, but by the same token, you don't want to have license taken. When a composer specifically says that she wants everyone equidistant from each other, then respect that. But there is give and take. A composer doesn't always think of everything. Or maybe there's some way that a piece can be done that works better.

JK: So you're open to that—that maybe there's something you didn't think of that's in the music.

MJL: Oh, yeah. Just like turning the speakers to the wall. You think you've learned all the tricks, but there's always something new.

JK: So a performer does have some creative license when they play the piece?

MJL: Yeah, it's a performance. It's really boring to be so straitjacketed that you can only do it one way. And a performer is not a machine. You want to be able to express yourself as a performer. The trick is for the composer to create a piece that a performer can express, yet it remains with some of your personality as a composer.

JK: I've noticed that a lot of your works, scores, are on your Web site. Self-published. And then C. F. Peters publishes some as well?

MJL: I learned a lot from my experience with Peters. The first time I got a score back from Peters it was full of red marks. Things that I hadn't really been aware of before, like consistent punctuation. There are certain things I do that aren't standard. So we came up with a kind of protocol for dealing with the widowed syllables in words—the carefulness to details that I never would have realized, and I learned so much. Now my scores are better. It's harder to get choral scores out there. Chamber music has a network and a smaller group of people involved. Most of my music is self-published, and now that you can put so much information on the Web, it does make it a little bit easier.

JK: I have spoken to many composers who are either already self-publishing or going in the direction of self-publishing.

MJL: Yeah. I did take some time off from writing to get my scores to publishing quality. It can be frustrating, but it's necessary.

JK: Going back to the compositions themselves, how do you think about rhythm and form?

MJL: Rhythm depends on the key of the piece, because I try to work with the frequency when working on an idea. And I play around with the tempo because I find it makes a huge difference in the sound. As an aside, that's the tempo that works with the playback that I've got. There might be a tempo that would work better in different spaces. If you get the exact right tempo in a work, it's almost like hang gliding. The music floats, as opposed to flying away or plummeting to the ground.

JK: It's propelled on its own.

MJL: Yeah! It's like singing. You need that image of the ball on the fountain, balancing on the top of your breath. I usually find that there is a tempo that is exactly right for the situation and perfectly supports the sound. You have to think about what works in the space and not fight the space.

JK: How do you think about melody when you're writing?

MJL: It depends on the piece. I think I use a lot of melody. I also think a lot about silence, like Schubert uses silence. I went to a concert where Andras Schiff performed Schubert, and at one point, all of a sudden he let the sound die out and come up again. Many people don't think about rests that much. A rest does not actually connote silence, because there is usually sound that has just been sounded. And a rest is another way to open up your path of listening. What I mean is that many people listen with their eyes on the score rather than the actual sound they're hearing. The actual sound is composite. Sometimes, I'll write a whole measure of rest for everybody. I don't want it to be a pause; I want it to be precisely that amount of time. There is a reason I don't write "pause," because in the heat of performance, one tends to hurry up those silences. And Schubert often wrote *tutti* whole rests, as Mozart did. It's the sense of letting the sound settle and then starting it up again.

JK: Are you hopeful about the music that is being written today?

MJL: It seems like there is an awful lot of crappy music being written, but maybe it is just hard to find good things with all of the music being written. And today everything is multitracked, precise, and Auto-Tuned. They are compressing music so much that everything is equal. All the highs are being taken out, so the sound is actually distorted in order to have maximum volume impact.

JK: So do you think we're headed into another era where live music reigns again?

MJL: No, I don't think so. I think recorded is what's going to happen. Just speaking as a composer, it's really frustrating to spend lots of energy and money on a live concert that people may or may not attend. You can put almost that same amount of money into a recording, and lots of people can hear it. I mean, I love live concerts, but it's frustrating. For instance, New York. You pick a day, and everybody else has a concert that same day. Or it rains. You put all this work into something for a very small audience. In a recording, you can put the same amount in, and thousands of people can hear.

JK: Where does contemporary music thrive today?

MJL: I don't think there's any one place. I think it's anywhere where you look for it. I was reading a blog by Elodie Lauten one day. She was listing these concerts, saying, "The men get all of the concert halls, and the women get the churches." But I want a nice sounding space, so I don't consider that a demotion at all.

JK: How many concerts do you put on here?

MJL: Well, not that many, because of a few reasons: heat, location, funding reasons, and the fact that it's taking time away from my own work. There's a fine line between putting something on and then getting so absorbed with administration.

JK: It's a production. You want to make sure you're primarily a composer.

MJL: I was talking to Barbara Thornton [of Sequentia] when we were both in Cologne. She was saying, "If I were in America, I would be spending all of my time grant writing instead of researching the music."

JK: Lots of my musician friends talk about how the number of opportunities, jobs, grant money, what have you, has dropped out of the business. The top-tier musicians are dropping to the second-tier gigs because there are fewer top-tier gigs anymore. But where do the second-tier musicians go?

MJL: Yeah, it's fascinating, because I was living in Germany in 1989 and 1990, in a culture where they really esteem artists. You can say you're a composer in Germany, and that's really good. But when I came back here [to the United States], the arts were being demonized. If you say you're a composer here, people often think it's a synonym for freeloader. Also, my generation is sort of caught in between. The generation ahead of us, like Pauline [Oliveros], had opportunities available to them, and they've held on to all of those, like teaching. Today, everybody is going for doctorates and getting institutional gigs. Those things weren't available when I was around. So people my age are caught in between.

JK: What are you working on now?

MJL: A piano concerto. It's a commission [*laughs*].

JK: You're laughing. What's your reaction about?

MJL: Well, I just can't believe I'm doing this. It's short, about ten minutes. For some reason, I have a lot of fans in Italy. It happened through Facebook. It's a small world. So, this pianist "friended" me. He said, "I just love your music. Have you ever written for piano?" So I said, "If you ever commission pieces, think of me." A couple of weeks later, I get this email saying that he'd like to commission me to write a piano concerto for this Italian orchestra. The fee is ridiculously low, but I think it could be a good chance to get my toe in that world. The conductor and the pianist are very good, so it's for people I respect, and that makes it fun. And orchestral writing is so much broader than what I normally do.

JK: This is your first large orchestral work. How is the experience?

MJL: The hardest part is the large score and how to deal with it. I'm most worried about actually printing out the scores.

JK: The practical end of it.

MJL: Yeah, because I think I've got a handle on the music. I've worked pretty closely with almost every instrument and written for winds, strings, and everything else except timpani.

JK: Did schooling prepare you for this?

MJL: I have to say that most of it was stuff I did on my own, just experimenting. And what I was writing—working with sound phenomena and using multiples—wasn't taught anywhere or even written by that many other people at that time. It wasn't like I could go and learn it somewhere, because we were all doing it at the same time. So I just came upon working with sound phenomena just by accident. In college, I was a theater and music major. Through theater, I learned about incidental music in our Shakespeare festival, which led me into liking a lot of early music. At that time, a lot of early music was for recorders, because performance practice and scholarship of it was still being formulated. Now, early music is performed more vocal than instrumental. It's stunning to listen to recordings from that earlier era and listening to them now, because it's changed so much.

JK: Do you mean in terms of what's being performed or the performance practice itself?

MJL: The performance practice itself. I spent a summer after college doing early music in 1972, and there was a guest named Thomas Binkley from the Studio for Early Music in Munich. He played us tapes of his music, and it was just magical. He was incorporating vernacular music, getting the feel of the street, and not just having early music be so sterile. It was getting fleshed out. People like Binkley and David Munrow really transformed early music from sterile to vibrant—and acknowledging that a lot of it was vocal.

JK: So it sounds like you had your most inspirational training after college.

MJL: Yes, I did. Being a theater and music major were good things. I learned about lighting through theater.

JK: Did that influence your music? I think there would be a lot of similarities between theater lighting and music.

MJL: Yes, there are. Actually, the first job I had in New York was running a light board off-Broadway with this incredible lighting designer, Arden Fingerhut, and we talked about the similarities between music and light. Vibrations, combining notes, and getting a third note the way you do with light and color. At the same time, they both kind of deal with the abstract. There are a lot of similarities.

JK: So when you write a piece, how do you know when it's finished?

MJL: It's pretty organic. I used to really plan things out, especially when working with sound phenomena, but it's really organic. I start with the sound of the instrument, for instance. Then I do the studies and see what happens. At a certain point, if it's unison and you start hearing the octave, I'll add the octave. And then sometimes a certain note combination is created. No one is playing that; it's just happening. Then, I'll wonder what happens if I add something else, and then I'll notate that. It's very organic.

JK: It's very layered, too. Do you find that the more you add, some of the partials eventually disappear, or does all of the sound stay?

MJL: It depends. One of the reasons my pieces are so difficult to perform is because all the entrances are staggered so that the combined sound doesn't drop out. Staggered entrances keep the sound phenomena going. And it takes a little time for it to build up. A fellow, an osteopath, used to come to my concerts. He said, "You should see people. Sometimes they are just vibrating." Especially in my choral music.

JK: Is that a reaction you are consciously trying to achieve?

MJL: No, it just happens. That kind of took me by surprise. Live would be more effective, because you are immersed in the sound, especially if it is a nice space. A dead space is the worst to me.

JK: What inspires you?

MJL: Well, sometimes it doesn't feel like inspiration at the time, but when you hear it, you think, Wow, that's what it was all about. I think, as composers, you don't always feel inspired. And so sometimes you just have to play around until something happens, or keep plugging away and hope that something happens. Sometimes you can be really intimidated by the whole idea of perfection.

JK: Are you a perfectionist?

MJL: I used to be, but it was hard to get any music written that way. So that's what I meant being intimidated by perfection. It has to be the perfect note. I still kind of work that way, but I don't second-guess myself so much. One of the problems with mid-twentieth-century music was, you always had to be doing something different. There was always that worry, Has someone else already done this? You were always thinking in terms of outside the music rather than inside the music. And I tend to think inside the music, if that makes any sense. And one thing I do, especially with MIDI playback, is kind of dance to the music to see if it flows or not. Most of my music is so intricately constructed that I kind of do it note by note, and if something doesn't work, it's like having to unravel a sweater; I have to go back to the point where it got lost. I don't write chunks here and chunks there and then mush them together. They organically develop, and the instrument is the inspiration of the piece. I play around with the sounds until there is something that occurs to me.

JK: What about working with text?

MJL: Writing with words brings in a whole other element to it. All of a sudden, it's not so abstract. But usually I have several texts happening simultaneously. Although the words still make a difference in those kinds of pieces, I'm not writing sentences or lines. I feel it's okay to chop them up.

JK: So are you thinking text, or are you thinking vowels and consonants?

MJL: I'm thinking more vowels and consonants and a sense of the meaning.

JK: So if someone sits down to listen, they're not going to immediately understand the stream of text, but they'll experience the meaning. So do you rely on program notes with the text printed, so they can understand that, or does it not matter?

MJL: Hopefully it doesn't matter. Some of my best pieces, *Ceremony of the Bull* or *O Magna Vasti Creta,* I think you can get the sense of the words even though you don't know precisely what they are. The first time *O Magna Vasti Creta* was performed, I think they got the whole concept of god and goddess in the piece. What's a good word for it? Spiritual. A sense of grandeur, poly-grandeur. I think they got it, and they really reacted to it.

JK: Do you enjoy choral music now?

MJL: Yeah, I like it a lot. In some cases, it's easier to get choral music done because there are so many choruses. But some choral music is so limpid; I'm obviously not into that. I started from a different viewpoint. I didn't start writing my "choral music" as choral music. So that kind of got me off onto a whole other path.

JK: What's your favorite combination of sounds?

MJL: Voice and strings.

JK: I enjoy your use of string instruments as separate and equal voices, instead of as accompaniment or feature. I think that's one of the things that attracted me to your music.

MJL: Well, thank you. I really think they are equal partners. String instruments just don't have words.

JK: Now when you're writing a piece for eight or twelve parts, how do you handle vibrato?

MJL: Well, I'm not against vibrato. I am against wobbles.

JK: And using vibrato, can one still achieve the same partials?

MJL: Oh, yeah. The singers on my recordings are singing with vibrato. It has to be a tight vibrato. It's not healthy to sing without vibrato for long periods of time. When I started studying voice, I was writing vocal pieces, and I wanted to figure out how to sing louder and have more dynamics and sing lower without vibrato. And what I learned was the opposite, that it wasn't possible. You don't have a lot of dynamic range without vibrato. That's why early music is in small halls and not big halls. Sometimes I have a real problem with the "early music sound" because it can often sound pinched. I think most people think a wobble is a vibrato, but that isn't true. You can sing with vibrato so that most listeners don't even know it's happening. You can stay precisely in pitch and have vibrato.

JK: Does your compositional voice continue to evolve?

MJL: No, it hasn't really changed. I think the die has been cast. I feel lucky that I found my own voice compositionally. It doesn't mean that every piece is going to be exactly like every other piece, but there's kind of an aesthetic that I've developed. If you're reinventing the wheel every time you start a composition, a lot of uninspired music can happen, because you may be forcing it.

JK: How often do you write?

MJL: I'm not someone who feels I have to write X number of measures every day. That's a great way to end up with a lot of mediocre music. I'd rather have ten good pieces than a hundred crappy pieces. I work kind of slowly, because everything is so carefully constructed in terms of counterpoint, the way I overlap everything, and then dealing with sound phenomena. And I've gotten better. I can usually tell if something is going to work or not. But I still try new combinations and see if they will work.

JK: Moving from the hustle and bustle of New York City to a small town in upstate New York seems isolating.

MJL: If the internet weren't around, I would certainly feel a lot more isolated. For instance, if the internet had been around when I lived in Germany, it would have been a totally different experience. At that time, most people didn't have fax machines, telephone calls were incredibly expensive, and it look two weeks for letters to be delivered, so there was a sense of isolation. Today you can go there with your laptop and be in touch with everybody. So geographic differences are totally different now than they were before. I have a lot of friends all over. I don't physically see them as much, but I'm probably as in touch with them as I ever was. Technology really makes a huge difference. So living [in upstate New York] with village politics and things like that don't bother me because I have another world. And I don't know if you could do that without the internet. I'm in touch with people all over the world every day.

JK: When a student says to you they want to be a composer, what do you say?

MJL: I say, "Great!" and then give them reality lessons. Basic practical things. If someone asks you for something, send it immediately. Don't not send it. I think women are probably missing a lot of this. They are not proactive. I've learned this through experience, because over the years I have organized some things. The men always responded immediately, and about 75 percent of women I had to keep calling and prodding to even get a dub from them. It's disheartening. If someone wants to hear your music or see a score, send it to them! That's one reason I set things up on the internet, because it's a lot easier. You don't have to print out a score, burn a CD, or anything. It's just a lot easier. And it's okay if you choose not to make it easy in that way, but then don't complain that no one wants to do your music. There is that negative wish fulfillment with some women, unfortunately.

JK: Negative wish fulfillment?

MJL: Yeah: "I'm never going to get this, so why bother?" And then you don't do it, and then you don't get it. You're living up to your negative expectations. It's self-defeating. I think younger women are much better at it today because they don't have as much baggage.

JK: Has the gender barrier been broken?

MJL: No, but I think unless you have high-quality, name-brand composers on the bill, it just seems kind of "ghettoizing." People don't pay attention to it. And unfortunately, there are a lot of whiners who don't do anything for themselves. I get kind of impatient with some of the women on these kinds of things. There was a woman once who was complaining about not getting performances, so I offered to look at her score. There were so many notational problems I wanted to tell her about, but she ended up blowing me off. Then she went on a women's list-serve saying, "As a woman, I'm being discriminated against." No, you wrote badly, you asked for help, and then you didn't even accept it. There are some really great women composers out there, but there are also some who are doing us no favors.

JK: So don't program a composer just because she's a woman.

MJL: Exactly. It needs to be integrated. If it is ghettoized, there is always a backlash. If you can program all-women's concerts, you can program all-men's. When I program concerts, there are sometimes more men than women or more women than men. There is obviously discrimination against women, but it does no good to use that fact as a crutch.

JK: Is everything that a performer or conductor wants to know in your score?

MJL: No. Look beyond the score, or hear beyond the score. I think a lot of people hear only what they see on the page. Unfortunately, because they think they know what they are hearing, they shut themselves off from what is actually happening. For instance, my earlier instrumental music is simplistically notated. It looks like a lot of whole notes, and sometimes I almost don't want people to see those scores because they'll get the wrong idea.

JK: You'd rather have them just experience it.

MJL: Yes, and I've been on panels where colleagues look at scores, and they'll pooh-pooh them. But they're scores by Meredith Monk, Bob Ashley, La Monte Young—people who are doing phenomenal work! Yet the panelists quibble because they only hear what they see on the score.

JK: So when you are sitting on a panel deciding who gets what grant or fellowship or what have you, what is it you're looking for?

MJL: I am not looking for someone who is just cranking out nice, formulaic, in-the-middle pieces. I am looking for some kind of honesty and a voice. Music is a subjective field, and trying to describe it in objective terms is misleading and does it a disservice. Yet people continue to make it an objective study so that everything has to be compartmentalized. I think that's a real mistake. You have to allow room for some ambiguity. There isn't always only one right way of doing things, and you have to be open enough to experience multiple ways. One of the problems with so-called classical music is that it seems like a closed field with a right way and a wrong way. There isn't just one way.

***

Works by Mary Jane Leach

All works self-published by Ariadne Press unless otherwise noted.

ORCHESTRA

Piano Concerto for Emanuele (2010).

VOCAL AND VOCAL ENSEMBLE

Ariel's Song, for eight women's voices (1987).
Ariadne's Lament, for eight women's voices (C. F. Peters, 2000).
Bruckstück, for six women's voices (1989, 2002).
Call of the Dance, for soprano and eight women's voices (1997).
Call to the Ceremony, for SSAATB and string quartet (1999).
Ceremony of the Bull, for SSAATB and string quartet (C. F. Peters, 2002).
Copralalia, La La La, for two sopranos and tape (2002).
The Crane Dance, for soprano soloist and eight women's voices (2005).
Glorious Ariadne, for eight women's voices (2001).
The Great Goddess, for eight women's voices (2001).
Green Mountain Madrigal, for eight women's voices (1985).
Gulf War Syndrone, for piano, synthesizer, clarinet, voice, one to three other instruments, and tape (2004).
He Got Dictators, for soprano, piano, and bass (1993).
Hear My Voice, for soprano solo, eight women's voices, and string quartet (2001).
Held, Held, for live alto flute and voice, and taped alto flute and voice (1984).
Her Thousand and One Nights, for eight voices (1988).
I Sing of Warfare, for tenor, TTBB, and string quartet (2001).
Labyrinthus, for mixed chorus with multiple divisi and string quartet (2007).

Minos, for tenor and SSAATB (1999).
Mountain Echoes, for eight women's voices (1987).
Night Blossoms, for SATB (2001).
Note Passing Note, for solo woman's voice and two taped women's voices (1981).
Notes Passing Notes, for two women's voices and two taped women's voices (1981, 2007).
O Magna Vasti Creta, for eight women's voices and string quartet (C. F. Peters, 2002).
Piano E-tude, for piano, voice, and taped piano e-bowed tones (2009).
The Sacred Dance, for soprano and string quartet (1999).
Sephardic Fragments, for solo voice (1989).
Solar Spots, for solo woman's voice and two taped women's voices (1983).
Song of Sorrows, for SSAATB (C. F. Peters, 1999).
Theseus Arrives, for SSAATB and string quartet (2000).
Tricky Pan, for countertenor and eight taped tenors/countertenors (1995).
Trio for Duo, for live alto flute and voice, and taped alto flute and voice (1985).

CHAMBER ENSEMBLE OR SOLO INSTRUMENT WITH TAPE

4BC, for four bass clarinets (1984).
8 × 4, for alto flute, clarinet, English horn, and voice (1985).
Bach's Set, for solo cello and eight taped cellos (2007).
Bare Bones, for four trombones or bass trombones (1989).
By'm Bye, for piano (2001).
Corrina Ocarina, for harp and flute (1994).
Dido Remembered, for synthesizer and tape (2002).
Dowland's Tears, for nine flutes (2011).
Feu de Joie, for bassoon and six taped bassoons (1992).
Gulf War Syndrone, solo version for synthesizer and tape (2006).
Gulf War Syndrone II, for clarinet, ensemble, and tape (2006).
Guy de Polka, for guitar, cello, accordion, and marimba (1988).
Guy de Polka, for solo accordion (1987).
Kirchtraum, radio soundpiece for WDR (1992).
Lake Eden, for open instrumentation (1986).
Pipe Dreams, for organ (1989).
String Quartet (1998).
The Upper Room, for synthesizer (installation piece), (1990).
Windjammer, for oboe, clarinet, and bassoon (1995).
Wolff Tones E-tude, for piano, two sustaining instruments, two to four melody instruments, and tape (2004).
Xantippe's Rebuke, for oboe and eight taped oboes (1993).

25

Emma Lou Diemer

The prolific composer Emma Lou Diemer has been writing music for over seventy years, and she still exclaims, "I think I'm the happiest when I'm writing!" Born in 1927 and growing up in and around Kansas City, Missouri, Diemer was exposed to big-band music, the American Songbook, 1930s radio broadcasts of orchestral music, and music from the Christian church. She and her siblings were encouraged as children to pursue their artistic natures, and Diemer began composing music at age thirteen. She gravitated to the organ she heard in church as a large machine capable of innumerable shades of color and power. Like Mary Jane Leach, Diemer concerns herself with the acoustics of space and enjoys playing different organs in varied halls. During our conversation, she discusses her early passion for the organ and her disappointment that it is not a more popular instrument today.

With her early interest in this adaptable machine, it is no surprise that, like Laura Karpman, Svjetlana Bukvich, and Pamela Z, Diemer also gravitated toward technology when it was introduced to her as an adult. An early advocate of electronic possibilities in music, she began composing with electronics in her own music in the mid-1970s, pioneered the introduction of MIDI to the church organ, and founded the electronic and computer music center at the University of California at Santa Barbara (UCSB) in 1973. One of the few women composers in the mid-twentieth century to earn advanced degrees in music at Yale and Eastman, Diemer studied with Paul Hindemith, Ernst Toch, and Roger Sessions. She furthered her studies in Brussels on a Fulbright Fellowship in 1952–53 to study piano with André Dumortier and composition with Jean Absil at the Royal Conservatory. The composer in residence with the Santa Barbara Symphony from 1990 to 1992, Diemer has been honored with the Kennedy Center Friedheim Award in Orchestral Music for her 1991 piano concerto and named Composer of the Year by the American Guild of Organists in 1995.

Still a prolific composer, Diemer has over five hundred compositions in her catalog for organ, orchestra, chorus, chamber ensemble, band, voice, keyboard, solo instruments, and electro-acoustic repertoire. Celebrated for her organ music, she has also composed abundant works for choir, including her large settings *Mass* and *Songs of the Earth*. Having spent most of the twentieth century fusing traditional music with new developments and ideas, Diemer remains surprised that the simple and relatively easily written *Three Madrigals* became the choral piece for which she is most known.

While the nuances of Diemer's style have adapted with the times, she has stayed true to her core of tonality, explaining, "I came much earlier than some of the younger composers. There were different opportunities and different styles, and I've always leaned more towards a conservative style in some ways." Like Leach, she expresses how one's music "must make sense within its own being." Still rare for women composers even today, over one hundred of Diemer's compositions have been recorded. She believes that the challenge of being a working musician informs her writing and encourages her to compose for both amateur and professional musicians.

A natural teacher, Diemer has always combined composition and performance with teaching, and she was a professor of theory and composition at UCSB for twenty years. In fact, when I expressed my own trepidation at composing a melody that someone else may have already written, she became my teacher for the moment, encouraging me to continue and explaining technique to help me improve.

During our conversation, Diemer discusses her musical development, the important composer-performer relationship, her views on audience, and a life in music. After sweetly describing her earlier days, when she would place her working score under her pillow at night to guard it, she reflects upon her career: "My life has been very one-track. And if your whole eighty years or a hundred years has been one-track, you hope there's something that you can say, 'Well, it's done some good in the world.' And I think it has."

***

April 2010, at her home in Santa Barbara, California

EMMA LOU DIEMER: I was kind of a restless child who liked to play by ear, so my teacher would teach me things by ear. She would play, and then I would play and learn it that way. Consequently, I didn't learn to read music until I was nine or ten. Today, I still like to sit down and improvise. And really, I think being able to improvise is a way a lot of composers write.

JENNIFER KELLY: Do you still compose at the piano?

ELD: Yes, computer, piano, synthesizer. I have a clavinova, sometimes at the organ. Unfortunately, I've done more at the computer the last few years, written actual pieces, but that can be a kind of crutch in a way.

JK: A crutch?

ELD: I really was happy when they got computer notation, because it was so much easier. But if you're using Finale, for instance, you can be led down bad paths if you're not careful, such as everything in 4/4 time. It's good to stop for a while and go to the keyboard. On the other hand, you can hear what you're doing right away, and you can play the whole thing back to get an idea of the balances, mistakes, and things that need to be longer or shorter.

JK: That would be very helpful, especially when you're writing for multiple instruments. You aren't limited by your two hands and can hear it all rather than wait for it to be realized.

ELD: That's right. Also, the instruments in the computer are better now. They sound more like real instruments. But there are certain drawbacks to it, too, such as you're always going by what you're hearing, rather than what you're playing. A lot of composers, like Stravinsky, discovered things on the keyboard—sometimes mistakes—that became part of their pieces.

JK: How did you begin?

ELD: I started quite young. I had composed a few little things when I was about five, and my teacher would write them down. By the time I was twelve or thirteen, I was sure I was a composer. I got very interested in just the act of writing on score paper; I thought, Gee, it's fun to put those notes on a big score. It's very visual. And I played the baritone horn in band where we played a lot of marches and then a beautiful Bach chorale.

JK: So by the early 1940s, as a teenager, you knew you wanted to be a composer. Did your family support you?

ELD: Yes, they all were musical. My father could read music and sing because he came from a rather musical background. And my mother and grandmother. My brothers had a band, what you would call a dance band. One of them lived only to [age] twenty-three; he was a fighter pilot in the war. That was traumatic for me, because I was sixteen at the time. He was beginning to write more music. They would take their dance band and go around to different dances in communities in Missouri. I never thought of it much, but it was good for a young person to hear them rehearsing. So we weren't really surrounded by classical music—Mozart, Bach. I had to discover that later.

JK: So when you decided at twelve or thirteen that you wanted to be a composer, what were you playing and listening to at the time?

ELD: I was just beginning to play Mozart, but it was more Cole Porter, Gershwin, and the music we had in school. We had these books, like Cole Porter's music, things like *Night and Day*. I was accompanying the choruses and the groups that sang that. I remember I always liked that particular style. Porter is a very classical-type composer in his musical forms and the way he writes his melodies. And I would listen to the songs of the day we would sing. I didn't really like Mozart and Haydn and all that.

JK: So when you were first thinking about being a composer, it was more of the American Songbook material that you were exposed to.

ELD: Yes, and church music, because I had played the organ since I was thirteen, played in church. That's always been an influence. There are a lot of good hymns and a lot of good church music. But I never wanted to write four-part harmony, and that's about all you have in hymns.

JK: Did your father mind you listening to Cole Porter and Gershwin?

ELD: Oh no, they didn't mind anything. I can remember actually composing at home with people upstairs or in the kitchen. I did a lot of composing at home.

JK: Did you ever say, "How am I going to make a living with this?"

ELD: Yes, I certainly did. That's why I went ahead and got a degree in school, so I could have a university position and teach. I would be terrified to be a freelance composer with the kind of music I write. I would never create a living.

JK: Your catalog is so varied. Do you have a particular medium you like to write for the most part?

ELD: I like chorus and orchestra. And that's the most impractical medium [*laughs*].

JK: Well, between the American Songbook and the church hymns, you had a relationship with text almost from the beginning. So a love of choir makes sense. How would you describe your relationship with text?

ELD: In the beginning, a lot of them were biblical. I would usually look in the Psalms, most people knew the Psalms, and take what I liked from that. I didn't like the violent parts of the Psalms, so I would usually eliminate those. My sister was a poet and wrote a lot of poems I have set to music. I like only certain types of poetry—things that are not too wordy, or too long, and I of course gravitated to women poets, being a woman composer. And I liked Elizabethan text because it was light, about nature, and fun. The little madrigals that I have [*Three Madrigals*] that everybody sings, my only big hit, those are Shakespeare.

JK: Do you like those pieces—the short madrigals that are your big hit?

ELD: I did when I wrote them, which was, you know, probably in a few hours, and yes, I like them. I mean, you have to like anything you write, really. If you don't, you shouldn't write it [*laughs*]. But I had no idea that they would catch on in such a way.

JK: It's true. Just about everyone in the choral world knows them.

ELD: They know those if they know anything of mine, and I wasn't aware of that for a long time. I'll meet somebody sometimes, and they say, "Oh yeah, I sang your madrigals in high school."

JK: Do you conduct?

ELD: No, hardly ever. I just don't have the personality.

JK: So, when you hand over a score to a conductor, what kind of relationship do you like to have with the conductor?

ELD: First of all, you want them to recognize you're the composer. It's so funny: every once in a while I have gone to a rehearsal, and they don't even acknowledge the fact that the composer is there. The conductor is the main focus. So the composer is just someone that wrote this thing [*laughs*]. But usually, it's a good relationship if they like it, because it's really fatal if the conductor does not like what you have written. They don't present it well. Maybe they don't understand the music, so the singers guess as to what it should sound like. But that doesn't happen very often. I've heard some good performances of my music that were so sensitive, better than what I would have thought. For instance, I wrote something for Wayne State University a long time ago called *Prophecy.* I met the conductor before I had written this, and he turned out to be a very handsome black man. Not that that makes any difference, but in that day and age, 1968, you thought all conductors were white. I found a recording of it, and it was just marvelous. I recently looked up the school, and he had passed away a few years ago. I don't think he was that old, and I felt so sad about that, because it's just once in a while that somebody really knows what you had in mind when you wrote it. That's a nice experience.

JK: Do you get a lot of questions about your music from performers?

ELD: I get questions like, "How do I do this?" or, "Do you have some recordings?"

and so on. There are so many ways to do a piece of music, and you're lucky to have more than one recording of something—the recording of my *Fantasy* by two different pianists being an example. Hopefully, each recording would be quite different.

JK: You want each recording to be quite different from one another? To express different sides of a composition?

ELD: When we compose a work, we have an idea of how it should sound, and that is what we hope to hear, but performers and conductors may have their own interpretation, especially of tempo and dynamics. And sometimes their interpretation is just as, or more, effective. One wonders how Bach or Beethoven might have performed their own music. Would Bach have played his keyboard music at breakneck speed or lingered over the lush harmonies? Performance practice is an unending study, isn't it? Although I think one of the worst things is to have tempos that are too slow. That could be a problem for conductors doing a new piece. For instance, some of my pieces have meter changes, and it should be faster because, if you slow some things down too much, it loses the impetus that you had when you wrote it. Also, if I'm particularly tired of a mode or scale, I'll change it. That can be challenging because, as soon as you change key, people are thrown off balance.

JK: How quickly do you write?

ELD: I like to write really quickly. I've been writing for so many years, it is always there. I can sit down most anytime and write something. You know, in the earlier days, we made music all the time. I listened to the radio on Sunday afternoon, the New York Philharmonic or big-band music. But more than that, I wanted to make music myself. And I think that people should do that. For instance, I think everybody should have a piano in their house. You've got to be able to create sound.

JK: How do you begin?

ELD: Words can help, because you will have a mood set. Something is inspiring when you know what the words are. Then I approach rhythm, or maybe the structure of it. Emily Dickinson always has something that you are going to think about, and when you set it to music it becomes a little more meaningful. You know, I never started out wanting to be a choral composer. I guess maybe I am considered a choral composer, because I love text. But being a pianist, I wanted to be an instrumental composer, which is more about finding ideas that you like. With me, that idea often comes as some kind of an energetic idea, usually rhythmic, followed by the structure. I'm very interested in what happens with the material. Maybe begin with a little motive; maybe have two or three motives I am going to work with that are there from the beginning. You go on from there . . . develop those.

JK: So you tend to start at the beginning and go forward, rather than develop a large architecture and fill in?

ELD: I start at the beginning. At some point, I know what the rest of it is going to be like, but it is kind of fun to see how it develops. That's one way that the computer is so helpful, because you can tell how long something has been. Is this section long enough? Or what should be done with that section? For me, that's time-saving. Often, if I sit down at the piano, I tend to get caught up in one little idea, and I am deceived into feeling that it's longer than it is. Whereas in the computer, you can actually play it back and see that it's too short. I haven't done it much, but it really saves some time working on the computer. At the piano, I'll improvise, write things down in pencil. I'll sketch maybe a melodic line sometimes all the way through, and then I go back and fill it in.

JK: I envy that. I find myself humming melodies all the time, but then I convince myself that I've heard it somewhere before or it already belongs to somebody.

ELD: Well, you shouldn't, because a lot of composing is changing in little bits. Maybe what I'm writing now sounds too much like something else, so I change it. Because, unless we're working with microtones, we only have twelve pitches, and there are so many ways to rearrange them or change the rhythm or the chords. How long do you stay in this tonal center? When do you introduce something new? And it's always nice when there's a surprise. I mean, you can always develop material that's more interesting, but that can also become boring. You know the way some fugue writers are terribly predictable? And I think I am sometimes a bit predictable, too. I know when certain pieces are more imaginative or more inspired and those that are a little bit duller.

JK: Do you know that in the midst of writing it?

ELD: Yes, because if you have a really good idea, you're feeling kind of "sparky" [*laughs*]. Some ideas are just better.

JK: What inspires you? What gives you those ideas?

ELD: Very often it's a feeling about something. And books, poetry. When I was in my teens, I used to go to a movie and come home and write music because the film inspired me.

JK: Given that inspiration from film, as a composer, would you mind if someone was presenting a piece of yours and included some visual aspect to it, maybe adding some slides to accompany your *Mass*?

ELD: Oh yes! And dance, too. I've always thought that dance was probably closer to musical expression more than anything else. I think those kinds of ideas are very exciting.

JK: As a composer with such a large catalog of varying styles, mediums, and abilities, do you think classical music is in trouble?

ELD: I think it's mostly popular music that has taken over. Maybe that's always been the case. Maybe the most elite music has always been a small percentage of what people like. It certainly is the case now. But I think there will always be people that want something that demands a little more of the creator and the listener and the player. It would be too bad if we all became simple-minded. And it's a challenge to write things that are more difficult. You have to say, "Well, people are not really going to like this, but I'm going to write it anyway." On the other hand, I've known some student composers that write things so difficult or uncommunicative. There is a lot of music that doesn't really communicate, and the composers don't care that it doesn't really communicate. For me, I like to have people like what I write.

JK: So do you consider audience when you're writing?

ELD: Oh yes, very often. I've done some things for the symphony here [in Santa Barbara], and I tried to write pieces I thought they'd like.

JK: What would you like an audience member to leave with after hearing one of your pieces? What do you want them to remember about your piece?

ELD: Well, you'd like them to be moved in some way. You'd like for them to have been made happy or excited about it. When you write a lot of different types of music like I do, you're going to get different reactions. Also, many pieces are performed just once. The second performance is a rarity for some works.

JK: If you know there may be only one listening of a work, do you feel a responsibility to make sure it is accessible enough for an audience to be moved the first time they hear it? And how do you reconcile the fact that all of one's hard work may only have one listening?

ELD: Some of one's "best" works may be seldom performed or once performed and never again. So many factors are involved, not only the immediate favorable reaction that I, for one, like to try to ensure by introducing or incorporating musical elements that are not totally foreign. Next comes the interest from other performers who hear a work and want to perform it, and sometimes this is nil. Word of mouth, advertising, promotion. Most composers (myself included) don't engage a whole lot in these ways of disseminating our music. I recently wrote a chamber work for an ensemble in South Dakota. They premiered it and have actually performed it a number of times, mostly in surrounding areas. Imagine writing something and having the musicians for whom it was written tour all over the United States and beyond to the point that it would be known far and wide, as is much of popular music. Pop-music performers give concerts, record, tour, promote continually. It pays off, regardless of the relative worth of the music. So it's not always the attractiveness and accessibility of the music, but what comes after in terms of promotion.

JK: What kind of freedom of performance or creative license does someone have when they perform one of your pieces?

ELD: They have the various indications in the score, and sometimes they consult me for guidance—made much easier with the use of email now and the fact that we can be found on the Web. Other than that, it is up to the conductor's or performer's own sensibilities and experience and insight. This can be "right on" or not. The composer doesn't have any control without personal contact. Neither does a writer or artist or politician have any control over response and interpretation of her or his creations and utterances under the same circumstances.

JK: So when you write in something as subjective as a dynamic marking or as objective as a tempo marking, are those absolute? Or can a performer play with those to see what works and what they feel?

ELD: Oh yes, and I think they do. It's nice when performers become creative in studying a score. When you look at the way people play Chopin, it's so different. I know when I'm composing, there's a lot more freedom and nuance than you could possibly notate. You know the notation is kind of a compromise, so you hope that the conductor/performer is going to use a lot of creativity.

JK: You've written so much music for so long.

ELD: Hundreds of years [*laughs*].

JK: Do you find that you can keep up the same pace that you did perhaps fifty years ago?

ELD: I think I could, yes. But, when you get older, your mind seems to be split in many different ways. It's not as easy as when you are in college or right afterwards, when it's all focused, and you're totally self-centered usually, and maybe you don't have as many doubts about what you're writing.

JK: So the older you get, the more doubts you have. I guess the older you get, the more you realize you don't know.

ELD: That's right: you learn more, so you don't know much. But usually, if I think something isn't working that I am going to keep, I can turn it into something I like. At this point, I can make something out of almost nothing. Prokofiev can take a simple scale, and all of a sudden it's a whole piece. I think composers are inspired by what they are writing, and that continues.

JK: I must admit, I was a little surprised reading the level of credentials and the amount of schooling and formal training that you had as a woman in the middle of the twentieth century. Were other women studying with you?

ELD: A few. At Yale there was another woman, Violet Archer. She was thirty, and I was nineteen. She was the only other one there in my composition class. At Eastman, I only remember one other in the doctoral program when I was there. I was aware of how few of us there were and kind of proud of it. You know, you're proud of it in the beginning.

JK: There are many women in the field today. . . .

ELD: Yes, there are many more women composers now, in many kinds of genres, and some have achieved greater recognition than outstanding composers did in earlier times. Probably the smallest audience is for music in the academic, contemporary classical field.

JK: How do you feel when you're called a "woman composer"?

ELD: I would prefer to be called just a "composer." I've had different labels and reviews. One reviewer said, "Her music is wonderful, and she looks like a girl-scout leader" [*laughs*]. So there are a lot of things like that that still happen.

JK: What about a different label, like "American composer"?

ELD: "American composer," sure! But I don't think it's necessary, and I think it's increasingly uncommon to be labeled, really. I went into university teaching right away. So that's a different atmosphere. You're pursuing scholarly things, hopefully, and you're learning a lot as a teacher, and students are pretty good at accepting. For instance, when I taught [at UCSB], there were two women and two men teaching composition, and that was good.

JK: Wow—1971, and there were already two and two. That's great.

ELD: A composer, Peter Fricker, was chairman and hired me on the phone. I had a good resumé, and he was pro-woman. He had Thea Musgrave coming some to teach at that time. Very often, the person in charge is the defining factor, because of whom they hire. And teaching at a university is good because you learn more, and more is expected of you.

JK: I imagine that in the early seventies, there weren't many women composing and teaching composition at the university level.

ELD: It was certainly different if you were married or had children. Today, many women do it all and still write music. And now we have several Pulitzer Prize winners who are women. Actually, when I had my concerto performed in the Kennedy Center competition, Shulamit Ran's piece won. She had entered the piece that won her the Pulitzer. Thanks a lot! [*Laughs*] But I never really competed in the upper echelon.

JK: Why not?

ELD: There were a lot of different factors. I came much earlier than some of the younger composers. There were different opportunities and different styles, and I've always leaned more towards a conservative style in some ways. I keep coming back to something resembling tonality and theme and development. I don't use many ethnic ideas, and I don't bring in all the exotic instruments, and also I do a lot in the organ field, and the organ isn't as particularly popular as it should be.

JK: What is it you really like about organ? In some circles, you really are known as a fantastic composer for organ.

ELD: You can make a lot of noise on the organ [*laughs*]. And then the color. It's just a wonderful instrument; it's a machine. If you like machines, then you can deal with it very well. And I've always been a church organist. There's something very inspiring about church music and playing in different places, different acoustics, and the sound in a big cathedral.

JK: Do you find yourself composing on the organ for other instruments? Much like you might do on the computer because there are so many different colors?

ELD: Yes, because you do have the different colors—strings, flute, oboe.

JK: Do you think playing the organ early in your life informed your orchestral writing?

ELD: Oh yes, definitely. The importance of the pedal, the bass. You know, the bass has to be very prominent and have some good role. And then different colors.

JK: You were born in 1927 and decided you were going to be a composer by thirteen years old. There aren't very many people that can say they have composed music for so many decades, still widely performed, and still compose. And your experiences as a teacher have affected too many students to count. How do you think your path as a composer would be different if you were born in the twenty-first century?

ELD: Well, I'm sure it would be easier. There would be more of us. Because when I was growing up, even when I was teaching [at UCSB], I didn't know any women composers especially, and I certainly didn't play any—well [Cécile] Chaminade may have had a piece in an anthology of some kind. But it didn't bother me, because I loved the music. I didn't care who wrote it. Yes, there would be that difference; there would be more of us. I don't know that I personally would have been any different.

JK: As a composer, how have you experienced American music change over the decades?

ELD: Classical music? Well, we went through the serial period, and if you didn't write serial music, atonal music, you were out of it. But then there was a more romantic movement that came in the sixties, and it became all right to write music that was romantic and tonal. There always has to be some difference. You can't just write the way someone wrote in the nineteenth century, or earlier. Today, it's become so eclectic, you can have all kinds of influences in your music. And a lot of composers do that; they'll have a little jazz, a little folk music, a little serialism—it's kind of a melting pot, which is exactly what Charles Ives did in the beginning of the twentieth century. And he was really lambasted for it by some people. But he was already doing it.

JK: Now the lines have blurred so much that even commenting on it is becoming rare. So you like the direction it seems to be going in today?

ELD: Well, I think it should continue along these lines, and there's so much global interest in all kinds of music, and that's good. But I also think it's a mistake to go all the way just to change your style. There was a composer in the early periods of electronic music, [Vladimir] Ussachevsky. He might have very simple melodic music, and then he introduces electronic music—total, total change in style. There has to be some unity to what you write so that it's cohesive. It's okay to experiment, but I think it has to make sense within its own being. You can't take some of this, and some of that, and expect it to really be meaningful.

JK: When were you first introduced to technology with regard to composition?

ELD: When I was at the University of Maryland, I was really interested in the electronic production of sound. Then in 1970, I attended a workshop where someone was using synthesizers. When I came [to UCSB], I wanted to go on with electronic sound and got them started with an electronic music studio through a grant.

JK: That was quite a big deal in the early seventies.

ELD: Yes! I got them some Moog synthesizers and some other things, and then got some of my own, and started playing with them. It was fun to get different sounds. At different points in your life, when you live a long time, you feel like you're not expanding enough, developing enough, or learning enough, and so that was part of that phase. I also pursued it for the sake of the students. You know, they're going to be way ahead of you if you don't get in there and learn something. And I don't pretend to know an awful lot about it, but I did learn how to work analog synthesizers and make my own music.

JK: Do you think that technology is aiding the progression of classical music nowadays?

ELD: It must be, particularly with CDs and DVDs and so on, the recording of it. I don't think electronic music per se has become terribly popular. I mean it's there, it's in film music, and there are lots of synthesizers in popular music. Being an organist, the Hammond organ was a very interesting instrument, because you could create the harmonic series with that—you know, the fundamental and the overtones—and I've heard that used in church and gospel music very well. I added a synthesizer to the organ in the church where I played and began using it with the pipe organ. That was fun, because there wasn't anything that soft on the organ, and it was a different sound source.

JK: What can women do to continue being a part of the musical dialogue into the future?

ELD: I've been really pleased. People like you are writing. And it's the women musicologists that have really helped women because they've researched, and they've learned a lot and brought music out that people didn't know about before. I would hope that would continue, that women support other women in the arts, in music. The test for longevity of what composers write is still dependent on the appeal of their work, as well as its overall quality. Think of the appeal of certain works of Mozart, Tchaikovsky, and Prokofiev. What genius, innovation, and technique gives them that appeal? Whether the work of women composers, and men composers, will enter the repertoire more or less permanently is still a question of word of mouth, advertising, and promotion as well as being liked by many listeners. A composer may write music in which she or he was very emotionally involved in the writing. Milton Babbitt is said to have had tears in his eyes after the playing of some of his electronic works, and many composers have that experience in hearing their own music. Mathematicians speak of the beauty of formulas. I have sometimes been very moved in the writing of a piece, but that doesn't necessarily mean that what I am writing at the time is particularly good. A strict serial work of uncompromising dissonance will have its followers just as will a sentimental song. Just not as many.

JK: Are you thinking about legacy? Are you happy with the output you've got to leave behind?

ELD: I have a lot of things that are good, but people don't really know about them much. Most of it is in the library at the university [UCSB] in the special collections. I don't know what will happen to special collections in the centuries to come. The universities are a great repository. And then anything you publish is in the Library of Congress, and the New York Public Library has some things. I think it's important to get things into libraries, and I noticed that many of them do make a point of ordering women's music. I also have a lot of music [upstairs] that somebody is going to have to get rid of—all my choral music, most of it is up there. And saving the sound. I wonder how that is going to change. It's very interesting, because people in different fields have usually made it or not by their late forties and fifties. There's more attention paid now to older people—seventies, eighties, and nineties—remaining productive. That's certainly going to continue.

JK: Is writing still an enjoyable process?

ELD: Oh yes, it always is. I think I'm the happiest when I'm writing! I used to write a piece and at night put it under my pillow because it was so precious to me. Isn't that sweet? Anything you write for a while, it's the most important thing you're doing, something precious that you're guarding.

JK: What are you most proud of at this stage in your life?

ELD: Well, the music. My life has been very one-track. And if your whole eighty years or a hundred years has been one-track, you hope there's something that you can say, "Well, it's done some good in the world." And I think it has.

***

Works by Emma Lou Diemer

ORCHESTRA

Chumash Dance Celebration (C. Alan Publishing, 2004).
Concert Piece for Organ and Orchestra (Seesaw Music, 1977).
Concerto for Flute and Orchestra (Southern Music Company, 1982).
Concerto for Harpsichord and Chamber Orchestra (Seesaw Music, 1979).
Concerto for Piano and Orchestra (1953).

Concerto for Trumpet and Orchestra (1983).
Concerto for Violin and Orchestra (1983).
Concerto in One Movement for Marimba (C. Alan Publishing, 1994).
Concerto in One Movement for Organ and Chamber Orchestra: "Alaska" (MMB Music, 1995).
Concerto in One Movement for Piano (1991).
Fairfax Festival Overture (Seesaw Music, 1979).
Festival Overture (Theodore Presser/Elkan-Vogel, 1968).
Homage to Tchaikovsky (Hal Leonard, 2000).
O Viridissima, for keyboard and orchestra (Hildegard Publishing, 2000).
Pavane, for string orchestra (Carl Fischer, 1964).
Poem of Remembrance for Clarinet and Chamber Orchestra (MMB Music, 2006).
Rondo Concertante (Boosey and Hawkes, 1971).
Santa Barbara Overture (MMB Music, 1995).
Serenade, for string orchestra (Seesaw Music, 1988).
Suite for Orchestra (Seesaw Music, 1981).
Suite of Homages (Carl Fischer, 1985).
Symphonie Antique [Symphony No. 4] (Belwin Mills Music, 1966).
Symphony No. 1 (1953).
Symphony No. 2 (1955).
Symphony No. 2 on American Indian Themes (1959; Seesaw Music, 1981).
Youth Overture, for youth orchestra (Mills Music, 1962).

BAND

The Brass Menagerie: A Suite for Band (Mills Music, 1967).
La Rag (Carl Fischer, 1987).

CHAMBER ENSEMBLE

Aria, for flugelhorn and piano (Tap Music Sales).
Before Spring, for violin and piano (Seesaw Music, 1997).
Catch-a-Turian Toccata, for violin or flute and piano (Seesaw Music, 1991).
A Certain Slant of Light, Winter Afternoons, for flute and guitar (Seesaw Music, 1993).
Chorale on "Herzliebster Jesu," for eight trombones (Ensemble Publishing, 2000).
A Day in the Country, for clarinet and tape (1984).
Declamation, for brass and percussion (Theodore Presser/Elkan-Vogel, 1967).
Fanfare, for three trumpets, three trombones, and optional tuba (1959).
Four for Three (4-4-3): Suite for Brass Trio, for trumpet, trombone, and horn (1997).
Go Four It, for trumpet quartet (Tap Music Sales).
Homage to Paderewski, for viola and piano (Seesaw Music, 1997).
Homage to Poulenc, Mozart, and MacDowell, for cello, flute, and piano (MMB, 2004).
Improvisations for 'Cello and Piano (2000).
Indian Flute, for flute and narration (2003).
Laudate, for trumpet and organ (Seesaw Music, 1991).
Lovely Song, for violin and viola (one player) and piano (Seesaw Music, 1993).

Movement for Flute, Oboe, and Organ: "September 8, 1974" (Carl Fischer, 1977).
Movement for Flute, Oboe, Clarinet, and Piano (Seesaw Music, 1977).
Music for Woodwind Quartet, for flute, oboe, clarinet, and bassoon (Oxford University Press, 1972).
An Old Black and White Movie, for solo double bass and piano (2005).
Palm Sunday, for eight trombones (Ensemble Publishing, 2000).
Pianoharpsichordorgan, for one performer or three (Seesaw Music, 1976).
Psalm 1, for tenor or bass trombone and organ or piano (Ensemble Publishing, 2000).
Psalm 121, for organ, brass, and percussion (C. Alan Publishing, 2002).
Psalm 122, for bass trombone or tuba and organ (Ensemble Publishing, 1999).
Psalms for Flute and Organ or Piano (Seesaw Music, 1998).
Psalms for Trumpet (or Clarinet in B-flat) and Organ or Piano (Tap Music Sales, 2000).
Psalms for Percussion and Organ (C. Alan Publishing, 1999).
Quadralogue, for flute quartet and tape (1978).
Quartet for Flute, Viola, 'Cello, Harpsichord, and Tape (Seesaw Music, 1977).
Quartet for Trumpet, Horn, Trombone, and Piano (Hildegard Publishing, 2002).
A Quiet, Lovely Piece, for clarinet and piano (Seesaw Music, 1993).
A Requiem, for string quintet and woodwind quintet (MMB Music, 2004).
Serenade, for flute and piano (Seesaw Music, 1995).
Serenade, for woodwind quintet and tape (1989).
Serenade for Flugelhorn and Piano (Tap Music Sales, 2002).
Sextet, for flute, oboe, clarinet, cello, violin, and piano (Seesaw Music, 1993).
Sextet, for piano and woodwind quintet (Seesaw Music, 1968).
Six for Three, for flute, clarinet, and bassoon (arrangement of *Four for Three* for brass trio, 1997).
Solotrio, for xylophone, vibraphone, and marimba (one player) (Music for Percussion, 1982).
Sonata, for flute and piano or harpsichord (Southern Music Co., 1973).
Sonata, for violin and piano (Seesaw Music, 1976).
Sonatina, for two violins (Seesaw Music, 1994).
String Quartet No. 1 (Seesaw Music, 1990).
Suite for Flute and Piano: Homage to Hindemith (Oxford University Press, 1993).
Suite for Violin and Piano (Hildegard Publishing, 2009).
Suite Sunday, for organ and piano, harpsichord, or synthesizer (Sacred Music, 1997).
Summer of '82, for cello and organ (Seesaw Music, 1984).
Time Pieces, for trumpet and organ (Zimbel Press, 2009).
Toccata, for flute chorus (Carl Fischer, 1974).
Trio for Clarinet, Violin, and Piano: Summer Day (2003).
Trio, for flute, marimba, and cello (Seesaw Music, 1993).
Trio, for flute, oboe, harpsichord, and tape (Seesaw Music, 1976).
Toccata for Six, for six mallet percussionists (C. Alan Publishing, 2004).
Variations on "Antioch," for brass trio (Tap Music Sales, 2001).

Woodwind Quintet No. 1, for flute, oboe, clarinet, bassoon, and horn (Boosey and Hawkes, 1962).

PIANO/HARPSICHORD

Adventures in Sound, for piano (Summy Birchard Music, 1989).
Aria and Scherzo for C Instrument, for piano or keyboard/organ (Sacred Music, 1998).
Chromatic Fantasy, for piano (1946).
Encore, for piano (Arsis Press, 1984).
Fantasy, for piano (Plymouth Music, 1994).
Fiesta, for two pianos (original organ solo), (MMB Music, 1996).
Four on a Row, for piano (1966; New Scribner Music Library, 1972).
Funfest, for piano and tape (1984).
Hannukah Song, for piano (1999).
Holidays for Piano, (National Music Publishing/Emerson Music).
Holidays of the Year, for piano (National Music Publishing/Emerson Fred Bock).
Homage to Cowell, Cage, Crumb, and Czerny, for two pianos (Plymouth Music, 1983).
Norteamexispanicumsake, for two pianos (MMB Music, 2001).
Piano Trio, for three pianos (MMB Music, 2001).
Piano Trio No. 2, for three pianos (2008).
Piano Quartet (Seesaw Music, 1977).
Preludes, for piano (1945).
Psalms for Piano, for piano (Dixon/Broyles Productions, 2004).
Reaching Out, for piano (FJH Music, 2004).
Rite of Summer, for piano and tape (1986).
Seven Etudes, for piano (1965; Carl Fischer, 1965/1972).
Seven Pieces for Marilyn; or, A Little of This and That, for piano (1982).
Sonata in One Movement, for piano (1949).
Sonata No. 2, for piano (1955).
Sonata No. 3, for piano (1996–2000; Hildegard Publishing, 1999–2000).
Sound Pictures, for piano (1971; Boosey and Hawkes, 1971/1983).
Space Suite: Twelve Short Pieces, for piano (Colla Voce/Plymouth Music, 1989).
Spirituals, for piano (Santa Barbara Music Publishing, 2003)
Suite, for harpsichord (1982).
Suite No. 1 for Children, for piano (1952).
Suite No. 2 for Children: "At the Zoo," for piano (1952).
Suite No. 1: Landscapes, for piano (1947).
Suite No. 2, for piano (1948).
Suite "The Sea," for two pianos (1949).
Three Pieces, for piano (Colla Voce/Plymouth Music, 1992).
Time Pictures: Four Studies in Time, for piano (1961; Boosey and Hawkes, 1962/1983).
Toccata, for harpsichord (in *Contemporary Composers for Harpsichord,* vol. 2 Vivace Press, 1993).

Toccata, for piano (Arsis Press, 1980).
Two Pieces: Menuet and Polonaise, for piano (Hildegard Publishing, 2000).
Variations for Piano, Four Hands: Homage to Ravel, Schoenberg, and May Aufderheide (Colla Voce/Plymouth Music, 1989).

ORGAN

Adoring Praise: Two Hymn Settings (MorningStar Music, 2005).
Antioch and Galilee: Hymn Settings (Augsburg Fortress, 2003).
Aria (Zimbrel Press, 2002).
Aria and Scherzo (Sacred Music, 1998).
Beneath the Cross (Zimbel Press, 2003).
Bring Many Names (Westchase) (Zimbel Press, 1999).
Carols for Organ (Sacred Music, 1996).
Celebration "Marian's Piece" (Zimbel Press, 2004).
Celebration: Seven Hymn Settings (Zimbel Press, 1965).
Church Rock (1986).
Come, Come Ye Saints (National Music Publishing/Emerson).
Communion Hymns for Organ: Music for Celebration and Introspection (Sacred Music, 1996).
Contrasts (in *Preludes and Postludes,* vol. 4, Augsburg Fortress, 1976).
Declarations (Seesaw Music, 1976).
Deliger den Himmel Blaa (Bright and Glorious Is the Sky) (Conners Publications, 2000).
Diademata (1956).
Eight Hymn Preludes (Augsburg Fortress, 1993).
Elegy for Organ Duet (Seesaw Music, 1982).
Fantasie (Oxford University Press, 1967).
Fantasy (MorningStar Music, 2007).
Fantasy on "O Sacred Head" (Boosey and Hawkes, 1970).
Festival Voluntary for the Feast of St. Mark (St. Mary's Press, 1957).
Fiesta (1996).
Folk Hymn Sketches (Sacred Music Press, 1987).
Four Biblical Settings (MorningStar Music, 2001).
Glory and Praise: Familiar Praise and Worship Songs (Sacred Music, 2000).
God and Country: Organ Settings of Hymn Tunes for National Occasions (Sacred Music, 1997).
God with Us: Eleven Pieces for Organ (Sacred Music, 1994).
Hankey: I Love to Tell You the Story (Augsburg Fortress, 2003).
He Leadeth Me: Hymn Setting for Organ (Oxford University Press, 1969).
Hymn Preludes and Free Accompaniments (Augsburg Fortress, 1978).
I Danced in the Morning (Zimbel Press, 2007).
I Have Decided to Follow Jesus (Zimbel Press, 2002).
Jesus, the Very Thought of Thee (in *Quiet Reflections: An Organ Anthology,* ed. Dale Wood, Sacred Music, 1994).

Jubilate (in *Preludes and Postludes,* vol. 4, Augsburg Fortress, 1976).
Lac qui Parle: Many and Great, O God, Are Your Works, for organ (Augsburg Fortress, 2003).
Lauda Anima: Hymn Prelude (1956).
Little Suite (Augsburg Press, 1985).
Little Toccata (in *Jon Spong Collection of Organ Music: New Compositions for Worship and Recital,* Arvon Publishing, 1978).
A Mighty Fortress Is Our God [Eine Feste Burg] (in *Laudate!* vol. 4, Concordia Publishing, 1997]).
O Welt, ich muss dich lassen (in *A New Liturgical Year,* ed. John Ferguson, Augsburg Press, 1997).
Odes on Beethoven's Ninth and Simple Gifts (Zimbel Press, 2006).
Praise: Eight Hymn Preludes for Organ (Sacred Music, 1995).
Prelude on a Millennium Hymn Tune (St. Paul's Cathedral), (Gemini Press International, 2000).
Prelude on "Lobe Den Herren" (2000).
Preludes to St. Paul's Cathedral (Tritone Press/Tenuto Publications, 2000).
Preludes to the Past (in *Organ Settings of Enduring Nineteenth-Century Hymn Tunes,* vols. 1–3, Sacred Music, 1990–92).
Psalm 151 (MorningStar Music, 2001).
Psalm Interpretations, Vols. 1–2 (Sacred Music, 2000).
Psalms (Sacred Music, 1993).
Ragtime, for organ pedals alone (Zimbel Press, 2003).
Rejoice, Ye Pure in Heart (Zimbel Press, 2002).
Romantic Suite (1983).
Scherzo (MorningStar Music, 2001).
Seasonal Psalms, Vols. 1–2 (Sacred Music, 1999).
Seven Hymn Preludes (Shawnee Press/Harold Flammer, 1968).
St. Anne (O God Our Help in Ages Past) (Shawnee Press, 1951).
Suite of Easter Hymns (Sacred Music, 1984).
Ten Hymn Preludes for Meditation and Praise (Carl Fischer, 1967).
Three Carol Lullabies (Zimbel Press, 2011).
Three Fantasies on Advent/Christmas Hymns (Augsburg Publishing, 1979).
Toccata (Oxford University Press, 1967).
Toccata and Fugue (1969; Seesaw Music, 1976).
Valet will ich dir geben: All Glory, Laud, and Honor (Augsburg Fortress, 2003).
Variations on "Abide with Me" (Zimbel Press, 2001).
Variations on "Alleluia" (Zimbrel Press, 2003).
Variations on "Coatue" (Zimbel Press, 2002).
Variations on "Dove on Peace" (Zimbel Press, 2001).
Variations on "Old One Hundredth," for piano and organ (Zimbel Press, 2009).
Variations on "Reformation" (Zimbel Press, 2001).
Variations on "Rendez a Dieu" (Zimbel Press, 2001).

Wachet auf: Wake, Awake, for Night Is Flying, for organ (Augsburg Fortress, 2003).
We Praise Your Name: Suite on "Grosser Gott" (Sacred Music, 1996).
Were You There (Augsburg Fortress, 2003).
When John Was Baptized by Jordan's River (Rendez à Dieu), (in *Laudate!* vol. 4, Concordia Publishing, 1997]).
With Praise and Love, Vols. 1 and 2: Settings of Nineteenth-Century Hymn Tunes (Sacred Music, 1978).

ADDITIONAL SOLO INSTRUMENTS

Bell Song, for guitar (originally for carillon), (Seesaw Music, 1999).
Bells over Sydney for Carillon (Guild of Carillonneurs, 2009).
Bellsong, for carillon (in *Leuvens Beiaardboes,* 1983).
Echospace, for guitar (Seesaw Music, 1993).
Ice Rhythm, for solo marimba and optional electronics (C. Alan Publishing, 1998).
Reflections from the Tower, for carillon (Guild of Carillonneurs, 1992).
Three Pieces for Carillon (Guild of Carillonneurs; No. 10 in the series *Compositions for Carillon,* 1976).
Toccata for Marimba (Colla Voce, 1967).
Toccata for Timpani (C. Alan Publishing, 2002).

VOCAL

And I Saw a New Heaven and a New Earth, for medium high voice, trumpet, and piano (Arsis Press, 1991).
Away, Delights! for medium voice and piano (1950).
The Caller, for soprano and piano/organ (Southern Music Company, 2000).
Celebrate the Journey: The Hymns of Emma Lou Diemer, for voice and keyboard (Zimbel Press, 2005).
Create in Me a Clean Heart, O God, for medium voice and organ or piano (Arsis Press, 1990).
The Dogwood Tree, for high voice and piano (1985).
Four Chinese Love Poems, for voice and harp or piano (Seesaw Music, 1976).
Four Poems by Alice Meynell, for soprano or tenor and chamber ensemble (Carl Fischer, 1977).
The Four Seasons, for high voice and piano (Seesaw Music, 1981).
Four Songs, for high voice and piano (1948).
Frisch Gesungen, for voice and piano (2000).
I Will Sing of Your Steadfast Love, for high voice and organ (Arsis Press, 1987).
In You, O Lord, Do I Put My Trust, for medium high voice and piano or organ (Seesaw Music, 1993).
Lute Songs on Renaissance Poetry, for high voice and piano (Seesaw Music, 1988).
A Miscellany of Love Songs, for high voice and piano (1972–73).
O Wondrous Sight, O Vision Fair, for medium high voice and organ or piano (1996).
October Wind, for high voice and piano (1948; in *Art Songs by American Women Composers,* vol. 4, ed. Ruth Friedberg Southern Music Co., 1995).

One Perfect Rose, for high voice and piano (Southern Music Co., 2000).
On This Wedding Day, for voice and piano (National/Emerson Fred Bock).
Poems by Dorothy Diemer Hendry, for voice and piano (2000).
Psalm 121, for high voice and piano (Seesaw Music, 1981).
Psalm 137, for medium voice and piano (1950).
Seven Somewhat Silly Songs, for medium high voice and piano (1996).
Shall I Compare Thee to a Summer's Day? for high voice and piano (Southern Music Co., 1995).
Songs, for high voice and piano (1949).
Songs of Reminiscence, for soprano and piano (Seesaw Music, 1968).
Strings in the Earth and Air, for soprano and piano/organ (Southern Music Co., 2000).
Three Christmas Songs, for medium high voice and keyboard (Hal Leonard, 2004).
Three Mystic Songs, for soprano, baritone, and piano (1963; Seesaw Music, 1968).
To a Gypsy, for high voice and piano (1954).
The Twenty-third Psalm, for soprano, tenor, and piano (1943).
Wedding Song, for voice (National Music Publishers/Emerson Music).
Who Can Find a Virtuous Woman? for medium voice and organ or piano (Arsis Press, 1990).

CHORUS AND ORCHESTRA

Anniversary Choruses, for mixed voices and orchestra (or piano), (Carl Fischer, 1970).
Invocation, mixed voices and orchestra (or piano), (1985; Carl Fischer Rental Library, 1987).
There Is a Morn Unseen, for mixed voices and orchestra (or piano), (Seesaw Music, 1993).
To Come So, for mixed chorus, women's chorus, piano, organ, and large instrumental ensemble (1992).
To Him All Glory Give, for mixed voices and orchestra (Theodore Presser/Elkan-Vogel, 1962).

CHORUS

Agnus Dei, from *Mass,* for SATB and piano (Santa Barbara Music Publishing, 2001).
Alleluia, for SSA (Carl Fischer, 1962).
Alleluia! Christ Is Risen, for SATB with trumpet and organ (Harold Flammer, 1965).
And in the Last Days, for SATB and organ (Augsburg Publishing, 1987).
The Angel Gabriel, for divided SATB with piano or organ (Carl Fischer, 1965).
Anthem of Faith, for SATB and organ (G. Schirmer, 1972).
As a Hart Longs, for SATB (H. W. Gray, 1962).
At a Solemn Music, for SATB, (Boosey and Hawkes, 1970).
Aunt Sal's Song, for SSA and piano (1975).
Awake, My Glory, for SATB, organ or piano, and optional guitar (Abington Press, 1976).
Away, Delights, for TTBB (Tetra Music, 1979).
A Babe Is Born, for SATB, organ or piano, brass quartet, and tambourine (Sacred Music, 1969).
The Baptist Shouts on Jordan's Shore, for SATB and piano or organ (Pilgrim Press, 1995).
Bee, I'm Expecting You! for SATB and piano (Alliance Music Publishing, 1994).

Before the Paling of the Stars, for SATB and keyboard (Theodore Presser/Elkan-Vogel, 1964).

The Bells, for SATB and piano four hands (Boosey and Hawkes, 1961).

Billy Broke Locks, for SATB and accompaniment (1975).

Blessed Are You, for SATB with organ or piano, optional guitar (Carl Fischer, 1970).

Bless the Lord, O My Soul, for SATB, congregation, keyboard, and optional brass, percussion (SBMP, 1999).

Blow, Blow, Thou Winter Wind (from *A Feast for Christmas*), speech choir a cappella (Santa Barbara Music Publishing, 1991).

California Madrigals, for SATB and piano (Carl Fischer, 1977).

Cantata for Palm Sunday: "The Triumphal Entry," for SATB and organ (1963).

Caprice, for SATB and piano (Carl Fischer, 1988).

Choral Responses for Worship, for SATB (Sacred Music Press, 1990).

Choruses on Freedom, for SATB, strings, piano, and percussion (G. Schirmer, 1976).

Christ at Table There with Friends: A Hymn (in *The New Century Hymnal,* Pilgrim Press, 1995).

Christ the Lord Is Ris'n Today: An Easter Anthem, for SATB and organ, optional congregation and trumpets (Sacred Music, 1987).

Christian Women, Christian Men, for SATB (in *The New Presbyterian Hymnal,* Westminster/John Knox Press, 1990).

Christmas Carol, for SSA and piano or organ (Carl Fischer, 1962).

The Church's One Foundation, for SATB and congregation with organ, brass, and percussion (Hinshaw Music, 1981).

Clap Your Hands, for SATB and keyboard (Carl Fischer, 1984).

Come, Fill the Cup, and in the Fire of Spring, for SATB a cappella (Boosey and Hawkes, 2010).

Come Hither, You That Love, for SSA, piano, and flute (Piedmont Music, 1974).

Come, Said the Muse, for SATB (National/Emerson Fred Bock).

Consider the Lilies, for SATB divisi (MorningStar Music, 2006).

Counting-Out Rhyme, for SSAA (Plymouth Music Co, 1986).

Dance, Dance My Heart, for SATB and piano (Carl Fischer, 1973)

Dance for Spring, for SSA, strings, flute, oboe, and clarinet (1960).

Dear God, Bestow on Us Your Grace, for SATB and keyboard (Theodore Presser, 2002).

A Description of Love, for TTBB (1972).

Drop, Drop, Slow Tears, for SATB and narrators (Gemini Press, 1979).

Eleven Limericks by Lear, for SSA (Carl Fischer, 1991).

A Feast for Christmas, for SATB and brass (Santa Barbara Music Publishing, 1991).

For the Fruit of All Creation, for SATB (Hope Publishing/Agapé, 1970).

For Ye Shall Go Out with Joy, for SATB and piano or organ (Carl Fischer, 1968).

Four Carols, for SSA (Theodore Press/Elkan-Vogel, 1962).

Fragments from the Mass, for SSAA (Marks Music, 1961).

Geronimo, for SATB and piano (in *New Dimensions in Music, American Book Company Choral Art Series,* Gemini Press, 1970).

The Gift, for SSAA and piano (1956).

Give Thanks for God is Good (in *Hymns from the Bible,* Gemini Press, 2000).

Glorious the Day, for SATB (in *A New Hymnal for Colleges and Schools,* Yale University Press, 1992).

Glory to God (Sacred Music, 1988).

God Is Love, for divided SATB and electronic tape (Sisra Publishing, 1982).

God of Love and God of Power, for SATB and congregation with organ, brass, and percussion (Hinshaw Music, 1981).

Hallelujah! for SATB (Santa Barbara Music Publishing, 2001)

Hast Thou Not Known? for SATB, organ, brass quintet, and timpani (Roger Dean Publishing, 1984).

Here with a Loaf of Bread beneath a Bough (from *Verses from the Rubaiyat*), for SATB (Boosey and Hawkes, 2010).

Hey, Boys! Hi, Girls! for SATB and piano (Santa Barbara Music Publishing, 1994).

The Holy Child: A Cantata for Christmas, for SATB, organ or piano with additional vocal and instrumental ensemble (Sacred Music, 1990).

Honor to Thee, for SATB and organ (H. W. Gray, 1963).

How Firm a Foundation, for SATB and congregation with organ, brass, and percussion (Hinshaw Music, 1981).

How Lovely Is Your Dwelling, for SAB, keyboard, and flute (Santa Barbara Music Publishing, 1995).

How Majestic Is Thy Name, for unison voices and accompaniment (H. W. Gray, 1962).

I Know a Bird (from *More Madrigals*), for SATB (Santa Barbara Music Publishing, 1991).

I Sing, for SATB and keyboard (Hinshaw Music, 1992).

I Stand beside the Manger Stall, for SATB (Carl Fischer, 1962).

I Will Extol You, for SATB and organ (Augsburg Fortress, 1992).

I Will Give Thanks, for SATB and keyboard (Sacred Music, 1968).

I Will Give Thanks to the Lord, for SATB and keyboard (Hinshaw Music, 1987).

I Will Sing of Mercy and Judgment, for SATB with piano or orchestral accompaniment (Carl Fischer, 1970).

In Hope We Sing: Alleluia, for SATB and organ (Zimbel Press, 2001).

Is It a Dream? for SATB and keyboard (Santa Barbara Music Publishing, 1992).

Jesus, Lover of My Soul, for two-part voices with optional C instrument (Lorenz, 1974).

Jesus, Still Lead On, for SATB, congregation, organ, and optional brass (Sacred Music, 1998).

Joy to the World, for SATB and keyboard (in Hymnal Supplement, *Ecumenical Praise,* Agapé, 1976).

Laughing Song, for SSATB with optional four-hand piano (Shawnee Press, 1974).

The Legend of Sleepy Hollow, for SATB and piano (Carl Fischer, 2001).

Let Thy Steadfast Love, for SATB and keyboard (Hinshaw Music, 1987).

Let Us Hope When Hope Seems Hopeless, for choir, organ, and optional flute (in *New Century Hymnal,* Pilgrim Press, 1995).

Lift Up Your Heads, O Mighty Gates, for SATB and organ (Tenuto Publishing, 1995).

A Little Song of Life, for SATB or SA and piano (Tenuto Publishing, 1964).
The Lord Is Mindful, for SATB with keyboard (Hinshaw Music, 1979).
The Lord Is My Light, for SATB with organ or piano (Hinshaw Music, 1977).
The Lord's My Shepherd, for unison choir and congregation and keyboard with optional brass quartet (Hinshaw Music, 2000).
The Lord's Prayer, for SATB, tape, and organ (Van Ness/Broadman Press, 1985).
Love Is a Sickness Full of Woes, for SAB (in *American Book Company Choral Art Series,* Gemini Press, 1977).
Madrigals Three, for SATB and piano (Carl Fischer, 1972).
The Magnificat, for SA and piano or organ (Piedmont Music, 1963).
Mary's Lullaby, for SSA and piano (Boosey and Hawkes, 1961).
Mass, for SATB, two pianos, percussion and optional organ (Santa Barbara Music Publishing, 1996, 2000).
May God Bestow on His Grace, for unison voices and accompaniment (1998).
Men Are Fools That Wish to Die, for SATB (in *American Book Company Choral Art Series,* Gemini Press, 1977).
A Mighty Fortress Is Our God, for SATB and keyboard (Tenuto Publishing, 2002).
More Madrigals, for SATB and piano (Santa Barbara Music Publishing, 1984).
A Musical Instrument: A Choral Cycle, for women's chorus and two pianos (1978).
Myself When Young Did Eagerly Frequent, for SATB a cappella (Boosey and Hawkes, 2010).
Noel-Rejoice and Be Merry, for SATB and keyboard (Carl Fischer, 1967).
Now God Be Praised: An Anthem, for choir, adult choir, trumpet, and organ, with optional additional instruments (1988).
O Come, Let Us Sing unto the Lord, for SATB or TTBB with piano or organ (Carl Fischer, 1961).
O Give Thanks to the Lord, for SATB, congregation, and keyboard (Sacred Music Press, 1999).
O Shenandoah, for TTBB and piano (Carl Fischer, 1964).
O to Make the Most Jubilant Song, for SATB and piano (Carl Fischer, 1972).
O Viridissima Virga: "Song to the Mother," for SSAA, optional keyboard, and percussion (Hildegard Publishing, 1998).
On Christmas Eve, for SATB (Santa Barbara Music Publishing, 1991),
Outburst of Praise, for SATB and keyboard (Theodore Presser, 1968).
Peace Cantata, for SATB, narrators, organ, brass, and timpani (1985).
Persimmon Tree, for SATB (Santa Barbara Music Publishing, 1990).
Prairie Spring, for SSAA and piano or synthesizer (Plymouth Music Co., 1988).
Praise of Created Things, for SATB and keyboard (Belwin Mills, 1964).
Praise the Lord, for SATB and keyboard (1958).
Praise the Lord, for SATB with brass quintet, organ, optional timpani (Carl Fischer, 1975).
Praise Ye the Lord, for SATB and piano, four hands (Shawnee Press, 1964).
Proclaim the Day, for SATB, organ, and brass quartet (Harold Flammer, 1964).
The Prophecy, for SSAA a cappella (Boosey and Hawkes, 2010).
Psalm 100, for SATB, organ, drum, and optional brass quartet (Sacred Music, 1996).

Psalm 113 (Praise the Lord), for SATB and keyboard (Carl Fischer, 1992).
Psalm 134, for SATB (Seesaw Music, 1977).
Psalm 148: Praise the Lord from the Heavens, for SATB and organ with optional handbells (Sacred Music, 1995).
Psalm 150, for SATB and organ (Oxford University Press, 1999).
Psalms for Chorus, for SATB, congregation, and organ (2005).
Reasons Briefly Set Downe by th' Auctor to Perswade Euery One to Learne to Sing, for TTBB and piano (Seesaw Music, 1993).
Rejoice in the Lord, for SATB, keyboard, and optional flute (Santa Barbara Music Publishing, 1998).
Rejoice in the Lord, for SATB, organ, and optional flute (Seesaw Music, 1998).
Responses in the Passion Gospel According to Matthew, for chorus (Gemini Press, 1979).
Romance, for SATB and piano with optional triangle (Carl Fischer, 1974).
The Sea, for SATB and chamber ensemble (1987).
A Service in Music and Poetry, for congregation, choir, soloists, organ piano, percussion, and narrator (1967).
The Shepherd to His Love, for chorus, flute, and piano (Marks Music, 1963).
Show and Tell, for SATB (Santa Barbara Music Publishing, 1990).
Sing a Glory: Cantata for Chorus, Orchestra, and Band (1965).
Sing, O Heavens, for SATB (Carl Fischer, 1975).
Sing Praises to the Lord, for SATB and keyboard (Hinshaw Music, 1987).
Sing to the Lord New Songs (in *Hymns from the Bible,* Gemini Press, 2000).
So Have I Seen a Silver Swan, for SATB, a cappella (Tenuto Publishing, 1977).
Song of Praise, for SATB and organ (Sacred Music, 2000).
Songs for the Earth, for SATB and orchestra (Seesaw Music, 2003).
Spring, for SATB and piano (Heritage Music Press, 1969).
A Spring Carol, for SATB and piano (Carl Fischer, 1962).
St. Chrysostom Cantata, for choir, soloists, and organ (1956).
Strong Son of God: Hymn for Chorus and Organ, (Agapé Music, 1977).
Sweet Dreams, Form a Shade, for SATB (Santa Barbara Music Publishing, 1991).
Tell Me Dearest, What Is Love? for SATB (Tetra Music, 1979).
There Was the Door to Which I Found No Key (from *Verses from the Rubaiyat*), for SATB a cappella (Boosey and Hawkes, 2010).
Thine, O Lord, for two-part voices and accompaniment (Harold Flammer, 1966).
Three Carols for Spring, for SATB and piano (1961).
Three Madrigals, for SATB and piano (Boosey and Hawkes, 1962).
Three Poems by Alice Meynell, for SATB, woodwind quintet, percussion, marimba, vibraphone, piano, and organ (1976).
Three Poems by Oscar Wilde, for SATB and piano (Carl Fischer, 1989).
Three Poems for Chorus, for SATB (1955).
Three Poems of Ogden Nash, for TTBB (Harold Flammer, 1965).
Thy Holy Wings, for SATB, keyboard, flute, and cello/bass (MorningStar Music, 2009).

To Praise God Again, for SATB (Carl Fischer, 1972).
Two Haiku, for SATB and piano (in *New Dimensions in Music, American Book Company Choral Art Series,* Gemini Press, 1970).
Two Madrigals for Young Singers, for two-part chorus and accompaniment (Hinshaw Music, 1975).
Two Poems by Edgar Allan Poe, for SATB and piano or electric piano (Hinshaw Music, 2001).
Two Poems by Emily Dickinson, for SATB and piano (Alliance Music Publishing, 1994).
Verses from the Rubaiyat, for SATB and piano (Boosey and Hawkes, 1970).
Verses on the Birth of Christ, for SATB, tubular chimes, and organ (Zimbel Press, 2009).
The Visionary, for SSA and piano (Seesaw Music, 1993).
Weep No More, for SSA (Tetra Music Corp, 1979).
Weep You No More, Sad Fountains, for SAB (Gemini Press, 1977).
What Child Is This? for SATB and organ (Sacred Music Press, 1990).
When in Man's Music, for SATB and organ (Augsburg Publishing, 1976).
Who Gave Us the World, for unison voices and keyboard, optional flute (Pilgrim Press, 1997).
Why So Pale and Wan? for SATB (Gemini Press, 1977).
Wild Nights! Wild Nights! for SATB and piano (Hinshaw Music, 1978).
Winds of Spring, for unison voices and accompaniment (Harold Flammer/Shawnee Press, 1967).
With Them the Seed of Wisdom Did I Sow (from *Verses from the Rubaiyat*) for SATB (Boosey and Hawkes, 2010).
Your Friends Shall Be the Tall Wind, for SATB or SSA and piano (Tenuto Publishing, 1960).

ELECTRONIC (SEE CHAMBER ENSEMBLE FOR WORKS COMBINING INSTRUMENTS AND TAPE)

Add One No. 1, for electronic piano and tape (1980).
Add One No. 2, for live synthesizer (optional) and tape (1981).
Add One No. 3, for electric piano or synthesizer or tape alone (1981).
Harpsichord Quartet, for two- or four-channel tape (1980).
Patchworks, for two- or four-channel tape (1978).
Presto Canon, for two- or four-channel tape (1980).
Scherzo, for two- or four-channel tape (1980).
Three Poems by Emily Dickinson, for tape (1984).
Untitled, for two- or four-channel tape (1980).

Notes

Chapter 9. Pauline Oliveros

1. Deep Listening Institute, "Pauline Oliveros" (accessed February 6, 2012), http://deeplistening.org/site/content/pauline-oliveros.

Chapter 12. Pamela Z

1. The BodySynth, created by Chris Van Raalte and Ed Severinghaus in 1994, is a MIDI controller that transforms movement, gestures, and other muscle efforts into sounds. The performer attaches electrodes to the body over various muscles. The tiny electrical signals generated by muscle contractions are measured and analyzed by a microprocessor. A variety of processing algorithms are available through the keypad on the processor unit. These algorithms translate effort into MIDI commands, thus causing the body to become a controller for an electronic-sound module such as a synthesizer or a sampler.

2. The "Wiimote" (Wii remote) is the primary controller for Nintendo's Wii console. Through a built-in accelerometer and optical sensor, it allows users to interact with and manipulate digital media.

3. Pro Tools is a digital audio workstation system that is considered an industry standard for recording and editing music and sound.

4. Auto-Tune is software that uses a phase vocoder to alter pitch. Originally invented by the research scientist Dr. Harold (Andy) Hildebrand, who founded Antares Audio Technologies, Auto-Tune was designed in the late 1990s to subtly correct pitch inaccuracies in recording. Popular-music artists such as T-Pain later used Auto-Tune technology as a much more obvious sound tool, making the fluidity of a slurred line sound like digital leaping between stepwise pitches.

Chapter 13. Toshiko Akiyoshi

1. V-discs, often called Victory discs, were produced during World War II in a program designed to boost the morale of soldiers overseas. The American Federation of Musicians, on strike at the time, made a deal with the U.S. military to volunteer their musicians as long as no commercial profit was made from the discs. Twelve inches in diameter, the longer playing records were pressed by record companies and packed by the military to ship overseas. See "V-Discs Boosted Troop Morale during World War II," Record Collectors' Guild (accessed June 6, 2012), http://www.recordcollectorsguild.org/index.php?name=Sections&req=viewarticle&artid=11&page=1.

Chapter 22. Beth Anderson

1. Beth Anderson, "Beauty Is Revolution," *EAR* 6.3 (April/May 1981): 6.
2. "Beth Anderson, Composer" (accessed February 6, 2012), http://www.beand.com/.

Selected Resources

These published books help to identify women composers beyond journal articles, or the perusal of various nonpublished documents, such as concert series and programs; university music-department rosters, ensembles, and courses; online sources; and conference-circuit presentations and information. The list of publications below is provided as a resource and is not a comprehensive bibliography for this book.

Ammer, Christine. *Unsung: A History of Women in American Music.* Century Ed. Portland, Ore.: Amadeus Press, 2001.

Anderson, Ruth, ed. *Contemporary American Composers: A Biographical Dictionary.* Boston: G. K. Hall, 1982.

Appleby, Rosalind. *Women of Note: The Rise of Australian Women Composers.* Freemantle, Australia: Freemantle Press, 2012.

Bailey, Candace. *Music and the Southern Belle: From Accomplished Lady to Confederate Composer.* Carbondale: Southern Illinois University Press, 2010.

Bedford, Frances. *Harpsichord and Clavichord Music of the Twentieth Century.* Berkeley, Calif.: Fallen Leaf Press, 1993.

Block, Adrienne Fried, and Carol Neuls-Bates. *Women in American Music: A Bibliography of Music and Literature.* Westport, Conn.: Greenwood Press, 1979.

Boenke, Heidi M. *Flute Music by Women Composers: An Annotated Catalog.* Westport, Conn.: Greenwood Press, 1988.

Bowers, Jane, and Judith Tick, eds. *Women Making Music: The Western Art Tradition, 1150–1950.* Urbana: University of Illinois Press, 1986.

Briscoe, James R., ed. *Contemporary Anthology of Music by Women.* Bloomington: Indiana University Press, 1997.

———. *New Historical Anthology of Music by Women.* Bloomington: Indiana University Press, 2004.

Claghorn, Gene. *Women Composers and Songwriters: A Concise Biographical Dictionary.* 2d ed. Metuchen, N.J.: Scarecrow Press, 1996.

Cohen, Aaron I. *International Discography of Women Composers.* Westport, Conn.: Greenwood Press, 1984.

———. *International Encyclopedia of Women Composers.* 2d ed. New York: Books and Music, 1987.

Coleman, Bud, and Judith A. Sebesta, eds. *Women in American Musical Theatre.* Jefferson, N.C.: McFarland, 2008.

Dees, Pamela Youngdahl. *A Guide to Piano Music by Women Composers.* Vol. 1: *Composers Born before 1900.* Westport, Conn.: Greenwood Press, 2002.

———. *Piano Music by Women Composers.* Vol. 2: *Women Born after 1900.* Westport, Conn.: Praeger, 2004.

Enstice, Wayne, and Janis Stockhouse. *Jazzwomen: Conversations with Twenty-One Musicians.* Bloomington: Indiana University Press, 2004.

Floyd, Samuel A., Jr., ed. *International Dictionary of Black Composers.* 2 vols. Chicago and London: Fitzroy Dearborn, 1999.

Fuller, Sophie. *Pandora Guide to Women Composers.* London: Pandora Press, 1994.

Gann, Kyle. *American Music in the Twentieth Century.* New York: Schirmer, 1997.

Glickman, Sylvia, and Marthia Furman Schleifer. *From Convent to Concert Hall: A Guide to Women Composers.* Westport, Conn.: Greenwood Press, 2003.

———. *Women Composers: Music through the Ages.* 8 Vols. New York: G. K. Hall, 2003.

Gray, Anne. *The World of Women in Classical Music.* La Jolla, Calif.: WordWorld, 2007.

Gray, John, ed. *Blacks in Classical Music: A Bibliographic Guide to Composers, Performers, and Ensembles.* Westport, Conn.: Greenwood Press, 1988.

Green, Mildred Denby. *Black Women Composers: A Genesis.* Boston: Twayne, 1983.

Heinrich, Adel. *Organ and Harpsichord Music by Women Composers: An Annotated Catalog.* Music Reference Collection 30. Westport, Conn.: Greenwood Press, 1991.

Hinkle-Turner, Elizabeth. *Women Composers and Music Technology in the United States: Crossing the Line.* Burlington, Vt.: Ashgate, 2006.

Jackson, Barbara Garvey. *Say Can You Deny Me: A Guide to Surviving Music by Women from the Sixteenth through the Eighteenth Centuries.* Fayetteville: University of Arkansas Press, 1994.

Jezic, Diane Peacock, ed. *Women Composers: The Lost Tradition Found.* 2d ed. (Prepared by Elizabeth Wood.) New York: Feminist Press, 1994.

Johnson, Rose-Marie. *Violin Music by Women Composers: A Bio-Bibliographical Guide.* Westport, Conn.: Greenwood Press, 1989.

LePage, Jane Weiner, ed. *Women Composers, Conductors, and Musicians of the Twentieth Century: Selected Biographies.* 3 Vols. Metuchen, N.J.: Scarecrow Press, 1980–88.

Letzter, Jacqueline, and Robert Adelson. *Women Writing Opera: Creativity and Controversy in the Age of the French Revolution.* Berkeley: University of California Press, 2001.

MacAuslan, Janna, and Kristan Aspen. *Guitar Music by Women Composers: An Annotated Catalog.* Westport, Conn.: Greenwood Press, 1997.

McVicker, Mandy. *Women Composers of Classical Music: 369 Biographies from 1550 into the Twentieth Century.* Jefferson, N.C.: McFarland, 2010.

Meggett, Joan, ed. *Keyboard Music by Women Composers: A Catalog and Bibliography.* Westport, Conn.: Greenwood Press, 1981.
Patterson, Willis, ed. *Anthology of Art Songs by Black American Composers.* New York: E. B. Marks, 1977.
Pendle, Karin. *Women and Music: A History.* 2d ed. Bloomington: Indiana University Press, 2001.
———. *Women in Music: A Research and Information Guide.* New York: Routledge, 2005.
Rodgers, Tara. *Pink Noises: Women on Electronic Music and Sound.* Durham, N.C.: Duke University Press, 2010.
Roma, Catherine. *The Choral Music of Twentieth-Century Women Composers: Elisabeth Lutyens, Elizabeth Maconchy, and Thea Musgrave.* Lanham, Md.: Scarecrow Press, 2005.
Sadie, Julie Anne, and Rhian Samuel, eds. *The Norton/Grove Dictionary of Women Composers.* New York: W. W. Norton, 1995.
Slayton, Michael K. *Women of Influence in Contemporary Music: Nine American Composers.* Lanham, Md.: Scarecrow Press, 2011.
Stewart-Green, Miriam. *Women Composers: A Checklist of Works for the Solo Voice.* Boston: G. K. Hall, 1980.
Tick, Judith. *American Women Composers before 1879.* Ann Arbor, Mich.: UMI Press, 1983.
Walker-Hill, Helen. *From Spirituals to Symphonies: African-American Women Composers and Their Music.* Westport, Conn.: Greenwood Press, 2002.
———. *Music by Black Women Composers: A Bibliography of Available Scores.* CBMR Monographs No. 5. Chicago: Center for Black Music Research, 1995.
———. *Piano Music by Black Women Composers: A Catalog of Solo and Ensemble Works.* Westport, Conn.: Greenwood Press, 1992.
Williams, Ora. *American Black Women in the Arts and Social Sciences: A Bibliographic Survey.* 2d ed. Metuchen, N.J.: Scarecrow Press, 1978.
Zaimont, Judith Lang, and Karen Famera, eds. *Contemporary Concert Music by Women: A Directory of the Composers and Their Works.* Westport, Conn.: Greenwood Press, 1981.
Zaimont, Judith Lang, Catherine Overhauser, and Jane Gottlieb, eds. *The Musical Woman: An International Perspective.* 2 Vols. Westport, Conn.: Greenwood Press, 1987.
Zaimont, Judith Lang, Jane Gottlieb, Joanne Polk, and Michael J. Rogan, eds. *The Musical Woman: An International Perspective.* Vol. 3. Westport, Conn.: Greenwood Press, 1991.

Selected List of Publishers Featuring Women Composers

Ars Femina (focused on music before 1800)
Arsis Press/Sisra Publications
ClarNan Editions (historical music)
Furore Verlag
Hildegard Publishing Co.
Independent Music Publishers Cooperative
I Resound Press
Oceanna Music Publications (emphasizing educational purposes)
Treble Clef Music Press (choral music for treble voices, principally by women composers)

Index

JENNIFER KELLY is director of choral activities and asssociate professor of music at Lafayette College, Pennsylvania, and the artistic director of Concord Chamber Singers.

The University of Illinois Press
is a founding member of the
Association of American University Presses.

University of Illinois Press
1325 South Oak Street
Champaign, IL 61820-6903
www.press.uillinois.edu